Mac® OS X Version 10.3 Panther™ *fast&easy*®

Lisa A. Bucki

A DIVISION OF COURSE TECHNOLOGY

© 2004 by Premier Press, a division of Course Technology. All rights reserved. No part of this book may be reproduced or transmitted in any form or by any means, electronic or mechanical, including photocopying, recording, or by any information storage or retrieval system without written permission from Premier Press, except for the inclusion of brief quotations in a review.

Premier Press™

The Premier Press logo and related trade dress are trademarks of Premier Press and may not be used without written permission.

SVP, Professional, Trade, Retail Group: Andy Shafran
Publisher: Stacy L. Hiquet
Senior Marketing Manager: Sarah O'Donnell
Marketing Manager: Heather Hurley
Manager of Editorial Services: Heather Talbot
Senior Acquisitions Editor: Kevin Harreld
Book Packager: Justak Literary Services, Inc.
Technical Reviewer: Mark Abdelnour
Retail Market Coordinator: Sarah Dubois
Interior Layout: William Hartman
Cover Designer: Mike Tanamachi
Indexer: Sherry Massey
Proofreader: Janette Lynn

Apple, Macintosh, Mac OS X, and Panther are trademarks or registered trademarks of Apple Corporation.

All other trademarks are the property of their respective owners.

Important: Premier Press cannot provide software support. Please contact the appropriate software manufacturer's technical support line or Web site for assistance.

Premier Press and the author have attempted throughout this book to distinguish proprietary trademarks from descriptive terms by following the capitalization style used by the manufacturer.

Information contained in this book has been obtained by Premier Press from sources believed to be reliable. However, because of the possibility of human or mechanical error by our sources, Premier Press, or others, the Publisher does not guarantee the accuracy, adequacy, or completeness of any information and is not responsible for any errors or omissions or the results obtained from use of such information. Readers should be particularly aware of the fact that the Internet is an ever-changing entity. Some facts may have changed since this book went to press.

ISBN: 1-59200-344-3

Library of Congress Catalog Card Number: 2003115740

Printed in the United States of America

04 05 06 07 08 BH 10 9 8 7 6 5 4 3 2

Premier Press, a division of Course Technology
25 Thomson Place
Boston, MA 02210

To Mac fans everywhere,
who tend the flame so well.

Acknowledgments

The *Fast & Easy* series continues to be one of my favorites for bringing novice users up to speed with a new piece of technology. I thank Senior Acquisitions Editor Kevin Harreld of Premier Press for giving me the opportunity to update this book to cover Panther, the latest cool version of Mac OS X. I also extend my appreciation to Mike Shebanek at Apple, who sent me an early "seed" version of Panther. Thanks for your support, Mike.

Please also join me in offering kudos to the real heroes of this venture. Book packager Marta Justak and technical reviewer Mark Abdelnour kept the text on point to ensure that this book would be the best. The production team of Bill Hartman and Jan Lynn and indexer Sherry Massey also did a beautiful job in composing the pages for this book, yielding a terrific looking, easily read book.

About the Author

An author, trainer, and publishing consultant, **Lisa A. Bucki** has been involved in the computer book business for more than 12 years. She wrote *iTunes 4 Fast & Easy, iPhoto 2 Fast & Easy, Adobe Photoshop 7 Fast & Easy, Adobe Photoshop 7 Digital Darkroom, Managing with Microsoft Project 2002*, and a number of other titles for Premier Press. She also has written or contributed to dozens of additional books and multimedia tutorials, as well as spearheading or developing more than 100 computer and trade titles during her association with Macmillan. Bucki currently serves as a consultant and trainer in western North Carolina.

Contents

PART II
WORKING WITH APPLICATIONS AND DISKS 83

PART III
CUSTOMIZING MAC OS X VERSION 10.3 135

PART IV GETTING CONNECTED 209

PART VII BASIC MAINTENANCE AND TROUBLESHOOTING . . . 405

Introduction

This *Fast & Easy* guide from Premier Press will introduce you to the latest version of the innovative operating system from Apple—Mac OS X Version 10.3 Panther. This book will show you how to master the many and diverse features built into the Mac OS X Version 10.3 operating system--including some of the 150 new features added to the operating system--so you can work effectively with your Macintosh.

Mac OS X Version 10.3 Panther Fast & Easy teaches the steps that will enable you to navigate the Mac OS X interface (called the *Aqua interface*), manage your files and disks, and customize your Mac. Learn to surf the Web, chat with friends, handle your email and addresses, and schedule your time. You also will learn how to import and catalog your digital images, produce better home movies, enjoy your music files, recover from common emergencies, and use security features to protect your valuable files.

If you want to get the most from your Macintosh hardware, Mac OS X Version 10.3 Panther and this book provide everything you need to exploit your system's resources.

Who Should Read This Book?

This book is geared for novices who are new to all versions of the Mac OS X operating system, including first-time Macintosh users, as well as users upgrading from earlier Mac OS X versions who want to learn more about new features.

Because nearly every step in this book includes a clear illustration, you won't have to struggle to learn a process or find the right tool onscreen. The non-technical language also helps smooth the transition from newbie to comfortable user.

With each task clearly identified by a heading, you'll also find it easy to use the table of contents to find the steps you need. So, whether you want to work through the book from beginning to end or find just the tricks that you need, this book will accommodate your style and enhance your results.

Added Advice to Make You a Pro

Once you get started, you'll notice that this book presents many steps, with little explanatory text to slow you down. Where warranted, however, the book presents these special boxes to highlight a key issue:

TIP

Tips give shortcuts or hints so you learn more about the ins and outs of Mac OS X Version 10.3.

NOTE

Notes offer more detailed information about a feature, food for thought, or guidance to help you avoid problems or pitfalls in your work.

CAUTION

Cautions alert you to pitfalls and problems you should avoid.

An appendix at the end of the book highlights additional issues to consider before installing Mac OS X Version 10.3, if you haven't done so already. Finally, the glossary explains key terms that you need to understand to work effectively in Mac OS X Version 10.3.

Whether you have used a Macintosh before or not, you'll have fun as you dive in now with *Mac OS X Version 10.3 Panther Fast & Easy*!

PART I

Meet Panther

1

Getting Started with Mac OS X Version 10.3

Apple developed the original Mac OS X as a brand new OS (*Operating System*). When you start Mac OS X Version 10.3 Panther, you are greeted with the friendly Aqua user interface, which enables you to work with programs, files, communications, and other functions and content. This latest version of the Macintosh operating system offers even more easy and elegant functionality. In this chapter, you will learn how to:

- Start up your Macintosh.
- Recognize the parts of the interface.
- Start using the programs, utilities, and features included in Mac OS X Version 10.3.
- Work with the Sleep feature.
- Shut the system down or simply log out.

Starting Up

Macintosh systems have historically offered an easy startup process. Press a button on the keyboard or system; the Apple logo and the spinning starburst make their appearances; and then the OS finishes loading. With Mac OS X Version 10.3 Panther, the process works just about the same. (See Appendix A for more on setting up Mac OS X Version 10.3.)

Press the Power button, found near the upper-right corner of the keyboard or on the computer's case to start up the Macintosh. The system will power up. If you've previously set up multiple users under Mac OS X (see Chapter 23), a log-on screen will appear. Click on the desired user name, enter the Password, and click on Log In. The desktop will appear.

NOTE

To click with the mouse, move the mouse on your desk until the mouse pointer moves over the desired item on-screen. Then press and release the button on the mouse.

Looking at the Desktop

The Mac OS X Version 10.3 desktop provides functionality similar to previous Macintosh operating systems. Later chapters will review the specifics of working with various features of the Mac OS X Version 10.3 interface. Here, take a first glimpse at its features:

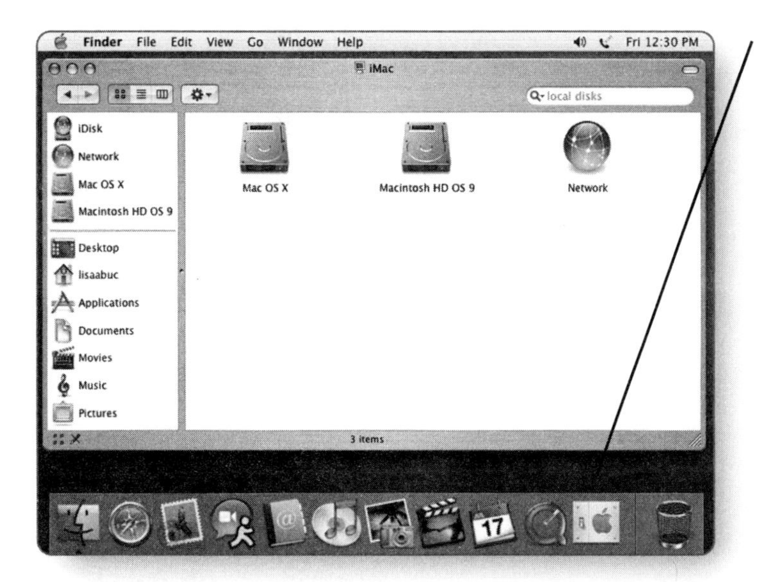

- **Desktop**. The entire screen area, which presents the features of the OS, is the desktop. The program and file windows with which you will work appear on the desktop. You also can store files, post notes called *Stickies*, and even add a custom picture to change the appearance of the desktop.

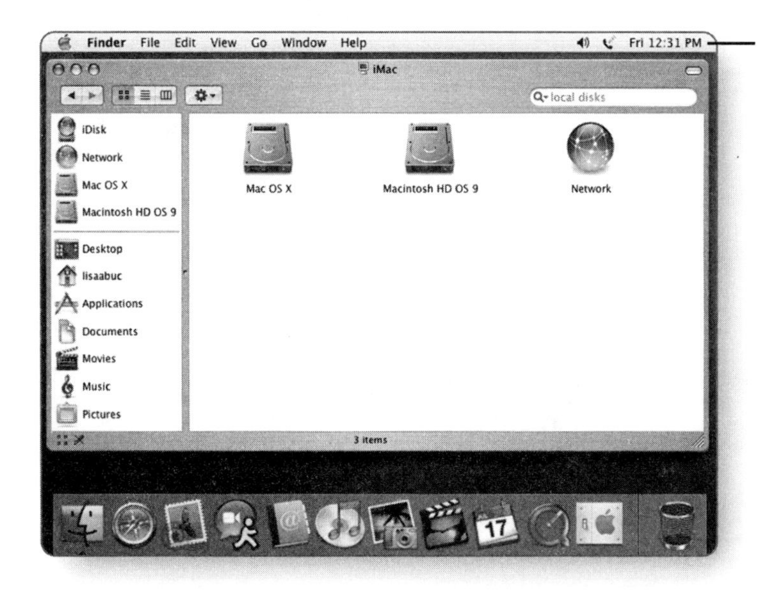

- **Menu bar**. The menu bar at the top of the screen holds pull-down menus. When you're working with the Finder, the menu bar shows the Finder application menus. When you later open or switch to another application (program), the menu bar changes to display the menus for that application.

> **NOTE**
>
> Many menu commands have keyboard shortcuts. Chapter 2, "Working with Menus and Dialog Boxes," will teach you more about using both the mouse and the keyboard to work with menus.

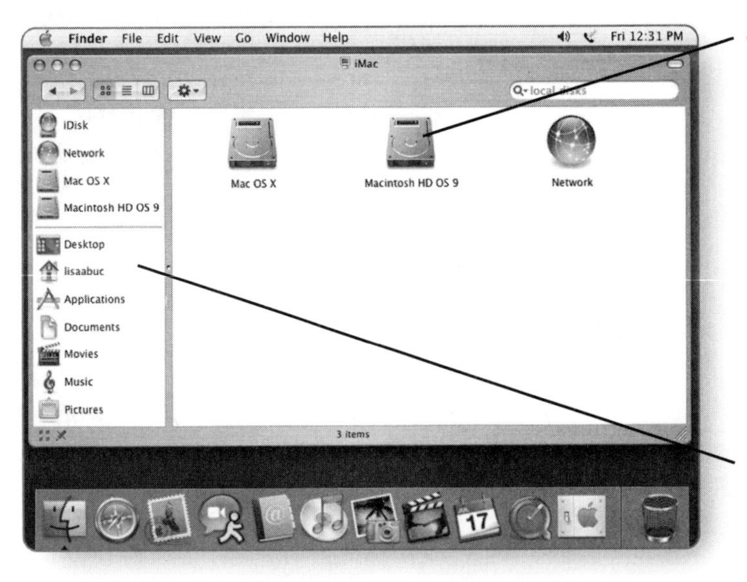

- **Finder**. The Finder application enables you to work with the desktop and the folders, files, and applications on the system's hard drive and any other disks connected to the system. When you switch to the Finder, its menu bar appears at the top of the desktop.
- **Finder window Sidebar**. The pane at the left side of the Finder window enables you to navigate quickly to key folders and locations on the system's hard drive. See the section called "Customizing the Finder Window Sidebar" in Chapter 8 to learn how to set up this pane as you prefer. The buttons above the Sidebar, technically said to be on the Finder window Toolbar even though it doesn't look like a toolbar, also enable you to navigate and to change the way you view files and folders in the Finder

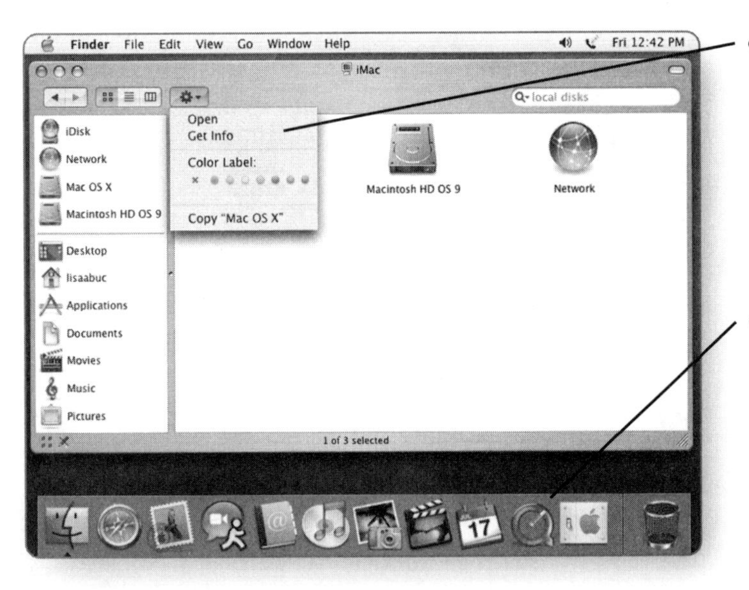

- **Action pop-up menu.** This pop-up menu offers choices for working with the item that's currently selected in the Finder window. Click on the far right button above the Sidebar to open this menu.
- **Dock**. The Dock appears along the bottom of the screen. Use the icons in the left section of the Dock (to the left of the dividing line) to start programs and switch between running programs.

The icons in the right section represent minimized document files, document or server shortcuts that you can click to open or go to the document or server, and Trash, which you can use to delete files and eject disks.

NOTE

Mac OS X uses a graphics technology called *Quartz Extreme* along with powerful video cards on many Macs shipped starting in 2001 to render fonts and graphics more quickly and with more precision. With Quartz Extreme, screen images appear even crisper, windows resize and scroll more quickly, and the OS can use special effects such as fading and cube animation.

Reviewing Mac OS X Version 10.3 Features

Mac OS X Version 10.3 offers a wide variety of programs, utilities, and features that you can use to perform tasks and set up the system as you prefer. Again, you'll learn more about many of these features in later chapters throughout the book. The following table summarizes the basic programs, utilities, and features you're most likely to use for now. (As you work further in Mac OS X Version 10.3 and this book, you'll discover even more!)

NOTE

Macintosh HD is the default name for the system's hard disk drive. (The following table references disk locations.) If you partitioned your system's hard drive in order to preserve an earlier OS version, you may have named the disk holding Mac OS X Version 10.3 something else, instead, such as Mac OS X.

Name	Location	Description
Finder	Dock	Opens a new Finder window.
Safari	Dock or Macintosh HD> Applications	Uses Apple's new Web browser to view pages of information from the World Wide Web.
Mail	Dock or Macintosh HD> Applications folder	Manage your email.
iChat AV	Dock or Macintosh HD> Applications folder	Chat online in real time with friends and colleagues.
Address Book	Dock or Macintosh HD> Applications folder	Track and update your list of contacts in the Address Book.
iTunes	Dock or Macintosh HD> Applications folder	Organize and play your digital music files.
IPhoto	Dock or Macintosh HD> Applications folder	Organize digital photos or order prints with this application.
iMovie	Dock or Macintosh HD> Applications folder	Save video clips, organize clips into a movie, add transitions and titles, and export finished productions with this application.
iCal	Dock or Macintosh HD> Applications folder	Manage your schedule with this application, included with the OS for the first time.
QuickTime Player	Dock or Macintosh HD> Applications folder	View QuickTime movies (digital video) and work with still images.
System Preferences	Dock or Macintosh HD> Applications folder	Enables you to choose many aspects of how Mac OS X looks and works.
Acrobat Reader	Macintosh HD> Applications folder	Read and navigate lengthier PDF (Adobe Acrobat) files.
Calculator	Macintosh HD> Applications folder	Check your math with this application.
Chess	Macintosh HD> Applications folder	Play chess against your Mac by using the Chess application.
DVD Player	Macintosh HD> Applications folder	Play your DVD videos with this handy tool.

Name	Location	Description
Font Book	Macintosh HD> Applications folder	Manage fonts on your system.
Image Capture	Dock or Macintosh HD> Applications folder	Download images from a compatible digital camera to your Mac.
Internet Connect	Macintosh HD> Applications folder	Set up a dial-up connection to use for the Internet.
iSync	Macintosh HD> Applications folder	Synchronize Address Book and iCal information with a Bluetooth phone, iPod, or Palm OS device (new to OS). If you join .Mac, you also can use iSync to synchronize information between multiple Mac systems.
Preview	Macintosh HD> Applications folder	Open and print graphics and .PDF (Adobe Acrobat) files.
Sherlock	Macintosh HD> Applications folder	Search for files on your system or to find information from the World Wide Web.
Stickies	Macintosh HD> Applications folder	Create electronic "sticky notes" that you can place on your Desktop to remind yourself of important tasks or items.
TextEdit	Macintosh HD> Applications folder	Create, save, and edit .RTF (text) files.
Disk Utility	Macintosh HD> Applications> Utilities folder	Format and repair disks.
Grab	Macintosh HD> Applications> Utilities folder	Take pictures of your screen.
Keychain Access	Macintosh HD> Applications> Utilities folder	Enhance system security with this utility.
Multiple Users	Macintosh HD> Applications> Utilities folder	Manage user access to the system with this utility.
Print Center	Macintosh HD> Applications> Utilities folder	Set up and manage printers to work with Mac OS X.
Stuffit Expander	Macintosh HD> Applications> Utilities folder	Expand a compressed file.

Putting the Mac to Sleep and Waking It Up

The sleep feature enables your Mac to conserve power when it's not in use. After a designated time of inactivity (which you can adjust in Mac OS X Version 10.3 System Preferences, as described in Chapter 9, "Changing Essential System Preferences"), the hard disk and monitor will go into the power- or battery-conserving sleep mode. Sleep mode also helps extend the life of flat panel displays. You can put the system to sleep at will, such as when you need to be away from your desk for a designated period of time. Using sleep mode creates less wear and tear on the system than repetitively turning the system off and on. That's because sleep mode keeps a small supply of power flowing to system components, so that they stay warm and can ramp up more smoothly when the system leaves sleep mode. In contrast, starting the system zaps a higher amount of electricity to the system all at once, taxing the components.

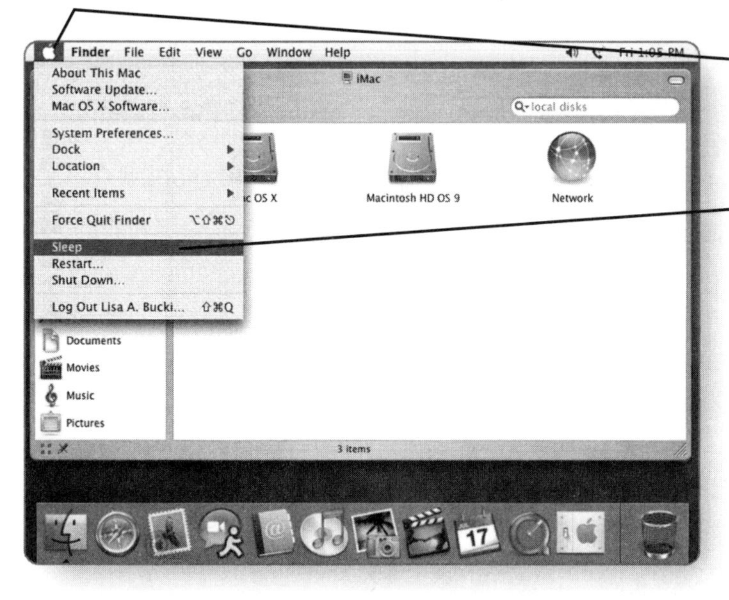

1. **Click** on the **Apple icon** (Apple menu) on the menu bar. The Apple menu will appear.
2. **Click** on **Sleep**. The screen will turn black as the system goes to sleep.
3. **Press a key, wiggle the mouse**, or **click the mouse button**. The Mac will wake up, and the desktop will reappear.

Shutting Down

While during the workday, it's best to use sleep mode to preserve the system hardware, there may be circumstances where you want to turn your Mac off, such as when you're leaving on vacation or want to protect the system during an electrical storm. (In the latter case, you also should unplug the system and all components, including disconnecting the modem from the phone jack.) When you want to turn off your Mac, you need to close any open applications and the OS and then power down the system. This ensures a safe shutdown that won't in any way damage the system or software settings.

> **NOTE**
>
> If you encounter a system problem, you also can restart the system. See the section called "Restarting the System" in Chapter 21 to learn more.

Using a Menu to Shut Down

You can use a menu command to shut down your Macintosh.

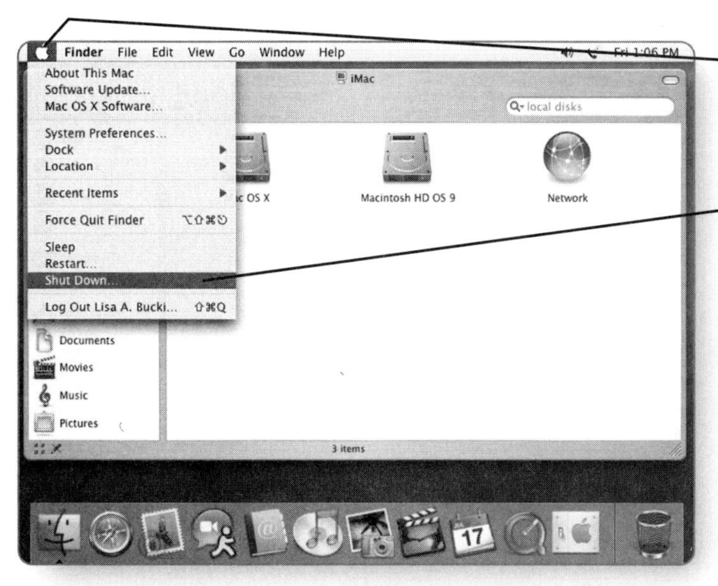

1. Click on the **Apple icon** on the menu bar. The Apple menu will appear.

2. Click on **Shut Down**. On some systems, the desktop will disappear from the screen, and the system will shut down. In other cases, an alert box will open to prompt you to verify that the system did shut down.

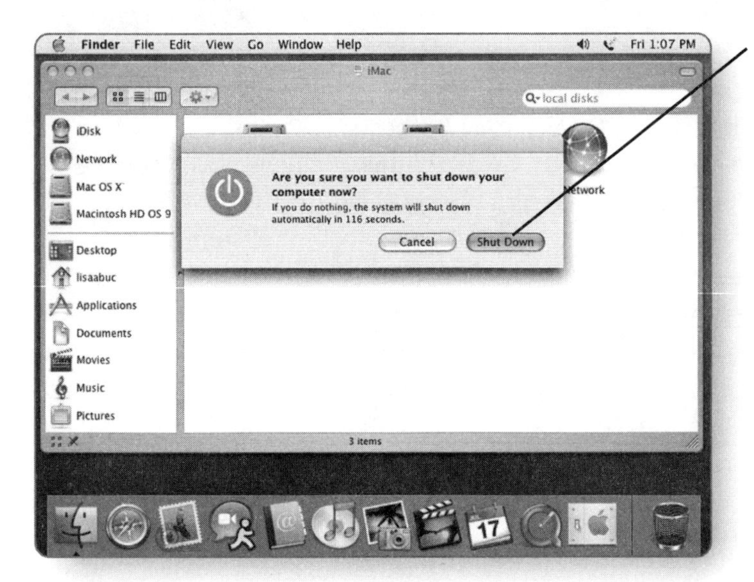

3. Click on **Shut Down**. The desktop will disappear from the screen, and the system will shut down.

> **NOTE**
>
> If you forgot to save any document or file on which you were working before choosing the Shut Down command, a dialog box appears to remind you to save your work. You can click on Save to display a Save As dialog box (if needed) so that you can save the file, or click on Don't Save to continue shutting down without saving your work.

Using the Power Button to Shut Down

If you prefer a single button approach to shutting down the system, you can use the Power button on some Macintosh models.

1. **Press** the **Power button**. An alert box will open to prompt you to verify that the system shut down.

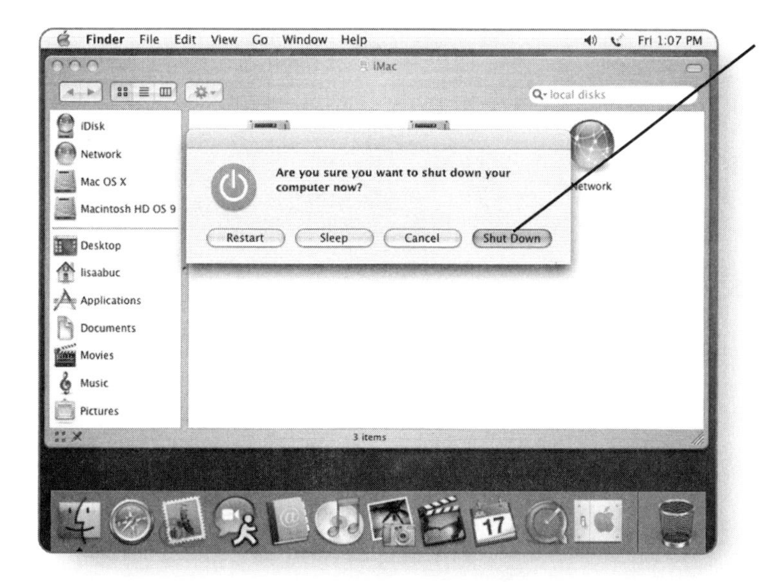

2. **Click** on **Shut Down**. The desktop will disappear from the screen, and the system will shut down.

> **NOTE**
>
> If your Mac is frozen, try pressing ⌘+Control+Power or ⌘+Option+Shift+Power to restart or shut down. Also, depending on your Mac model and keyboard, pressing Control+Return may display a dialog box with options for restarting or shutting down.

2

Working with Menus and Dialog Boxes

Early Apple personal computers shook up the computer industry by adding a new input device called a *mouse*. With the mouse and the graphical user interface created for the Apple systems, users no longer had to remember arcane commands or tricky keyboard combinations. The mouse made selecting a command almost as easy as moving a finger. In this chapter, you will learn how to:

- Recognize the Finder pull-down menus.
- Choose a menu command.
- Use a contextual menu when you need it.
- Work with dialog box choices.
- Get Help from the system.

Reviewing the Desktop Menus

Virtually every computer program includes a set of commands and options you can find and access via menus. Like other programs, the Finder offers a series of pull-down menus that are found on the menu bar that spans the top of the desktop. When you click on the name of a pull-down menu on the menu bar, the menu appears, listing its commands. When you start or choose another application in Mac OS X Version 10.3, its menu bar will replace the Finder menu bar at the top of the desktop.

> **NOTE**
>
> If you've used a prior Macintosh operating system, you may be tempted to skip over this introduction to the Mac OS X Version 10.3 menus. However, the menus have changed substantially in all versions of Mac OS X, so you should pause to review this section.

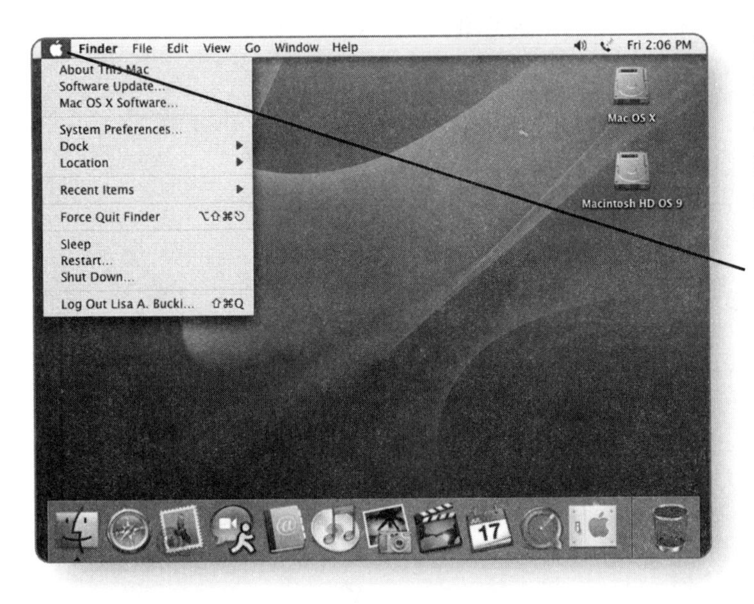

Learning the menus available via the Finder menu bar in Mac OS X Version 10.3 is a good starting point for learning your way around your Macintosh.

- The **Apple menu** enables you to review basic information about your Mac, log out, shut down, restart, and put your Macintosh to sleep. The Apple menu remains the same regardless of which application you are using.

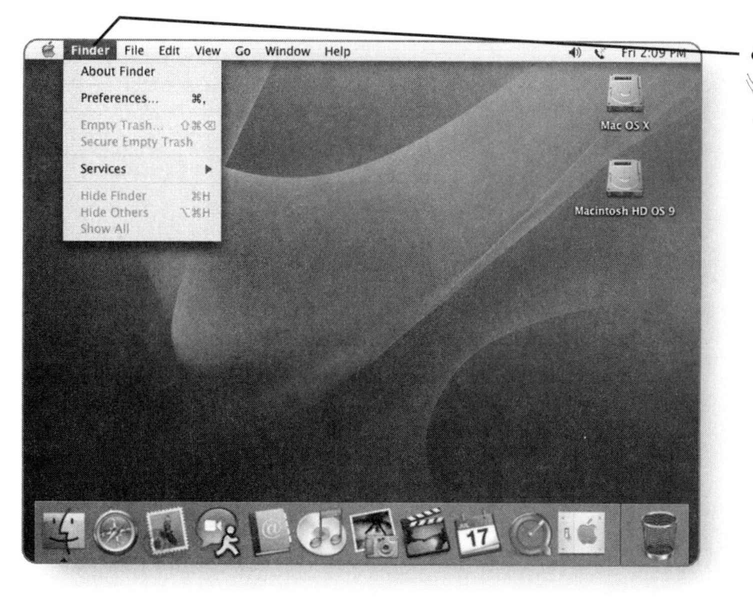

- The **Application menu** always appears to the right of the Apple menu. The name of the menu changes depending on the application that you're currently working with. For example, when you're working with the Finder, the Finder menu appears here and enables you to hide any open Finder windows or hide any other windows that may be open. You can also change the picture on your desktop and empty your Trash by using the commands available on the Finder menu.

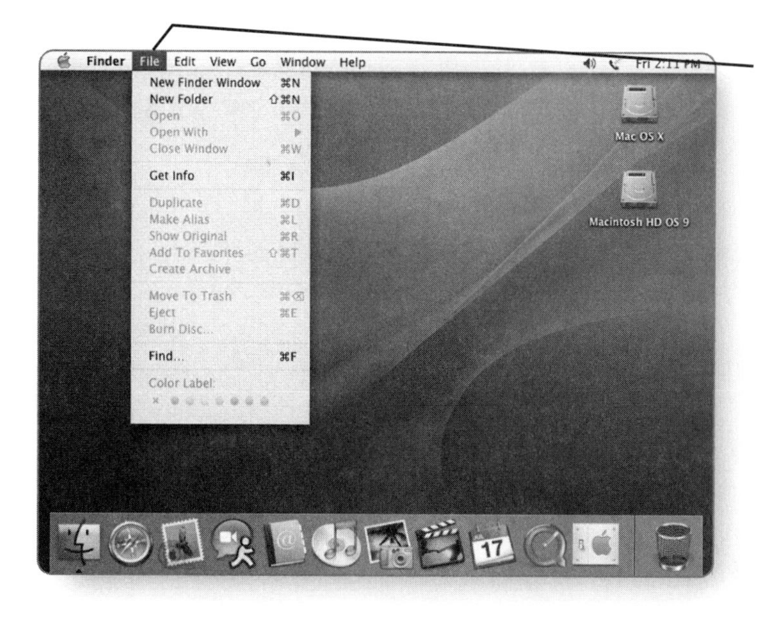

- The **File menu** enables you to work with files, and it includes file management tools. For example, you can open another Finder window, create a folder, open a selected file or folder, close the current window, view file information, trash and duplicate files, add a favorite file to the Sidebar, add a color label to a file or folder, or find files. You also can burn a CD-R (see the section called "Burning a CD-R" in Chapter 6 to learn more) if you have a CD-R drive installed with your system.

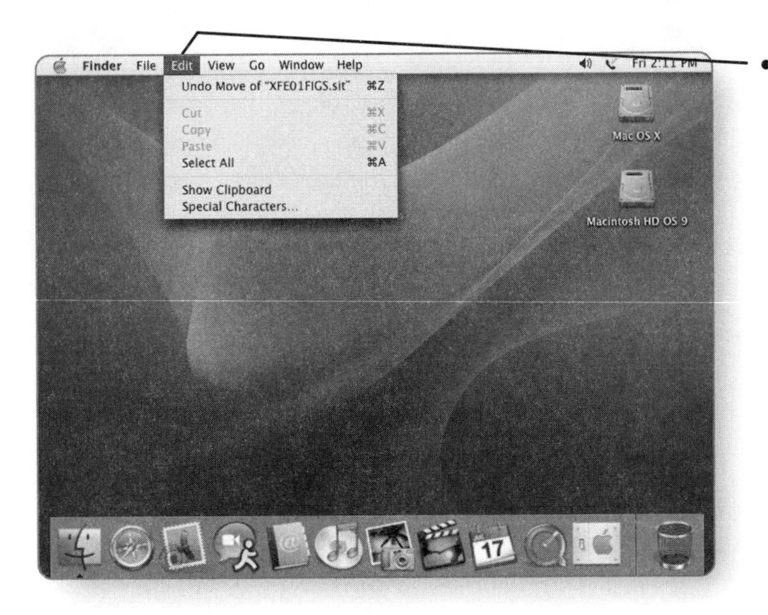

- The **Edit menu** enables you to work with the contents of a folder. You can cut, copy, and paste file and folder name information; select all the icons in a folder; and even undo your mistakes! You also can select files, copy them, and then paste them into another folder location.

- The **View menu** enables you to change the way files and folders are listed in a window. In addition, you can arrange window contents, show and hide a Finder window toolbar, or even display the options for changing overall view settings.

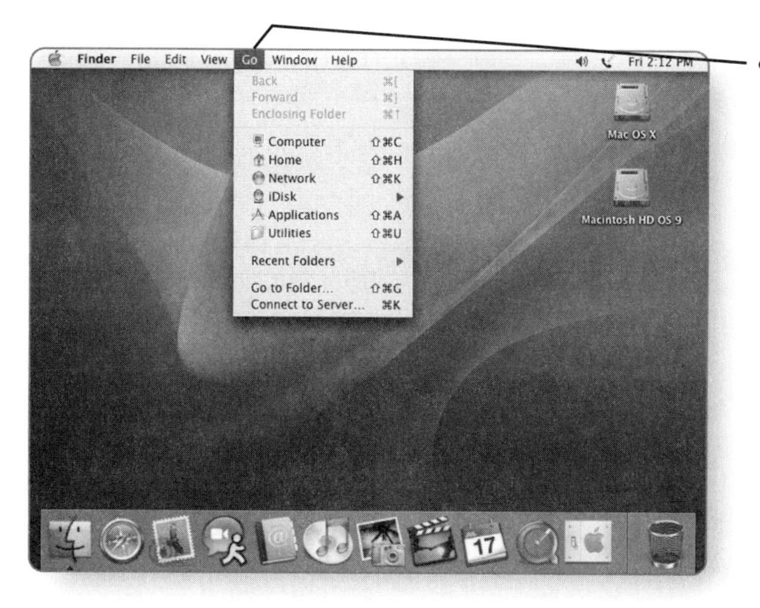

- The **Go menu** helps you navigate more quickly in Mac OS X Version 10.3. You can open a specific folder in a Finder window, display a default Finder window such as your Home folder, jump to a favorite or recently used folder, or connect to a network server.

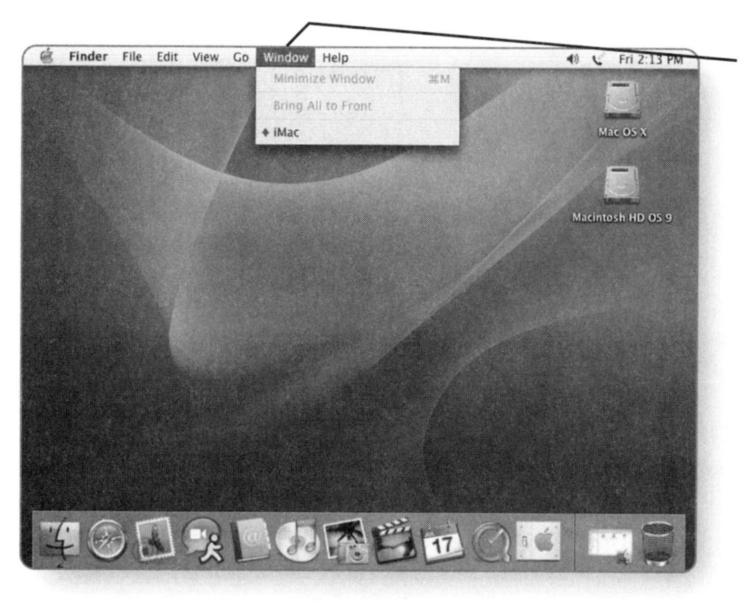

- The **Window menu** enables you to reduce a window to an icon on the Dock or switch to a particular window.

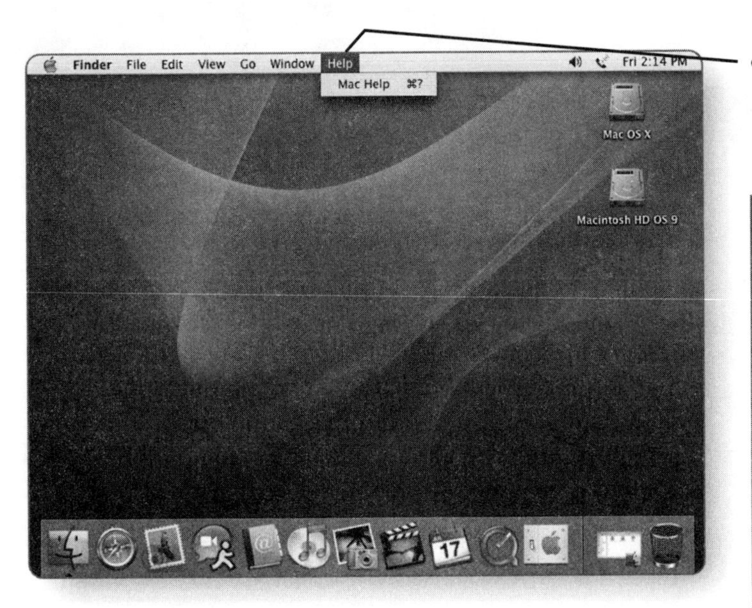

- Use the **Help menu** to launch Help Viewer and get Mac OS X help.

> **NOTE**
>
> Different icons may also appear near the right end of the menu bar, such as the small speaker and phone handset icons shown in this chapter's illustrations. You can use these icons to accomplish actions such as adjusting system volume, connecting to the Internet, and displaying your iChat status. You can control whether icons appear by using preference settings in the applicable programs and utilities.

Choosing a Menu Command

Using the mouse to choose a command is a rather simple operation. Further, knowing the ins and outs of working with menus makes you much more efficient in working with Mac OS X Version 10.3. The techniques described in this section apply not only to menus in Mac OS X 10.3 and earlier Mac OS X versions, but also to Mac applications with which you'll be working.

1. **Click** on the **menu name** on the menu bar. The menu will open.

> **TIP**
>
> With a menu already open, press the left or right arrow keys to move to and open another menu instead.

2. **Drag** the **mouse** down the menu (or use the up and down arrow keys) to the command you desire. The command will be highlighted.

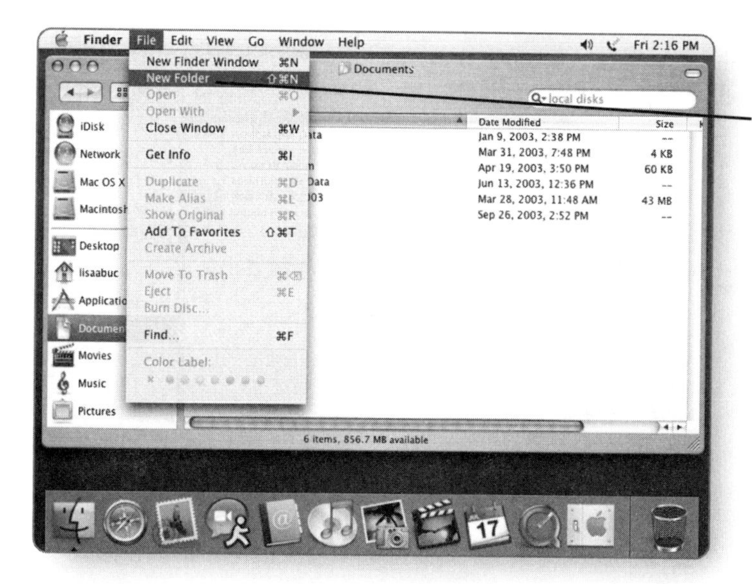

3. **Click** on the **command** to select it. The command will be executed.

> **TIP**
>
> If you press and hold the Option key while the File or Window menu is open, a command on the menu changes. On the File menu, the Close Window command changes to the Close All command. On the Window menu, the Bring All to Front command changes to the Arrange in Front command.

Identifying Special Commands in Menus

Mac OS X Version 10.3 makes it easy to recognize special commands that are available from pull-down menus.

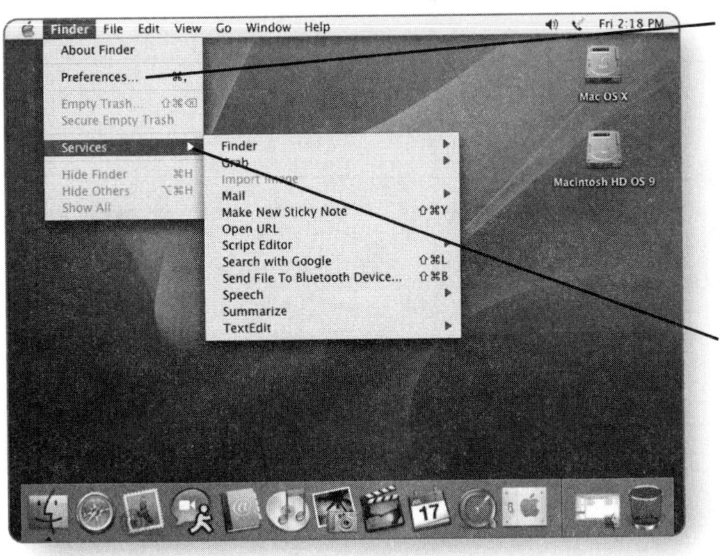

- A command that has an ellipsis (...) following its name will open a dialog box to ask you for more information. See the section "Responding to a Dialog Box" later in this chapter to learn more about working with dialog boxes.
- A command that has an arrow to the far right of its name will display a submenu with additional commands when you highlight it. Drag the pointer down the submenu to highlight the desired command; then click on the command name.

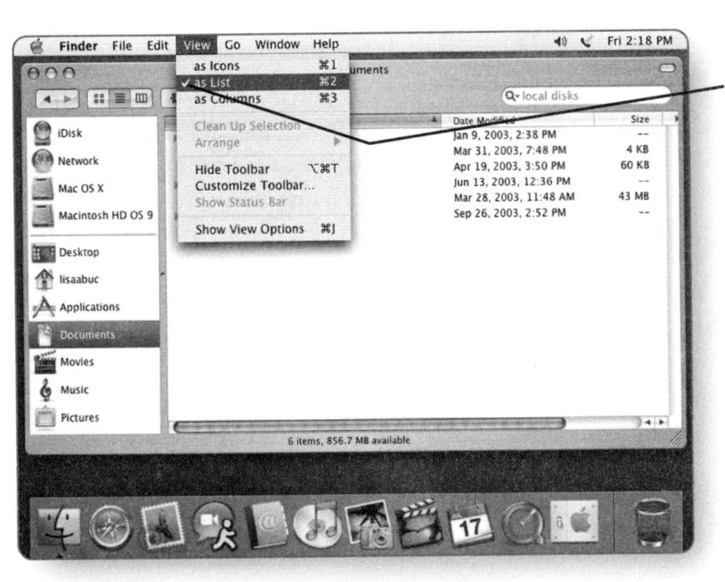

- A command that has a check to the left of its name is the currently selected choice among a group of related choices. Click on another choice in the group to choose it instead.

> **NOTE**
>
> Click away from the menu on the desktop or press the Escape (esc) key to close or cancel a menu without making a selection.

Using a Keyboard Shortcut to Choose a Command

Using a keyboard shortcut saves time because you don't have to complete multiple steps—clicking on a menu and then clicking on a command. Plus, if you're typing in a document, it's generally faster to keep your hands on the keyboard and use a shortcut key combination rather than taking a hand off the keyboard to grab the mouse.

To learn a shortcut key for a particular command, look at the command on its menu. If a shortcut key combination is available for a command, "shorthand" characters to the right of the command name tell you what keys to press as the shortcut. For a command to work, you need to press all the keys together. Usually, it's easier to press and hold the first key, or press and hold any others, and then release them all. (This book uses a + symbol between the keys to press when it presents a shortcut key combination.) Following are the characters you'll see on the menu to represent special keyboard keys:

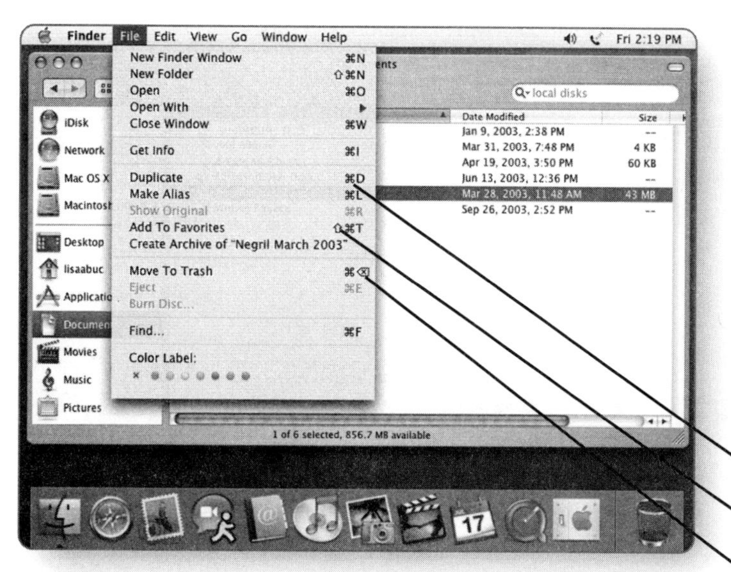

- Command key
- Shift key
- Delete key

You also may need to choose the tilde (~) key by pressing Shift+` on the keyboard when called for by a keyboard shortcut. Finally, some keyboard combinations may call for the Control key or Option key. (Note that some applications refer to the Alt key; press the Option key whenever the Alt key is called for.)

Using a Contextual Menu

A contextual menu offers commands for dealing with a particular selection or item. Because the contextual menu applies to only the selected command or location, it displays a more limited range of commands that pertain specifically to that selection or location. This means you can more quickly identify and choose the appropriate command to use. In Mac OS X Version 10.3, you'll use contextual menus often for working with files and folders in a Finder window, or for working with items on the desktop. (You also can display a contextual menu within an application or file to see commands for working with the current selection.)

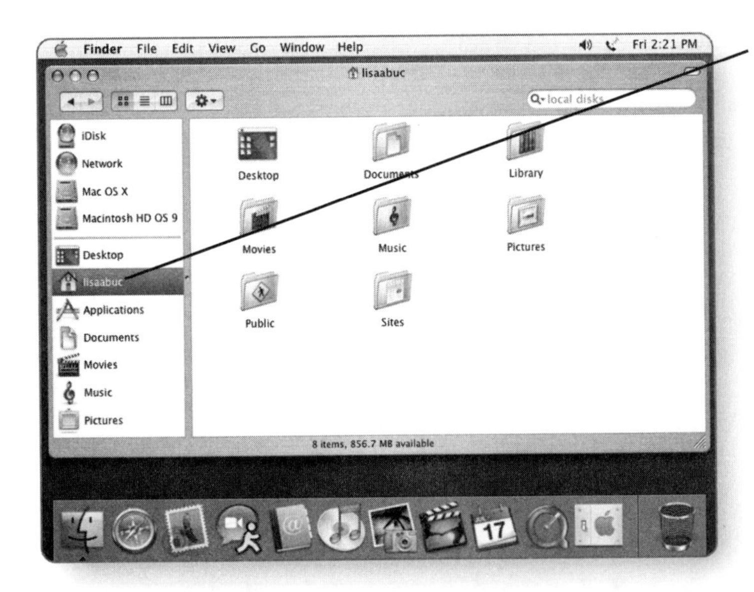

1. **Navigate** to the **folder** that holds the file or folder to work with. For example, **click** on the **folder** with the House icon and your user name (your Home folder) in the Finder window Sidebar. The Finder window will display the contents of your Home folder—the folder set up for your files in Mac OS X Version 10.3. This folder already contains a number of predefined folders (subfolders) for you.

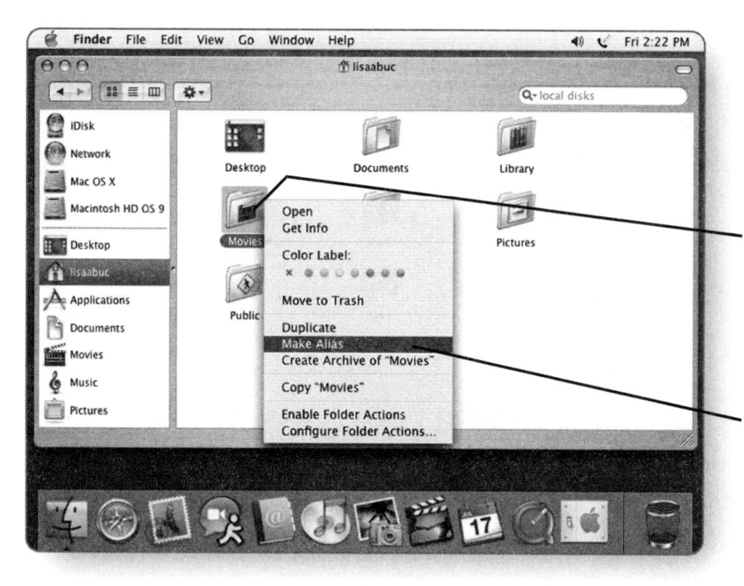

2. **Press** and **hold** the **Control key**. The mouse pointer will change to include a small menu icon.

3. **Click** on the **desired file** or **folder**, such as the Movies folder in this example. The contextual menu will appear.

4. **Move** the **mouse pointer** down the contextual menu to highlight the command you want to perform and then **click** the **command**.

Responding to a Dialog Box

Remember that if a command on a menu includes an ellipsis (...), selecting the command opens a dialog box so that you can provide further information about how the command should work. Dialog boxes and some specialized windows in Mac OS X Version 10.3 include a number of different types of options.

> **NOTE**
>
> The controls described next also appear in *sheets* throughout Mac OS X Version 10.3 and Mac OS X applications. Rather than opening in its own floating window, a sheet drops down from the title bar of another window, such as a file window title bar. The sheet stays attached to the window, so you can move to other documents or applications, leaving the sheet open until you decide what options to select.

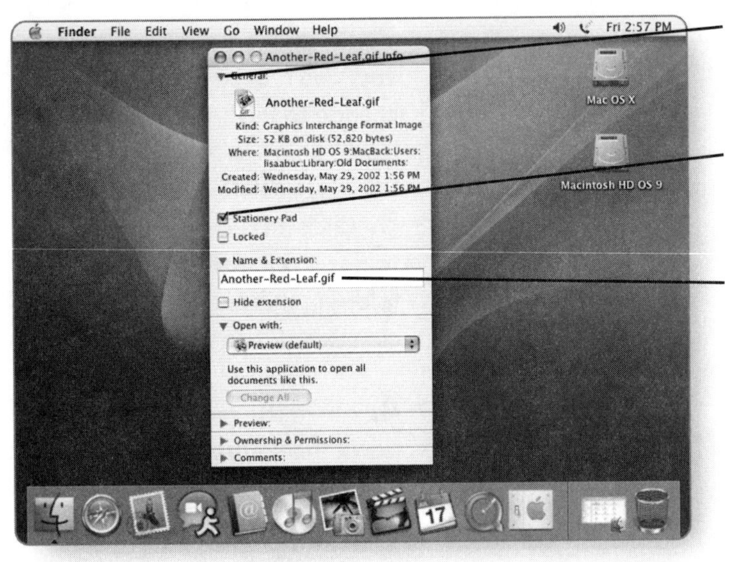

- **Arrow.** Click to display or hide the choices in a section of a dialog box.
- **Check box.** Click on a check box to check (enable) it or uncheck (disable) it.
- **Text box.** A text box or entry box enables you to type in and edit an entry, such as a file name. Click in the text box and type an entry as needed. Or, select the contents of the text box by dragging over the existing entry and type a new entry to replace the previous entry.

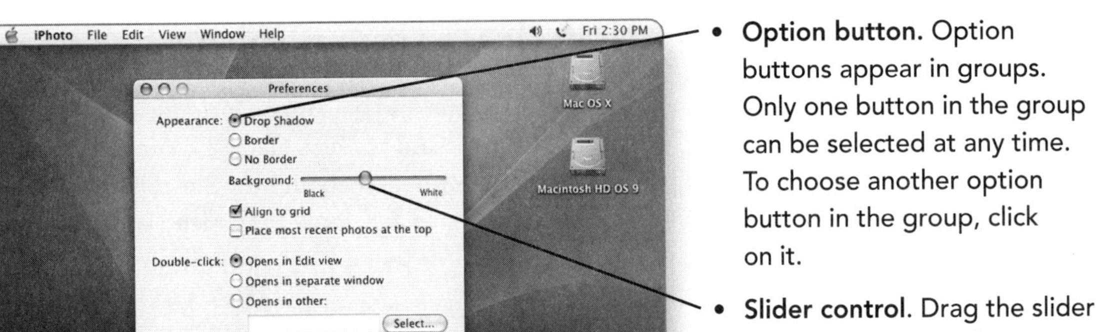

- **Option button.** Option buttons appear in groups. Only one button in the group can be selected at any time. To choose another option button in the group, click on it.
- **Slider control.** Drag the slider on the slider control to change a setting.
- **Pop-up menu.** Click on the double-arrow button to display a pop-up menu; then click on the desired choice in the menu.

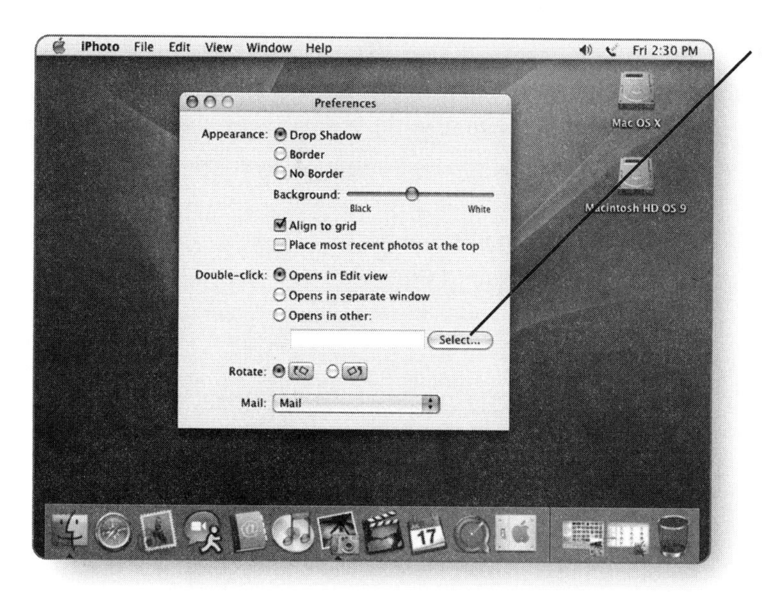

- **Command button.** Click on a command button to display another dialog box (if an ellipsis follows the button name) or to continue with the dialog box choices. Many dialog boxes include Cancel and OK command buttons. Click on Cancel to close the dialog box without applying its choices or executing the command. Click on OK to finish the command, apply the dialog box choices, and close the dialog box.

NOTE

Some dialog boxes in Mac OS X Version 10.3 actually work as windows that you can resize and close. If this is the case, you'll see special red, yellow, and green buttons in the upper-left corner of the window. Chapter 3, "Working with Finder (and Other) Windows," describes the techniques for using these buttons. Also note that some dialog boxes include a question mark or Help button on which you can click to display help about the dialog box choices.

Getting Help When You Need It

Macintosh systems and software have long had a reputation for being virtually idiot-proof. Computer novices, users making a shift from another type of system, and even grade school children could always jump right in and click and peck their way through nearly any operation. That being said, however, today's Macintoshes are more sophisticated than ever, accommodating a wide variety of hardware add-ons, communications connections, and more. Given the wide variety of features in Mac OS X Version 10.3, even experienced Macintosh users may need to review some helpful information now and then. Follow these steps to get help in Mac OS X Version 10.3:

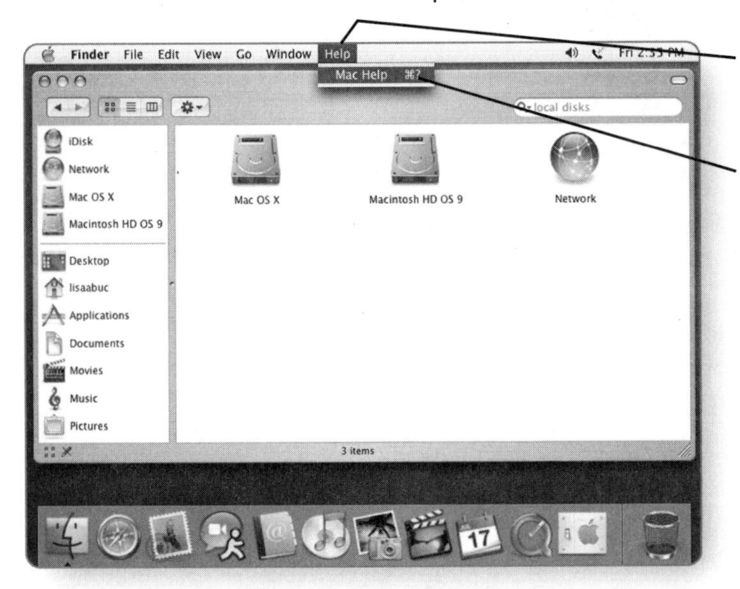

1. **Click** on **Help**. The Help menu will appear.

2. **Click** on **Mac Help**. The Help Viewer will open.

> **NOTE**
>
> You also can get help within an application by choosing Help, (Application Name) Help. Or, to get help in a dialog box, click on the ? button.

3. Click on a **category**. The Help Viewer window will display subcategories in that category.

> **NOTE**
>
> To return to general help about Mac OS X or to switch to help about another installed application, click the Library menu and then click on Mac Help or the choice for help about the desired application.

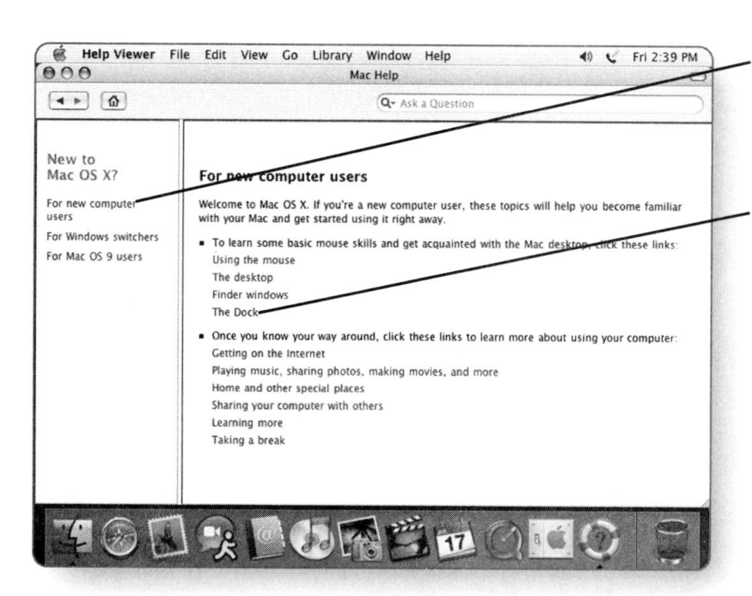

4. Click on a **subcategory link** on the left pane. The right pane will display a list of help topics.

5. Click on the **desired topic.** Help about that topic will appear.

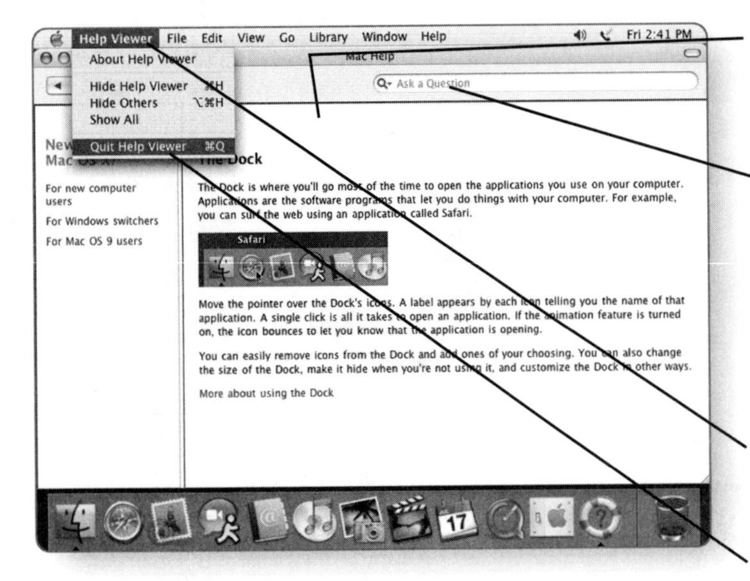

6. **Read** the **help** as needed.

> **TIP**
>
> To search for help, enter a word or phrase to search for in the Ask a Question text box and then press Return.

7. **Click** on **Help Viewer**. The Help Viewer menu will appear.

8. **Click** on **Quit Help Viewer**. Help Viewer will close.

3

Working with Finder (and Other) Windows

As in prior Macintosh operating systems, windows on the Mac OS X Version 10.3 desktop hold applications, files (documents), and folders. You perform all your work within windows. The use of windows also provides an elegant solution to the need to work on multiple tasks at (nearly) the same time. You can move seamlessly between windows and tasks to handle your work in the order you prefer. This chapter builds your Mac OS X skills by leading you through a number of window management tasks. In this chapter, you will learn to:

- Identify the parts of the new Finder window.
- Display another Finder window when needed.
- Choose the window in which you want to work.
- Navigate in a Finder window and change the view.
- Move, resize, dock, or close a window.
- Use Exposé to arrange windows with a single key press.

Reviewing the New Finder Window

As you learned in Chapter 1, the Finder enables you to work with the folders and files on the system's hard disk and any other disks connected to the system. To understand how to work with a Finder window, you need to understand the parts of a window in Mac OS X Version 10.3.

Many of the features described here appear only in Finder windows. However, some of the features in this list also appear in application and file (document) windows.

- **Title bar.** The title bar area displays the name of the folder, application, or document in the window. You also can use the title bar to position the window as described in the later section "Moving a Window."

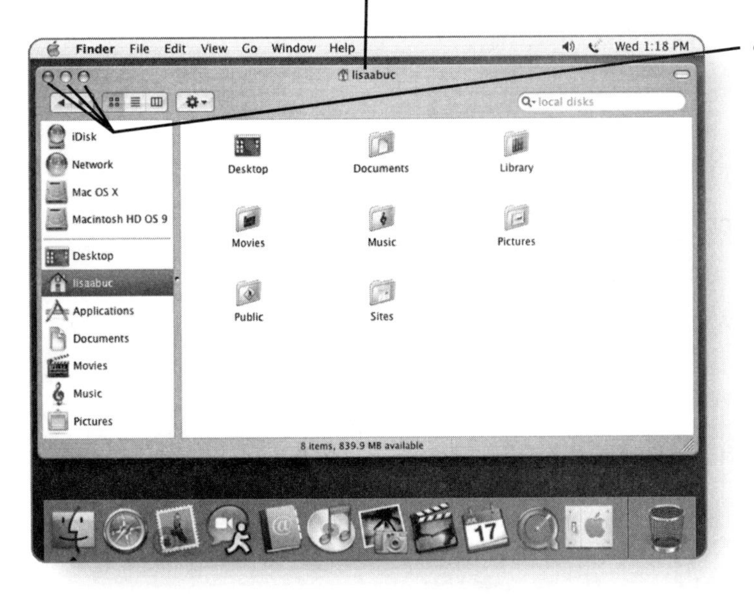

- **Close, Minimize, and Zoom buttons.** These buttons appear in the upper-left corner of Finder windows, application windows, document windows, and some dialog boxes. You can click on the buttons to manipulate the window; for example, to reduce the window to an icon on the Dock. Later sections of this chapter cover these buttons in more detail.

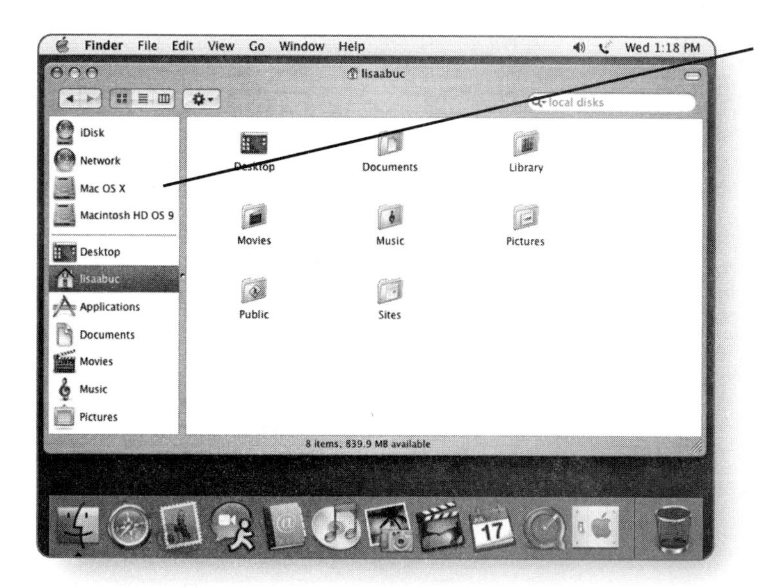

- **Finder window Sidebar.** The pane at the left side of the Finder window enables you to navigate more quickly to particular folders. The section later in this chapter called "Using the Finder Window Sidebar" explains the destination for each button, and the section called "Finding a File from the Finder Window" in Chapter 6 describes how to find a file using the Search text box in the Finder window.

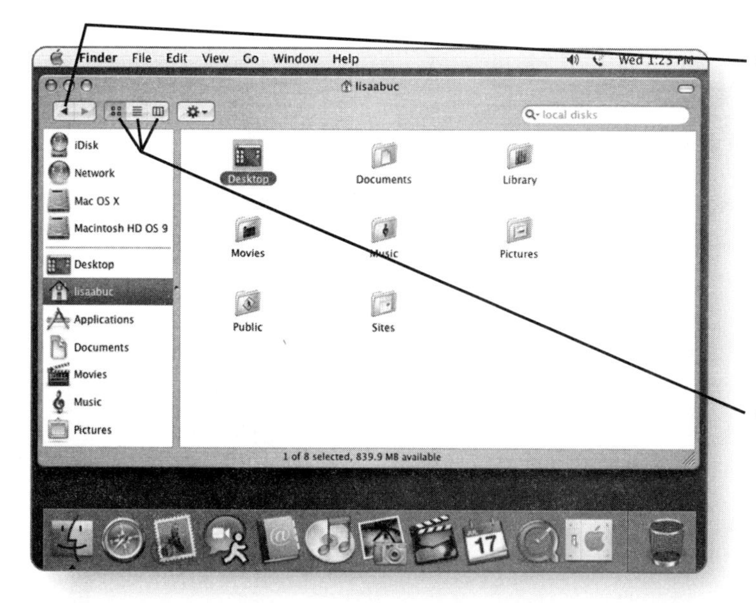

- **Back button.** After you've used a Finder toolbar button or another method to display the contents of a particular folder in the Finder window, you can click on this button to return to a previous location or folder where you were working.
- **View buttons.** By default, the Finder window contents appear in a large icon format. You can click on one of these buttons to change to another one of the views available in Mac OS X Version 10.3. See the section called "Changing a Finder Window View" later in this chapter to learn how the view buttons work.

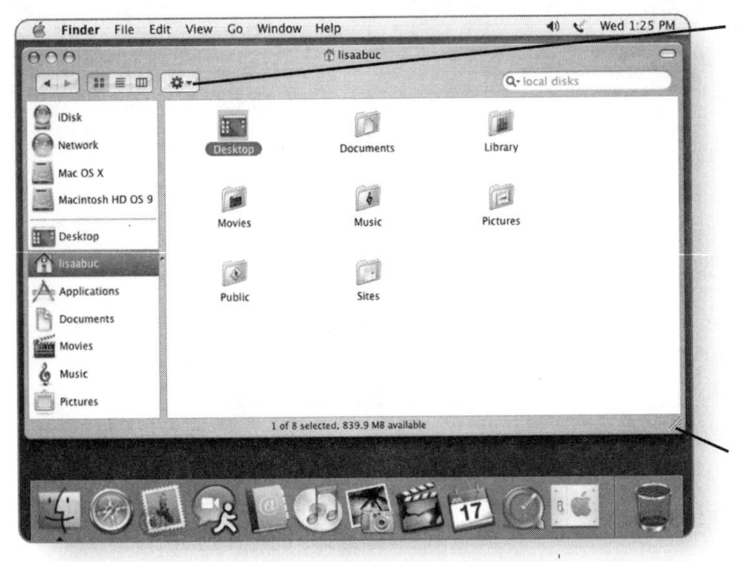

- **Action pop-up menu button.** Click on this button to open a pop-up menu that offers choices for working with the item that's currently selected in the Finder window. For example, you can get information about the selected item, assign a color label to it, or duplicate the item.
- **Size box.** You can use the size box to change the size of the window, as described in the later section "Resizing a Window."

> **TIP**
>
> You can change the Finder preferences so that each disk or folder you open appears in its own new window. To do so, click on the Finder; then click on Preferences. Click on the General button at the top of the window; then click on the Always open folders in a new window check box to check it.

Opening Another Finder Window

In Macintosh operating systems before the original Mac OS X release, each folder appeared in its own window. By contrast, Mac OS X enables you to navigate to a particular location within a single Finder window. As you make your way through various folders, the contents of the current Finder window simply change. This streamlined approach helps reduce clutter on the Desktop, making it easier for you to select a particular window.

On the other hand, there will be instances where you need to see multiple Finder windows onscreen, such as when you want to move a file from one folder to another. The following steps show you two different methods for opening another Finder window:

1. **Click** on **File.** The File menu will appear.

2. **Click** on **New Finder Window**. An additional Finder window will open.

> **TIP**
>
> Press ⌘+N to open a new Finder window. Press Shift+⌘+N to create a new folder.

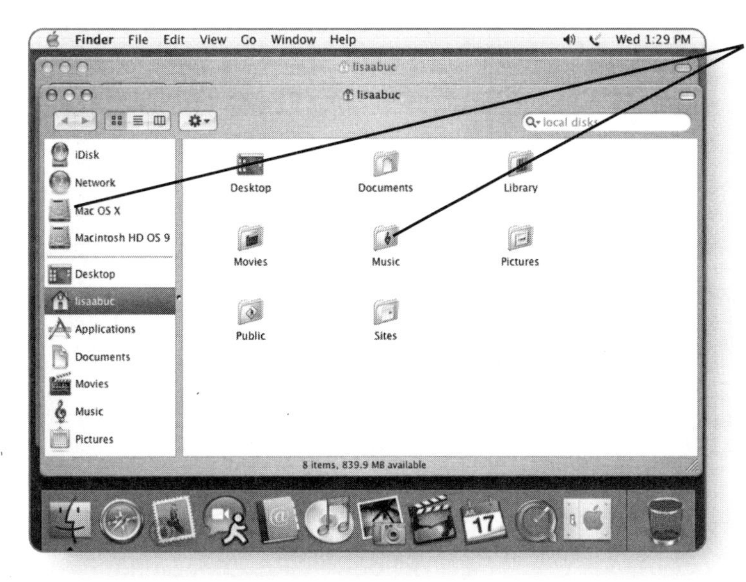

3. ⌘+ **click** a **Sidebar button** or **⌘+double-click** a **disk** or **folder icon**. A new window for the disk or folder appears.

Choosing a Window

Before you can work with the files or folders in a window, you must make the window the active window on your desktop. An active window is the frontmost window among all the windows on your desktop. Any command or action you take next will apply to the contents of the active window. There are several ways to move between open windows.

1. **Click** on **Window.** The Window menu will appear.

2. **Click** on the **name of the window** to display. The window will move in front of (on top of) other open windows.

OR

3. **Click** on a **visible portion of the window** you want to choose. The window will move in front of (on top of) the other open windows.

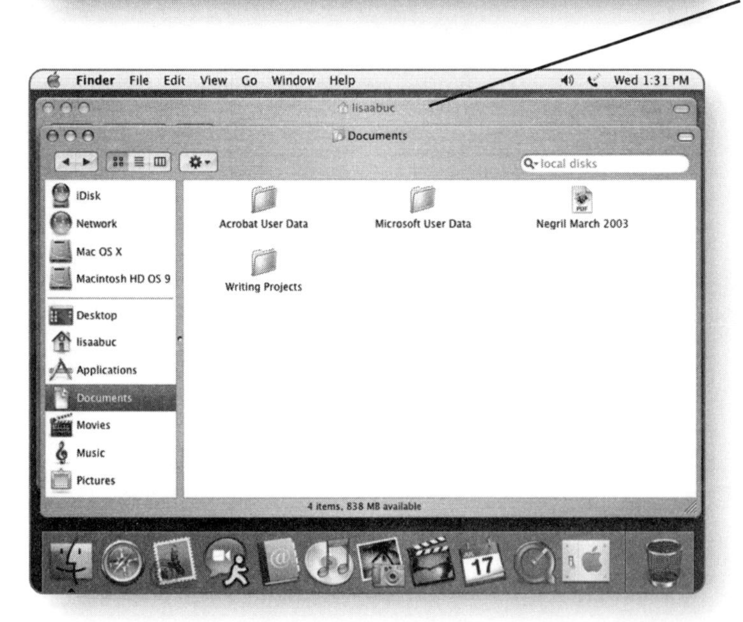

TIP

Most application menu bars also include a Window menu. Click on the Window menu and then click on the name of the document to make it the active document or window in the application.

Using the Finder Window Sidebar

Mac OS X Version 10.3 organizes applications and information for you in specific folders corresponding to the buttons in the Finder window Sidebar. For example, for each user (user name) set up for the system, Mac OS X Version 10.3 creates a Home folder to hold that user's working files. Clicking a Finder window Sidebar button opens a window that displays the contents of the corresponding folders or locations.

> **TIP**
>
> Resizing a Finder window may hide some of the Sidebar buttons. If you don't see the desired button, a scroll bar will appear so that you can scroll down the Sidebar.

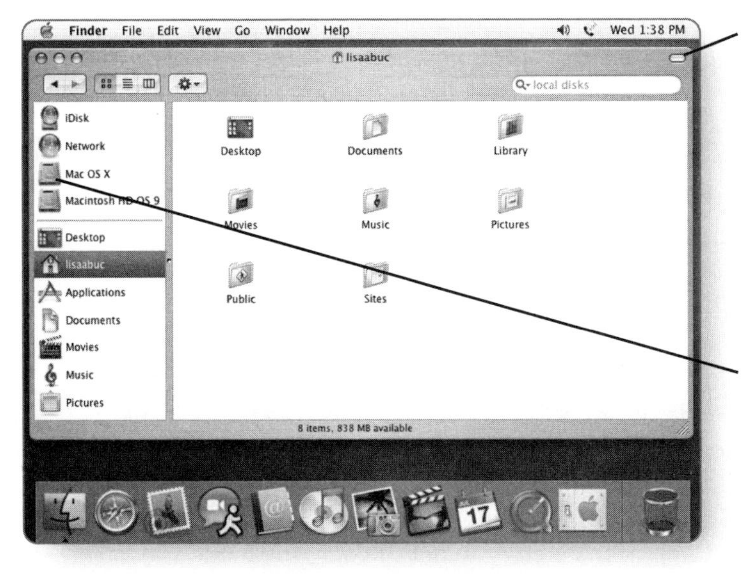

1. If you don't see the Finder window Sidebar and toolbar, **click** on the **oblong button** in the upper-right corner of the Finder window or **choose View, Show Toolbar**. The Finder window Sidebar and toolbar will appear.

2. **Click** on the **button for your boot disk.** The Finder window will display the contents of the disk that holds the Mac OS X operating system files.

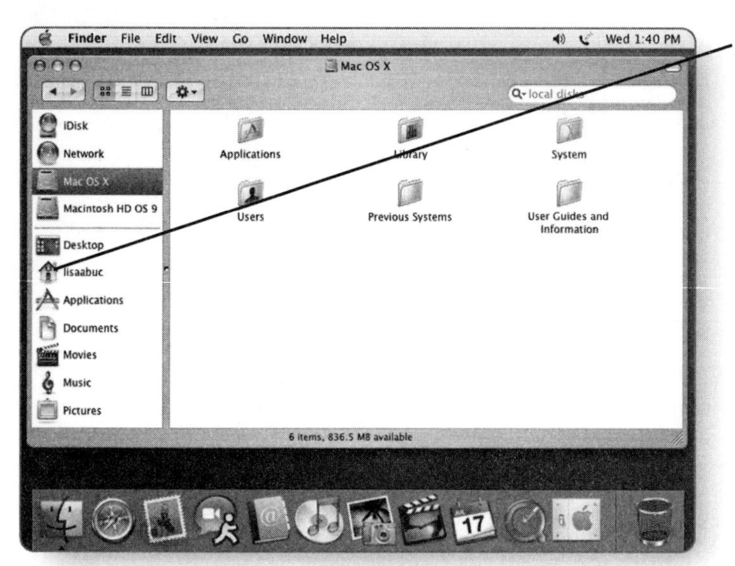

3. Click on the **Home button.** The Finder window will display the contents of the Home folder set up for your user name. By default, the Home folder contains additional folders for your documents, pictures, movies, and more.

TIP

Your home folder is not called "Home." Instead, Mac OS X Version 10.3 names your Home folder by using the first eight letters of the user name you specified when you used the Setup Assistant the first time you used Mac OS X. You also can use the Accounts pane of System Preferences to set your user name and password.

TIP

You can add an icon for a particular folder or file to the Finder window Sidebar by dragging the folder or file icon onto the Sidebar. Drag the icon back off the Sidebar to remove it at any later time. Note that the Sidebar doesn't offer a button for your Favorites folder (stored in the Library folder of your Home folder). You can use the drag-and-drop technique to add the Favorites folder to your Sidebar if you prefer.

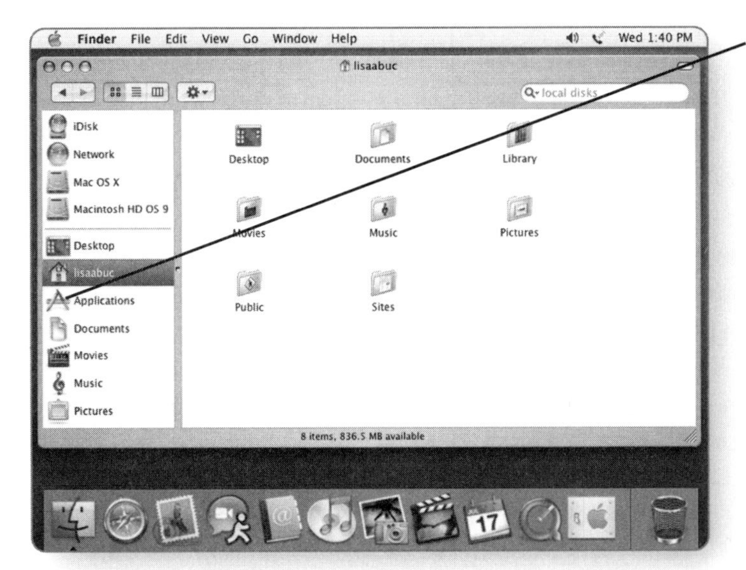

4. Click on the **Applications button**. The Finder window will display the Applications folder content. The Applications folder holds the applications that come with Mac OS X, as well as folders containing additional utilities and tools.

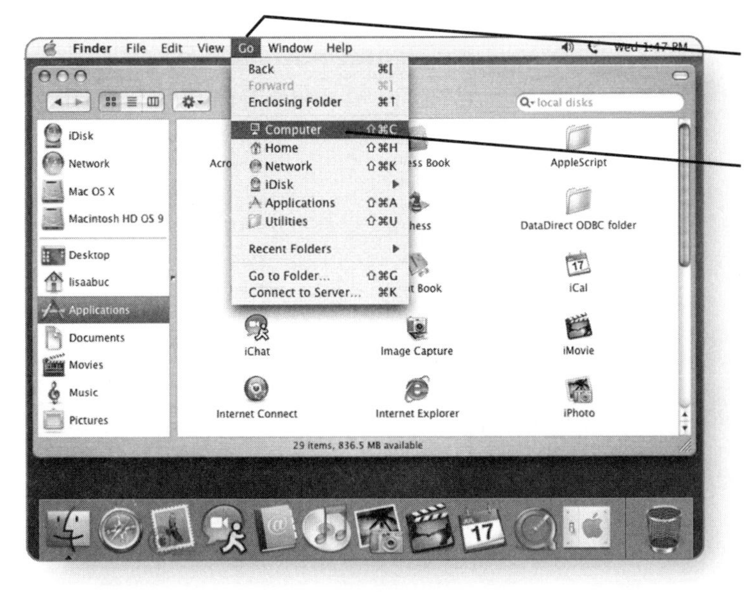

5. Click on **Go**. The Go menu will appear.

6. Click on **Computer**. The Finder window will display the disk drives (both internal and removable) connected to your system, as well as the Network choice you can use to view and connect with network servers.

Changing a Finder Window View

By default, Mac OS X Version 10.3 represents disks, files, and folders as large icons within a Finder window. This default view is called the *icon view*. You can change the way a Finder window lists its contents so that you can work in the most convenient view. In addition to the icon view, you can choose the list view, which presents a single list of file and folder names along with brief information about the file; or the column view, which illustrates the path or various folders within which the currently selected file or folder is located. The steps that follow show you how to choose a particular view.

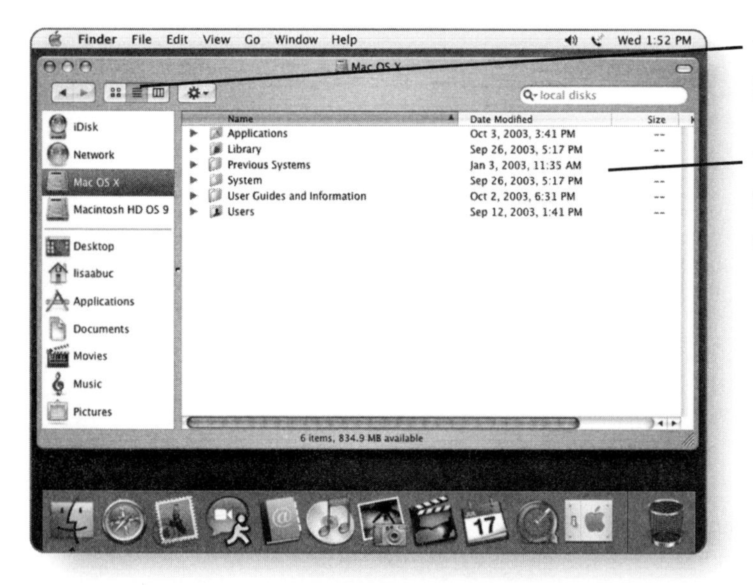

1. Click on the **List View button.**

The Finder window will display the contents of the folder (or disk) in the list view.

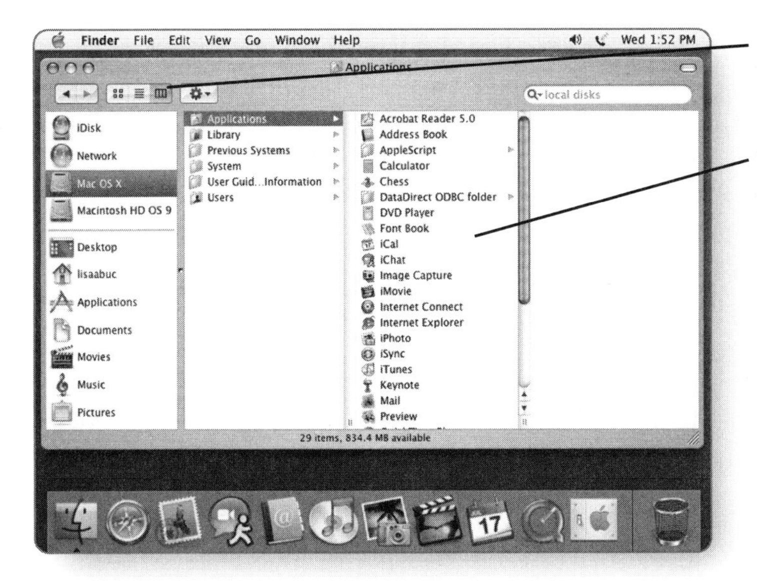

2. **Click** on the **Column View button**.

The Finder window will display the contents of the folder (or disk) in the column view. The Finder window displays the contents of the folder (or disk) in the column view.

3. **Click** on **View**. The View menu will appear.

4. **Click** on the **desired view**. The Finder window will display the contents of the folder (or disk) in the view you specified.

> **NOTE**
>
> If the commands for the various views are disabled (dimmed) on the View menu, it means that you haven't selected a Finder window. In that case, click on the desktop to close the View menu, click on a Finder window to make it active, and then choose the appropriate View menu command.

Manipulating Windows

We all like a nice, large desk so that we can organize our files and printouts into neat piles and still have a large workspace for the current task. As you switch from one task to another, typically you'll set aside one stack of paper, grab another stack, and carry on with your business. Similarly, you can work with the windows on the Mac OS X Version 10.3 desktop to arrange them as your work needs dictate. (This is why many computer users love a large monitor, which provides a great deal of room for arranging various windows.) The remainder of this chapter reviews the various techniques you can use to work with the Finder, disk, and file windows on your Mac OS X Version 10.3 desktop.

Moving a Window

When you move a window, you change its location. The following steps illustrate how to "make your move" with a Finder window, but the technique applies to any type of window or dialog box (but not sheets).

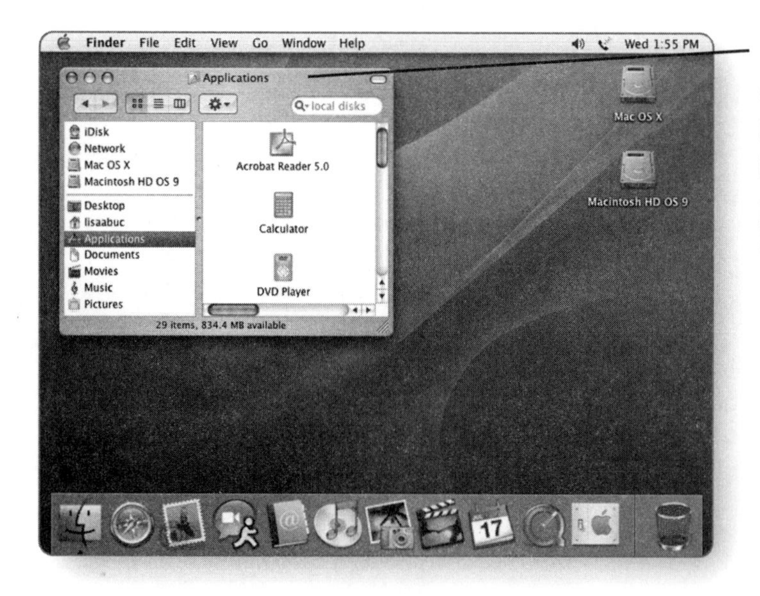

1. **Move** the **mouse pointer** over the active window's title bar. (Click the window to make it active first.) The mouse pointer will appear on the title bar.

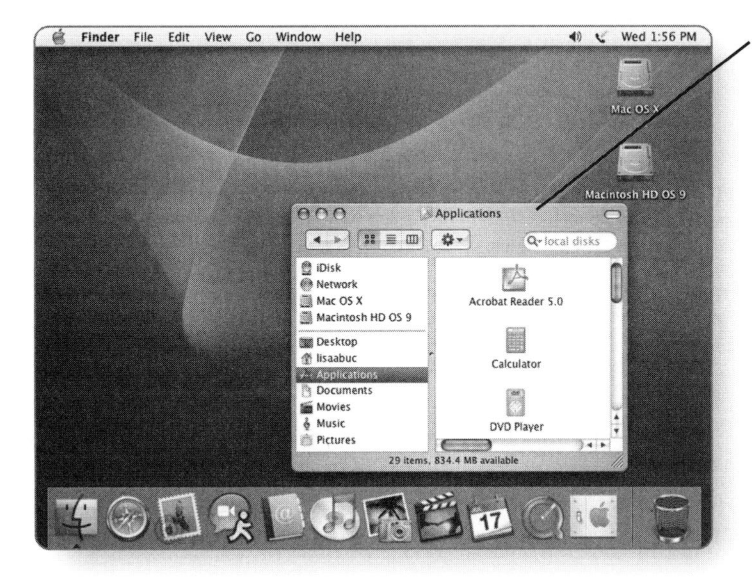

2. **Drag** the **window** and **release** the **mouse button** when the window reaches the desired location. The window will appear in its new location.

Resizing a Window

If you want to fit a number of windows on-screen and perhaps view their contents simultaneously, you'll probably need to resize one or more of the windows to facilitate the fit. These steps present techniques you can use to manage a window's size:

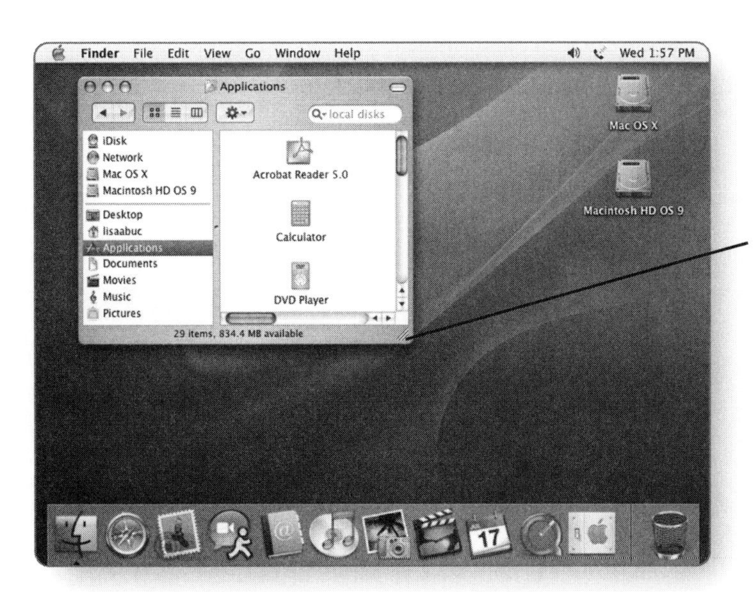

1. **Drag** the **size box** in any direction and **release** the **mouse button** when the window reaches the desired size and shape. The window will appear in its new shape.

2. Click on the **Maximize button** near the upper-left corner of the window. The window will snap back to a previous, larger size or, if possible, to a size large enough to display the icons in the window.

> **NOTE**
>
> If you're working in an application and want to have quick access to all your open Finder windows, click on the desktop to display the Finder's menu bar. Then click on a Window and click on Bring All To Front.

Scrolling a Window

When you make a window too small to display all of its contents, a scroll bar appears at the bottom, and sometimes the right side, of the window. To use a scroll bar to view additional folder contents, use the techniques described in the following steps:

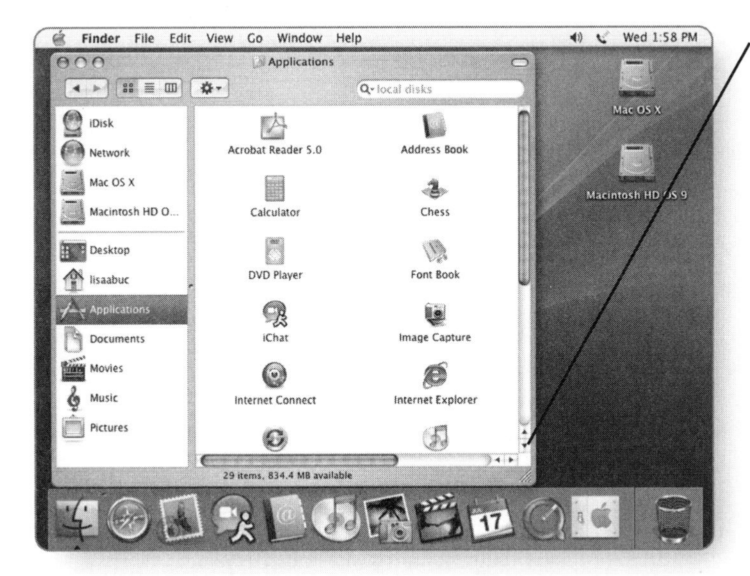

1. **Click** on the **desired scroll arrow** at the end of the scroll bar. The window contents will scroll slightly in the direction of the arrow each time you click.

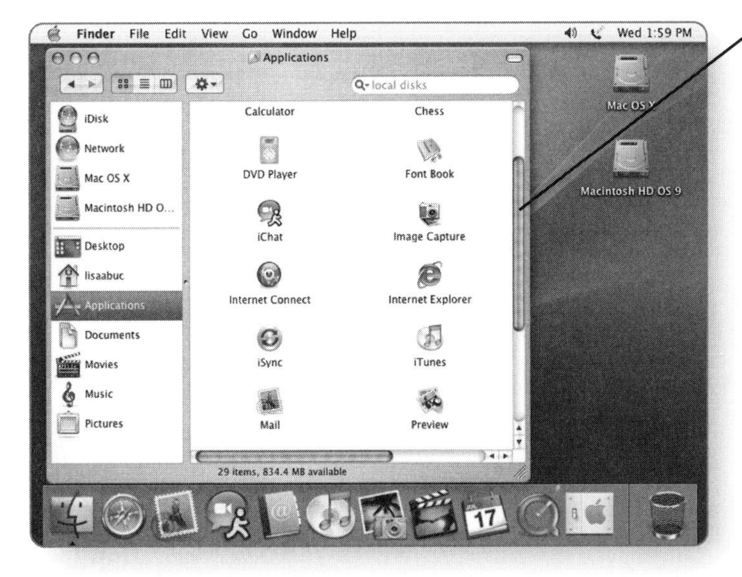

2. **Drag** the **scroller** on a scroll bar in the desired direction. The window contents will scroll more quickly in the direction in which you drag.

> **TIP**
>
> You can press and hold the Option button and then drag within a window to scroll the window to scroll the window's contents. When you use this technique, a gray bar appears to the left of the mouse pointer.

Closing a Window

Closing a window removes it from the screen altogether. There are two easy ways to close the active window on your screen.

> **NOTE**
>
> You also can minimize a Finder window to park it on the Dock. The process works the same for application windows and is covered in the section titled "Minimizing and Expanding Windows" in Chapter 5.

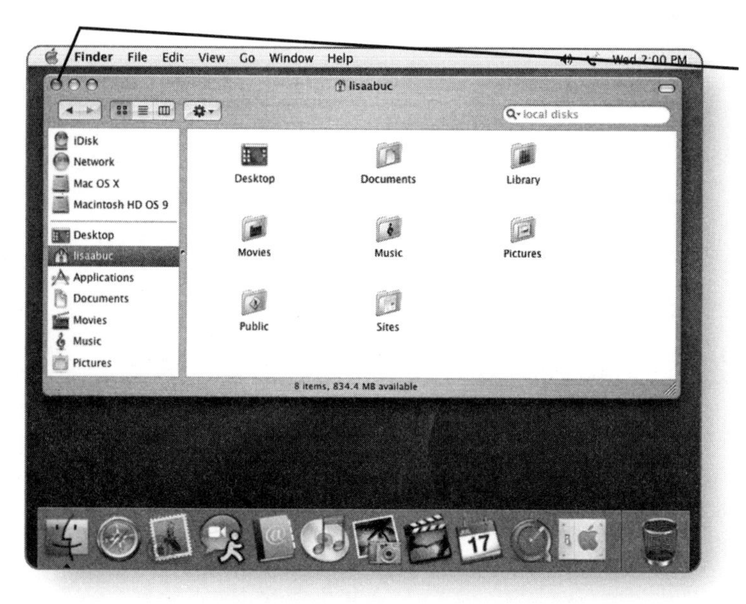

1. Click on the **Close button** near the upper-left corner of the window. The window will close immediately.

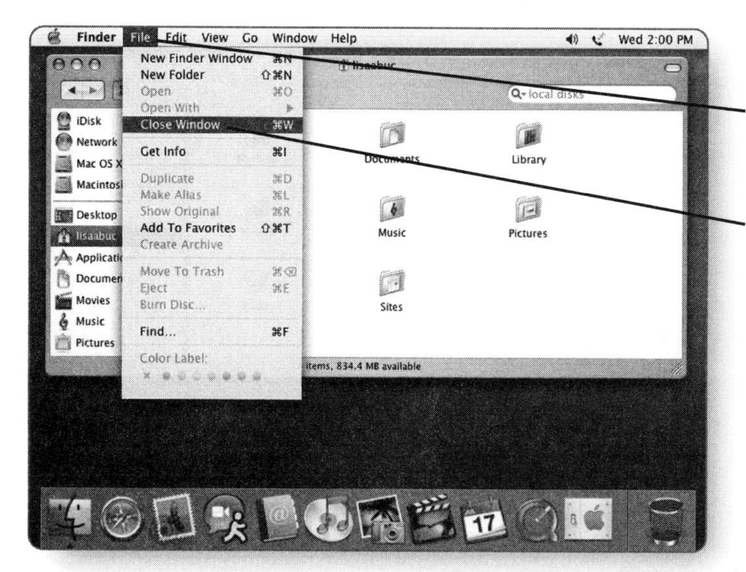

OR

2a. Click on **File**. The File menu will appear.

2b. Click on **Close Window**. The active window will close immediately.

NOTE

If you're working in an application, closing a window closes the file (document) in the window. If you haven't saved any work or changes in the document whose window you're closing, a dialog box will prompt you to do so. You can click on Save to save (and name) the file, click on Don't Save to close the document without saving it, and Cancel to return to working in the document window. Closing the documents in an application does not close the application itself, however. Chapter 6, "Using the Dock and Applications," provides more details about working with applications.

Using Exposé to View Open Windows

Mac OS X Version 10.3 Panther includes a new Finder feature called Exposé. Exposé provides a fast way to hide and display all the Finder and document windows on the desktop. By default, Exposé uses the three function keys to perform specific actions:

- **F9.** Press F9 to rearrange Finder and document windows on the desktop so that you can see each window.
- **F10.** When you have multiple documents open in an application, press F10 to hide Finder windows but rearrange the document windows on the desktop so that you can see each window.
- **F11.** Press F11 to hide all open windows, giving you a clear view of the items on the desktop.

If you're having trouble visualizing how Exposé works, the following example steps will give you a better idea. The steps assume that you have at least two Finder windows and two document windows from an application open.

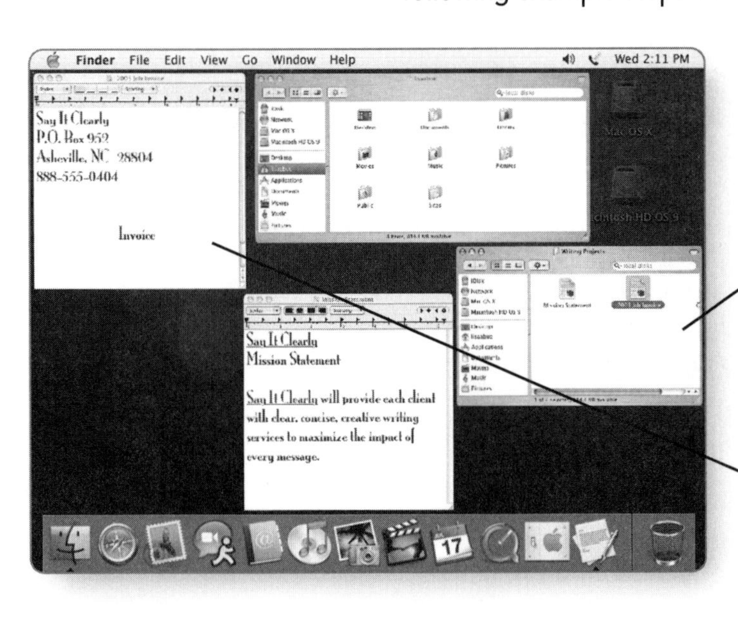

1. Press F9.

Exposé will resize all open windows to a smaller size and arrange them so that you can see each window onscreen.

2. Click on **one** of the **document windows**. The document will be selected, and its application will become active.

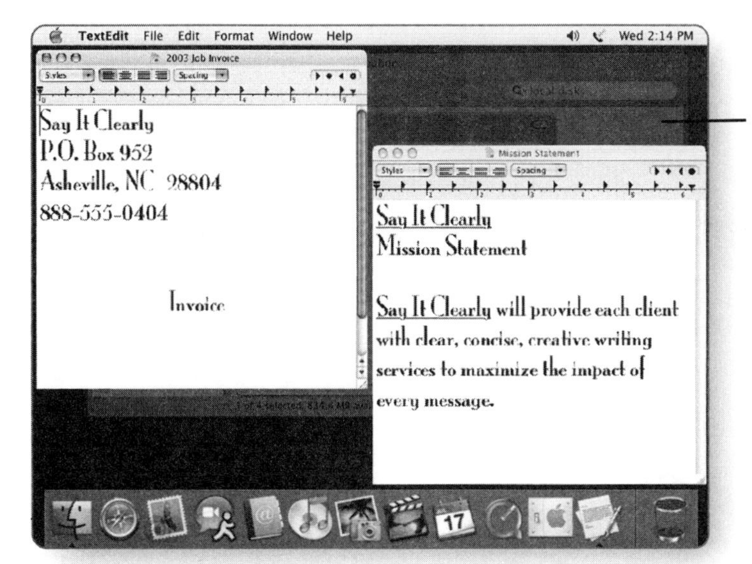

3. Press F10.

Exposé will resize all open windows to a smaller size and arrange them so that you can see each window onscreen.

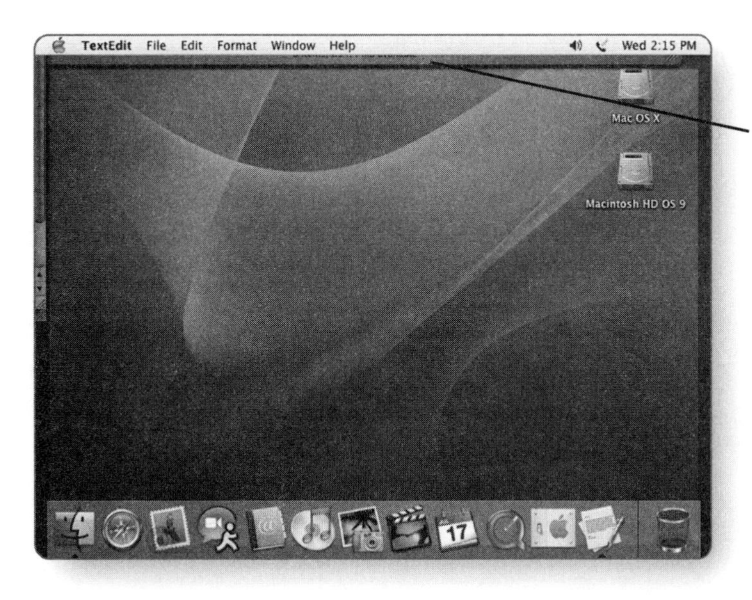

4. Press F11.

Exposé will hide all open windows.

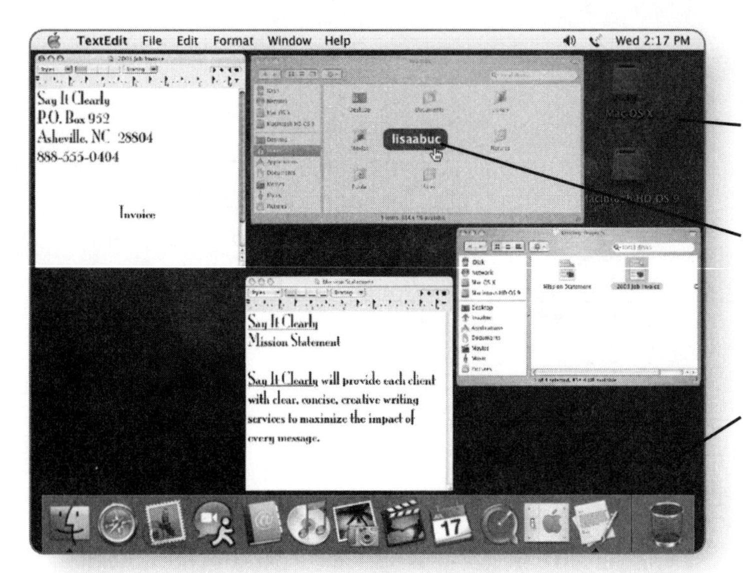

5. Press F9.

All open windows will appear onscreen again.

6. Place the **mouse pointer** on a **window**. A label with the folder or document name will appear.

7. Click on the **desktop**. The folders will return to their normal appearance.

4

Working with Folders and Files

In this chapter, you'll learn how to:

- Locate your home folder.
- Open, make, or move a folder.
- Copy or duplicate a file.
- Throw a file in the trash and retrieve it.
- Erase a file securely.
- Review file information.
- Change a file or folder name.
- Apply a color label to a file or folder.
- Create an alias or favorite.

Files and folders flesh out the framework of your computing organization. You must store your work in each program as a file on a disk. (Programs or applications also run from files that are stored on the Mac's hard disk.) To enable you to find files more easily when you need them, you organize the files in folders. Mac OS X Version 10.3 Panther conveniently sets up a few storage folders for you. If you're a beginner, you'll find this chapter particularly useful. If you have a little Mac time under your belt, this chapter will help you identify where Mac OS X Version 10.3 differs from earlier operating systems such as Mac OS 9 in terms of file management—and there are differences.

Understanding Home Folders

In older Macintosh operating systems, you could save your files in virtually any location on the hard disk. This made for a great deal of flexibility in organizing your files, but also created a housekeeping issue—having files and folders scattered all about made it more difficult to find a file or folder when needed.

All versions of Mac OS X take a different approach toward user files and folders, which was touched upon in earlier chapters. For each user name set up under Mac OS X (and there is always at least one user by default—you), Mac OS X creates a Home folder. The Home folder, in turn, contains several folders that are organized to hold your personal files and data. The following list touches on the folders that you'll use most often.

- **Desktop.** The Desktop folder holds items you've saved to the Mac OS X Version 10.3 desktop.
- **Documents**. Store all the documents (files) you create in this folder so that they can be found when you need them. You can create additional folders within this folder to further organize your work.

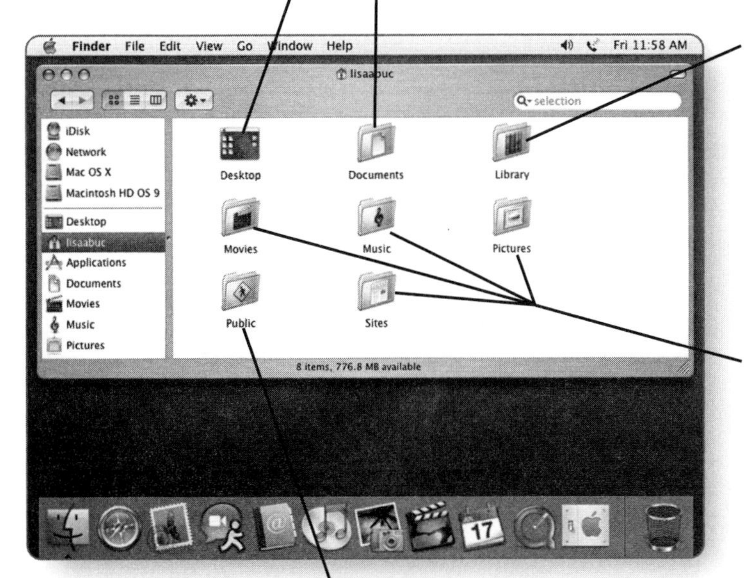

- **Library**. This folder holds several predefined folders for special uses. Several of the folders hold your specific user preferences. The Favorites folder holds the aliases to favorite files and folders that you use frequently.
- **Movies, Music, Pictures, and Sites.** These other folders enable you to store various types of content you create, view online, and download to your Mac. Later chapters will cover these folders as they apply.
- **Public.** If your Mac is connected to a network and you enable the file-sharing feature in OS X Version 10.3, other users can copy files into this folder. Likewise, this is the only folder that other users of your Mac can place files into. (For more on sharing your Mac OS X Version 10.3 system among multiple users, see Chapter 23, "Managing Users.") This technique helps you more clearly identify files you need to handle in the near future and helps prevent others from tampering with your more vital files in the Documents folder (found within your Home folder).

Mac OS X Version 10.3 doesn't just create your Home folder to be your organizational helper. It actually forces you to use the Home folder (unless you are a system administrator, which the first user always is). If you try to save a file or create a folder in another user's folder or the System folder in the root (top level) of the hard disk, an alert box appears. The error message reads "An error occurred while trying to save." What that message really means is that you don't have permission to save information in the specified location. Instead, use your Home folder or one of the folders it contains. (Users with administrator privileges can create folders in some other locations, such as folders elsewhere in the root of the hard disk.)

NOTE

Your Home folder is actually a subfolder of the Users folder in the root (top level) of the hard drive.

Using Folders

Computer disks, especially hard disks and CD-ROMs, can hold thousands of files. Some files work together to produce a running program or application. Other files hold documents and data that you create. If all these files were just dumped randomly onto a system's hard disk, you'd have a hard time finding what you need. Worse yet, if you mistakenly deleted a file needed by a particular program (or the Mac OS X Version 10.3 operating system), your program or the system itself might stop working.

Folders serve as containers for related files. For example, a folder might hold all the files for a program, as well as subfolders with additional files for the program. An install routine usually sets up the folders for a program and places the program files in those folders. You can use and create other folders to hold your document files and data, separating them from the program file information.

The rest of this section describes how to manage your folders in Mac OS X version 10.3. This latest version of Apple's breakthrough operating system incorporates some changes in how you work with folders, so even more experienced users of older Mac operating systems should take care to spin through the next few topics.

NOTE

For most of the procedures in this chapter (and the rest of the book, for that matter), you must be working on the desktop or in a Finder window. If a command doesn't work or you hear a beep and nothing happens, click on the desktop or the appropriate Finder window title bar and then try again.

Navigating to a Disk or Folder

Every disk has a *root*, which is its base location or folder that holds all other folders on the disk. In Mac OS X Version 10.3, you can display the root of the hard drive by clicking on the disk icon for the hard disk where you installed Mac OS X in the Finder window Sidebar. As was noted earlier in the section titled "Understanding Home Folders," you generally cannot save information or create new folders in any location except your Home folder and its subfolders. However, you can navigate to any folder, starting from the root, as described here. Navigating to a folder means moving to a folder so that its contents can be displayed in a window on the desktop.

TIP

If you've hidden the Sidebar, you can choose Go, Computer to display icons for your system's disks in the Finder window. Then you can double-click on the desired disk.

In general, double-clicking a disk icon will open the disk; double-clicking a folder icon will open the folder. In previous Mac operating system versions, a new window opened each time you double-clicked on a disk or folder icon. In Mac OS X Version 10.3, the process works a bit differently by default. After you double-click on a disk or folder icon, the current Finder window changes to display the contents of that disk or folder. In addition, you can navigate to some folders by using the Go menu and Back button on the Finder window, as well as the toolbar buttons, which display a particular folder when clicked.

> **NOTE**
>
> When you're using the column view of a Finder window or are working with the From or Where list when using a dialog box or sheet to open or save a file, you only need to single-click a disk or folder icon to display its contents. The contents of the selected item appear in the next column to the right.

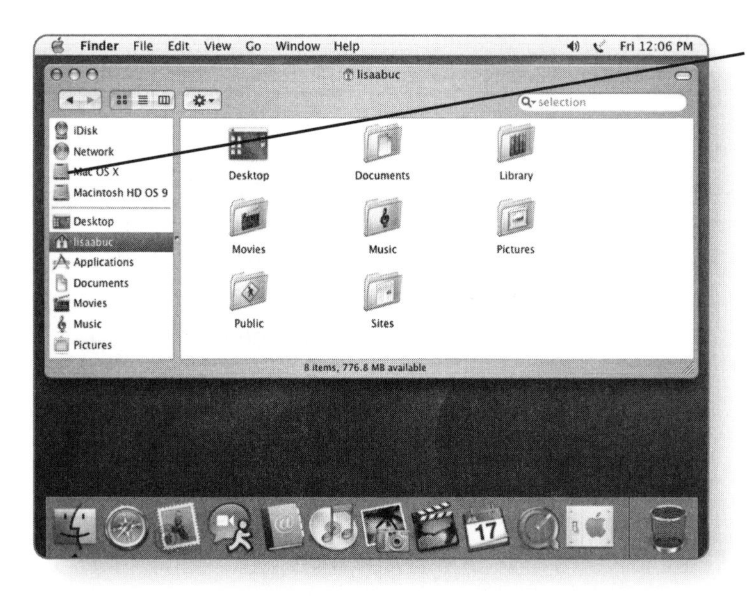

1. **Click** on the **icon** for the hard disk where you installed Mac OS X in the Sidebar. The contents of the root of the hard disk will appear in the Finder window.

NOTE

By default, Mac OS X names your hard disk "Macintosh HD" when you install to a drive with a single hard disk partition. If you installed on a system where the hard disk has multiple partitions, you may have chosen another name such as "Mac OS X." In cases where this book uses the more general term "Mac OS X," the advice presented applies to all releases of Mac OS X.

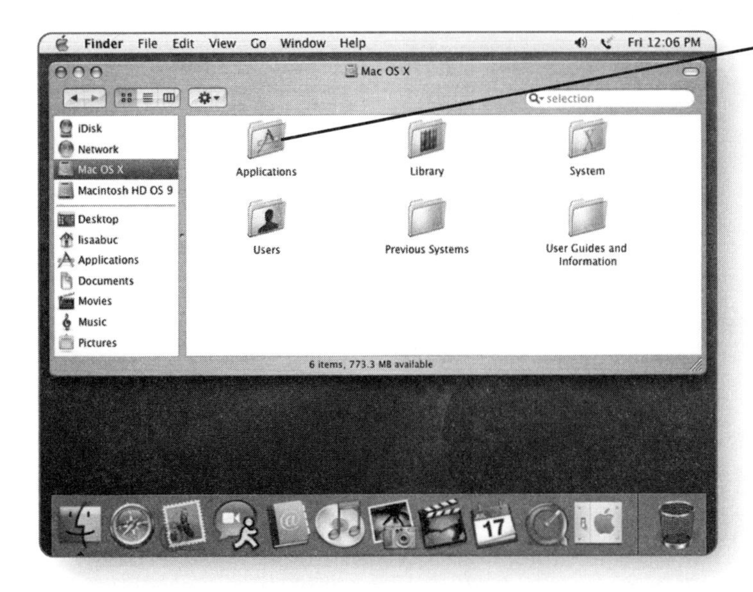

2. Double-click on the **Applications folder**. The contents of the Applications folder will appear in the Finder window. This folder holds the applications (programs) and utilities that come with Mac OS X Version 10.3, as well as many applications that you may subsequently install.

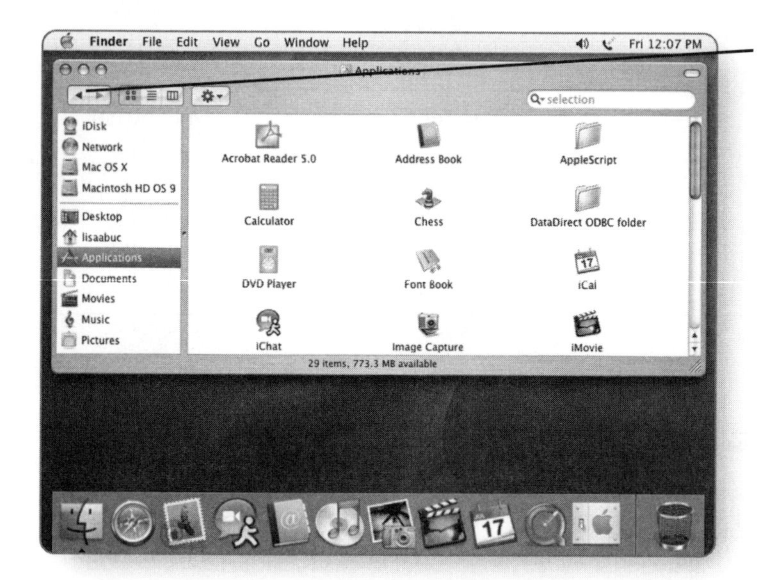

3. Click on the **Back button**. The Finder window will redisplay the contents of the root (top level) of the hard disk.

TIP

You can click on the Back button multiple times to continue backing up to prior folders or locations that you've displayed in the Finder window.

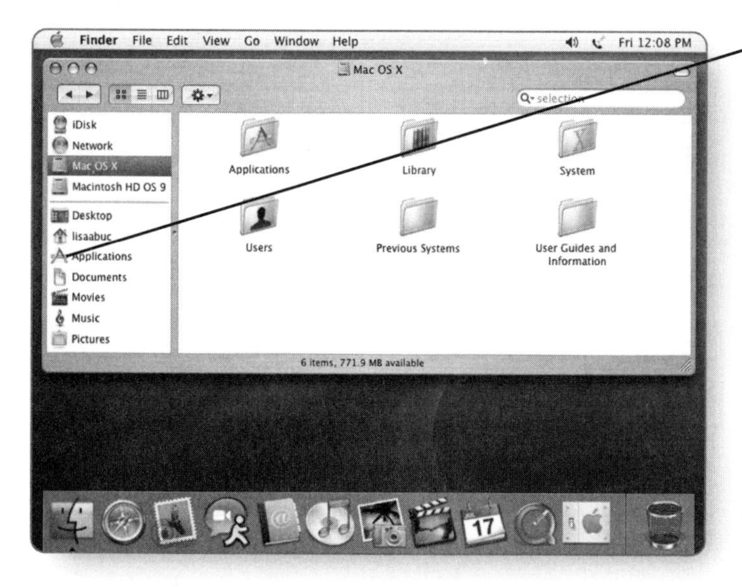

4. Click on the **Applications icon** in the Sidebar. The contents of the Applications folder will appear in the Finder window.

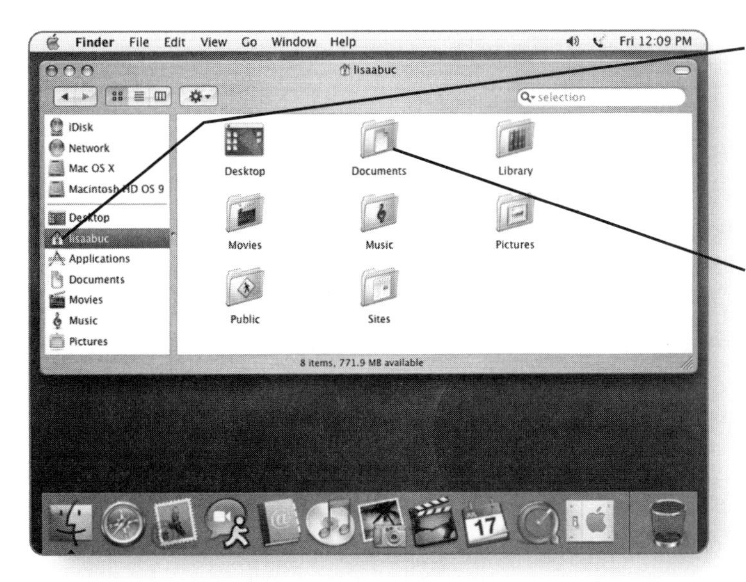

5. **Click** on the **Home folder icon** in the Sidebar. The contents of your Home folder will appear in the Finder window.

6. **Double-click** on the **Documents folder** in the Finder window. The contents of your Documents folder will appear in the Finder window.

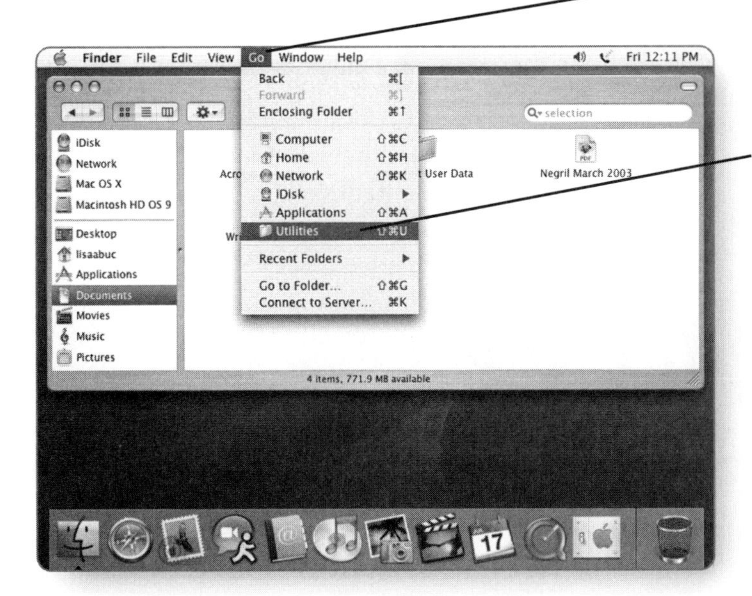

7. **Click** on **Go**. The Go menu will appear and display a list of locations to which you can navigate.

8. **Click** on a **folder** or **location** in the menu. The contents of the selected location will appear in the Finder window.

> **TIP**
>
> You can use the Recent Folders submenu of the Go menu to navigate to a folder you've used recently. Choosing Go, Enclosing Folder moves up one level in the folder hierarchy; that is, it displays the folder that holds the currently selected folder.

Creating a Folder

If needed, you can create your own folder within your Home folder or one of its subfolders to further organize your work. (Remember that Mac OS X Version 10.3 only enables most users to create new folders or store files within your Home folder. Users with administrator privileges can create folders anywhere except in the System folder of the hard disk root or in other users' Home folders and subfolders.) For example, you could create a folder within the Documents folder to hold the files related to each of your projects or clients.

1. **Open** the **folder** in which you want to create a new folder. The contents of the folder will appear in the Finder window.

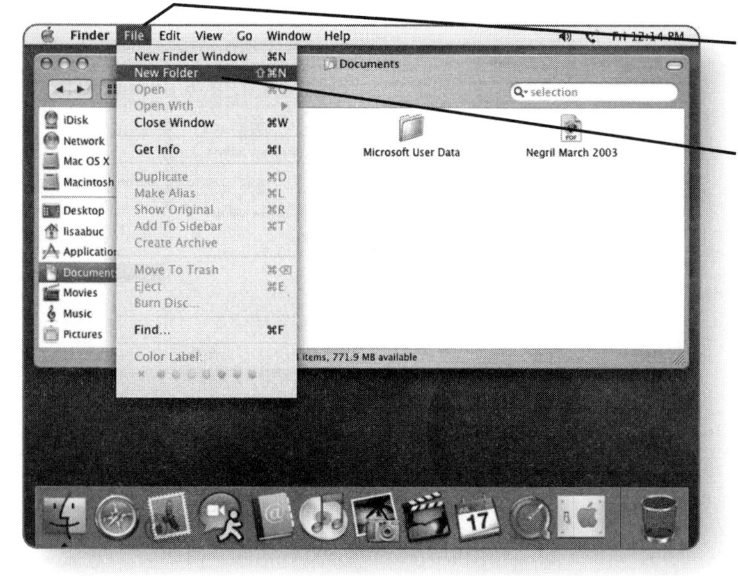

2. **Click** on **File**. The File menu will appear.

3. **Click** on **New Folder**. A new folder will appear, and its name will be selected so that you can enter the name of your choice.

> **TIP**
>
> You also can press Shift+⌘+N to create the new folder.

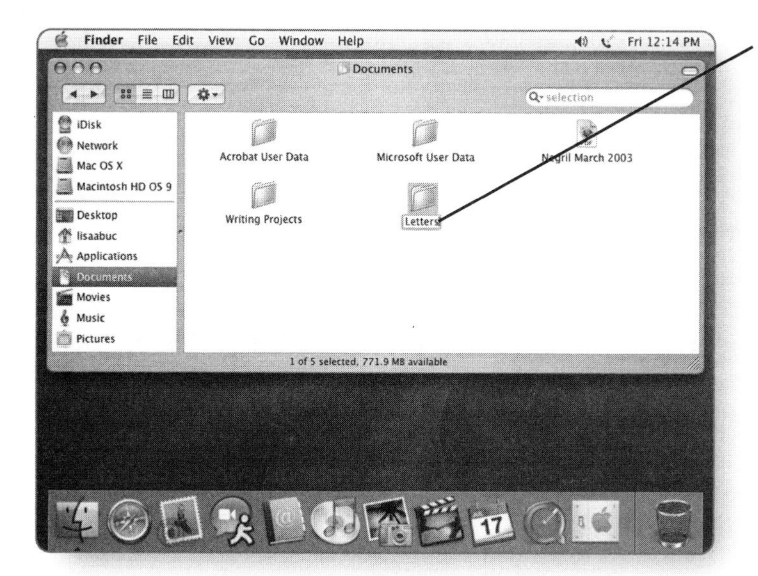

4. **Type** a **name** for the new folder and **press Return**. The name for the new folder will appear below the folder's icon.

> **NOTE**
>
> Folder names can use spaces and capitalization, and they can be more than 100 characters long, even though you probably won't see the full name listed below the icon. Do not start a folder name with a period or the # (pound) sign; doing so can create problems. It's also best to avoid including a / (slash) character because some programs may have problems recognizing a folder name that includes a / character. Note that the full folder name may not be displayed in the Finder window due to limited space. See "Changing View Options" in Chapter 8 to learn about adjusting view settings, which may alleviate the problem.

Moving a Folder Within the Current Folder

You may need to change a folder's location from time to time as part of maintaining your system. For example, you may want to organize several folders with information pertaining to a particular client into a new folder that is clearly identified by the client's name. Mac OS X Version 10.3 enables you to drag a folder and its contents to a new location.

Mac OS X Version 10.3 includes a feature called *spring-loaded folders*. When you drag a file or folder (or a group of selected files or folders) over a folder icon and pause, a window springs open to display the contents of the destination folder. This enables you to verify whether you want to complete the move. If not, drag the item(s) back over the original (source) folder and release the mouse button.

The steps used to move a folder from one location to another differ slightly, depending on where the original folder and the destination folder exist.

Moving a folder into another folder that resides in the same folder location is the easiest.

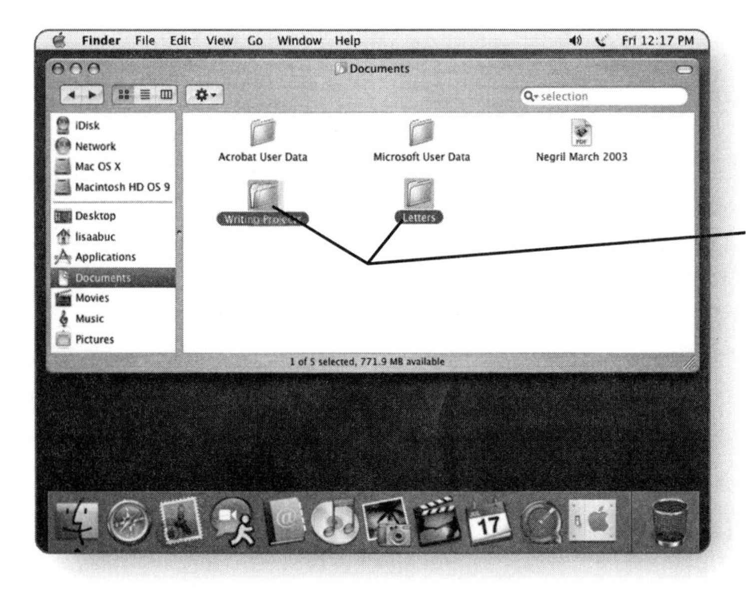

1. **Open** the **folder** containing both the destination and the target folders. You will see both folders in the Finder window.

2. **Drag** the **folder** to be moved over the destination folder; then **release** the **mouse button**. The icon for the moved folder will disappear from the current Finder display because it is now within the destination folder.

Moving a Folder to a New Location

If the folder to be moved and the destination folder are in different locations, the process for moving a folder gets a little more complicated.

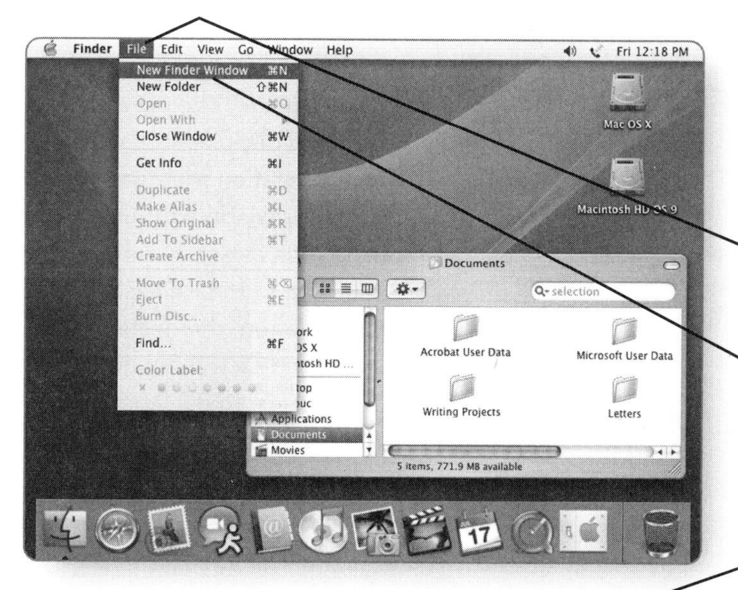

1. Open the **folder** in which the folder to be moved resides. You will see the subfolder displayed in the Finder window.

2. Click on **File**. The File menu will appear.

3. Click on **New Finder Window**. Another Finder window will appear.

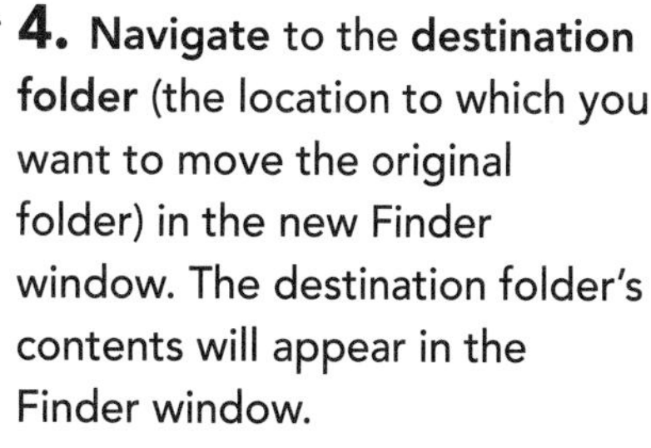

4. Navigate to the **destination folder** (the location to which you want to move the original folder) in the new Finder window. The destination folder's contents will appear in the Finder window.

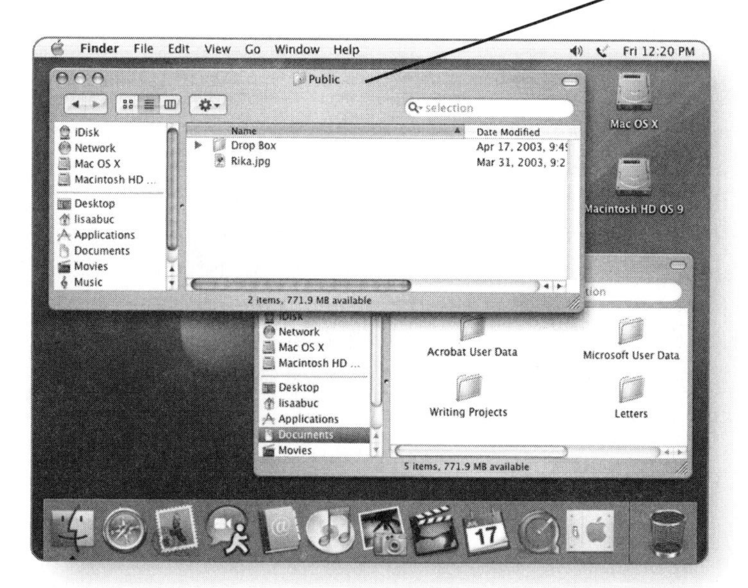

CAUTION

If you do not have administrator privileges, the destination folder must be located within your Home folder. Mac OS X Version 10.3 won't let you move a folder out of the Home folder.

5. **Move** the **Finder windows** so that you can see both the folder to be moved and the destination folder. The windows will appear in the desired positions onscreen.

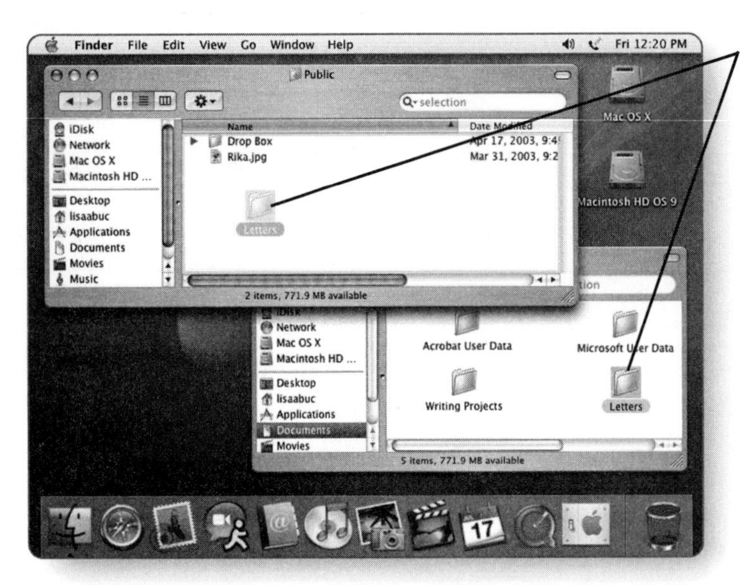

6. **Drag** the **folder** over the destination folder's Finder window; then **release** the **mouse button**. The moved folder will disappear from its original location and reappear in the Finder window for the destination folder. Note that if you pause before releasing the mouse button, the destination folder window will pop in front of the source folder; this is the spring-loaded folders function.

> **TIP**
>
> If you press and hold the Option key while dragging a folder to a new location on the same disk, Mac OS X Version 10.3 will copy (rather than move) the folder and its contents. You also can use Edit, Copy to copy a selected folder and then use Edit, Paste item to paste it into a destination folder. If you drag a folder between locations (folders) on the same disk, Mac OS X Version 10.3 moves the folder and its contents by default. However, if you drag a folder to a different disk (such as a removable disk like a Zip disk rather than the system hard disk), Mac OS X Version 10.3 will copy the folder.

Using Files

A file holds a particular document or set of data. Other types of files include program files or data files used by program files. This section covers the basics of managing your files in the Finder.

Opening a File

Mac OS X Version 10.3 tracks the program used to create each document file. Then, if you open a particular file, Mac OS X Version 10.3 knows which application or program to launch to display the file. (You can use the File, Get Info command as described in the later section called "Showing Disk, File, or Folder Information" to change the application used to open a particular file.) The program files that come with Mac OS X Version 10.3 reside in the Applications and Utilities folders.

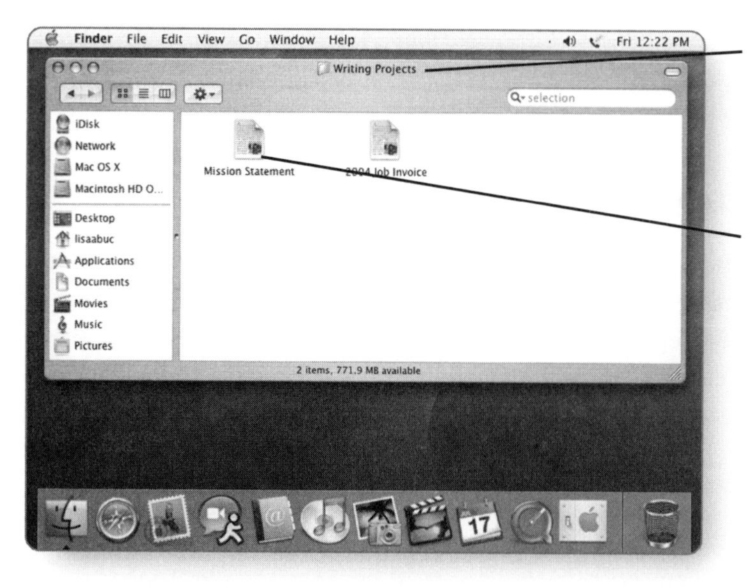

1. **Open** the **folder** that holds the file you want to open. The folder contents will appear in the Finder window.

2. **Double-click** on the **file**.

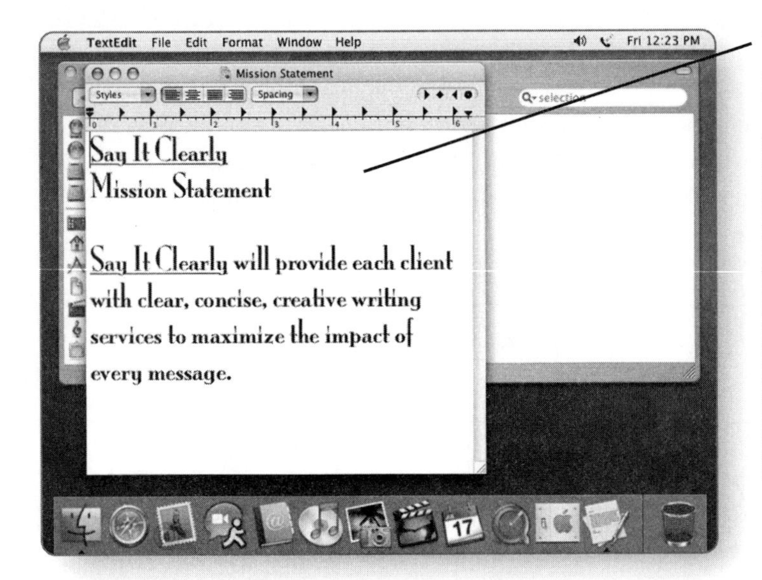

The file will open in the correct program.

> **NOTE**
>
> To choose a specific program in which to open the file, Control+click on the file and then use the Open With submenu to select the desired application.

> **NOTE**
>
> Once the file is open, you can press ⌘+Q to quit the program and close the file.

Duplicating and Moving a File

Moving a file uses the same process as moving a folder, which was described in the earlier sections, "Moving a Folder with the Content Folder" and "Moving a Folder to the New Location." Making a copy of the file is almost as easy, as these steps demonstrate.

> **TIP**
>
> You also can use the Duplicate command on the Finder's File menu to make a copy of the selected file. Then drag the copied file into another folder's Finder window to move the file. Or select a number of files and choose Edit, Copy (#) items; then navigate to the destination folder and choose Edit, Paste item.

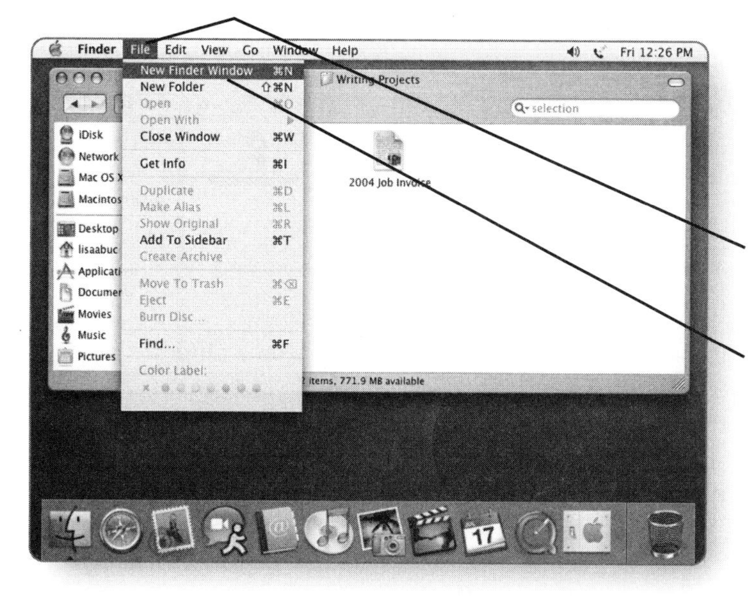

1. Open the **folder** that holds the file to be duplicated. You will see the folder's contents in the Finder window.

2. Click on **File**. The File menu will appear.

3. Click on **New Finder Window**. Another Finder window will appear.

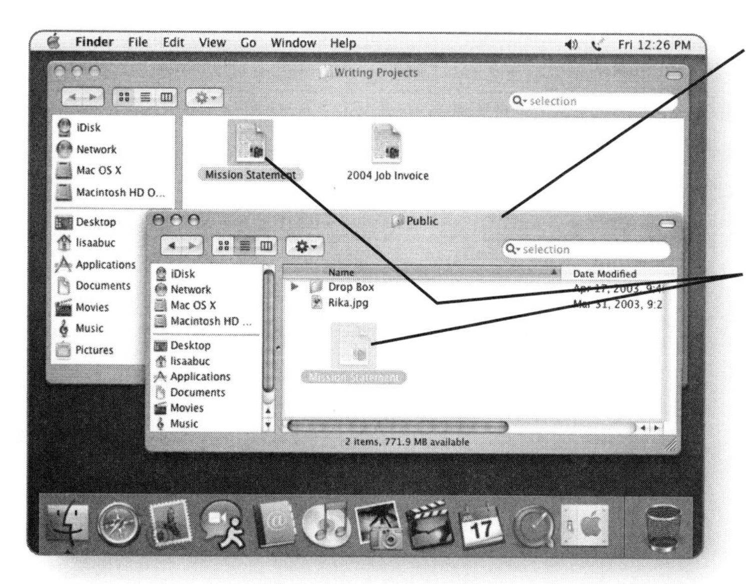

4. Open the **folder** into which you want to copy the file in the new Finder window. The destination folder's contents will appear in the Finder window.

5. Move the **Finder windows** so that you can see both the file to be copied and the destination folder. The windows will appear in the desired positions onscreen.

6. Press and **hold** the **Option key**. This will instruct the Finder to copy the item(s) you drag.

7. **Drag** the **file** over the destination folder's Finder window; then **release** the **mouse button**. As you drag, a plus sign appears beside the mouse pointer. When you release the mouse button, the copied file appears in the destination folder.

> **NOTE**
>
> If the destination location or folder is on a different disk (such as a Zip disk or other removable disk rather than the system hard disk), Mac OS X will copy any file that you drag automatically, so that you don't have to duplicate it first or use the Option key.

Selecting Multiple Files or Folders

You can perform several operations for managing files and folders on multiple files and folders at once. For example, you can move, copy, or trash multiple files and folders that you've previously selected. The following steps demonstrate techniques you can use for selecting multiple files and folders.

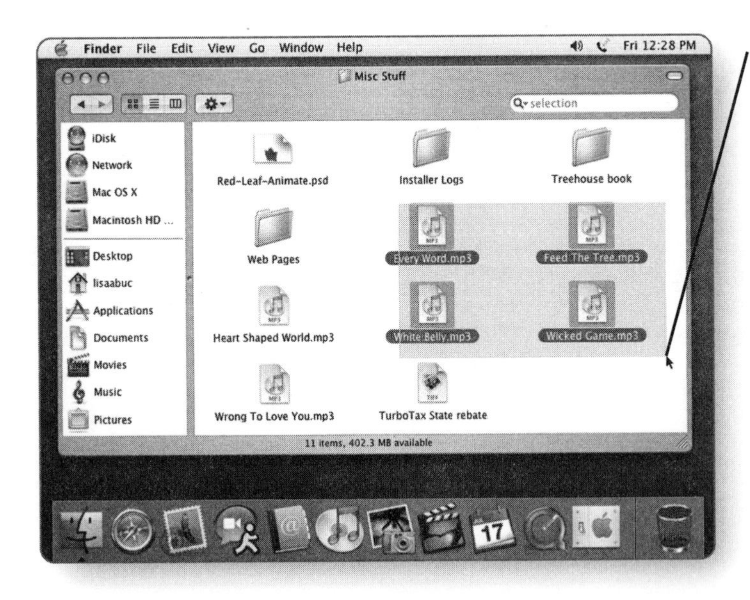

1. **Drag** over the **files** and **folders** to select them. Their icons will appear highlighted to indicate that they are selected.

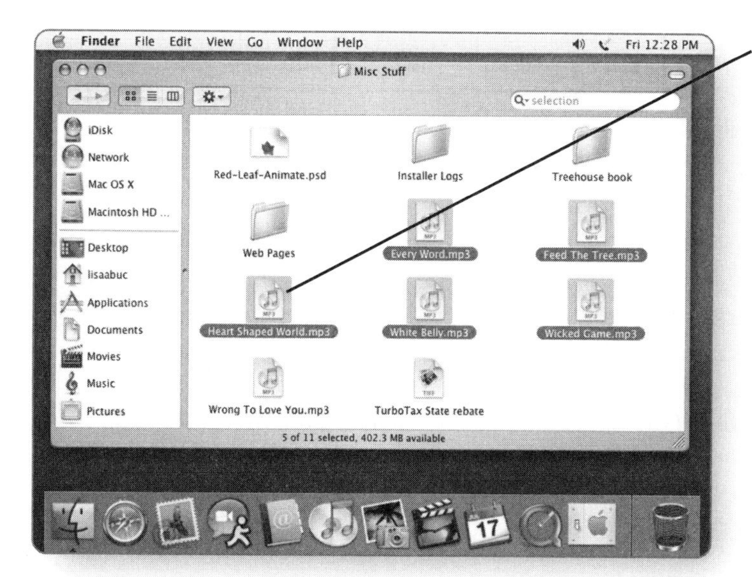

2. **Shift+click** on **additional adjacent files** and **folders**. They will be added to the selected group of items.

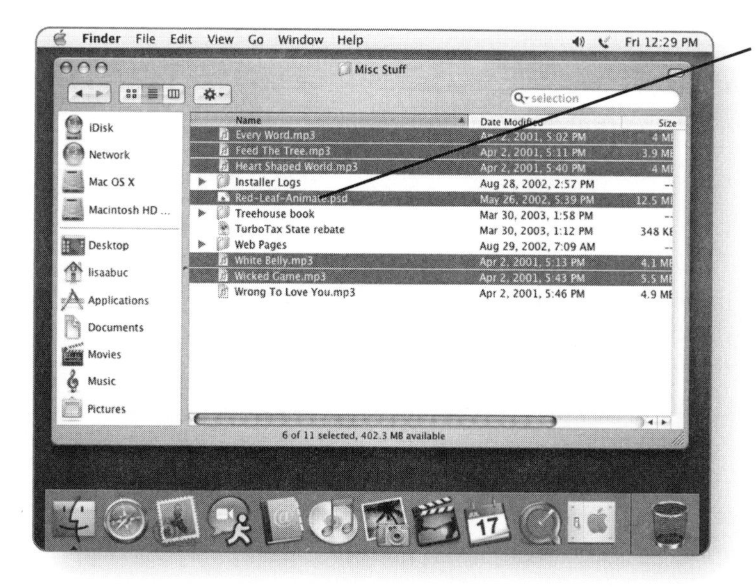

3. **⌘+click** on **additional nonadjacent files** and **folders** in list or column view. They will be added to the selected group of items.

Working with the Trash

Today's computer hard disks—and even other removable types of disks—store many more files than was possible on disks even a few years ago. A Zip disk, for example, has ten times the space of the hard disks first offered in computers in the late 1980s. That being said, you should get rid of files and folders that you no longer need in order to keep your Home folder well organized. As in previous Mac operating systems, Mac OS X Version 10.3 includes the Trash, which is used to delete files temporarily or permanently.

Trashing a File or Folder

When you no longer need a document in your office, you wad it up and drop it in the round file. Throwing a whole folder into the wastebasket removes both the folder and its contents from your desk or filing cabinet. Similarly, dropping a computer file or folder from a Finder window into the Trash on the Dock removes it from action.

> **NOTE**
>
> To eject a CD-ROM, floppy disk, or other removable media from the drive, you can drag its icon from the desktop to the Trash. This technique also dismounts disk images.

1. **Open** the **folder** that holds the file or folder you want to delete. You will see the folder's contents in the Finder window.

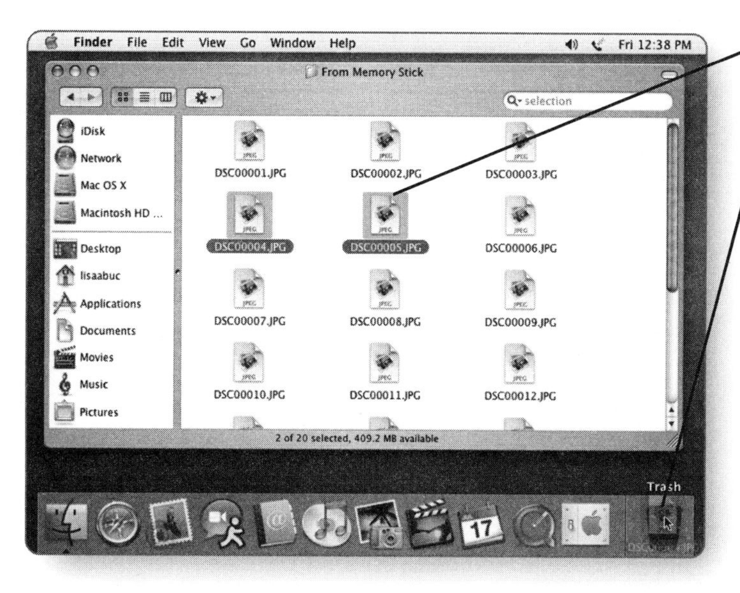

2. **Select** the **item(s) to be deleted**. The item(s) will appear highlighted.

3. **Drag** the **selected item(s)** over the Trash; then **release** the **mouse button**. The items will disappear from the Finder window, and an image of wadded up paper will appear in the Trash icon.

NOTE

You also can press ⌘+Delete to delete a selected file or folder. Alternatively, Control+click on the file and then click on Move to Trash in the contextual menu.

CAUTION

If you move a program file into the Trash, Mac OS X Version 10.3 does not warn you in any way. Press ⌘+Z to undo the move immediately. If you mistakenly trash a program file and don't immediately undo the move or retrieve the file later and replace it in the correct folder, the program may not run, and you may have to reinstall it.

Retrieving a File or Folder

Just as you can reach into a wastebasket and pull a file or folder back out if you've mistakenly thrown it away, you can retrieve a file or folder unless you've permanently deleted it.

1. Open the **folder** into which you want to place the deleted file. You will see the folder's contents in the Finder window.

2. Double-click on the **Trash icon**. A Finder window for the Trash will open.

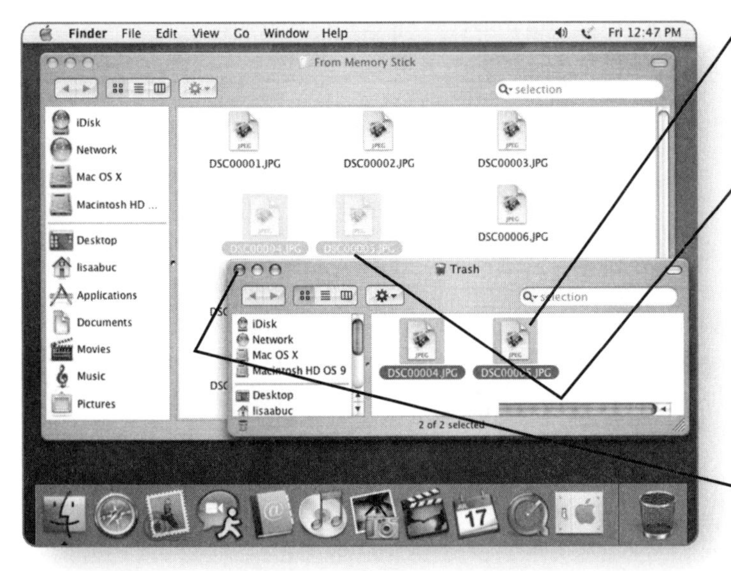

3. Select the **item(s) to restore**. The item(s) will appear highlighted.

4. Drag the **selected item(s)** from the Trash Finder window to the folder you opened; then **release** the **mouse button**. The selected item(s) will move into the Finder window for the specified folder.

5. Click on the **Close button** in the upper-left corner of the Finder window for the Trash. The Trash Finder window will close.

Emptying the Trash

Emptying the Trash in Mac OS X Version 10.3 is akin to having the garbage man haul your bags away from the curb: you pass the point of no return and can no longer retrieve your files and folders. However, you do want to empty the Trash on your Mac from time to time because it does consume storage space. Mac OS Version 10.3 also offers the ability to perform a secure erase. This more permanent type of erase prevents others from using undelete utilities to retrieve the deleted files; use this type of erase for greater information security.

> **CAUTION**
>
> Remember, you *cannot* retrieve files when you use the Secure Empty Trash command, so only use that command when you want to permanently erase files with sensitive information, such as your Social Security Number. If you use the Empty Trash command, instead, you can use third-party utilities to retrieve the deleted files.

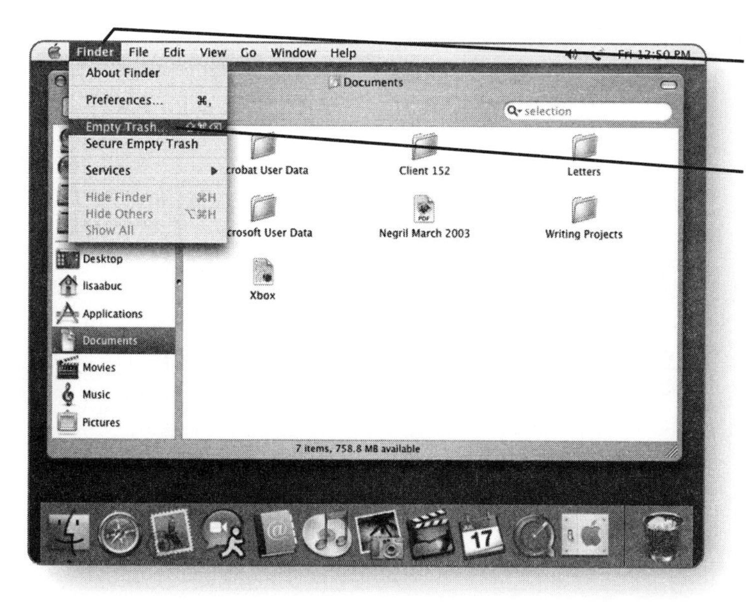

1. **Click** on **Finder**. The Finder menu will appear.

2a. **Click** on **Empty Trash**. A dialog box will open to prompt you to confirm the deletion.

OR

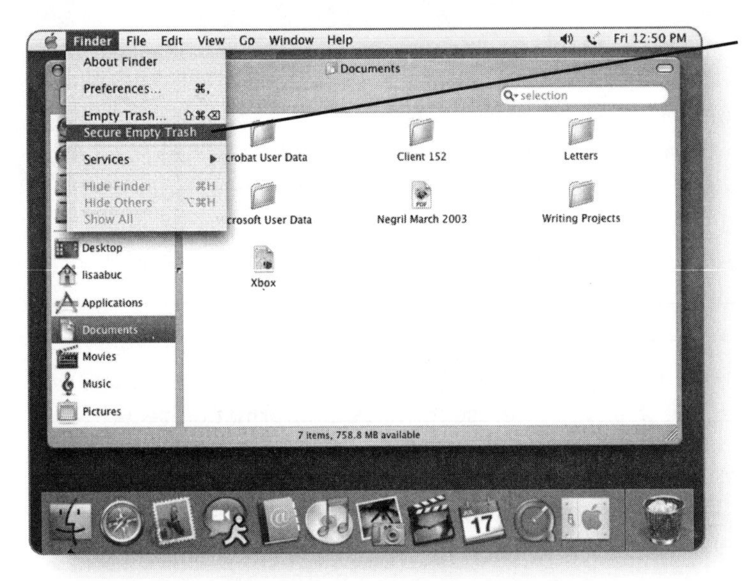

2b. Click on **Secure Empty Trash**. A dialog box will open to prompt you to confirm the deletion.

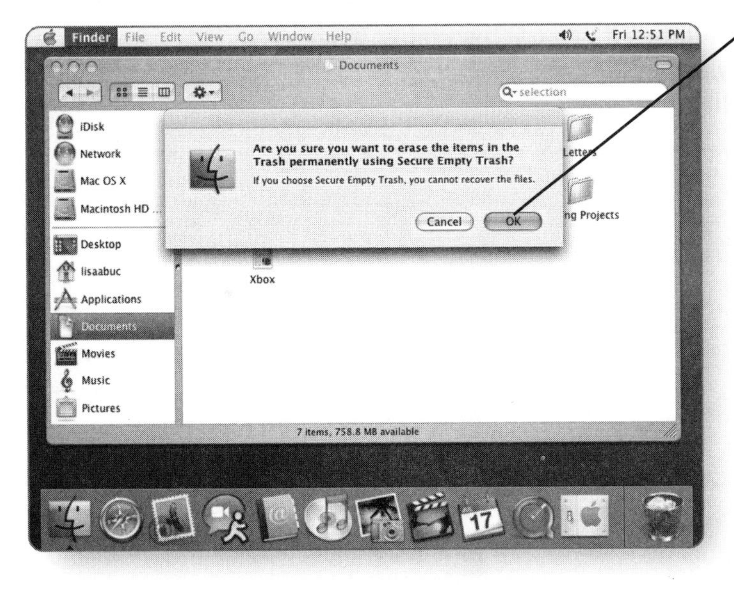

3. Click on **OK**. Mac OS X Version 10.3 will empty the Trash (and perform a secure erase if you chose the Secure Empty Trash command in Step 2), and the wadded up paper will disappear from the Trash icon on the Dock.

Showing Disk, File, or Folder Information

The Get Info command in Mac OS X Version 10.3 enables you to view and change certain information about files and folders. For example, you can see the storage space occupied by the file or folder (the file or folder size). You can lock a file or folder to prevent others from making changes to it, add a comment, and more.

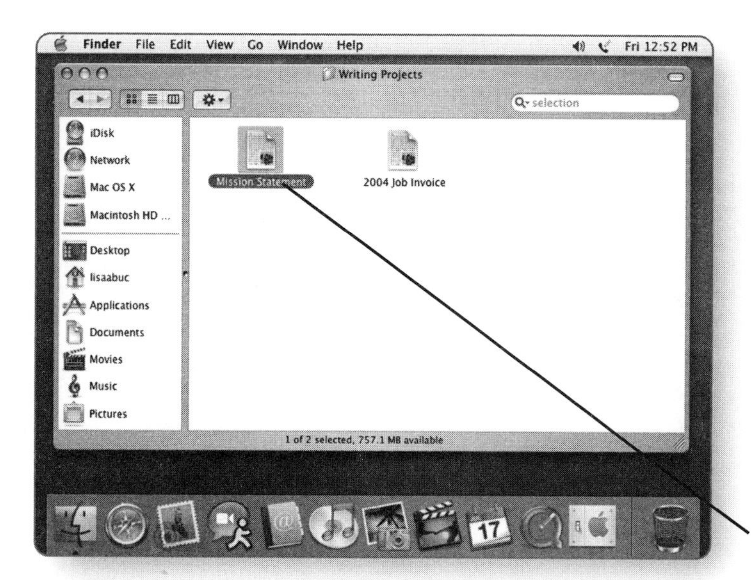

1. **Open** the **folder** that holds the file or folder you want to examine. You will see the folder's contents in the Finder window.

2. **Click** on the **file** or **folder**. The file or folder will be selected.

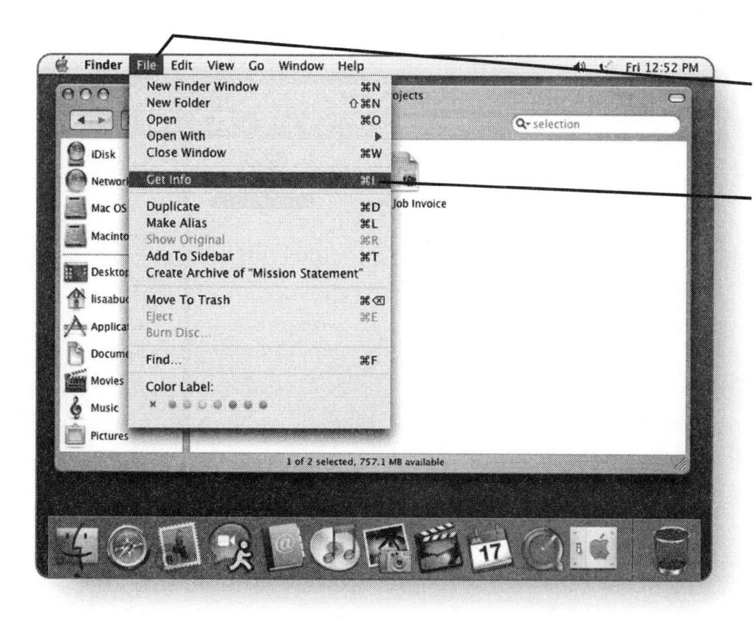

3. **Click** on **File**. The File menu will appear.

4. **Click** on **Get Info**. The Info window showing the file information will open.

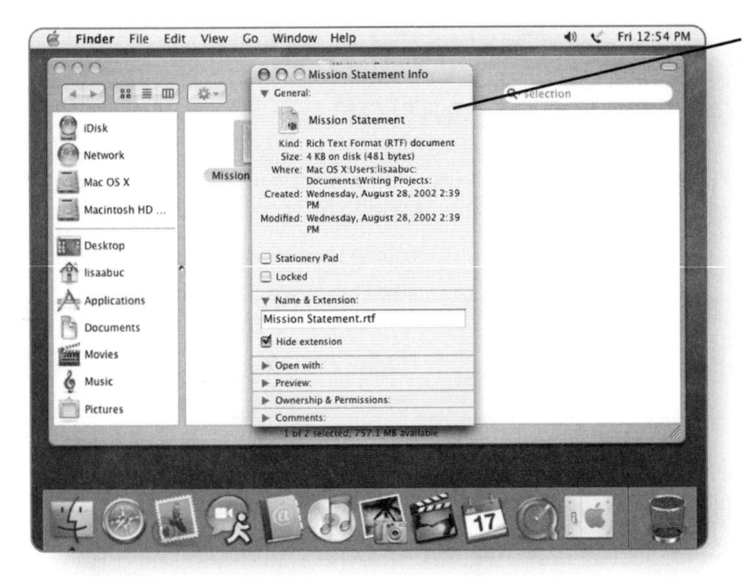

5. **Review** and **change file** or **folder information** in various window sections as needed. (Note that the contents of the window vary depending on the file or object selected in Step 2.) The Info window will apply your changes to the file.

- **General.** Review overall file information such as file location, have a file act as stationery by clicking Stationery Pad, or lock the file to prevent it from being moved or deleted.
- **Name & Extension.** Edit the file name and choose whether to hide the file name extension in Finder windows.
- **Open With.** Change the program used to open the file when you double-click on the file icon in a Finder window.
- **Preview.** See the type of icon that represents the file in Finder windows.
- **Languages.** Specify which languages can be used in the application when you're working with the application file's info.
- **Plug-ins.** Add plug-ins for an application to extend the program's functionality or compatibility with devices when you're working with the application file's info.
- **Memory.** Specify how much memory the application can use while running when you're working with the application file's info.

- **Ownership & Permissions.** Specify user rights, identifying whether groups of users may open the file as read-only or can make changes to the file.
- **Comments.** Type a descriptive comment about the file, helping other users to identify the file's purpose.

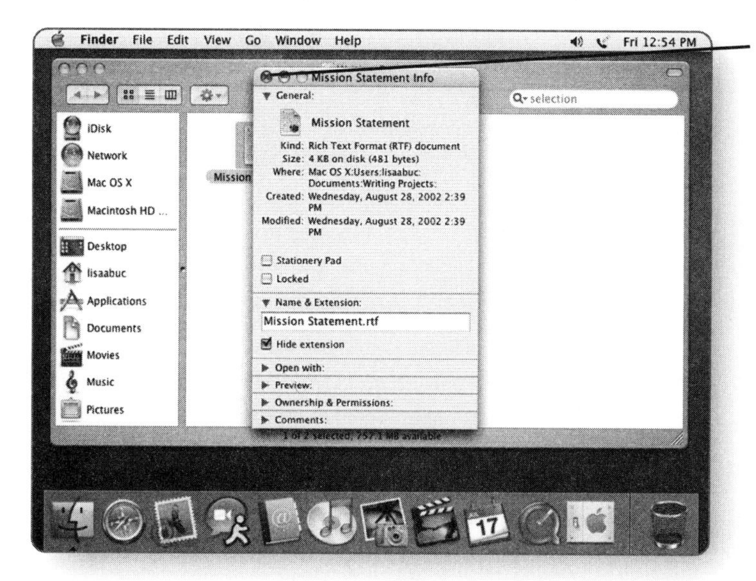

6. Click on the **Close button**. The Info window will close.

Renaming a File or Folder

As noted in the last section, you can type a new name for a file or folder by using the Info dialog box. However, it's handier to rename a file or folder right in a Finder window.

1. Open the **folder** that holds the file or folder you want to rename. You will see the folder's contents in the Finder window.

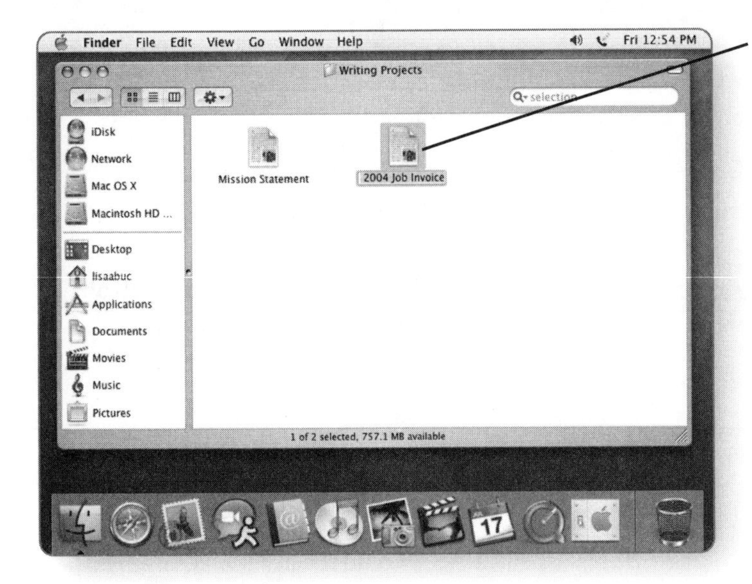

2. Click on the **file** or **folder name** you want to change. (The name appears either below or beside the icon for the file or folder, depending on the Finder window view you're using.) The file or folder name will appear highlighted, and a border will appear around the name.

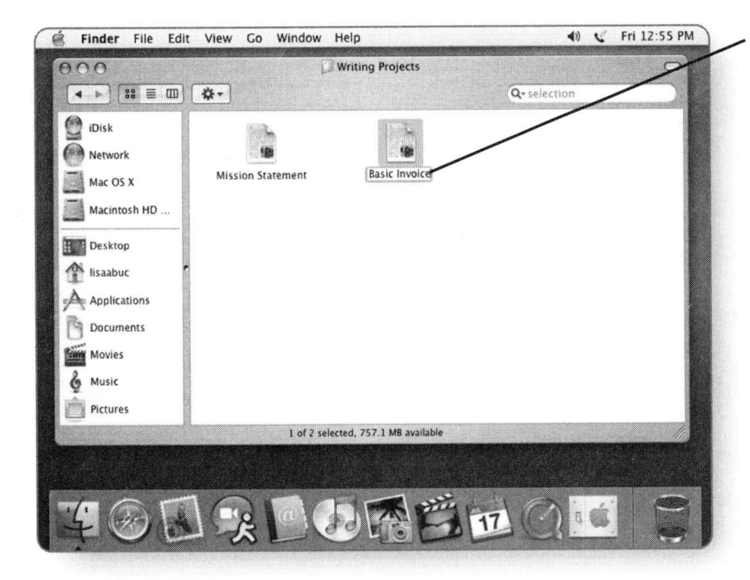

3. Type a **new name**; then **press Return**. The new file or folder name will appear immediately in the window.

NOTE

If a file name includes a period and a three-letter file name extension, such as .rtf, retype the period and file name extension. Alternatively, after you click on the file name, drag over the text preceding the extension to replace only that portion of the file name. This advice also applies to an alias you create for a file, as described next.

Choosing a Color Label

Mac OS X Version 10.3 provides an easy way to color-code file and folder names. If you're using the default Mac OS X color scheme, then only selected files and folders have colored labels—blue by default. You can assign one of several other color labels to a file or folder label. After you've color-coded labels, you can use the View, Arrange, by Label command to sort the contents of any Finder window by label color. To assign a color label:

1. Open the **folder** that holds the file or folder you want to color code. You will see the folder's contents in the Finder window.

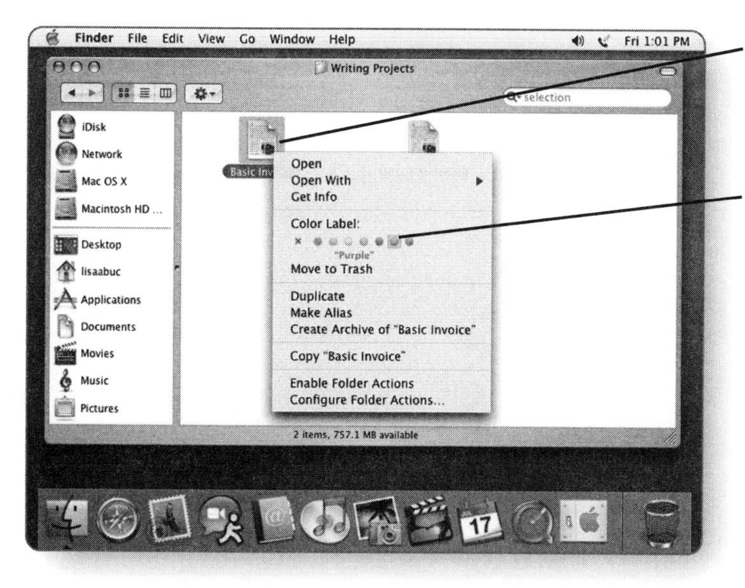

2. Control+click on the **file** or **folder name**. A contextual menu will appear.

3. Click on the desired **color dot** under Color Label. (To remove an assigned color, click on the gray x at the far left.) The label color will be applied to the file or folder.

Using Aliases

In Mac lingo, an alias is a shortcut link to a file or folder that you can double-click to open the file or folder. By creating and moving aliases to different folders (within your Home folder), you can set up numerous ways to access your files and folders.

> **TIP**
>
> For fastest access to a file or folder, create an alias for it and drag it from the Finder window to the desktop. Then you can use the alias to access the file or folder directly from the desktop.

You can move an alias to a variety of locations, such as the desktop, but you have to create it first.

1. **Open** the **folder** that holds the file or folder for which you want to create an alias. You will see the folder's contents in the Finder window.

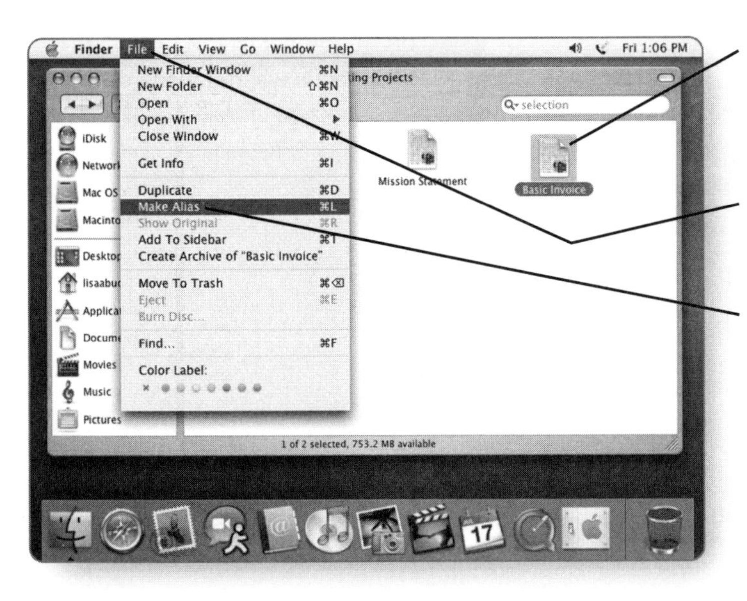

2. **Click** on the **file** or **folder**. The file or folder will appear selected or highlighted.

3. **Click** on **File**. The File menu will appear.

4. **Click** on **Make Alias**. The alias will appear immediately, with the file or folder name selected for renaming.

NOTE

You also can Control+click on the file or folder; then click on Make Alias in the contextual menu that appears.

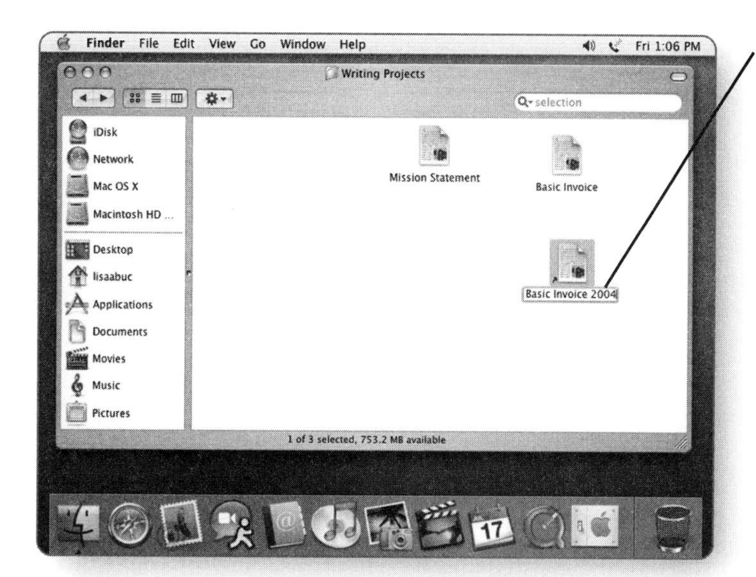

5. Type a **new name** and **press Return**. The new alias name will appear immediately below the alias icon. You can then move the alias to the desired location, just as you would any other file or folder.

TIP

The icon for an alias includes a small, angled, black arrow in the lower-left corner, so that you can distinguish the alias from the original file or folder. (Its text is not italicized or highlighted in any way, as in pre-Mac OS X operating systems.)

Part I Review Questions

1. How do I start up my Mac and Mac OS X Version 10.3 Jaguar? *See "Starting Up" in Chapter 1.*
2. How do I shut down my Mac and Mac OS X? *See "Shutting Down" in Chapter 1.*
3. How do I choose a command? *See "Choosing a Menu Command" in Chapter 2.*
4. How do I work with a dialog box? *See "Responding to a Dialog Box" in Chapter 2.*
5. What is a Finder window? *See "Previewing the New Finder Window," "Using the Finder Window Sidebar," and "Changing a Finder Window View" in Chapter 3.*
6. What's the fastest way to see open windows on the desktop? *See "Using Exposé to View Open Windows" in Chapter 3.*
7. What's my home folder? *See "Understanding Home Folders" in Chapter 4.*
8. How do I open a file? *See "Opening a File" in Chapter 4.*
9. How do I use the trash? *See "Working with the Trash" in Chapter 4.*
10. Can I label files and folders with color? *See "Choosing a Color Label" in Chapter 4.*

PART II

Working with Applications and Disks

5

Using the Dock and Applications

The Dock stands out as one of the most important new features of the Aqua interface in all versions of Mac OS X. You can use the Dock to start applications in Mac OS X. You also can temporarily "park" open files and windows on the Dock. In this chapter, you will learn how to:

- Start a program and select the current program.
- Save a file on disk.
- Find preference settings in an application.
- Hide and redisplay an application.
- Use the Dock as a parking place for files and folders.
- Quit an application.
- Go back to the desktop when needed.

Starting an Application from the Dock

The icons to the left of the vertical dividing line on the Dock represent applications, utilities, and key features of Mac OS X Version 10.3. The Dock icons provide easy access for starting a program or utility; click a Dock icon once to launch the associated program or utility. You can start as many applications or utilities as the amount of memory in your Mac allows. The following steps illustrate an example of using the Dock to start applications.

> **NOTE**
>
> You also can customize the Dock to include icons for other programs, as described in Chapter 8 "Setting up the Desktop."

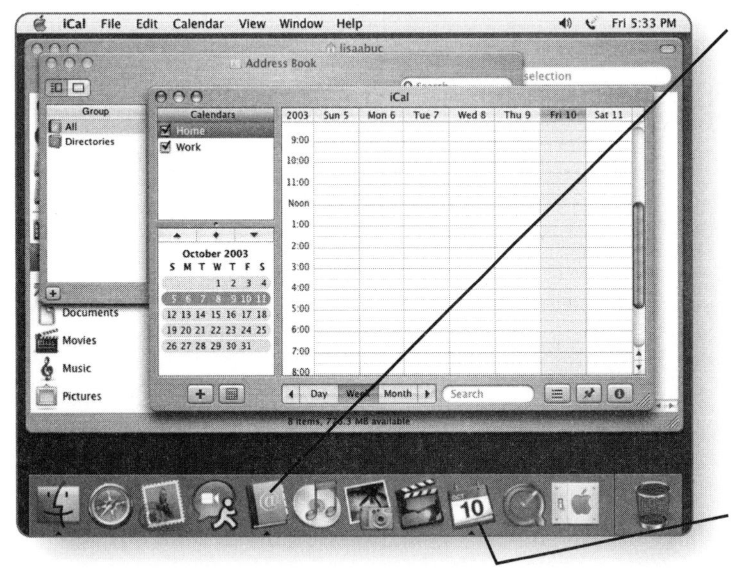

1. **Click** on the **Dock icon** for the application or utility you want to start. The application will launch, and its window will open. (You may be prompted to connect to the Internet or perform some other action when starting certain applications.) A small, black triangle will appear below the Dock icon to tell you that the application or utility is running.

2. **Click** on **another icon**. The next application or utility will start, and its window will open.

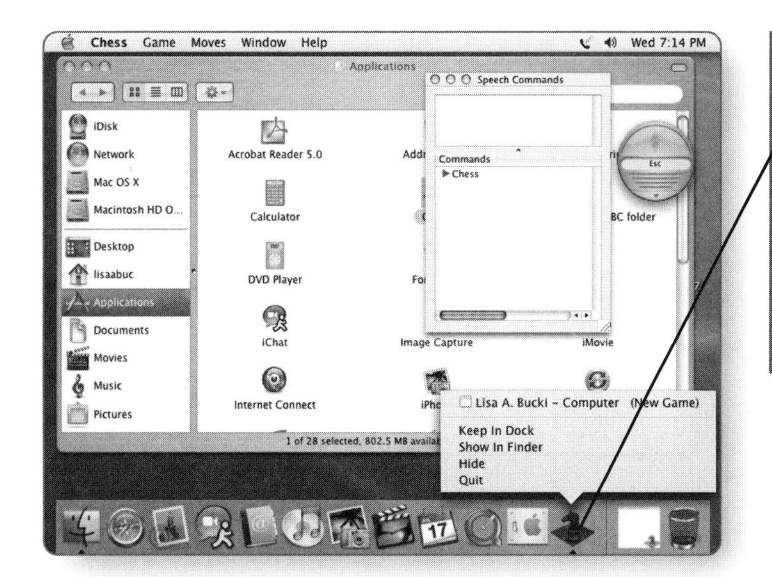

NOTE

Once an application is running on the Dock, you can Control+click on its icon to see a contextual menu of commands for working with the application.

Switching to an Application Using the Dock

After you start an application or utility, a small black triangle appears below its icon on the Dock. You can use such Dock icons to switch between running applications and utilities. As you learned in Chapter 4, "Working with Folders and Files," you can double-click an application or utility in a Finder window to start the application or utility. After you do so, an icon for the application or utility appears on the Dock so that you can switch back to the application or utility.

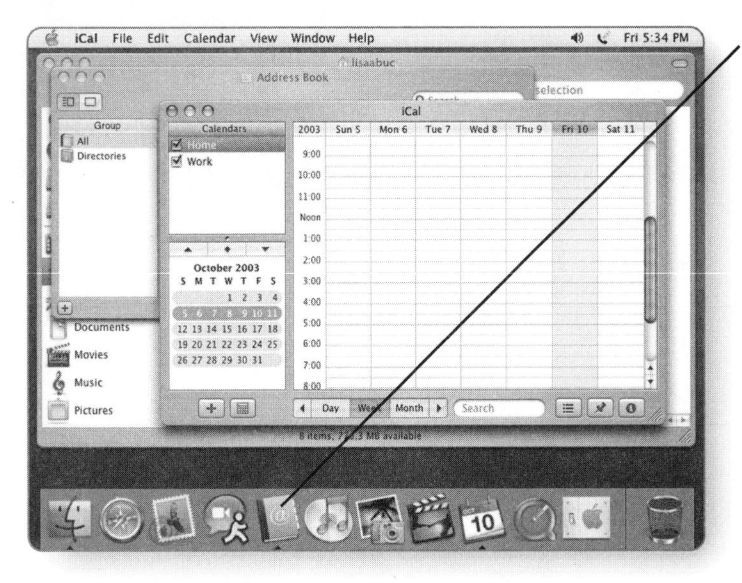

1. **Click** on the **icon** for the application or utility to which you want to switch. The application or utility window will jump to the front of other open windows, meaning that it has become the active application.

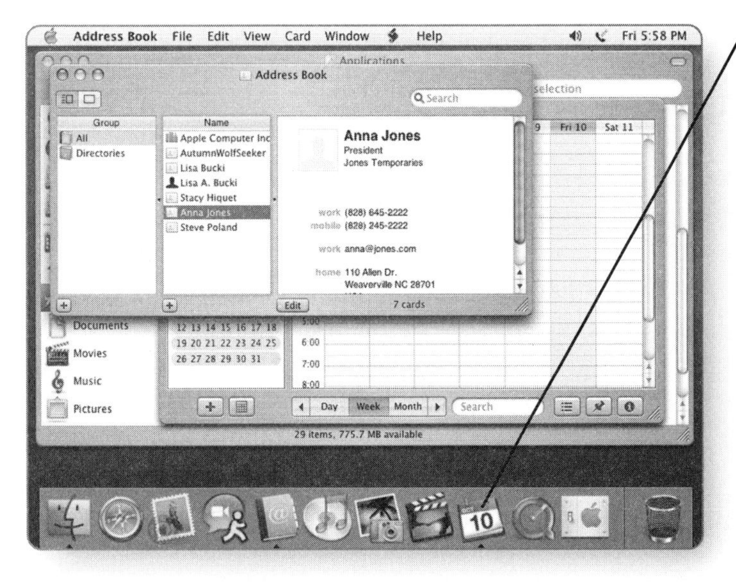

2. **Click** on **another icon**. The next application or utility will become the active application.

> **TIP**
>
> You also can press ⌘+Tab to cycle through the icons on the Dock. Each time you press ⌘+Tab, the next icon for a running application or utility on the Dock will be selected, thus enabling you to switch easily to the application or utility you want to use.

Saving a File in an Application

For utilities and features of Mac OS X Version 10.3, you generally change settings in a window or dialog box and then close the window to apply your changes. In other types of programs, such as the TextEdit word processor that you can start by double-clicking its icon in the Applications folder, you need to save your work to a particular file before closing your work or the application. The following steps illustrate how to save a file in an application, when required.

> **NOTE**
>
> Remember that if you've set up multiple accounts under Mac OS X Version 10.3, a user without administrator privileges can only save files within his or her Home folder.

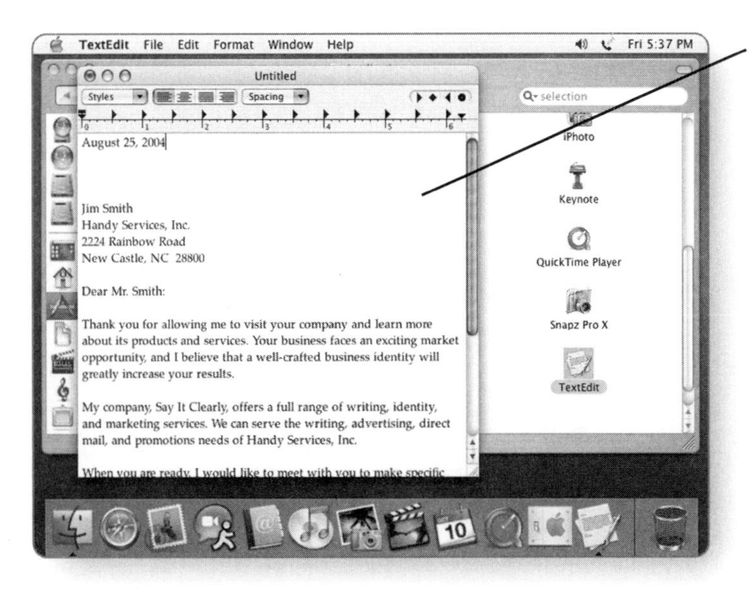

1. **Start** the **application** and **create** your **file**. Your work will appear in a window for the application.

> **TIP**
>
> Generally, a new, blank file is created for you the first time an application is started. After that, use the File, New menu command within the application to create another new file.

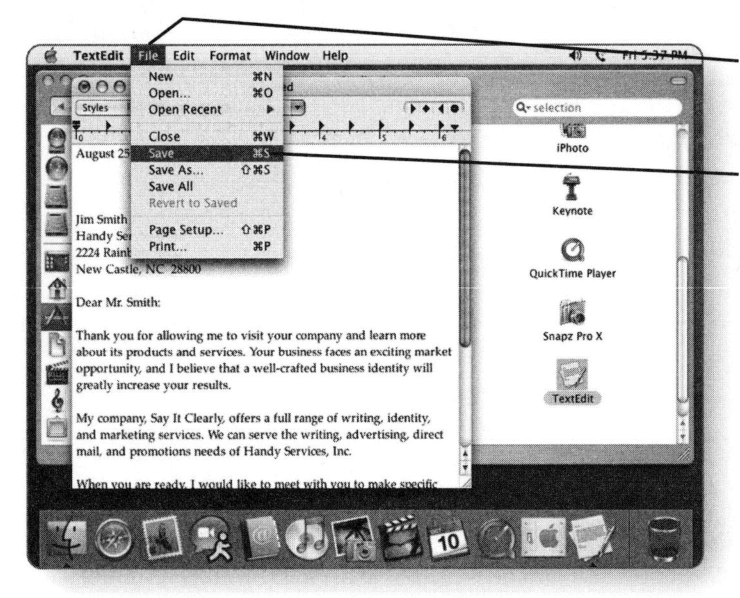

2. **Click** on **File**. The File menu will appear.

3. **Click** on **Save.** (In some applications, you may need to click on Save As.) The Save As sheet will open. By default, it will suggest that you save the file in the Documents folder within your home folder.

> **TIP**
>
> If you've already saved a file once but want to save a copy under a new name, choose File, Save As instead. If the application offers the File, Save As command rather than File, Save, choose File, Save As.

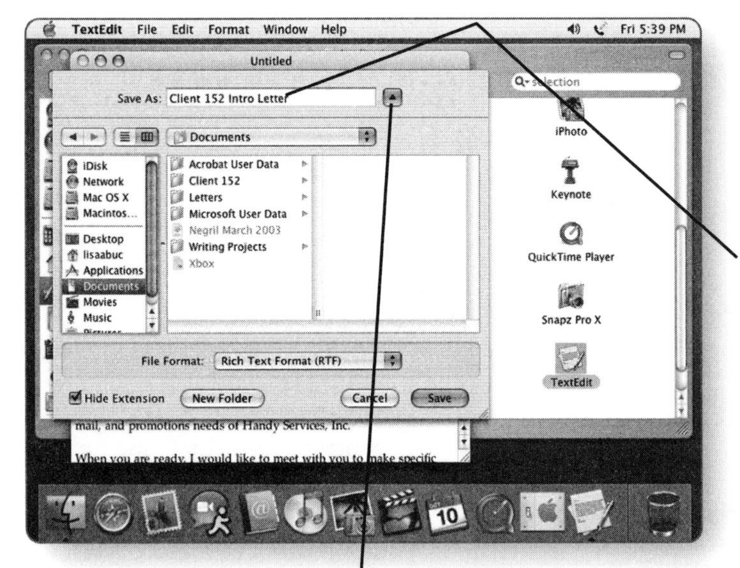

4. **Type** a **name** for the file in the Save As text box. Do not start a file name with the # sign or a period and avoid the / (slash) character, although you can use capitalization and spaces. The name will appear in the text box.

5. **Skip** to **Step 7** if you want to save the file in the current folder. Otherwise, **click** on the **Arrow button** to the right of the Save As text box. The sheet will expand to show a list of folders, so you can select or navigate to the folder that you need.

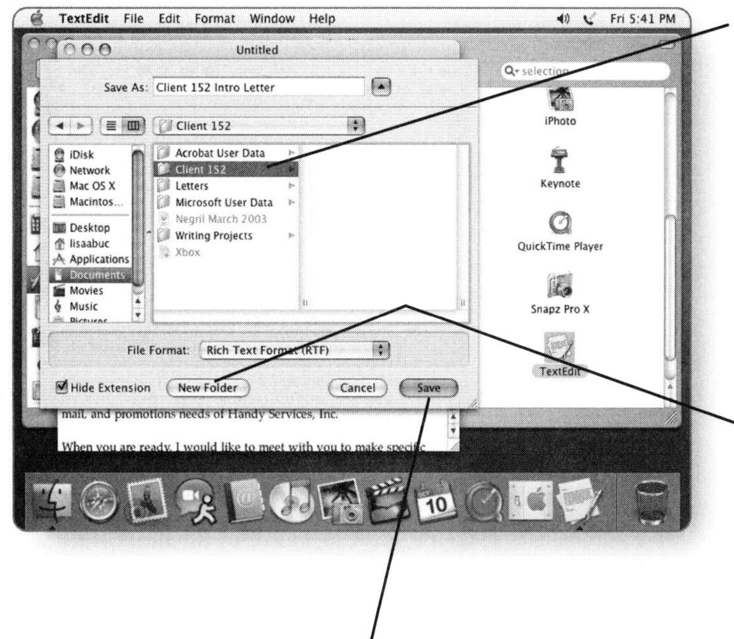

6. Click on a **folder name** in the center column. (Repeat the process to navigate to a desired location.) The new folder will be selected as the destination folder for the newly-saved file. To back up to a previous folder, click on the Back button.

> **TIP**
>
> Click on the New Folder button to create a new folder to hold the file you're saving. In the New Folder dialog box that opens, type a name for the new folder and then click on Create.

7. Click on **Save.** The Application saves the file in the location you specified, and the file name will appear in the title bar for the document window.

> **TIP**
>
> Choose File, Close or click on the Close button in the upper-left corner of the file window to close your document.

Setting Application Preferences

In Chapter 9,"Changing Essential System Preferences," you'll learn about a number of the preferences that you can set to control how Mac OS X Version 10.3 operates. Similarly, many applications offer a number of preferences that enable you to set basic parameters about how the application works, as the following example illustrates.

1. Start the **application**. It will appear onscreen, and its menu bar will appear at the top of the Desktop.

> **TIP**
>
> To start TextEdit, for example, click on Applications in a Finder window Sidebar. Scroll down in the window; then double-click on the TextEdit icon.

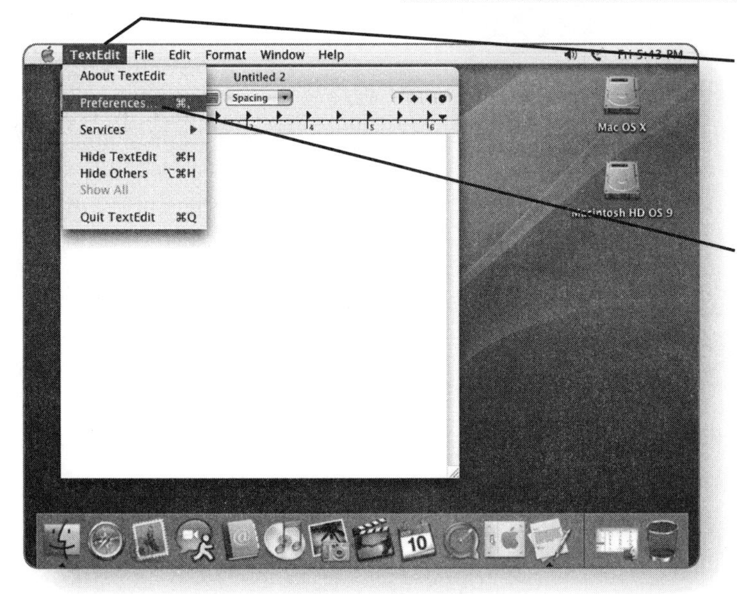

2. Click on the **application menu** (with the application or utility name). The application menu will appear.

3. Click on **Preferences.** The Preferences dialog box will open. The Preferences dialog box includes settings appropriate to the application or utility.

> **TIP**
>
> The applications included with Mac OS X Version 10.3 typically present the Preferences command on the application menu. However, applications by other software publishers may place the Preferences command on another menu. Consult the application's Help system to identify the correct menu.

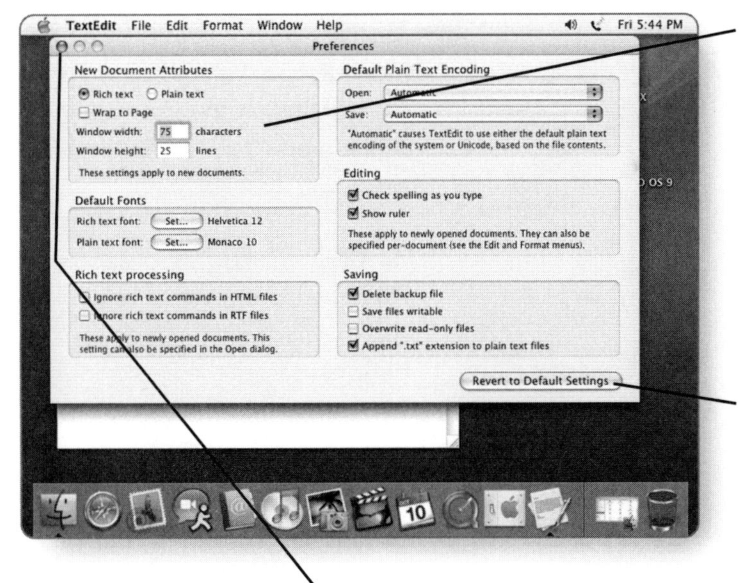

4a. Make changes to the settings, as needed. Consult the application's Help before making a particular change if you're unsure of how that change may affect the application's operation.

OR

4b. Click on **Revert to Default Settings**, if available. All the settings will return to their original state.

5. Click on the **Close button**. The dialog box will close, and the new preference settings will take effect.

Hiding and Redisplaying an Application

Hiding an application or utility removes its windows and menu from view without closing (quitting) it. The icon for the application or utility remains on the Dock, still displaying the black triangle that indicates that it's running. Hiding an application merely provides a way to reduce the number of open windows so that you have an easier time choosing the one you want to use.

1. Switch to the **application**. It will appear onscreen in a window, and its menu bar will appear at the top of the Desktop.

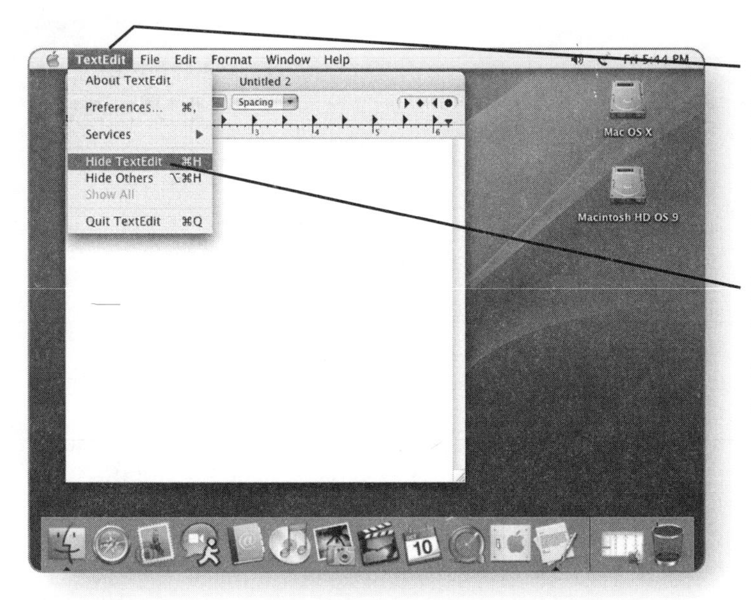

2. Click on the **application menu** (it has the application or utility name) at the far-left end of the menu bar. The application menu will appear.

3. Click on **Hide** (Application Name). The application or utility and its windows and menu will disappear from the Desktop.

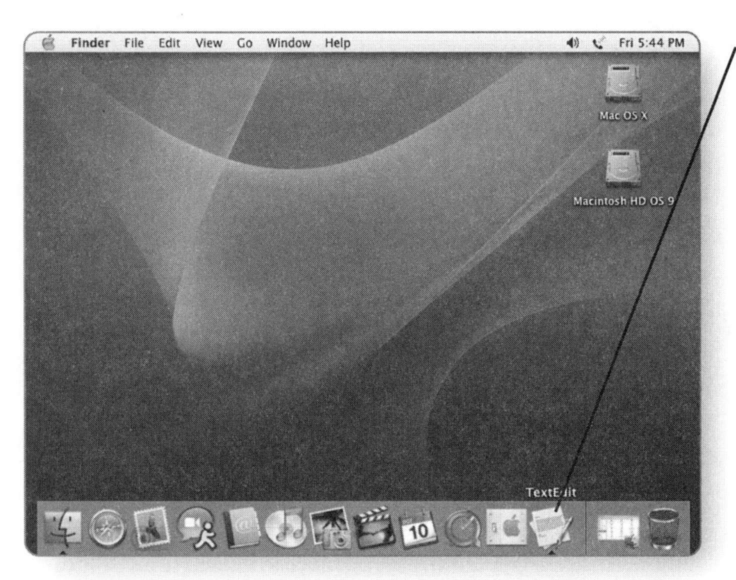

4. Click on the **icon** for the **application** or **utility** to redisplay on the Dock. The application window will reopen and will become the current application.

> **TIP**
>
> When you move the mouse pointer over any icon on the Dock, the name of the application, utility, file, or folder (for a Finder window) appears above the icon. If you've minimized multiple files or Finder windows, the pop-up name can help you make sure you're clicking on the right icon.

Minimizing and Expanding Windows

Rather than leaving multiple Finder or document windows onscreen and sizing and dragging them around, you can use the Dock as a convenient parking place for files and folders that you're not currently using but may need during the current work session. In such an instance, the icon for the Finder window or document window appears to the right of the vertical divider.

1. **Switch** to the **window to dock**. It will appear onscreen as the active or current window.

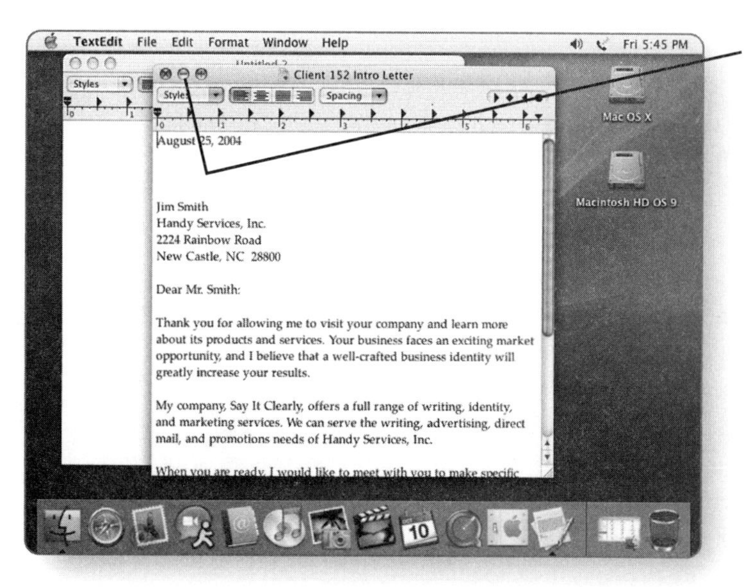

2. **Click** on the **Minimize button**. The window will minimize to an icon on the Dock.

> **TIP**
>
> You also can double-click on a window's title bar or choose Minimize Window from the Window menu to reduce the active window to an icon on the Dock.

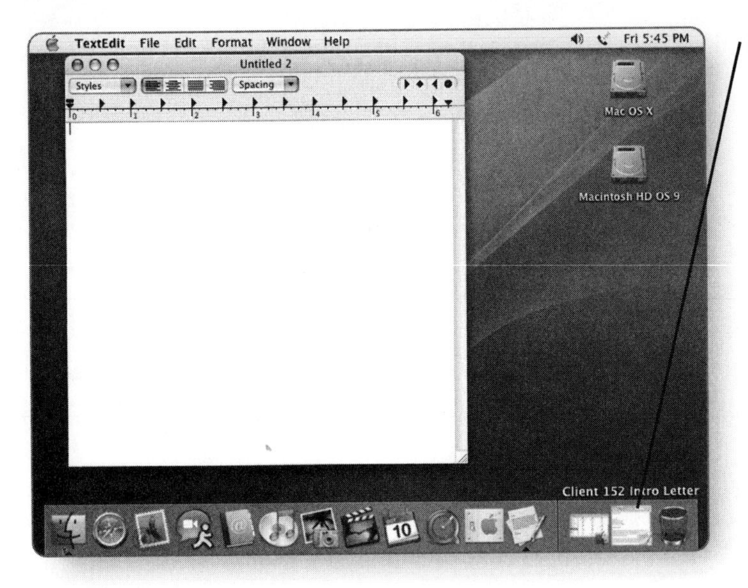

3. Click on the **icon** on the Dock. The window will expand, becoming the current window. If you opened a file window, its application also becomes the current application.

> **TIP**
>
> Alternatively, open the Window menu and click on the window name to reopen the window.

Quitting an Application

When you've finished working with an application or utility, it's a good practice to quit the application or utility. This frees up the system memory and other system resources that the application or utility was using, enabling the system to apply those resources to another function. For example, playing video in the QuickTime Player requires a lot of memory, so you'll want to close any other open programs or utilities to ensure the best video playback, especially if your Mac system is a bit low on memory. Fortunately, quitting an application is a quick process, as shown in the following steps:

1. Switch to the **application**. Its window will appear, and its menus will appear on the menu bar.

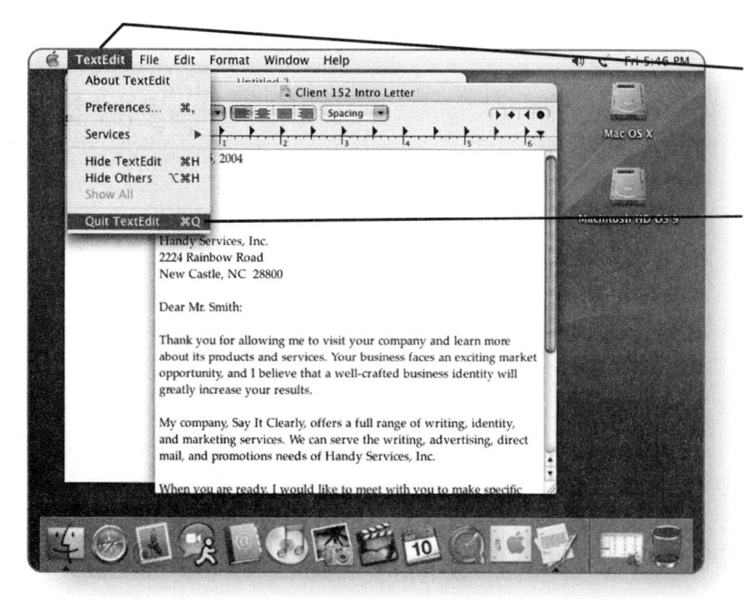

2. Click on the **application menu.** The application menu will appear.

3. Click on **Quit** (Application Name). The application or utility will close.

> **NOTE**
>
> If you made changes to a file that's open in the application and you didn't save the changes before quitting the application, a Close dialog box appears to ask whether you want to save the file. You can click on Don't Save to quit the application without saving the file, or Save to display the Save As dialog box so that you can use it to save the file.

Forcing an Application to Quit

If you encounter a situation where an application has "locked up" so that you cannot switch to it or use its menu to quit the program, Mac OS X Version 10.3 offers an alternate way to force a program to quit. Follow these steps to select an application or utility and force it to quit:

1. **Press ⌘+Option+Escape**. (You also can click on the Finder button on the Doc, click on the Apple menu, and then click on Force Quit.) The Force Quit Applications window will open, listing the running applications and utilities.

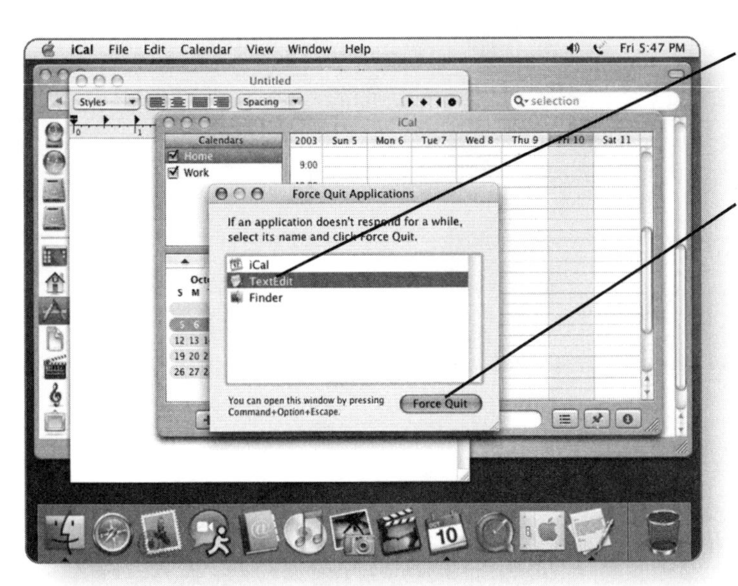

2. **Click** on the **application** or **utility name** in the list. The name will be selected.

3. **Click** on **Force Quit**. An Alert sheet will appear, asking you to confirm that you want to force the application to quit and noting that you will lose any unsaved work in the selected application.

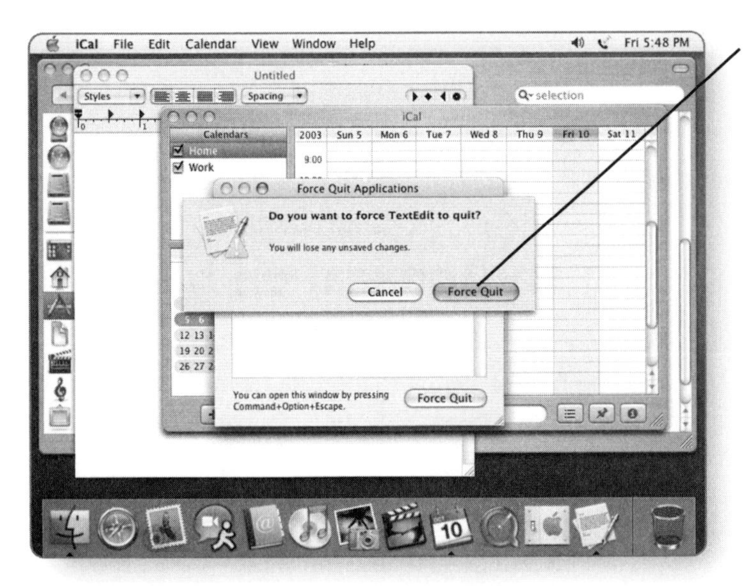

4. **Click** on **Force Quit**. The application or utility will quit, and its icon will be removed from the Dock, if applicable.

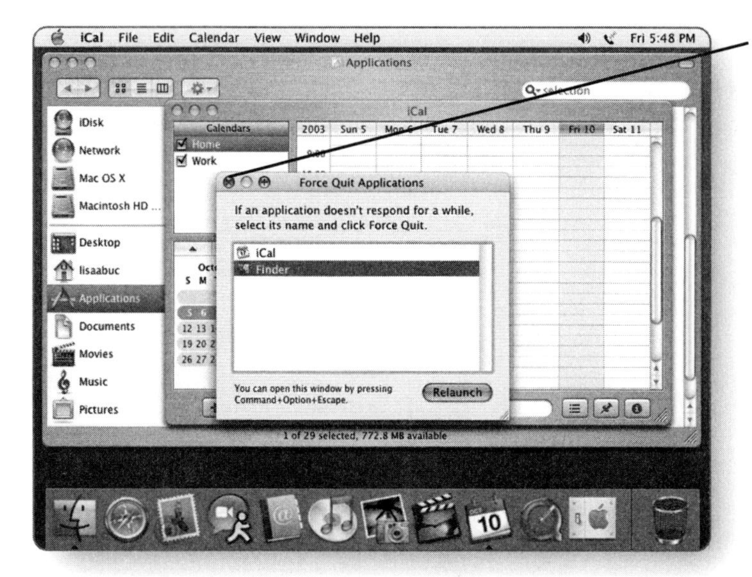

5. Click on the **Close button**. The Force Quit Applications window will close.

> **NOTE**
>
> If you force quit a Classic application (one designed to run under Mac OS 9), the Classic environment that Mac OS X Version 10.3 uses to run such applications may also hang or quit. See Chapter 7, "Working in the Classic (Mac OS 9) Environment" to learn more about quitting or restarting Classic and Classic apps.

Redisplaying the Desktop

If you have been working with many applications, you may want to quickly return to the desktop and display only Finder windows and the Finder menu bar.

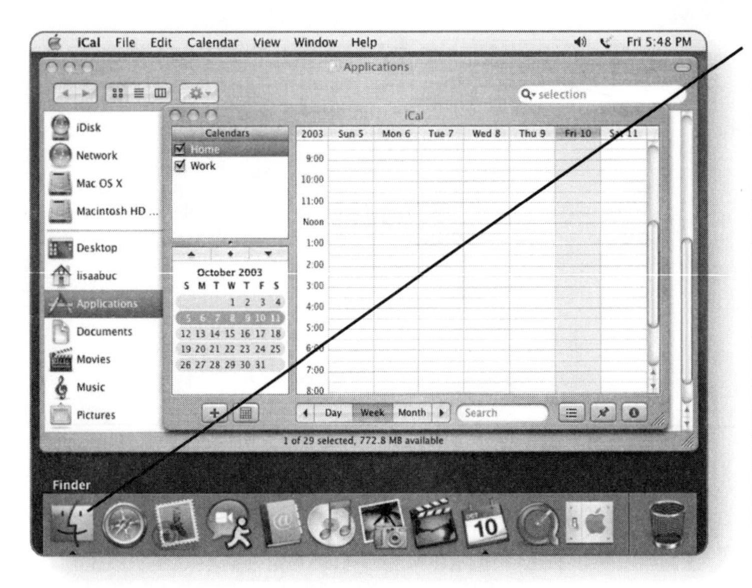

1. Click on the **Finder icon** on the Dock. The Finder will become the active application.

TIP

If you return to the Finder and don't see any open windows, they may have been hidden. Click on Finder on the menu bar, and the Finder windows will reappear.

6

Finding and Preserving Files

Today's computers feature large hard disks and, typically, CD writing capabilities. All this space is wonderful—until you need to find one of the thousands of files stored on a disk. That's why the Finder in Mac OS X Version 10.3 offers enhanced capabilities to help you protect files, find files when you need them, and burn files to CD-Rs for backup and storage. In this chapter, you'll learn how to:

- Encrypt your Home folder with the new FileVault.
- Index the contents of files in a specified disk or folder.
- Make a .zip archive of files.
- Perform a quick find.
- Use more advanced find options.
- Burn files to a CD-R.

Using FileVault to Protect Your Home Folder

With a more connected computer world, you have better access to files and information, whether on your own computer, on a network, or on the Internet. But recent problems with identity theft and other cyber crimes have spotlighted the need to prevent unwanted access to personal data or sensitive business information stored on your computer, especially when your computer is lost or stolen. You can use the new FileVault feature in Mac OS X Version 10.3 Panther to protect all the files and folders in your Home folder.

FileVault encrypts (scrambles) your files by using Advanced Encryption Standard 128-bit (AES-128) encryption. Once you log in to the system with your user password, FileVault will automatically decrypt files as you need them. When you turn on the FileVault protection, you also set up a master password for your Mac. Another user, such as a system administrator, can use the master password to log on to your system if you forget your user password or if you're unavailable to provide access to a crucial file on your system.

CAUTION

Apple's Help information about FileVault includes a warning that bears additional emphasis here. If you forget or lose both your user login password and the master password set for FileVault, you will not be able to retrieve the contents of your Home folder. Make sure to keep a record of your passwords somewhere!

Follow these steps to turn on the FileVault security feature:

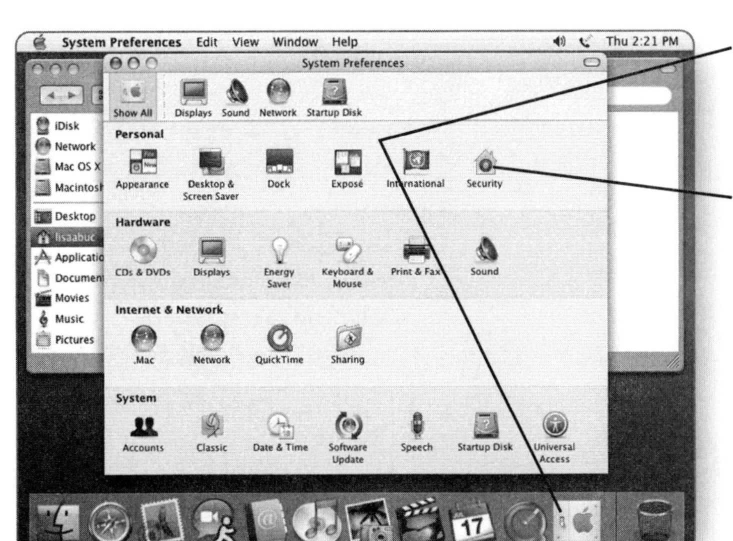

1. **Click** on the **System Preferences icon** on the Dock. System Preferences will launch.

2. **Click** on the **Security icon**. The Security pane will appear in the System Preferences window.

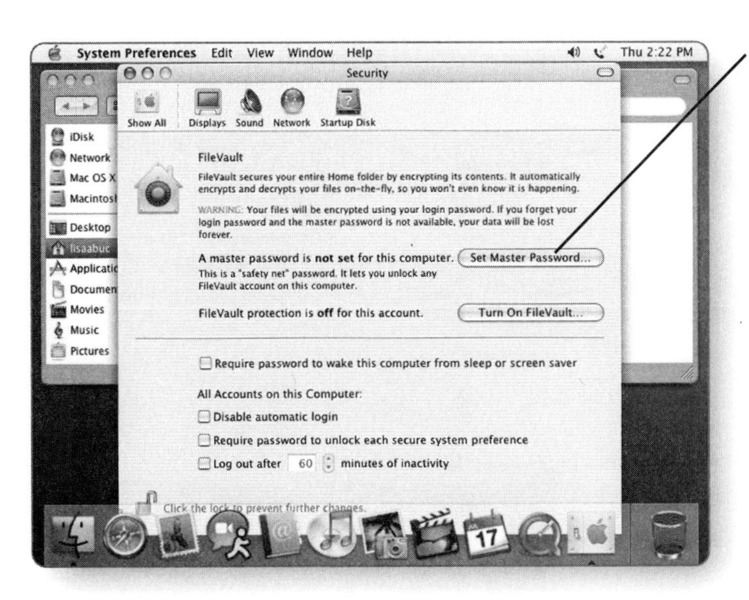

3. **Click** on **Set Master Password**. A sheet for creating the master password will appear.

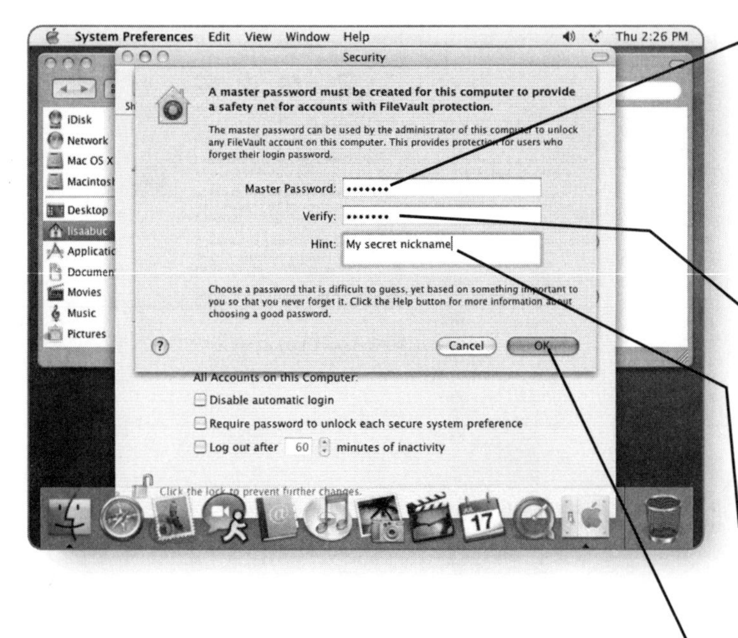

4. Type a **password** into the Master Password text box and **press Tab**. A dot will appear in the text box for each letter you type, and the insertion point will move to the Verify text box.

5. Type the **password again** in the Verify text box and **press Tab.** The insertion point will move to the Password Hint text box.

6. Type a **hint** in the Password Hint text box. If a user tries to log in to Mac OS X and fails three times, the password hint will appear.

7. Click on **OK**. The master password sheet will close.

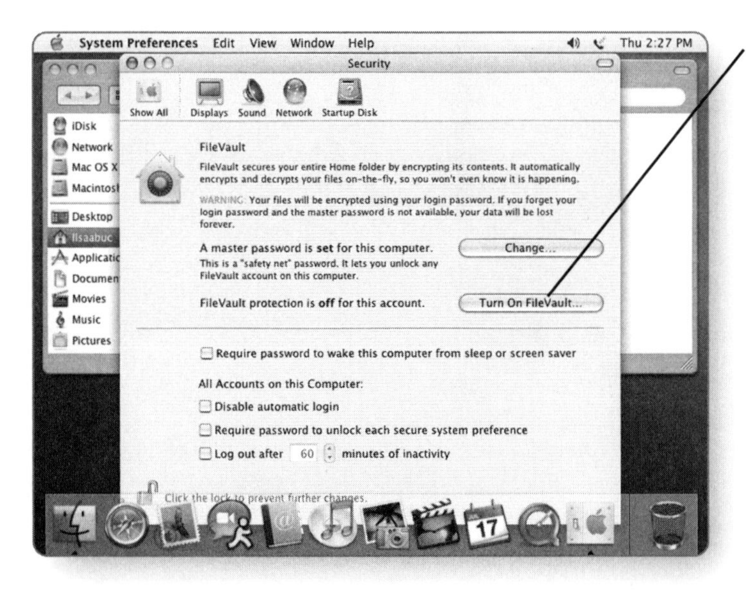

8. Click on **Turn On FileVault.** A sheet prompting you to enter your user password will appear.

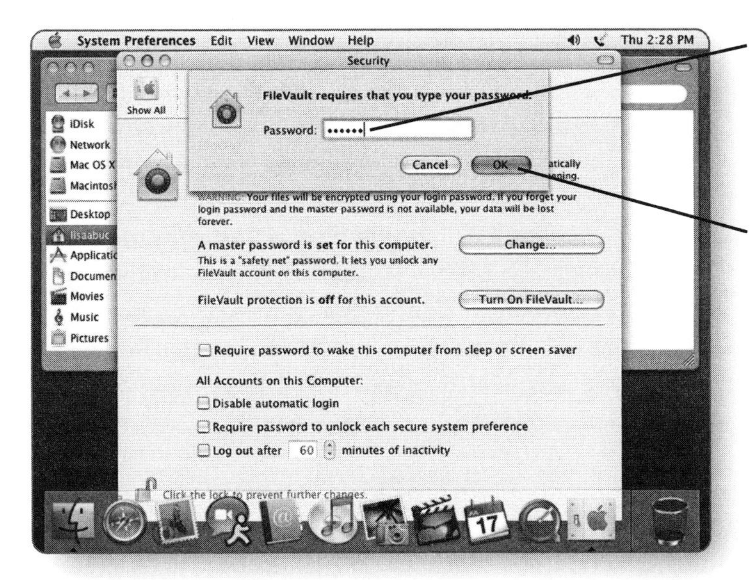

9. Type your **password** into the Password text box. A dot will appear in the text box for each letter you type.

10. Click on **OK**. The password sheet will close, and a warning sheet will appear.

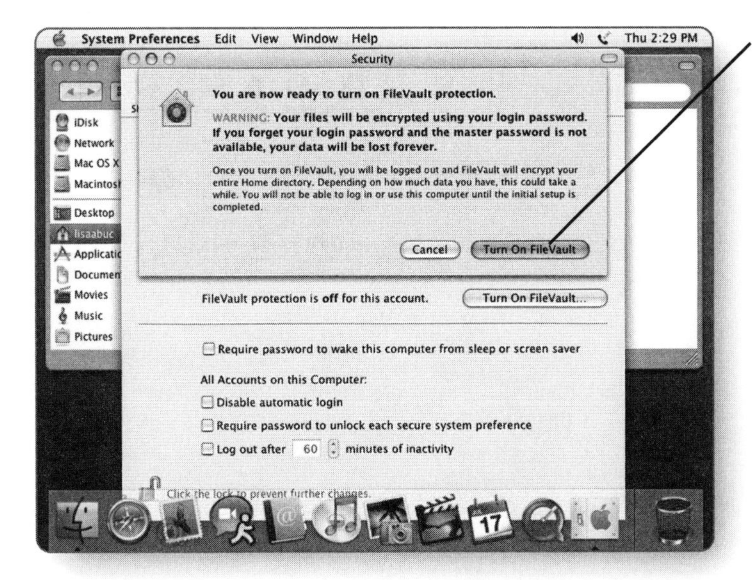

11. Review the warning carefully and then **click** on **Turn On FileVault.** The warning sheet will close, and FileVault will encrypt your Home folder. The process will take several minutes. When FileVault finishes, you will be prompted to log back in to your system.

You can turn off the FileVault protection at any time by redisplaying the Security pane of System Preferences and clicking on Turn Off FileVault.

> **NOTE**
>
> If you're using FileVault, you must be logged in to your system for other users to have access to your shared folders over a network.

Indexing Files

Its indexing capability helps Mac OS X Version 10.3 identify the contents of individual files in a specific folder or on a disk. The process works something like a book index. Finder builds its behind-the-scenes list of keywords and identifies the file in which each is located. Then, if you search for one of those keywords, the Finder can identify the relative files more quickly. Finder does index on its own when you perform a search, but you should also index your hard disks periodically to keep the index current. To create an index:

> **TIP**
>
> The indexed information includes file properties or info.

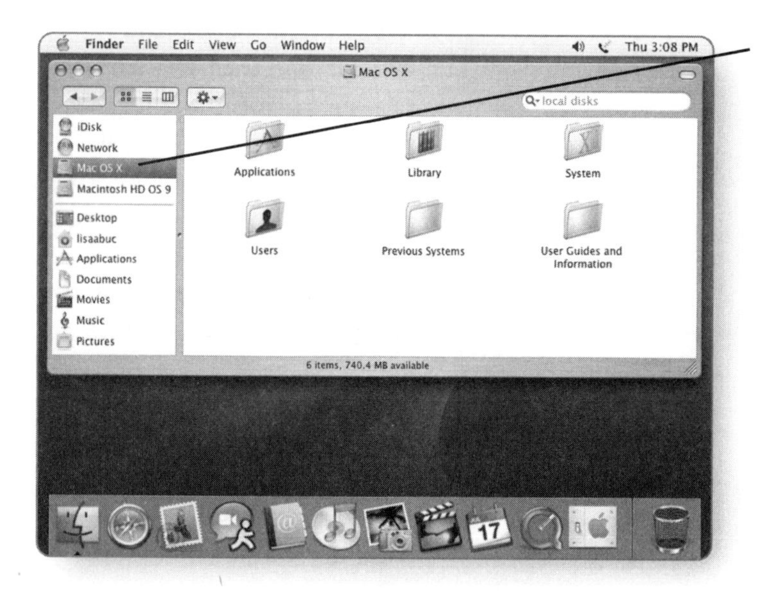

1. In a Finder window Sidebar, **click** on the **disk** or **folder** for the item to index. The disk or folder will be selected.

2. Click on **File**. The File menu will appear.

3. Click on **Get Info**. The Info window for the selected disk or folder will open.

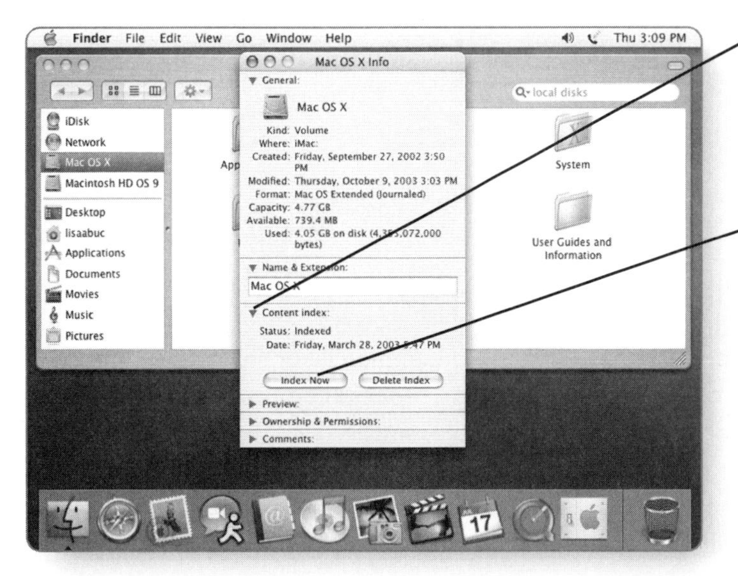

4. Click on the **Content index section divider**. The section will expand to display its information and choices.

5. Click on **Index Now**. The Finder will build the index, which may take a few minutes for a large hard disk. When the process finishes, the Status displayed in the Content index section will change to Indexed.

TIP

Click on Stop Indexing if you need to terminate the process and index the selected location later. You also can use the Delete Index button to discard the existing index and build a new one.

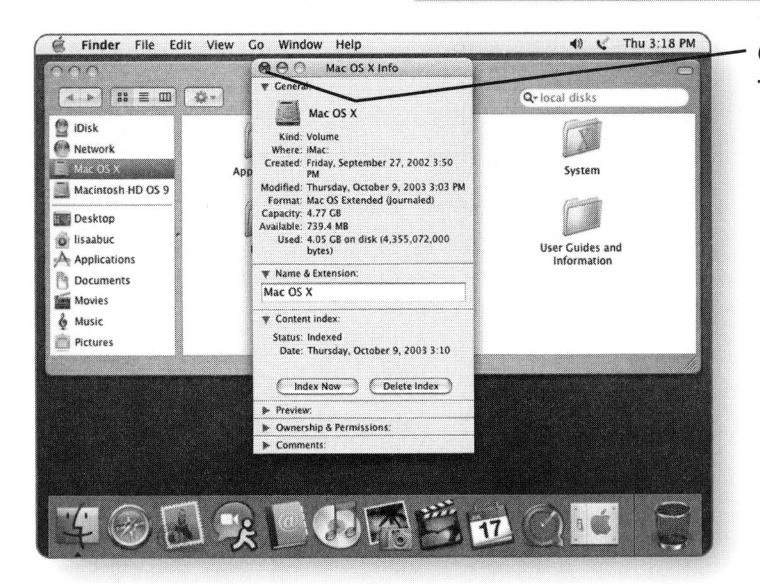

6. **Click** on the **Close button.** The Info window will close.

Archiving (Zipping) Files

Mac users have long used commercial or shareware software to archive files. The archive process compresses several files that you select into a single, smaller file. The single archive file can be emailed or otherwise shared more easily than multiple files. Mac OS X Version 10.3 Panther now offers archiving as a built-in feature. You can create an archive (with the .zip file extension) of any files that you select in a Finder window. Follow these steps to create and open an archive:

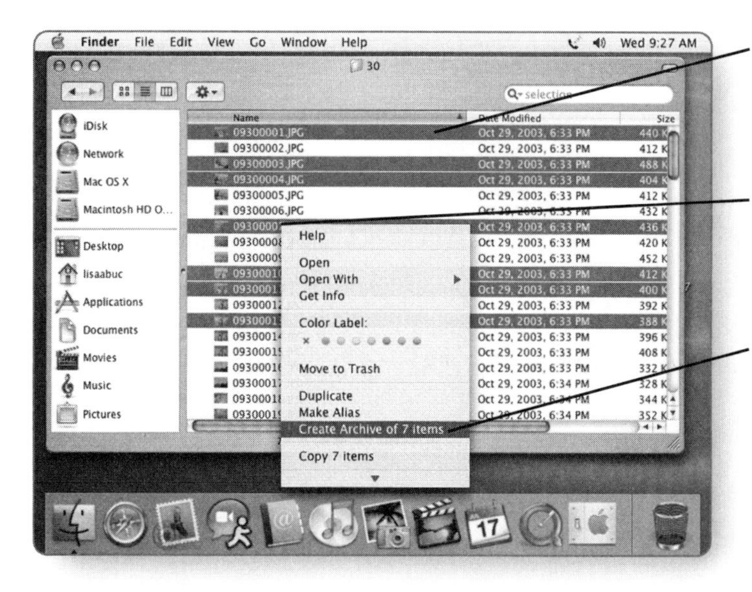

1. In a Finder window, **select** the **files to archive.** Selection highlights will appear.

2. **Control+click** on the **selected files**. A shortcut menu will appear.

3. **Click** on **Create Archive of (X) items**. Mac OS X will create the archive file, naming it Archive.zip.

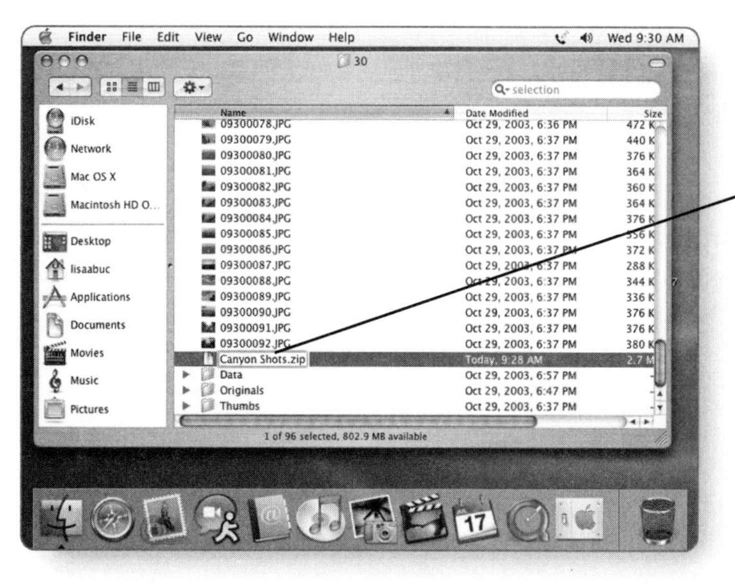

4. **Click** on the **archive file** and then **click** on **its file name**. The file name will be selected.

5. **Edit** the **file name** and **press Return**. The new file name will appear.

CAUTION

I suggest that you leave the ".zip" file name extension unedited. This ensures that other users will know the file is an archive and that other systems will recognize the archive file format.

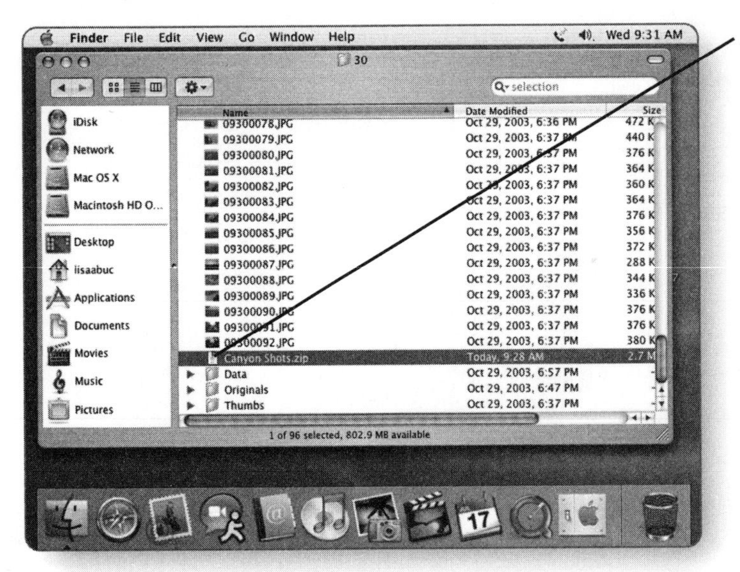

6. Double-click on the **archive file**. A folder for the archive file contents will be created (it will have the same name as the archive file), and the individual files from the archive will be expanded and placed in the folder.

Finding a File from the Finder Window

If you need to find a file or folder whose name contains a particular word or phrase, you can do so by using a tool on the Finder window. The Search tool enables you to find Files or folders.

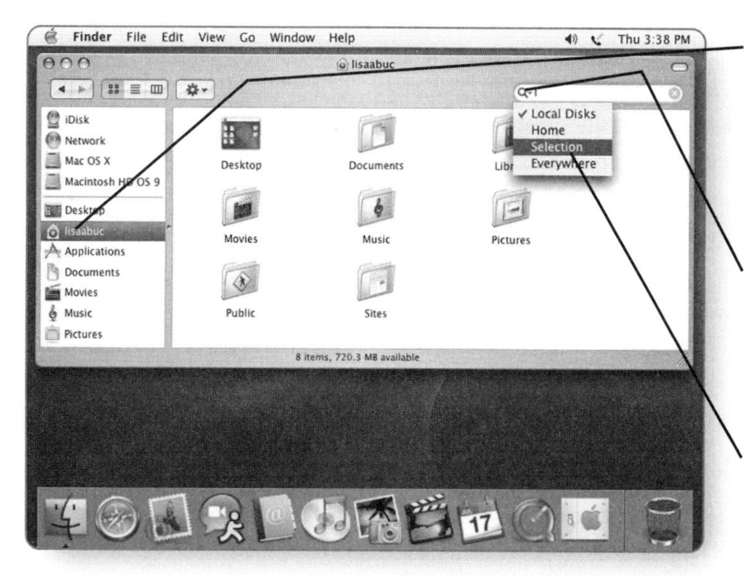

1. To search within a particular folder, **navigate** to the **disk** or **folder to search.** The contents of the disk or folder will appear in the Finder window.

2. **Click** on the **magnifying glass icon** in the Search text box. A menu of search locations will appear.

3. **Click** on **Selection**. The Search tool will then search only the selected disk or folder.

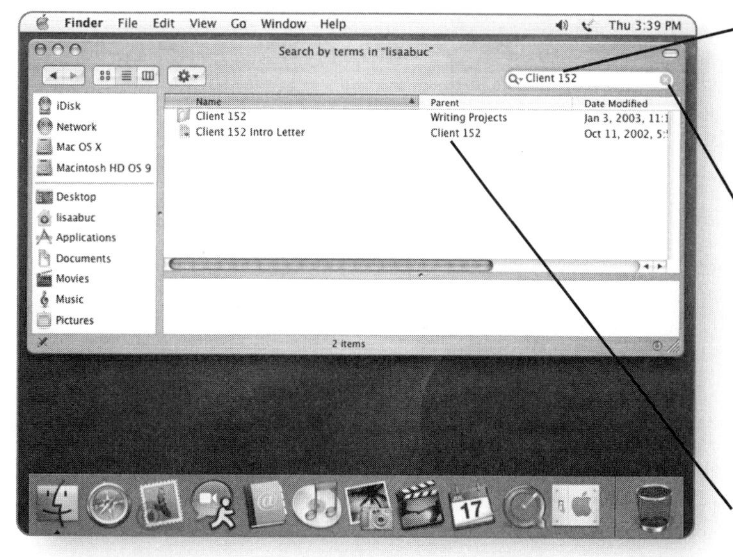

4. **Click** in the **Search text box** and **type** the **search word** or **phrase**.

> **TIP**
>
> Click on the x button to remove the search word or phrase and redisplay all the contents of the selected disk or folder.

The Finder will perform the search and will display the matching files and folders in the Finder window.

Performing an Advanced Find

The Search tool won't return the results you need if the content you'd like to search for is within a particular file rather than part of the file or folder name. Not to worry. Finder also now offers more advanced search capabilities, so you can search for a file based on a word or phrase it contains, based on part of its name, or based on the date it was last modified.

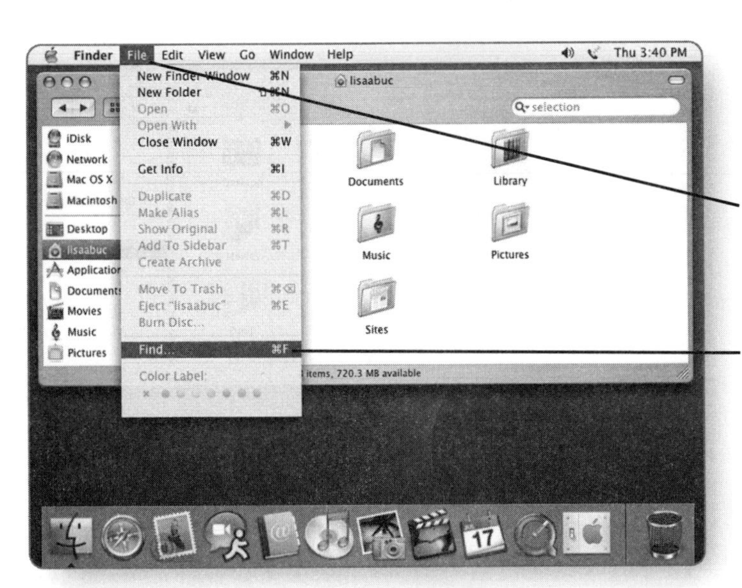

1. With a Finder window open, **click** on **File**. The File menu will appear.

2. **Click** on **Find**. The Find window will open.

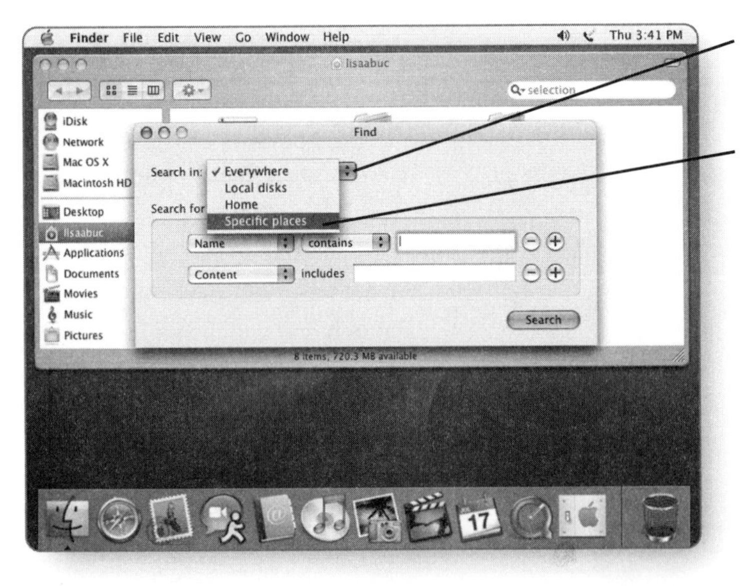

3. **Click** on the **Search in pop-up menu**. The menu will appear.

4. **Click** on the **location to search**. Your choice will appear.

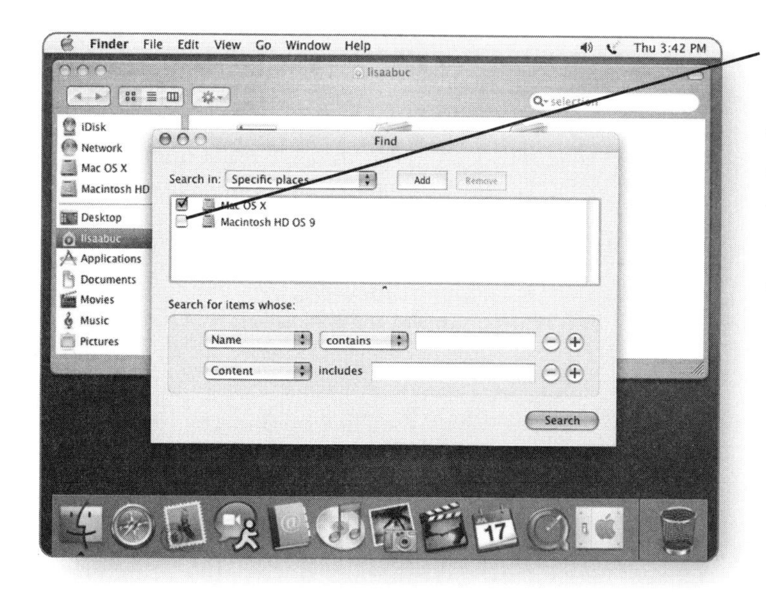

5. If you chose Specific places in Step 4, **click** on the **check box** to check or clear the desired disk check boxes that appear in the Search in list as needed. The Finder will search only checked disks.

6. Specify the **desired search criteria**. The default choices include:

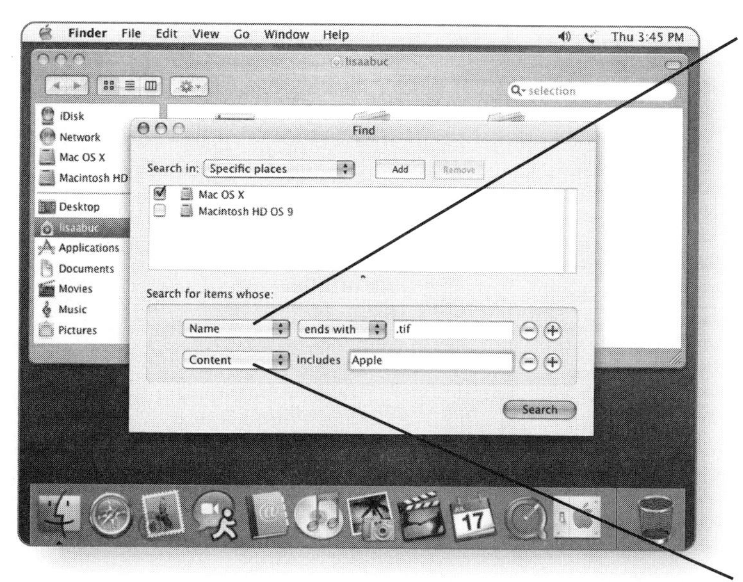

- **Criterion.** Use the first pop-up menu to choose a criterion such as file Name or Date Created. Then use the accompanying pop-up menu (and text box if any) that appears to indicate what to search for. For example, if you're searching for a file name, specify whether the file name starts with, ends with, contains, or is the word or phrase you enter in the accompanying text box.
- **Content.** Type the word or phrase that is found in the file(s) (or in the descriptive file info for the file) that you're searching for.

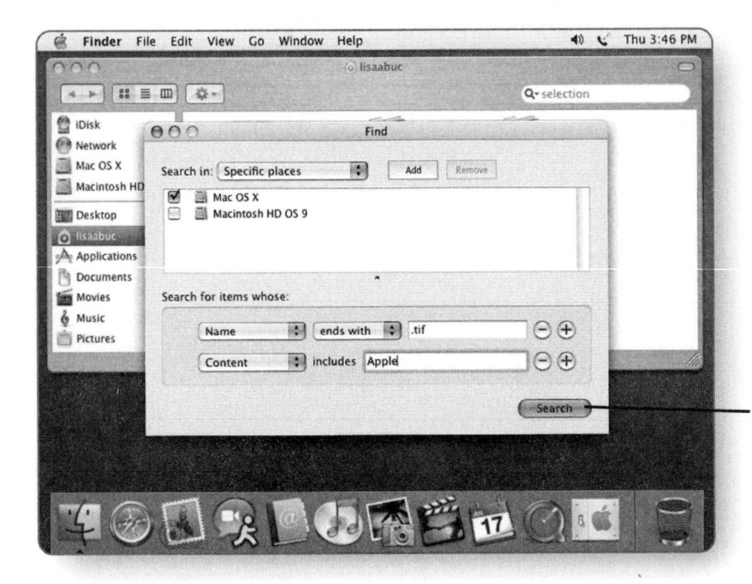

NOTE

To remove a criterion from the Find window, click on the minus icon to the right of it. To add additional criteria, click on the plus icon.

7. Click on **Search**. The Finder will open the Search Results window. After the find process finishes, which may take a moment or two, the Search Results window will list matching files so that you can work with them.

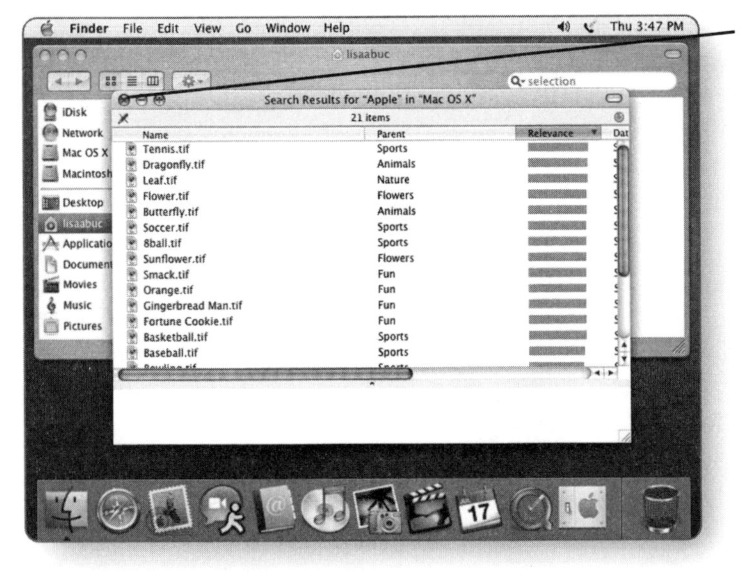

8. Click on the **Close button** for the Search Results window when you've finished working with the found files. The window will close. Back in the Find window, you can perform an additional find or close down Find.

> **NOTE**
>
> When you enter multiple criteria in the Find window, the found files must match *all* the criteria. So, if the find operation doesn't list the desired file in the Search Results window, you can try returning to the Find window and remove one or more criteria to broaden the search results.

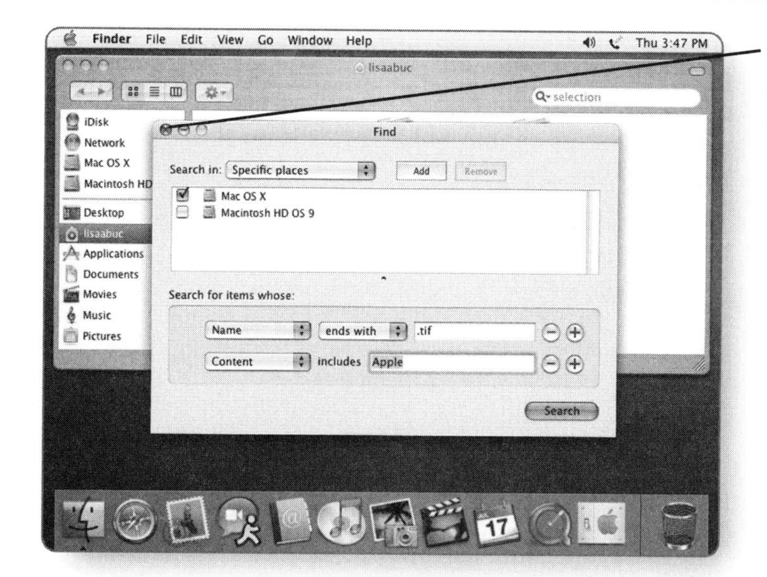

9. Click on the **Close button** for the Find window. The window will close.

Burning a CD-R

Even if you judiciously delete old files from time to time, you may still find your hard disk filling up. In such a case, you can copy old files to a CD-R (Compact Disc-Recordable) or CD-RW (Compact Disc-ReWriteable), assuming that you have a drive for one or both of those media installed with your Mac. After you've preserved the old files on a CD-R, you can delete those old files from the hard disk to free up space.

> **NOTE**
>
> You can erase CD-RW discs by using Mac OS X Version 10.3's Disk Utility. The section called "Erasing a Disk" in Chapter 22 describes the process for erasing all types of disks.

New Macs (with the exception of iBooks) ship with built-in CD-R drives, but you also can add a high-speed external drive that connects to an older Mac via USB or FireWire (or both) for around $200. Of course, you'll need to install the appropriate drivers so that Mac OS X Version 10.3 can run the drive, but you don't need to install any specific CD-burning software as was once required. Mac OS X Version 10.3 includes technology to enable it to recognize blank writeable media and enable you to burn files to that media.

> **NOTE**
>
> I like to make it a practice to burn all the files related to a particular project to a CD-R after I finish, so I can then remove the files from the hard disk. You also can organize CD-R content by category, such as photos of wildlife, .MP3s by your favorite band, and so on.

1. Make sure the drive is connected and turned on; then **insert** a **blank CD-R** or **CD-RW** into the drive. The Finder will display a message dialog box prompting you to specify how you want to proceed with the inserted media.

> **NOTE**
>
> Depending on the age of your drive and its drivers, you may see additional prompts at this point to guide you through the process of preparing the disc for content.

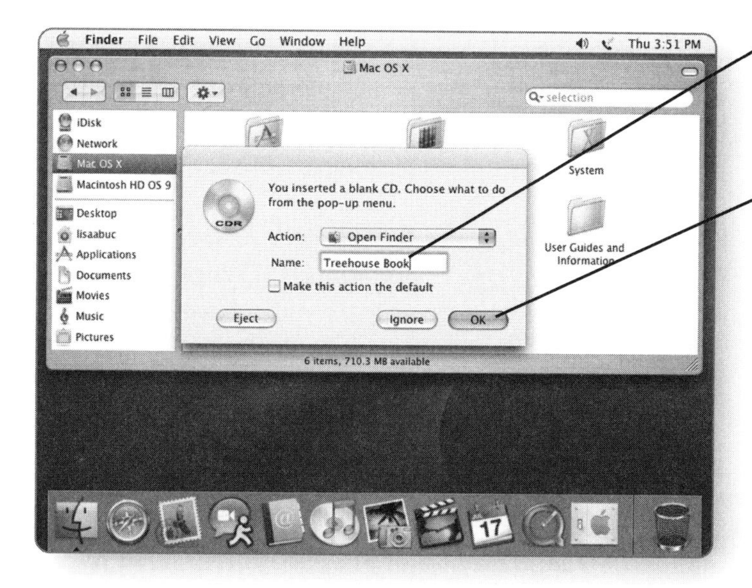

2. Type a **volume name** for the CD-R in the Name text box. The name will appear.

3. **Click** on **OK**. Mac OS X will prepare the disk to receive files and will display an icon for the CD-R on the desktop and in the Finder Sidebar.

NOTE

If you want to burn music files, you can click on the Action pop-up menu and then click on Open iTunes. To copy a whole disk, you can click on the Action pop-up menu and then click on Open Disk Copy.

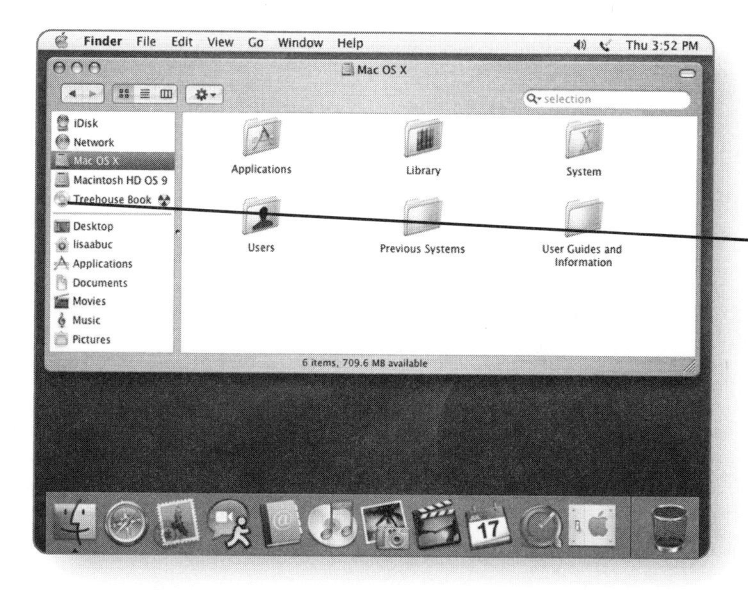

4. **⌘+click** on the **CD-R icon** in the Sidebar. A Finder window for the CD-R will open.

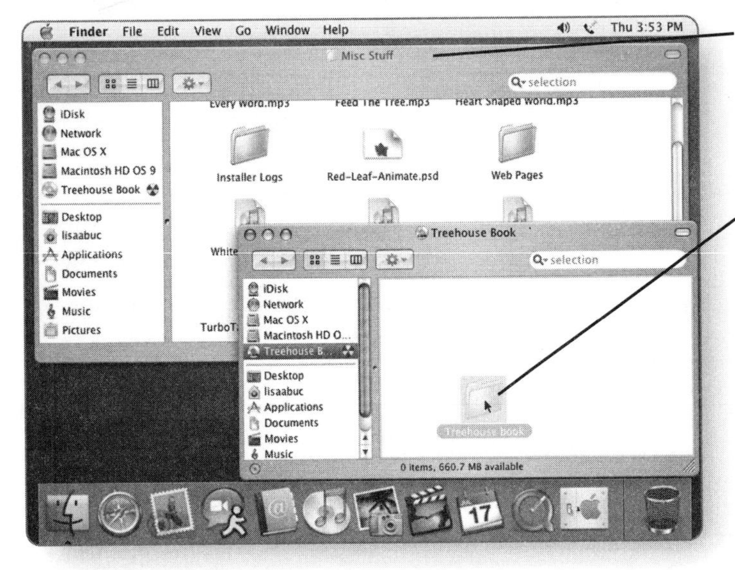

5. Return to or **open another Finder window** and **navigate** to the **location** holding the files to burn to the CD-R.

6. Select the **item(s)** to **copy** and **drag them** onto the CD-R window. A Copy window informs you of the progress of the copy operation. When the operation finishes, the items appear in the Finder window for the CD-R.

NOTE

If there is not enough free space on the CD-R to hold the items to be copied, a message will inform you. Click OK to close the message and deselect some of the items.

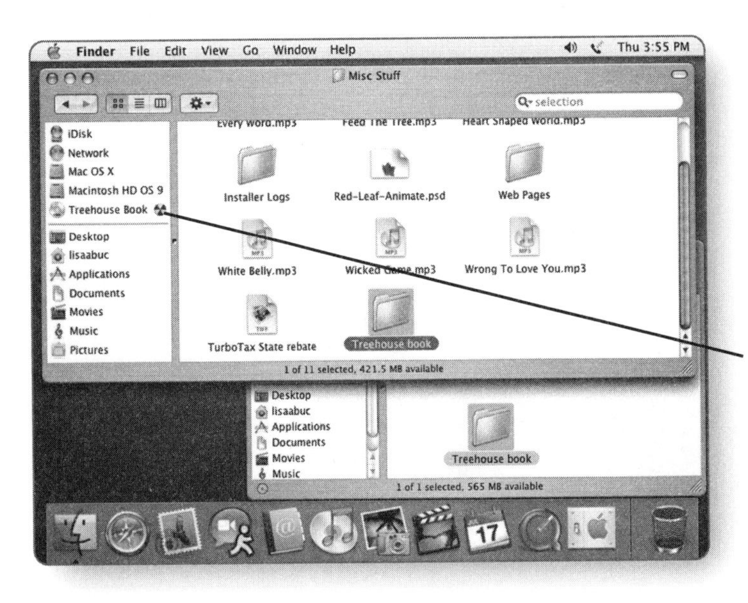

7. In any open Finder window, **click** on the **Burn Disc button** beside the CD-R icon in the Sidebar. A confirmation dialog box will open.

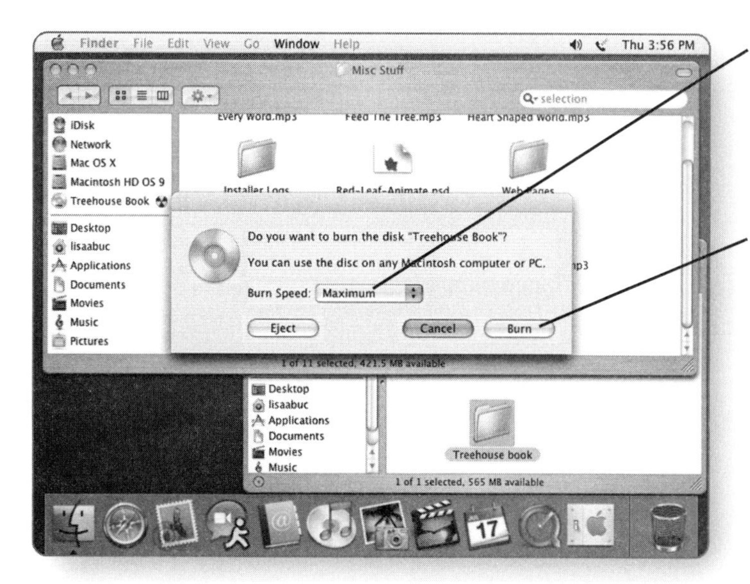

8. **Choose** an **alternate burn speed** from the Burn Speed pop-up menu. The selected speed will appear.

9. **Click** on **Burn**. The Finder window for the CD-R will close, and the Burn window will appear to illustrate progress as Mac OS X Version 10.3 burns and verifies the files. When the process finishes, an icon for the finished CD-R will appear on the desktop and in the Sidebar.

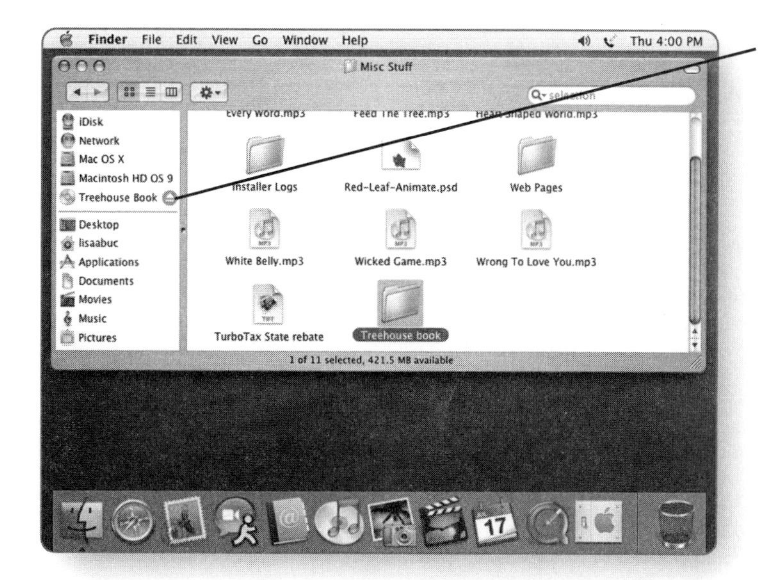

10. In any open Finder window, **click** on the **Eject button** beside the CD-R icon in the Sidebar. The drive will eject the disc.

> **CAUTION**
>
> For good measure, always test a new CD-R (preferably in another drive, if possible) before you Trash the original files or folders from the hard disk. Despite the ever-improving quality of drives and media, burn errors do sometimes occur. So you want to make sure the final CD-R is good before you permanently delete any files.

7

Working in the Classic (Mac OS 9) Environment

In this third major release of the Unix-based Mac OS X operating system, Apple continues to accommodate those of us who use programs written for Mac OS 9. You might stick with your trusty OS 9 app because you can't find an equivalent OS X app, prefer the features of the OS 9 app, or are just being a little frugal. Whatever the reason, Apple's answer is the Classic environment, which enables you to seamlessly use older software while working in Mac OS X Version 10.3. In this chapter, you'll learn how to:

- Enter and exit the Classic Environment.
- Start a Classic application.
- Move between Mac OS X applications and Classic applications.

Starting the Classic Environment

Mac OS X has built-in software that enables it to run applications designed for the older Mac OS 9 (referred to as *Classic applications*). The Classic environment in Mac OS X offers this capability. This important feature enables you to continue using your favorite Mac applications until upgraded versions designed for Mac OS X become available.

The Classic environment starts automatically when required, running Mac OS 9.2, which installs automatically with Mac OS X Version 10.3. However, you also can start the Classic environment at any time.

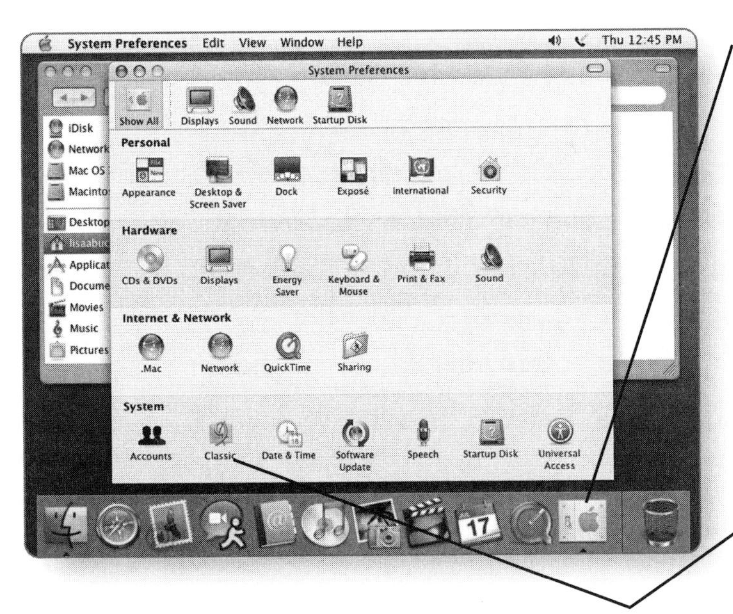

1. Click on the **System Preferences icon** on the Dock. System Preferences will launch.

> **NOTE**
>
> Read more about using System Preferences in Chapter 9, "Changing Essential System Preferences."

2. Click on the **Classic icon.** The Classic pane will appear in the System Preferences window.

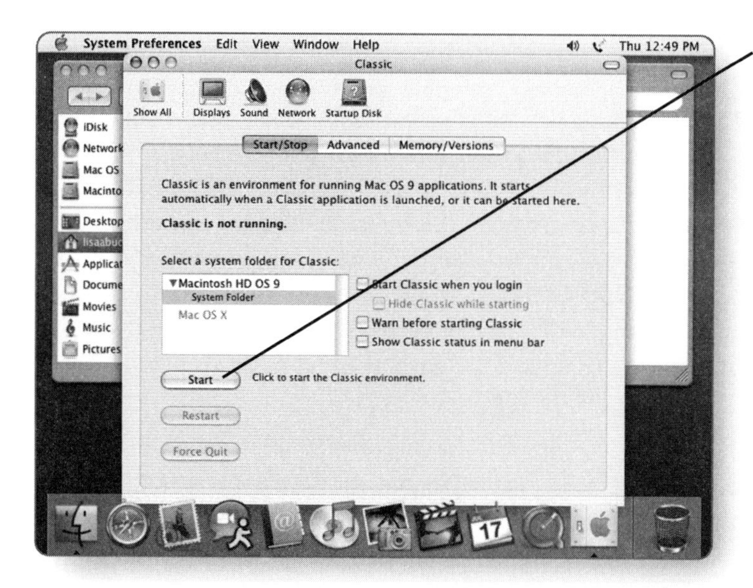

3. Click on **Start**. The Classic icon will appear briefly on the Dock, and the other choices for working with Classic will be enabled in the Start/Stop group of the Classic pane in the System Preferences window.

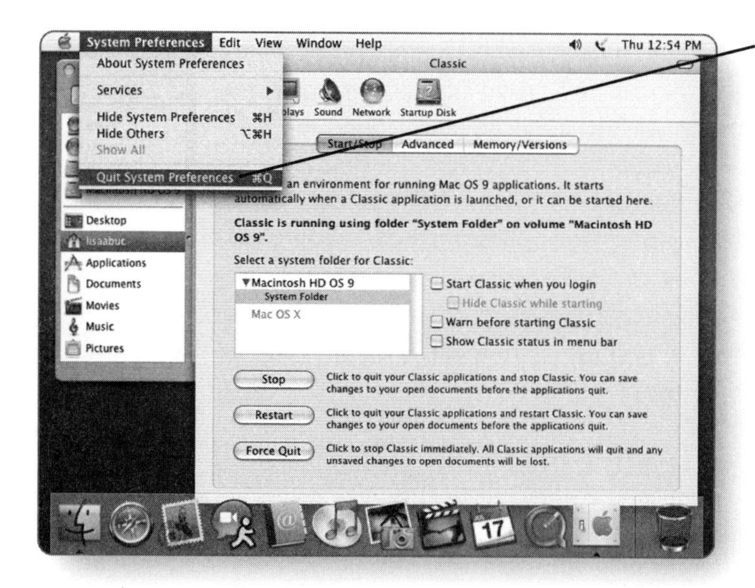

If you want, you can close the System Preferences window by choosing System Preferences, Quit System Preferences. You can start Classic applications as needed, and the Classic menus will appear.

TIP

The Start/Stop settings in the Classic pane also include options for starting the Classic environment automatically when you log in under Mac OS X Version 10.3 (the Start Classic when you log in check box) and for displaying a warning asking you to confirm whether or not to load when you attempt to start a Classic application (the Warn before starting Classic check box). Enable these options as needed to have greater control over when Classic loads.

Starting and Quitting a Classic Application

As noted earlier, the Classic environment enables you to run an application designed for older Mac operating systems. To start a Classic application, you use the same method as you would to start an application designed for Mac OS X. Once you start a Classic application, the desktop changes a bit to include the Mac OS 9 menu bar. You can then use that menu bar to work in the application, just as you would have done in Mac OS 9. The following example illustrates how this works with the SimpleText application, which appears on your system as part of the support system for the Classic environment.

TIP

If you didn't start the Classic environment prior to starting a Classic application, the Classic environment will launch automatically unless some problem prevents it from doing so.

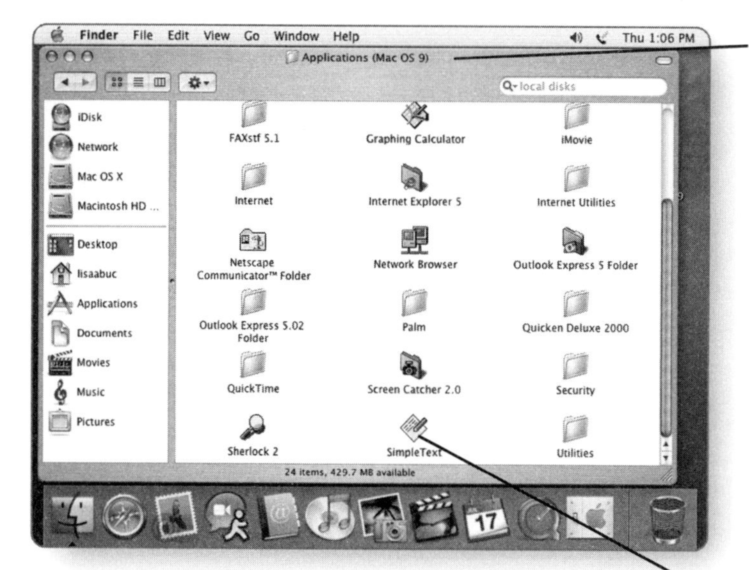

1. Open the **Applications (Mac OS 9) folder** in the Finder. You will see the folder's contents in the Finder window.

> **NOTE**
>
> The Applications (Mac OS 9) folder may appear on a separate disk volume if you installed Mac OS X to a new partition on the system's hard disk.

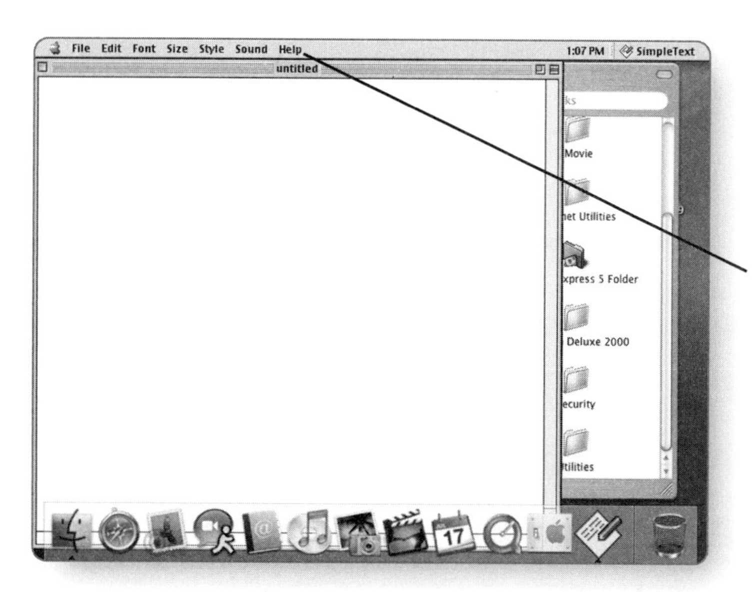

2. Double-click on **SimpleText**. (Of course, you would double-click on the icon for another Classic application to start it rather than SimpleText.) The application will launch, and its icon will appear in the Dock.

3. Review the **menu bar**. It will change to look like a Mac OS 9 menu bar, and it will offer the menus for SimpleText. Dialog boxes for the application also will look and work just as they did in Mac OS 9.

NOTE

When you're using a Mac OS X application, the Mac OS X menu bar appears at the top of the Desktop. When you're using a Classic application, its Classic menu bar appears. This visual clue helps you ensure that you've made the correct application active. You can use the Dock to switch between Classic applications and Mac OS X applications.

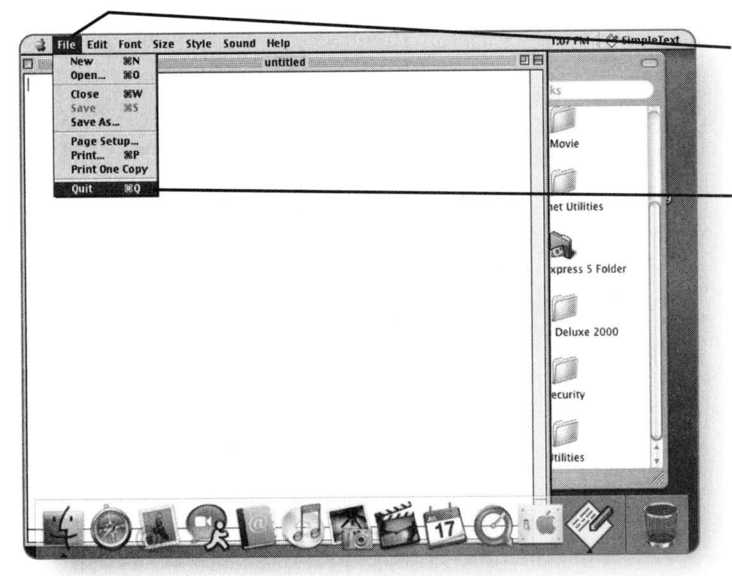

4. To close a Classic application like SimpleText, **click** on **File**. The File menu will appear.

5. **Click** on **Quit**. The Classic application will quit, but the Classic environment will continue to run, while the Mac OS X menu bar will return. If you have any unsaved work in a Classic application, the application will prompt you to save that work before it quits.

NOTE

Not all older applications will run in the Classic environment. If you think you might need to use all your Classic applications, then you should have Mac OS 9.x installed on another partition on your system so you can boot to Mac OS 9.x. Appendix A, "Installation Notes," gives you pointers about how you can set up your system to run both Mac operating systems. Systems purchased after January 2003 can boot into Mac OS X only, however.

Adjusting Classic Preferences and Checking Usage Stats

You can control just a few aspects of how the Classic environment behaves, as well as checking the amount of system memory being used by Classic environment applications and background processes. You accomplish these operations in the System Preferences pane you used earlier to start the Classic environment. The following steps show you how to find the Classic preferences and check memory usage to troubleshoot problems.

1. Click on the **System Preferences icon.** The System Preferences window will open, and its menu will appear.

2. Click on the **Classic icon.** The Classic pane will appear in the System Preferences window.

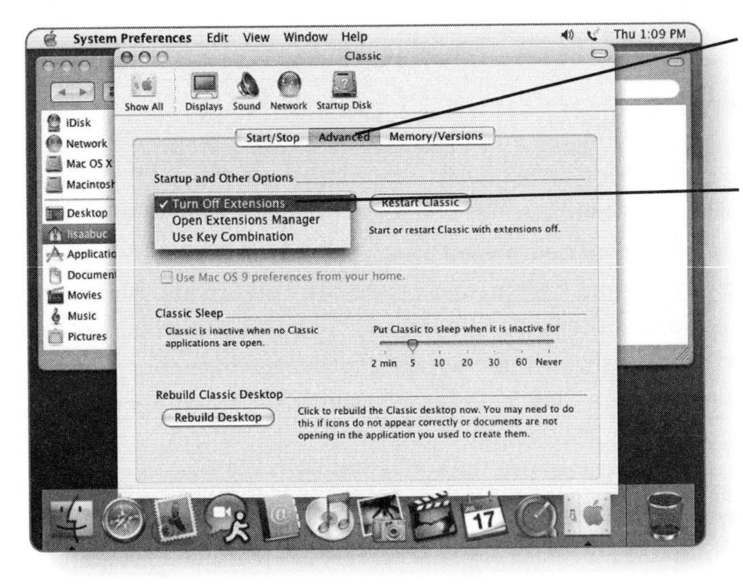

3. Click on **Advanced**. The Advanced settings will appear in the window.

4. Click on the **Startup Options** pop-up menu and then **click** an **option**. The option will appear in the pop-up menu.

The choices in the Startup Options pop-up menu designate which system extensions load when the Classic environment starts under Mac OS X. Use the choices to troubleshoot Classic applications and improve overall Classic environment performance.

NOTE

Checking Use Mac OS 9 preferences from your home, when available, instead loads preferences stored in your Home folder. These preferences are stored each time you change the settings on the Advanced tab of the Classic pane, so choosing this option saves you the trouble of resetting preferences each time you use the Classic environment.

5. **Click** on **Restart Classic** to activate your Startup Options pop-up menu choice. Classic will restart with the newly designated setting.

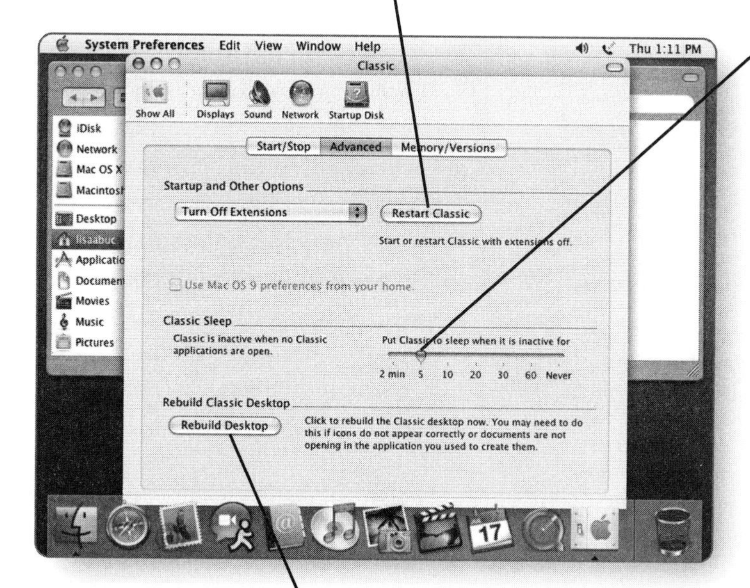

6. **Drag** the **Put Classic to sleep when it is inactive for slider**. This will specify the amount of time Classic can remain inactive before Classic sleeps. Your system performance will improve when the Classic environment is in sleep mode.

> **CAUTION**
>
> If Classic applications hang when the Classic environment sleeps, change the Put Classic to sleep when it is inactive for setting to Never.

7. **Click** on **Rebuild Desktop** if you are having trouble with files opening with the incorrect application in Classic. A dialog box will appear; use it to update the application bindings (the application associated with files of a particular type) on a disk volume.

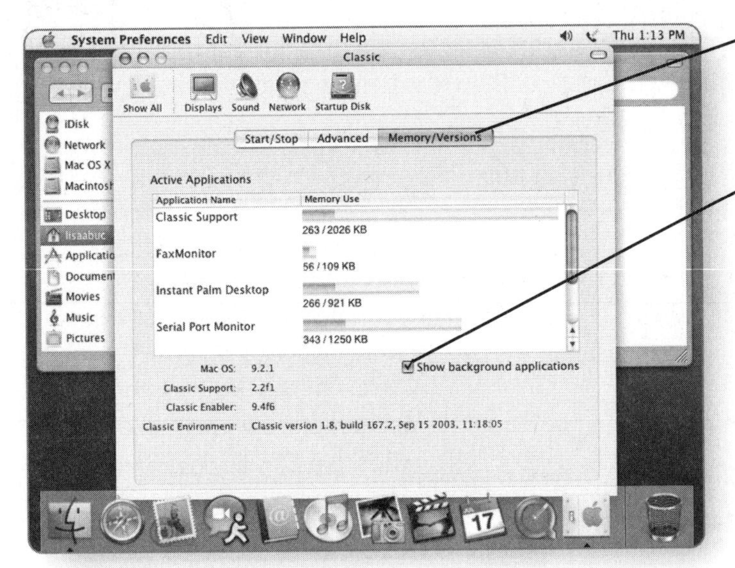

8. **Click** on **Memory/Versions.** The Memory/Versions settings will appear in the window.

9. **Click** on the **Show background applications check box.** The application processes will appear in the Active Applications list, along with any Classic applications that are running, so you can check memory consumption.

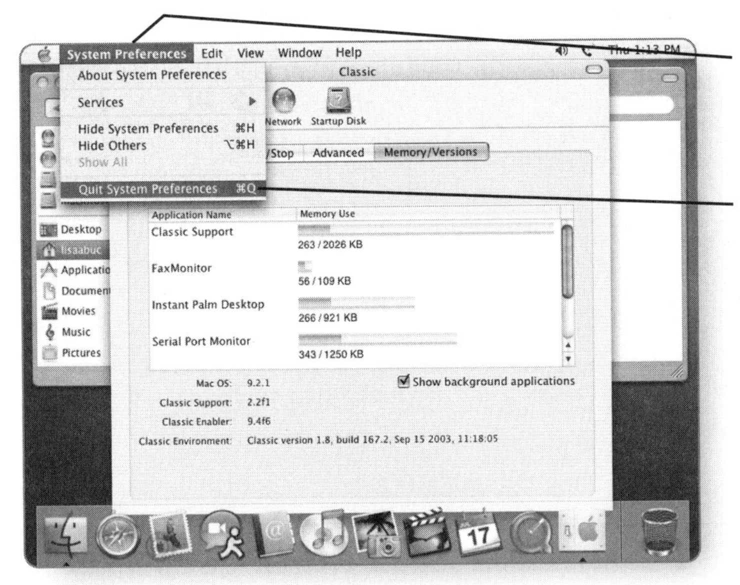

10. **Click** on **System Preferences.** The System Preferences menu will appear.

11. **Click** on **Quit System Preferences.** System Preferences will close and will apply the selected new Classic environment settings.

> **NOTE**
>
> Closing the System Preferences window while the Classic environment is running does not shut down or exit the Classic environment.

Closing the Classic Environment

If you've finished working in your Classic applications for the current work session and have quit those applications, it's a good idea to quit the Classic environment as well. Like any other application or utility, the Classic environment consumes system memory. Quitting the Classic environment releases that memory so that your Mac can use it for other applications.

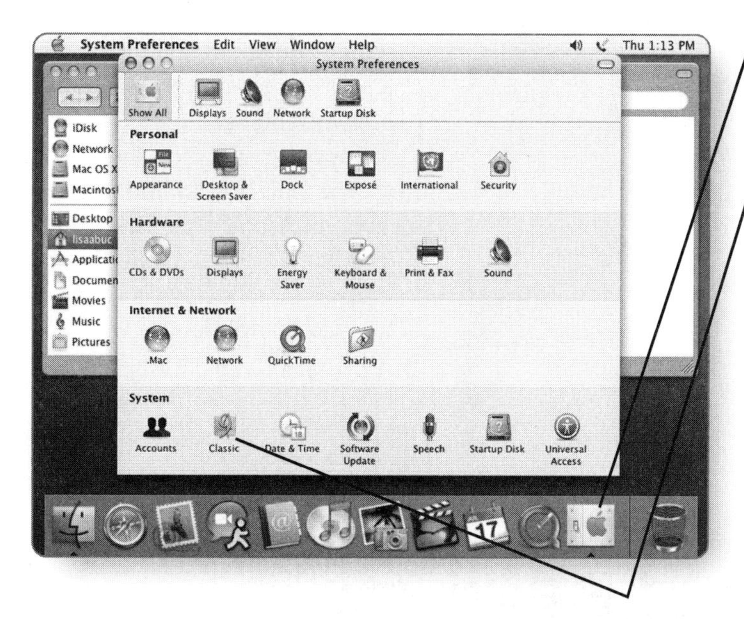

1. **Click** on the **System Preferences icon** on the Dock. System Preferences will launch.

2. **Click** on the **Classic icon**. The Classic pane will appear in the System Preferences window, with the Start/Stop tab selected.

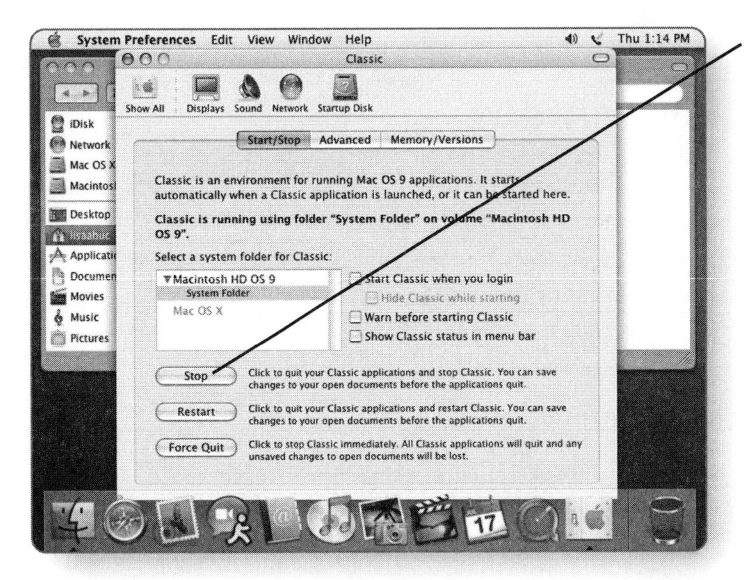

3. Click on **Stop**. The Classic environment will shut down. If any Classic applications were still running, they will also close when the Classic environment shuts down.

> **NOTE**
>
> It may take some seconds for the Classic environment to stop. You'll know it has stopped completely when the Mac OS 9 menu bar disappears. Click on the Force Quit button and then click on Force Quit in the warning sheet that appears if Classic fails to unload completely.

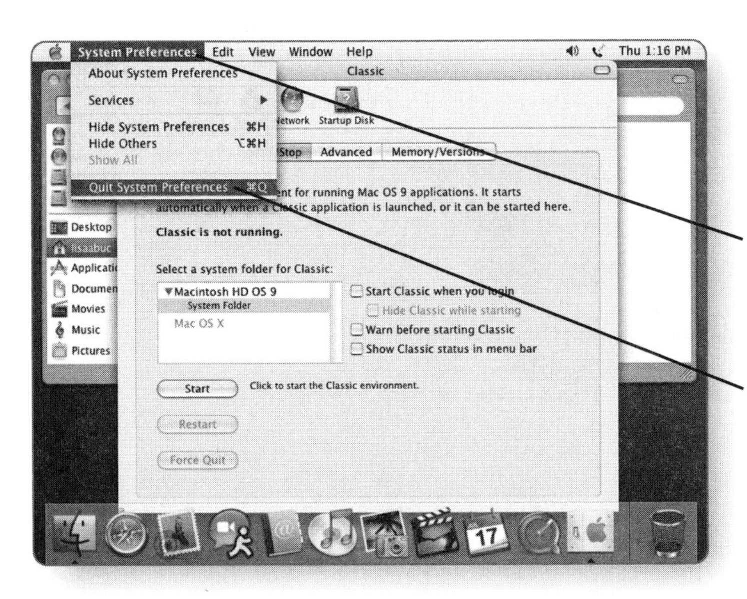

4. Click on **System Preferences**. The System Preferences menu will appear.

5. Click on **Quit System Preferences**. System Preferences will close.

Part II Review Questions

1. How do I start a Dock application? *See "Starting an Application from the Dock" in Chapter 5.*
2. How do I move between running applications? *See "Switching to an Application Using the Dock" in Chapter 5.*
3. How do I save a file? *See "Saving a File in an Application" in Chapter 5.*
4. How do I work with preferences in an application? *See "Setting Application Preferences" in Chapter 5.*
5. How do I dock a file or Finder window? *See "Minimizing and Expanding Windows" in Chapter 5.*
6. My application hung. How can I force it to quit? *See "Forcing an Application to Quit" in Chapter 5.*
7. How do I find a file based on its contents? *See "Indexing Files" and "Performing an Advanced Find" in Chapter 6.*
8. How do I burn my files to a CD? *See "Burning a CD-R" in Chapter 6.*
9. How do I start a Classic application? *See "Starting the Classic Environment" in Chapter 7.*
10. How do I finish using Classic? *See "Closing the Classic Environment" in Chapter 7.*

PART III

Customizing Mac OS X Version 10.3

Setting Up the Desktop

It's more fun to use a computer when you can personalize the desktop or customize a few settings to meet your needs. You can control a number of settings affecting how Mac OS X Version 10.3 works and appears. This chapter focuses only on those settings pertaining to the appearance and function of the Finder, Dock, and desktop. In this chapter, you'll learn how to:

- Change the way disks and Finder windows appear.
- Customize the Finder window Sidebar.
- Choose a Desktop picture.
- Adjust how the Dock looks.
- Control which icons appear on the Dock.
- Set up the Clock to work the way you want it to.

Changing Basic Finder Preferences

By default, Mac OS X Version 10.3 Panther places an icon on the desktop whenever you insert a new disk into a CD-ROM, DVD-ROM, or removable disk drive. It also, by default, displays the contents of a folder in the same Finder window when you double-click on a folder (rather than opening a new window) and uses spring-loaded folders. You can change these and other settings by adjusting the Finder's preferences.

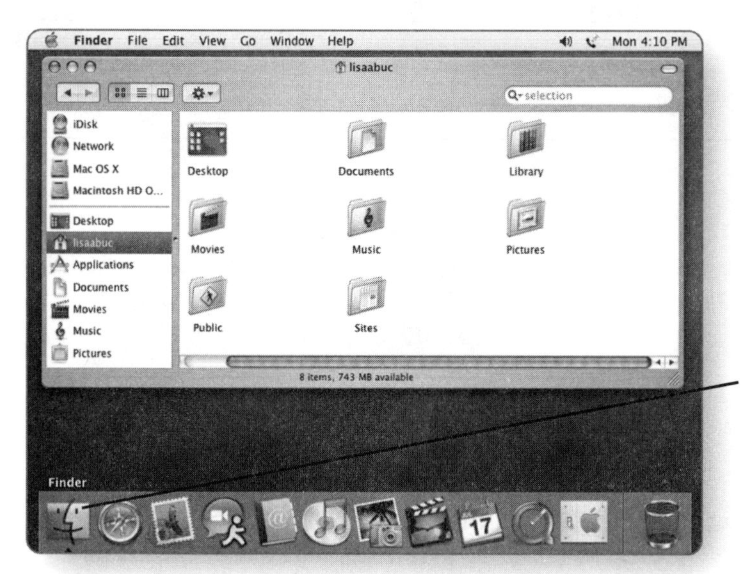

1. **Click** on the **Finder icon** on the Dock. The Finder will become active, and its menus will appear on the menu bar.

2. **Click** on **Finder**. The Finder menu will appear.

3. **Click** on **Preferences**. The Finder preferences dialog box will open.

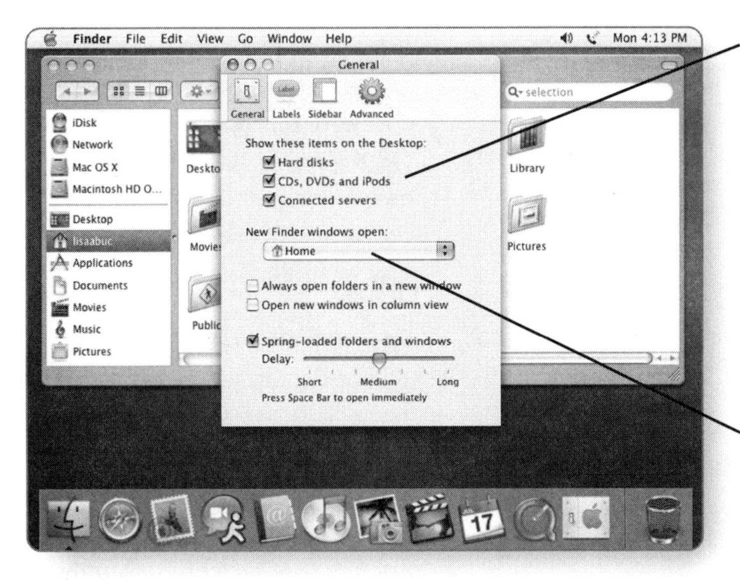

4. With the General button selected, **click** on the **desired options** under **Show these items on the Desktop**. When checked, these check boxes will tell Mac OS X to display a desktop icon for each of the Hard disks, for each inserted Removable media (such as CDs), or Connected servers on the network.

5. **Choose** an **option** from the **New Finder windows open pop-up menu**. If you select Home, Mac OS X Version 10.3 will display the contents of your Home folder in each new Finder window you open. If you select Computer, Mac OS X Version 10.3 will display the contents of the Computer folder, which shows icons for each disk and the Network.

6. **Click** on **Always open folders in a new window**. When checked, this option will tell Mac OS X Version 10.3 to open a new Finder window each time you double-click on a disk or folder icon.

7. **Click** on **Open new windows in column view**. When checked, this option will tell Mac OS X Version 10.3 to display the contents of each new Finder window you open in the Column view rather than the default Icon view.

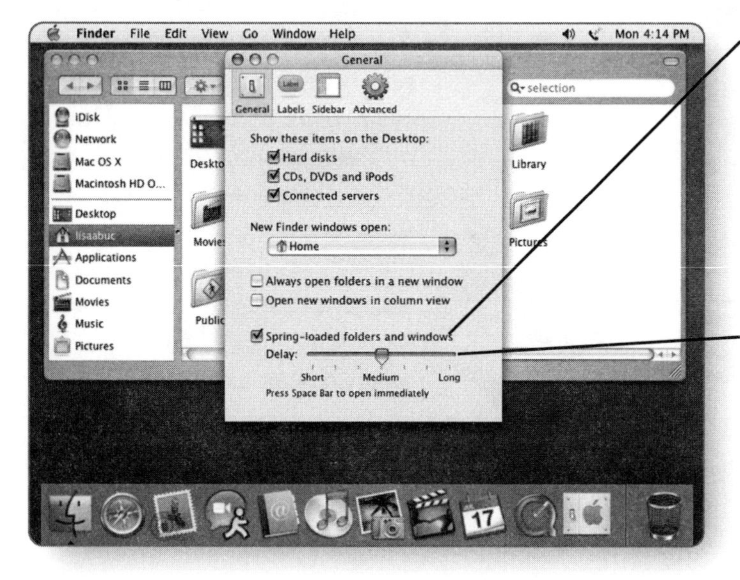

8a. Click on **Spring-loaded folders and windows.** When checked, this option will tell Mac OS X Version 10.3 to open a new Finder window when you hover the mouse pointer over a disk or folder icon.

8b. If you've enabled the Spring-loaded folders and windows check box, **drag** the **Delay slider.** This option will tell Mac OS X Version 10.3 how long you must hold the mouse pointer over an icon before the spring-loaded Finder window opens.

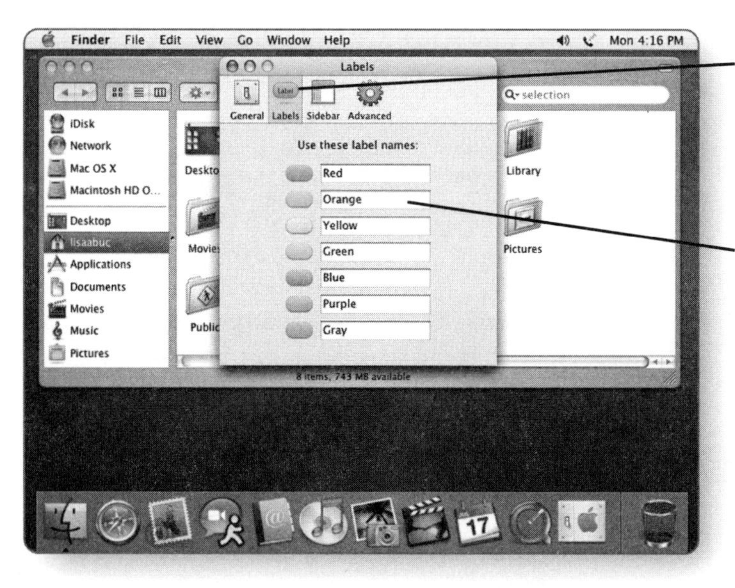

9. Click on **Labels.** The text boxes for changing the names of the color file and folder labels will appear.

10. Edit label names. (For example, you could change "Red" to "Highest Priority," to remind yourself that every file with a red label needs immediate or frequent attention.) The new label names will appear in the window.

11. Click on **Advanced**. The advanced Finder preferences will appear.

12. Click on **Show all file extensions**. When checked, this option will tell Mac OS X Version 10.3 to display the file extension (which helps identify the file type) for each file in a Finder window.

13. Click on **Show warning before emptying the Trash**. When checked, this option will tell Mac OS X Version 10.3 to display a warning message asking you to confirm that you want to permanently delete files by emptying the Trash.

14. Click on **Select** under Languages for searching file contents if you need to change the languages you can use to search file contents in the Finder window. The Languages dialog box will open.

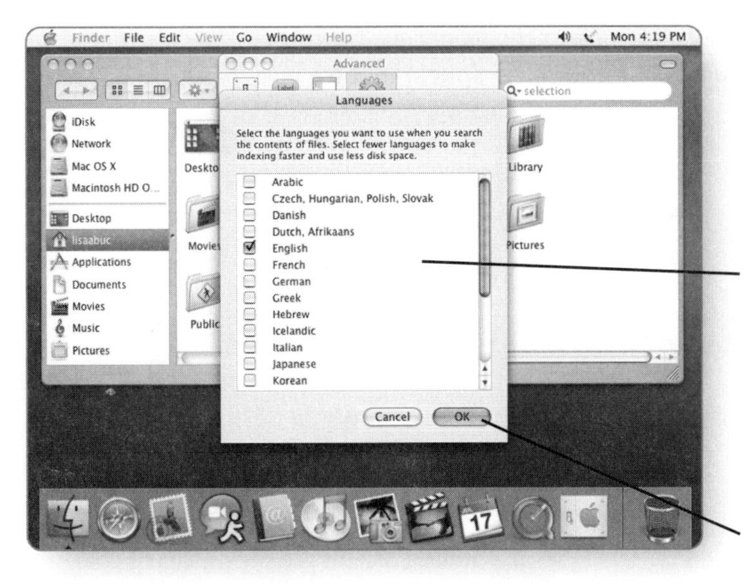

15. Click on **languages.** Each language you check will be selected and enabled for searching. Each language that you deselect will no longer be used.

16. Click on **OK**. The Languages dialog box will close.

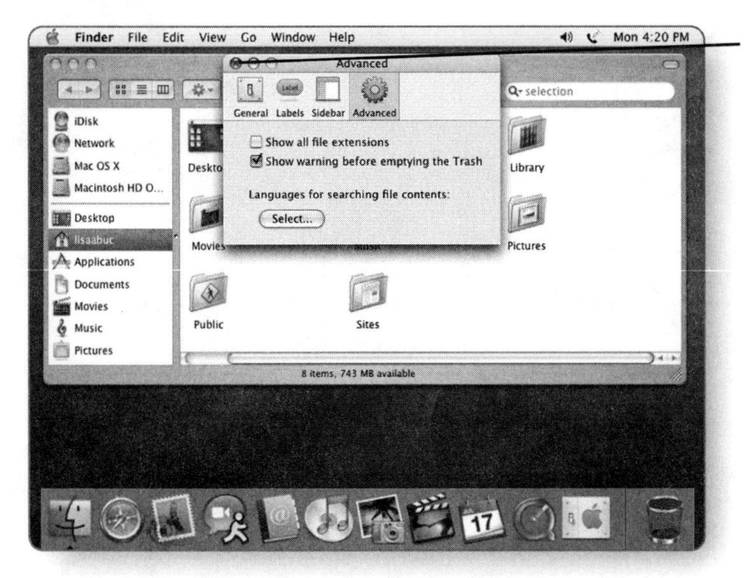

17. **Click** on the **Close button** in the upper-left corner of the Finder preferences dialog box. The dialog box will close, and Mac OS X Version 10.3 will apply the settings you specified.

Changing View Options

In addition to changing the Finder window functionality, you can change aspects of how Finder windows display files. For example, you can adjust the size of the icon and text used to identify each file in the Icon view. Or you can choose which columns of information appear in the List view.

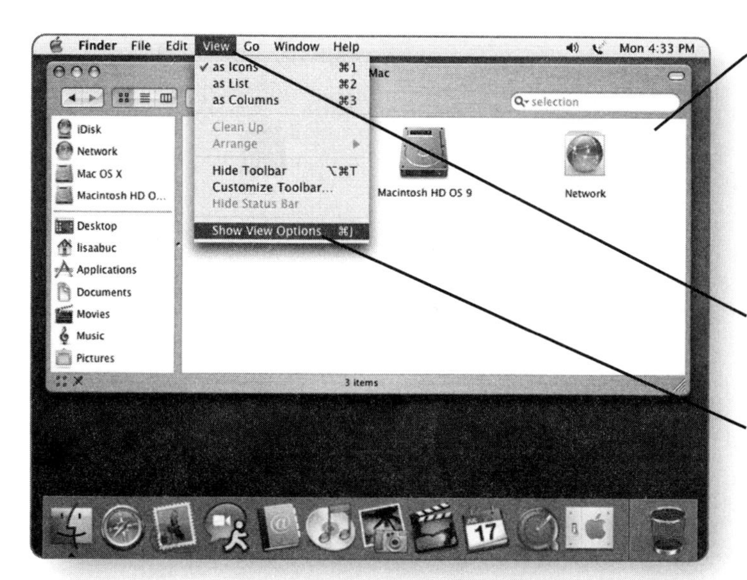

1. **Open** the **desired Finder window** and **choose** the **desired view**. The Finder window will become active, so the view changes you make will apply to it.

2. **Click** on **View**. The View menu will appear.

3. **Click** on **Show View Options**. A dialog box with options for the current Finder window and view will open.

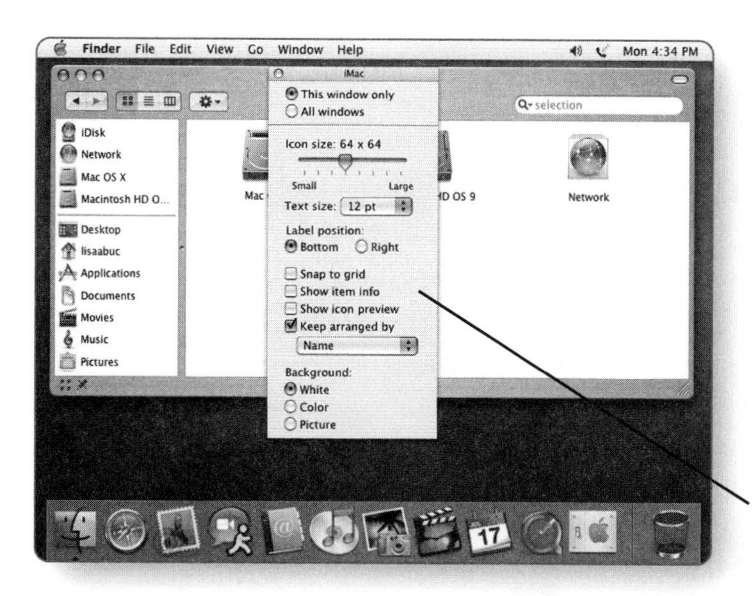

NOTE

The options available in the dialog box will vary depending on the current view of the selected window. You can change the window view to change the options displayed, or even click on the desktop to see choices for changing the desktop view.

4. **Choose** the **desired options**. They will be selected in the dialog box. The table that follows details the available options, depending on the currently selected view.

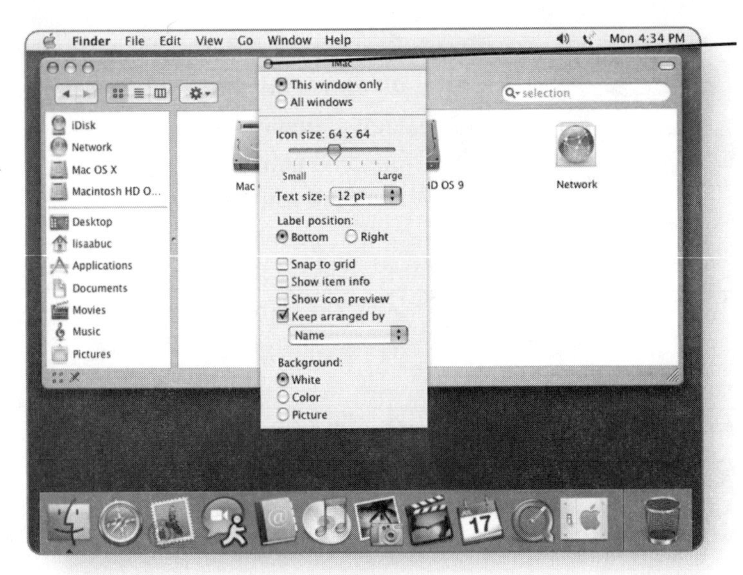

5. **Click** on the **Close button** in the upper-left corner of the dialog box. The window will close, and Mac OS X Version 10.3 will apply the settings you specified.

Desktop options

Option	Description
Icon size	Drag the slider to determine the size of the icon used to identify each disk, folder, or file in the Finder window.
Text size	Use this pop-up menu to specify the size of the text used to display the name of each disk, folder, or file in the Finder window.
Label position	Choose Bottom or Right to specify where the name of the disk, folder, or file appears relative to its icon.
Snap to grid	Check this option if you want icons to snap to an invisible grid, yielding neater window contents.
Show item info	Check this option to display additional information, such as the size of the file, along with the label (name) for each disk, folder, or file.
Show icon preview	Check this option to ensure that the Finder window displays an icon that previews the file contents, if the application can be recognized by Mac OS X Version 10.2's Preview application.
Keep arranged by	Make a choice from this pop-up menu to specify whether the Finder arranges the window contents by Name, Date Modified, Date Created, Size, or Kind.

Icon view options

Option	Description
This window only/ All windows	Choose one of these option buttons to specify whether the other settings you choose apply to the current Finder window only or all Finder windows.
Icon size	Drag the slider to determine the size of the icon used to identify each disk, folder, or file in the Finder window.
Text size	Use this pop-up menu to specify the size of the text used to display the name of each disk, folder, or file in the Finder window.
Label position	Choose Bottom or Right to specify where the name of the disk, folder, or file appears relative to its icon.
Snap to grid	Check this option if you want icons to snap to an invisible grid, yielding neater window contents.
Show item info	Check this option to display additional information, such as the size of the file, along with the label (name) for each disk, folder, or file.
Show icon preview	Check this option to ensure that the Finder window displays an icon that previews the file contents, if the application can be recognized by Mac OS X Version 10.2's Preview application.
Keep arranged by	Make a choice from this pop-up menu to specify whether the Finder arranges the window contents by Name, Date Modified, Date Created, Size, or Kind.
Background	Make a choice here to control how the window background appears. Choose White for a plain white (default) background. Click on Color, click on the color box that appears, click on the desired color in the Colors window, and then click on OK to apply a new background color for the window. Click on Picture, click on the Select button, and use the Select a Picture dialog box that appears to select an image as the background for the Finder window.

List view options

Option	Description
This window only/ All windows	Choose one of these option buttons to specify whether the other settings you choose apply to the current Finder window only or all Finder windows.

Icon size	Click one of the two available sizes to determine the size of the icon used to identify each disk, folder, or file in the Finder window.
Text size	Use this pop-up menu to specify the size of the text used to display the name of each disk, folder, or file in the Finder window.
Show columns	Click on choices here to control which columns of information appear for each disk, folder, or file listed in the window. You can include any of the following columns by checking its check box: Date Modified, Date Created, Size, Kind, Version, Comments, and Label.
Use relative dates	When checked, the Date Modified and Date Created columns display **Today** or **Yesterday** in place of the date for recently created or modified folders and files.
Calculate all sizes	When checked, the Size column displays a size for each disk, folder, and file. The first time you check this option, Mac OS X Version 10.3 may take a few minutes to perform all the calculations.

Column view options

Option	Description
Text size	Use this pop-up menu to specify the size of the text used to display the name of each disk, folder, or file in the Finder window.
Show icons	Check this option to include an icon beside the name of each disk, folder, or file listed in the Finder window.
Show preview column	When this option is checked and you click on a file in one of the columns, a column with a preview icon (assuming the document can be recognized by the Preview application) and document information appears at the far right side of the Finder window.

TIP

If the Finder seems sluggish, turn off the Calculate all sizes and Show icon preview options.

Customizing the Finder Window Toolbar

The toolbar area on a Finder windows offers handy access to the commands you use most. In Mac OS X, you can customize the Finder window toolbar to add and remove tools as needed. The toolbar changes you make apply to all Finder windows.

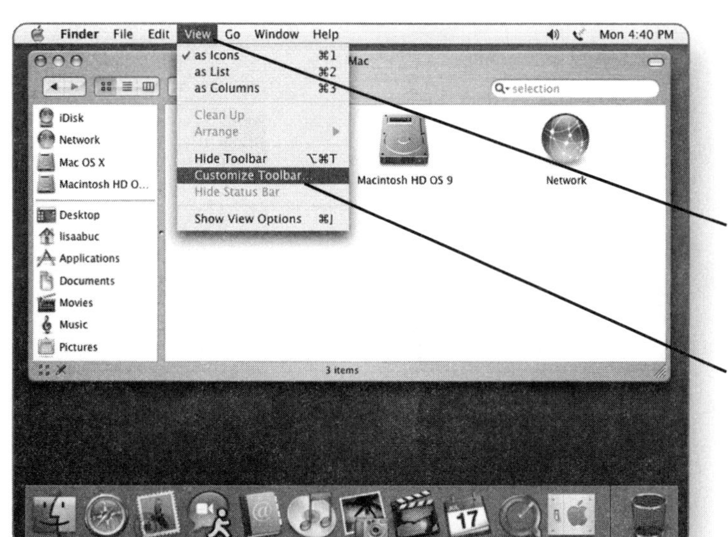

1. With a Finder window open, **click** on **View**. The View menu will appear.

2. **Click** on **Customize Toolbar**. A sheet with choices for customizing the toolbar will appear.

3. **Drag** an **icon** to the desired toolbar position. When you release the mouse button, the icon will be added to the toolbar.

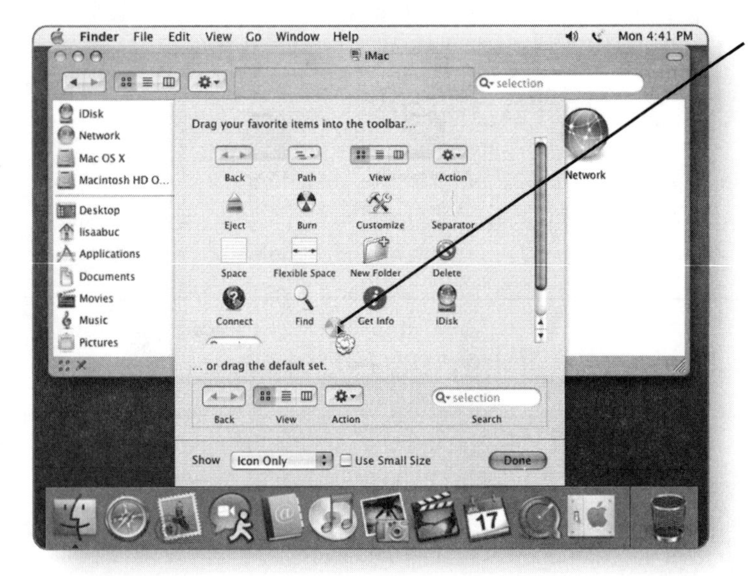

4. Drag an **icon** off the toolbar. When you release the mouse button, the icon will be removed from the toolbar.

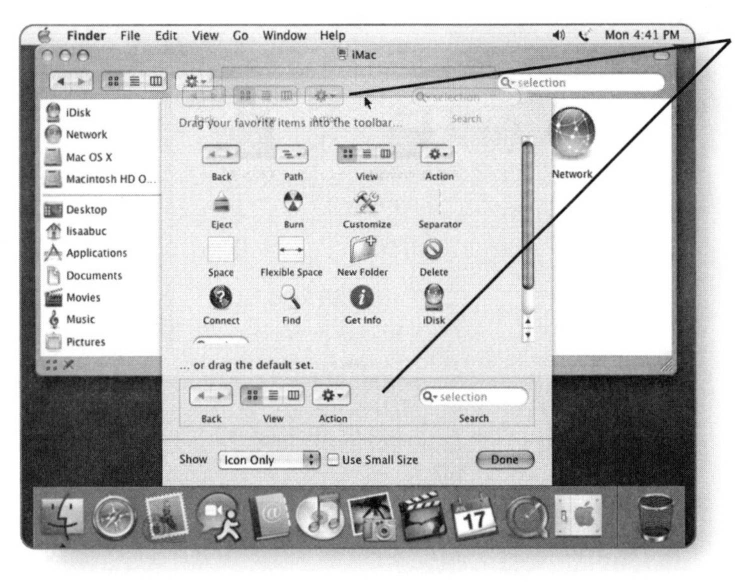

5. Drag the **default set** onto the toolbar. When you release the mouse button, the toolbar will redisplay the default set of buttons.

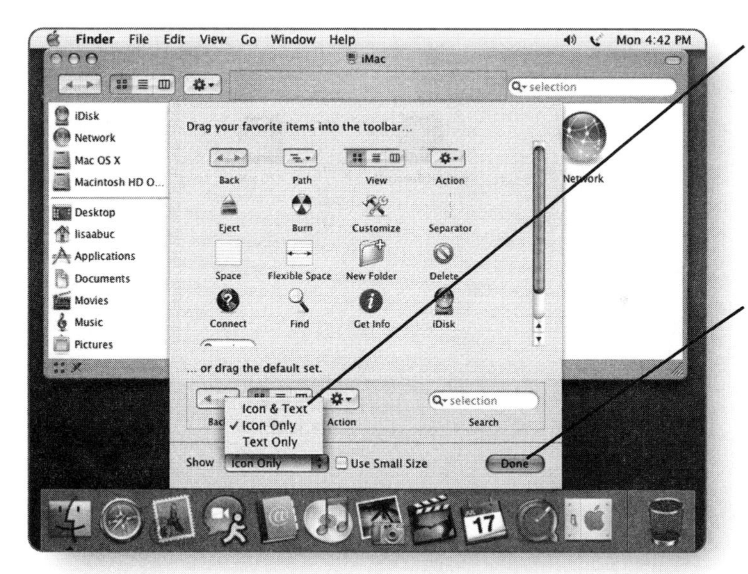

6. Click the **Show pop-up menu** and then **click** on a **menu option**. The Finder toolbar icons will change according to your choice: Icon & Text, Icon Only, or Text Only.

7. Click on **Done**. The choices for customizing the toolbar will disappear, and the changes will appear on the Finder window toolbar.

Customizing the Finder Window Sidebar

The Sidebar for a Finder window gives you a quick way to navigate to folders you use most frequently. If you prefer, you can customize the Sidebar to include other folders, as well as frequently-used files. This makes favorite locations even more accessible than they were from the Favorites folder in the last major release of Mac OS X. Use these steps to customize the Sidebar.

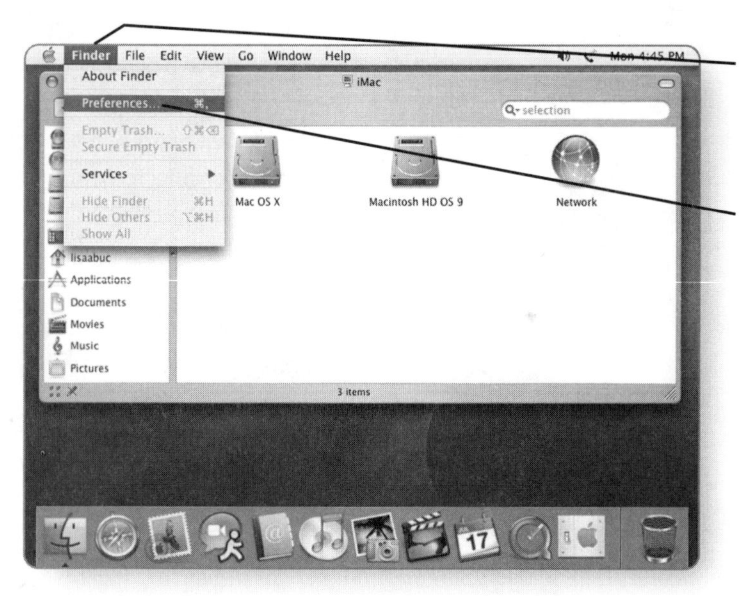

1. With the Finder active, **click** on **Finder**. The Finder menu will appear.

2. **Click** on **Preferences**. The Finder preferences dialog box will open.

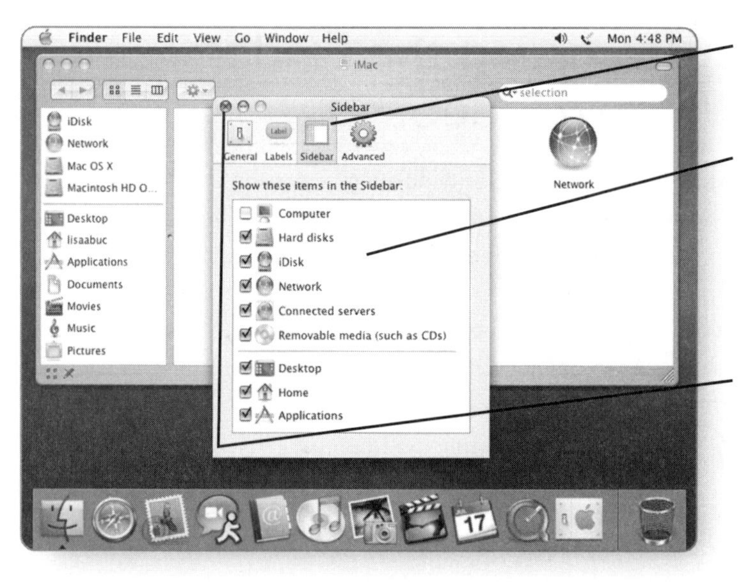

3. **Click** on **Sidebar**. The Sidebar choices will appear.

4. **Click** on **locations**. When you check a location, it will be listed in the Sidebar. When you uncheck a location, it will be removed from the Sidebar.

5. **Click** on the **Close button** in the upper-left corner of the Finder preferences dialog box. The dialog box will close, and Mac OS X Version 10.3 will adjust the Sidebar as specified.

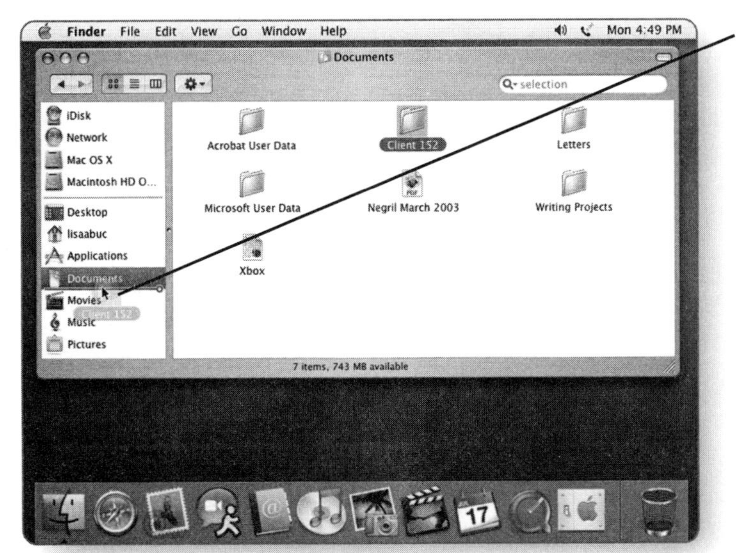

6. Alternatively, **drag** a **file** or **folder icon** to the desired Sidebar position. When you release the mouse button, the icon will be added to the Sidebar.

> **TIP**
>
> If you've added a file icon to the Sidebar, click on the icon once to open the file in its source application.

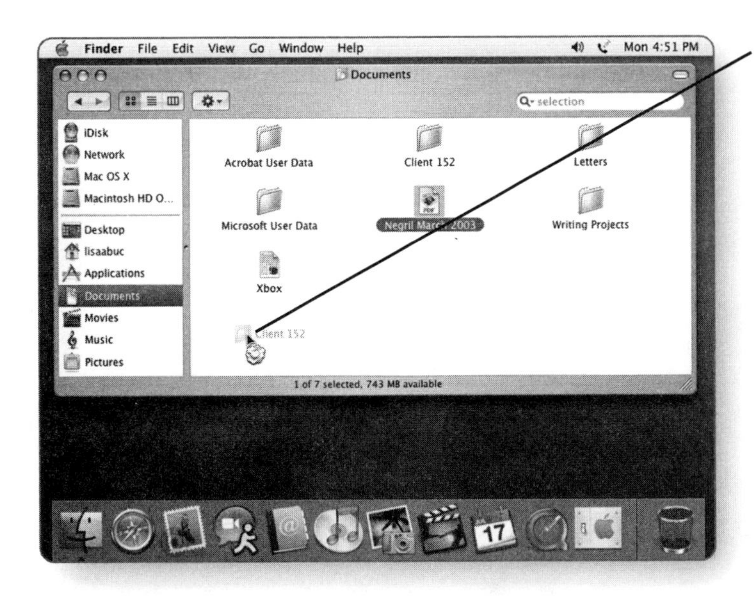

7. **Drag** an **icon** off the Sidebar. When you release the mouse button, the icon will be removed from the Sidebar.

Choosing a Desktop Picture

Mac OS X Version 10.3 enables you to use a graphic file in one of a variety of formats (such as .gif and .jpg images) as a new desktop picture. You can jazz up your desktop with a downloaded image, a shot from your digital camera, or an original digital drawing that you've created.

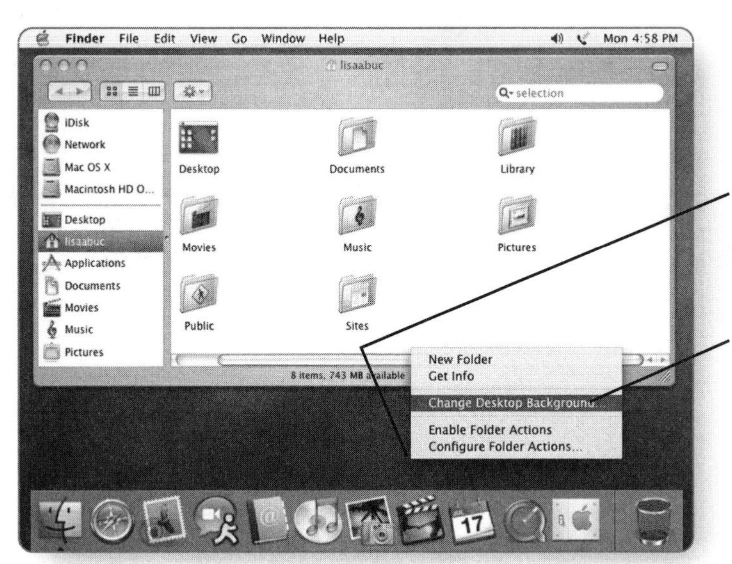

1. **Control+click** on the **desktop**. The desktop's contextual menu will appear.
2. **Click** on **Change Desktop Background**. System Preferences will start and display the Desktop & Screen Saver panel.

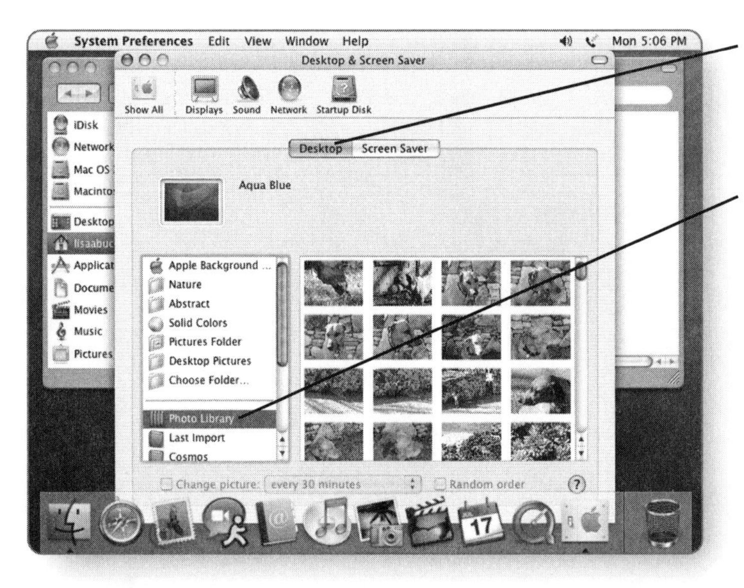

3. **Click** on **Desktop**. The desktop picture settings will appear.
4. **Click** on the **photo source** in the left pane. For example, you can click on the Pictures folder or Photo Library to choose one of the pictures that you've imported from a digital camera. Choose Folder enables you to navigate to any other folder. The images in the specified collection or location will appear in the scrolling list at the right.

5. Scroll to **examine** the **available images.** Thumbnails of different images will appear as you scroll.

6. Click on the **desired image.** System Preferences immediately applies it to the desktop.

> **NOTE**
>
> Use the choices in the pop-up menu beside the current desktop picture thumbnail to control the size of the image on the desktop.

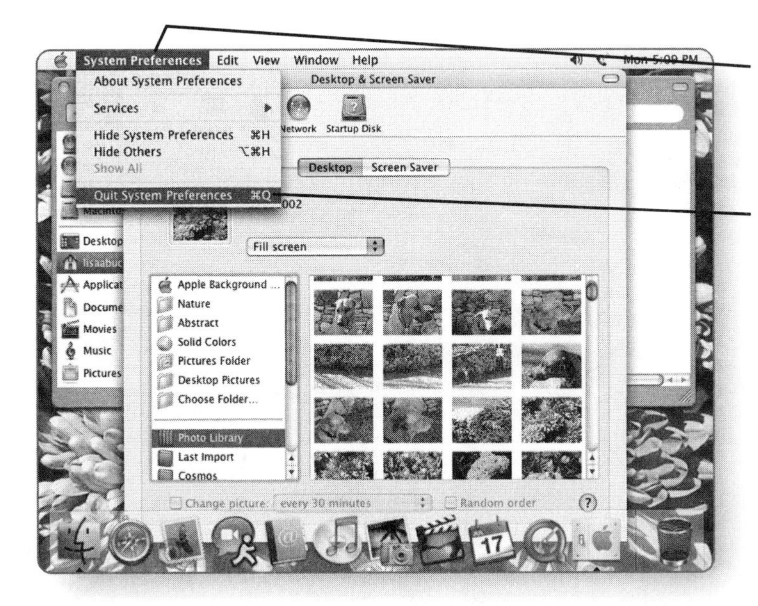

7. Click on **System Preferences.** The System Preferences menu will appear.

8. Click on **Quit System Preferences.** System Preferences will close.

> **NOTE**
>
> To display all the images in a collection or folder over a period of time, check the Change picture option in the Desktop panel of System Preferences. Use the pop-up menu to specify the interval for changing to the next image.

Changing Dock Settings

If you're not quite satisfied with how the Dock looks, you can make a few cosmetic changes, as well as some functional ones. For example, you can:

- Alter the size (height) of the Dock.
- Add magnification (which causes a Dock icon to zoom to a larger size when you position the mouse pointer over the icon).
- Change the Dock's position onscreen for your convenience.
- Turn off the animation effect when you open an application, undock a window from the Dock, or choose an animation style for minimizing.
- Turn on the auto hide feature (which hides the Dock until you move the mouse pointer to the bottom of the screen or to the location where you've placed the Dock).

Making changes to the Dock is simple.

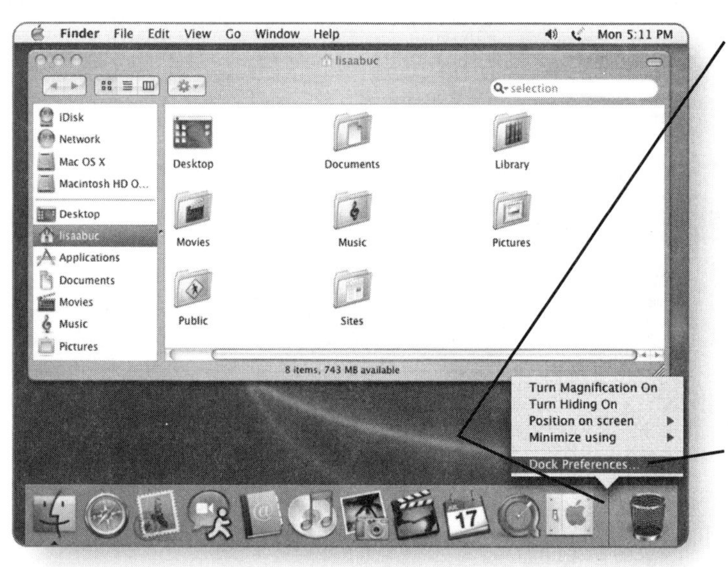

1. Control+click on the **Dock**. The Dock's contextual menu will appear.

> **TIP**
>
> It's easiest to Control+ click just to the right of the divider bar.

2. Click on **Dock Preferences**. System Preferences will start and display the Dock panel.

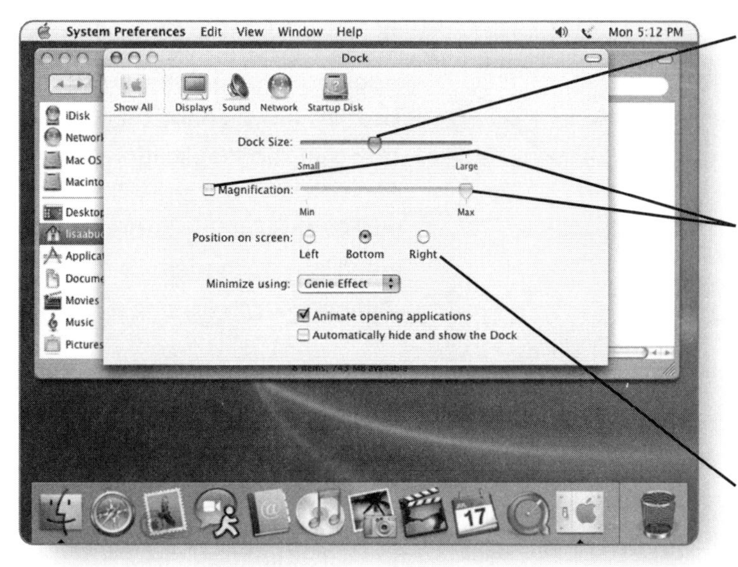

3. **Drag** the **Dock Size slider**. The Dock will appear smaller or larger, depending on the slider position you ultimately select.

4. **Click** on the **Magnification check box** to enable or disable the feature; then **drag** the **accompanying slider.** Your setting changes will appear in the dialog box.

5. **Click** a **Position on screen option button**. The Dock will move to the specified location.

> **NOTE**
>
> Both the Dock submenu of the Apple menu and the Dock contextual menu also offer choices for working with Dock magnification, hiding, and positioning.

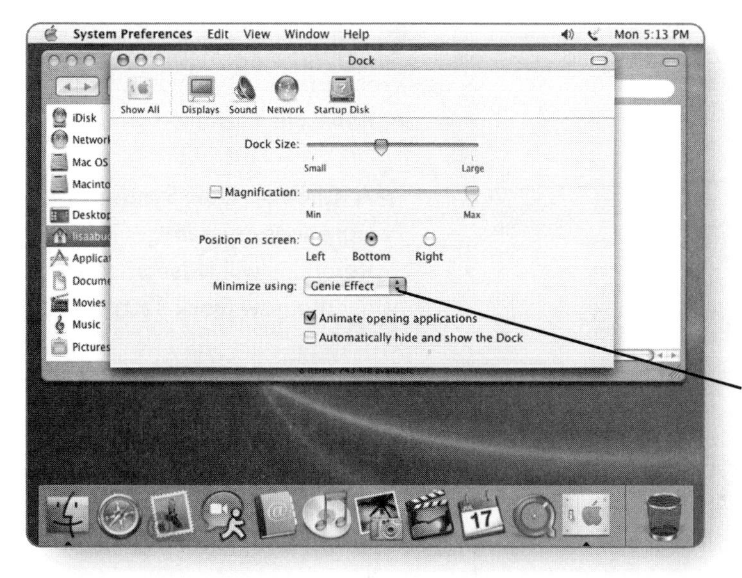

6. **Choose** a **Minimize using option**. Your choice specifies how file and application windows will act when you minimize them to the Dock.

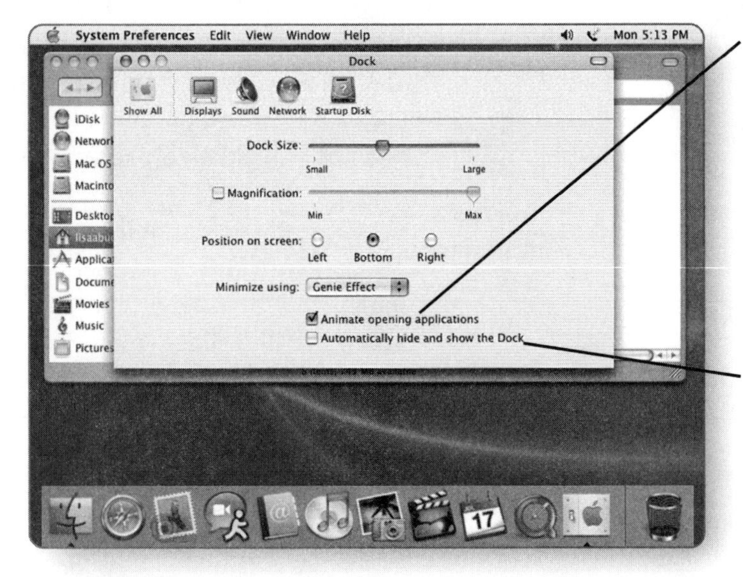

7. Click on the **Animate opening applications check box**. When you have this check box checked, application (and file) windows will zoom in size (rather than simply appearing) when you open them or minimize them.

8. Click on the **Automatically hide and show the Dock check box**. When you have this check box checked, you will not see the Dock unless you move the mouse pointer down to the bottom of the desktop.

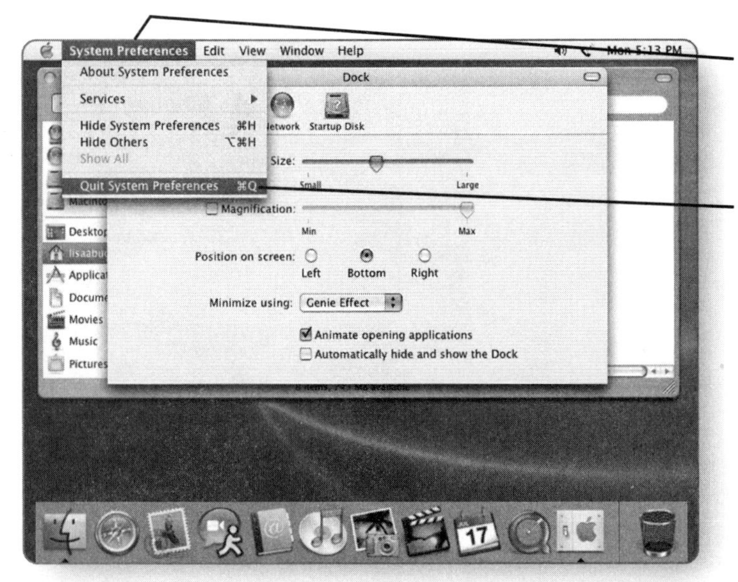

9. Click on **System Preferences**. The System Preferences menu will appear.

10. Click on **Quit System Preferences**. System Preferences will close and will apply the new Dock settings.

> **NOTE**
>
> You also can use the mouse to resize the Dock. Move the mouse pointer over the vertical divider line on the Dock until the resizing pointer appears. (The pointer is a vertical double-headed arrow with a horizontal bar through it.) Then drag the divider line up or down to adjust the Dock size

Adding and Removing Dock Icons

The Dock offers a great deal of convenience, but you can make it even more functional by adding Dock icons for your favorite programs and files.

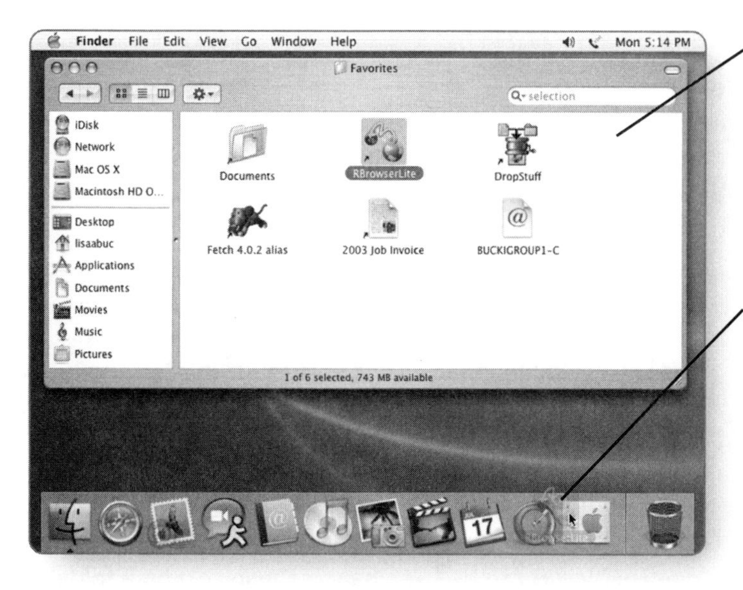

1. **Open** the **folder** that holds the application or file (or alias for either) that you want to place on the Dock. You will see the folder's contents in the Finder window.

2. **Drag** the **icon** from the folder to the desired Dock location; then **release** the **mouse button**. The icon will appear in the specified location on the Dock.

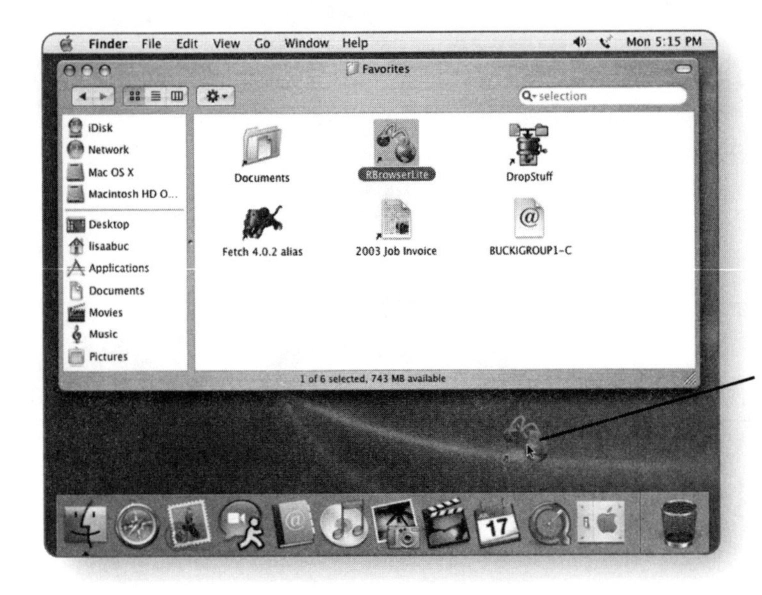

NOTE

You can only place application icons to the left of the vertical divider line and file, document or folder icons to the right.

3. To remove a Dock icon, **drag** the **icon** from the Dock to the Desktop; then **release** the **mouse button**. The icon will disappear from the Dock.

CAUTION

You can remove the default Dock icons by dragging them off the Dock as well. If you do so mistakenly, click on the Applications toolbar icon in a Finder window and look in the resulting folder (and its subfolders) for the desired application or utility. Then drag its icon back onto the Dock.

Adding a Folder Icon and Viewing Its Contents

If you add a folder icon to the right section of the Dock, you can use a shortcut to open the folder's contents in a Finder window. This setup can be even handier than adding a folder icon to the Finder window toolbar. Use these steps to create and use a Dock folder icon:

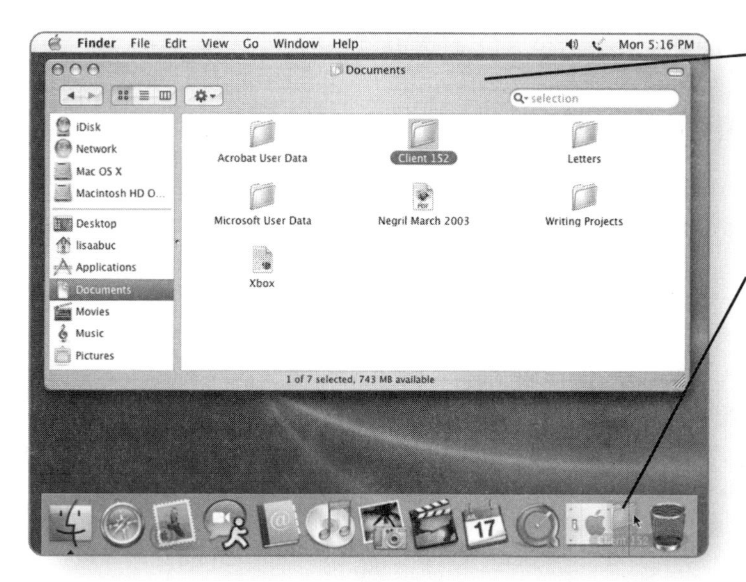

1. **Navigate** to the **disk** or **folder** that holds the folder that you want to place on the Dock. You will see the folder's contents in the Finder window.

2. **Drag** the **icon** from the folder to the **desired Dock location**; then **release** the **mouse button**. The icon will appear in the specified location on the Dock.

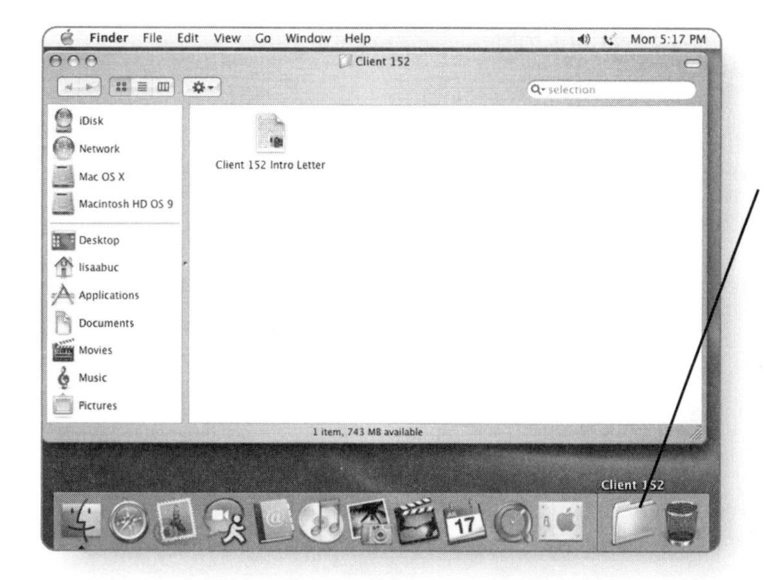

Once the folder icon is on the Dock, you can use it as a shortcut in one of two ways:

- **Click** on the **folder icon**. A Finder window showing the folder's contents will appear.
- **Control+click** on the **folder icon**. A contextual menu listing the folder's contents will appear. If needed, you can click on a file listed in that menu to open the file in its application.

Changing the Clock Appearance

If you start the Mac OS X Version 10.3 Clock application, its icon appears on the Dock and displays the actual system time as set in Mac OS X version 10.3. (This clock supplements the clock on the Finder menu bar. Click on that Finder clock to switch between the current date and the current time.) You can change the Clock application so that it displays as a digital clock or appears in its own floating window instead of the Dock. (The "Setting Date & Time Preferences" section in Chapter 9 explains how to change the actual system time.) Follow these steps to set up the Clock display, as you prefer:

> **NOTE**
>
> Start the Clock by double-clicking on the Clock icon in the Applications folder.

1. **Control+click** on the **clock** in the menu bar. The contextual menu will appear.
2. Click on **Open Date & Time.** The Date & Time panel of System Preferences will open.

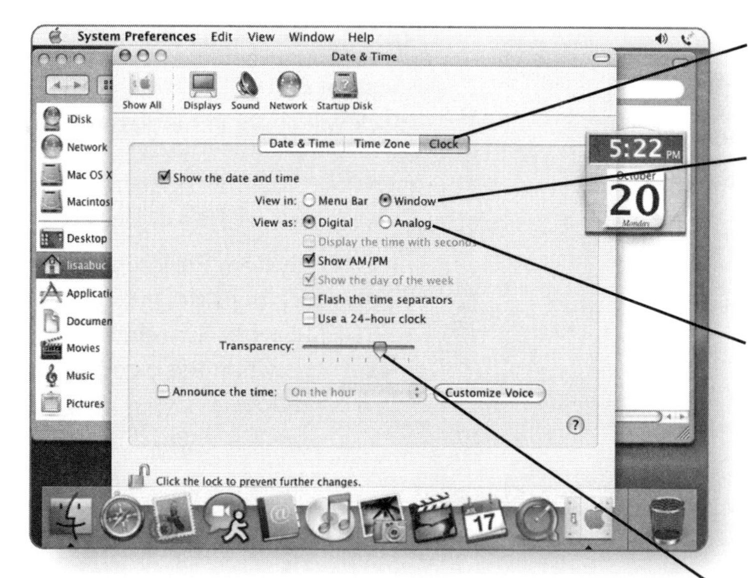

3. Click on **Clock**. The clock settings will appear.

4. Click on the **Menu Bar** or **Window option button**. The clock will be displayed in the specified location.

5. Click on the **Analog** or **Digital option button**; then **click** on the **accompanying check boxes**. The settings you select will immediately adjust the Clock's appearance.

6. Drag the **Transparency slider** if you opted to place the clock in its own window. The Clock will become more or less transparent.

7. Click on **System Preferences**. The System Preferences menu will appear.

8. Click on **Quit System Preferences**. System Preferences will close and will apply the new Dock settings.

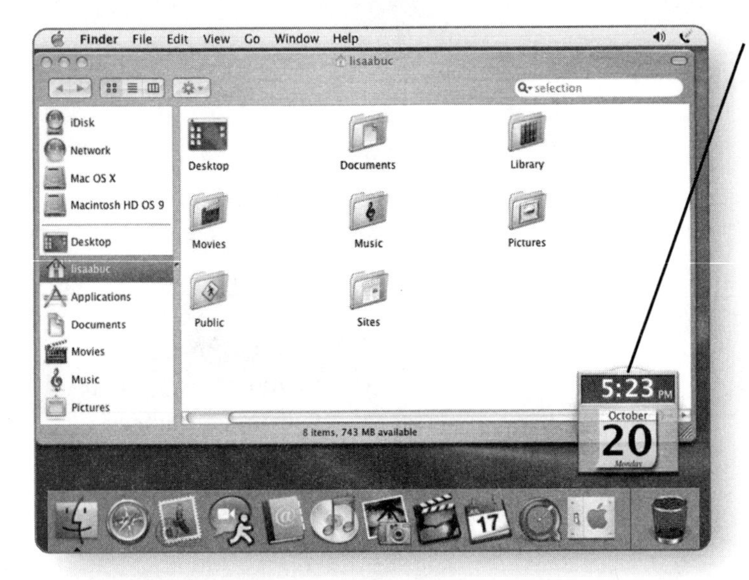

9. **Drag** the **Clock** to a new location on the Desktop. The clock will move immediately.

> **TIP**
>
> Open System Preferences and click on Date and Time to work with clock settings when the clock is in a window.

9

Changing Essential System Preferences

Early computers from Apple had a killer selling point: they were easy to set up and adjust. You didn't have to be a programmer to change the monitor display or choose different settings in programs. The new Mac OS X Version 10.3 Panther continues this tradition, organizing its numerous preference settings in a central location. Anyone can easily find and change system preferences. This chapter serves as a reference to the most commonly used preferences in Mac OS X Version 10.3. In this chapter, you'll learn how to:

- Launch System Preferences.
- Display a pane of preferences.
- Unlock and re-lock a pane of preferences.
- Set the most important preferences.

Displaying System Preferences

Mac OS X Version 10.3 includes System Preferences, which organizes the settings that control how the system operates. System Preferences replaces the control panels found in Mac operating systems prior to the initial release of OS X. When you start System Preferences, its menu appears and the System Preferences window opens. The window holds an icon for each pane of settings and has a toolbar at the top that you can use to navigate in System Preferences. This section explains how to find the settings pane that you need and how to lock and unlock a pane of preferences.

Displaying a Preferences Pane

To change a particular preference setting, you need to start System Preferences. After you do so, display the particular pane (group of preferences) in which you want to make changes by clicking on the icon for that pane.

1. **Click** on the **System Preferences icon** on the Dock. The System Preferences window will open and its menu will appear.

TIP

You also can click on the Apple menu icon and then click System Preferences to start System Preferences.

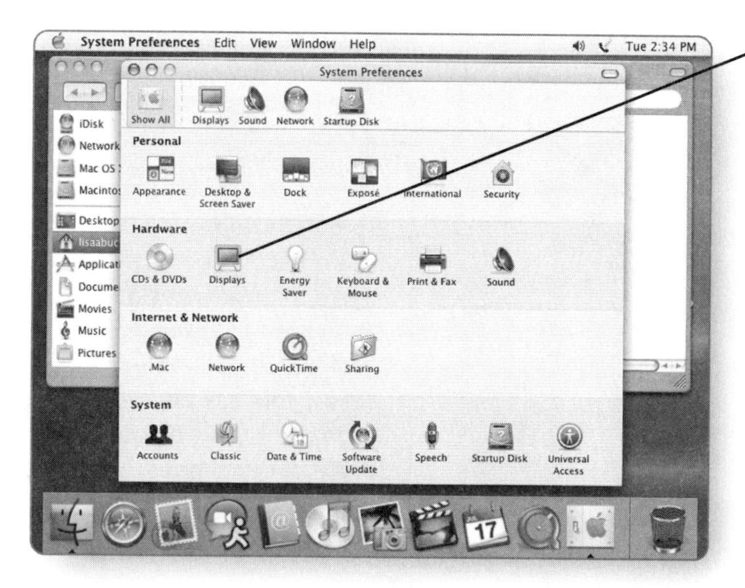

2. Click on the **icon** for the preference pane of your choice. The pane will appear in the System Preferences window. Some panes contain a collection of settings that appear immediately. Others offer multiple tabs of settings.

> **TIP**
>
> You also can click on View in the menu bar and then click on the name of the desired pane. Or click on an icon on the System Preferences window toolbar.

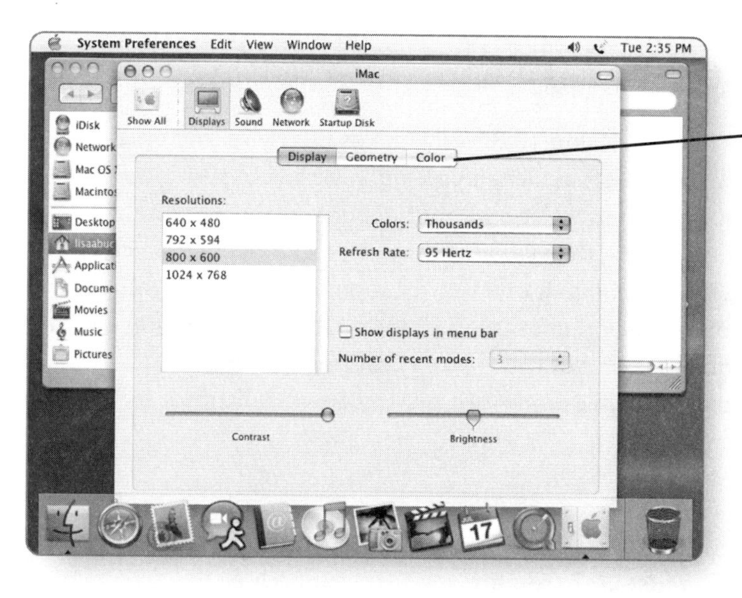

3. Click on the **button (tab)** that holds the settings you want to use.

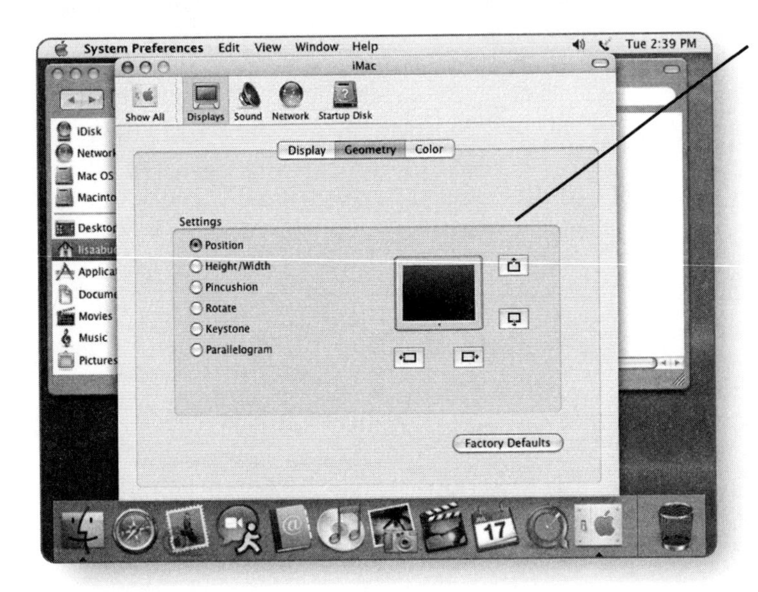

The settings will appear in the pane.

> **NOTE**
>
> To quit System Preferences, open the System Preferences menu and choose Quit System Preferences. In some cases, you may be prompted to save your preference changes.

Unlocking and Locking a Preferences Pane

Mac OS X Version 10.3 really makes it easy for multiple users to share a system. When you log in with your user name, you can work on your files without disrupting the work of any other user on the system. However, sharing a system can create a problem if one user changes a preference without the knowledge and consent of other system users. To prevent this problem, some of the System Preferences panes can be locked and unlocked—but only by an administrator for the system.

> **NOTE**
>
> The first user created when you set up Mac OS X Version 10.3 is always an administrator account, so the user name and password for that account can be used to unlock preferences. Chapter 23, "Managing Users," explains how to add users to the system and designate which users have administrator privileges.

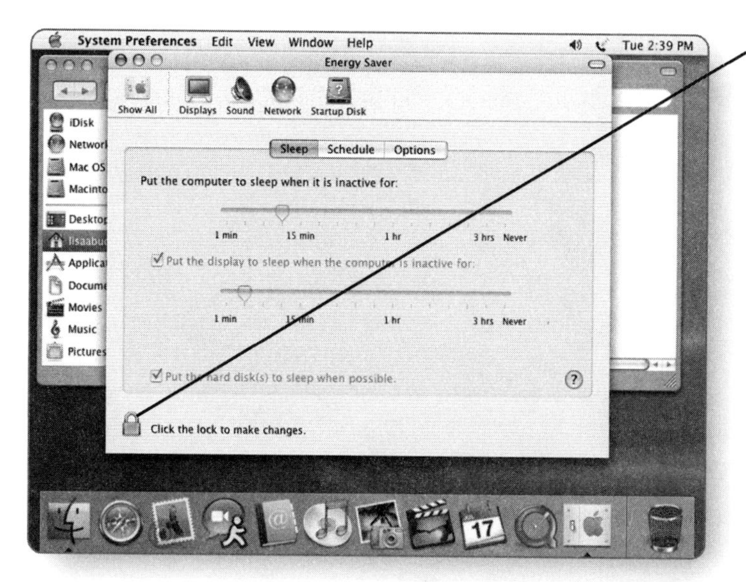

1. Click on the **small locked lock icon**. An Authenticate dialog box will open to prompt you to enter the administrator password.

> **NOTE**
>
> At smaller screen resolutions, you may have to hide the Dock to see the lock icon.

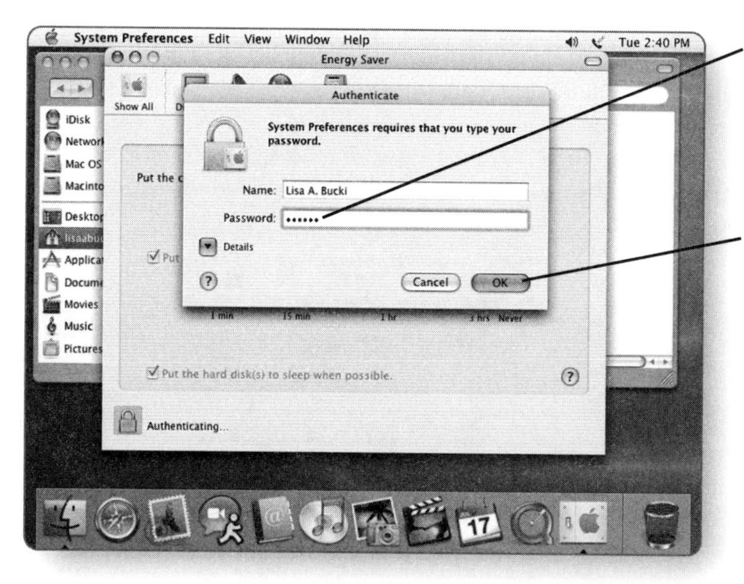

2. Type the **password** into the Password text box. A dot appears in the text box for each letter you type.

3. Click on **OK**. Mac OS X will verify that you have administrator privileges and will then unlock the pane. The locked lock icon will change to an unlocked lock icon, and you can then change settings on the pane.

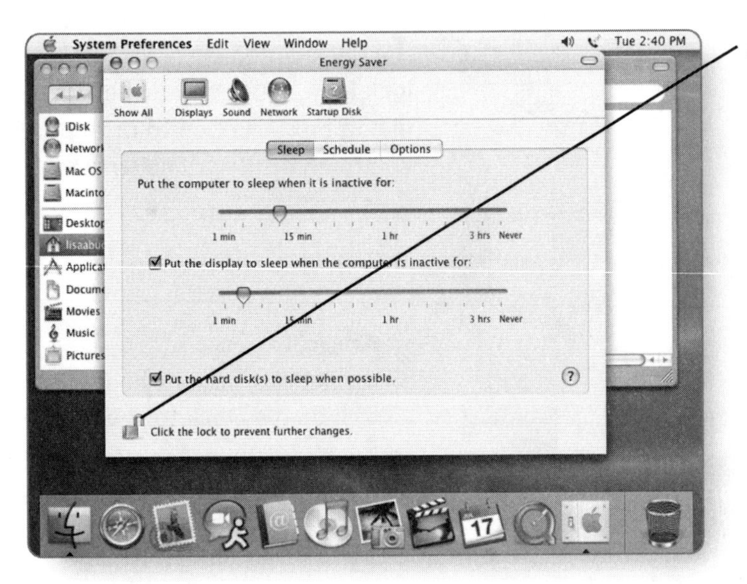

4. **Click** on the **unlocked lock icon**. The icon will change to a locked lock, and changes will be prevented until you unlock the pane again.

Redisplaying All the Preferences

Once you display a particular pane of preference settings, you may notice there's no back button to redisplay all the icons. There are two simple techniques to redisplay all the icons.

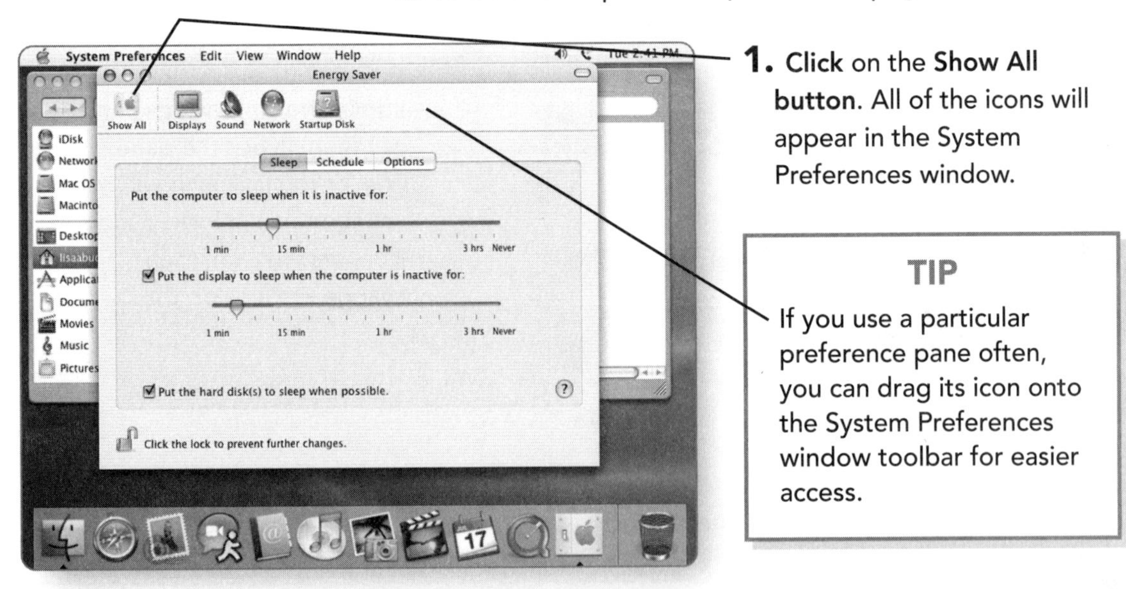

1. **Click** on the **Show All button**. All of the icons will appear in the System Preferences window.

TIP

If you use a particular preference pane often, you can drag its icon onto the System Preferences window toolbar for easier access.

Reviewing Key System Preferences

Now that you've learned how to find the settings that you need in System Preferences, you can take a little time to familiarize yourself with what's available. This section reviews some of the more general panes in System Preferences. (Other, more specific preference panes, such as Internet settings, are covered in the chapters where they apply.) After you've read this section, you can keep it in mind to use as a reference.

The controls on a System Preferences pane work just like those in dialog boxes. You can click on option buttons and check boxes, drag sliders, and so on to make the changes you want. For the most part, your changes will take effect immediately.

NOTE

The descriptions in this section assume that you've unlocked preference panes as needed to change settings.

Setting Appearance Preferences

The Appearance pane offers settings to control the colors used for screen elements like menus. It also enables you to adjust how scroll bars function in Finder and application windows, how many recently used files and applications appear on the Apple menu, and how the system smoothes fonts for display.

- **Appearance.** Open this pop-up menu and click on a color to change the color used for buttons, menus, and windows.

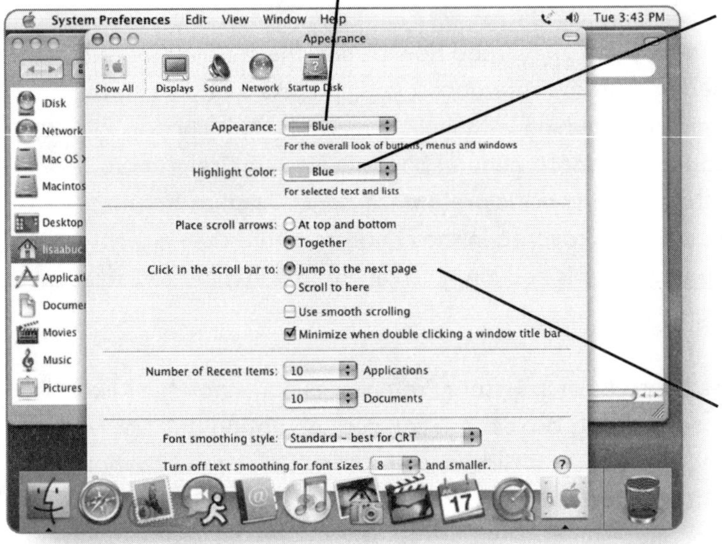

- **Highlight Color.** Open this pop-up menu and click on a color to change the color used for items that you highlight or select in documents and lists. This is the surrounding color that appears when you drag over text in a document or click an item in a list or window.
- **Place scroll arrows and Click in the scroll bar to.** These choices control where scroll arrows appear on scroll bars and how far window (or list) contents scroll when you click on the scroll bar above or below the scroll box.

NOTE

When the Jump to next page option button is selected, each click scrolls the window contents a full page. When the Scroll to here option button is selected, the window contents scroll a distance that's approximately proportionate to the location where you click above or below the box.

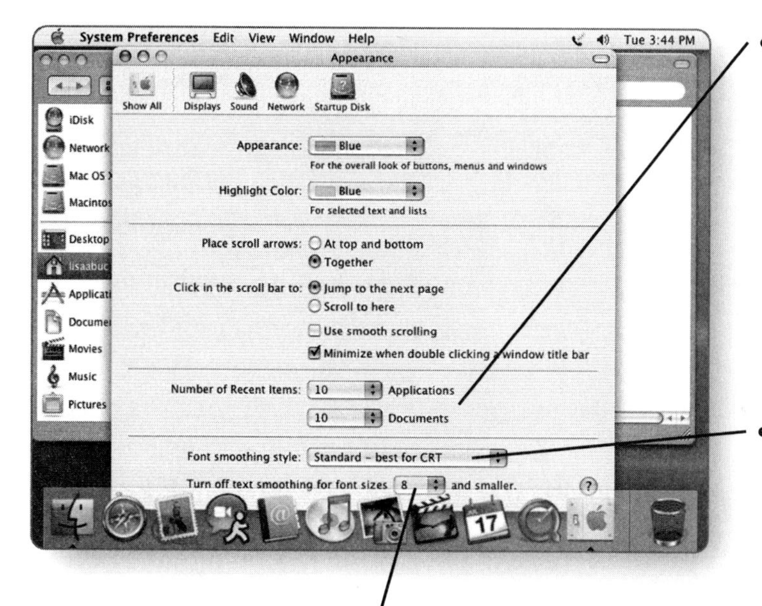

- **Number of Recent Items.** The Recent Items submenu of the Apple menu lists the applications and documents you've most recently opened. You can control how many of each type of item appear on that submenu by using the Applications and Documents pop-up menus here.
- **Font smoothing style.** Select the style to use—such as Medium (best for Flat Panel)—from this pop-up menu.
- **Turn off text smoothing for font sizes (size) and smaller.** Improve the apparent speed of the display by increasing this setting; however, return to a larger setting if you subsequently have difficulty reading the smaller type.

Setting CDs & DVDs Preferences

The CDs & DVDs pane offers pop-up menus you can use to specify how Mac OS X Version 10.3 should respond when you insert a CD, CD-R, DVD, or DVD-R into an appropriate drive connected to the system. Each of the pop-up menus here offers similar options, including:

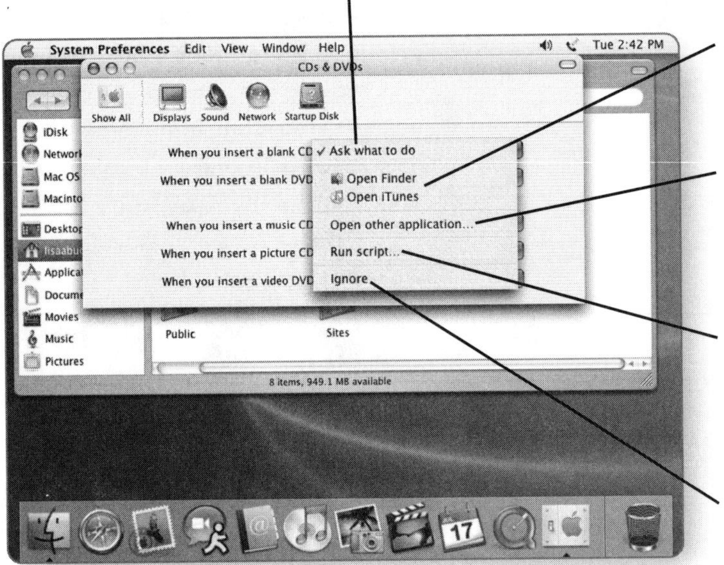

- **Ask what to do.** Displays a dialog box prompting you to specify what action to take on the inserted media.
- **Open (application).** Tells Mac OS X Version 10.2 to launch the specified application.
- **Open other application.** Enables you to browse and choose the application to open.
- **Run script.** Enables you to specify an AppleScript script to run when the media has been inserted.
- **Ignore.** Takes no action.

Setting Date & Time Preferences

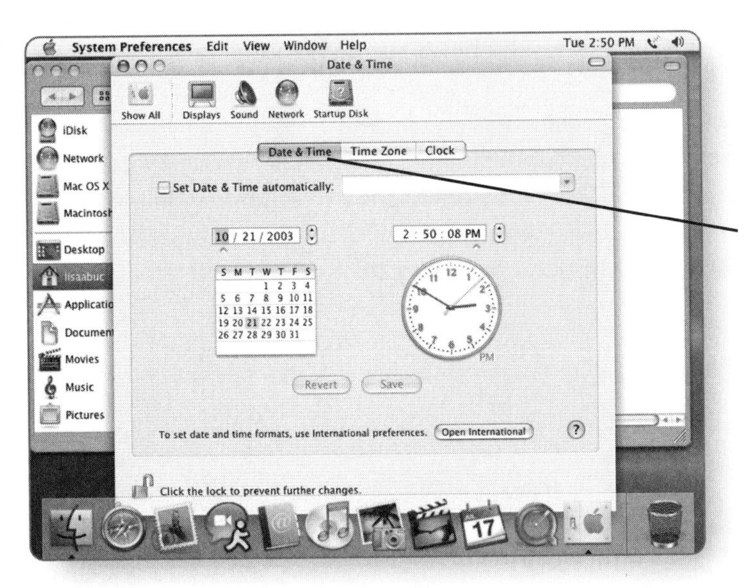

The Date & Time pane includes three tabs of settings that you use to adjust how your Mac displays the time and date.

- **Date & Time.** Change the system date by clicking on the calendar and using the arrow buttons on either side of the month and year. Change the system time by dragging the hands on the clock. After you make your changes on this tab, click on the Save button to save your changes or the Revert button to undo your changes.

> **NOTE**
>
> To have the time set automatically, check Set Date & Time automatically and then choose the desired Apple server from the accompanying drop-down list.

- **Time Zone.** After choosing this tab, click on the map or use the pop-up menu to specify a new time zone.

- **Clock.** Choose whether to display the clock in the Menu Bar or a Window. Use the View as option buttons and the check boxes below it to control how the time appears. You can choose Display the time with seconds, Show AM/PM with the time, Show the day of the week, Flash the time separators, or Use a 24-hour clock. You also can adjust clock Transparency and have your Mac Announce the time.

Setting Desktop & Screen Saver Preferences

In the section called "Choosing a Desktop Picture" in Chapter 8, you learned how to choose the picture to appear on your Mac OS X Version 10.3 desktop. The Desktop & Screen Saver pane in System Preferences also enables you to choose whether or not to use a screen saver. Click on the Screen Saver button in the pane to display the screen saver settings. Today's screen savers mostly serve to entertain and as a security measure to hide sensitive data displayed onscreen.

This works if you have activated the screen saver to begin when the system is unattended and only deactivate with a password that you set up. To deactivate a screen saver once it displays, wiggle your mouse or press a key.

- **Screen Savers.** Click on the screen saver that you want Mac OS X to use in the Screen Savers list at the left. Your selection will appear in the Preview screen. If you would like to preview the screen saver at full-size, click on the Test button. The screen saver will run until you interrupt it. Click on the Options button if you would like to display the available options for the selected screen saver (these vary). A dialog box will appear. Make your choices in the dialog box that appears and click on OK. Your screen saver settings will be configured.

TIP

Check Use random screen saver if you want Mac OS X to choose a screen saver each time your system is idle.

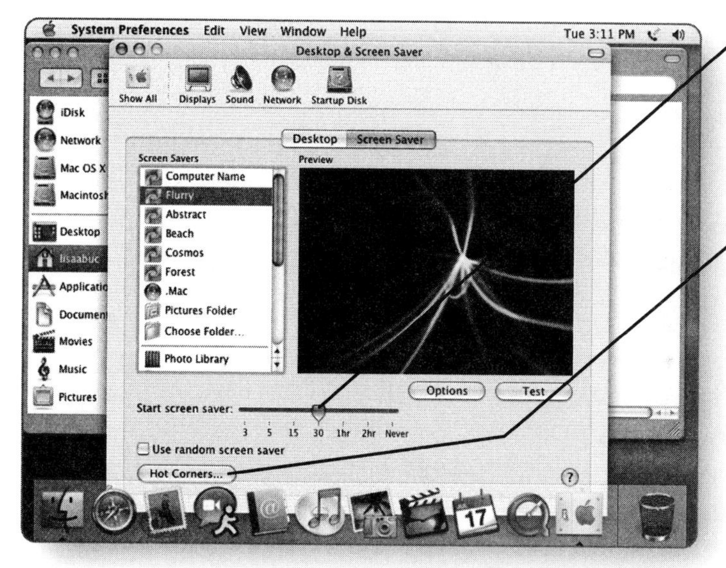

- **Start screen saver.** Drag this slider to specify how much idle time should elapse before the screen saver activates.
- **Hot Corners.** If you want to be able to trigger the screen saver without a wait period, click to check one or more of the corners shown in the screen image on this tab. Moving the mouse pointer to one of the corners you specified will then activate the screen saver. Clicking a corner twice until a minus sign appears means that you can move the mouse pointer over that corner to turn off the screen saver (change its Start screen saver setting back to Never).

NOTE

The screen saver does not appear when your Mac goes to sleep, based on the preferences you've chosen on the Energy Saver pane (nor is the screen saver an energy-saving feature). The time you select using the Start screen saver slider should be shorter than the inactivity periods you specify on the Energy Saver pane. Otherwise, your computer will always go to sleep before it displays the screen saver.

Setting Displays Preferences

All current Mac models can connect with standard VGA monitors with the appropriate adapter. PowerBook G4 (with DVI connectors) and Power Mac G4 systems also can connect with Apple's digital flat panel displays. The Display pane offers three tabs used to specify the proper display connected to your system and the settings you prefer.

> **NOTE**
>
> Depending on the monitor connected to your Macintosh, additional tabs may appear in the Displays pane.

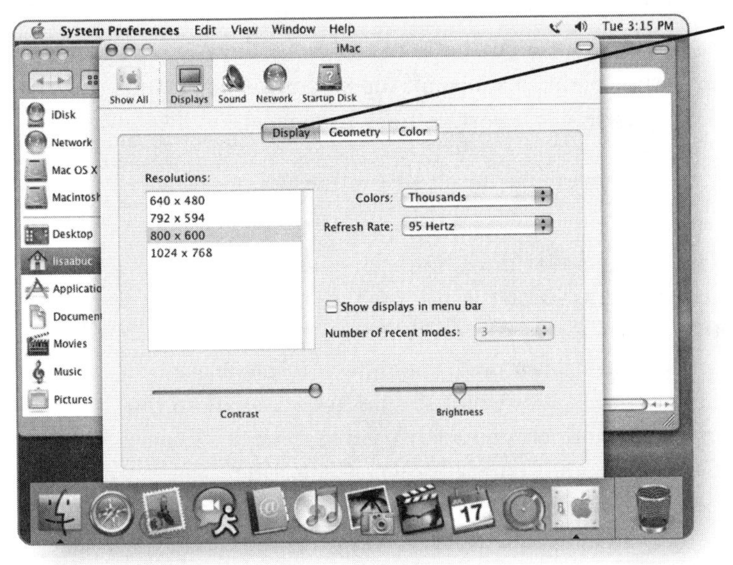

- **Display.** You can change the display resolution (number of pixels in width and height), number of Colors displayed, the Refresh Rate (the speed at which the monitor redraws its image—a higher value reduces any flicker you may perceive), contrast, and brightness. You also can drag sliders to adjust Contrast and Brightness.

> **TIP**
>
> If you want faster access to the Displays settings, check Show displays in menu bar to place an icon for display settings at the right end of the menu bar.

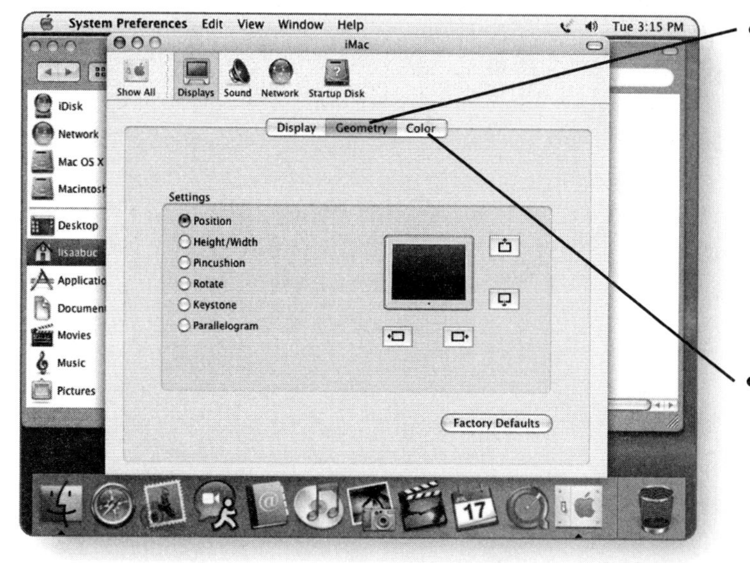

- **Geometry.** You can set how the image appears within the actual boundaries of the screen. Click one of the option buttons to the left; then drag the monitor image to the right (or click one of the accompanying buttons) to adjust the image positioning.
- **Color.** Choose a Display Profile from the list on this tab; then click on the Calibrate button to start the Display Calibration Assistant, which will help you create a ColorSync profile for that display.

Setting Energy Saver Preferences

The Energy Saver pane provides settings to take full advantage of your Mac's power-saving capabilities. The settings enable you to control the timing for when the system automatically enters the power-conserving sleep mode.

> **NOTE**
>
> If you display the Energy Saver pane and don't see any settings, click on the Show Details button.

- **Put the computer to sleep when it is inactive for.** Drag the slider to adjust the specified period of inactivity. When the system has been inactive for the period, both the display and hard disk will sleep unless you override this setting by enabling one of the other two settings.

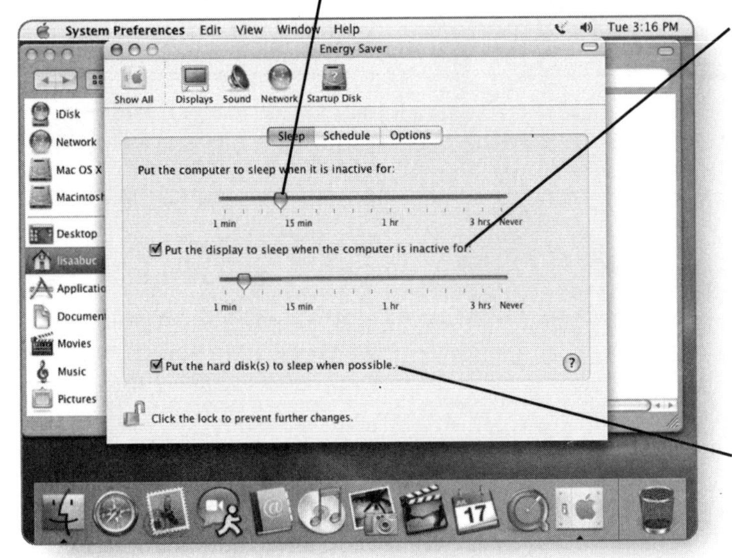

- **Put the display to sleep when the computer is inactive for.** When this setting is enabled (checked), drag the slider to adjust the specified period of inactivity triggering when the display or monitor should sleep. Note that when this feature is enabled, it overrides the general Sleep setting.
- **Put the hard disk(s) to sleep when possible.** When this setting is enabled (checked), the hard disk will be put to sleep, if possible for the hardware, according to the general sleep setting.

NOTE

The Energy Saver panel offers additional settings for PowerBooks and iBooks. That's because sleep settings help conserve battery power for notebook computers. While increasing or turning off sleep settings can improve system performance, using shorter sleep settings for notebook models is essential for good battery life, and also helps prolong the life of flat panel displays used with other systems.

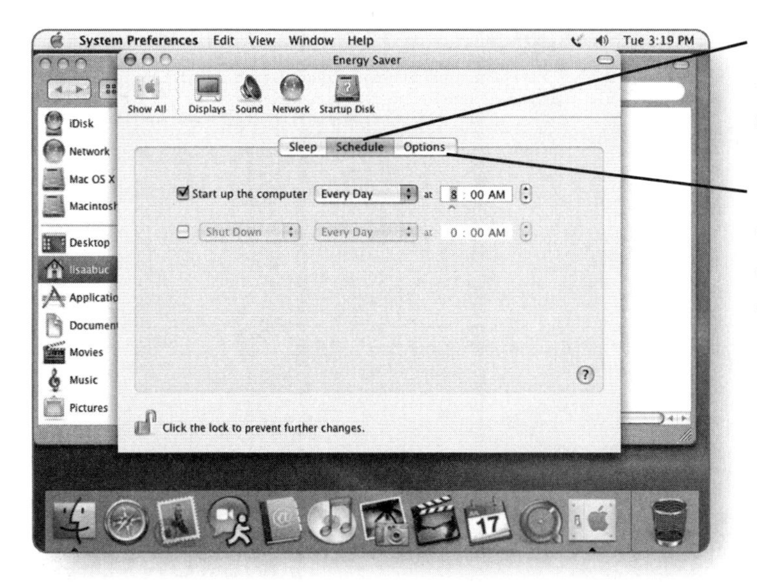

Use the Schedule tab settings to automatically schedule system startup and shutdown.

Use the Options tab settings to control wake-up behavior or automatically restart the system after a power failure.

Setting Exposé Preferences

The new Exposé feature enables you to rearrange open windows on your screen with a single keystroke. The Exposé preferences pane enables you to both change the Exposé shortcut keys and add special functionality to corners of the screen.

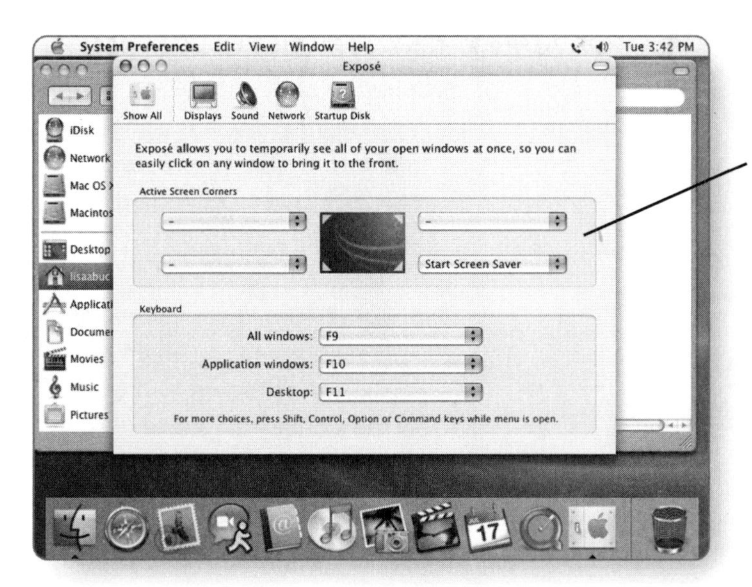

- **Active Screen Corners.** Open the pop-up menu for a corner and choose the functionality that you want to apply whenever you move the mouse pointer over the specified corner. For example, Start Screen Saver will display the currently selected screen saver when you move the mouse pointer over the designated corner.

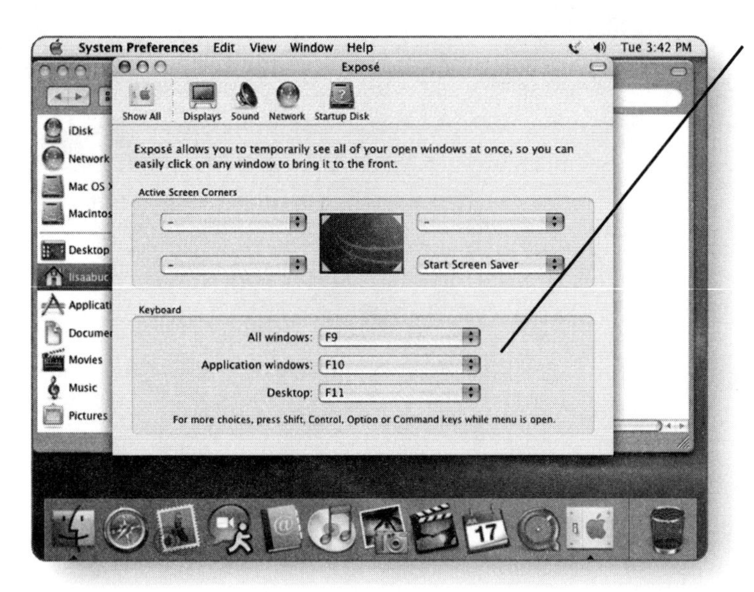

- **Keyboard.** Choose the keyboard shortcut to use when arranging All windows or Application windows, or when hiding open windows so that the Desktop is visible.

Setting International Preferences

If you create or work with documents not written in English, then you can change a variety of settings in the International pane. You can control how the menus appear, how dates and times appear, how numbers and currency values appear, and whether or not Mac OS X Version 10.2 displays a keyboard menu to enable you to switch quickly between keyboard layouts.

- **Language.** In the Languages list, you can drag an entry to the top of the list to make it the primary language used in Mac OS X, as well as any applications that support this feature. (Document contents are not translated, however.) You can add additional languages by using the Edit button. To control how Mac OS X treats issues like sort order for items shown in menus, click on Customize Sorting; in the sheet that appears, click on one of the choices in the Script list, and then open the Behaviors pop-up menu and click on the desired behavior style (German versus English, for example, when you've selected the Roman script).

- **Formats.** Make changes as needed on this tab to adjust how dates, times, and numbers appear. Click on the Customize button for one of these elements and then use the settings in the sheet that appears to select the desired format.

- **Input menu.** If you check the On check box beside more than one language on this tab, a keyboard menu (identified by a small flag icon) appears on the menu bar on the desktop. You can make a selection from this keyboard menu to choose which language layout the keyboard uses. If you click the Options button, you can specify whether the ⌘+Option+Space keyboard combination also cycles through the specified keyboard layouts and whether or not the font script onscreen always changes to match the selected keyboard layout.

Setting Keyboard & Mouse Preferences

We all type at different speeds and have varying levels of dexterity. Because of this, you may want to adjust how the keyboard and mouse respond as you press a key or move the mouse on your desk.

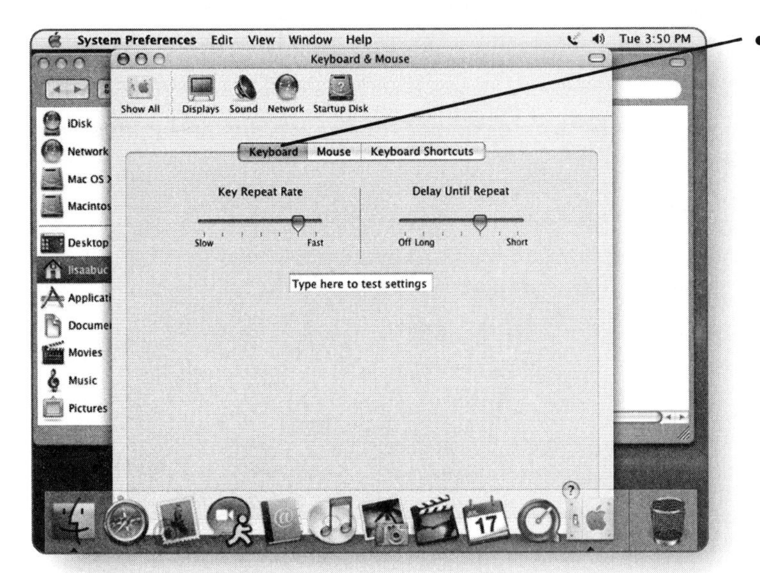

- **Keyboard.** Change the Key Repeat Rate to control how quickly Mac OS X Version 09.2 repeats a character when you press and hold a key. Change the Delay Until Repeat setting to control how long Mac OS X Version 10.3 pauses before repeating a character once you press and hold a key.

> **TIP**
>
> Less experienced typists or folks whose fingers may have been slowed down by arthritis or other illness may be more comfortable using a slower Key Repeat Rate setting.

- **Mouse.** Adjust the Tracking speed, or the resulting speed at which the mouse pointer moves when you move your mouse on your desk. When you increase the speed, the mouse pointer moves farther faster in response to a mouse movement on the desktop, and vice versa. You also can change the Double-Click Speed, how quickly you must double-click the mouse button in order for Mac OS X Version 10.3 to recognize the double-click.

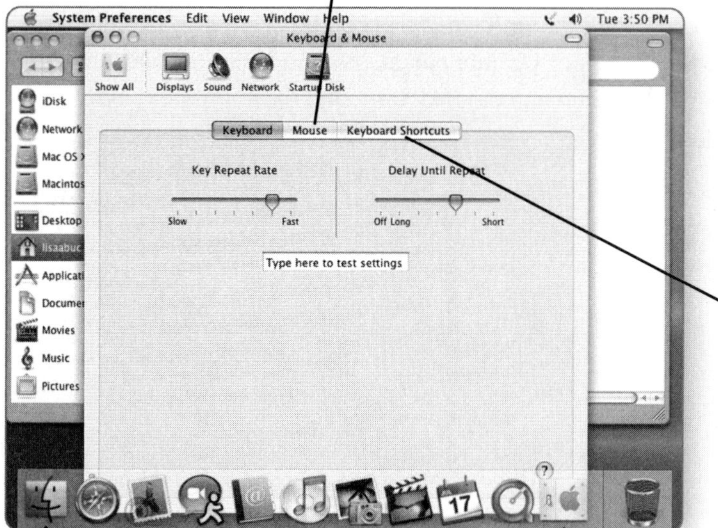

- **Keyboard Shortcuts.** Activate, deactivate, and change the keyboard shortcuts you want to use with Mac OS X Version 10.3.

> **TIP**
>
> If you're less experienced with your Mac and using a mouse, slower Tracking Speed and Double-Click Speed settings can help you have greater control until you're comfortable. On the other hand, a faster Tracking Speed setting coupled with a slower Double-Click Speed setting can be useful if your physical range of motion is limited.

Setting Software Update Preferences

The Software Update application enables Mac OS X Version 10.3 to connect to the Internet periodically, check for updates to the system software, and download and install those updates. You can use the choices on the Software Update pane to control how frequently you want to use System Update.

- **Check for updates.** Choose this option as well as a frequency setting from the accompanying pop-up menu to have Software Update run at the specified interval.

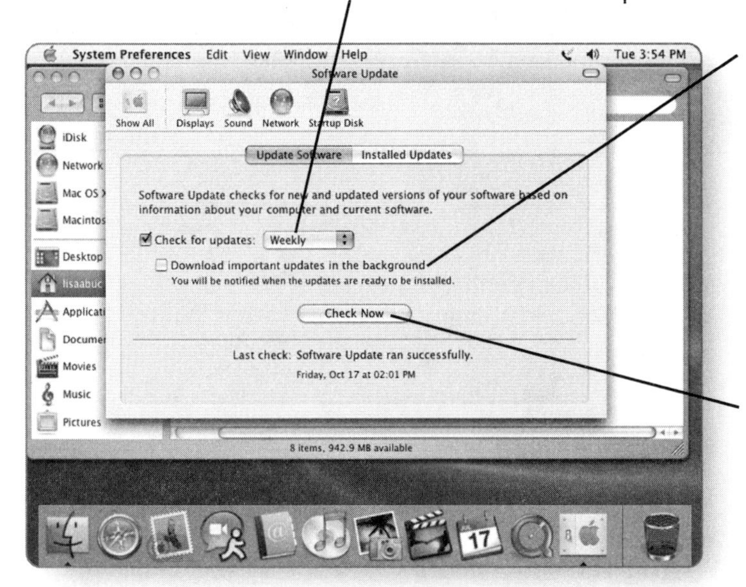

- **Download important updates in the background.** Have Mac OS X Version 10.3 automatically download the updates in the background so that you can do other work. A message will then inform you when the download is finished.
- **Check Now.** Click this button to run Software Update now.

NOTE

If you have a dial-up Internet connection, leave the Check for updates option unchecked. Software updates are typically several megabytes in size, and can take hours to download over a dial-up connection. Thus, users with a dial-up connection might prefer to start Software Update manually in the evening, so the download doesn't interfere with other work. See the section called "Using Software Update" in Chapter 15 to learn how to perform a manual update.

Setting Sound Preferences

Newer Macs have pretty slick sound capabilities, and the settings on the Sound pane enable Mac OS X Version 10.3 to take full advantage of those capabilities. Here are the basics.

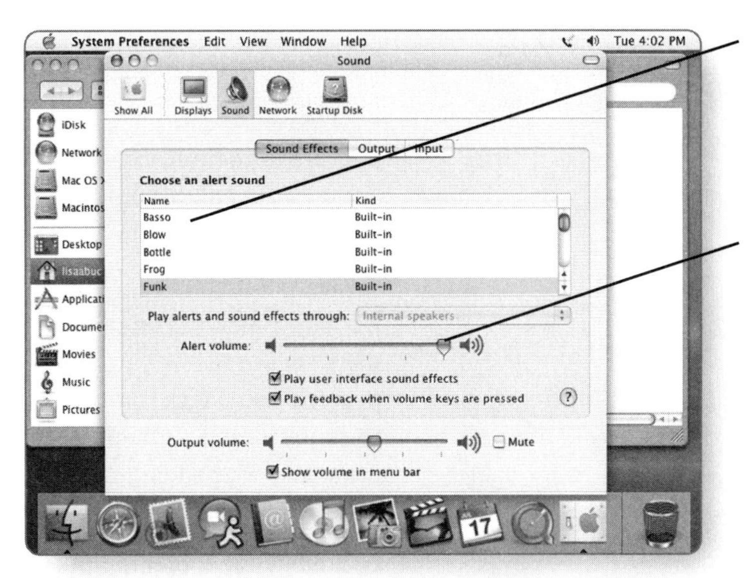

- **Choose an alert sound.** Click on the sound you prefer to use for system alerts in this list box. The sound will be selected.
- **Alert volume.** Drag this slider to the left to decrease alert volumes or right to increase alert volumes.

> **NOTE**
>
> If you have additional sound devices installed on your system, use the Output and Input tabs to choose various devices and adjust their settings such as balance.

Setting Security Preferences

With the growing prevalence of software viruses, Mac OS X Version 10.3 features new security settings to help keep your system safe. The section called "Using FileVault to Protect Your Home Folder" in Chapter 6 explained one of the new security features that you can work with in the Security pane of System Preferences. Here's the lowdown on the other security features:

- **Require password to wake this computer from sleep or screen saver.** If you want to be forced to enter the password for the user currently logged into the system to wake up the system or stop the screen saver, check this option.

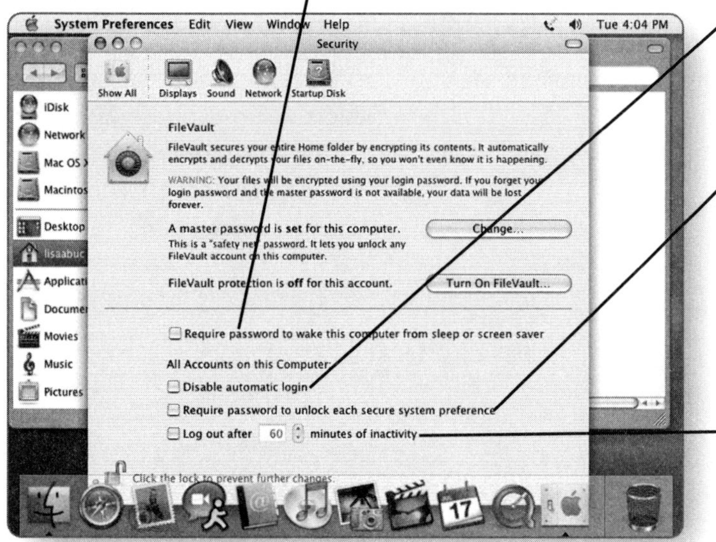

- **Disable automatic login.** When checked, this option prevents the use of the automatic login feature.
- **Require password to unlock each secure system preference.** Check this option to require extra Authenticate requests for changing sensitive preferences.
- **Log out after (time) minutes of inactivity.** Check this option and specify a time to have your system automatically log a user off after the designated period of activity. This prevents unauthorized access to the system.

10

Working with Printers, Faxes, and Fonts

Despite its capabilities for play, chances are that your Macintosh will serve as a working tool for you during a significant portion of its life. While the technology world has made great strides in sharing digital content in recent months, most of us still need to generate a fair amount of printed matter for both our jobs and our personal lives. In this chapter, you'll learn how to:

- Install a printer to work with Mac OS X Version 10.3.
- Choose which printer to use and print from an application.
- Specify a default printer.
- Remove a printer that you've set up.
- Send a fax from the print sheet.
- Manage the fonts you use in your printed documents.

Setting Up a Printer

Setting a printer up to work under Mac OS X Version 10.3 can be a multi-step process. First, you set up the printer's connections as described in the printer documentation. You'll have to plug in the power for the printer and then plug in the cable that enables the printer to communicate with the Macintosh. Newer Mac models connect with a printer via a USB port, but Mac OS X Version 10.3 also supports printers connected via other types of connections.

NOTE

Some printers aren't supported yet by Mac OS X. If this is the case for your printer and you're using an older Mac that you've upgraded to Panther, you can still set the printer up under Mac OS 9.2 (boot to Mac OS 9.2 by restarting while holding down the Option key); then reboot to Mac OS X Version 10.3 and use the printer with Classic applications. In other cases, even when Mac OS X supports a particular printer model, it may not support all features of that model, such as custom paper sizes. Using the Software Update feature regularly can help you check for printer support improvements for Mac OS X. See the section called "Setting Software Update Preferences" in Chapter 9 to learn more about downloading Mac OS X Version 10.3 updates. Finally, if you upgraded to Mac OS X Version 10.3 from an earlier Mac OS X version, you may need to delete and reinstall a printer to make sure it works and to take advantage of the latest drivers included with Mac OS X Version 10.3. Also check your printer manufacturer's Web site for updated drivers and help with using your printer with Mac OS X Version 10.3.

Mac OS X Version 10.3 supports a number of printers directly. All you have to do is connect such a printer to your system and turn it on (many of them are USB or network printers), and Mac OS X automatically sets up the printer. To verify whether Mac OS X can automatically set up your printer, visit the following page on Apple's Web site:

http://www.apple.com/macosx/upgrade/printers.html.

Print Setup Utility serves as the printer management utility for Mac OS X Version 10.3. It enables you to set up other printers that don't set up automatically, select a default printer, and control printing. The steps presented here are a generalization showing you how to set up a printer using Printer Setup Utility. Be sure to read the documentation for your printer prior to installation and follow its directions if they differ from the steps presented here.

1. Connect your printer to its power source and to the Mac (via the appropriate cable) and then **turn** on the **printer**. The printer will start up and be ready for setup.

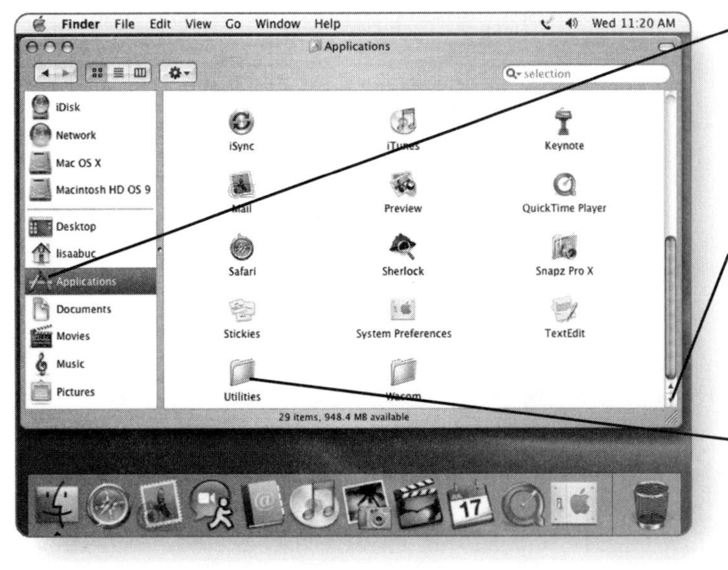

2. Click on the **Applications icon** on a Finder window Sidebar. The Applications folder contents will appear in the window.

3. Click on the **down arrow** of the vertical scroll bar. The Utilities folder will scroll into view.

4. Double-click on the **Utilities folder**. The contents of the folder will appear in the Finder window.

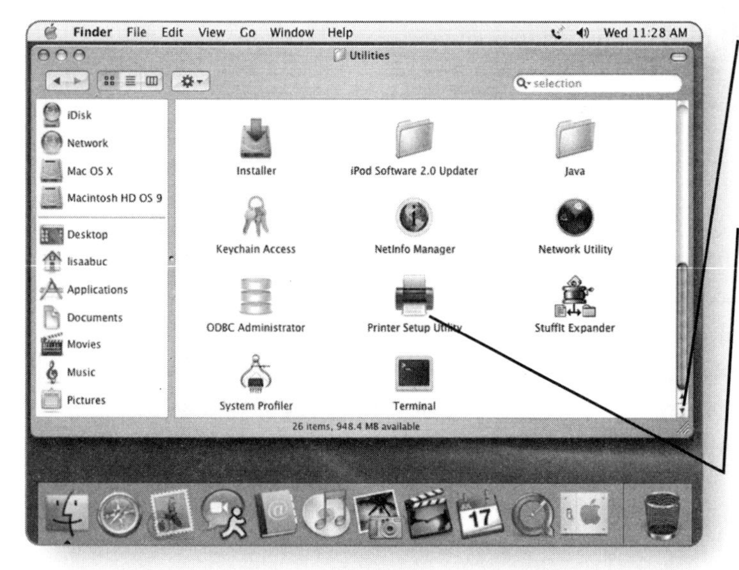

5. Click on the **down arrow** of the vertical scroll bar. The Printer Setup Utility icon will scroll into view.

6. Double-click on the **Printer Setup Utility icon**. Printer Setup Utility will start, and the Printer List window will open.

> **NOTE**
>
> The first time you set up a printer, a dialog box informs you that you have no printers available. In this case, click on the Add button and then skip to Step 7.

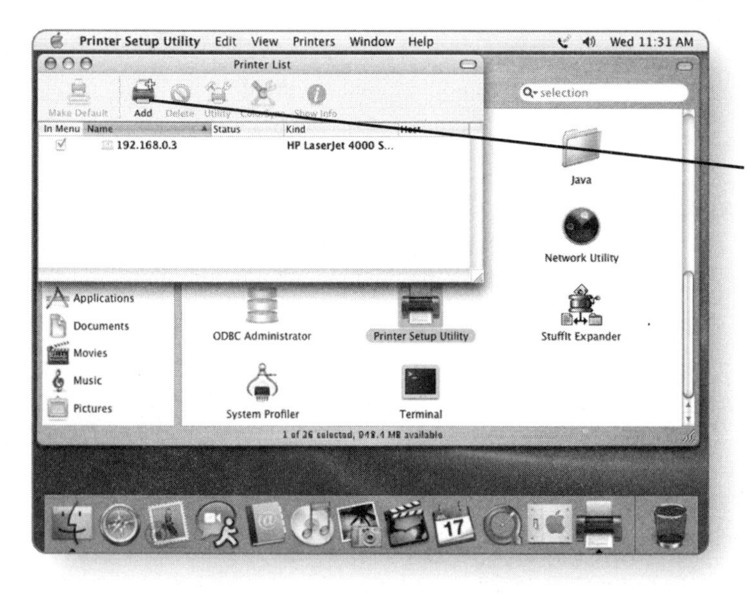

7. Click on the **Add button** on the window toolbar. A sheet for adding printers will appear.

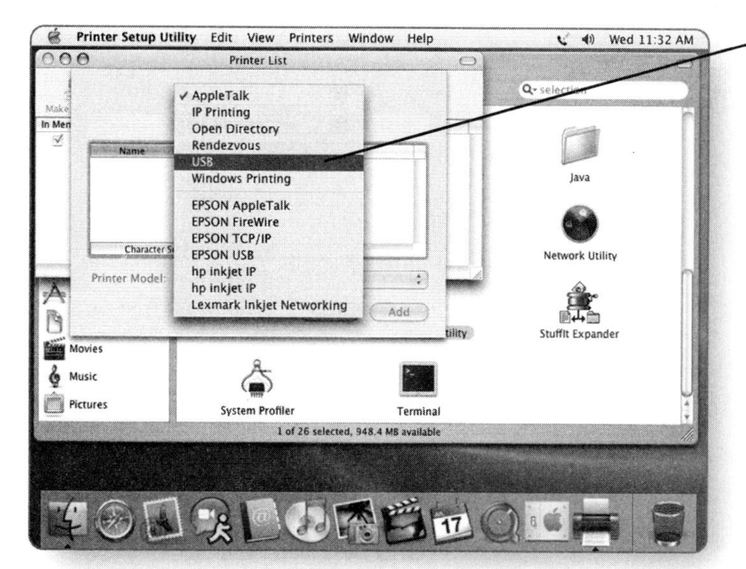

8. Click on the **pop-up menu** near the top of the sheet and then **click** on the **type of connection** your printer uses. (Choose one of the EPSON choices or Lexmark Inkjet Networking if you're using a newer Epson or Lexmark printer to take advantage of the latest drivers built into Mac OS X Version 10.3.) A list of printers available via that connection type will appear in the sheet.

NOTE

To choose a printer connected to a network or on an older Mac system that uses AppleTalk connections, AppleTalk must be enabled. Click on the System Preferences icon on the Dock; then click on the Network icon. Open the top Show pop-up menu and click on Built-in Ethernet. Then click on the AppleTalk tab and use it to enable AppleTalk. The section called "Connecting to a Network Printer" in Chapter 11 will cover how to set up computers on an IP network.

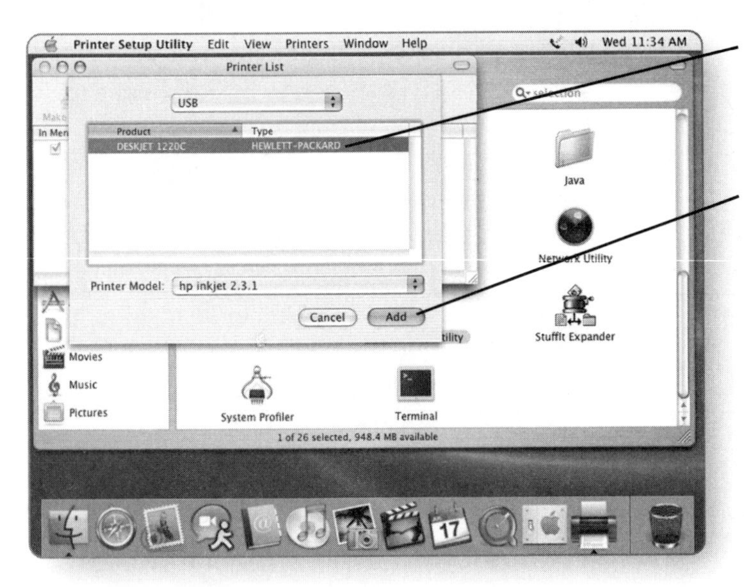

9. Click on the **desired printer** in the list. The printer will be selected.

10. Click on **Add**. The sheet will close, and the printer will appear in the Print List and be available for printing from your applications.

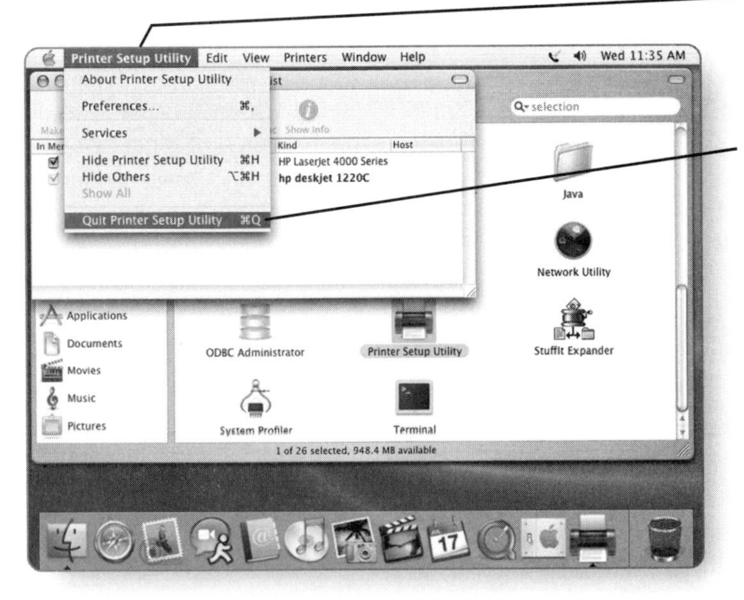

11. Click on **Printer Setup Utility**. The Print Setup Utility menu will appear.

12. Click on **Quit Print Center**. The Print Center utility will close.

Now you can resume your work in other applications, as you're ready to print.

> **NOTE**
>
> You can add a printer on-the-fly via the print sheet in some applications. Open the Printer pop-up menu and click on Edit Printer List to go to the Printer Setup Utility and add a printer.

Selecting a Printer and Printing

You do not need to open Print Center every time you want to print a document. Any application you're using provides the capability for you to select a printer and choose settings for the printout. You should note, however, that the settings will vary depending on your printer model, its driver software, and the capabilities of the application from which you're printing.

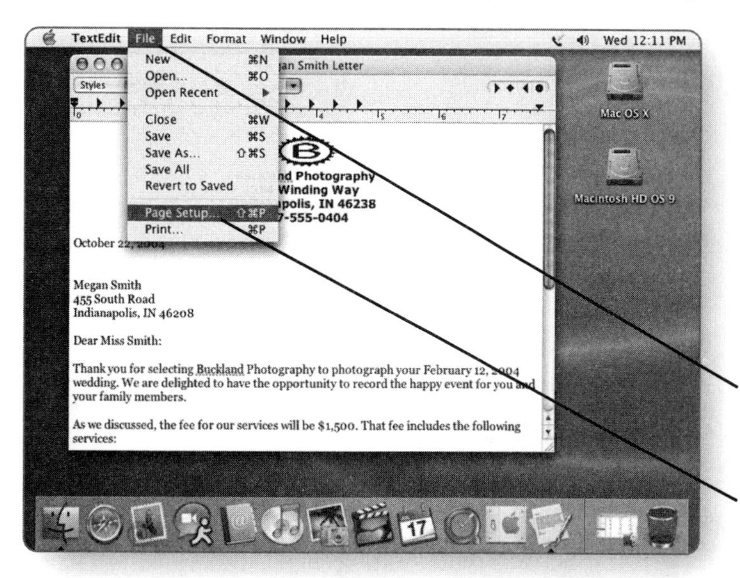

1. **Open** a **document** or **create** a **new document** in the preferred application. You will see an approximation of how your printout will look.

2. **Click** on **File**. The File menu will open.

3. **Click** on **Page Setup**. A page setup sheet will appear.

Here you can make changes to the overall layout of your document for printing. The available settings will vary depending on your application and the selected printer.

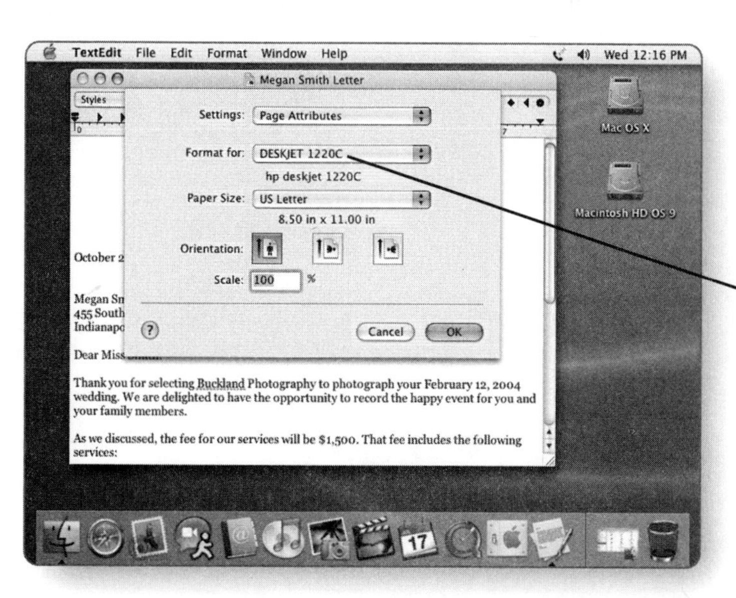

4. **Click** on the **Format for pop-up menu** and **click** on the **printer** to use for the print job. The available Page Setup choices may change depending on the printer that you've selected.

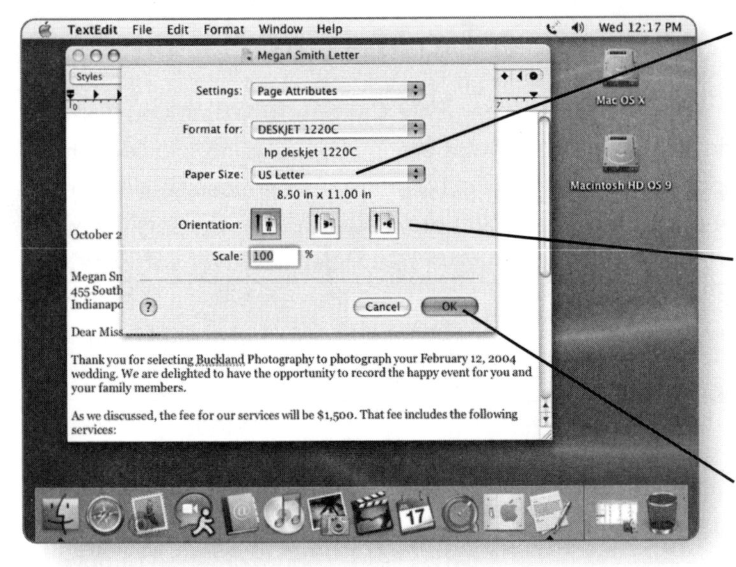

5. Click on the **Paper Size pop-up menu** and **click** on the **paper size** to use for the print job. The document will be reformatted for that paper size.

6. Click on the **desired orientation button**. The printer will print the document on the paper as specified by that orientation.

7. Click on **OK**. The dialog will close, and the settings will be applied.

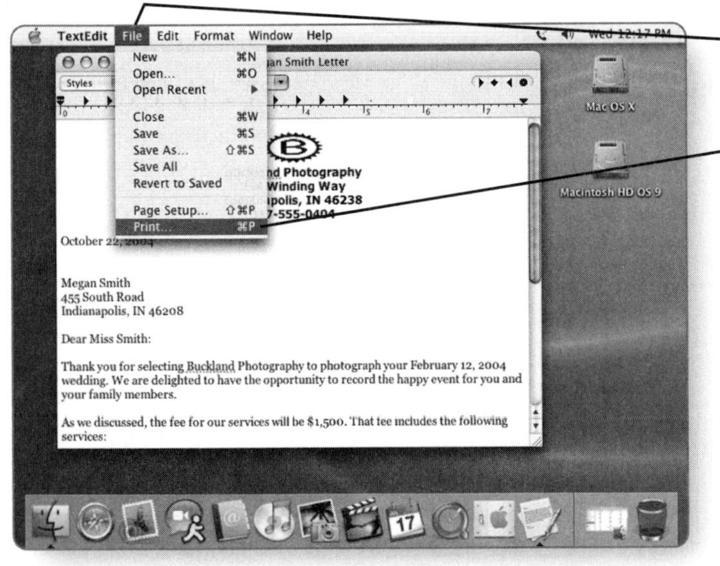

8. Click on **File**. The File menu will open.

9. Click on **Print**. A print sheet will appear. The available settings will vary depending on your application and the selected printer.

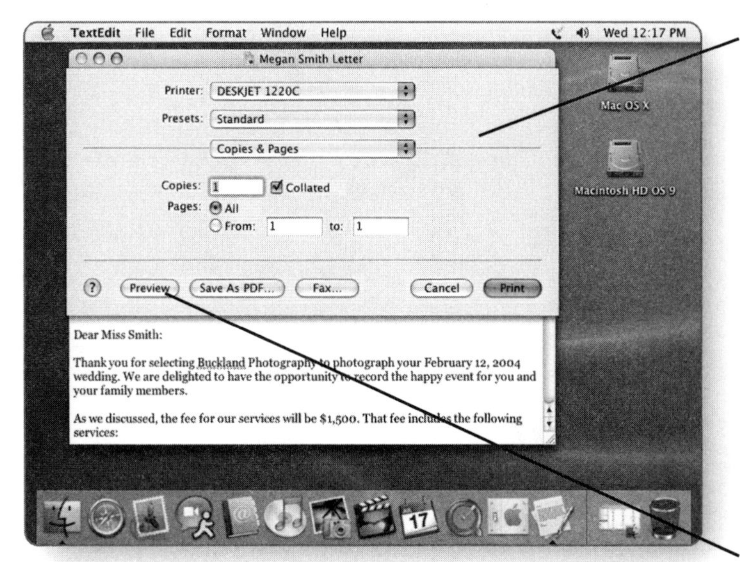

10. **Verify** and **change other settings** as needed. Any changes will become active.

> **NOTE**
>
> In this example using the TextEdit application, you can view additional printing options by clicking on the Copies & Pages pop-up.

11. Click on the **Preview button**. Preview will open and display your document.

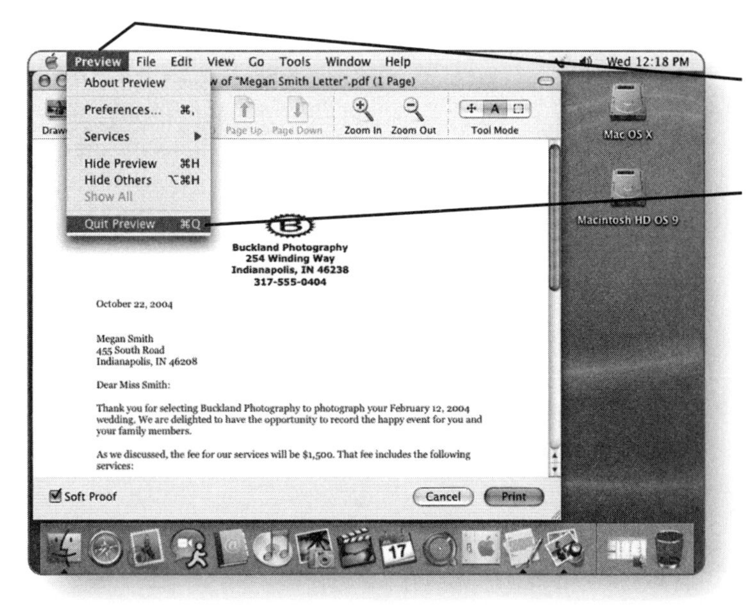

12. Click on **Preview**. The Preview menu will appear.

13. Click on **Quit Preview**. Preview will close.

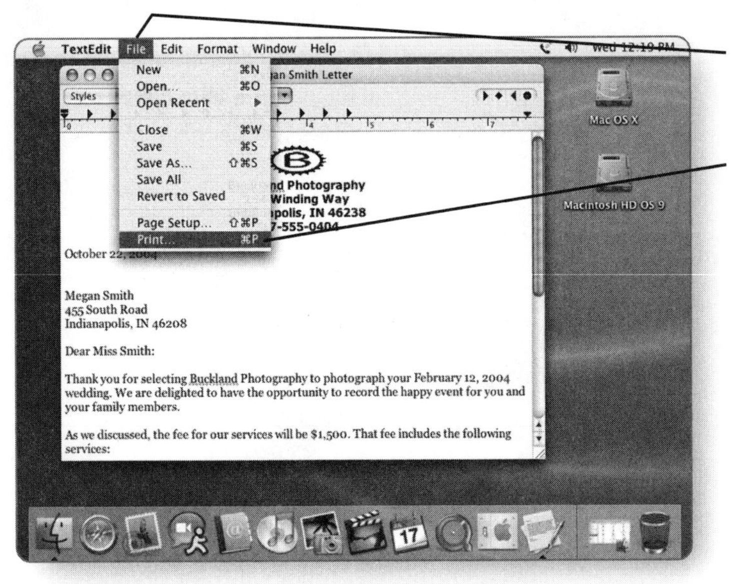

14. **Click** on **File**. The File menu will appear.

15. **Click** on **Print**. A print sheet will open. The settings you selected earlier will still be active.

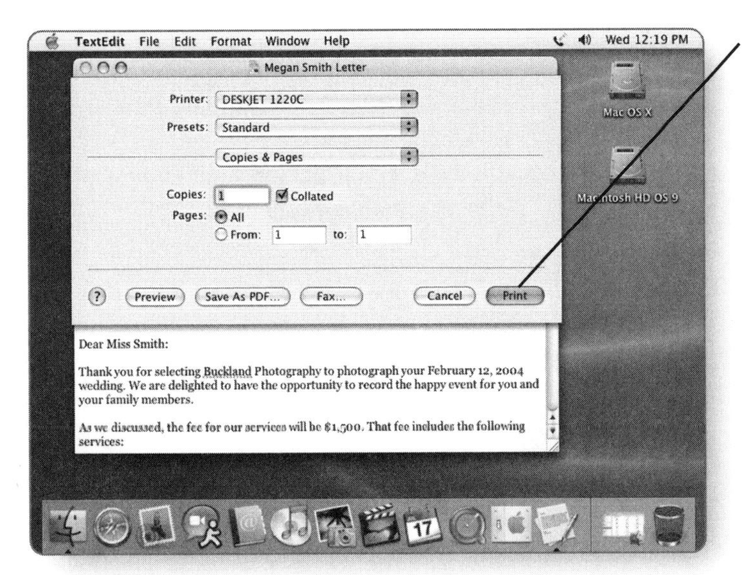

16. **Click** on **Print**. An icon for the printer will appear on the Dock as Mac OS X sends the document to the printer. After the print job finishes, the icon will disappear.

> **NOTE**
>
> You can click on the printer icon to open a window where you can stop or delete a print job. If the printer icon doesn't disappear automatically, click it on the Dock. Click the (printer name) menu and then click on Quit (printer name).

Choosing the Default Printer

Printers today offer a wide range of benefits and features; therefore, you can install multiple printers for use with your Macintosh. For example, you may have a color inkjet printer for printing family photos, cards, or business promotional materials. But because the inkjet ink can be a little pricey and the printer itself is slow, you may also have an inexpensive laser printer for a speedier and less costly method of printing. Use Printer Setup Utility to designate which printer to use as the default printer—the printer that is first suggested in your applications. Choosing the proper default printer reduces how often you need to change the printer selection and settings before printing.

> **NOTE**
>
> Printers set up under Mac OS 9.2 (the Classic environment) don't show up in Print Center, and vice versa. When you are working in the Classic environment (see Chapter 7, "Working in the Classic (Mac OS 9) Environment), use the Chooser to install the OS 9 printer drivers and to configure printers.

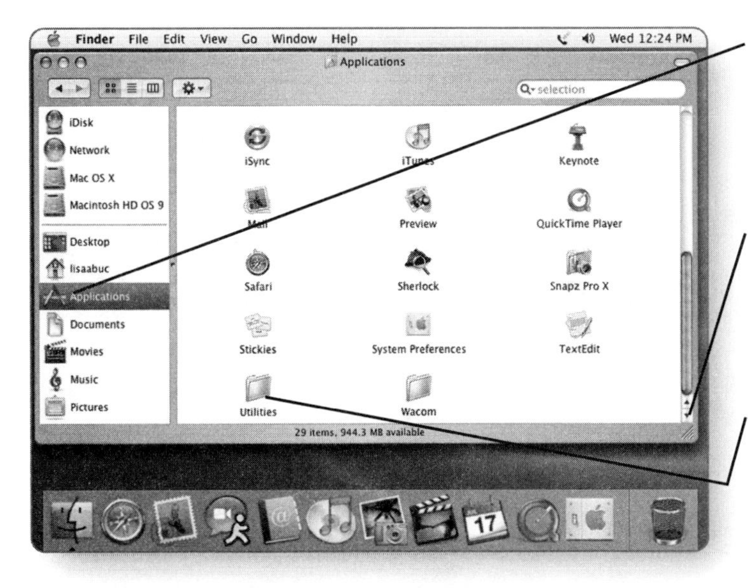

1. **Click** on the **Applications icon** in a Finder window Sidebar. The Applications folder contents will appear in the window.

2. **Click** on the **down arrow** of the vertical scroll bar. The Utilities folder will scroll into view.

3. **Double-click** on the **Utilities folder**. The contents of the folder will appear in the Finder window.

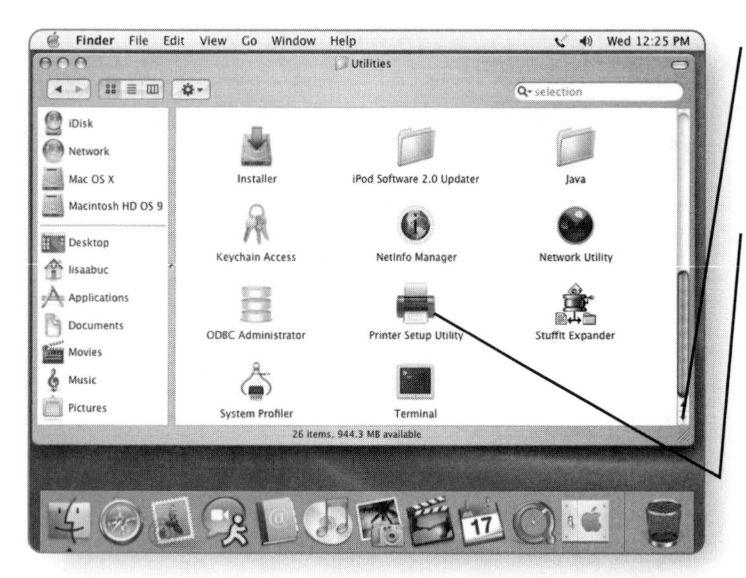

4. Click on the **down arrow** of the vertical scroll bar. The Printer Setup Utility icon will scroll into view.

5. Double-click on the **Printer Setup Utility icon**. Printer Setup Utility will start.

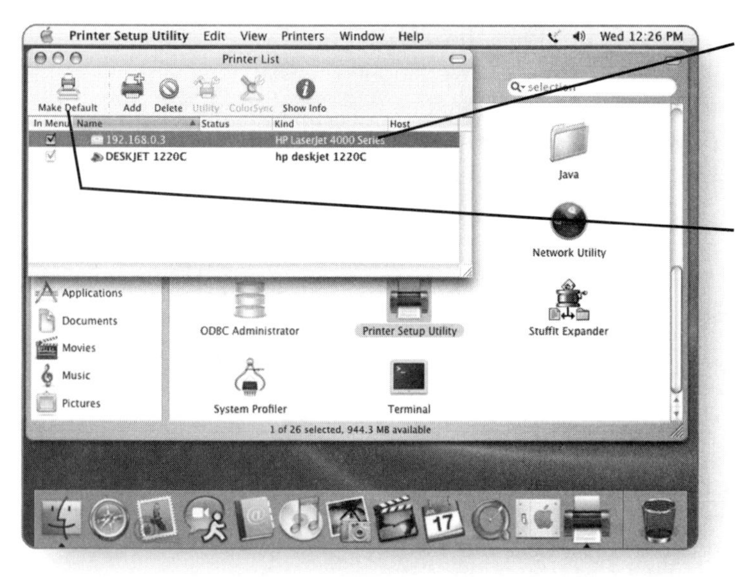

6. Click on the **desired printer** in the Printer List window. The printer will be selected in the list.

7. Click on **Make Default**. The selected printer will be immediately designated as the default printer.

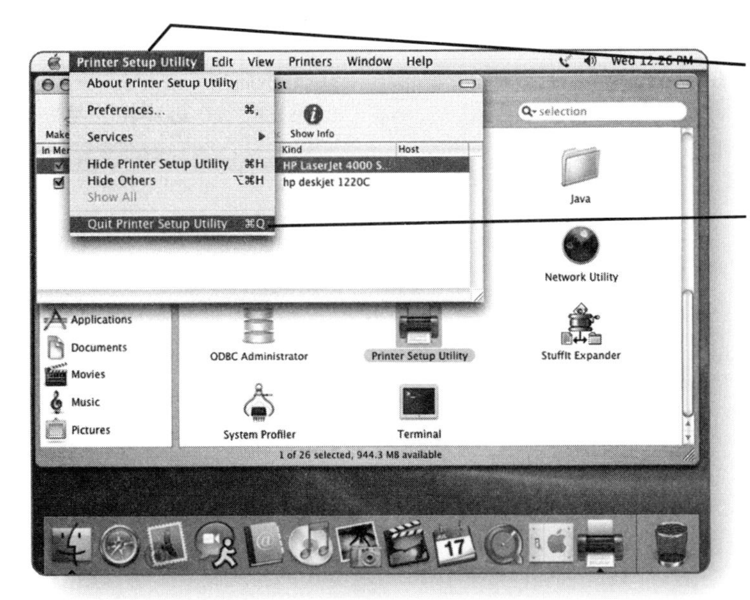

8. **Click** on **Printer Setup Utility**. The Printer Setup Utility menu will appear.

9. **Click** on **Quit Printer Setup Utility**. Printer Setup Utility will close.

NOTE

If you've started a number of lengthy printouts, notice that you can use the Print Center to control the print queue—the list of documents sent to the printer. Select a printer in Printer Setup Utility and choose Printers, Show Jobs. Click on a print job in the window that appears and then click on toolbar icons. The Stop Jobs button stops printing to the printer, but does not cancel the remaining pending print jobs. Hold and Resume pause and restart the selected print job. Delete removes the selected job from the queue. Click on the window close icon when you've finished manipulating print jobs.

Removing a Printer

You may need to remove a printer that's been set up for your system if you no longer plan to use it. Pruning out old printers is part of a good practice of keeping your system streamlined and working well.

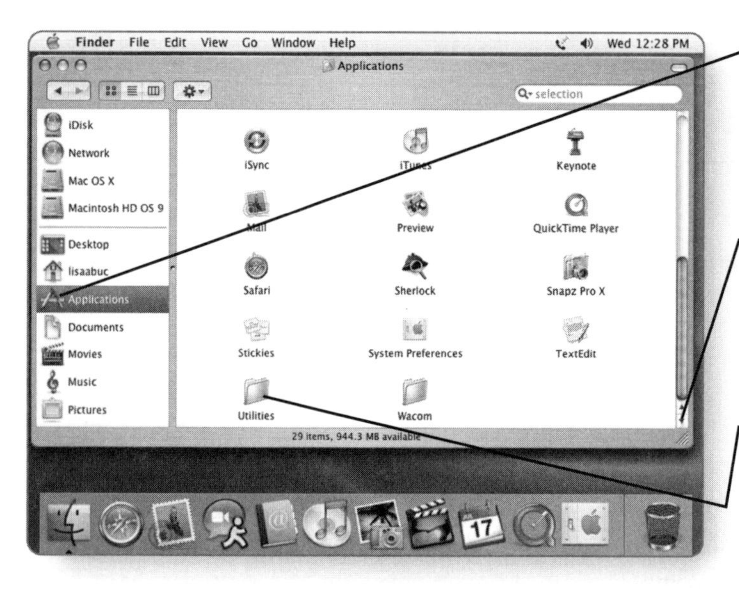

1. **Click** on the **Applications icon** in a Finder window Sidebar. The Applications folder contents will appear in the window.
2. **Click** on the **down arrow** of the vertical scroll bar. The Utilities folder will scroll into view.
3. **Double-click** on the **Utilities folder**. The contents of the folder will appear in the Finder window.

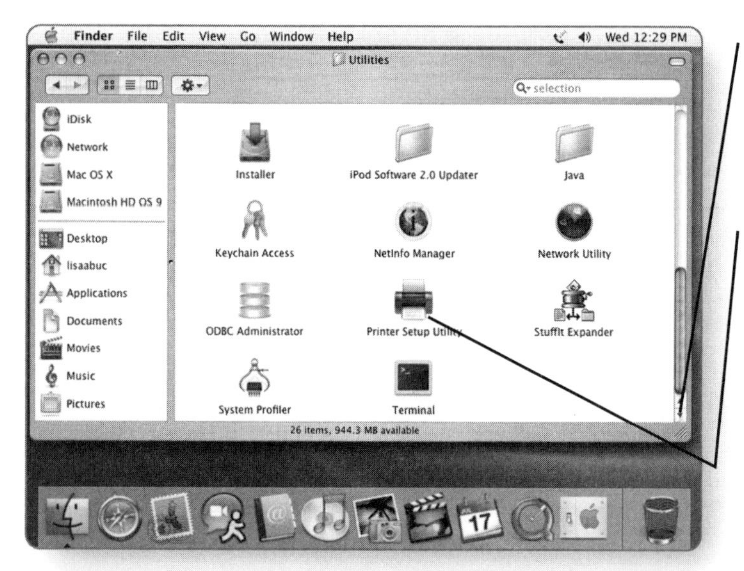

4. **Click** on the **down arrow** of the vertical scroll bar. The Printer Setup Utility icon will scroll into view.
5. **Double-click** on the **Printer Setup Utility icon**. Printer Setup Utility will start.

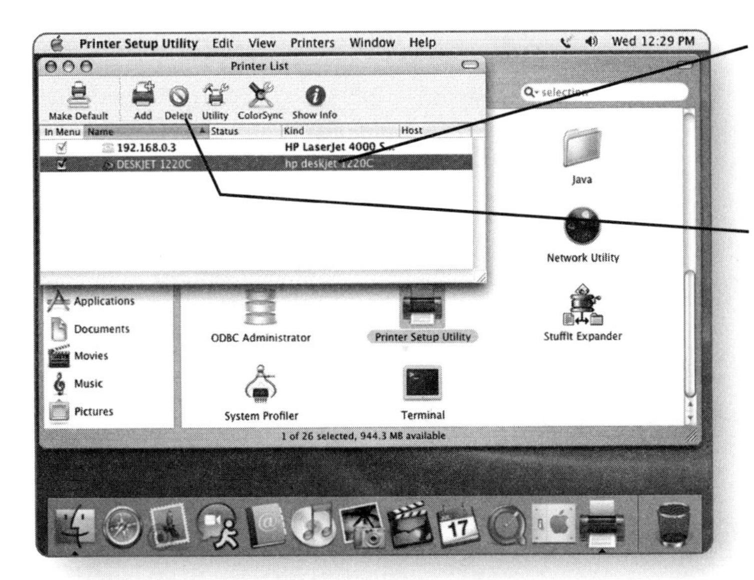

6. Click on the **printer name to be deleted** in the Printer List window. The printer will be selected in the list.

7. Click on the **Delete button**. The printer will be removed from the list.

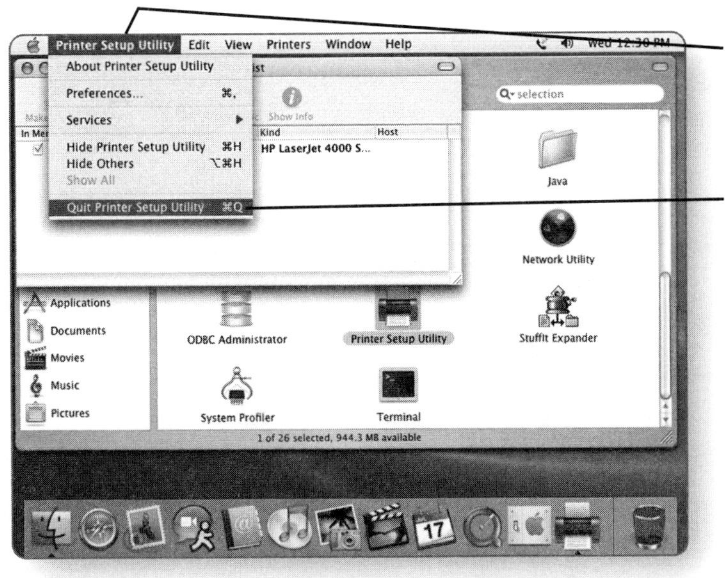

8. Click on **Printer Setup Utility**. The Printer Setup Utility menu will appear.

9. Click on **Quit Printer Setup Utility**. Printer Setup Utility will close.

Sending a Fax

For your convenience, you can now fax a document from within applications used in Mac OS X version 10.3 Panther. The process works much like printing a document:

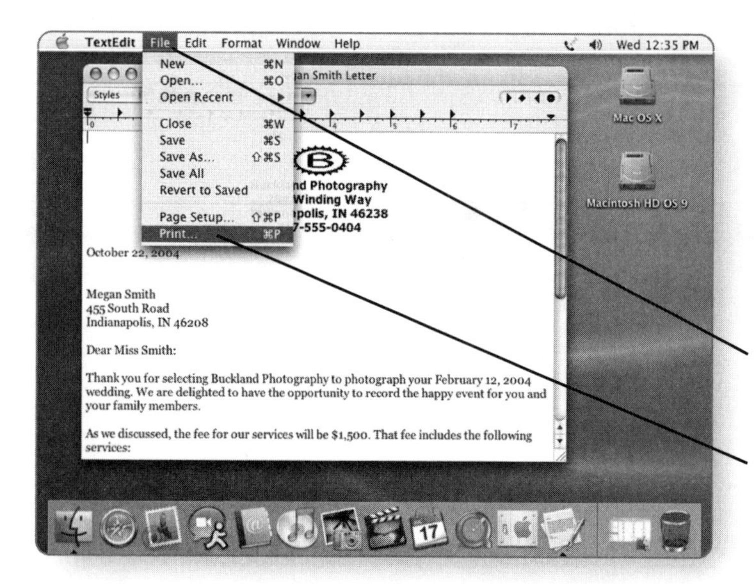

1. **Open** a **document** or **create** a **new document** in the preferred application. Also adjust the page setup as preferred. You will see an approximation of how your faxed document will look.

2. **Click** on **File**. The File menu will open.

3. **Click** on **Print**. A print sheet will appear.

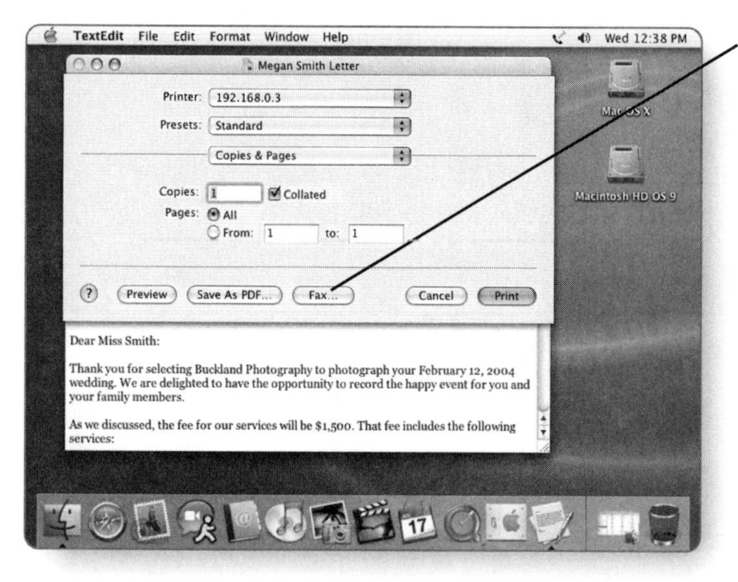

4. **Click** on **Fax**. The print sheet will change to a fax sheet.

5. **Enter** the **fax number** to send to in the To text box. The number will appear.

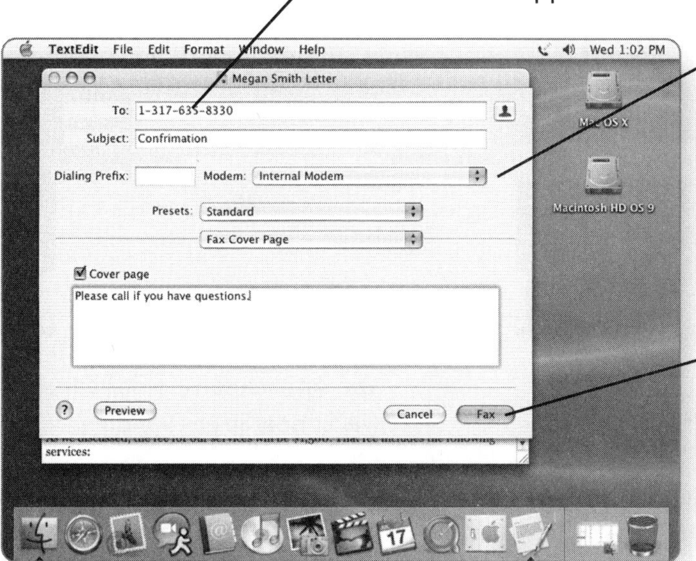

6. **Enter other cover page information.** (If you have to dial 9 to access an outside line from your location, enter the 9 in the Dialing Prefix text box.) The specified information will appear.

7. **Click** on **Fax**. Your system's modem will dial the specified line and send the fax. An icon for the modem will appear on the Dock while the fax sends. You can click on that icon to open a window for your modem that you can use to check on fax status, or stop, delete, or resume a fax.

NOTE

To receive faxes on your Mac, you need to use the Print & Fax panel in System Preferences. Click on the Faxing button in the panel, check the Receive Faxes on this computer check box, and then enter your fax number in the My Fax Number text box.

Managing Fonts with the Font Book

Mac OS X Version 10.3 Panther includes a new font management program called Font Book. With Font Book, you can install and remove fonts for use with your Mac OS X applications and with Classic applications. You can purchase more fonts (usually TrueType fonts) online or through computer catalogs. Some clip art collections also include fonts that you can install. On the other hand, many program installers install additional fonts automatically. If you have no use for these added fonts, you may want to delete them to free up disk space.

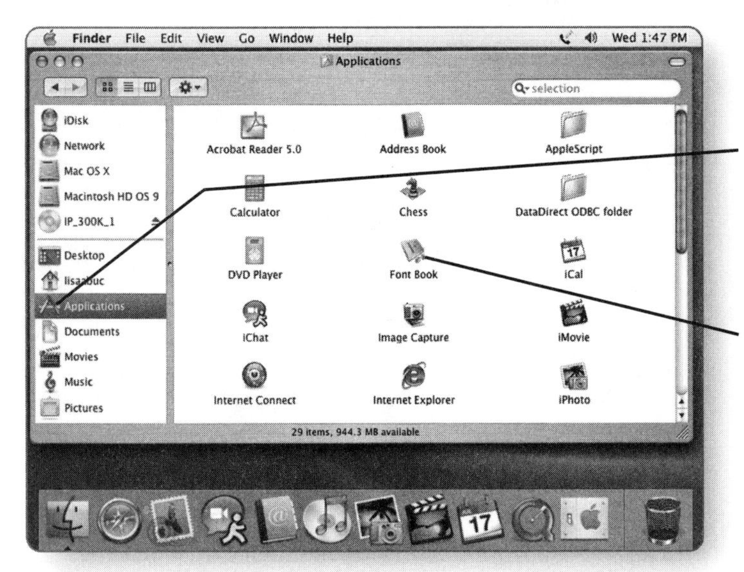

Follow these steps to use Font book to add or remove a font:

1. **Click** on the **Applications icon** in a Finder window Sidebar. The Applications folder contents will appear in the window.

2. **Double-click** on the **Font Book icon**. The Font Book application window will open.

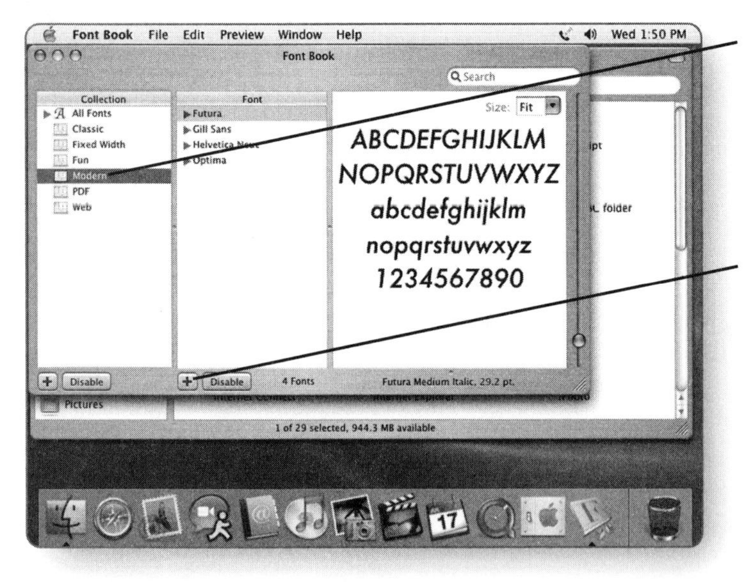

3. **Click** on the **collection** to which you want to add the font in the Collection list. The fonts in that collection will appear in the Font list.

4. **Click** on the **add (+) button** under the Font list. A sheet for selecting the font to add will open.

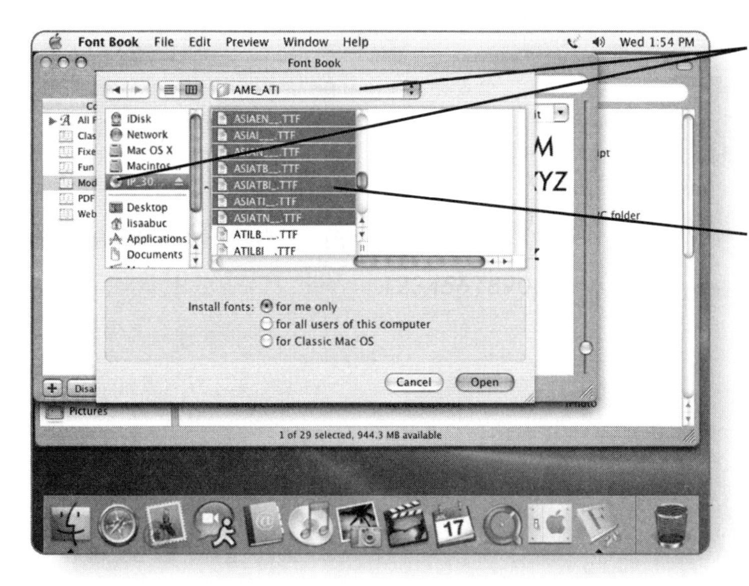

5. Navigate to the **disk** and **folder** holding the font to add. The fonts in that location will appear in the list at the right.

6. Select the **font(s) to add**. You can Shift+click or Control+click to add multiple fonts. The specified fonts will be selected.

> **NOTE**
>
> Usually, to get the bold, italic, and other versions of a particular letter style, you will need to install several font files.

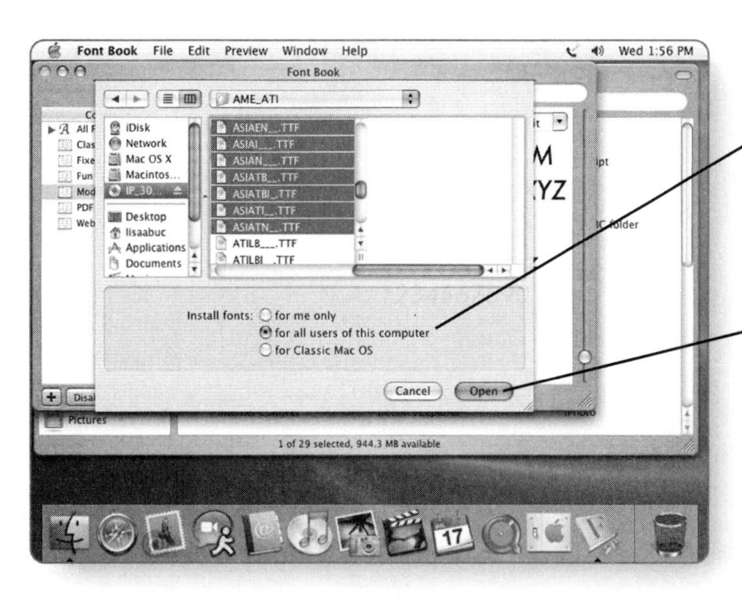

7. Click on the **desired Install fonts choice**. The selected font(s) will be installed as specified by your choice.

8. Click on **Open**. The font(s) will be installed and will appear in the Font list in the Font book.

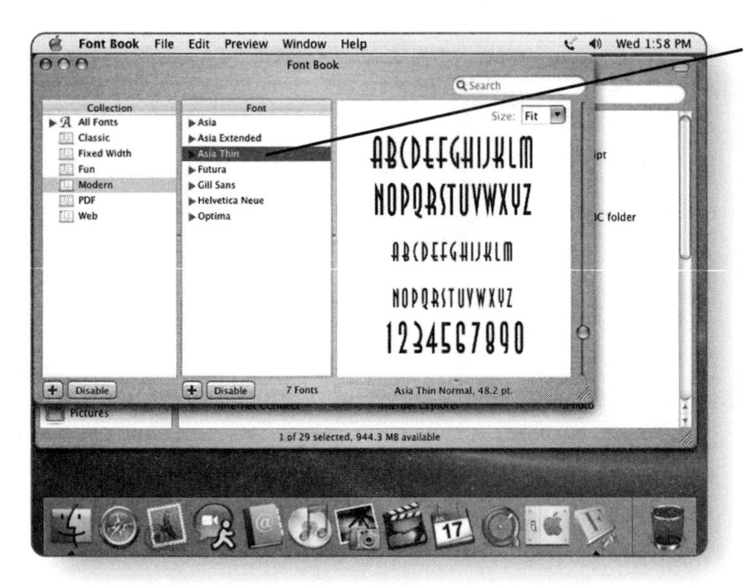

9. To remove a font, **click on it** in the Font list. The font preview will appear at the right side of Font Book.

10. Press Delete. A sheet will open to prompt you to confirm the deletion.

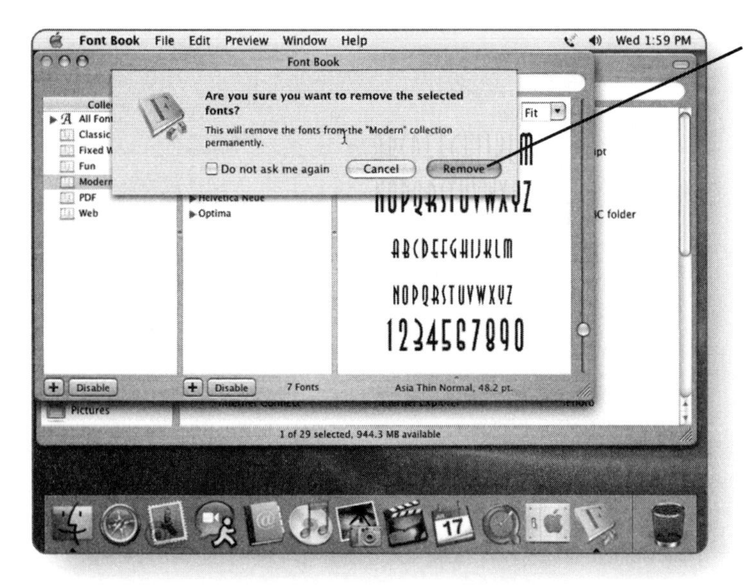

11. Click on **Remove**. The font will be deleted.

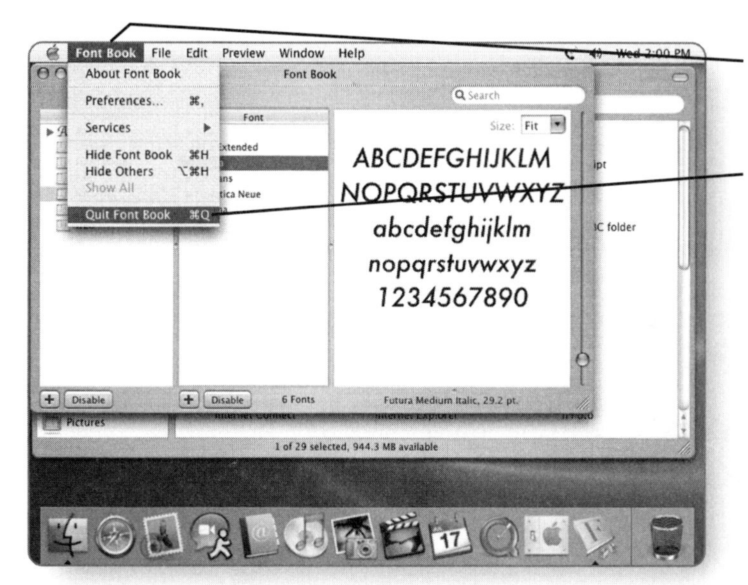

12. **Click** on **Font Book**. The Font Book menu will appear.

13. **Click** on **Quit Font Book**. The Font Book will close.

Part III Review Questions

1. How do I change Finder settings? *See "Changing Basic Finder Preferences" in Chapter 8.*
2. How do I use another graphic on my Desktop? *See "Choosing a Desktop Picture" in Chapter 8.*
3. Can I customize the Dock? *See "Changing Dock Settings" and "Adding and Removing Dock Icons" in Chapter 8.*
4. Where are the System Preferences? *See "Displaying System Preferences" in Chapter 9.*
5. The Preferences are asking me for an administrator password. What gives? *See "Unlocking and Locking a Preferences Pane" in Chapter 9.*
6. How do I get back to the full list of preferences? *See "Redisplaying All the Preferences" in Chapter 9.*
7. How do I reset the time? *See "Setting Date & Time Preferences" in Chapter 9.*
8. My system keeps going black. What is that? *See "Setting Energy Saver Preferences" in Chapter 9.*
9. I try to print, but there's no printer. How do I add one? *See "Setting Up a Printer" in Chapter 10.*
10. How do I print or fax my file? *See "Selecting a Printer and Printing" and "Sending a Fax" in Chapter 10.*

PART IV

Getting Connected

11

Making Network and Internet Connections

In this chapter, you'll learn how to:

- Prepare for networking with the right hardware and settings.
- Enable your system to share its files with other users on the network.
- Set up a network printer.
- Share your Mac files to a Windows system on the network.
- Enter or adjust Internet preferences for Mac OS X Version 10.3.
- Use Internet Connect to specify a connection phone number and other connection details.
- Connect and disconnect when needed.
- Set up a broadband connection.
- Connect to an online iDisk.

Most small businesses—and even many households—now have more than one computer. In such an instance, the need to share files becomes frequent but need not be cumbersome. After a small investment in network hardware, you can use capabilities built into the Mac OS X Version 10.3 software to network multiple computers to share files, printer access, and more. In addition, the majority of home computer users connect to the Internet in some way for work, entertainment, or study. Making your online connection takes just a few minutes.

Setting Up for Networking

Mac OS X Version 10.3 includes Rendezvous networking technology. You won't really see Rendezvous in action, but you'll know it's working because it will make networking computers virtually pain-free. Rendezvous helps Mac OS X more easily recognize computers connected to your LAN (*Local Area Network*). You create a LAN to connect two or more computers primarily to share files, storage space, printers, or even an Internet connection between systems, although other functionality can be added to more sophisticated LANs. The LAN can consist of two or more Macs connected via special cabling.

In addition to the networking capabilities in the operating system, most Macintoshes today ship with an Ethernet network installed. At a minimum, you will need to purchase an Ethernet cable to connect two Macs. (If you're connecting two iMacs or iBooks, you need to purchase a crossover Ethernet cable.) To connect multiple computers and other devices like network-capable printers, you will need multiple Ethernet patch cables as well as a switch, hub, or router—all are devices that enable multiple connections on the network.

Whether you choose a switch, hub, or router depends on the type of devices you want to connect to your network. For a simple network where you connect a couple of Macs and perhaps a printer, you can typically use a hub, the most simple connection device. For a more robust network, a switch might be preferred because a switch takes a more active role in directing network traffic. To share an Internet connection over your network, you may need a router, a connection device that can include such additional features as firewall protection (for keeping other users from hacking into your system over the Internet). While there's not room in this book for a detailed discussion of network hardware, you can find plenty of additional information about the type of hardware you need on the Internet or by contacting a computer store or consultant in your area.

From there, making the physical connection takes only moments:

- When connecting two Macs, plug each end of the crossover cable into the network interface port (on newer Macs, it has a symbol that looks something like <•••> near it) of one of the Macs.

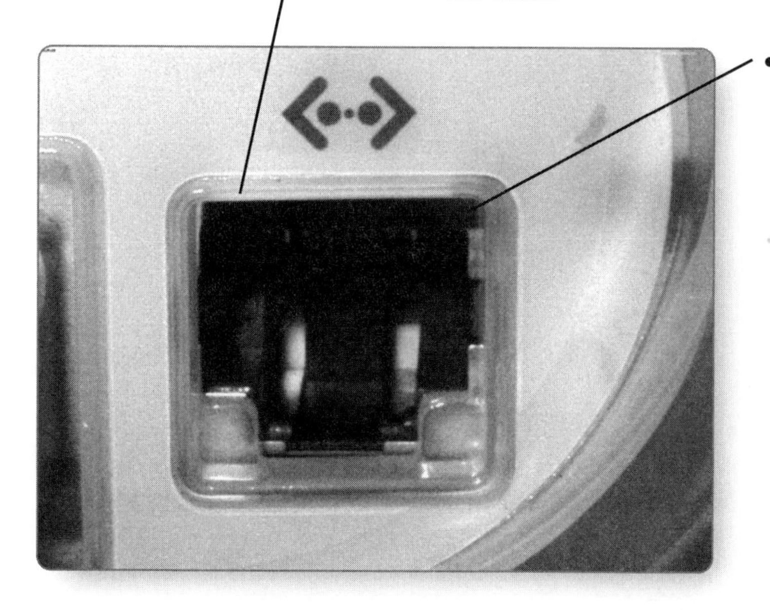

- When connecting multiple computers and/or printers, plug one end of each patch cable into the network interface port on the Mac or printer; then plug the other end of the cable into one of the ports on the switch, hub, or router. When using some switches and routers, you may need to install additional software to enable all of the device's capabilities. Refer to the device documentation to learn more about installing and using any included software.

In a simple network, chances are all you need to do is make the physical connections and power up the connected Macs. Rendezvous will help the systems "talk" to each other. However, for a more complicated setup, you may need to work with the TCP/IP networking settings on each Mac. You can identify each system with a unique IP address, in the format 000.000.000.000. (Each segment between the periods of the IP address can have one to three digits.) Apple recommends you start with simple addresses like 10.0.0.X (10.0.0.1, 10.0.0.2, and so on) for a small network.

1. Turn on the **power** to the switch, hub, or router and **boot** the **computers**. The devices will all be active and ready to network.

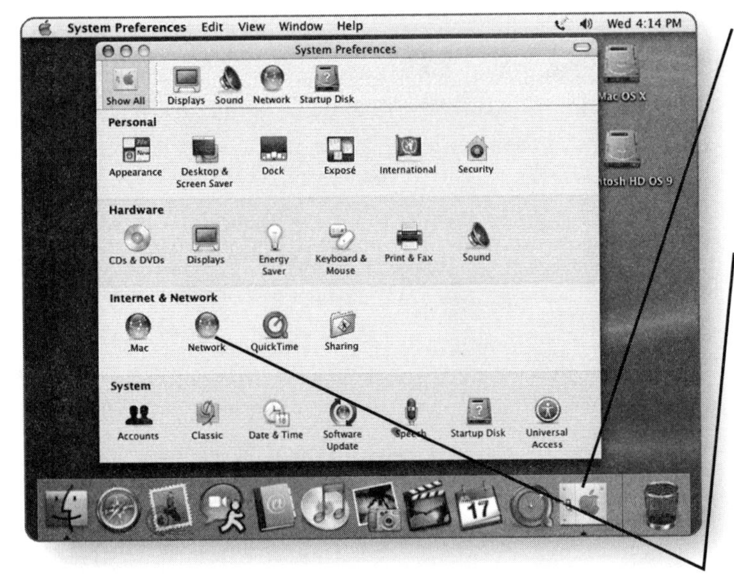

2. Click on the **System Preferences icon** on the Dock. The System Preferences window will open and its menu will appear.

3. Click on **Network**. The Network pane will appear in the System Preferences window.

NOTE

You can save each collection of network settings as a location in the Network pane of System Preferences. (The default location is called *Automatic*.) This helps you avoid deleting a set of settings you might need for one

(continued)

device when you're adding new settings for another. To add a location, click on the Location pop-up menu in the Network pane and click on New Location. Type a name for the location in the sheet that opens and then click OK. The new location will be selected, and any new settings you specify will be added to that location without disturbing the settings in any other location that's been defined.

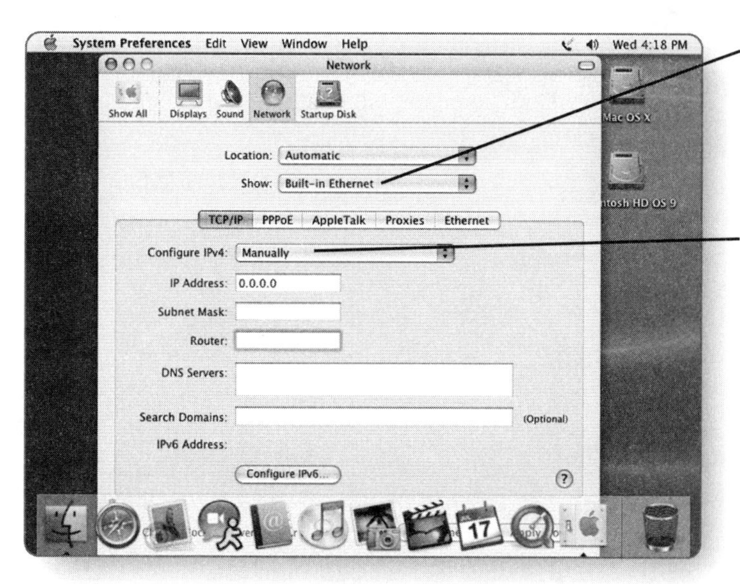

4. Choose Built-in Ethernet from the **Show pop-up menu.** The settings for Ethernet networking will appear.

5. Choose Manually from the **Configure IPv4 pop-up menu.** The choices for manually configuring networking will appear.

NOTE

If you're connecting an older Mac or printer that doesn't support TCP/IP to your network, you will likely need to enable AppleTalk Networking. Display the Network Pane in System Preferences, select Built-In Ethernet from the Show pop-up menu, click the AppleTalk button, and then check Make AppleTalk Active.

NOTE

If you're connecting to a network offering a server or using a router that supplies IP addresses, you may need to choose another configuration method. Consult your network administrator or your device documentation to learn more.

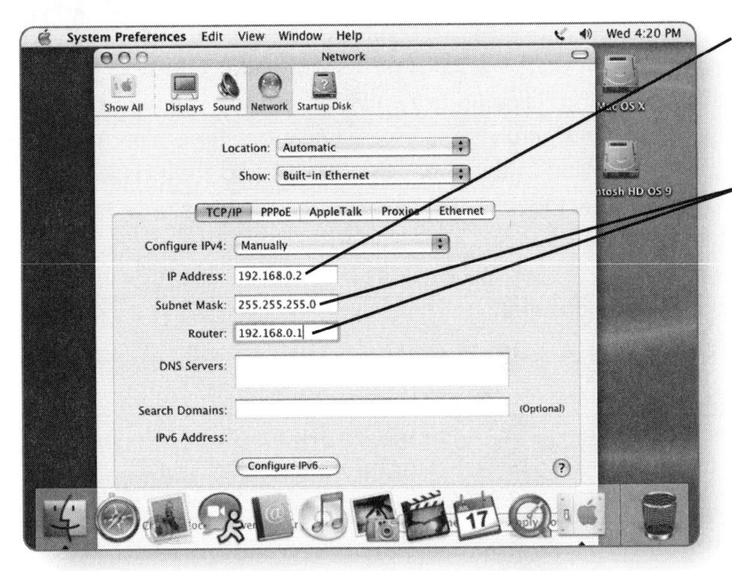

6. **Type** an **IP Address** in the IP Address text box. The IP address will appear.

7. If required by your network and hardware, also **type Subnet Mask** and **Router entries.** The entries will appear.

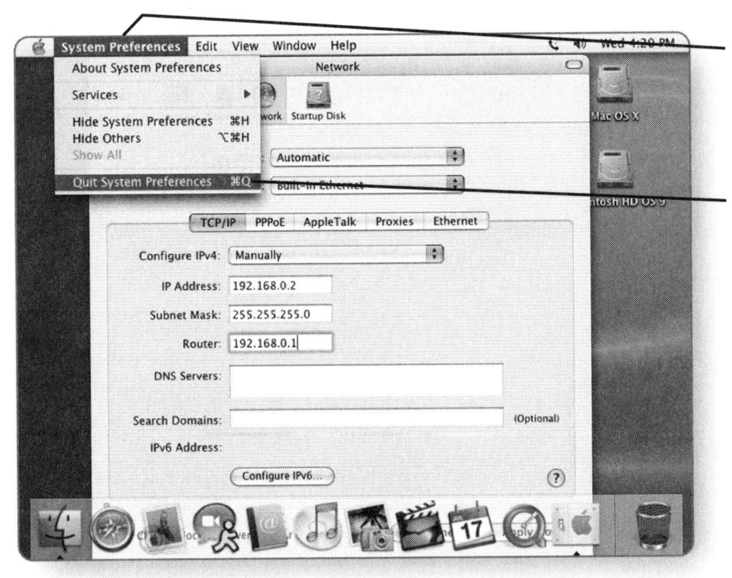

8. **Click** on **System Preferences**. The System Preferences menu will appear.

9. **Click** on **Quit System Preferences**. A sheet prompting you to apply your configuration changes will appear.

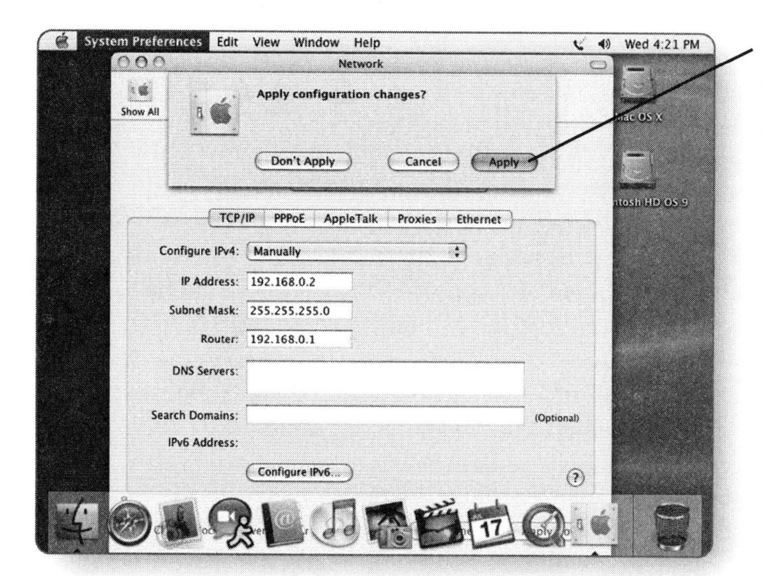

10. Click on **Apply**. System Preferences will apply your changes and close.

Turning On File and Printer Sharing

You're not quite ready to work on your network yet! In addition to setting up basic networking settings as just described, you need to turn on file sharing for each Mac on the network so that users can access each other's files. (Only the files in each user's Public folder will be shared by default.)

You also need to turn on printer sharing on any Mac that has a directly connected printer that you'd like to share.

> **NOTE**
>
> During this process, you also assign a name for the computer. Each computer on the network must have a unique name. Otherwise, other computers won't be able to access it on the network.

CAUTION

You may not want to leave file sharing turned on all the time, especially if your system or network uses an always-on Internet connection, such as a DSL connection. When file sharing is on, other users on the Internet (or your network) have the potential to hack into your system. So, consider disabling file sharing whenever you don't really need to have it working to share files. Also, click on the Firewall button in the Sharing pane of System Preferences, check services for which you want to restrict incoming network communication, and click the Start button to turn on Firewall protection.

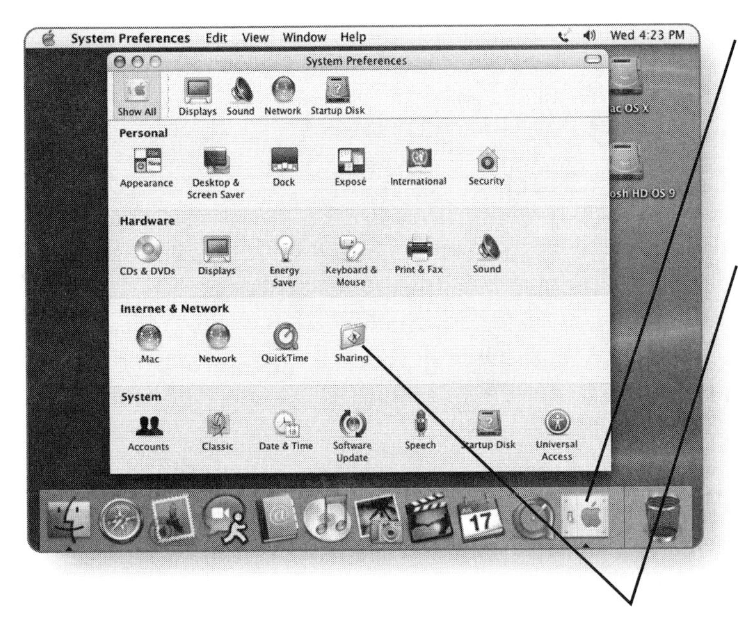

1. Click on the **System Preferences icon** on the Dock. The System Preferences window will open, and its menu will appear.

2. Click on **Sharing**. The Sharing pane will appear in the System Preferences window.

NOTE

Take note of the Network Address name assigned to your computer. Other users can use that name to access your computer over the network. Its full network address is *afp://networkaddress/*, where *networkaddress* is the actual Network Address for your computer shown on the Sharing pane.

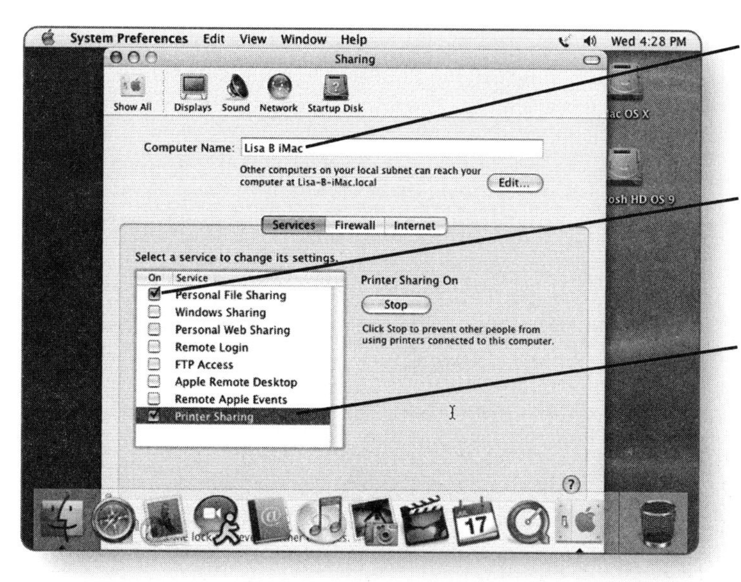

3. **Type** an **alternate computer name** in the Computer Name text box. The name will appear.

4. **Click** on the **Personal File Sharing check box**. File sharing will start for the Mac.

5. **Click** on the **Printer Sharing check box**. Printer sharing will start for the Mac.

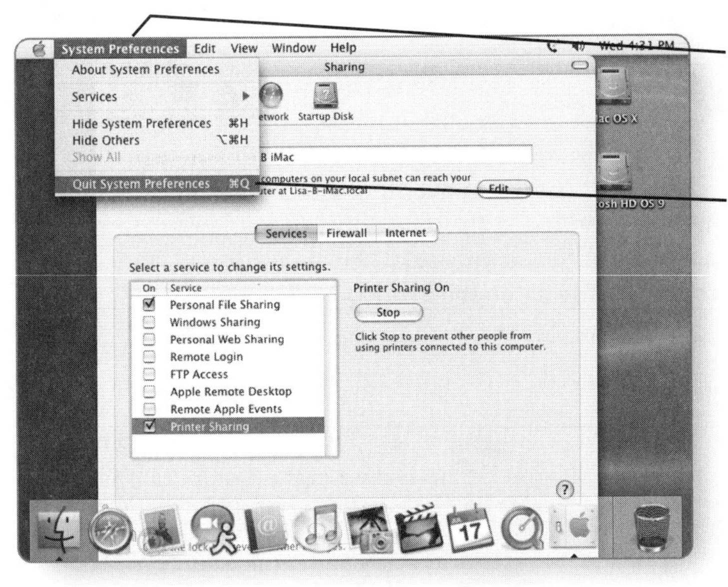

6. Click on **System Preferences**. The System Preferences menu will appear.

7. Click on **Quit System Preferences**. System Preferences will apply your changes and close.

> **NOTE**
>
> There's no need to reboot the system. The networking changes apply immediately.

Connecting to Other Computers

After you've set up your network, you're ready to work with the files on other users' systems. One way to find connected servers and the contents of other users' Public folders is to use the Network Browser. You find it by clicking on Computer in a Finder window toolbar and then double-clicking on Network. From there you can browse through locations and folders as normal. However, if a particular location or server isn't showing up, or you want to go to a favorite network location, use the Connect to Server command.

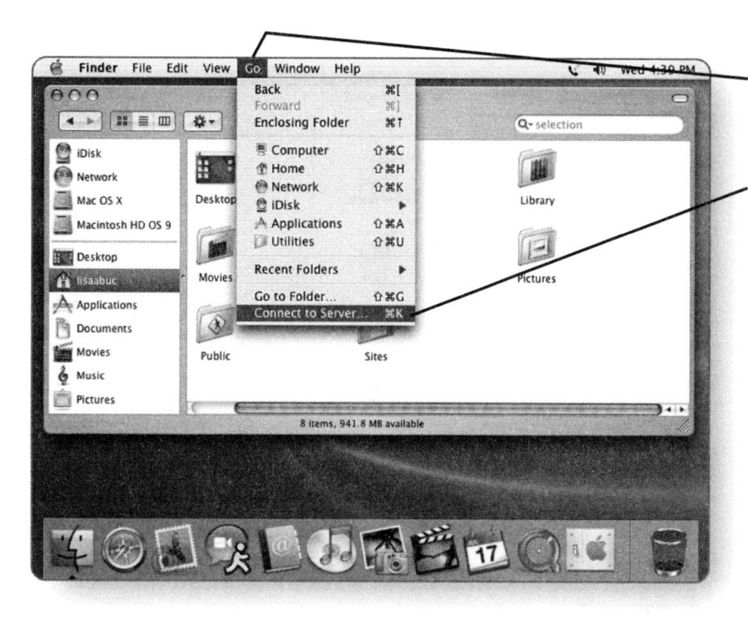

1. **Click** on **Go**. The Go menu will appear.

2. **Click** on **Connect to Server**. The Connect to Server dialog box will appear.

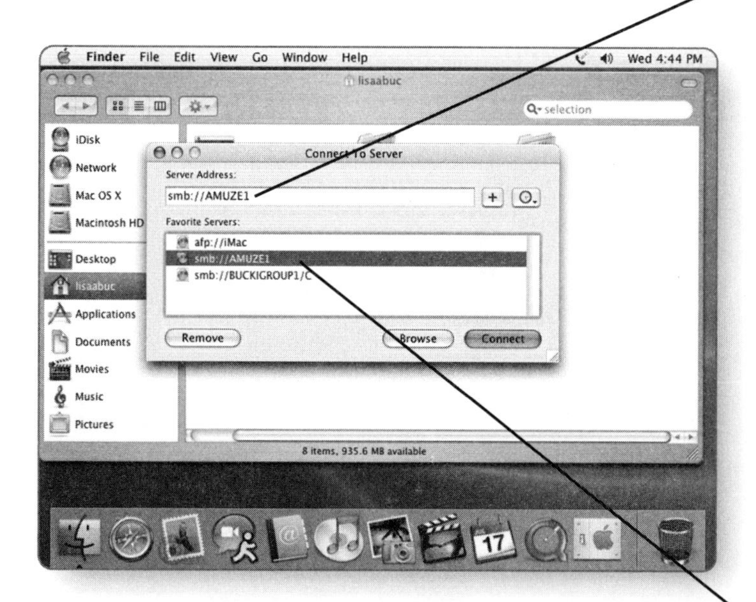

TIP

You can type a server address in the Server Address text box of the Connect to Server dialog box and then click on Connect. Use the format *afp://localhostname/* for Mac locations and *smb://computername/shared-location/* for Windows location. After you type in an address, click the Add button. You can later return to that location by double-clicking on the favorite in the Favorite Servers list.

3. **Double-click** on the **desired server (computer)**. If the selected server has multiple shared locations, a dialog box opens to prompt you to select a share.

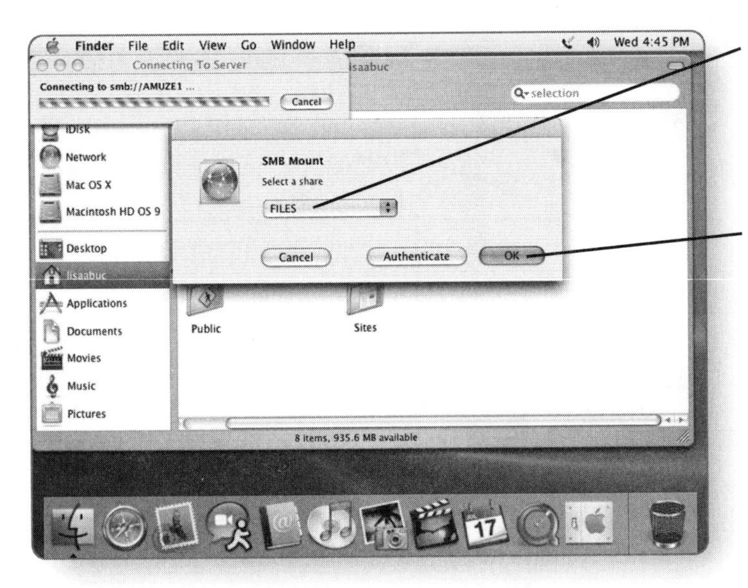

4. **Select** the **desired share** from the pop-up menu at the top of the dialog box. Its name will appear in the pop-up menu.

5. **Click** on **OK**. If the server requires a password for logon, an Authentication dialog box will open.

> **CAUTION**
>
> Avoid connecting to more than one shared Windows network drive at a time. Doing so can cause Mac OS X Version 10.3 to have a kernel panic—OS X's version of a crash—in which case, you'll need to reboot.

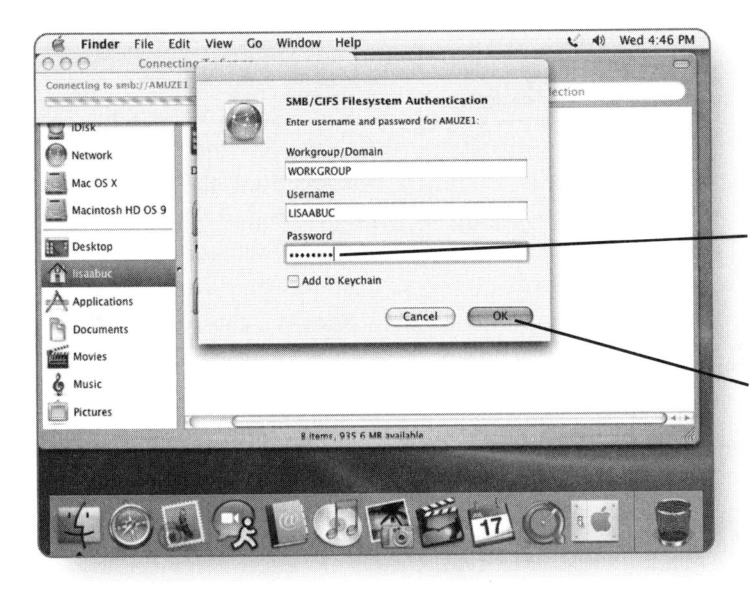

6. **Type** in the **password** in the Password text box. A dot will appear for each letter.

7. **Click** on **OK**.

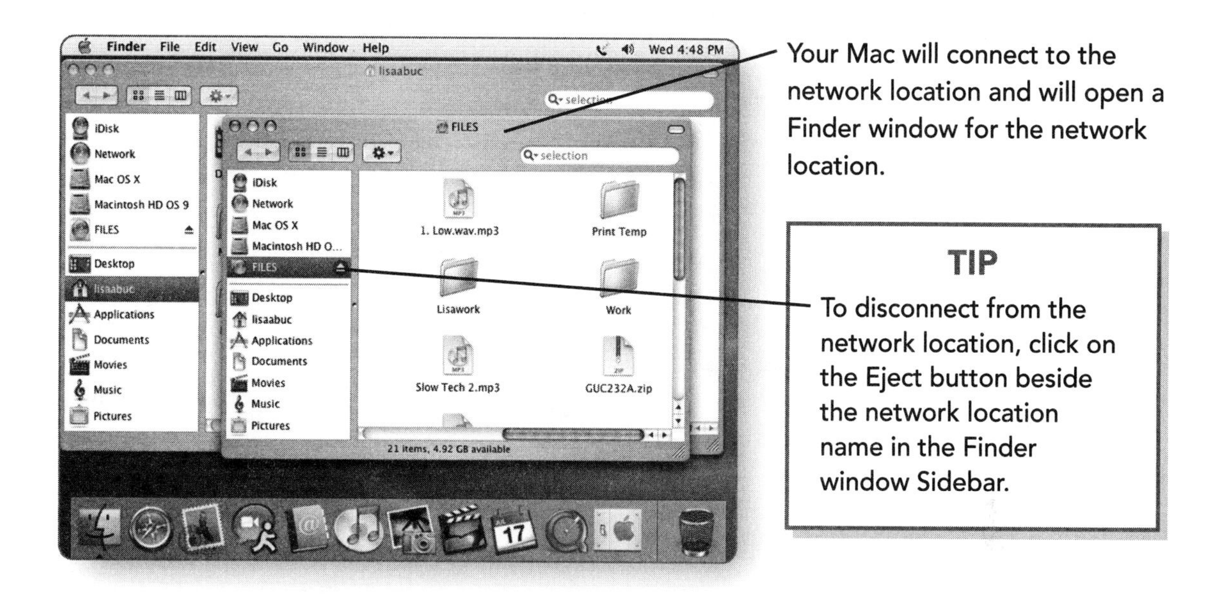

Your Mac will connect to the network location and will open a Finder window for the network location.

> **TIP**
>
> To disconnect from the network location, click on the Eject button beside the network location name in the Finder window Sidebar.

Connecting to a Network Printer

> **TIP**
>
> Most networkable printers have an option or can generate a printout to determine what IP address the printer is using. Consult your printer's documentation to learn how to find this information.

Some printer manufacturers—notably Epson, Lexmark, and HP—are working with Apple to provide automatic printer networking for printers that can connect via Ethernet and communicate via TCP/IP. (Refer back to Chapter 10, "Working with Printers, Faxes, and Fonts," for more on USB printers, which don't support TCP/IP communication and thus must be connected directly to a computer rather than being used as a network printer.) Rendezvous therefore recognizes and sets up some of their newer models automatically. However, for older printers attached to your network, you'll need to set the printer up manually using its IP address.

1. **Connect your printer** to its power source and to the network switch, hub, or router and then **turn** on the **printer**. The printer will start up and be ready for setup.

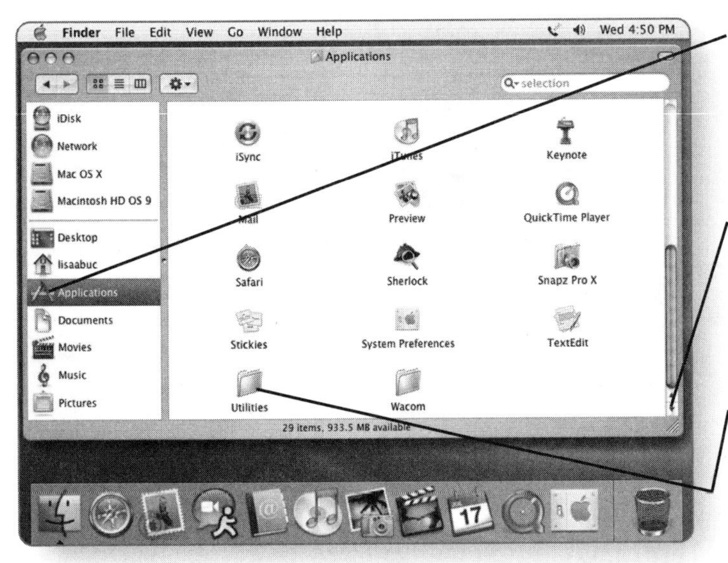

2. **Click** on the **Applications icon** in a Finder window Sidebar. The Applications folder contents will appear in the window.

3. **Click** on the **down arrow** of the vertical scroll bar. The Utilities folder will scroll into view.

4. **Double-click** on **Utilities folder**. The contents of the folder will appear in the Finder window.

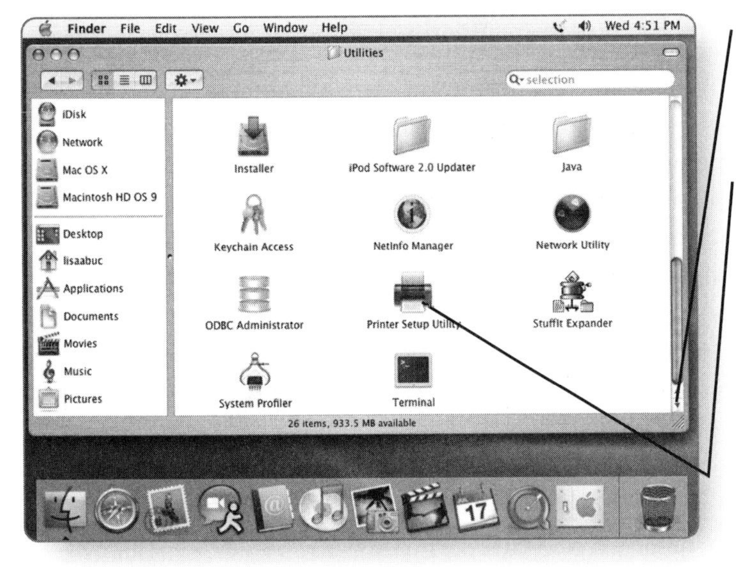

5. **Click** on the **down arrow** of the vertical scroll bar. The Print Center icon will scroll into view.

6. **Double-click** on the **Printer Setup Utility icon**. Printer Setup Utility will start, and the Printer List window will open.

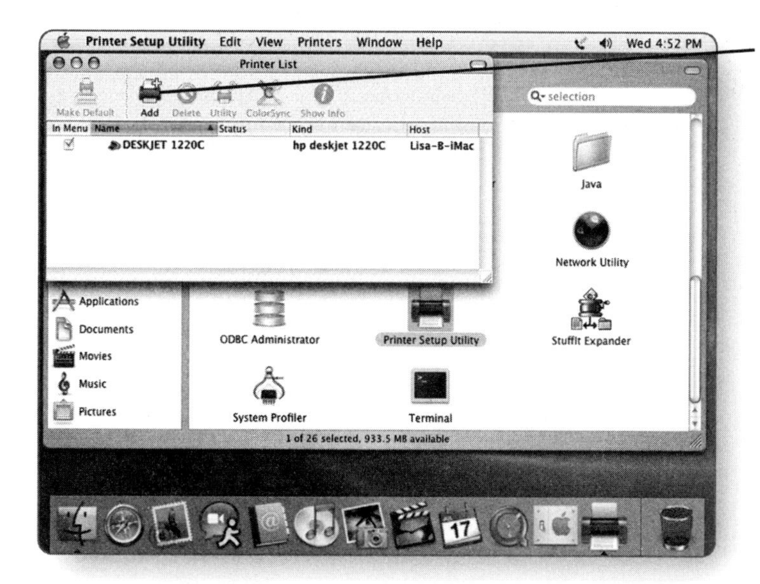

7. **Click** on the **Add button** on the window toolbar. A sheet for adding printers will appear.

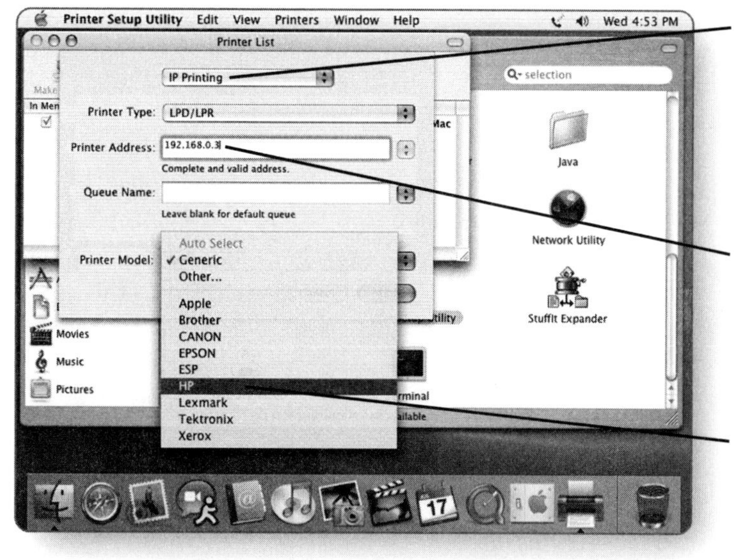

8. **Click** on the **pop-up menu** near the top of the sheet; then **click** on **IP Printing**. Settings for adding a printer using its IP address will appear in the sheet.

9. **Type** the **printer's IP address** in the Printer's Address text box. The IP address will appear.

10. **Click** on the **Printer Model pop-up menu**; then **click** on your **printer's brand**. The bottom of the sheet will expand to display a list of printer models.

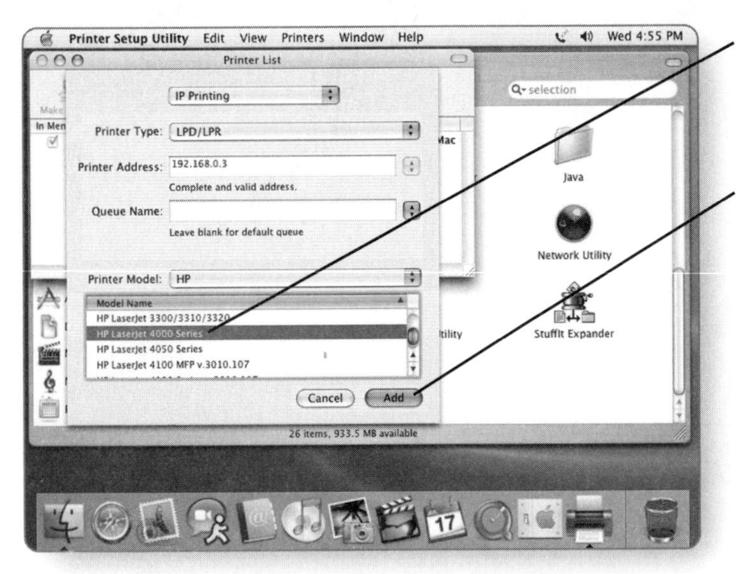

11. Scroll down and **click** on **your printer model**. It will appear highlighted.

12. Click on **Add**. Printer Setup Utility will add the printer to the list in the Printer List window and will designate the new printer as the default printer.

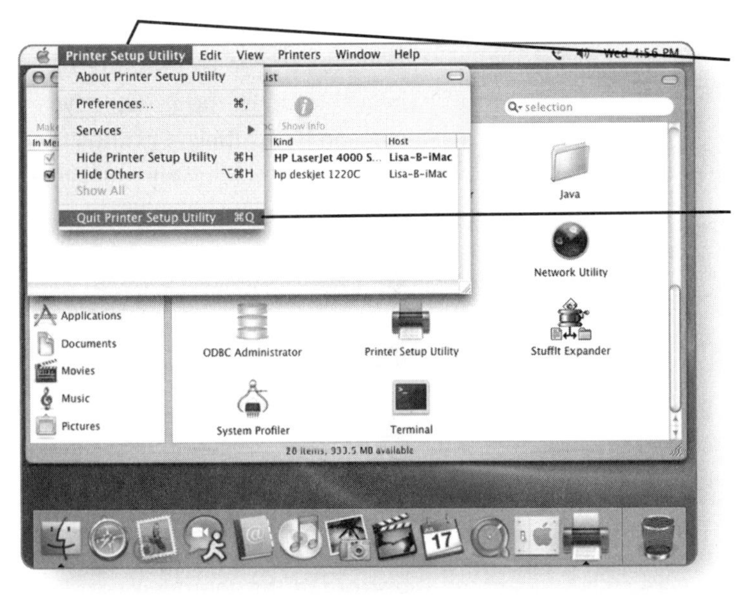

13. Click on **Printer Setup Utility**. The Printer Setup Utility menu will appear.

14. Click on **Quit Printer Setup Utility**. The Printer Setup Utility will close, and you will now be able to print to the newly added network printer.

Viewing Your Mac Folders from a Windows Network

Windows can use a generic method of file sharing called *SMB sharing*, as can Mac OS X Version 10.3. The trick is that you have to turn on a file sharing option in Mac OS X to enable a Windows system to connect to your Mac on the network. Here's a look at how to enable that sharing and how to connect to your newly shared Mac from a Windows XP machine.

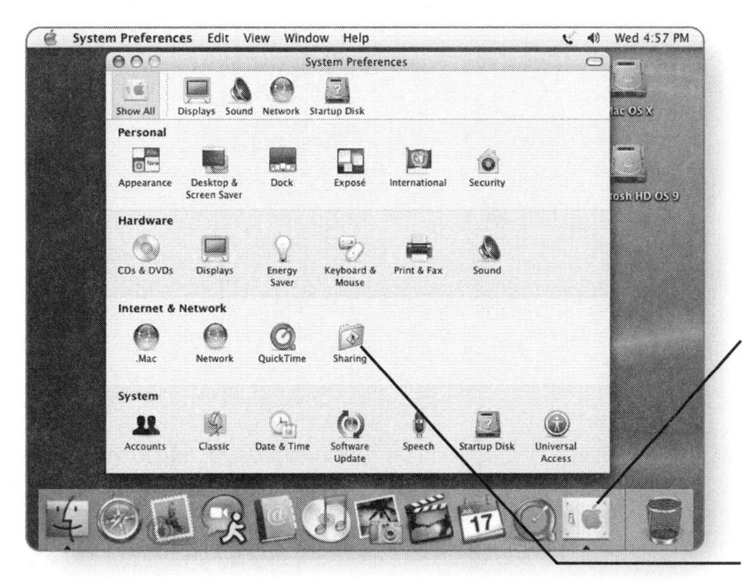

1. **Click** on the **System Preferences icon** on the Dock. The System Preferences window will open, and its menu will appear.

2. **Click** on **Sharing**. The Sharing pane will appear in the System Preferences window.

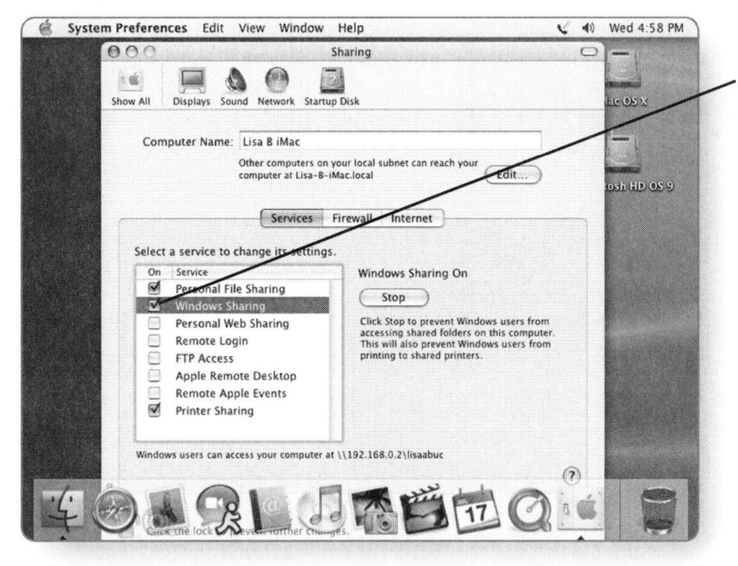

3. **Click** on the **Windows Sharing check box**. Windows file sharing will start.

> **NOTE**
>
> Take note of the login address listed for your computer. In this example it's *\\localhost\lisaabuc*. You often can use this address to log in to the Mac from Windows.

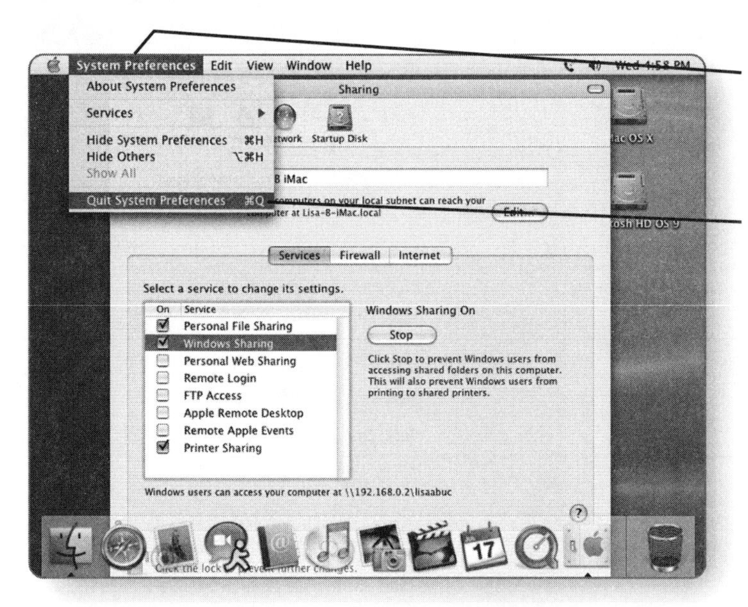

4. **Click** on **System Preferences**. The System Preferences menu will appear.

5. **Click** on **Quit System Preferences**. System Preferences will apply your changes and close.

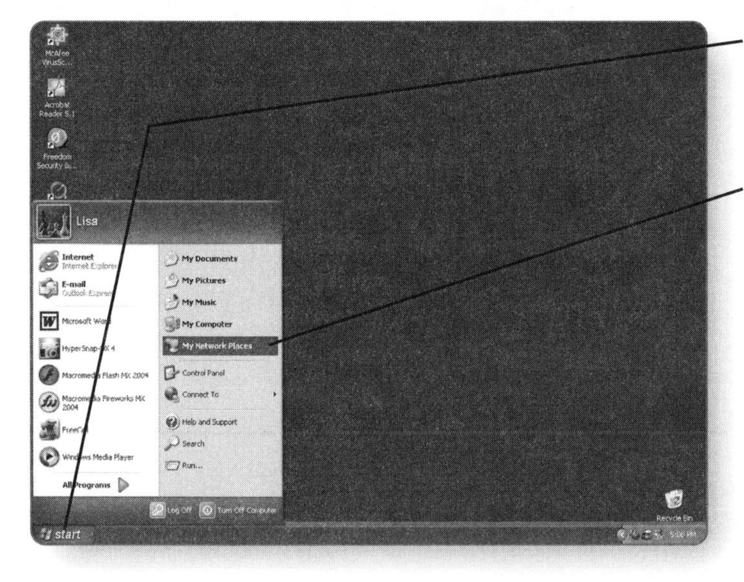

6. In Windows XP, **click** on **Start**. The Start menu will appear.

7. **Click** on **My Network Places**. The My Network Places window will open, and after a second or two, the icon for the Mac will appear.

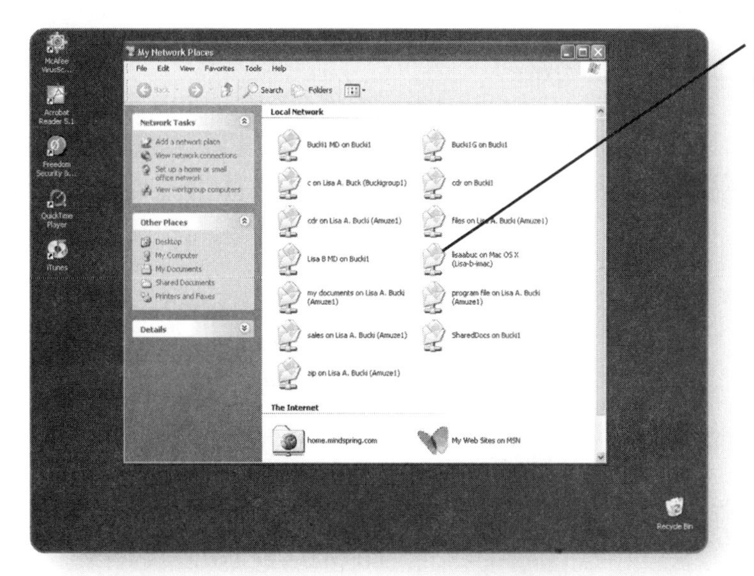

8. Double-click on the **Mac icon**.

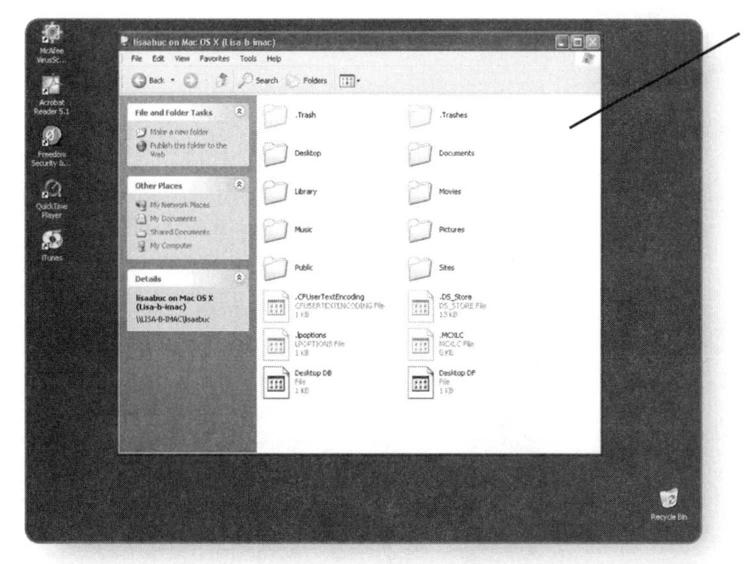

The folders on the shared Mac will appear.

In some cases, a Connect To dialog box will open to prompt you to enter your user name and password. Type your user name and password in the applicable text boxes and click on OK.

If the My Network Places window doesn't list your networked Mac, you can map the network drive. Use the following steps to do so:

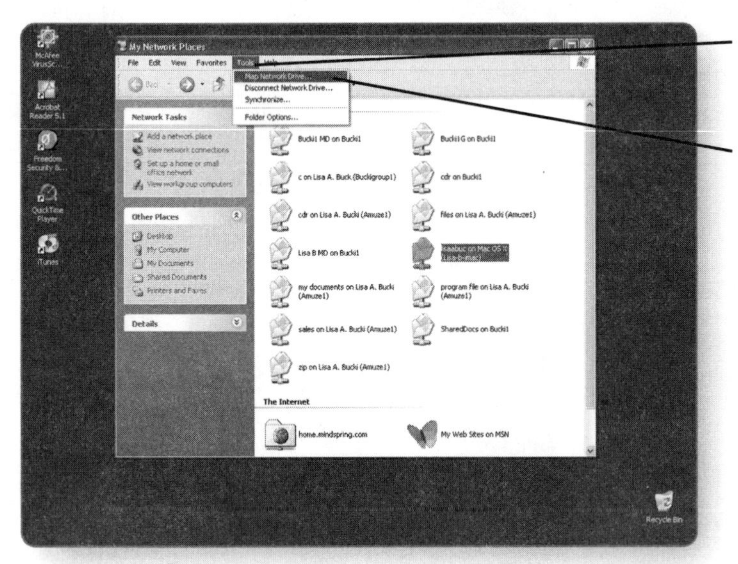

1. **Click** on **Tools**. The Tools menu will appear.
2. **Click** on **Map Network Drive**. The Map Network Drive dialog box will open.

> **NOTE**
>
> Use the Tools, Disconnect Network Drive command to disconnect from a network drive that you've mapped.

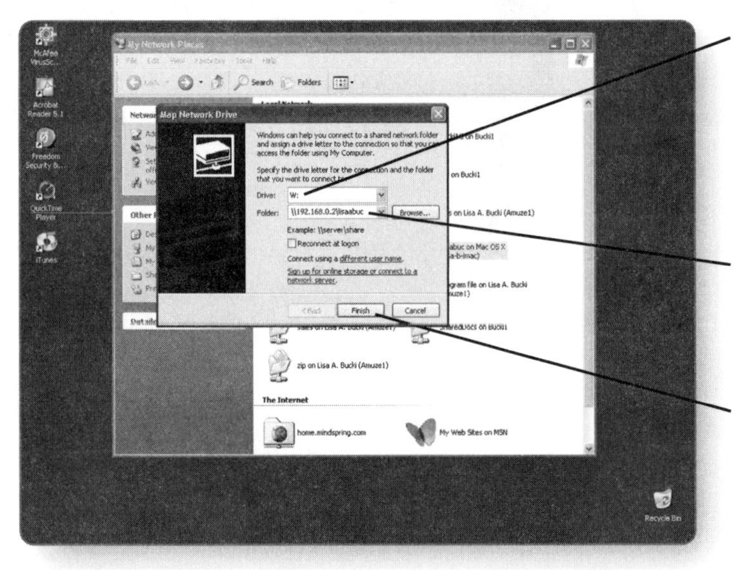

3. **Choose** the **desired drive letter** from the Drive list. The mapped network disk will appear with the specified drive letter.
4. **Type** the **Mac's server and share address** in the Folder text box. The address will appear.
5. **Click** on **Finish**. A Connect To dialog box will open to prompt you to enter your user name and password.

NOTE

Use the *servername**sharename* format you saw earlier in the Sharing pane of System Preferences, or use the format *IPaddress**sharename* as shown here. If you open My Network Places in Windows XP, you can choose Add a Network Place from the list of Network Tasks at the left and then use the Wizard that starts to save the Mac's server and share address as a network connection in My Network Places.

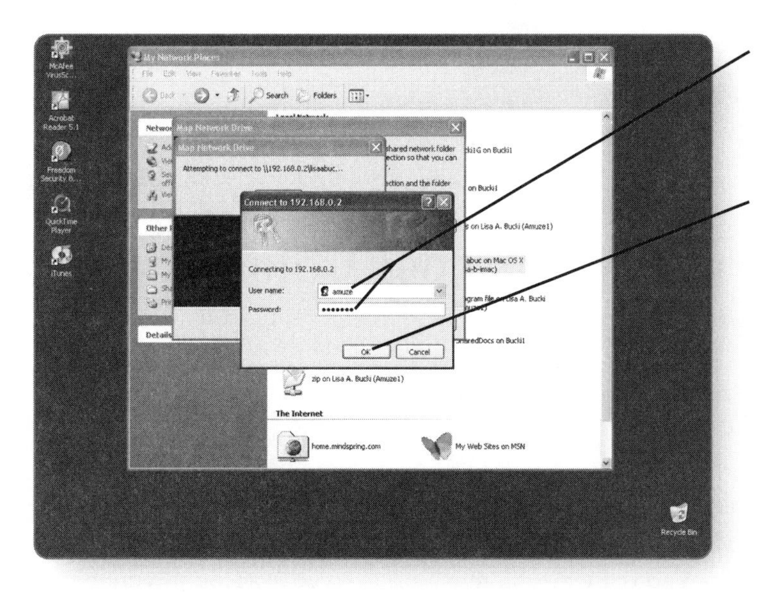

6. **Type** your **user name** and **password** in the text boxes. The information will appear.

7. **Click** on **OK**.

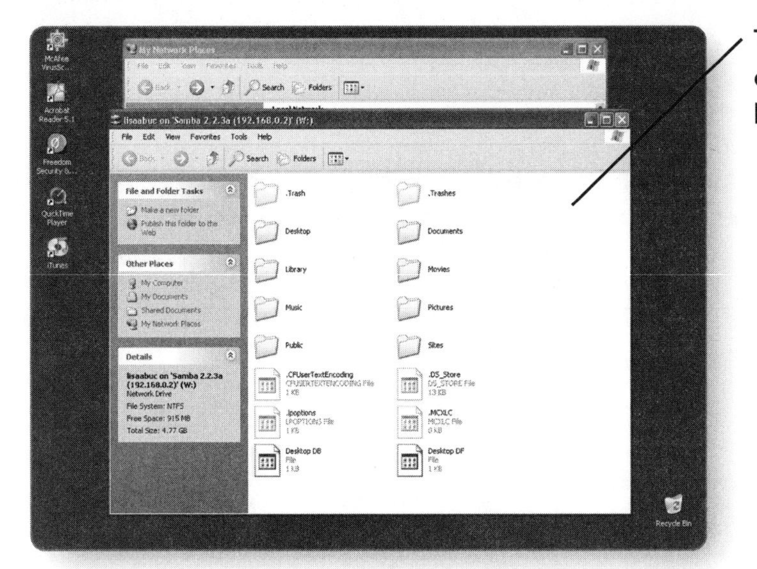

The contents of the mapped drive will appear. You can then browse the contents.

Entering Internet Connection Information

If you used the Setup Assistant the first time Mac OS X Version 10.3 was started on the system or ran it at a later time, you provided Mac OS X with some basic information about the account you have with your ISP *(Internet Service Provider)*. If you change ISPs or if your ISP makes some changes to the way you must log in to your account, you may need to alter the Internet settings used by your system. Here's how to alter the specific dial-up information:

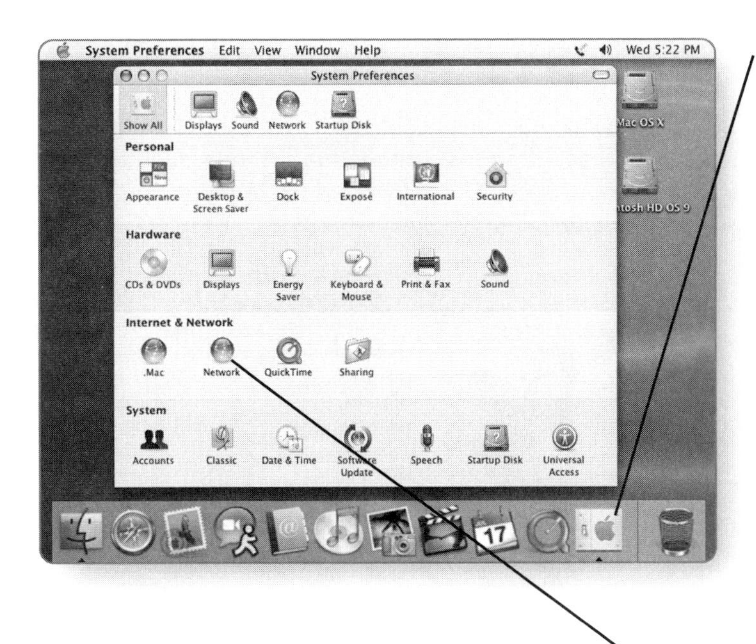

1. **Click** on the **System Preferences icon** on the Dock. The System Preferences window will open.

> **NOTE**
>
> You can use the .Mac icon to enter your .Mac account information or to sign up for a .Mac account if you wish. With .Mac, you can get email service via Mac.com, take advantage of your iDisk online storage space, and more.

2. **Click** on the **Network icon**. The Network pane will appear in the System Preferences window.

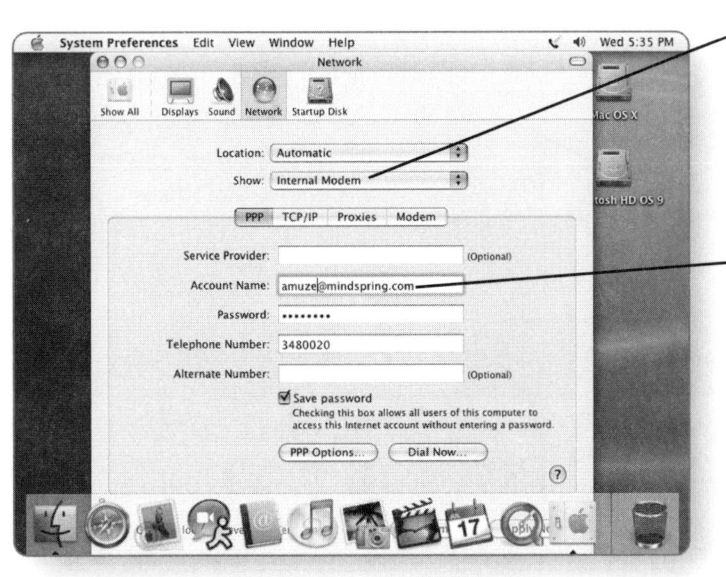

3. **Choose Internal Modem** from the Show pop-up menu. PPP settings will appear by default. (If not, click on the PPP button.)

4. **Type your Account Name** (usually your e-mail address), **Password**, and **Telephone Number.** These settings are provided by your ISP, and will appear when you type them. You also can enter additional settings if you prefer.

TIP

Click on the PPP Options button to open a sheet where you can choose additional connection settings, such as having your modem dial the Internet to Connect automatically when needed.

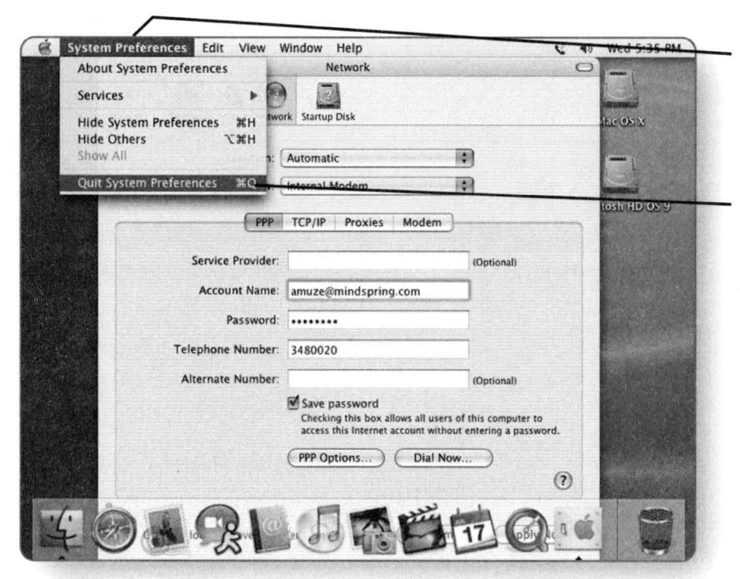

5. Click on **System Preferences**. The System Preferences menu will appear.

6. Click on **Quit System Preferences**. A confirmation sheet will appear.

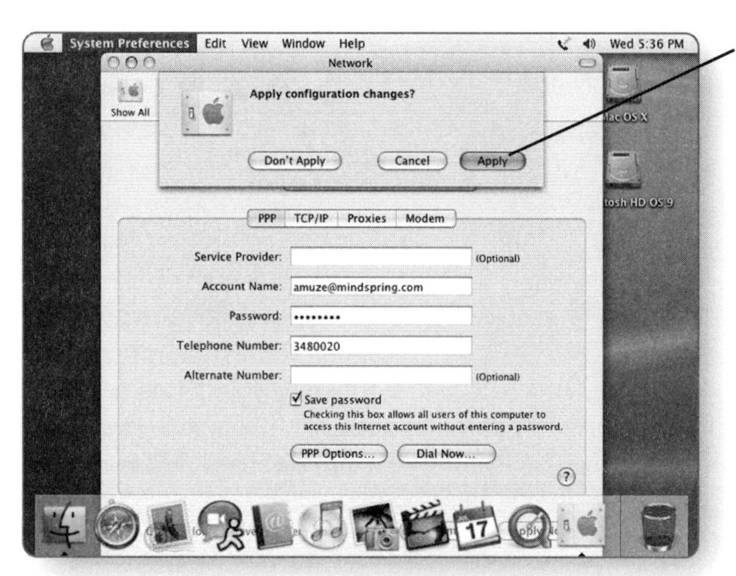

7. Click on **Apply.** Mac OS X Version 10.3 will apply your new settings and close System Preferences immediately.

Connecting to and Disconnecting from the Internet

Even if you configured Mac OS X to dial your Internet connection automatically, you still may encounter times when you want to connect on demand. Further, since Internet Connect won't automatically disconnect, it's a good practice to always check for an active connection and disconnect it.

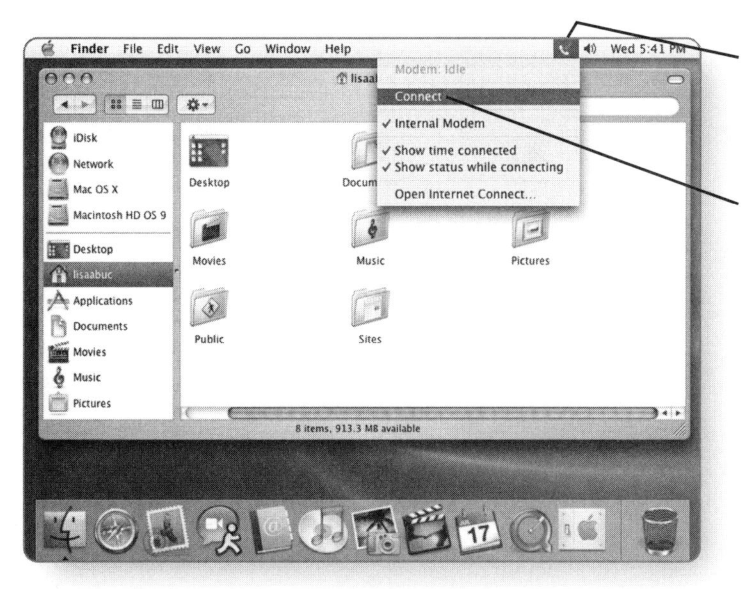

1. **Click** on the **modem (phone) icon** on the menu bar. A menu will appear.

2. **Click** on **Connect**. Your modem will dial the ISP number you specified, as described in the previous section.

> **NOTE**
>
> If you don't see the modem icon, click on the Applications icon in a Finder window Sidebar, scroll down, and double-click on Internet Connect. Click on the Internal Modem button in the window toolbar; then check Show modem status in menu bar. Quit Internet connect to apply the change.

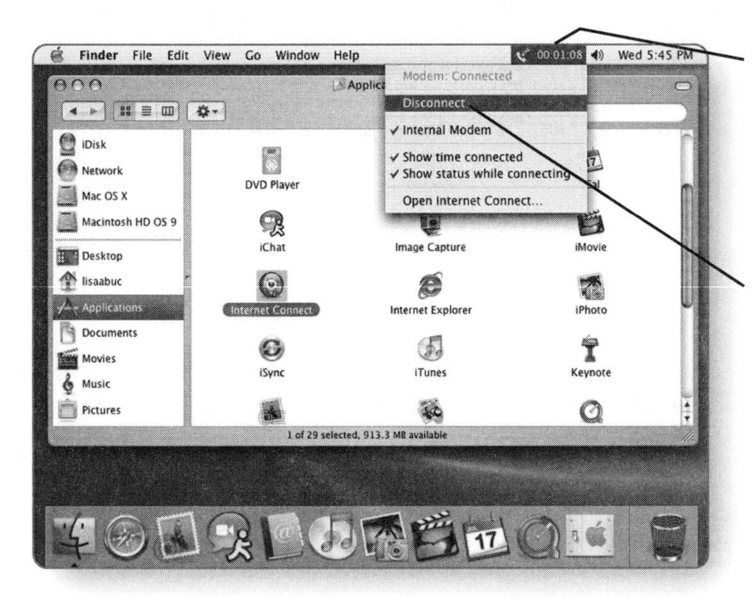

3. After you've finished working in the Internet application of choice, **click** on the **modem (phone) icon** on the menu bar. A menu will appear.

4. **Click** on **Disconnect**. Your system will hang up the Internet connection.

Setting Up a Broadband Connection

If you will be connecting to the Internet via a cable modem or DSL, setup may be fairly easy because your ISP typically will configure your Mac for you via an in-home visit or installation software. These types of connects are called *broadband* or sometimes *always on* connections.

> **NOTE**
>
> As not all cable modem and DSL connections are the same, the steps you need to follow may differ based on your ISP's requirements and your particular connection hardware. Be sure to follow your ISP's instructions and the hardware documentation, if required.

Cable, DSL, and ISDN modems (also called *routers*) connect to your Mac's Ethernet port. You can configure most of these modems as a specific network setting by using DHCP, as follows.

1. **Click** on the **System Preferences icon** on the Dock. The System Preferences window will open.
2. **Click** on the **Network icon**. The Network pane will appear in the System Preferences window.

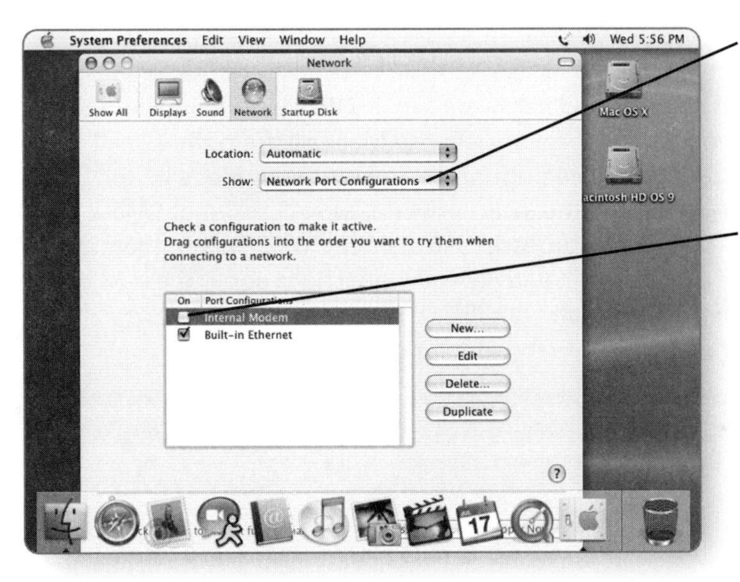

3. **Choose Network Port Configurations** from the Show pop-up menu. The configured ports will appear.
4. **Uncheck Internal Modem.** This will force your system to connect via the network rather than via dial-up.

5. Choose Built-in Ethernet from the Show pop-up menu. The settings for Ethernet networking will appear.

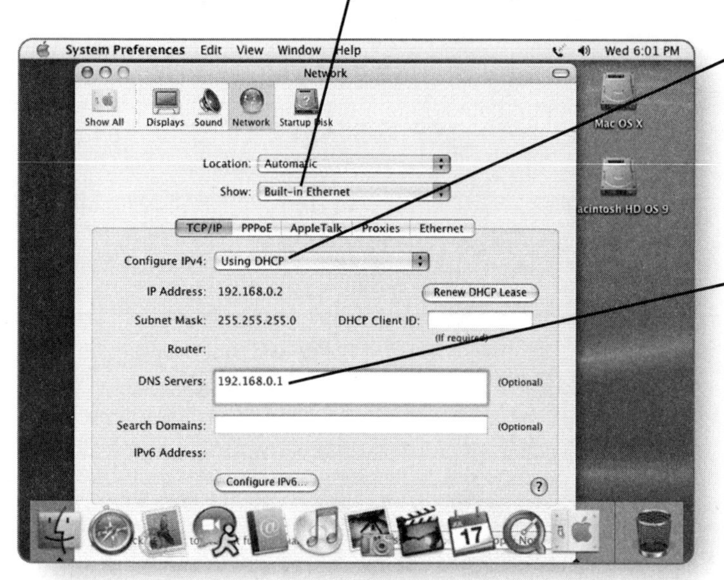

6. Choose Using DHCP from the Configure IPv4 pop-up menu. The active network IP address and Subnet Mask settings should appear.

7. Enter a **DNS Server** address, if required. For example, because my ISDN modem serves as a router so that all my networked computers can share the Internet connection, I must enter the first address on my TCP/IP network (the address that must be assigned to the router), as the DNS Server.

NOTE

If your ISP and hardware require that you set up the connection manually, choose Manually from the Configure IPv4 pop-up menu. Enter your Mac's IP Address (on the local network), as well as Subnet Mask and Router addresses. Also enter a DNS Server address, if applicable. If you have any questions about these entries, consult your ISP's technical support and the documentation for your modem hardware.

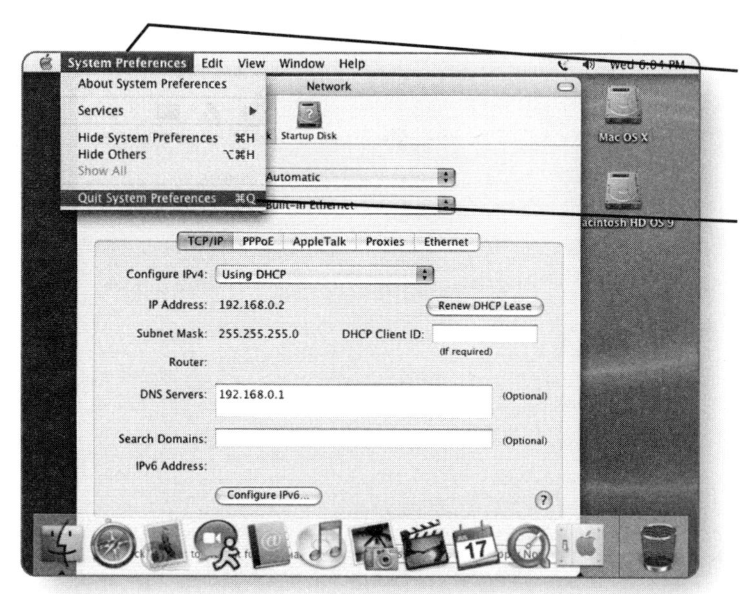

8. **Click** on **System Preferences.** The System Preferences menu will appear.

9. **Click** on **Quit System Preferences.** A confirmation sheet will appear.

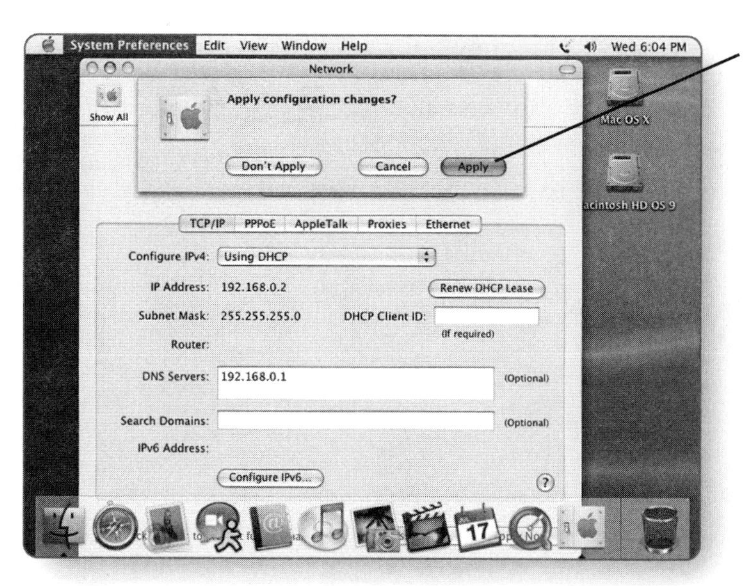

10. **Click** on **Apply.** Mac OS X Version 10.3 will apply your new settings and close System Preferences immediately.

Connecting to Your iDisk and Storing Files

Your iDisk is an online storage area that comes when you purchase a .Mac membership. You can use your iDisk not only to store copies of important files, but also to share files with other users.

NOTE

You can sign up for .Mac or get a 60-day free trial at *http://www.mac.com*. For $99.95 per year, .Mac members get an e-mail address usable from any Internet connection, an online HomePage, 100M of online iDisk storage, and more.

Once you've signed up for .Mac, click on System Preferences in the Dock and then click on the .Mac icon. Click on .Mac in the .Mac pane and enter your account information. You can then click on the iDisk button to access settings for working with the iDisk. When you finish, close System Preferences.

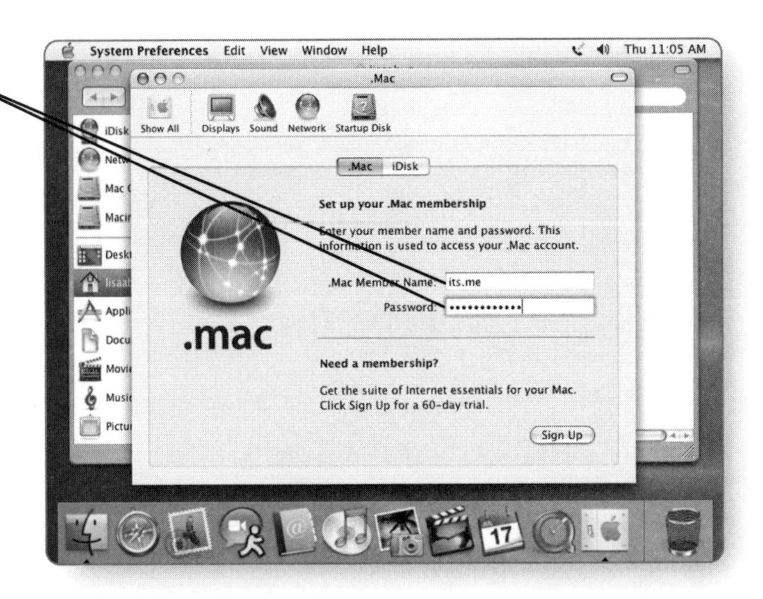

By default, the Finder window Sidebar enables you to access your iDisk and store files there, as follows:

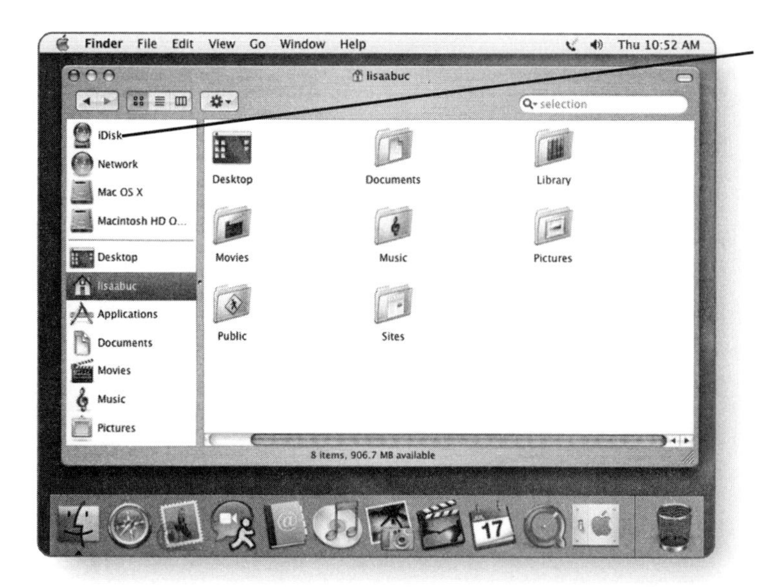

1. **Click** on the **iDisk icon** in a Finder window Sidebar. (Connect to the Internet if prompted to do so.) The contents of your iDisk (its folders) will appear in the window.

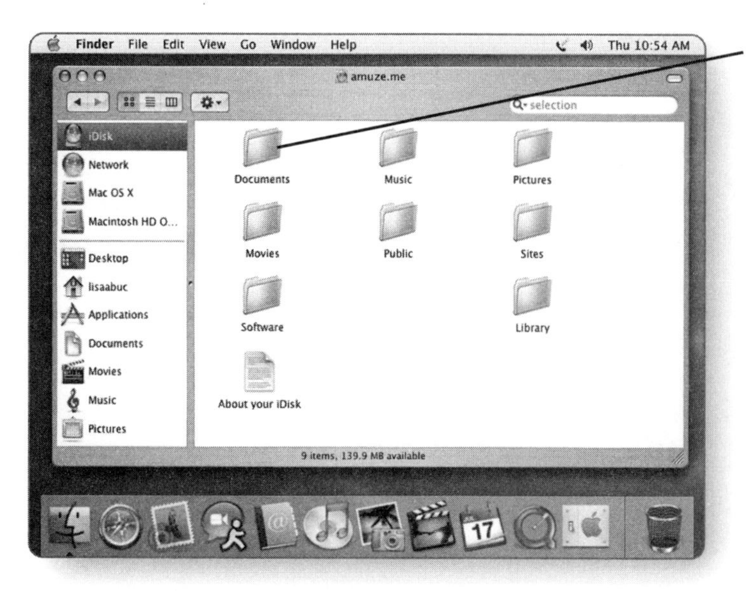

2. **Double-click** on the **folder to open**. Use the Documents folder to store your files online or the Public folder to share files.

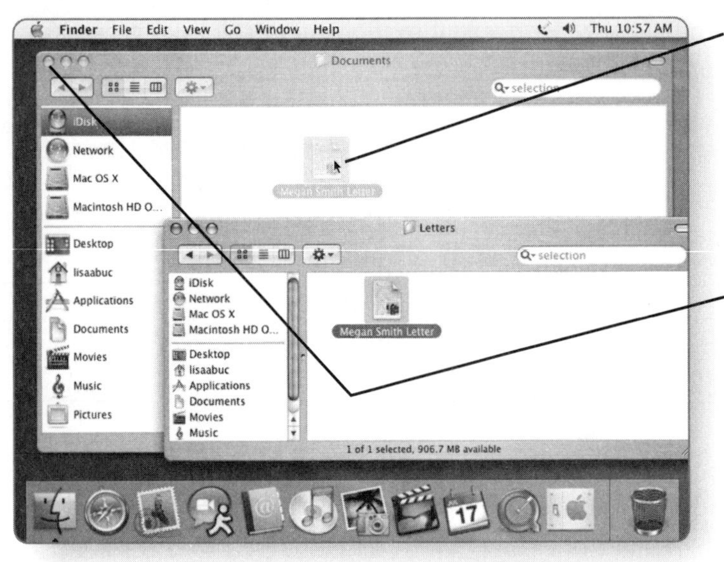

3. **Open** a **Finder window** and **navigate** to the **folder** that holds file(s) to store on the iDisk. **Drag** the **file(s)** to the iDisk window. Mac OS X will copy the file(s) to the iDisk.

4. **Click** on the **Close button** for the iDisk window. The window will close.

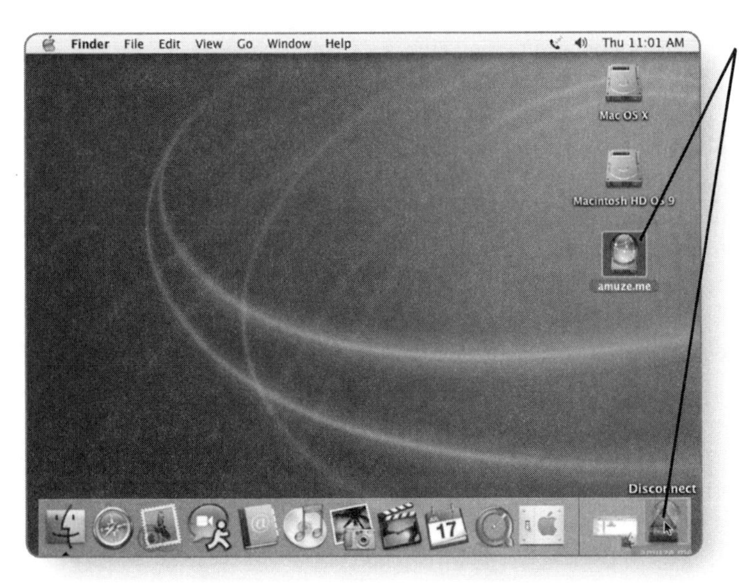

5. **Drag** the **icon** for the iDisk to the Trash. The Trash icon will change to the Disconnect icon. When you release the mouse button, Mac OS X will disconnect from the iDisk. You can then hang up the Internet connection, if required.

12

Corresponding with Mail

Email has become an important tool in both home and business settings. In the home, email lets you share information more easily with friends and relatives, while economizing on long distance charges. In an office, email not only enables fast, responsive communication but also maintains a record of your correspondence. Mac OS X Version 10.3 provides the Mail application to send, receive, and store email messages. This chapter introduces you to using the key features in the Mail application. In this chapter, you'll learn how to:

- Launch and close the Mail program.
- Set up an email account and control how Mail works by changing settings.
- Write and send email messages.
- Receive, respond to, and file email.
- Automatically discard junk mail.
- Organize your email addresses in the Address Book.

Starting Mail

Mac OS X offers easy access to the Mail program via the Dock.

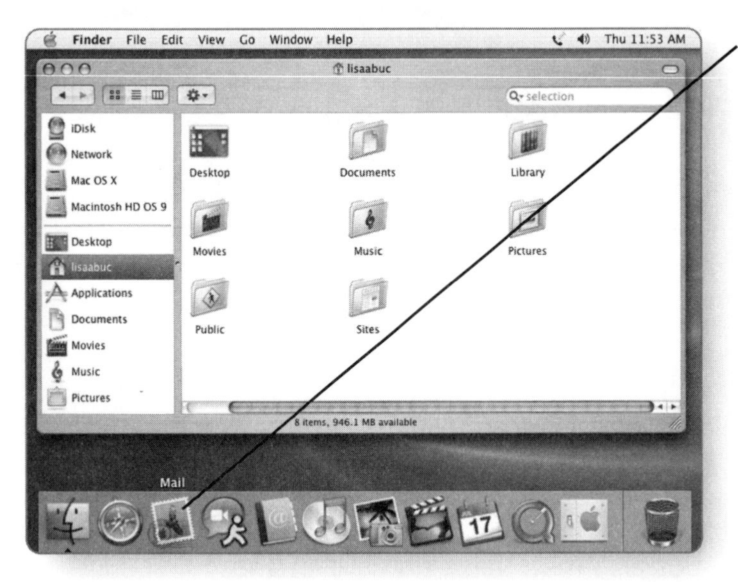

1. Click on the **Mail icon** on the Dock. The Mail application window will open and its menus will appear. You will see a main viewer window that displays the list of messages as well as a mailboxes window at the left that lists folders for working with email messages.

> **NOTE**
>
> If your system connects to the Internet via a dial-up connection and you have configured the system to connect automatically as explained in Chapter 11, "Making Network and Internet Connections," Internet Connect will launch and your modem will dial your Internet connection when you get mail. If you need to find out how to connect manually, see the section called "Connecting to and Disconnecting from the Internet" in Chapter 11.

Creating a Mail Account

Before the advent of computers and email, it was common for people to have personalized stationery, for reasons of practicality (not having to hand-write a return address) and to express individuality. You can personalize some of the settings used in the Mail application, to set up your Mail account (if you didn't complete the Setup Assistant when you installed Mac OS X or first used your system), customize some of its key behaviors to meet your needs, and put a custom stamp on your correspondence.

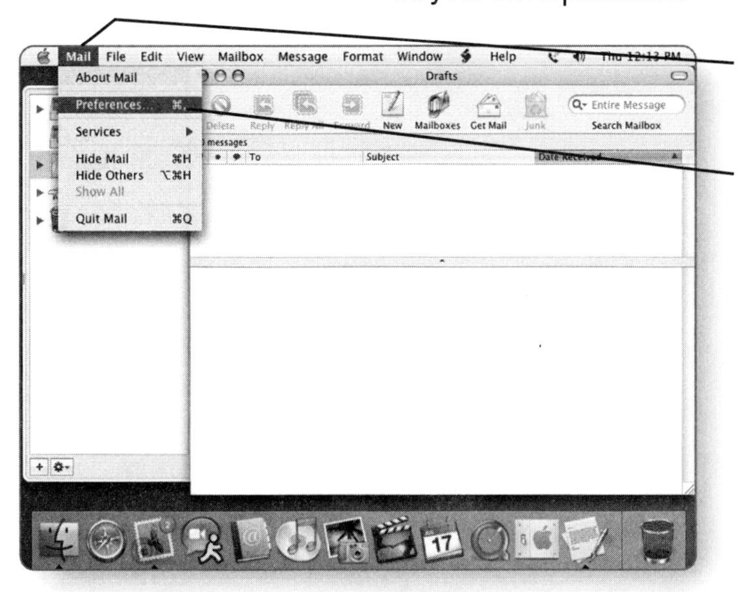

1. **Click** on **Mail**. The Mail menu will appear.
2. **Click** on **Preferences**. The Mail Preferences window will open.

> **TIP**
>
> Click on the Mail icon on the Dock any time that you need to start Mail.

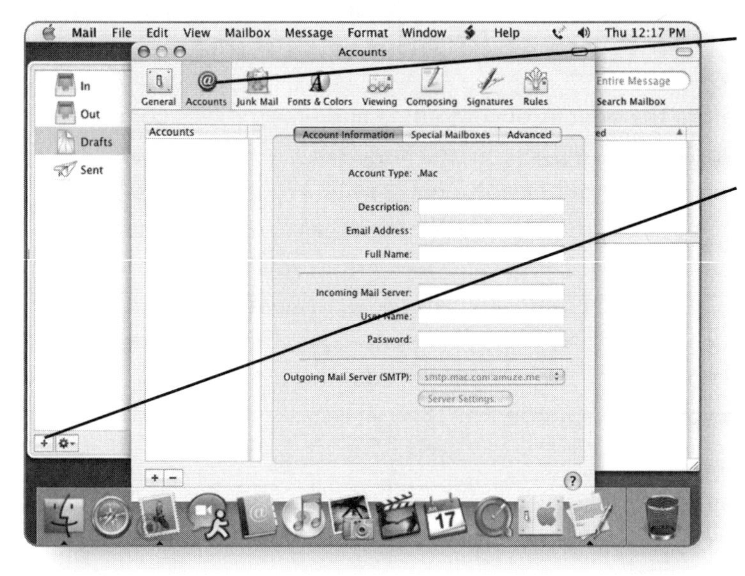

3. Click on the **Accounts icon**. The Accounts pane will appear in the window.

4. Click on the **add (+) button** below the Accounts list. Text boxes for creating the account will appear in the Account Information area.

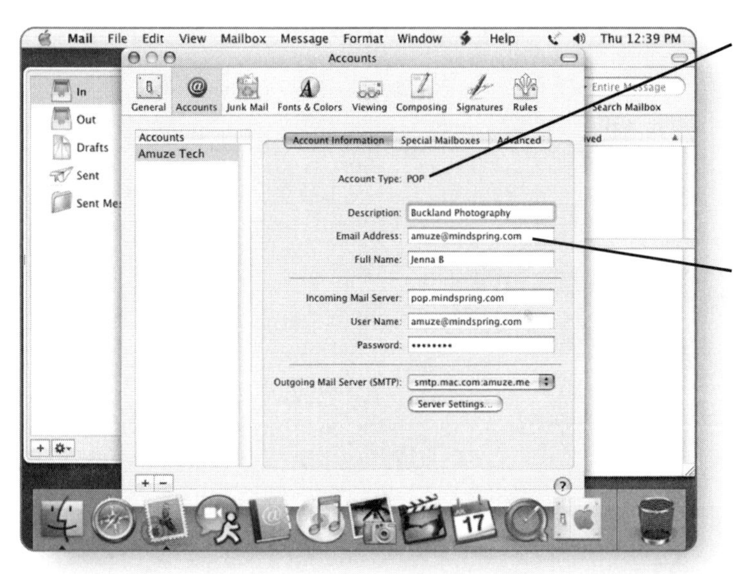

5. Choose an **Accounts Type**. (Choose POP for non-.Mac email accounts.) Example entries will appear for the other text boxes.

6. Enter account information as specified by your ISP. The account information will appear.

> **TIP**
>
> The Description that you enter will become the account name.

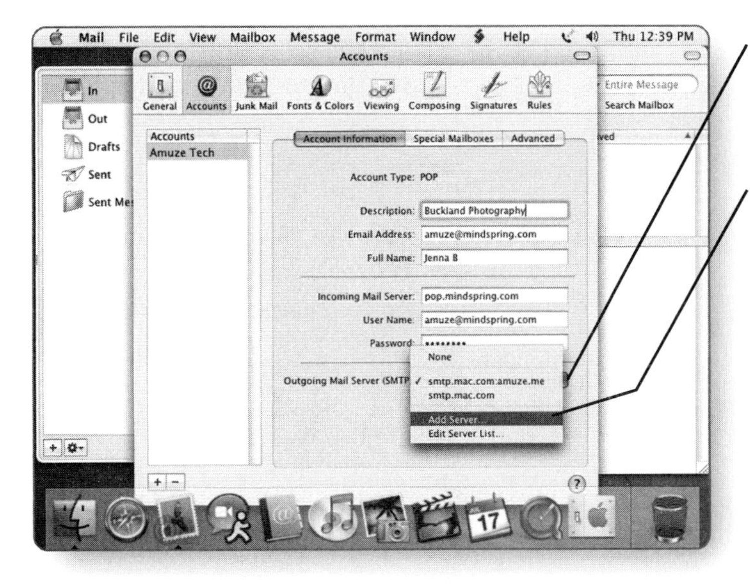

7. Click on **Outgoing Mail Server (SMTP)**. A pop-up menu will appear.

8. Click on **Add Server**. The SMTP Server Options dialog box will appear.

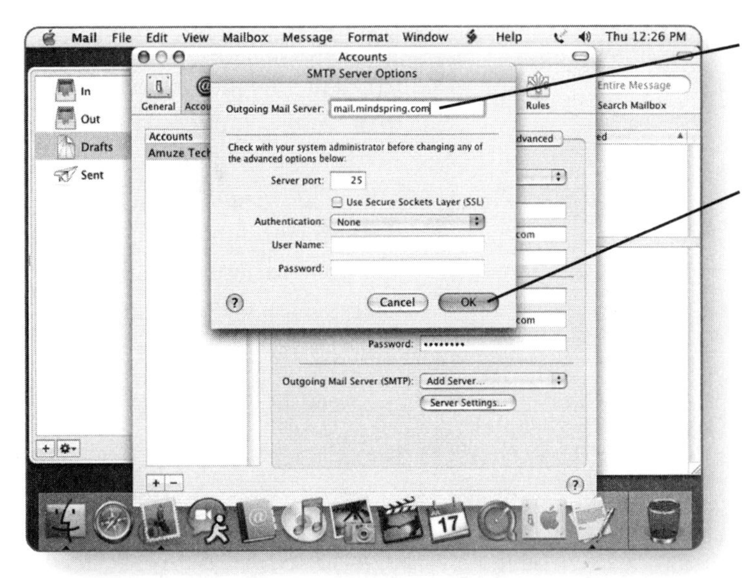

9. Enter the **server address** in the Outgoing Mail Server text box. The address will appear.

10. Click on **OK**. The dialog box will close, and the new server will be selected for the Outgoing Mail Server (SMTP) choice.

> **TIP**
>
> You can repeat Steps 3 through 10 to add additional accounts if needed.

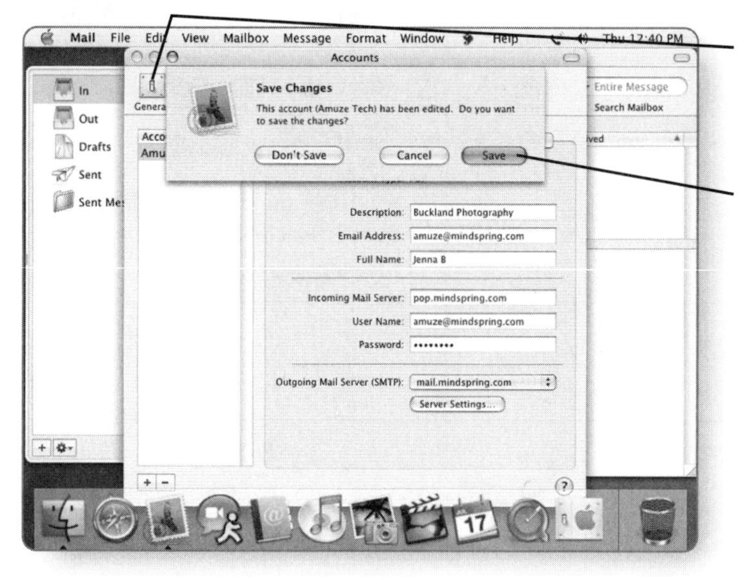

11. Click on **General**. A sheet will prompt you to save the new account.

12. Click on **Save**. Mail will save the new account and display general mail preferences.

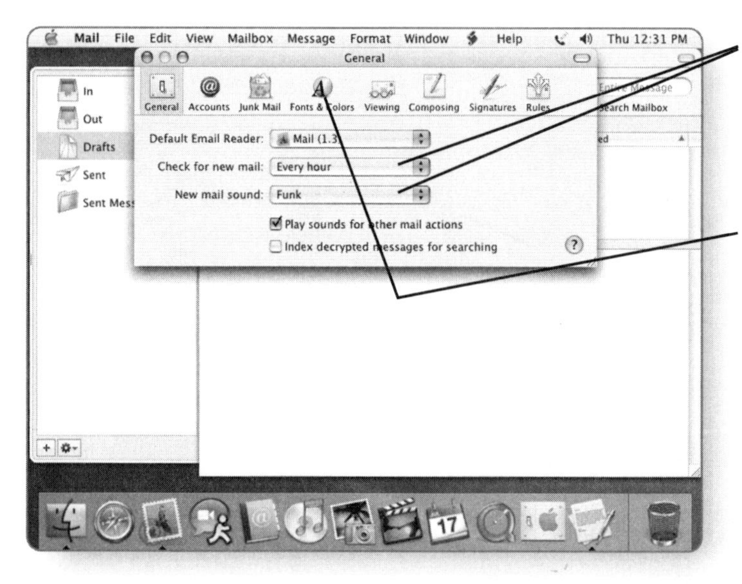

13. Specify the desired **Check for new mail interval** and **New mail sound**. Your choices will appear in the window.

14. Click on the **Fonts & Colors icon**. The Fonts and Colors pane will appear.

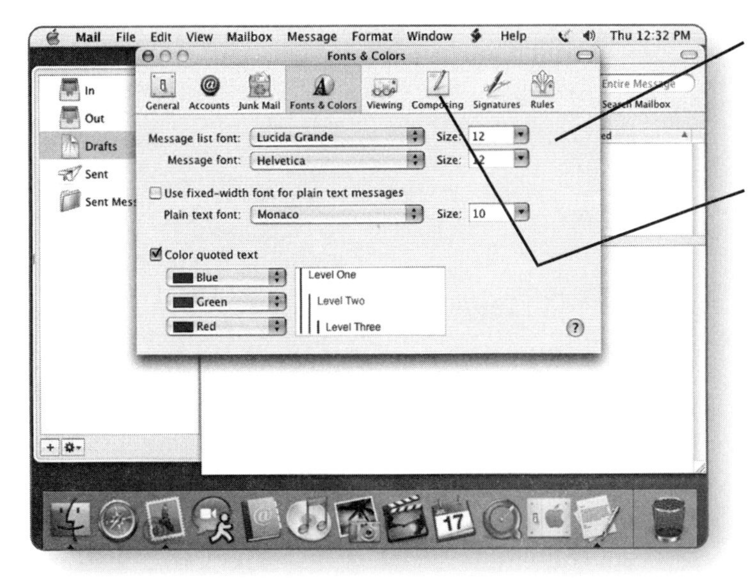

15. Change settings. Mail will use the new settings when you create email messages.

16. Click on the **Composing icon**. The Composing pane will appear in the window.

17. Change settings. Mail will apply your new settings. Important settings include:

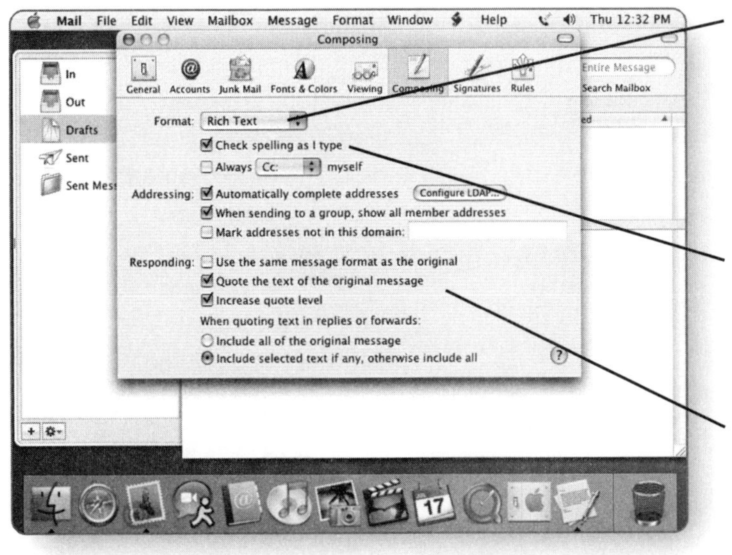

- **Format.** Use this pop-up menu to specify whether you want to use the Rich Text (default) or Plain Text format for messages you create and send.
- **Check spelling as I type.** Leave this check box checked to have your messages spell-checked automatically.
- **Responding.** Check Use the same message format as the original if you want Mail to always use the same text format (Rich Text or Plain Text) as the message to which you're replying. Also specify whether to Quote the text of the original message.

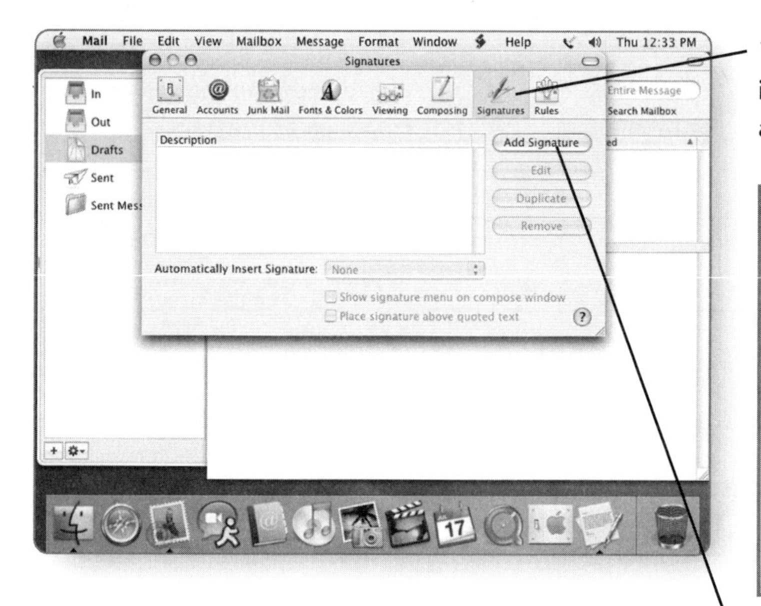

18. **Click** on the **Signatures icon**. The Signatures pane will appear in the window.

> **TIP**
>
> A signature is information that you want Mail to automatically tack on to the end of every message you send, such as your title or contact information. Some users like to include quotations or jokes in signatures.

19. **Click** on **Add Signature**. A sheet for creating a signature will appear.

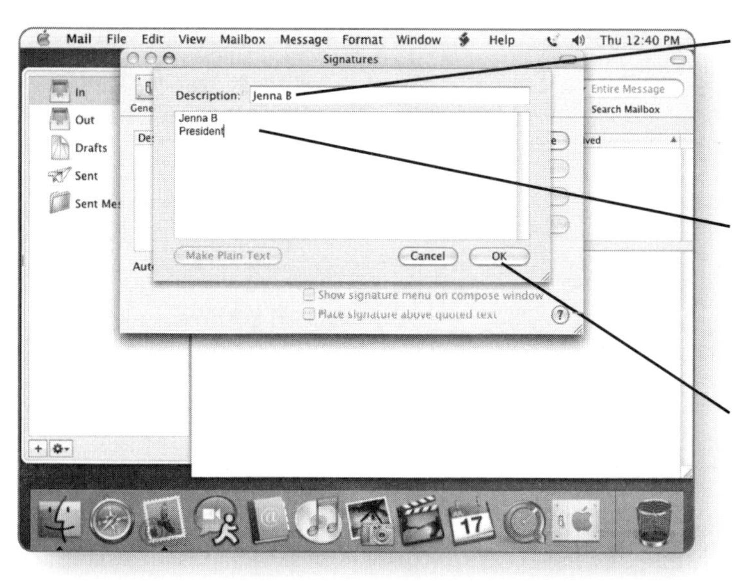

20. **Type** a **name** for the signature in the Description text box. The name you enter will replace the text there.

21. **Press Tab** and **type** the **signature content.** The information you type will appear in the text box.

22. **Click** on **OK**. The sheet will close, and the choices in the Signatures pane will reappear.

NOTE

Click on a signature in the Description list; then click on the Edit, Duplicate, or Remove buttons to change, copy, or delete the signature, respectively.

TIP

If you want to choose a signature when composing the message, click on the Show signature menu on compose window to check it. Then you can choose a signature for each message in the Compose window.

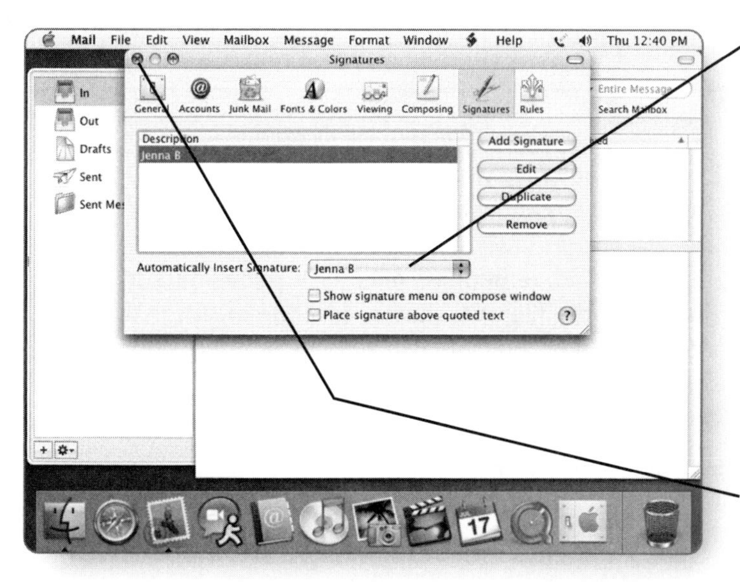

23. If you've created multiple signatures and want to specify which one to use, **choose it** from the **Select Signature pop-up menu.** Choose Randomly or Sequentially to have Mail automatically select and include a signature, or None to omit a signature. Mail will include a signature (or not) according to your choice.

24. Click on the **Close button.** The window will close, and the settings you selected will take effect.

Sending Mail

Sending an email message requires two basic steps. You compose the message and then send your mail to the Internet. (You may need to connect to the Internet to actually send your mail.) This section walks you through the ins and outs of each of these operations so that you'll be "emailing away" in no time!

Mail calls the message creation process *composing* your message. You start the message, specify one or more recipients, enter a subject, type message text, attach any files you want to send along with the message such as digital photos or word processing documents, and then perform the send function.

CAUTION

Don't go too crazy when you compose your message. The more bells and whistles like fancy fonts that you use, the longer it will take to send and receive the message. And, remember, most ISPs put a limitation on the size of the files attached to any one message. Large attachments or multiple attachments not only slow the send and receive, but also may cause the ISP to abort delivering the message.

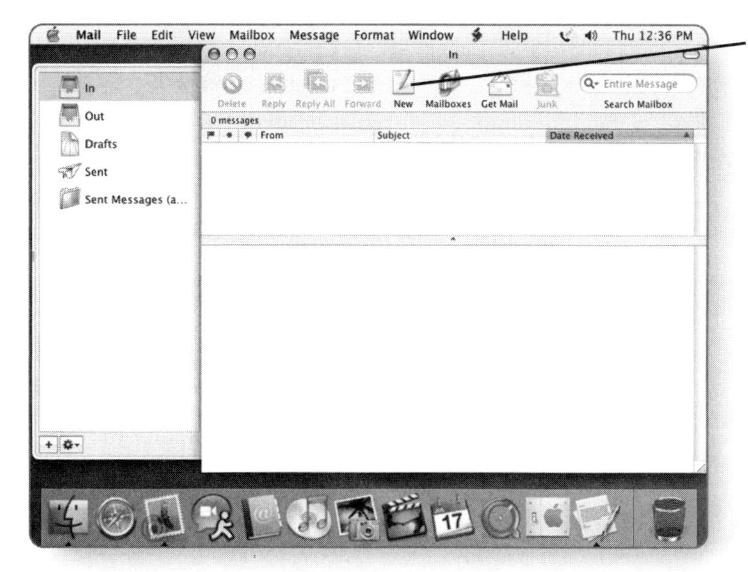

1. Click on the **New icon** in the toolbar of the main Mail window. The New Message window will open.

> **TIP**
>
> If you don't want to see the mailbox list to the left of the main Mail window, choose View, Hide Mailboxes. Or click on the Mailboxes icon in the Mail window.

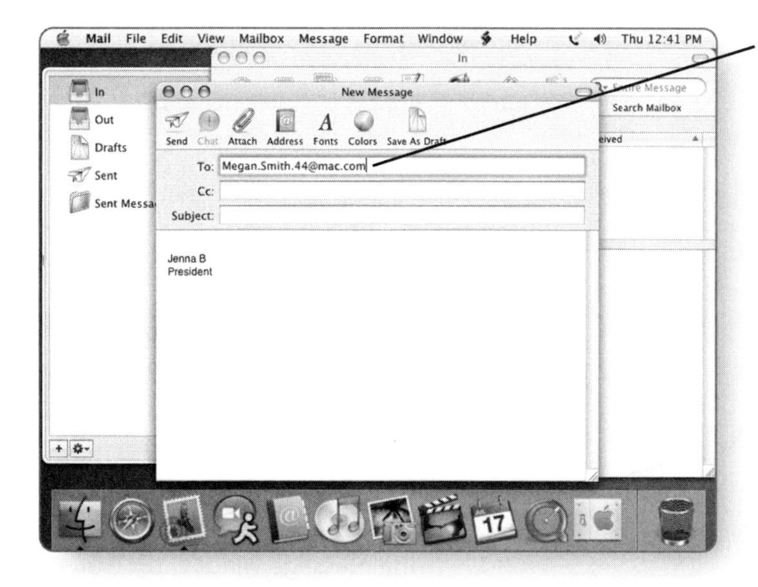

2. Type a **recipient's email address** in the To text box; then **press Tab**. The insertion point will move to the Cc text box. (If you've used the current email address in a previous message, the rest of the address may appear. Press Tab to accept the suggested entry or continue typing to finish your entry.)

> **TIP**
>
> If you want to include more than one email address in the To or Cc text box, type the first address followed by a comma and a space, and then type the next one.

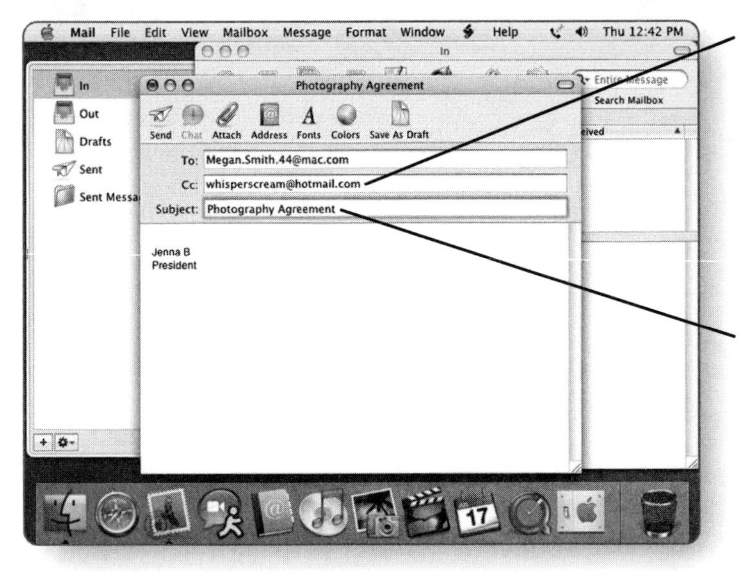

3. Type a **copy recipient's email address** in the Cc text box; then **press Tab**. (Or simply press Tab to continue without specifying a copy recipient.) The insertion point will move to the Subject text box.

4. Type the **message subject** in the Subject text box; then **press Tab**. The insertion point will move to the message text area in the message window.

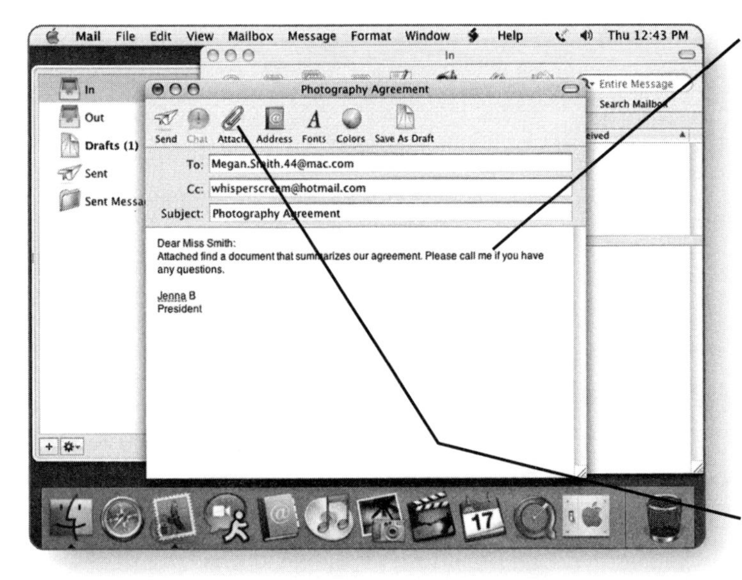

5. Type your **message text.**

> **TIP**
>
> You can select text in the message body and then use the Fonts and Colors icons on the message window toolbar to apply alternate formatting to the selected text.

6. Click on the **Attach icon** on the message window toolbar. A sheet will open so that you can select a file(s) to attach to the message.

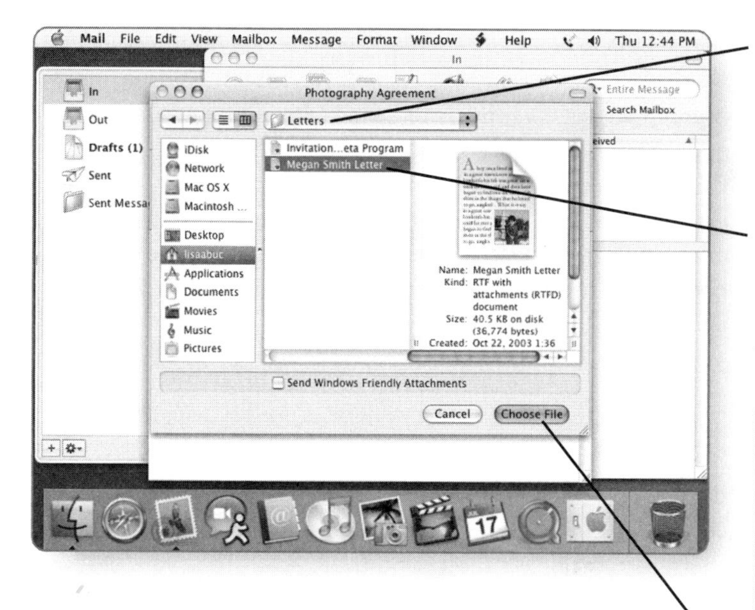

7. **Navigate** to the **folder** that holds the file(s) you want to attach. The folder's contents will be listed in the dialog box.

8. **Click** on the **file** to attach. The file will be selected, and a preview icon will appear in the far-right column.

> **TIP**
>
> To select multiple files to attach, Shift+Click on additional files in the list.

9. **Click** on **Choose File**. The dialog box will close, and an icon for the attached file will appear in the message window.

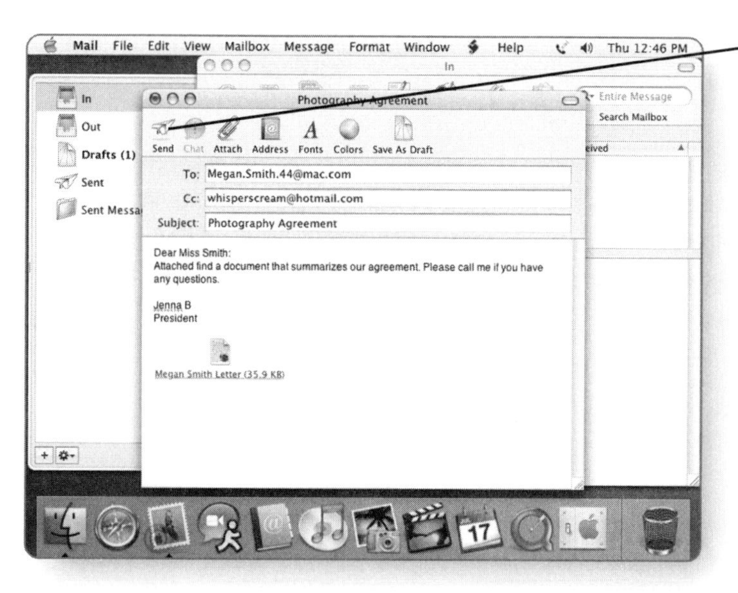

10. **Click** on the **Send icon** on the message window toolbar. Mail will use Internet Connect to connect to the Internet, if needed, and then send the message. (At the same time, any incoming messages addressed to you will be received.) A copy of the message will be placed in the Sent folder.

CAUTION

If you attempt to send your email without having first connected to the Internet or configuring Internet Connect to connect automatically as described in the last chapter, you will see an Error message that the message can't be delivered. Click on Close Window, connect to the Internet, and send the message from your Out folder.

NOTE

To reduce connect time, you can create messages, save them as drafts, and then send them later. To save a message as a draft, click on the Save As Draft icon in the message window toolbar. To later send a draft, click on the Drafts folder. The Viewer window will list your message drafts. Double-click on a message in the list to open the message. Then click on the Send button on the window toolbar.

Checking Mail

If you didn't choose to set up Mail to check for incoming email automatically, you can do so manually at any time. When you get your email, Mail connects to the Internet, if needed, checks for messages, and downloads messages into the In (inbox) folder for your account, which appears in the Drawer window to the right of the main window.

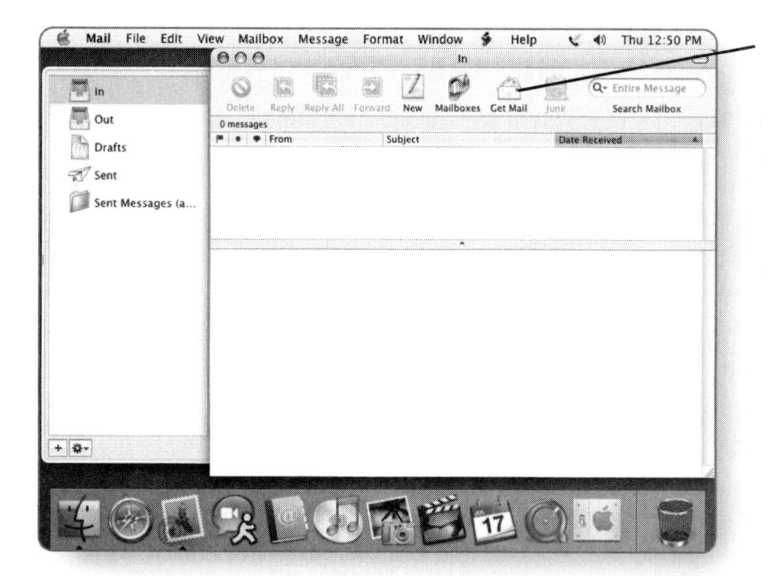

1. Click on the **Get Mail icon.** Mail will prompt you to connect to the Internet, if required, and then will check for messages addressed to you. A copy of the message will be placed in the In folder.

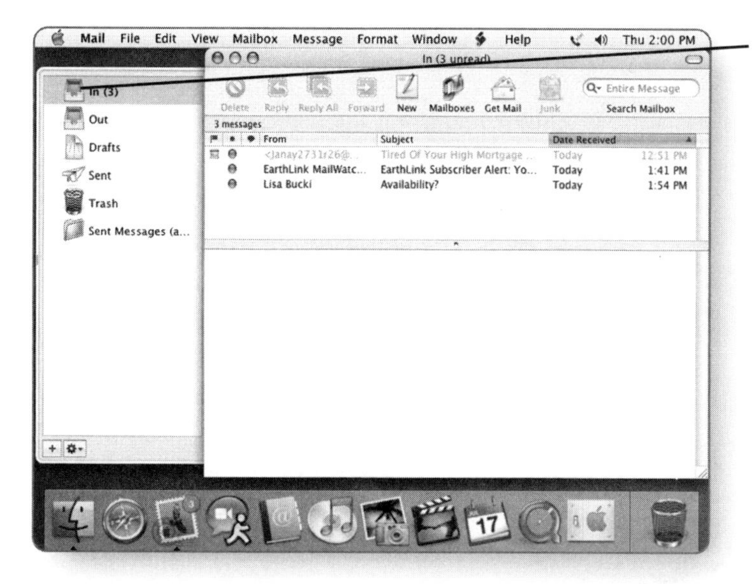

2. Click on the **In folder** in the mailbox list. The new message or messages will also be listed in the viewer window.

> **NOTE**
>
> If you have Mail set up to check multiple email accounts, you can check a particular account by clicking on the Mailbox menu, moving the pointer over the Get New Mail in Account choice, and then clicking on the account you want to check.

Reading and Responding to a Message

Any time you need to read your messages, you can display the list of messages in your In box in the main Viewer window in Mail. By default, that window will list the messages in chronological order, with the most recently composed message appearing at the bottom of the list. You can see who sent the message and its subject at a glance. After you read a message, you can decide how to respond to it, such as replying to the sender.

> **NOTE**
>
> Even though you can read messages while your system is connected to the Internet, it's not necessary. I prefer to disconnect after getting email and then reconnect to send any responses.

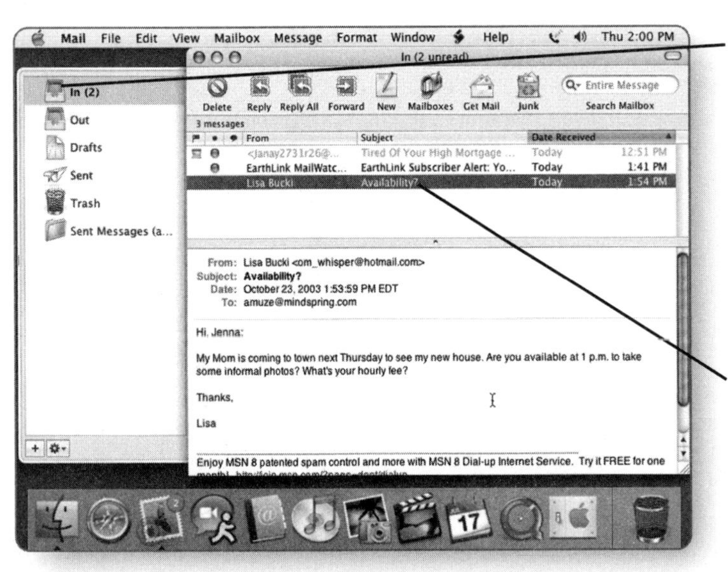

1. **Click** on the **In folder** in the mailbox list. This will ensure that your received messages appear in the viewer window. The bottom message in the list will be selected, and its text will appear in the bottom pane of the viewer window.

2. **Click** on the **message** you want to read in the list. Its text will appear in the bottom pane.

> **TIP**
>
> You also can double-click on a message in the list to open it in its own window.

3. To respond to the message, **click** on the **appropriate toolbar icon:**

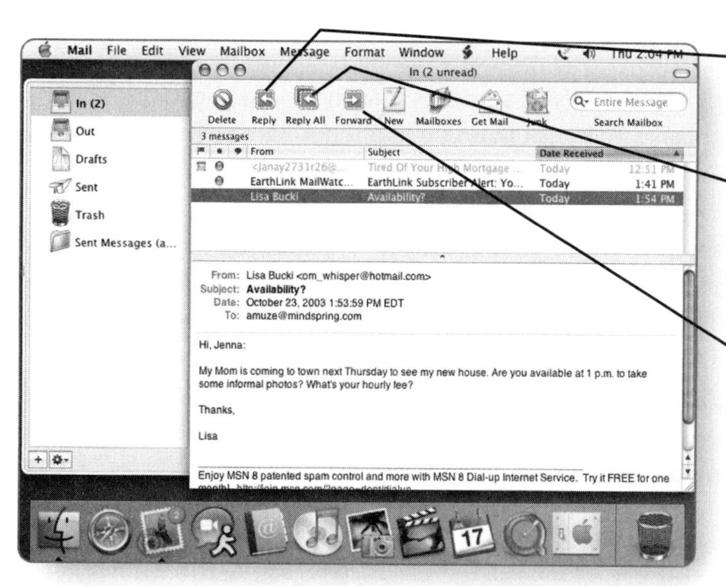

- **Reply**. Addresses the return message to the original sender only.
- **Reply All**. Addresses the return message to the original sender as well as all other recipients.
- **Forward**. Enables you to specify a recipient to whom you want to send a copy of the message and its attachments. Enter the recipient(s) in the To and Cc text boxes.

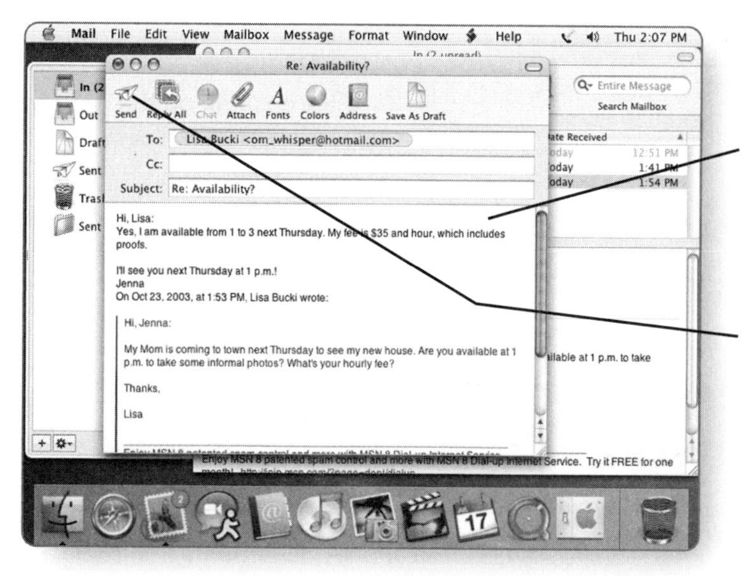

A message window will open so you can type your response.

4. **Type** your **response** and **change** any other **message information** (including recipients and attachments).

5. **Click** on the **Send button**. Mail will use Internet Connect to connect to the Internet and send the message, as well as receiving any incoming messages addressed to you. A copy of the message will be placed in the Sent folder.

Filtering Spam

> **CAUTION**
>
> The junk filter can incorrectly identify messages as junk, such as online newsletter messages. Be sure to mark these messages as "not junk," otherwise they will mistakenly be filtered out in the future.

You may have noticed that the listings for some of the messages you've received appear in brown-colored text. That's because Mail suspects that those messages are *spam*—electronic junk mail that you might not care to receive or read. Mail's junk mail filtering can automatically identify junk mail messages (based on the address of the sender) and delete them or move them to a special folder. When you initially use Mail, the junk mail features are in a training mode. To help the junk mail filter correctly, identify which messages are junk or not by using the Junk (Not Junk) icon on the toolbar to mark messages. You also can set a preference to tell Mail what to do with mail identified as junk mail, such as deleting it immediately.

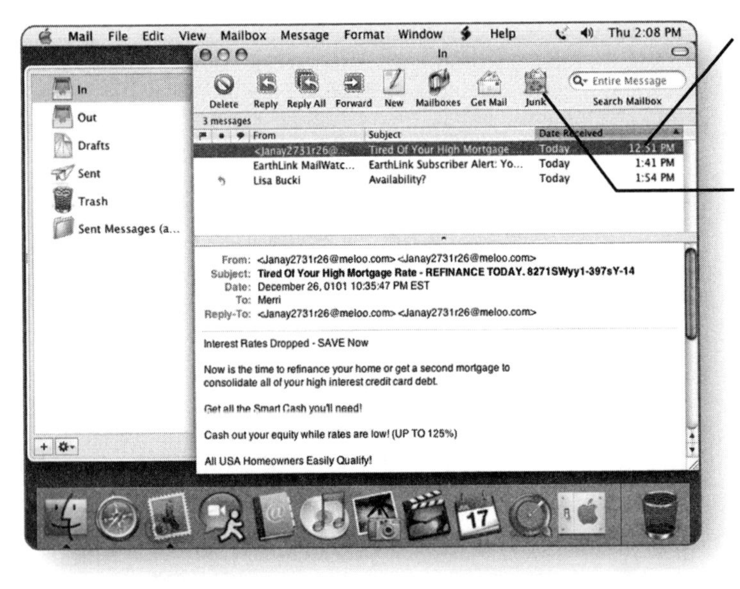

1. **Click** on the **message to mark.** Mail will select the message.
2. **Click** on **Junk** on the window toolbar. Its listing will appear in brown text, indicating it is junk mail.

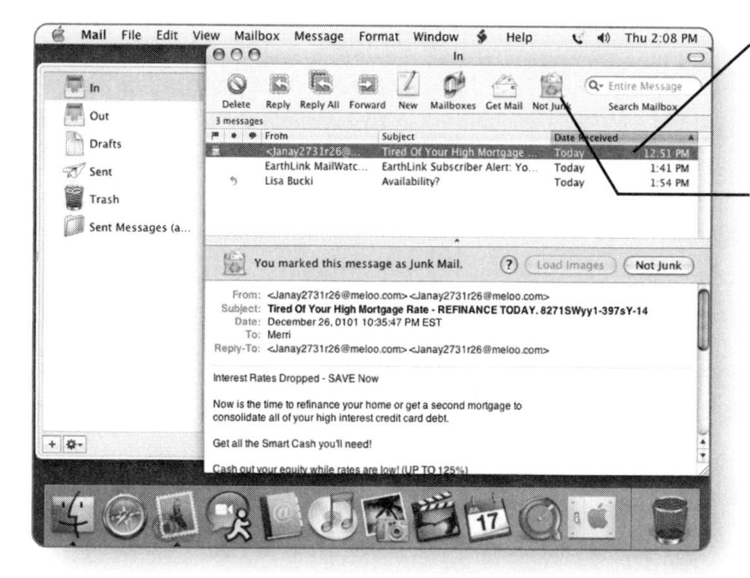

3. Click on the **message to mark**. Mail will select the message.

4. Click on **Not Junk** on the window toolbar. Its listing will appear in black text, indicating it is not junk mail.

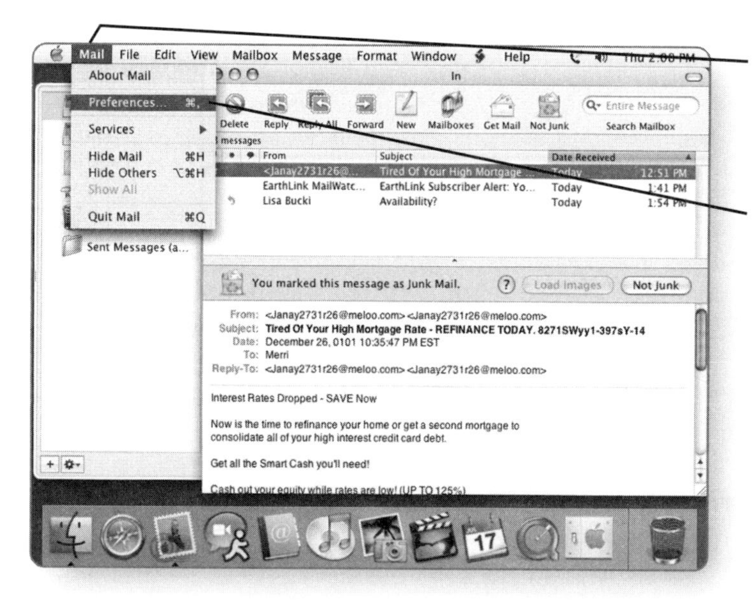

5. After you've marked all the messages, **click** on **Mail**. The Mail menu will appear.

6. Click on **Preferences**. The Mail Preferences window will open.

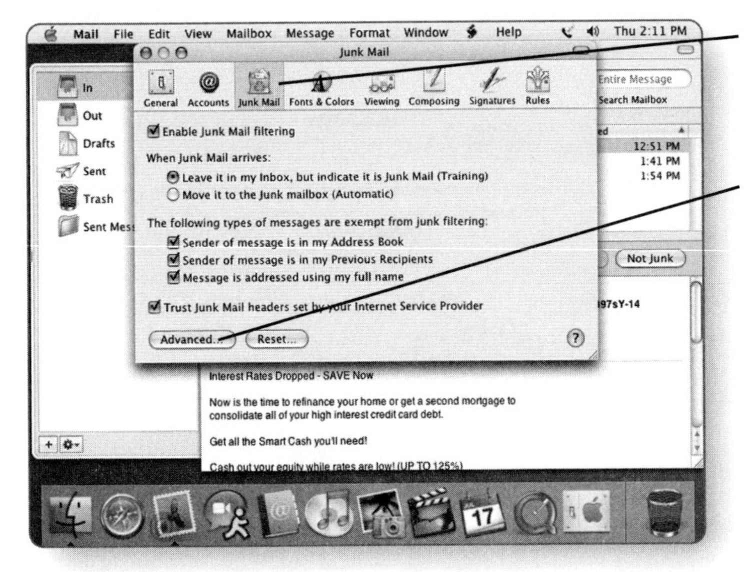

7. **Click** on the **Junk Mail icon.** The Junk Mail pane will appear in the window.

8. **Click** on **Advanced**. The settings for handling junk mail will appear.

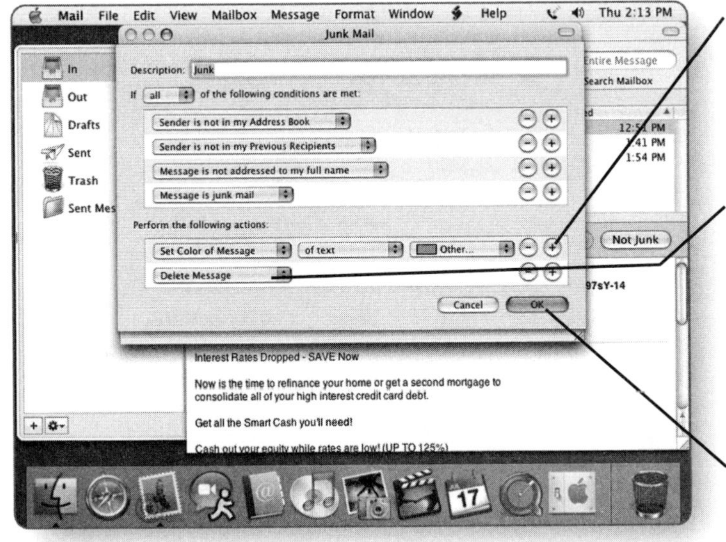

9. **Click** on the **add (+) button** under Perform the following actions. New criterion settings will appear.

10. **Choose** the **desired criterion settings**. In this case, the new rule will automatically delete the junk, but you could opt to move it to another folder, instead.

11. **Click** on **OK**. The new junk mail setting will become active.

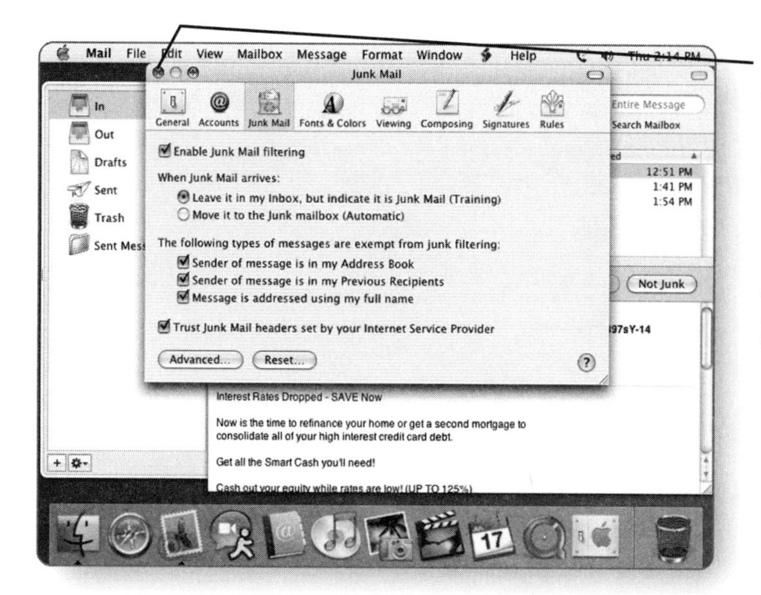

12. Click on the **Close button.** The window will close, and the rule you created will take effect. The next time you get your messages, any messages identified as junk will be deleted or dealt with according to the junk settings.

Bouncing a Message

We all want to respond to spam by sending a little message right back to the spam sender. However, that's not a great idea, because it will verify that your email address is a "live" address. The latest iteration of Mail, however, enables you to *bounce* a message—that is, to send it back in such a way that your email address appears invalid, with the hope of discouraging further messages from the sender. Follow these steps to bounce a message:

1. Click on the **message to bounce.** Mail will select the message.

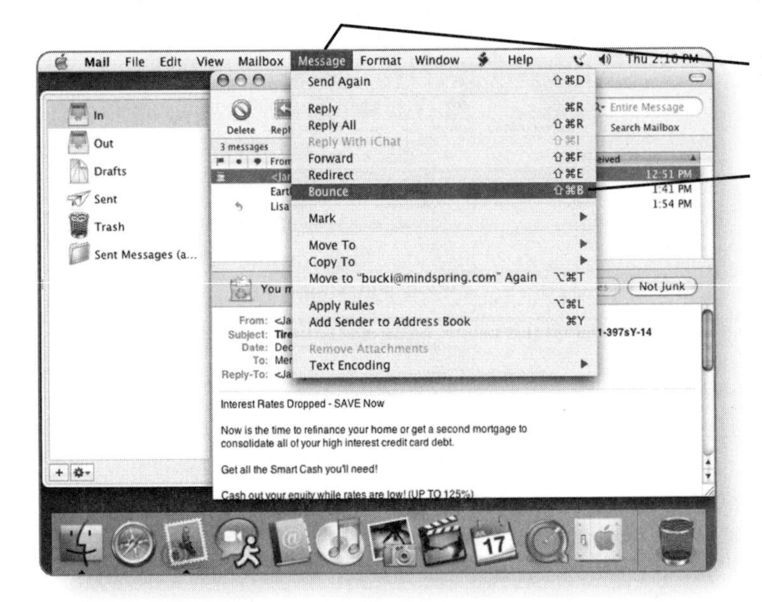

2. Click on **Message**. The Message menu will appear.

3. Click on **Bounce**. A confirmation prompt will appear.

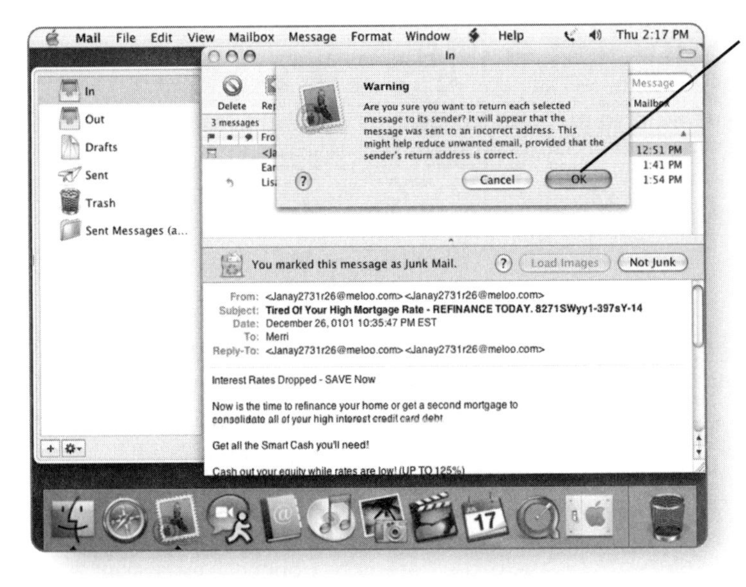

4. Click on **OK**. Mail will return the message to its sender.

Working with the Address Book

The Address Book application in Mac OS X Version 10.3 enables you to store contact information, especially email addresses, to help you address your Mail messages more easily. Remember that Mail, to some degree, remembers email addresses that you type into your outgoing messages. Address Book, however, enables you to capture much more information about a contact, such as a physical address and phone number, which you can use whenever needed. This section introduces you to the Address Book application so that you can begin to take advantage of its capabilities.

Starting and Quitting Address Book

You can start the Address Book application on its own or in conjunction with Mail. Start and exit Address Book, as follows:

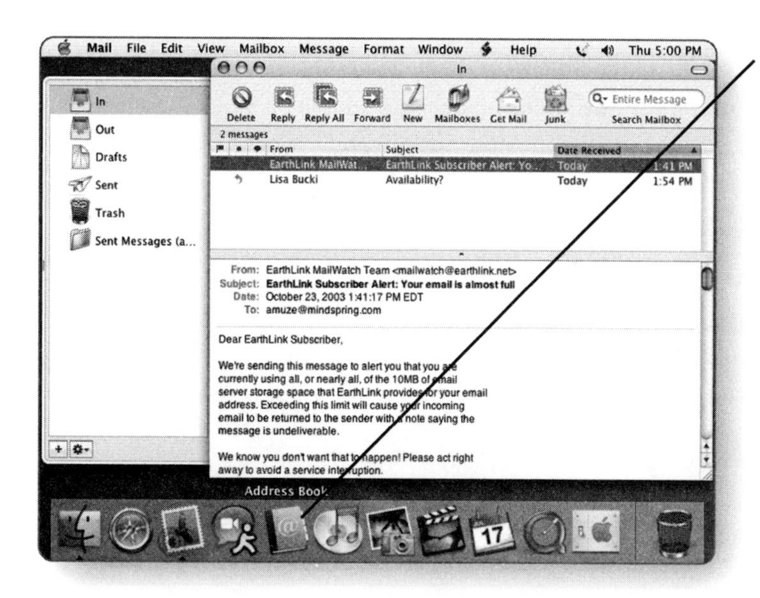

1. **Click** on the **Address Book icon** on the Dock. The Address book Window will open.

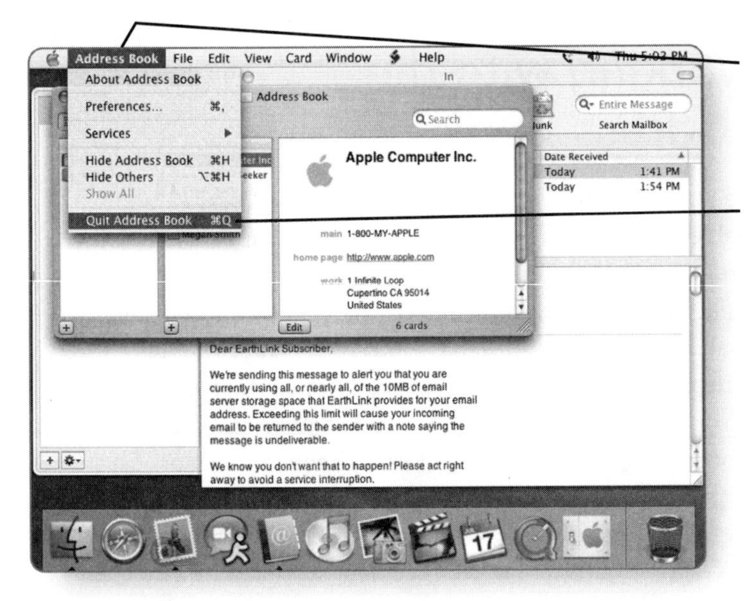

2. To close the Address Book, **click** on **Address Book**. The Address Book menu will appear.

3. Click on **Quit Address Book**.

Adding a Contact

When you add contacts, you store information about them in the Address Book. The process works much like adding contact information into a paper address book. You display the proper window (form or page) and type (write) the applicable information.

> **TIP**
>
> If you've received an email message from a sender whom you'd like to add to your Address Book, click on the message in Mail and then choose Message, Add Sender to Address Book.

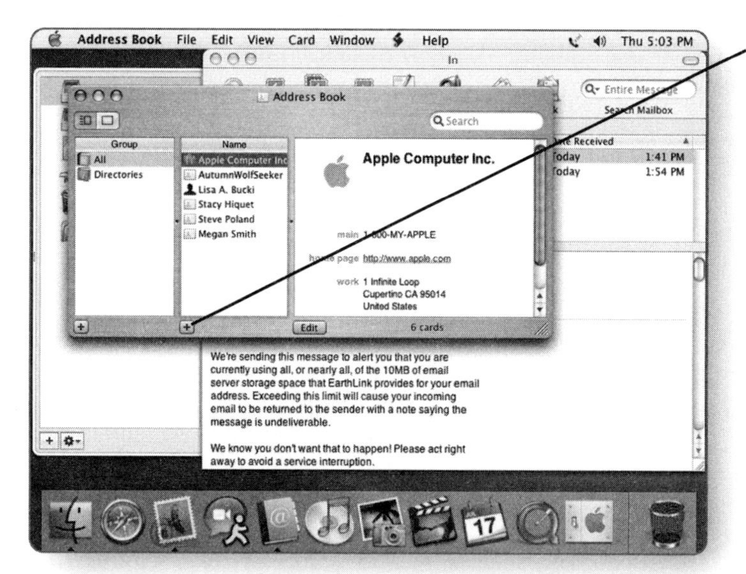

1. Click on the **Add New Person button** at the bottom of the middle column in the Address Book window. The Untitled Address Card window will open.

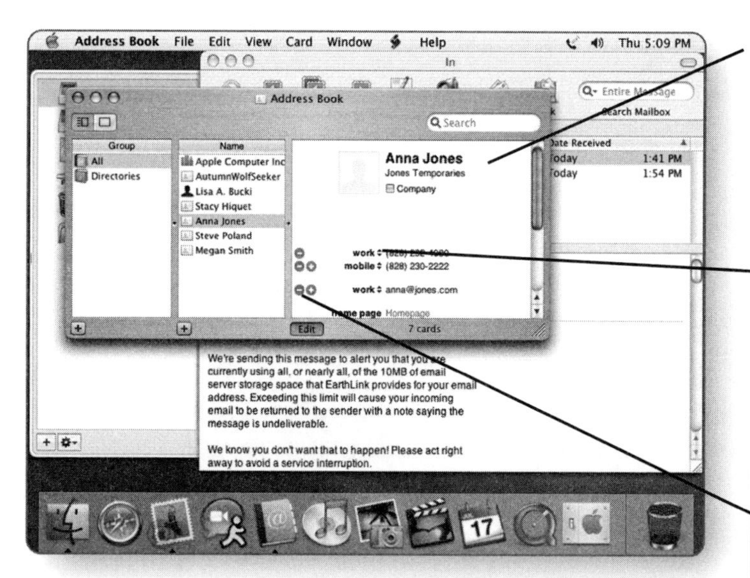

2. Make entries in any fields you require, **pressing Tab** to move from field to field.

> **NOTE**
>
> When a field has a pop-up menu button beside it, you can use the pop-up menu to choose a different field name or create a custom field name.
>
> When a field has a minus icon beside it, you can delete it. Click on a plus icon to add another field in a category, such as another phone field.

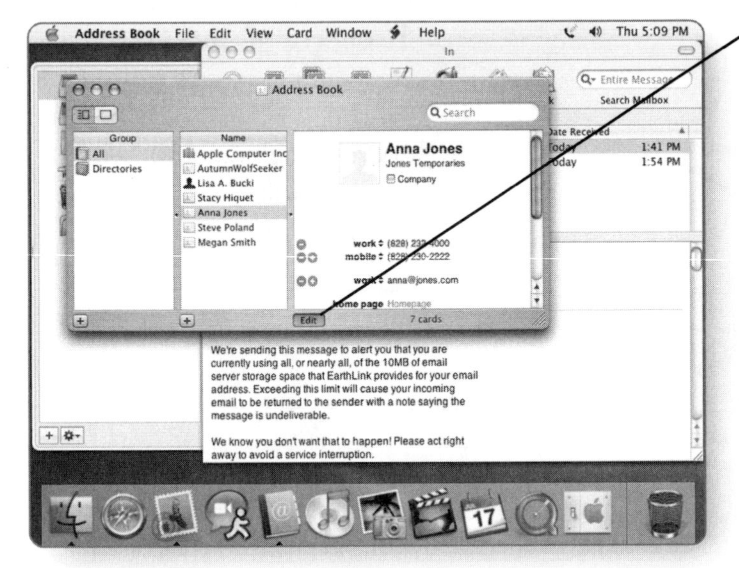

3. Click on the **Edit button**. Address Book will save the new contact and disable editing for it.

> **NOTE**
>
> Once you've created a contact, you can click on the contact in the middle column in the Address Book window and then use the Edit button to resume making changes. Or choose Edit, Delete Person to remove the contact from the list.

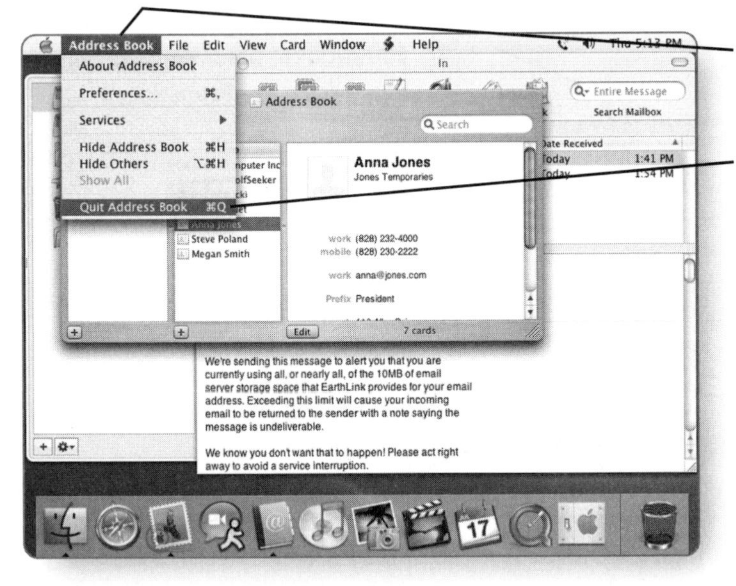

4. Click on **Address Book**. The Address Book menu will appear.

5. Click on **Quit Address Book**. Address Book will close.

> **NOTE**
>
> You can organize two or more contacts into a group. Then you can send an email message to everyone in the group by using the group listing in the Address Book. To create a group, use Shift+click to select contacts appearing contiguously on the list or ⌘+click to select non-contiguous entries. Then click on File and click on New Group from Selection. Type a Group Name and press Return. The group will be listed in the first column of the Address Book window.

Addressing a Message to a Contact

Sending a message to an Address Book recipient works quickly and easily.

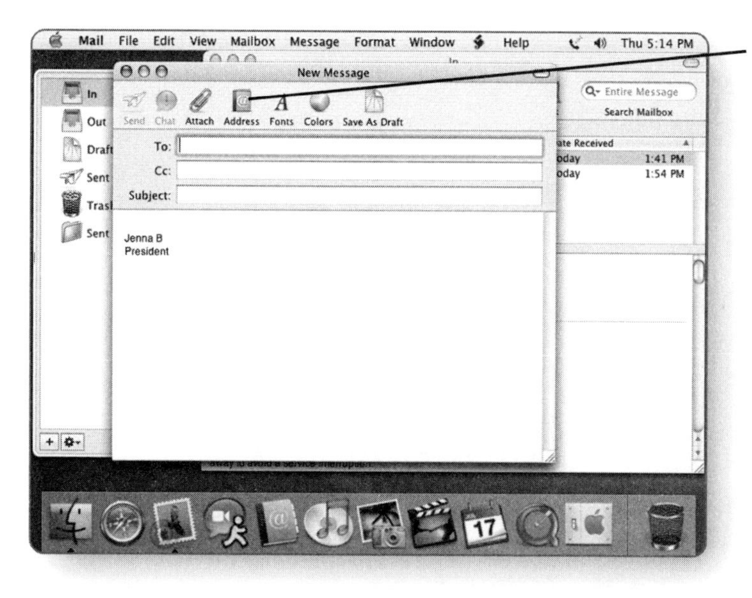

1. **Click** on the **Address icon** in the New Message window. The Addresses window will appear.

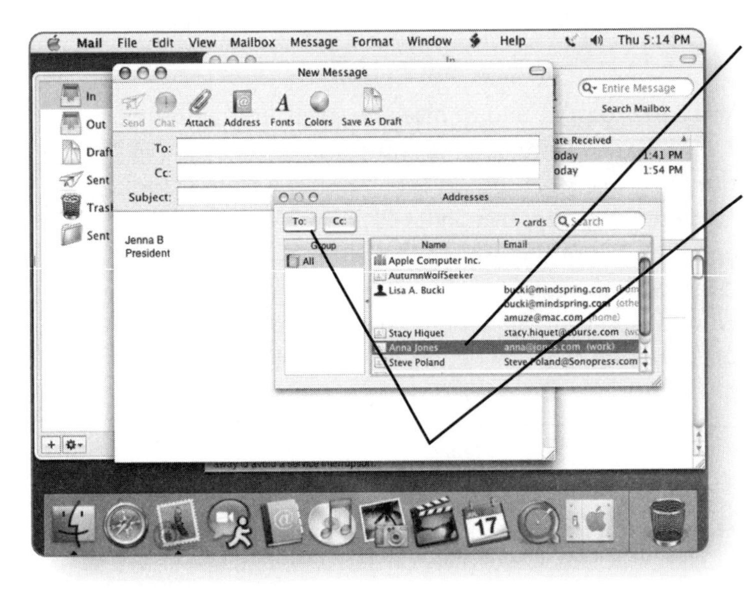

2. **Click** on a **message recipient** in the list of contacts. The recipient will be selected.

3. **Click** on either **To:** or **CC:**. The selected recipient will be added to the list of main recipients (To:) or carbon-copied recipients (CC:) for the message.

> **TIP**
>
> Use Shift+click to select contacts listed contiguously or ⌘+click to select non-contiguous contact entries. The message will then be addressed to all of the selected contacts.

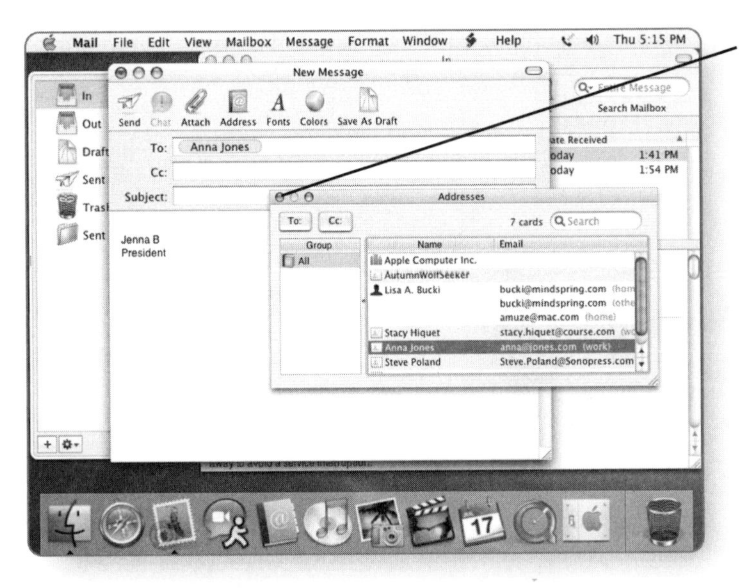

4. **Click** on the **Close button** for the Addresses window. The window will close, and the designated recipients will appear in the To: and Cc: text boxes of the Compose window.

Exiting Mail

When you've finished managing your email with the Mail program, use the following steps to exit Mail.

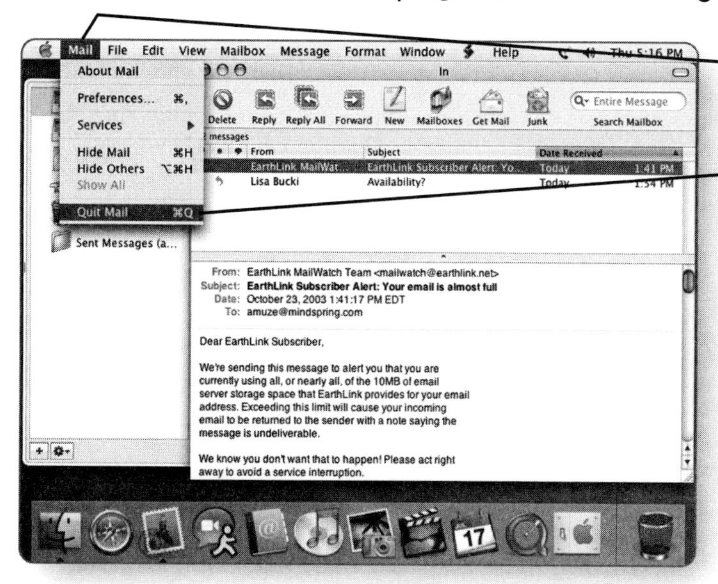

1. **Click** on **Mail**. The Mail menu will appear.

2. **Click** on **Quit Mail**. The Mail application window will close. If you need to disconnect from the Internet manually, you can do so at this time.

13

Chatting with Friends

If you've never tried instant messaging, you're in for a blast. With instant messaging, you can chat (by typing in messages) in real time with another user connected anywhere on the Internet. My niece—who lives in Cairo, Egypt—messages friends all over Europe for free. When my Mother first tried instant messaging, she messaged me so often during the day that I couldn't get anything done. Once you see how fun and useful it is to be instantly in touch, you'll be addicted, too. In this chapter, you'll learn how to:

- Sign up for an account to use with instant messaging.
- Start and set up iChat AV.
- Add buddies to your list of contacts.
- Send and respond to messages.
- End a chat.
- Understand iChat AV's audio and video capabilities.

Getting an Account

Mac OS X Version 10.3 includes the improved iChat AV program for instant messaging over the Internet. In addition to the software, however, you'll need access to the specific network online that handles instant messaging traffic. You actually have two options. If you already have a screen name for AOL Instant Messaging (AIM), you can use it with iChat. If you don't have an AIM screen name, you can sign up for a .Mac account instead. In addition to providing you with messaging capabilities, a .Mac account offers an email account, software for building Web pages, online iDisk storage, and backup and virus protection software.

> **NOTE**
>
> As of this writing, a .Mac membership was priced at $99.95 per year. (You can add up to 10 additional email-only accounts to enable more family members to chat.) However, a free 60-day trial was available for new users. You also can go to *http://www.aim.com*, the AIM home page, to sign up for a free AIM account and download the latest version of the AIM software.

The signup process only takes a few minutes. Be sure to have a credit card handy if you plan to sign up for a full membership rather than a free trial.

1. **Use Internet Connect** to connect to the Internet, if you haven't set up your system to do so automatically or if you don't have a cable modem or DSL connection. Your modem will dial your Internet connection and log on.

> **NOTE**
>
> Refer to Chapter 11, "Making Network and Internet Connections," to review how to use Internet Connect.

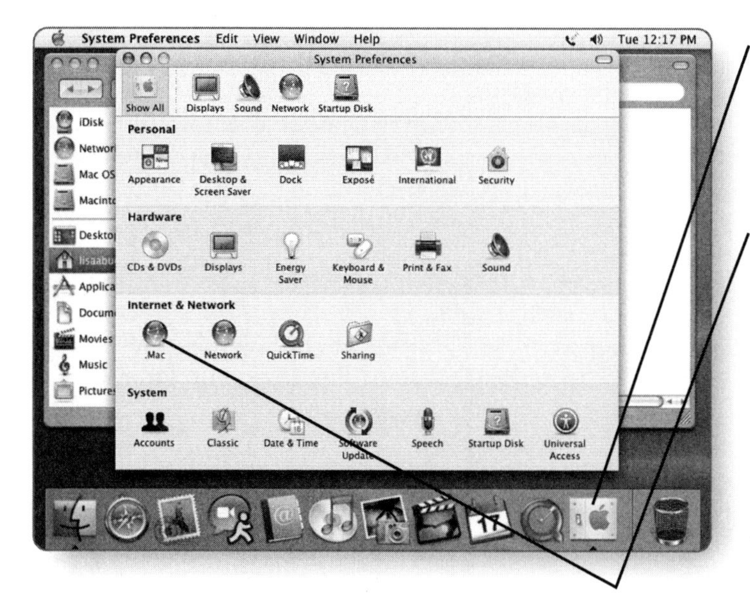

2. Click on the **System Preferences icon** on the Dock. The System Preferences window will open.

3. Click on **.Mac**. The .Mac pane will appear.

4. Click on **Sign Up**. Your Web browser will launch, and the sign-up page will appear.

> **NOTE**
>
> When various Security Notice dialog boxes open, click on OK to continue the sign-up process.

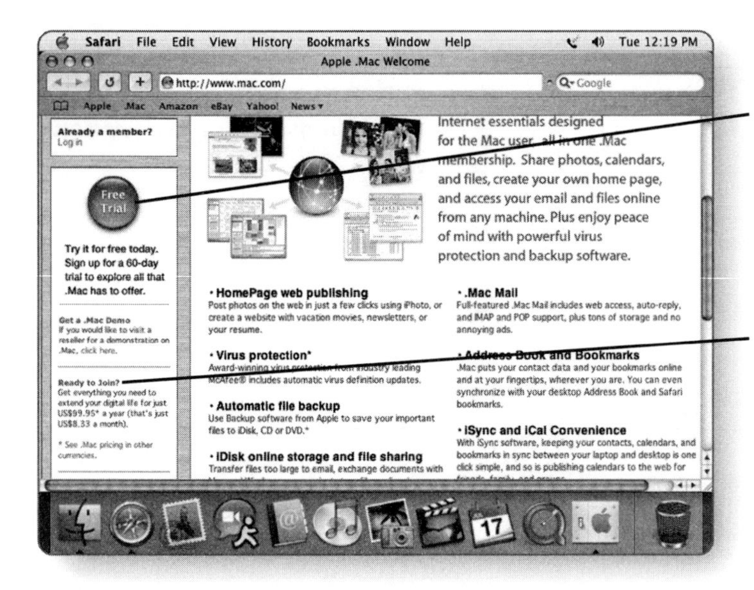

You can then do the following:

5a. **Click** on the **Free Trial button** to register for the free trial.

OR

5b. **Click** on the **Ready to Join? link** to sign up for a full year.

No matter which method you choose, follow the online instructions to continue. (I'm not showing the full sign-on process to protect my confidential information.) You will specify the .Mac member name (which becomes your email address, as in membername@mac.com) and password that you want to use.

> **CAUTION**
>
> One of the final Web pages during the sign-up process will show your account information. Be sure to print that page and store it in a safe location for future reference.

6. When you finish signing up, **close** your **Web browser**, **disconnect** from the **Internet**, and **quit Internet Connect**.

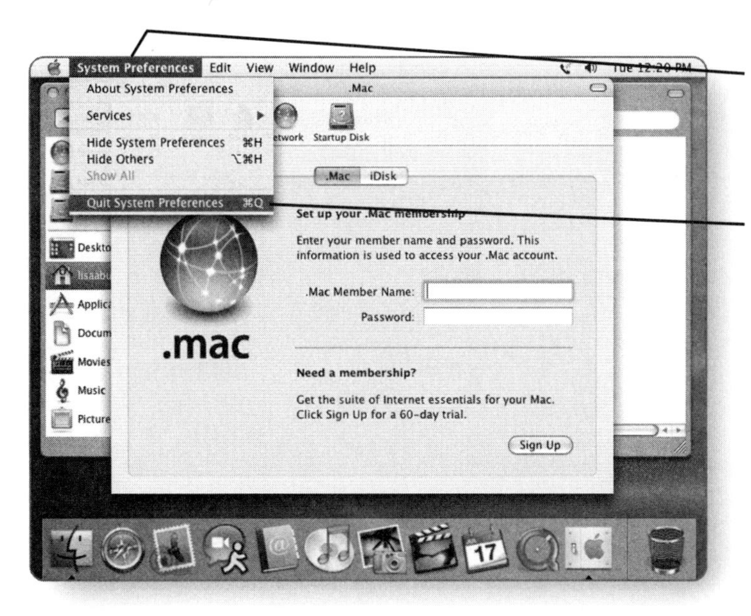

7. Click on **System Preferences**. The System Preferences menu will appear.

8. Click on **Quit System Preferences**. System Preferences will close.

Setting Up iChat AV

Once you've got a screen name and password, you need to enter that information into iChat, and you're almost ready to rumble. The first time you start the iChat application, you need to specify your name, user name (screen name), and password, as well as the account type.

1. Click on **iChat** on the Dock. The Welcome to iChat AV window will open.

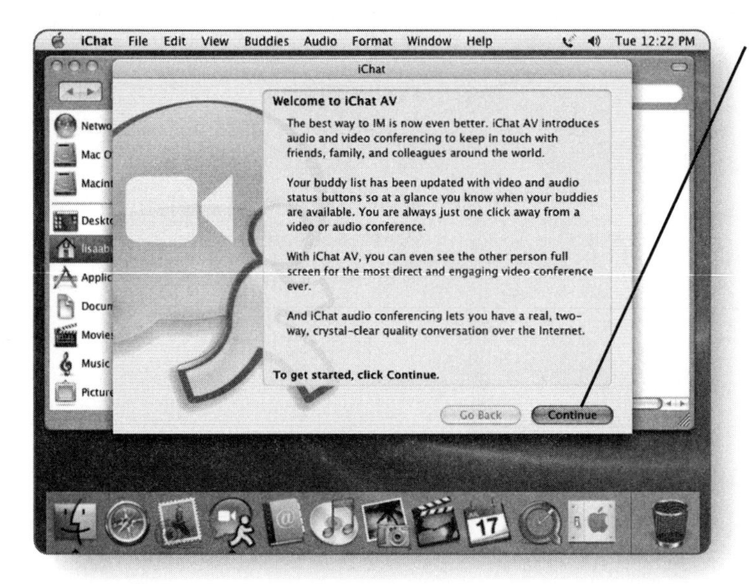

2. Click on **Continue**. The Welcome to iChat AV window will open.

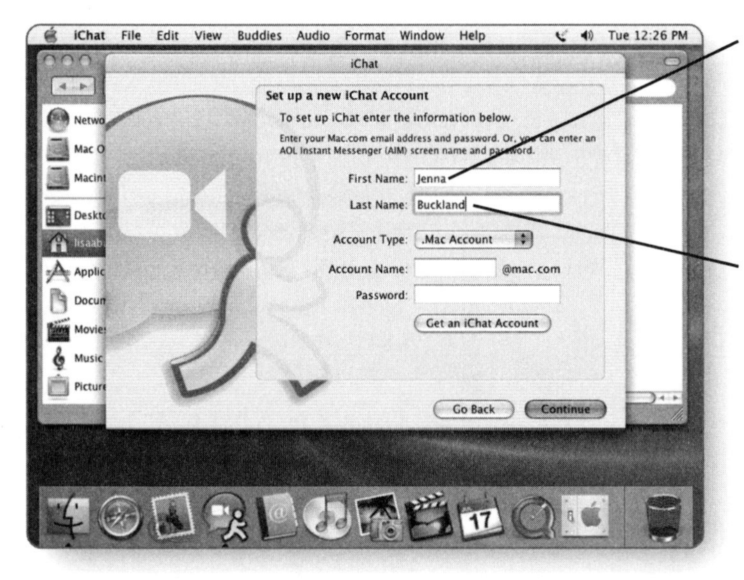

3. Type your **first name** in the First Name text box and then **press Tab**. The insertion point will move to the Last Name text box.

4. Type your **last name** in the Last Name text box. It will appear in the box.

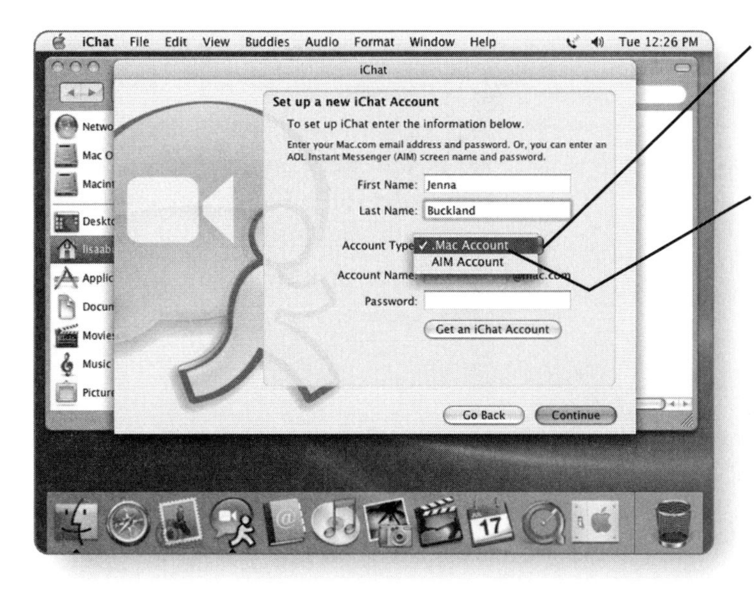

5. **Click** on the **Account Type pop-up menu**. The menu will appear.

6. **Click** on the **desired account type**. It will be selected.

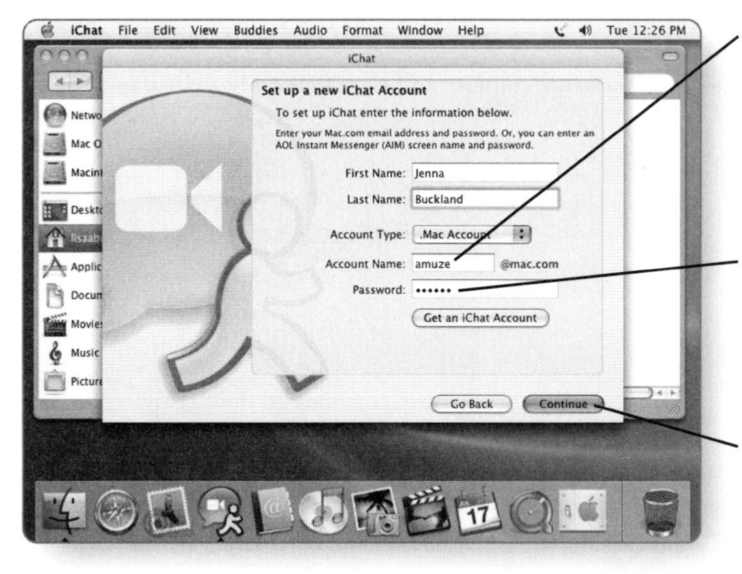

7. **Type** your **account name (member name)** in the Account Name text box and then **press Tab**. The insertion point will move to the Password text box.

8. **Type** your **password** in the Password text box. A dot will appear in the box for each letter you type.

9. **Click** on **Continue**. A Rendezvous message box will appear, asking if you want to turn on Rendezvous messaging. (Only do so if you want to use iChat AV over a local area network, or LAN.)

NOTE

When you are chatting, your screen name is your full .Mac email address, as in membername@mac.com, or your AOL screen name.

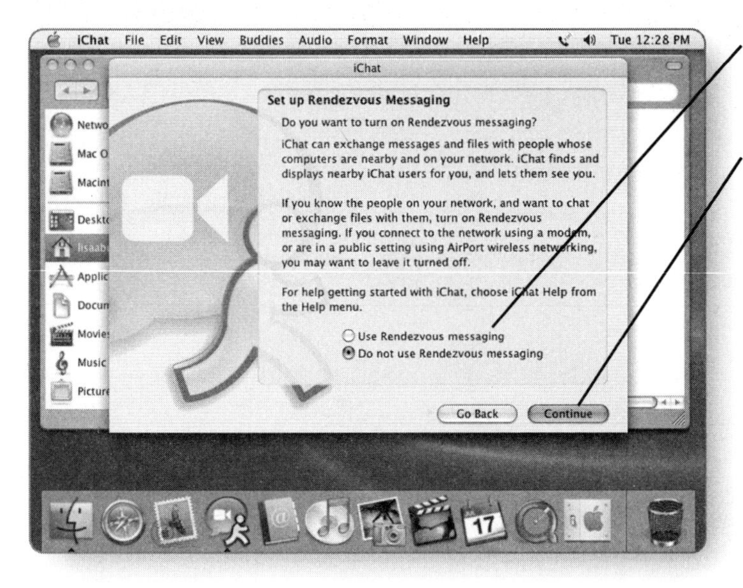

10. Click on the **desired option**.

11. Click on **Continue**. The next setup screen will appear, offering video conferencing settings, if supported by your system.

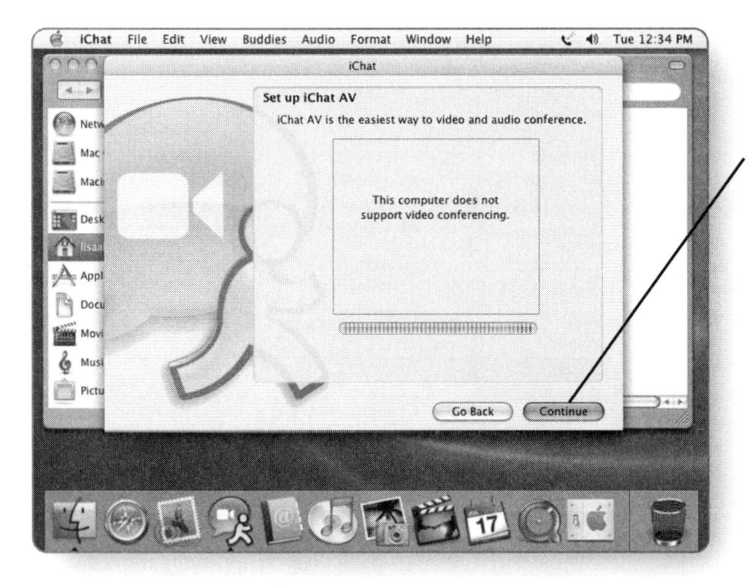

12. Click on the **desired option**.

13. Click on **Continue**. The final setup screen will appear.

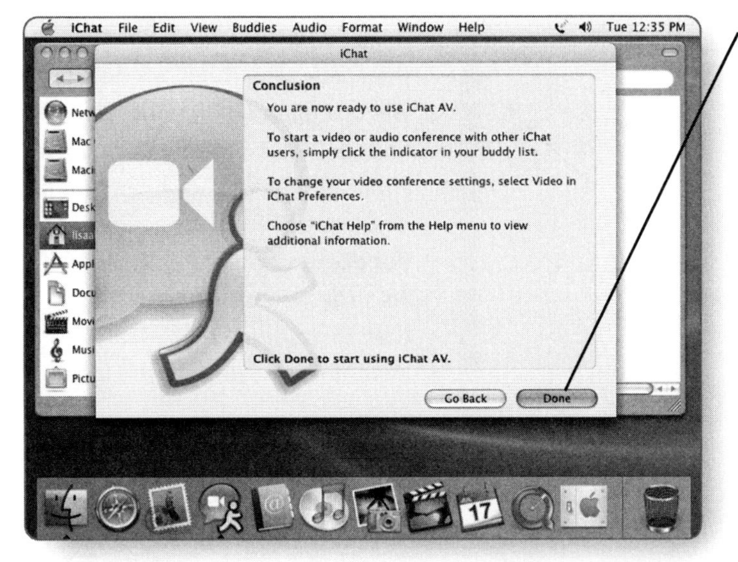

14. **Click** on **Done**. The Buddy List window will appear, along with a Rendezvous window if you enabled Rendezvous messaging.

> **NOTE**
>
> After you set up iChat AV, an indicator for iChat AV (it looks like a word balloon) may appear on the Finder menu bar. You can click on that indicator to see your current iChat status or even go offline.

Starting iChat AV and Logging On

As with other applications, you must start or run the iChat AV application to use it. In addition, however, you can log into and out of both AIM messaging and Rendezvous messaging when you don't want to use them. You also can close iChat when you no longer want to use it.

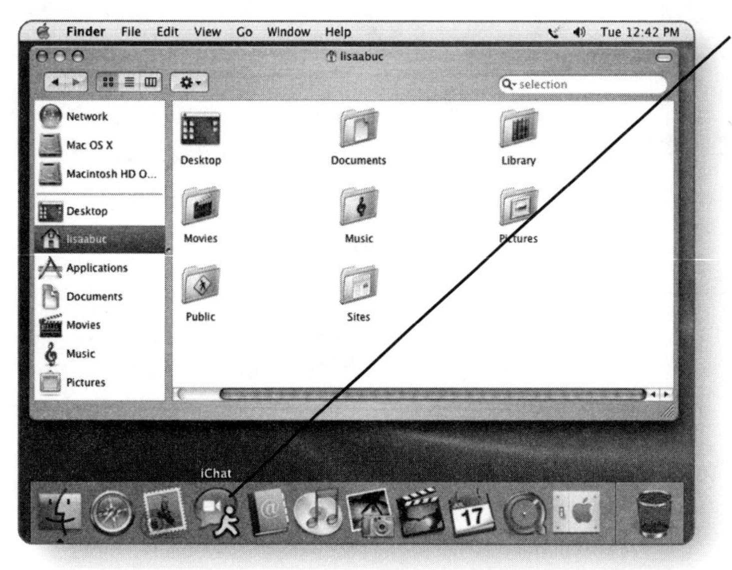

1. Click on the **iChat icon** on the Dock. The iChat window(s) will open, and its menus will appear. You will see a Buddy list window that will hold your list of chat partners. If you enabled Rendezvous messaging, you will also see a Rendezvous window that lists others logged in to instant messaging on the local network.

NOTE

If your system connects to the Internet via a dial-up connection and you have configured the system to connect automatically as explained in Chapter 11, "Making Network and Internet Connections," Internet Connect will launch and your modem will dial your Internet connection when you get mail. If you need to find out how to connect manually, see the section called "Connecting to and Disconnecting from the Internet" in Chapter 11.

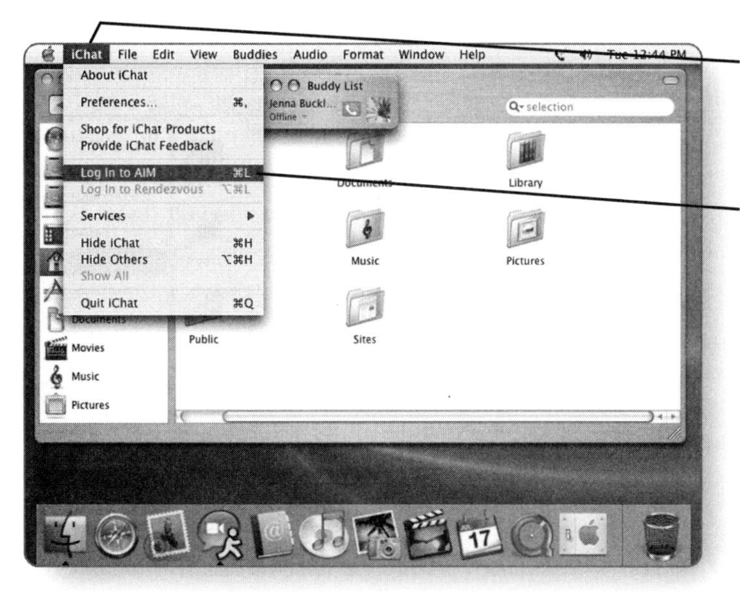

2. If iChat AV doesn't log you on automatically, **click** on **iChat**. The iChat menu will appear.

3. **Click** on **Log In to (Messaging Server)**. You will be logged into the appropriate server, depending on whether you chose Log in to AIM or Log in to Rendezvous.

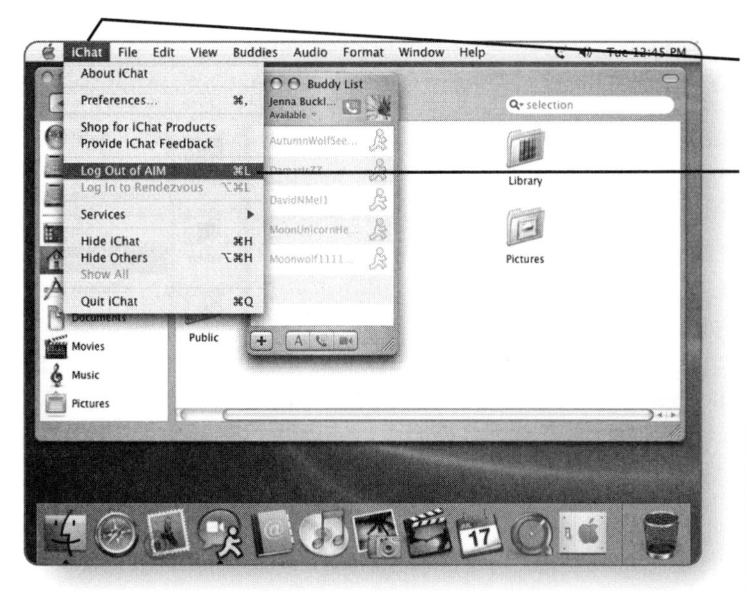

4. **Click** on **iChat**. The iChat menu will appear.

5. **Click** on **Log Out Of (Messaging Server)**. You will be logged off of the appropriate server, depending on whether you chose Log Out of AIM or Log Out of Rendezvous.

> **NOTE**
>
> The iChat windows will expand and collapse as needed and indicate your log-on status.

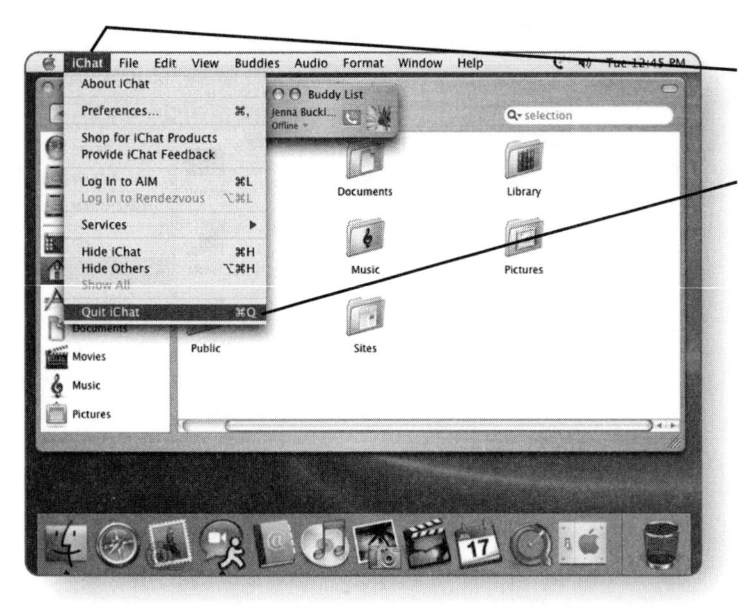

6. **Click** on **iChat**. The iChat menu will appear.

7. **Click** on **Quit iChat**. The iChat application will close. You can then disconnect from the Internet manually.

Adding Buddies

The AIM network now has millions of users. So, when you're using iChat AV with the AIM network, you need a way to identify only those persons you message with and a way to know whether your friends are online or not. You accomplish this via the Buddy List in iChat AV. You add the .Mac account (screen) name or AIM screen name for each person you want to chat with to your Buddy List. Then, when you go online, you can see at a glance whether your buddy is there and available to chat. To work with your Buddy List, you must be signed on to AIM messaging.

> **NOTE**
>
> In addition to adding buddies as described here, you can customize many aspects of how iChat AV looks and works. For example, you can choose another font and alternate formatting for your message text and change other defaults by choosing iChat, Preferences. You can use the View, Set Chat Background to choose a background picture for the message window. Experiment with the available settings until you find the look that you like.

1. **Click** on **Buddies**. The Buddies menu will appear.

2. **Click** on **Add a Buddy**. A sheet for adding a buddy will drop down from the Buddy List window title bar.

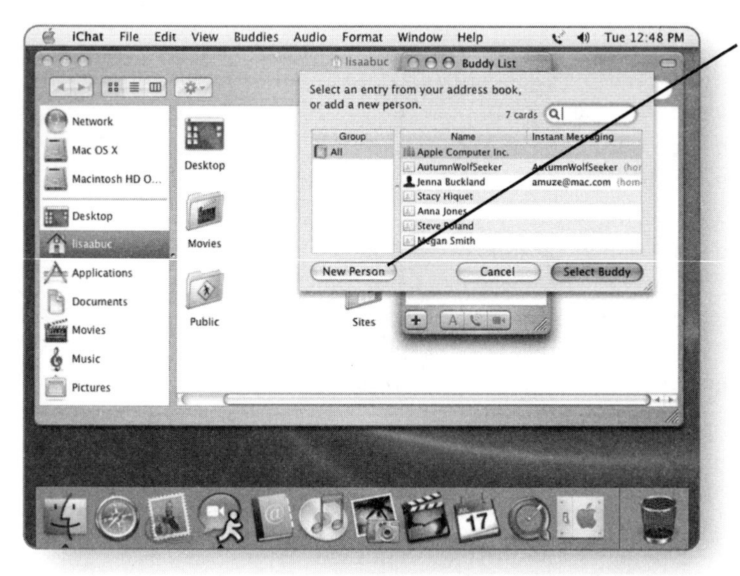

3. **Click** on **New Person**. The sheet will change with text boxes so you can enter information about your buddy.

> **NOTE**
>
> If your buddy's name already appears in the Address Book list, click on the name and then click on Select Buddy (instead of New Person). You can then supply the buddy's .Mac account name or AIM screen name, just as you would for a new buddy.

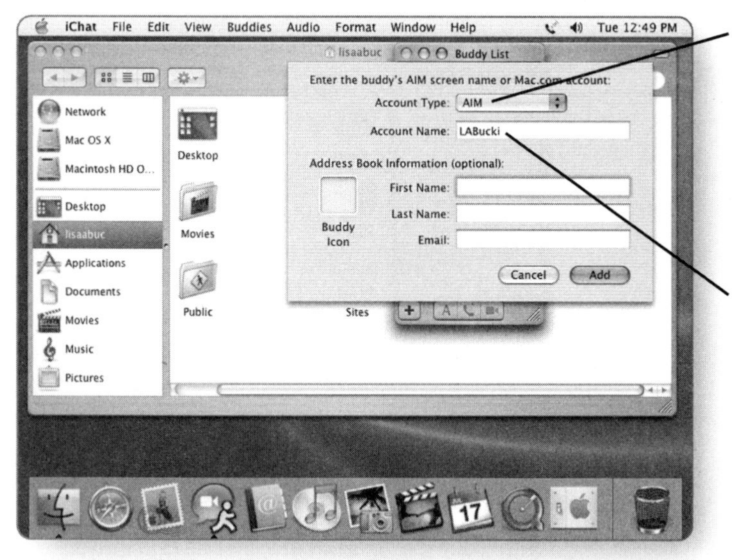

4. If needed, **make another choice** from the Account Type pop-up list. Your choice here specifies the type of account that your buddy uses to log onto the messaging network.

5. **Type** your **buddy's account (screen) name** in the Account Name text box. A sheet for adding a buddy will drop down from the Buddy List window title bar.

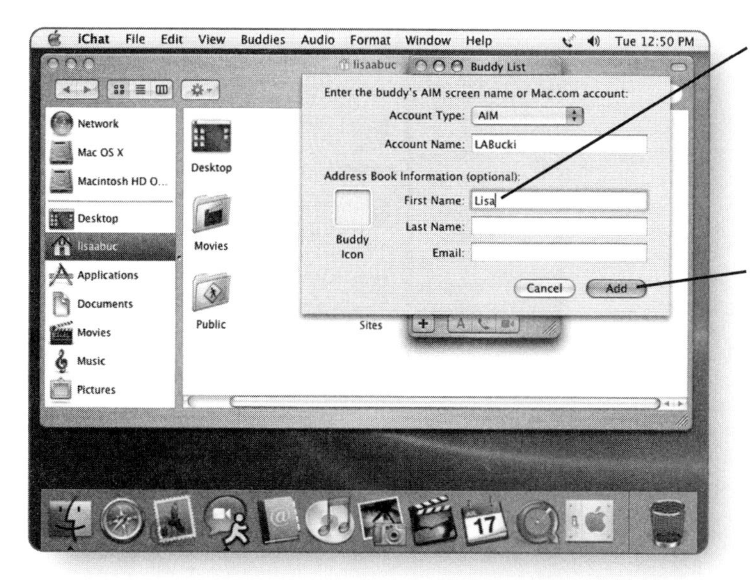

6. If desired, **enter additional information** about your buddy. This added information identifies your buddy in your Address Book.

7. **Click** on **Add**. The sheet will close, and the name of your new buddy will appear in the Buddy List window. If the buddy is online, his or her name will appear in bold text.

> **TIP**
>
> If you want to use a different picture to represent yourself in your Rendezvous and Buddy List windows, edit the listing for your name in Address Book. Click on the picture box and use the sheet that appears to select the picture to use. You can find additional pictures in the subfolders of the Library: User Pictures folder of the hard disk where Mac OS X Version 10.3 is installed. The next time you start iChat, the picture will appear.

Having and Ending a Chat

When you're ready to chat, you and your buddy both need to be connected to the Internet or network, and signed in to AIM messaging (or Rendezvous messaging for an internal network). At that point, initiating a chat takes seconds.

1. Click on the **buddy** to chat with in the Buddy List window. The buddy will be selected.

2. Click on the **Start a Text Chat button** at the bottom of the Buddy List window. The Instant Message window will appear.

> **TIP**
>
> For greater privacy, use the Buddies, Send Direct Message command to initiate a chat. If both connections are capable, this method enables your computer to connect directly with your buddy's rather than routing your messages through a messaging server.

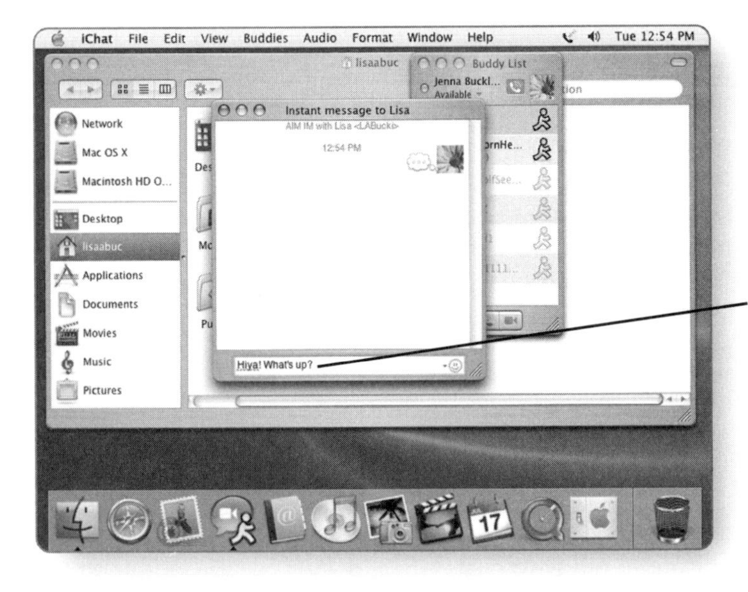

3. Type your **message** and **press Return**. Your message will appear in the window and will be sent to your buddy.

TIP

If you want to add a smiley to the end of your message, choose Edit, Insert Smiley (or click on the Insert a Smiley button in the message window), and then click on the smiley to use before you press Return. iChat AV offers a variety of different smileys, including Kiss, Sticking out tongue, Gasp, Wink, and Frown, so you can express a variety of emotions in your messages.

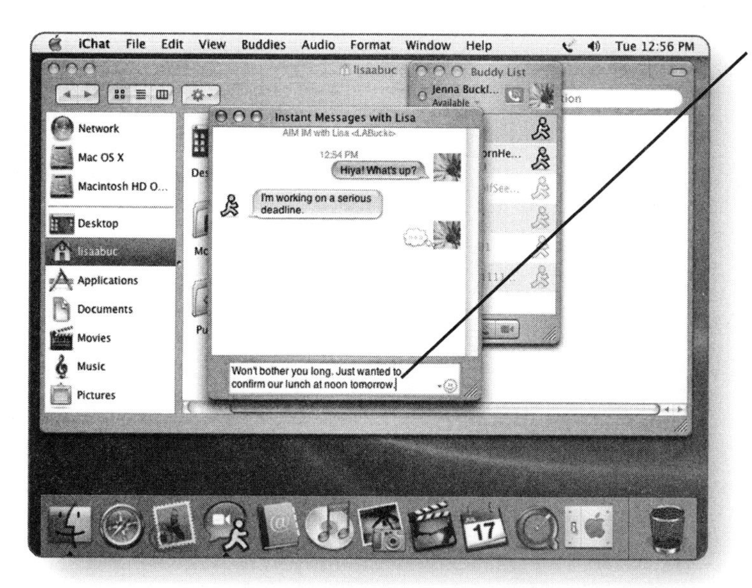

4. After your buddy responds, **type another message** and **press Return**. As you and your buddy send messages back and forth, they will appear in the Instant Message window.

NOTE

You also can use iChat AV to send a file directly to a buddy who is logged on. Send an instant message to the buddy and then use the Buddies, Send File command to select and send the file.

TRICKS OF THE CHAT TRADE

You can keep up with the flow of an online chat a bit more effectively if you try some of the shortcuts that chat "pros" use. For starters, keep each message you send short. You don't even have to send full sentences, which will particularly help if there's a lot of chat traffic and messages are moving slowly. Also, don't get too hung up on spelling or punctuation, unless you're messaging in a professional setting.

Also, learn some of the short cut lingo (or even create your own shortcuts!), which can reduce typing time. Here are a few common ones to get you started:

2	Too or two
2morrow	Tomorrow
Bcuz	Because
C U	See You
C U L8 R	See You Later
GG	Gotta Go
IMO	In My Opinion
JAS	Just A Second
K	OK
LOL	Laughing Out Loud
PLS or PLZ	Please
U	You

Ending a Chat

As fun and useful as chatting can be, there comes a time when you have to end a friendly chat.

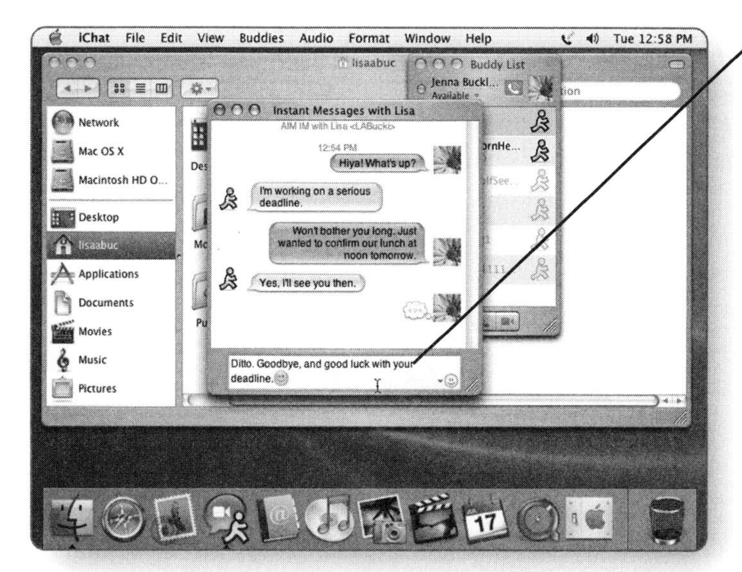

1. Type a **message** indicating it's time to sign off and **press Return**. Allow your buddy to acknowledge that the conversation is complete, as well.

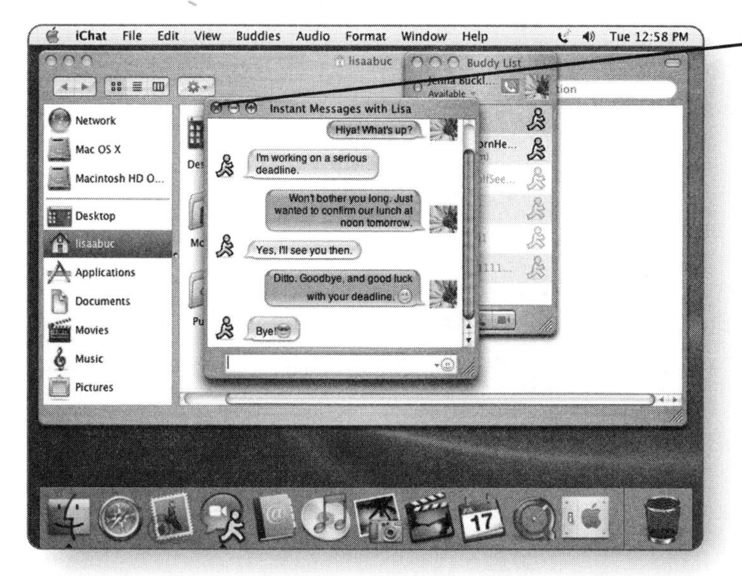

2. Click on the **Close button** on the Instant Message window. The window will close, and the chat session with that buddy will be terminated.

> **TIP**
>
> To invite additional buddies to a chat, use the Buddies, Invite to Chat command.

What About the AV Part?

The new iChat AV enables you to have both video and audio chats, as well as text chats. To have a chat that includes audio and video, you have to have a broadband (DSL or cable that connects at 128 Kbps or faster) Internet connection. You also must use an iSight Web camera or any other digital video camera or web camera that can connect via Firewire. You can buy the iSight camera for $149 at *http://store.apple.com*. Finally, your system must have a 600 MHz G3 or better processor to handle video conferencing.

After you connect the camera to your system's Firewire port, iChat AV should recognize it automatically. (In fact, if you connect an iSight camera, iChat AV should launch automatically.) You can ensure iChat AV is working with the correct camera by choosing iChat, Preferences and then clicking on the Video button in the toolbar of the window that appears.

Audio chats require only a 56K dial-up connection and a microphone, as well as the processing power described above.

To start a video chat, select your buddy in the Buddy List window and then click on the Start a Video Chat button at the bottom of the window.

To start an audio chat, select your buddy in the Buddy List window and then click on the Start an Audio Chat button at the bottom of the window.

14

Traveling the Web

Several years ago, my husband had a running joke with friends that the World Wide Web was "just a fad." Of course, his irony proved to be right on the mark and the World Wide Web evolved into a powerful and pervasive storehouse of information, products, and services. Twenty-four hours a day you can use the Web to perform research, get news, play games, shop for products, browse auctions, and more. Mac OS X Version 10.1 Panther includes Apple's new Safari browser program, which you can use to surf and search your way to the information you need. In this chapter, you'll learn how to:

- Start and exit Safari.
- Learn to navigate with links, URLs, and buttons.
- Visit and save favorite site locations.
- Search for more information about a particular topic.
- Download a file that you've found.

Starting and Exiting Safari

Mac OS X Version 10.3 offers easy access to the Safari program via the Dock.

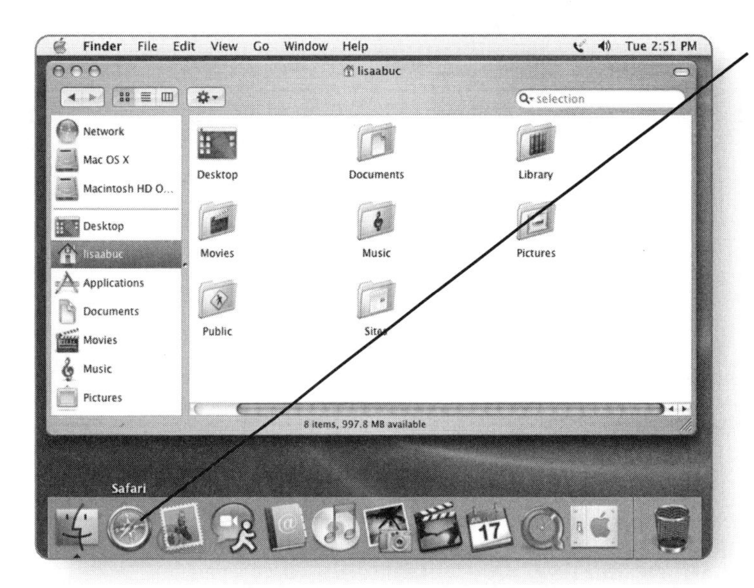

1. Click on the **Safari icon** on the Dock. The Safari application window will open, and its menu and toolbar will appear. An initial page called a *home page* will appear, and you can begin browsing the Web.

NOTE

If your system connects to the Internet via a dial-up connection, use the Internet Connect application to dial your Internet connection before starting Explorer. See Chapter 11, "Making Network and Internet Connections," to learn more about setting up your connection, dialing the connection, and configuring Internet Connect to dial automatically. Users with always-on Internet connections via DSL or cable don't need to connect or disconnect before or after using Safari.

2. **Click** on **Safari**. The Safari menu will appear.

3. **Click** on **Quit Safari**. The Safari application window will close. If you're using Internet Connect with a dial-up connection, you will need to disconnect manually when you exit Safari.

Navigating Online

The graphical nature of Web pages evolved to help users find and read information without having to remember esoteric commands and codes. Happily, Web page designs provide a lot of entertainment value and usually make pages more attractive and informative. They also provide you with a variety of ways to navigate between Web sites and pages. This section explains the various methods you can use to navigate online.

NOTE

A Web site includes a collection of individual Web pages that are published by a single source. For example, the Web address *http://www.premierpressbooks.com* leads to the main Web page for Premier Press, Inc. The Premier Press Web site includes many Web pages of information, such as *http://www.premierpressbooks.com/ptr_customerService.cfm* (a page with Premier Press contact information) or *http://www.premierpressbooks.com/downloads.asp* (a page where users can download practice and other files for books published by Premier Press).

Following a Link

Most Web pages feature distinctive text items that include special formatting such as underlining and special colors. This special formatting identifies the text as a link (or hyperlink) that leads to another Web page. Graphics, icons, or buttons on a Web page also often serve as links. Selecting a link is typically referred to as following a link or jumping to a link.

> **TIP**
>
> You can identify whether an item on the page is a link by moving the mouse pointer over the item. If the mouse pointer changes to a pointing hand, then the item under the pointer is a link.

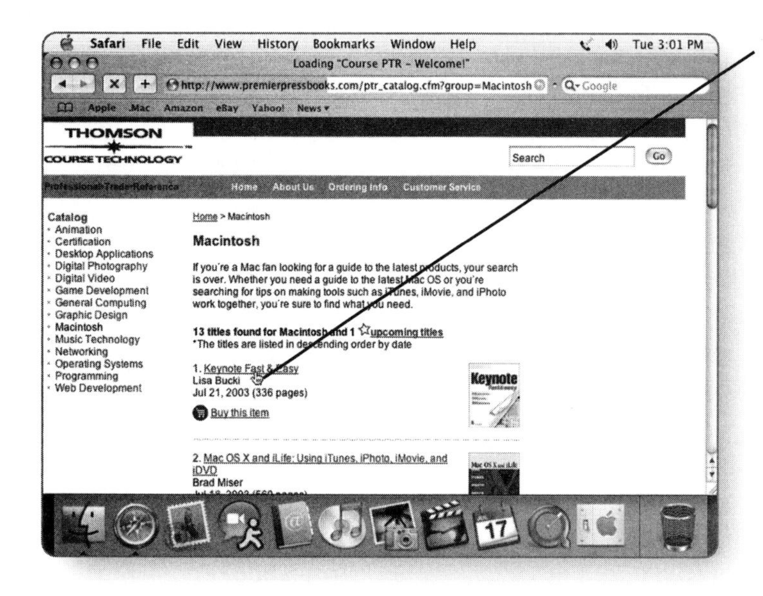

1. Click on a **text link**. The linked Web page will load in Safari.

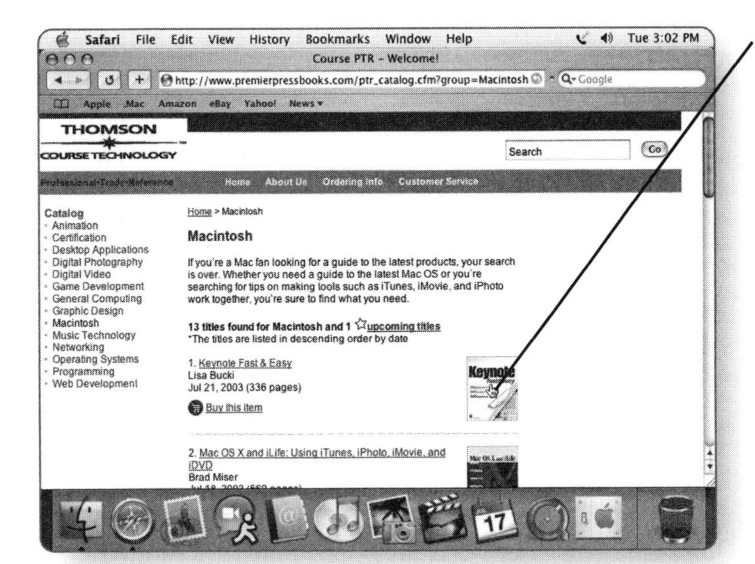

2. Click on an **image link**. The linked Web page will load in Safari.

3. Click on a **button** or **graphical link**. The linked Web page will load in Safari.

> **TIP**
>
> If a message box appears after you follow a link, respond to the message so that the linked Web page can load.

Entering a URL

Each Web page has its own online address called its Uniform Resource Locator or URL (pronounced "earl"). A full Web page address reads like this: *http://www.premierpressbooks.com/ptr_careers.cfm*, where http:// identifies the content type, www.premierpressbooks.com identifies the domain or main page of the site, and anything following the final forward slash identifies a particular Web page. You can go to a particular Web page by entering its URL directly in Safari.

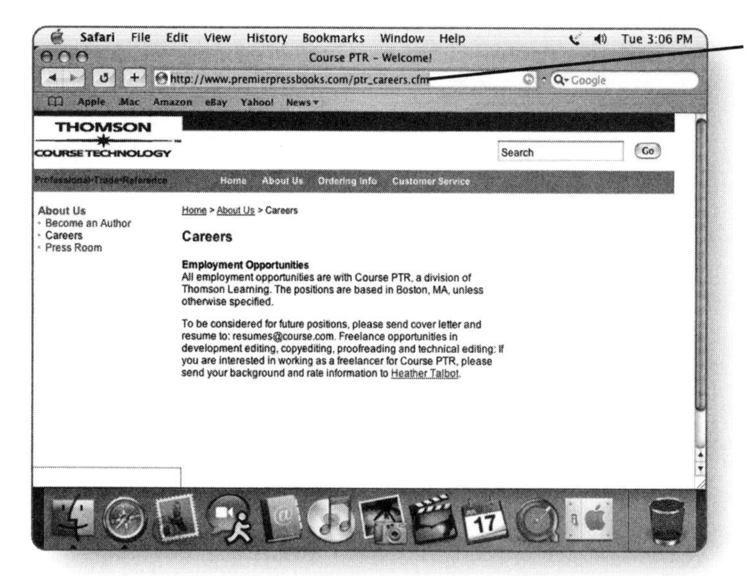

1. **Triple-click** on the **current URL** in the address text box. The entire contents of the text box should be selected. If not, drag the mouse pointer over the existing address to select it.

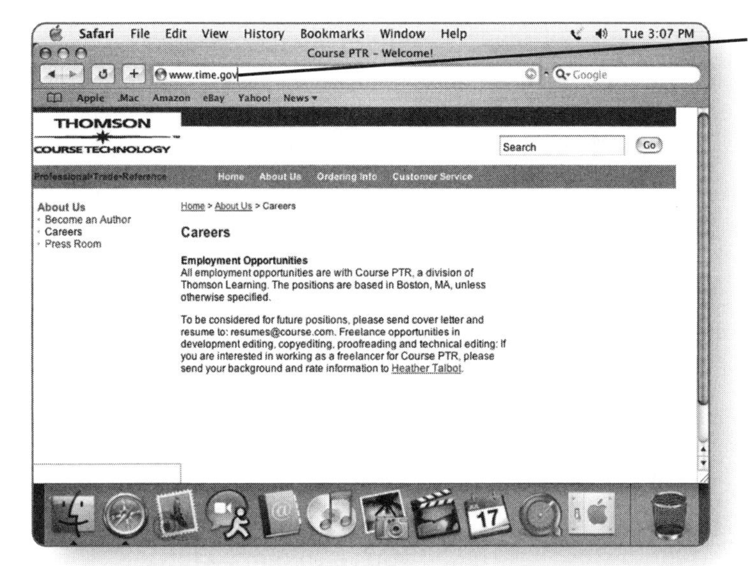

2. **Type** the **URL** to which you want to jump in the address text box. A suggested completion for your entry and/or a drop-down list with suggested addresses might appear.

3. **Press Return.**

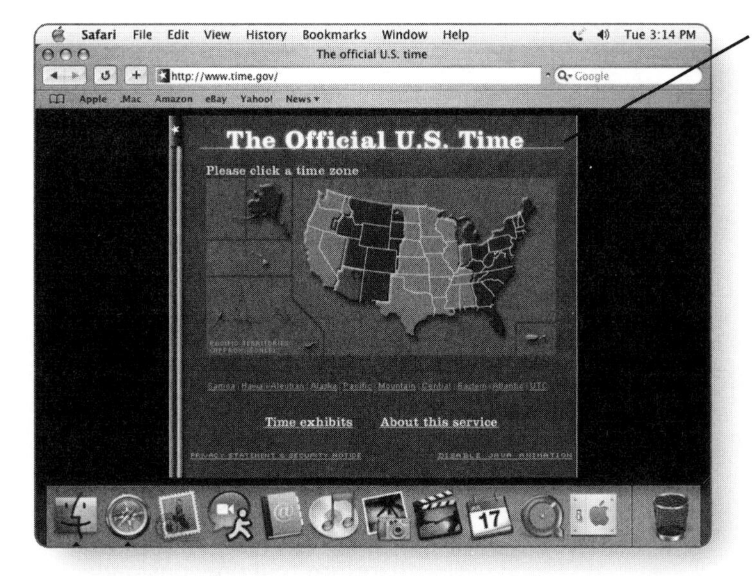

The Web page will load:

> **TIP**
>
> If the suggested entry that appears before you finish typing is the desired address, you can simply press Return. If the correct destination appears in the drop-down list, press the down arrow key to select it and then press Return.

Backing Up and Going Forward

At times, you may find that part of the information you want to view is on the current page, but other information you need is on a page you've viewed previously. The Safari toolbar offers icons you can use to back up and move forward through pages you've already viewed.

1. **Click** on the **back (Show the previous page) icon** on the toolbar. Safari will display the previous page you've viewed in the sequence of pages that you've currently browsed. The Forward icon will become enabled, as well.

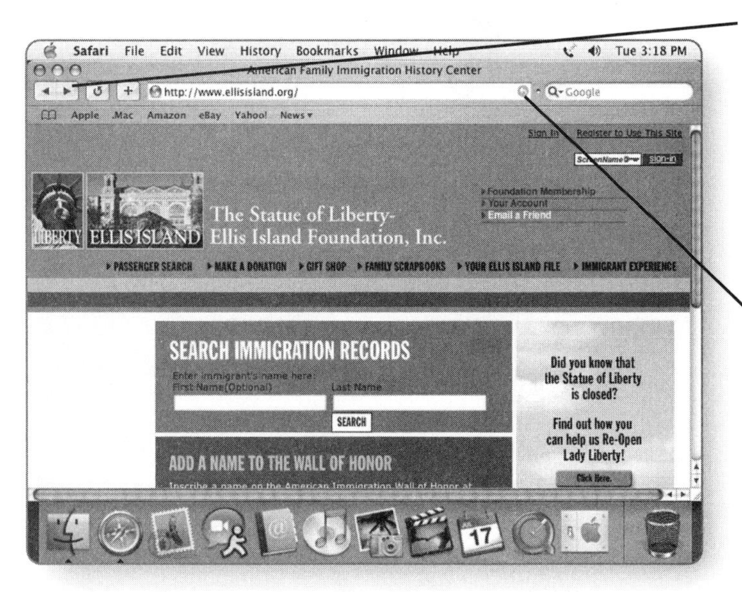

2. **Click** on the **forward (Show the next page) icon** on the toolbar. Safari will redisplay the page from which you previously backed up.

TIP

You also can click on the SnapBack button to return to a previous page. Move the mouse pointer over the button to display a tip with the name of the page that the button will take you to.

Working with Bookmarks

While Safari automatically remembers URLs that you've typed into the address text box, you generally have to remember to retype at least part of the URL to take advantage of this feature. Safari offers an even easier feature that you can use to mark and return to particular Web pages—the Bookmarks feature. (Other Web browsers offer a similar feature called *Favorites.*) This section shows you how marking and using a bookmark can save you time.

Marking a Page as a Bookmark

When you mark a Web page as a bookmark, you add it to the list in the bookmarks menu in Safari and the Bookmarks bar.

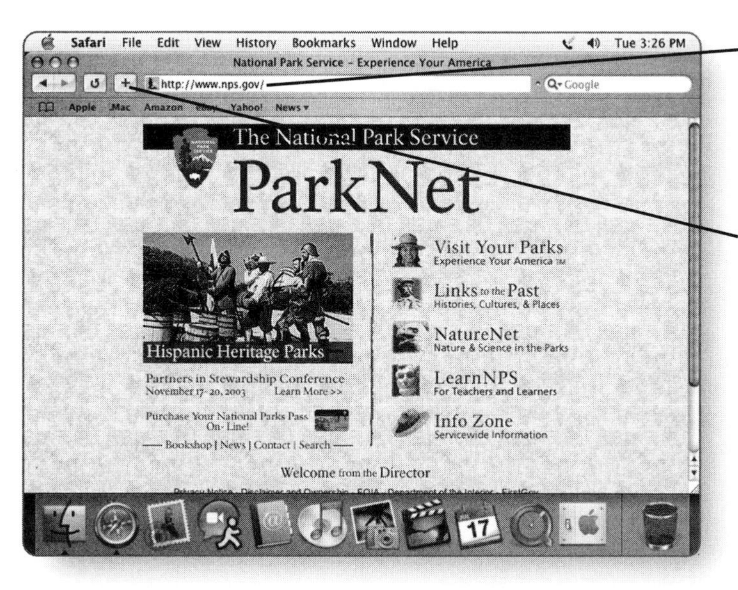

1. Navigate to the **Web page** that you want to mark as a bookmark. The page will appear in Safari.

2. Click on the **Add a bookmark for the current page button.** A sheet will prompt you to enter information about the bookmark.

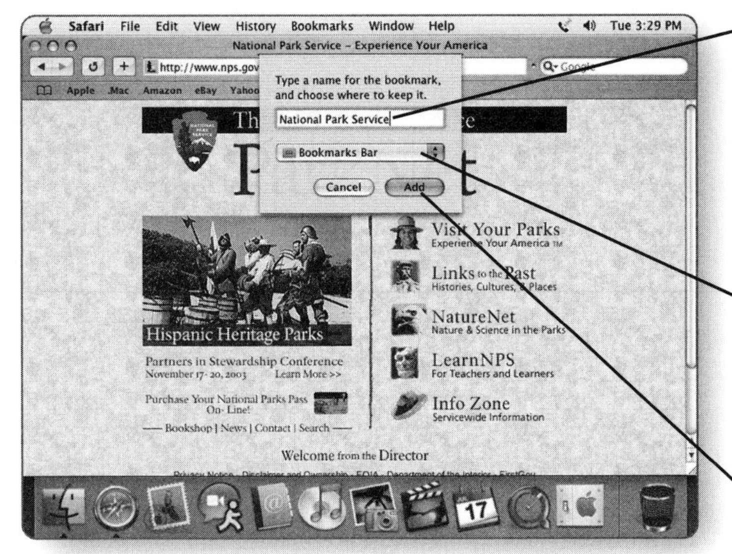

3. Type or **edit** the **bookmark name**. The specified name will appear.

The page will be marked as a bookmark.

4. Choose where to save the bookmark from the pop-up menu. The designated location will appear.

5. Click on **Add**.

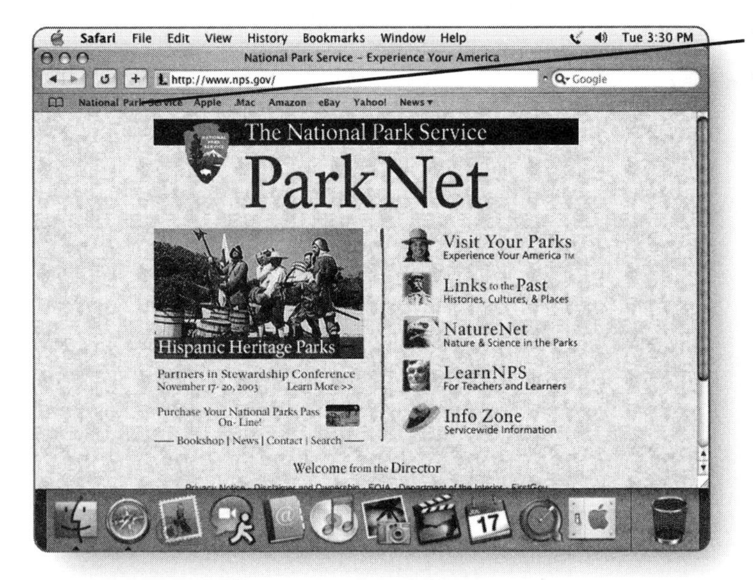

The Web page will be added to the Bookmarks menu or Bookmarks bar, according to the location you specified in Step 4.

Organizing Your Bookmarks

Adding a bookmark places it at the end of the list on the Bookmarks menu or in the Bookmarks bar. If you mark many Web pages as bookmark, these lists will quickly grow so long that it'll actually be harder to find a bookmark that you want to visit. For this practical reason, Safari enables you to better organize your bookmarks by grouping them into folders. You also can delete outdated bookmarks that you no longer use to keep the list trim.

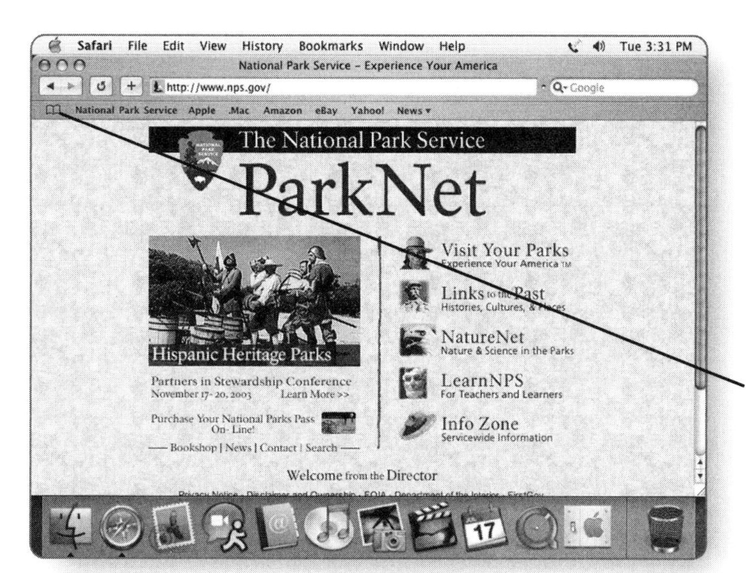

1. **Click** on the **Show all bookmarks button** at the left end of the Bookmarks bar. The Bookmarks window will open.

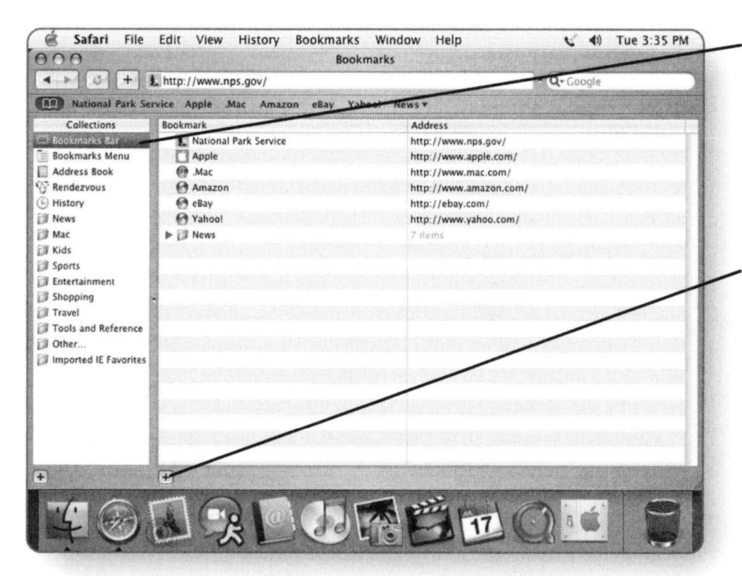

2. **Click** on **Bookmarks Bar** or **Bookmarks Menu.** The folder you create will be added to the bar or menu, depending on your choice.

3. **Click** on the **Create bookmarks folder button** below the list of bookmarks on the right. A new folder will appear at the bottom of the list, ready for you to name it.

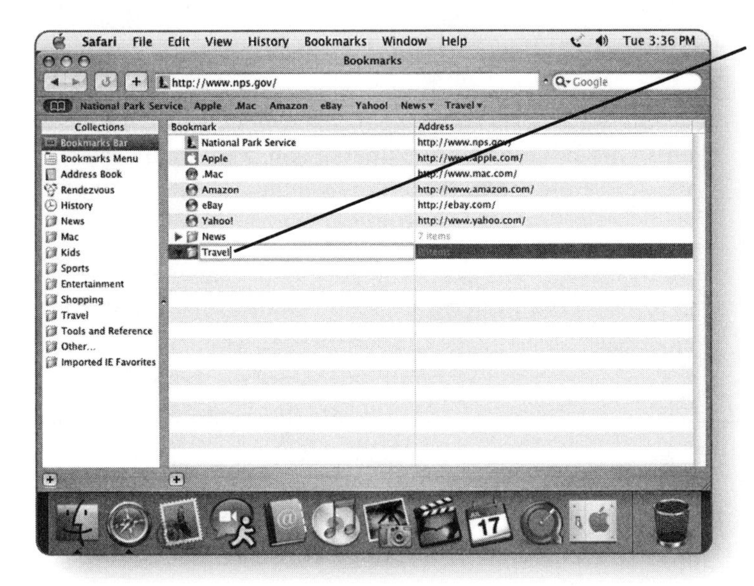

4. **Type** a **name** for the folder; then **press Return**. The finished folder will appear.

TIP

You can Control+click on bookmarks and folders in the Bookmarks window to display a context menu with commands for working with the selected bookmark or folder.

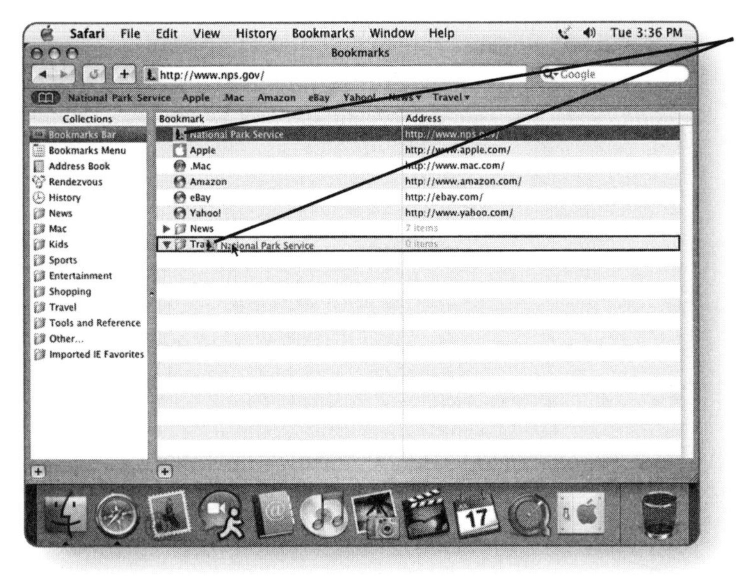

5. **Drag** a **bookmark** onto the **folder**. After you release the mouse button, the bookmark will be moved into the folder.

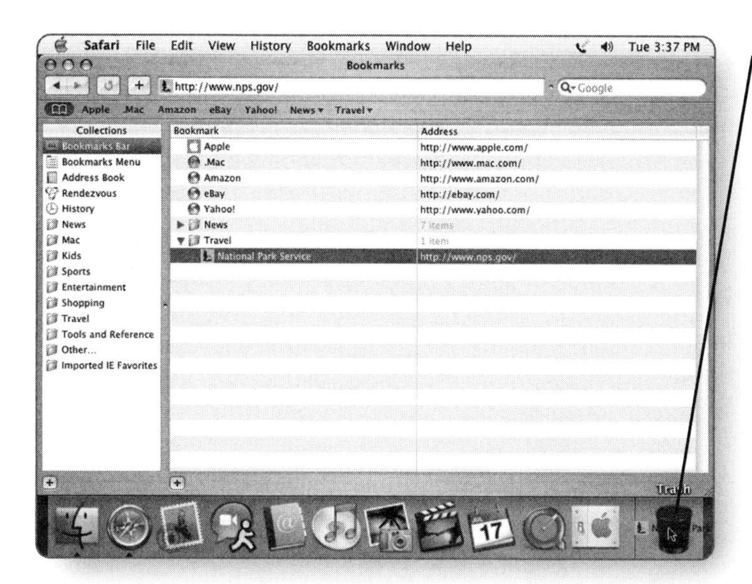

6. **Drag** a **bookmark** or **folder** to the **Trash icon** on the Dock. After you release the mouse button, the bookmark or folder (including its contents) will be deleted.

> **CAUTION**
>
> You cannot undelete a bookmark from the Trash.

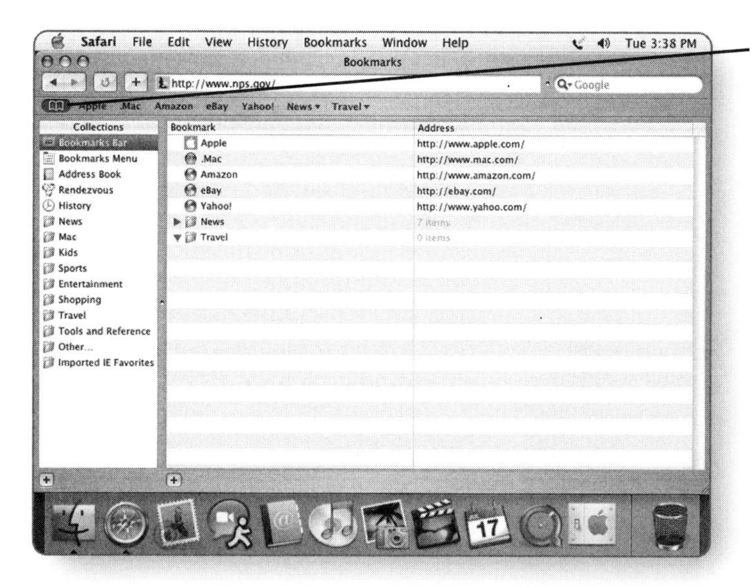

7. **Click** on the **Show all bookmarks button** at the left end of the Bookmarks bar. The Bookmarks window will close.

> **TIP**
>
> You also can drag bookmarks and folders to another position in the list.

Going to a Bookmark

Now that you've set up your bookmarks, you have two ways to use them: from the Bookmarks menu or the Bookmarks Bar.

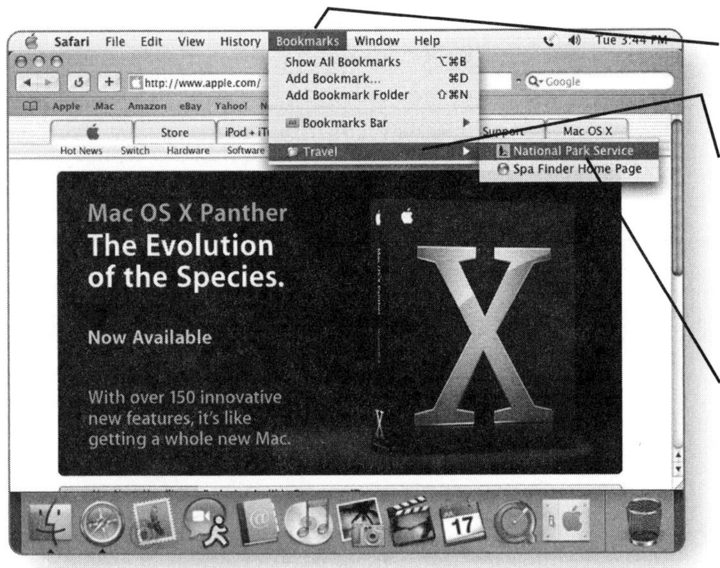

1. **Click** on **Bookmarks.** The Bookmarks menu will open.
2. If needed, **drag** the **mouse pointer** down to the folder holding the desired bookmark. A submenu listing the bookmark in that folder will appear.
3. **Click** on the **desired bookmark.** Safari will display the specified Web page.

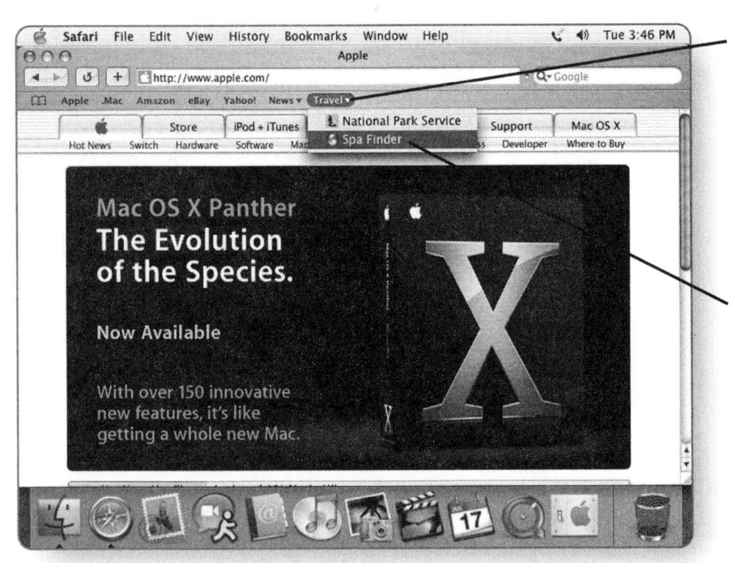

4. **Click** on the **folder button** for the folder that holds the desired bookmark on the Bookmarks Bar. The bookmarks in that folder will appear below the folder button.
5. **Click** on the **desired bookmark.** Safari will display the specified Web page.

Performing a Basic Web Search

As you might imagine, the early Web offered a lot of information but few easy roads for finding facts. You had to hear about the URL for a Web page of interest or browse and browse until you found the information you were after. Then some smart groups of people simultaneously developed search engine technology. Basically, a search engine indexes information on Web pages, so that you can perform a search for topics of interest. The search engine typically returns a list of links to potentially related Web pages, so you can review them and identify those that contain the information you need. Safari includes a search tool that you can use to locate information on the Web.

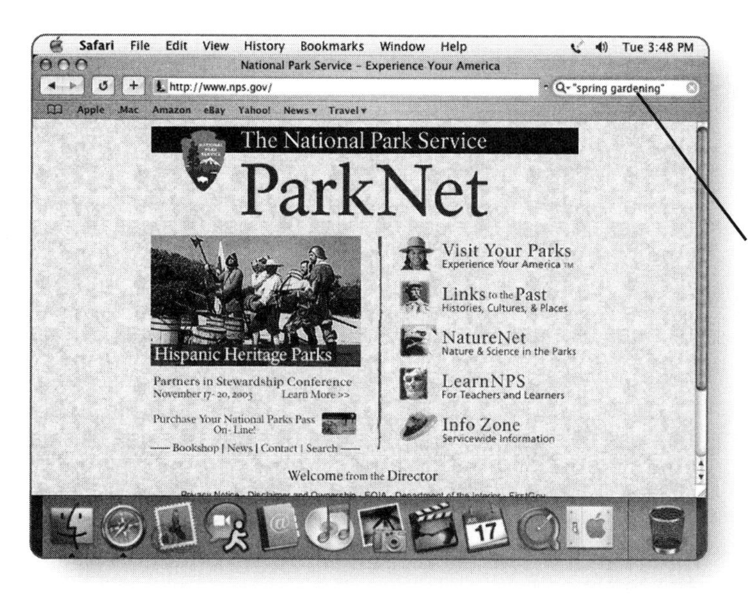

1. Click in the **search text box** that appears at the right side of the window. The insertion point will appear in the text box.

2. Type the **search term**. To search for an exact phrase, enclose the entire phrase in quotes.

3. Press Return. Safari will list links to potentially matching Web pages.

4. Click on a **link** in the results. Safari will display the specified Web page.

Downloading Files

From time to time, you may encounter files that you want to download from the Internet, such as .PDF files or software updates from a support Web site or graphics files from another Web site. Safari includes the Downloads window to enable you to do so.

> **NOTE**
>
> To download a graphic file shown on any Web page, Control+click on the image and then click on Download Image to Disk.

1. Start Safari, **connect** to the **Internet**, and **browse** to the **Web page** that holds the link for the file to download. The Web page will appear in your Web browser.

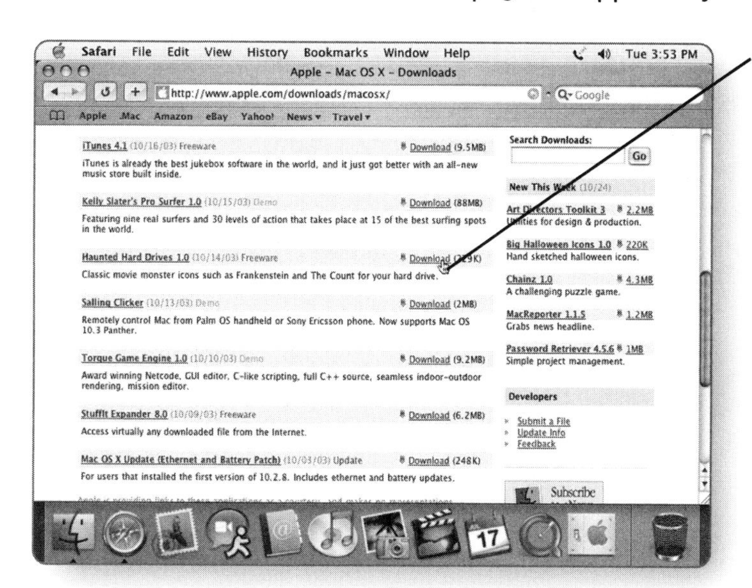

2. Click on the **download link** on the Web page. The Web browser may display the Downloads window and start the download immediately, or you may have to follow instructions on several more Web pages to choose a download site and/or provide payment information.

NOTE

In some cases, there may not be a Download link. You may click on the file name link or a Get and see the Unhandled File Type dialog box to ask you to specify how to handle the file. In most cases, you can click on the Save File As button and then use the Save dialog box that appears to specify the folder where you'd like to save the file, if different from the Default Documents folder. After you do so, click on Save.

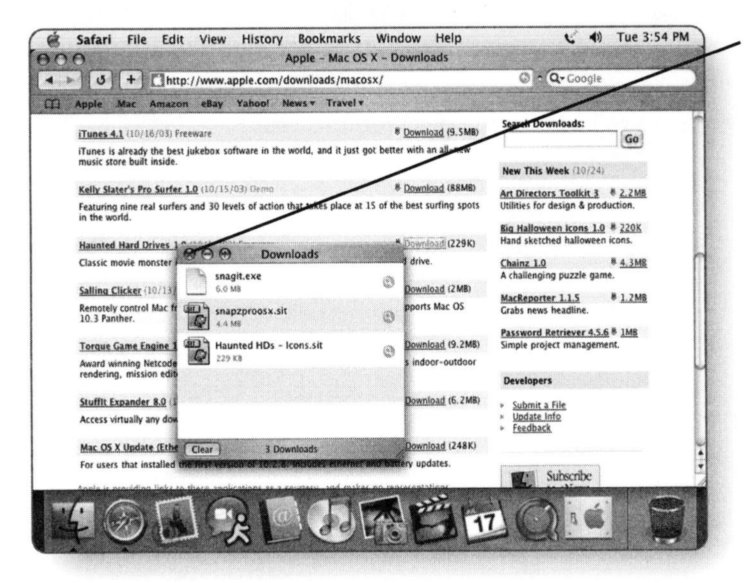

3. After Safari's Downloads tool finishes the download, **click** on the **window Close button.** The Downloads window will close.

After the download finishes, Mac OS X Version 10.3 may launch another application to decompress the downloaded file if it was an archive file.

NOTE

By default, the Downloads tool places downloaded files on the Desktop subfolder of your Home folder. To change this setting, click on Safari and then click Preferences. Click the General button and choose Other from the Save downloaded files to pop-up menu; then choose an alternate location for downloaded files in the sheet that appears.

15

Downloading and Installing Software

Every person has a distinct style for work and entertainment activities. For this reason, you can install new programs on your computer to get a job done more quickly, maintain the system, or just play around. (I won't tell!) Finding and installing a new program can be one of the most important skills for keeping your Mac useful. In this chapter, you'll learn how to:

- Find and download programs from online sources.
- Handle a program that's been compressed or "stuffed."
- Use the software installer.
- Run Software Update to keep Mac OS X Version 10.3 up-to-date.

Downloading Applications

Today, computer users can purchase software applications from a variety of sources. You can visit your local computer, electronics, or office supply store and typically find a nice selection of boxed software. Even major discount stores carry some software these days. You also can order your software from a number of catalogs or direct from a software company. You may receive software along with a new piece of equipment like a scanner and will need to install that software in order for the new hardware to work. Or, if you've set up the Internet connection for your Mac, you can go online to find and download software. Here are just a few resources to check out:

- ***http://www.apple.com /downloads/macosx.*** The Mac OS X Web downloads page includes links to a number of downloadable new programs and demo software that were written expressly for Mac OS X.
- ***http://www.download.com*, *http://www.tucows.com*, *http://www.macupdate.com*, and *http://www.pure-mac.com*.** A number of sites also enable you to download shareware, freeware, and commercial software that you purchase by providing credit card information online. You can find downloads via Mac-specific sites like *http://www.macupdate.com*, or go to a general download page like *http://www.tucows.com* or *http://www.download.com*.
- ***http://www.versiontracker.com/macosx/index.shtml.*** Enables you to download a variety of freeware and shareware programs for Mac OS X, as well as offering links to Mac news and help topics.

1. **Start Safari**, **connect** to the **Internet**, and **browse** to the **Web page** that holds the link for the software to download. The Web page will appear in your Web browser.

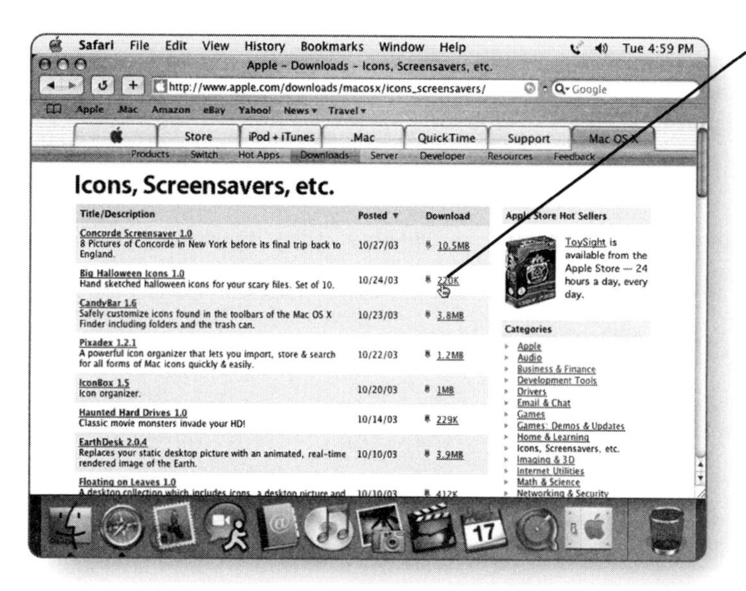

2. **Click** on the **download link.** Note that the download link may have a name other than "Download" and may be a button. The Web browser may display the Downloads window and start the download immediately, or you may have to follow instructions on several more Web pages to choose a download site and/or provide payment information.

> **NOTE**
>
> Keep in mind that with a dial-up connection, downloads may take seven to 10 minutes per megabyte of data. So, plan downloads for times when you don't need to be doing other work online.

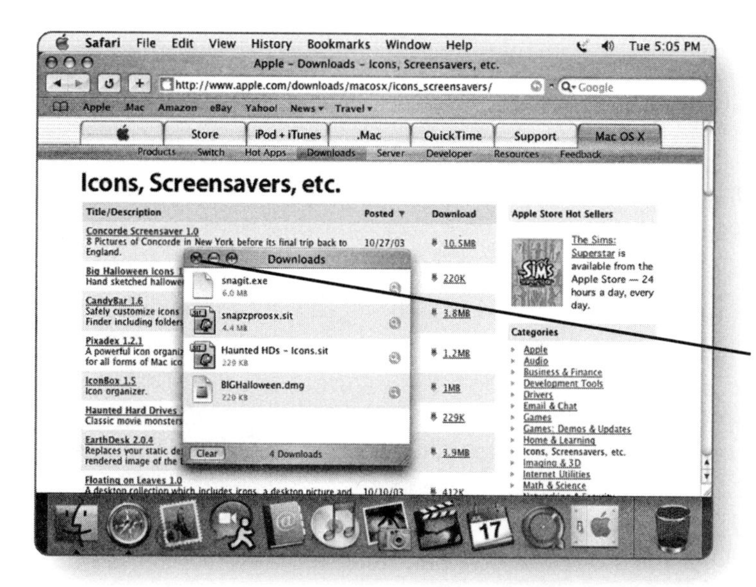

3. After Safari's Downloads' tool finishes its downloading task, **click** on the **Close button** in the upper-left corner of the Downloads window. The Downloads window will close.

You can then continue browsing the Web or quit Safari and disconnect from the Internet.

NOTE

By default, the Downloads tool places downloaded files in the Desktop subfolder of your Home folder. Change this setting in Safari's preferences.

Unstuffing Files

To speed download time, many program installation files (and other types of files) that you download will be compressed or *stuffed*. Basically, this means that special software has been used to reduce the file size and, in some cases, compress multiple files into a single file, creating an archive file that transfers more quickly or is easier to handle. The most common stuffing format results in an archive file with the .sit, .arc, or .lha file name extensions, or in some cases .hqx or .bin (for files that are encoded).

NOTE

If the file has the .img or .smi file name extension, it's a disk image file. You don't have to unstuff such a file, but you do have to handle it a bit differently, as described in the later section "Running an Install Program."

Often, Mac OS X Version 10.3 will unstuff the program or file immediately after download, placing the unstuffed (extracted) file or files on the desktop along with the downloaded archive. It uses the StuffIt Expander utility, which comes installed with Mac OS X Version 10.3. If the file doesn't unstuff automatically, you can do so manually. (Note that you can download the latest version of StuffIt Expander, as well as full compression programs such as StuffIt Standard, StuffIt Deluxe, and DropStuff from *http://www.aladdinsys.com.*)

1. **Open** or **navigate** to the **folder** into which you downloaded or moved the archive, or minimize open Finder and file windows so you can see the full desktop. You will see the icon for the archive file in the Finder window or on the desktop.

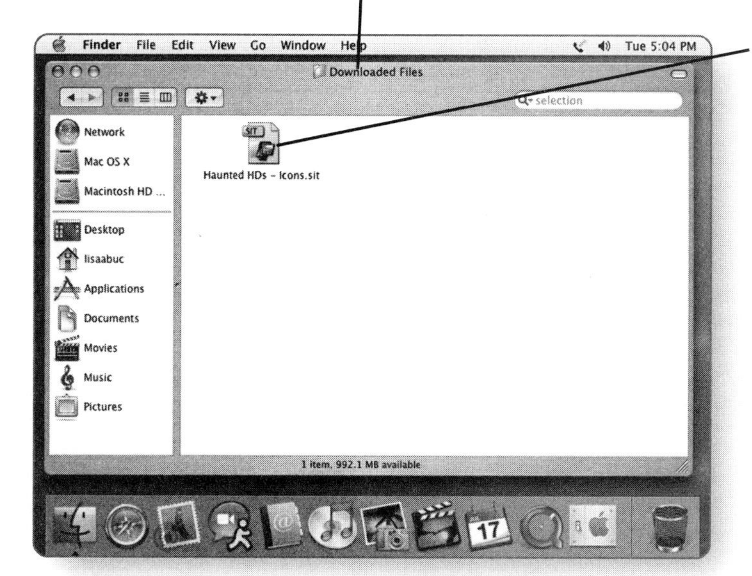

2. **Double-click** on the **icon** for the downloaded file. StuffIt Expander will open it automatically, unstuff the archive, and place the extracted file or files in the same location as the archive or in a new folder created by the unstuffing (decompression) process. StuffIt Expander will then close on its own.

Running an Install Program

Once you've downloaded and unstuffed a software program or have pulled the CD-ROM out of its packaging, you can begin the install process immediately. A single file is used to start the installer program, which, in turn, guides you through all the installation steps. The install process varies a bit from program to program, and the process starts out a bit differently depending on whether you're installing from a CD-ROM or a downloaded file. The following steps give you an overview of the process so that you can get started, no matter where the installer file is located:

> **NOTE**
>
> Not all downloaded programs require installation. In some cases, you can simply go to the folder that holds the unstuffed files and double-click on a startup icon to start the program.

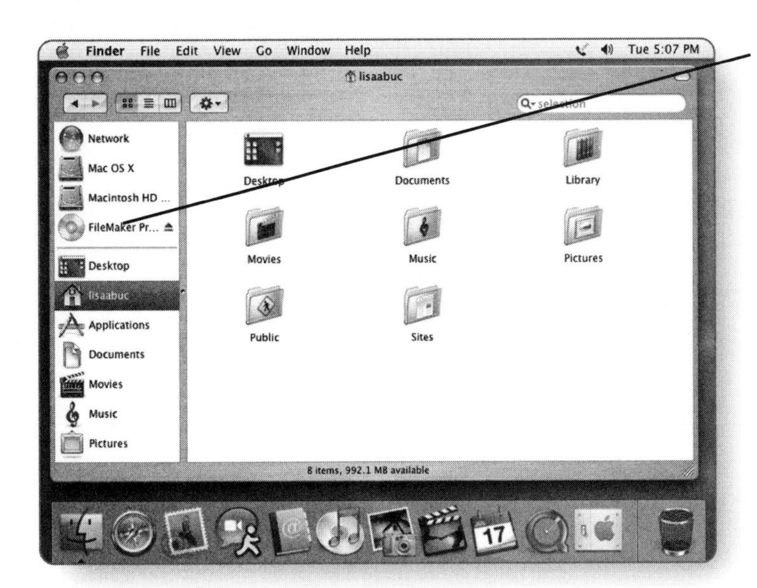

1a. Insert the **CD-ROM** into your Mac's CD-ROM or DVD-ROM drive. An icon for the disc (and perhaps also a volume) will appear on the Finder window Sidebar. A Finder window for the disc should appear automatically. (If not, click on the disc icon in the Sidebar. The resulting Finder window should contain the installer file.)

OR

1b. Open or **navigate** to the **folder** that holds the installer file you downloaded and unstuffed. The contents of the folder will appear in a Finder window.

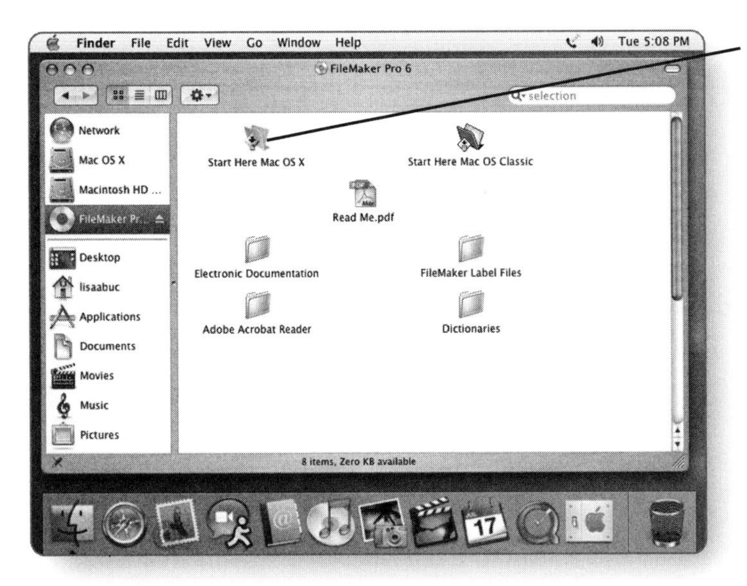

2. Double-click on the **installer file icon**. The install process will begin, and the opening installer screen will appear.

> **NOTE**
>
> You must be logged on as an administrator to install software. If that isn't the case, you will typically be prompted to enter an administrator password to continue the install process.

In some cases, a downloaded program file may create a .dmg or .smi file when unstuffed. This type of file is a self-mounting disk image file. To use such a file, double-click on it. Mac OS X Version 10.3 will use Disk Utility to mount the disk image. An icon for the mounted disk image will appear on the Desktop. Double-click on the disk image icon on the Desktop and then double-click on the installer file icon (or the program startup file icon) in the resulting Finder window to start the install process (or run the program).

> **NOTE**
>
> If the application is a Classic (Mac OS 9.x) application, the Classic environment will load so that the installation process can continue. This does not necessarily mean that the application itself will require the Classic environment; it may simply mean that the installer routine was written for the old environment.

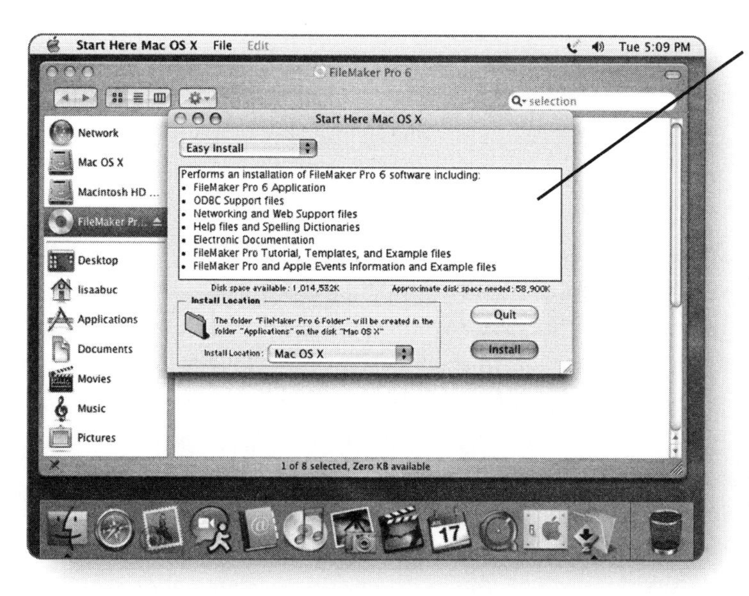

3. Follow the **instructions**, responding to each prompt. The installer may ask you for a valid registration number and your user information for registration. It also may ask you to specify the folder in which you want to install the application. In addition, many applications will prompt you to agree to an End User License Agreement. Very simple programs may have no further installation steps.

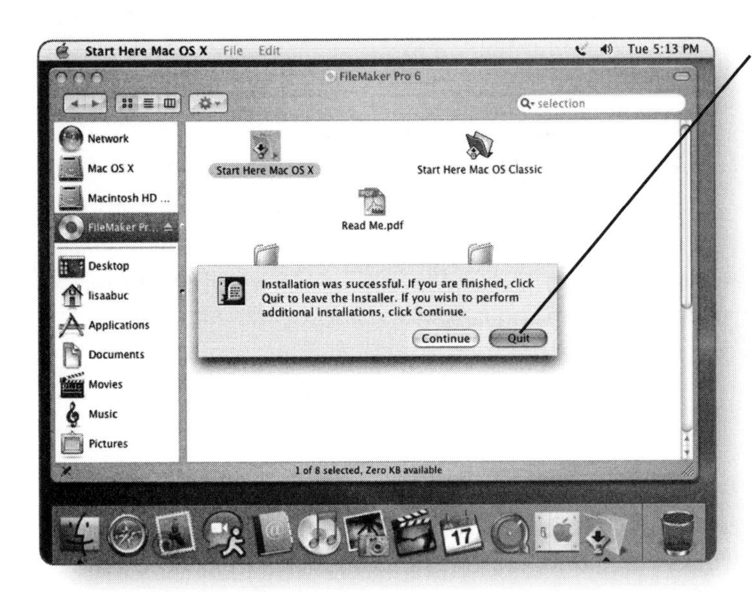

4. **Click** on **Close (or Quit)** when the installer informs you that it has completed the installation process. The installer will close. You can navigate to the folder where you installed the program and double-click on its program icon to begin using it.

> **TIP**
>
> The section called "Adding and Removing Dock Icons" in Chapter 8, "Setting up the Desktop," explains how you can add a program icon to the Dock for faster program access.

If the installer doesn't lead you through a registration process, you may be prompted to register the software the first time you start the application. (Or you can use the registration program icon in the folder where you installed the application.) Completing the registration helps the software developer keep you informed about product updates. For shareware, you should register the software and pay the shareware fee. Often, registering shareware and entering a registration number in the software enables features that are not available without registration. Remember that shareware developers bring you great software for a relatively cheap price!

Using Software Update

Mac OS X Version 10.3 includes the Software Update utility, which enables your system to connect with Apple's Web site, determines whether your Mac OS X Version 10.3 software requires any updates, and downloads and installs those updates automatically. In some cases, the Software Update utility will start automatically when you start up your system. If needed, you also can start the Software Update utility at any time as described in the steps that follow.

> **NOTE**
>
> The updates downloaded by software update typically are several megabytes in size. If you have a dial-up connection, consider running Software Update in the evening, when you wouldn't otherwise be using your Internet connection. Or, if you have an acquaintance with a faster connection, ask that person to download the updates for you and burn them to a CD-R.

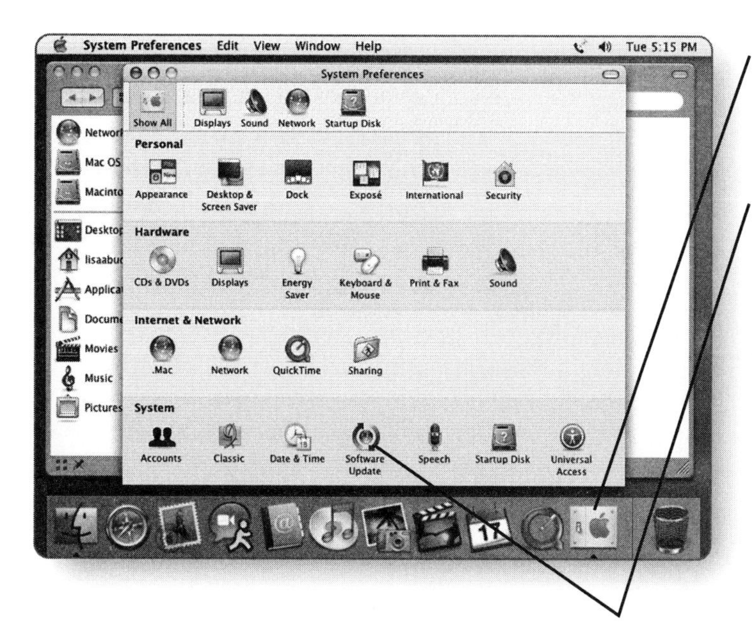

1. **Click** on the **System Preferences icon** on the Dock. System Preferences will open.

2. **Click** on the **Software Update.** The Software update pane will appear.

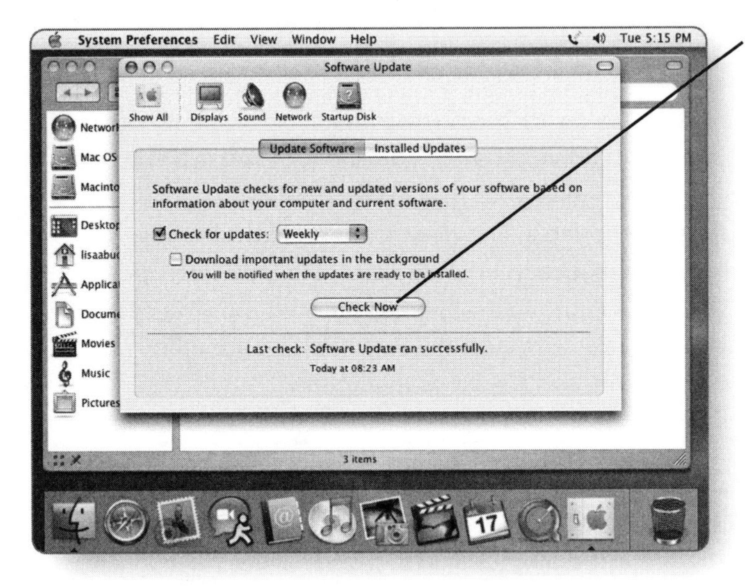

3. **Click** on **Check Now.** Software Update will connect to the Internet. (Or connect manually, if needed.) It will check the Apple Web site for updates and then download and install updates. You can click on the Software Update icon on the Dock if the Internet Connect application stays in front of Software Update.

4a. If no updates were required, the Software Update pane tells you that No new software updates were available. You can **jump** to **Step 6** at this point.

OR

4b. If the Software Update dialog box appears to alert you of an update, make sure all the desired updates are checked; then **click** on **Install (X) Items.** Software Update will continue.

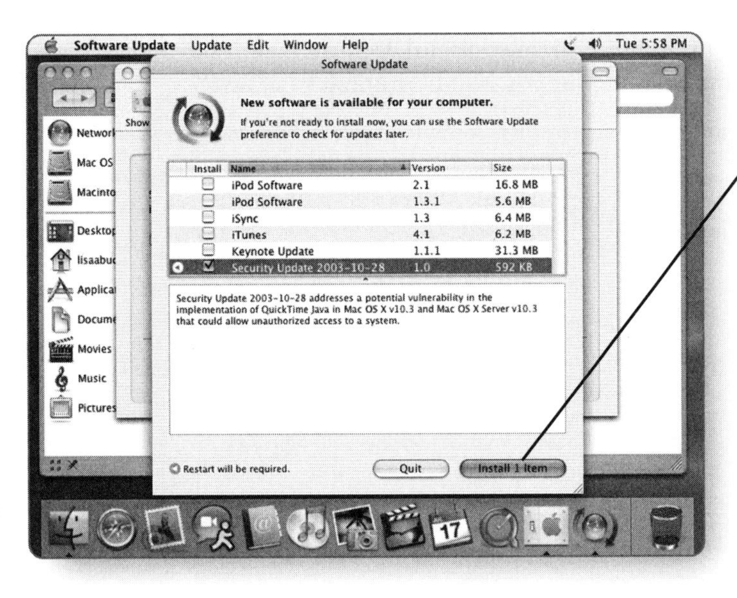

> **NOTE**
>
> The Authenticate dialog box may prompt you to enter an administrator password after Step 4b. Type the password in the Password or phrase text box and then click on OK. If the Software License sheet appears, read its contents and then click on Agree. Software Update will continue.

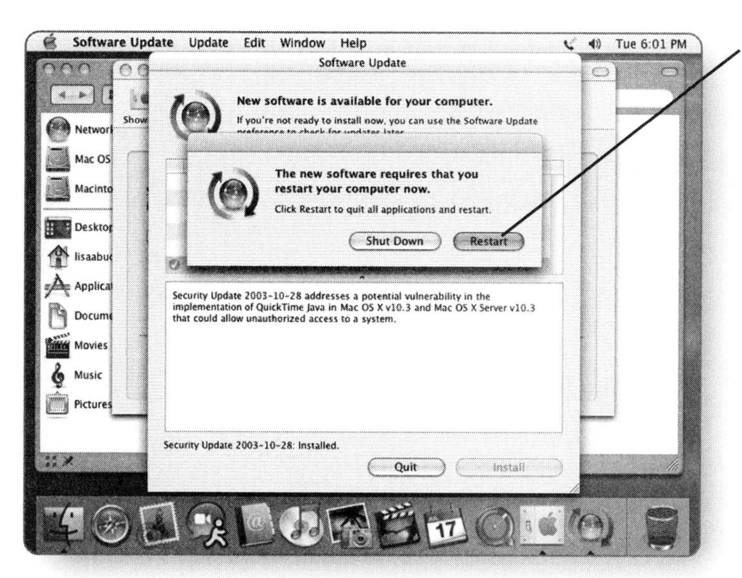

5a. When all updates are finished, **click** on **Restart** in the alert box, if prompted, to restart your computer. The alert box will close, and Software Update will close automatically.

OR

5b. When all updates are finished, **click** on **OK** in the alert box. The alert box will close and Software Update will close automatically. You can then close System Preferences and disconnect from the Internet, if needed.

> **NOTE**
>
> In some cases, a message box may appear when a download starts, reminding you that a particular update will require you to restart the system. Click on OK. Then, after the download completes and Software Update installs the downloaded software, another message box prompts you to restart the system. Click on Restart in the message box to do so.

> **NOTE**
>
> In some cases, Software Update does not list all the available updates in the Install Software dialog box. Clicking on Update Now again before you close Software Update will alert you if there are additional updates to download.

Part IV Review Questions

1. How do I work with files on another computer on my network? *See "Setting Up for Networking" and "Connecting to Other Computers" in Chapter 11.*
2. How do I set up for the Internet? *See "Entering Internet Connection Information" and "Setting Up a Broadband Connection" in Chapter 11.*
3. How do I hang up my Internet connection? *See "Connecting To and Disconnecting from the Internet" in Chapter 11.*
4. How do I send and receive Mail messages? *See "Sending Mail" and "Checking Mail" in Chapter 12.*
5. How do I deal with a message? *See "Reading and Responding to a Message" in Chapter 12.*
6. How do I discourage spam? *See "Bouncing a Message" in Chapter 12.*
7. I want to start chatting online, but I don't know if I can. *See "Getting an Account" and "Setting Up iChat AV" in Chapter 13.*
8. How do I jump directly to a Web site? *See "Entering an URL" in Chapter 14.*
9. How do I mark a good Web page so that I can go back? *See "Marking a Page as a Bookmark" in Chapter 14.*
10. Where can I get more software? *See "Downloading Applications" in Chapter 15.*
11. How do I install a downloaded application? *See "Running an Install Program" in Chapter 15.*
12. How do I use Software Update? *See "Using Software Update" in Chapter 15.*

PART V

Becoming a Multimedia Master

16

Jamming with iTunes 4

Even the programmers for earlier computers looked for ways to have fun, developing computerized versions of chess and the arcade game, Pong. Computers have evolved to include many more personal entertainment capabilities. With the advent of ways to digitize music, your Mac can even work as your personal jukebox serving up your favorite tunes any time. Mac OS X Version 10.3 includes iTunes 4 to play your audio CDs and other music files. In this chapter, you'll learn how to:

- Start and exit iTunes 4.
- Play an audio CD.
- Create an MP3 file.
- Buy music online.
- Create and use a playlist.
- Control music playback.

Starting and Exiting iTunes

As with other applications, you have to start iTunes to take advantage of its many features. By default, the Dock should include an icon for the iTunes application. (If it doesn't, you can always add it from the Applications folder as described in the section "Adding and Removing Dock Icons" in Chapter 8.

1. **Click** on the **iTunes icon** on the Dock. The iTunes program will open, and its menu and window will appear onscreen. The first time you start iTunes, a License Agreement and the iTunes Setup Assistant runs. If you see the License Agreement or iTunes Setup Assistant, proceed to the next step. Otherwise, go on to Step 6.

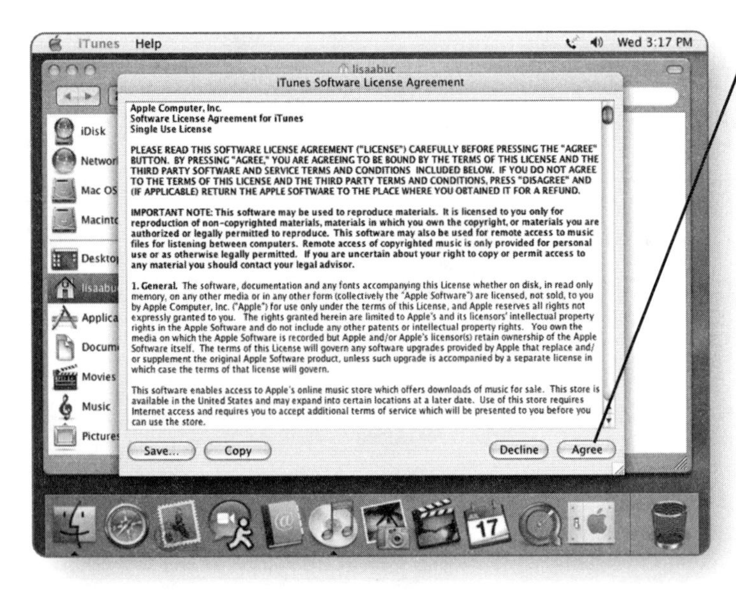

2. **Review** the **License Agreement** and then **click** on **Agree**. The iTunes Setup Assistant will appear.

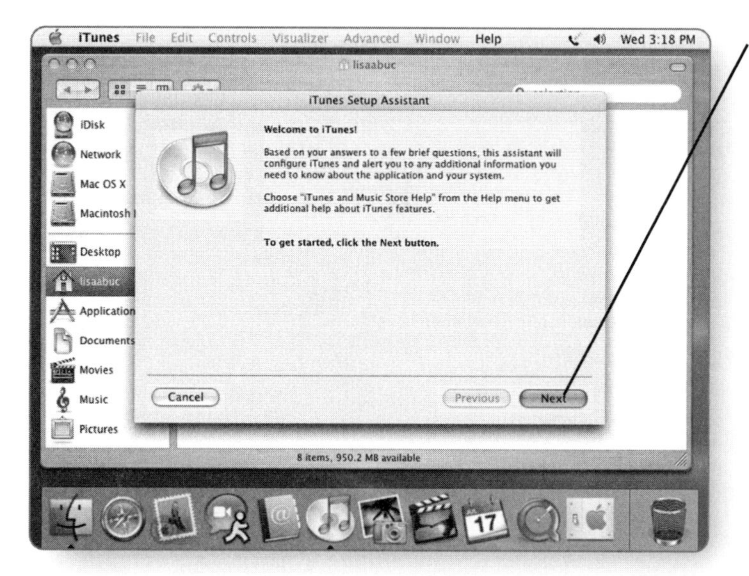

3. Click on **Next**. The iTunes Setup Assistant will ask you two questions regarding configuring your Internet connection for use with iTunes.

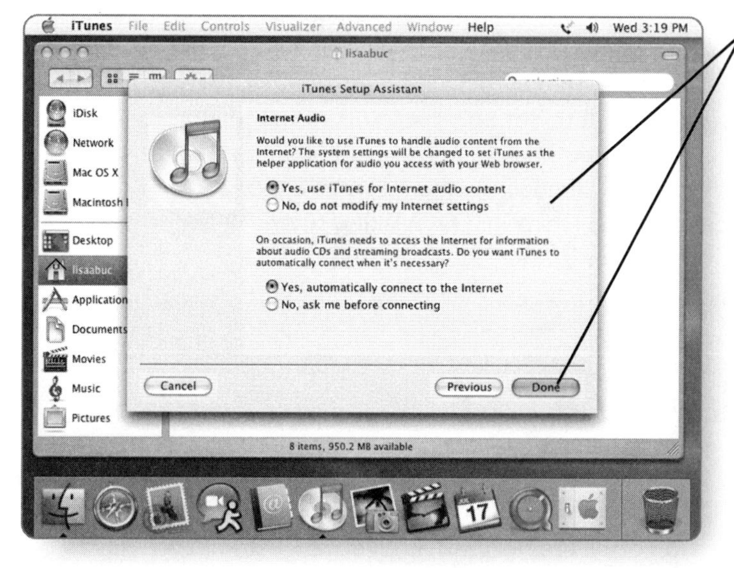

4. Choose options; then **click** on **Done**. The iTunes Setup Assistant will close, and you can start using iTunes.

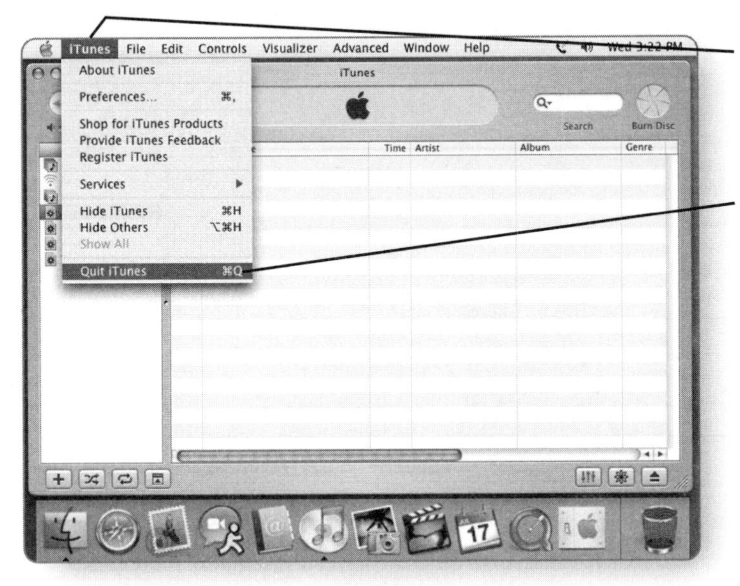

5. When you're ready to quit iTunes, **click** on **iTunes**. The iTunes menu will appear.

6. Click on **Quit iTunes**. iTunes will close.

NOTE

By default, the iTunes Setup Assistant suggests that you allow iTunes to connect to the Internet as needed. You still will need to set up your Internet connection to connect automatically, and you still will need to disconnect manually (using Internet Connect, as described in Chapter 11, "Making Network and Internet Connections") when you finish using iTunes.

Playing a CD

Many of us have made a substantial investment in an audio CD collection. The iTunes software doesn't make that collection obsolete. Instead, it gives you yet another way to listen to your music collection and even take advantage of extra playback features. Follow these steps to play an audio CD after you start iTunes:

1. Insert an **audio CD** into the CD-ROM or DVD-ROM drive. You will see a message that iTunes is accessing the CDDB database (an online database that helps software such as iTunes identify album titles, song titles, and artists). If the song names do not appear, choose Advanced, Get CD Track Names.

TIP

If iTunes doesn't automatically connect to the Internet, use the Internet Connect application to do so, as described in Chapter 11, "Making Network and Internet Connections."

TIP

If a dialog box appears and lists multiple matching CDs, click on the desired CD and then click on OK to continue.

2. Click on the **check box** beside a song to remove its check mark. iTunes will skip playback of any song that's not checked.

3. Click on a **button** to specify a playback mode. The buttons will work as follows:

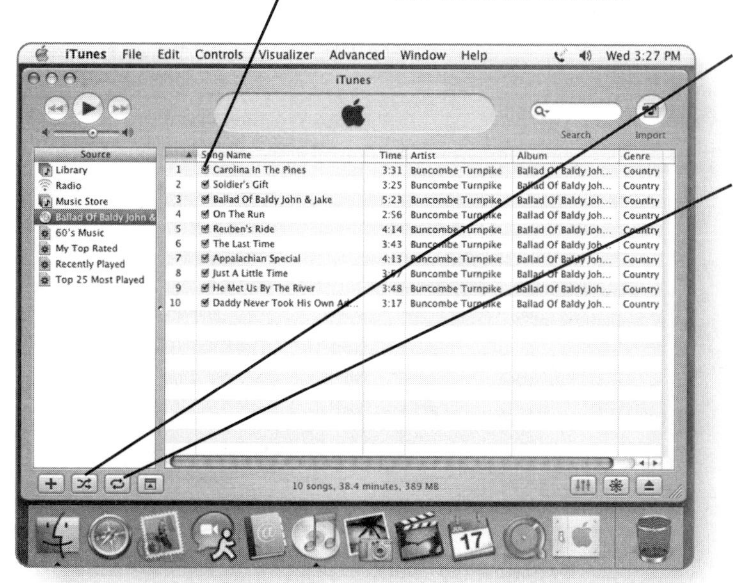

- **Shuffle the play order.** Click on this button to turn shuffle mode on or off.
- **Play once, repeat song, or repeat playlist.** Click on this button to advance through different repeat modes: repeating all the checked songs from the CD, repeating a single song on which you've previously clicked in the playlist, or playing the checked songs from the CD only once (repeat mode off).

4. Click on the **Play button** to start playing the CD. Music playback will begin immediately.

5. Drag the **volume slider**. The volume will be adjusted.

> **TIP**
>
> As a song plays, you can see information about the song in the small pane that appears at the top center of the iTunes window. Drag the small diamond in the timeline bar to back up or fast forward within the song that's currently playing.

6. After playback finishes, **click** on the **Eject button**. iTunes will eject the audio CD.

> **TIP**
>
> Once you play a CD or playlist, you also can display an animation file to accompany the music. To do so, choose Visualizer, Turn Visualizer On or click on the Turn Visual Effects On or Off button that appears to the left of the Eject button.

Making Digital Files and Adding Them to Your Library

If you want to build long playlists for your computer or to play music on portable devices, then you may want to convert your CD audio tracks to AAC or MP3 digital music files. When you use software like iTunes to convert a CD track to a digital file, the software eliminates certain file information that humans can't hear. The resulting file is about 11 percent of the size of the original file (the MP3 file for a typical song is 3-4M) and sounds great to most listeners using typical equipment.

You can convert an individual CD track to a digital by importing the songs into your iTunes Library. To prepare for the process, choose iTunes, Preferences and then click on the Importing button. Choose the desired format for the digital song files and then click on OK.

TIP

If you plan to add the digital songs to an iPod, stick with the AAC format. For other digital players, you may have to choose the MP3 format, instead.

Follow these steps to convert songs from a CD to digital files and add them to your library:

1. **Insert** an **audio CD** into the CD-ROM or DVD-ROM drive for your system. The iTunes window will list tracks by number in the playlist. You will see a message that iTunes is accessing the CDDB database. Your modem will dial your Internet connection (or do it manually with Internet Connect). Then the song information will appear.

> **TIP**
>
> Getting the track names from CDDB enables iTunes to name the tracks and folders for you, a huge timesaver. If iTunes doesn't automatically get the album and track information from CDDB, choose Advanced, Get CD Track Names. If a window lists possible matches, click on the name of the matching CD and then click on OK.

2. If needed, **click** on the **check box** beside a song to remove the check mark. iTunes will skip the import and digitization of any song that's not checked.

3. **Click** on the **Import button**. By default, iTunes starts simultaneously playing and converting the tracks.

The process of converting the songs and importing them into your Library actually takes less time than the playback. A small green check mark appears beside each song in the playlist after iTunes has successfully converted and imported the file.

> **NOTE**
>
> iTunes stores the digital files in subfolders of the Music: iTunes: iTunes Music folder in your Home folder, although the folders and files may not appear until you exit iTunes.

4. After the conversion and import operation is finished, **click** on the **Stop button.** iTunes will stop playing the CD.

5. Click on the **Eject button.** iTunes will eject the audio CD.

> **NOTE**
>
> iTunes also enables you to add other digital song files from your Mac's hard disk to the Library. To add songs, use the File, Add to Library command.

Buying Music from the iTunes Music Store

Since its introduction, the iTunes Music Store has sold tens of millions of digital songs. iTunes enables you to visit the store automatically to purchase digital music, which downloads into your iTunes Library. You can buy individual tracks or full albums.

Before you can purchase music from the iTunes Music store, you need to set up an Apple ID account and Apple's 1-Click Ordering service. These services not only store your contact and payment information in a secure way, but also enable you to save time if you order music, as well as photos prints, books, or other Apple products with frequency.

You can sign up for these services at *http://store.apple.com*. You'll need your contact and credit card information. After you sign up, follow these steps to find and purchase music:

1. Connect to the **Internet**, if your system doesn't have an always-on connection.

2. Click on **Music Store** in the Source list.

iTunes will connect with the Music Store and display its Home page.

3a. Browse to **find songs**. The Music Store will list tracks.

OR

3b. Enter an **artist, song** or **album** to find in the Search Music Store text box and **press Return**. The list of album or tracks will appear.

4a. Click on **Buy Album**. You will be prompted to sign in by using your Apple ID and password.

OR

4b. Scroll the **track list** to the right and **click** on **Buy Song**.

TIP

To preview a 30-second clip of a track, double-click on the track. The clip will download and then play.

5. Enter your **Apple ID** and **Password**. They will appear in the dialog box.

6. Click on **Buy**. iTunes will prompt you to verify your purchase.

> **TIP**
>
> The first time you make a purchase from the iTunes Music Store, you will be prompted to review your account information. Click on the Review button and then follow the prompts that appear to complete the review and agree to terms and conditions. Then click on Buy Song when the iTunes Music Store redisplays the song you wanted to purchase.

7. Click on **Buy**. iTunes will transmit your purchase information and commence downloading the song (or album) to a subfolder for the artist created within the Music:iTunes:iTunes Music folder of your Home folder.

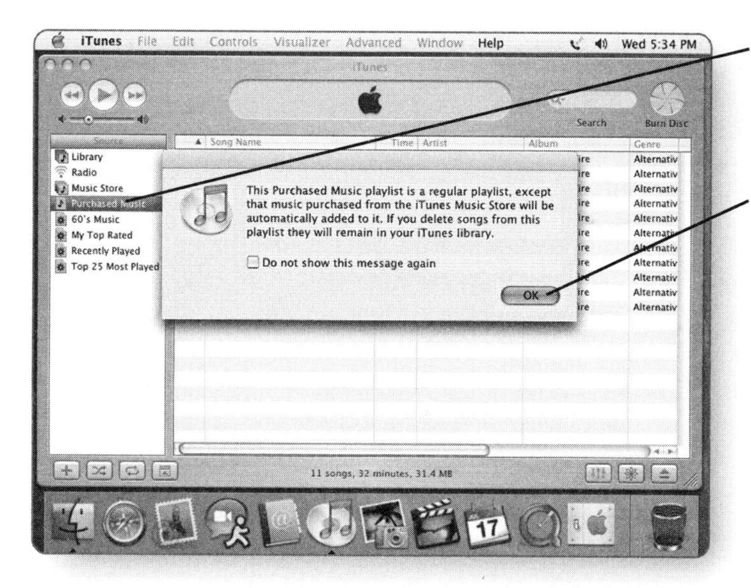

8. **Click** on **Purchased Music** in the Source list. A message box will appear.

9. **Click** on **OK**. (Check the Do not show this message again check box first, if you want to hide this message in the future.) The message box will close so that you can see your newly purchased song.

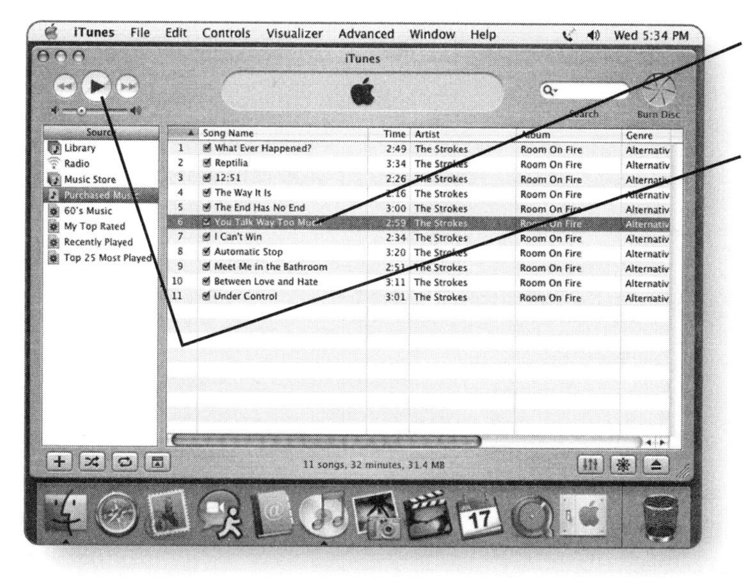

10. **Click** on a **new song**. A selection highlight will appear.

11. **Click** on the **Play button**. Your newly purchased song will play.

Building and Playing a Playlist

Most computers have a single CD-ROM or DVD-ROM drive, meaning you can play the contents of one audio CD at a time. When you've converted (or downloaded) and stored digital music files on your Mac's hard disk, you can mix and match songs from different sources as needed to develop your own playlist file. This gives you control over not only which songs play, but also how many songs play so that you don't have to swap CDs every hour or so. Follow these steps to build and play your own playlist of favorite songs:

1. **Click** on the **Create a playlist button.** A new playlist icon and file name will appear in the Source list at the left side of the iTunes window.

2. **Type** a **name** for the new playlist; then **press Return**. The new playlist name will appear in the Source list.

> **TIP**
>
> You also can open the File menu and then click on New Playlist to start a new playlist.

3. Click on **Library** in the Source list, if it isn't selected. The songs in your iTunes library will appear in the playlist area at the right.

4. Drag songs from the existing playlist onto the new playlist named in the Source list. As you release the mouse button to drop each song onto the new playlist, iTunes will add the song to the new playlist. Repeat this step, as needed, to build the new playlist.

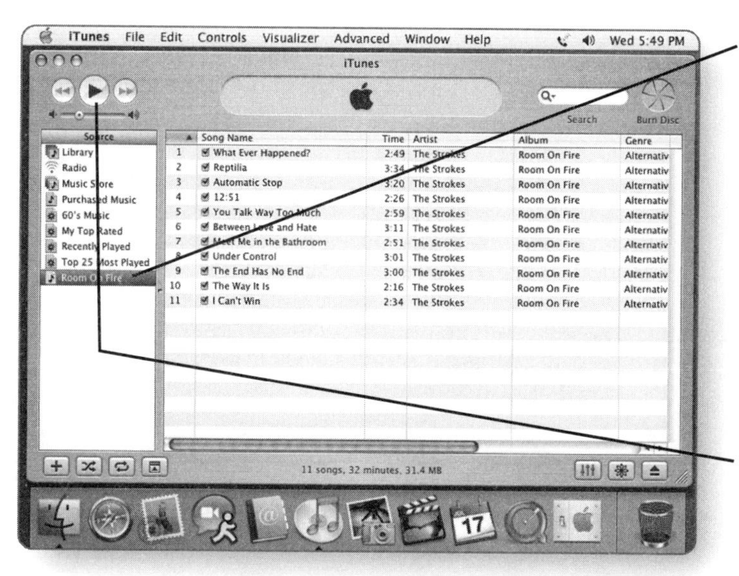

5. Click on the **playlist name** in the Source list. The playlist will be selected.

TIP

You can drag the songs in the playlist to change their order.

6. Click on the **Play button**. iTunes will play the playlist.

TIP

To delete a playlist, click on the playlist name in the Source list; then choose the Edit, Clear command. Click on Yes in the message box that appears to confirm the deletion.

Burning a CD-R of Your Tunes

If you have a CD-RW drive attached to your Mac, you can burn the contents of any playlist to a CD-R so you can take your music on the go. iTunes automatically converts the AAC or MP3 files to the AIFF format, so that your audio CD player need not have MP3 playback capability. (It does have to be able to play CD-Rs, however.)

1. Make sure the drive is connected and turned on; then **insert** a **blank CD-R** or **CD-RW** into the drive. The Finder will display a message dialog box prompting you to specify how you want to proceed with the inserted media.

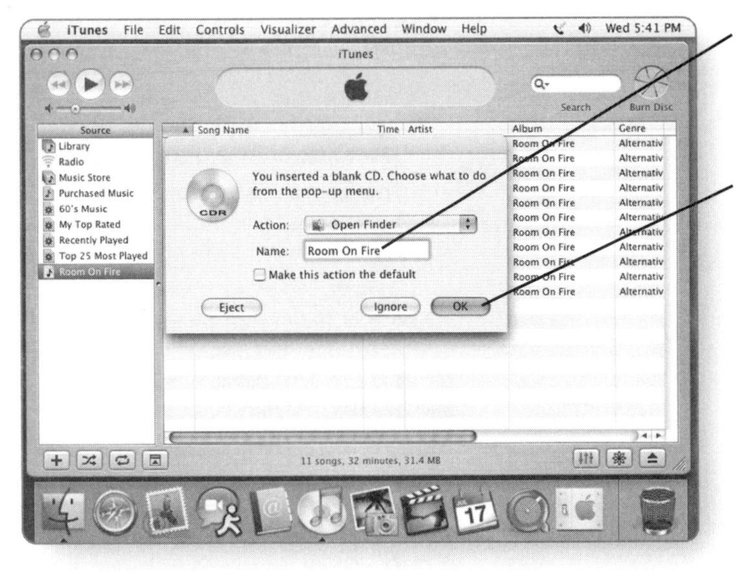

2. **Type** a **Name** for the CD. The name will appear in the dialog box.

3. **Click** on **OK**. Mac OS X will prepare the disk to receive files and will display an icon for the CD-R in the Finder window Sidebar.

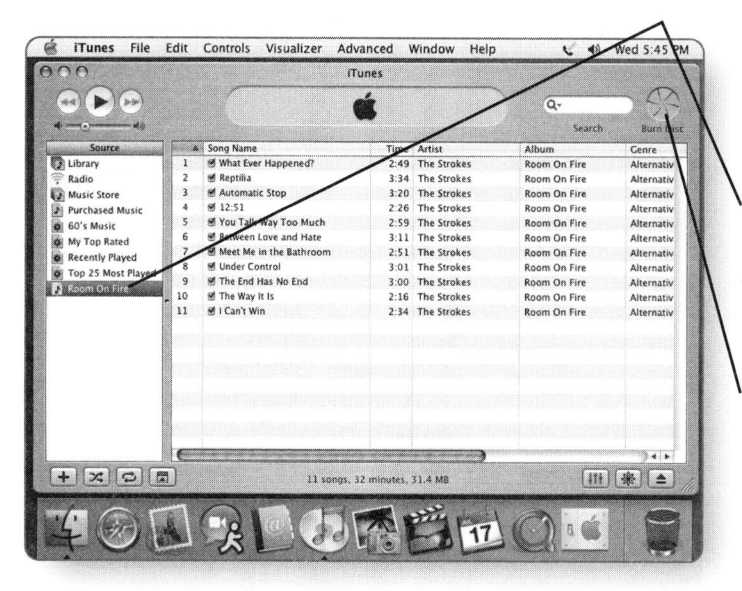

4. Click on **iTunes** in the Dock. The iTunes window will reappear.

5. Click on the **name of the playlist** to burn to CD-R in the Source list. The playlist will be selected.

6. Click on the **Burn Disc button.** The button will change in appearance, indicating the CD-R is ready.

7. Click on the **Burn Disc button** again. The small pane at the top center of the iTunes window will inform you of the burn progress. When the process finishes, an icon for the new CD-R will appear on the desktop.

8. Click on the **Eject button**. iTunes will eject the new disc.

TIP

You also can download your playlist to your iPod portable digital music player (or an MP3 Player). Connect the iPod to your Mac with its USB cable or dock, click on the player options button that appears at the bottom of the iTunes window, click on Manually manage songs and playlists, and click OK. Build the desired playlist in iTunes. Drag the playlist to the iPod icon in the Source list to complete the transfer. Click on the iPod icon in the source list and then click on the Eject button to disconnect it.

17

Managing Your Photos with iPhoto 2

Folks loved the original instant cameras from Polaroid. For the first time ever, they could see their pictures in minutes rather than days. Today's "instant cameras" are digital. With your digital camera, you not only see your pictures in an instant, but you also can use your computer to print, edit, publish, and otherwise share them in minutes. To handle all of these photo jobs, use iPhoto 2 in Mac OS X Version 10.3. In this chapter, you'll learn how to:

- Copy images from your camera with iPhoto.
- Create a photo album.
- Arrange and edit photos.
- Lay out a photo book.
- Print your photo book.
- Email, order prints, and otherwise share and view your photos.

Starting iPhoto and Importing Photos

Mac OS X Version 10.3 includes the iPhoto 2 application for importing, organizing, printing, and sharing your digital photos. Mac OS X Version 10.3 supports a number of digital cameras directly, but for others you may have to install the appropriate driver software. Connect the camera to your system via the USB or Firewire port and turn it on. iPhoto will recognize the camera and launch so that you can download images from the camera to any folder on your system. To verify whether Mac OS X Version 10.3 can work directly with your digital camera, visit the following page on Apple's Web site: *http://www.apple.com/macosx/upgrade/cameras.html*.

NOTE

Mac OS X Version 10.3 also includes the Image Capture application for downloading photos. You can specify whether to launch iPhoto or Image Capture when you attach your digital camera in Image Capture's preferences. The first time you load images in iPhoto, a dialog box appears to ask you to verify that you want iPhoto to launch automatically when a camera is attached. Click on Yes to have iPhoto launch automatically.

iPhoto also can import images from any disc attached to your system. That means you can import images already burned to a CD-R or stored on another system on your network. The following steps illustrate both how to import images from a digital camera and a folder on a disk.

1. **Connect** the **camera** to the system, **turn it on** or **plug in** its **power source**, and **switch** to its **playback** or **transfer mode**. iPhoto will launch.

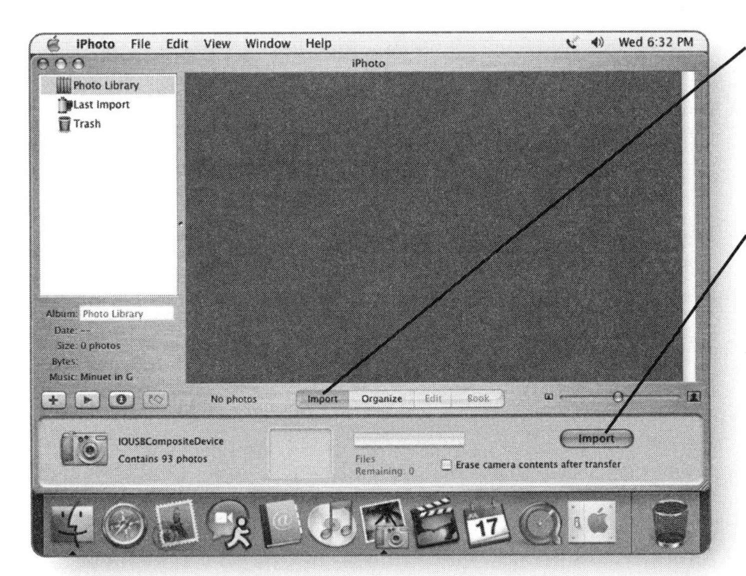

2. Click on **Import** in the bar of buttons for changing iPhoto panes. The Import pane will appear.

3. Click on the **Import command button** in the lower-right corner of the iPhoto window. iPhoto will import the image files from the camera's storage, add a thumbnail for each image into the iPhoto Photo Library, and switch to the Organize pane.

> **NOTE**
>
> iPhoto stores the actual imported image files in a subfolder it creates in the Pictures:iPhoto Library folder of your home folder.

4. Click on the **Minimize button** for the iPhoto window. iPhoto minimizes to an icon on the Dock.

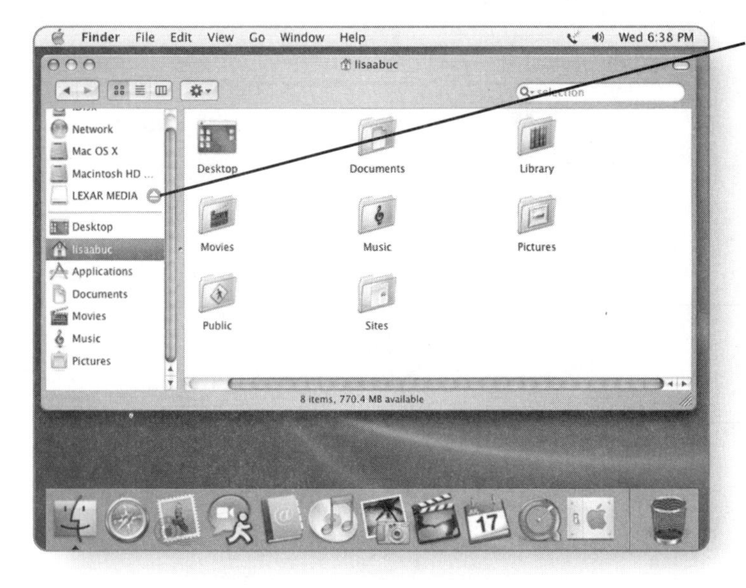

5. **Click** on the **Eject button** beside the storage media icon for your camera in a Finder window Sidebar. Mac OS X Version 10.3 will dismount (disconnect from) the disc, and its icon will disappear. You may now turn off and disconnect the camera.

> **CAUTION**
>
> Turning off and disconnecting the camera without first dismounting its media can damage the media. You also should click on the Stop button in iPhoto before disconnecting the camera if iPhoto has not yet finished importing images.

6. **Click** on the **iPhoto window icon** on the Dock. The iPhoto window will maximize so you can continue working.

7. **Click** on **File**. The File menu will appear.

8. **Click** on **Import**. The Import Photos dialog box will appear.

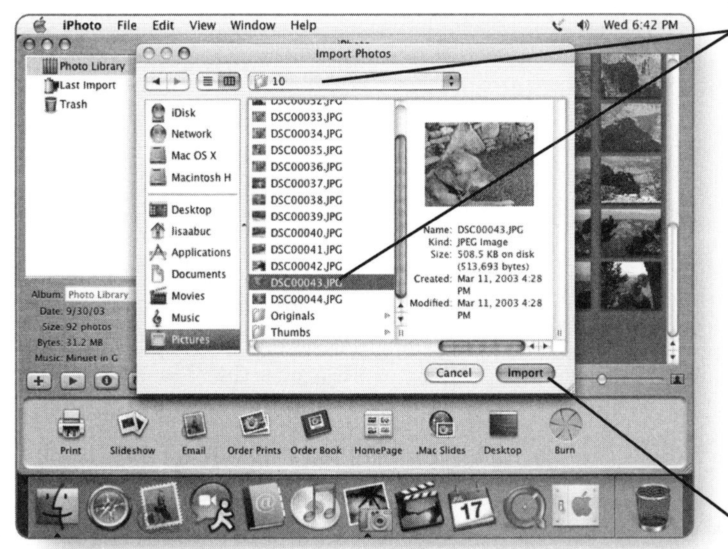

9. **Navigate** to the **disk** and **folder** that holds the photos to import and then **click** on the **photo** to import. Its preview will appear.

> **TIP**
>
> ⌘+click on multiple photos to select them for import.

10. **Click** on **Import**. Again, iPhoto adds the photo thumbnail into the Photo Library, and copies the image file to your Mac's hard disk.

Creating an Album

Over time, your photo library will grow to dozens—if not hundreds—of photos. iPhoto enables you to organize photos from the library into individual albums. Each album can hold a collection of photos with a particular theme, or simply a selection of photos that you want to print or share at a particular time.

1. **Click** on the **Add button** near the lower-left corner of the iPhoto window. The New Album dialog box will open.

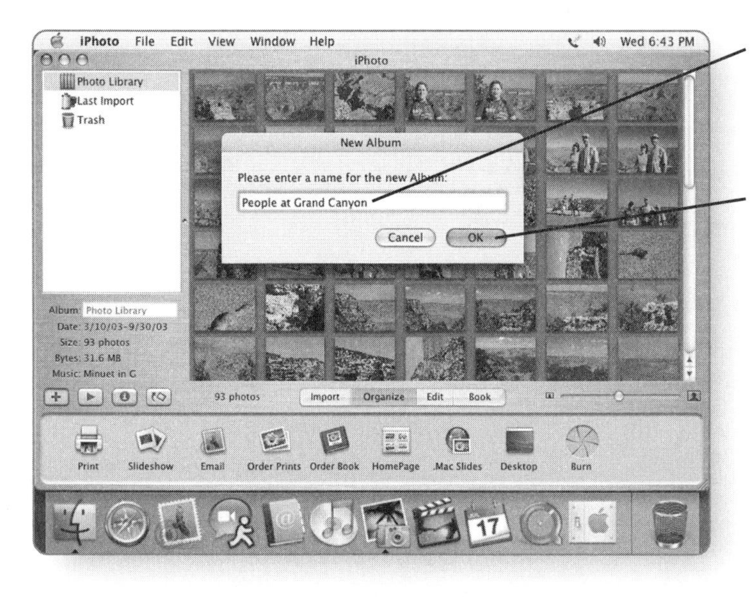

2. **Type** a **name** for the new album. It will appear in the dialog box.

3. **Click** on **OK**. The new album will appear in the list at the left side of the iPhoto window.

4. **Leave Photo Library selected** in the list at the left and **drag images** from the library onto the new album. Each time you release the mouse button, the photo(s) you dragged will be copied to the album.

> **CAUTION**
>
> Make sure the black selection marquee appears around the name of the desired album, not the whole list at the left, before you release the mouse button. Otherwise, your photo won't copy to the album.

Labeling and Organizing Photos

By default, iPhoto sorts photos in each new album according to the date when they were taken, and each photo is labeled with its file name. You can adjust the order of the pictures in the album, change each picture's title, and even add a comment for each picture.

> **NOTE**
>
> If needed, click on the Organize button to switch to the Organize pane before starting this operation.

1. **Click** on the **album** in the list at the left. The photos in the album will appear in the right pane.

2. **Drag photos** to alternate positions. As you drag, a vertical black bar will appear. Release the mouse button, and the photo will move to the bar's position.

> **TIP**
>
> You also can use the choices on the Edit, Arrange Photos submenu to sort the album contents by film roll (import) or date.

3. **Click** on the **photo** to label. A blue selection marquee will appear around the photo.

4. **Click** on the **Show Information about the Selected Photos button**. The information area in the lower-left corner of the iPhoto window will expand to include a comments text box.

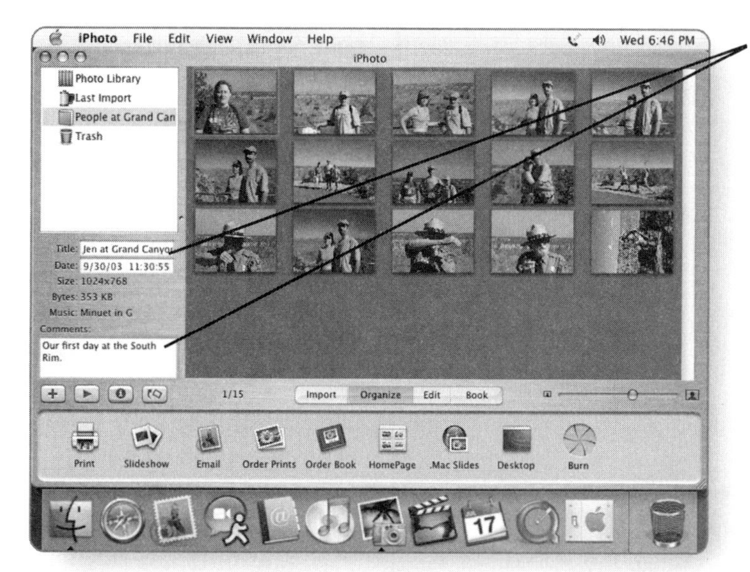

5. Edit the **Title** and **Date** and **enter Comments**. The information will appear and will be used by iPhoto to identify (or sort) the photos.

> **NOTE**
>
> You also can use the Commands on the Edit, Set Title To submenu to enter photo titles automatically. Albums enable you to make a book to print your images. Add comments so you can include them in the book to describe each photo in more detail.

Editing a Photo

While iPhoto isn't a full-fledged image editor like Adobe Photoshop, it does enable you to make some basic changes to the images in an album. For example, you may need to rotate pictures if you shot them in a portrait (tall) orientation with your digital camera. Or you may want to crop an image to eliminate extraneous content.

1. Click on the **album** in the list at the left. The photos in the album will appear in the right pane.

2. Click on the **photo to rotate** in the album. A blue selection marquee will appear around the photo.

3. Click on the **Rotate the Selected Photos button**. Each time you click, iPhoto will rotate the photo 90 degrees counter-clockwise.

4. After rotating photos as needed, **click** on the **photo to edit** in the album. A blue selection marquee will appear around the photo.

5. Click on the **Edit button**. The Edit pane will appear and display the selected photo.

6. **Drag** on the **photo**. The area to crop or correct will be selected.

7. **Click** an **editing button,** such as the crop button. Your change will be applied.

8. **Click** on **Next**. Other photos will appear so that you can make changes.

> **NOTE**
>
> You need not make a selection to adjust its brightness or contrast. Just display the photo in the Edit pane and then drag the Brightness/Contrast sliders.

Creating a Picture Book

By formatting your images as a picture book, iPhoto enables you to control the layout of printed pictures and share those pictures in a number of ways. By default, the Picture Book format is applied to each album. You can choose an alternate album format, control the number of pictures per page, and control the information that appears on each page.

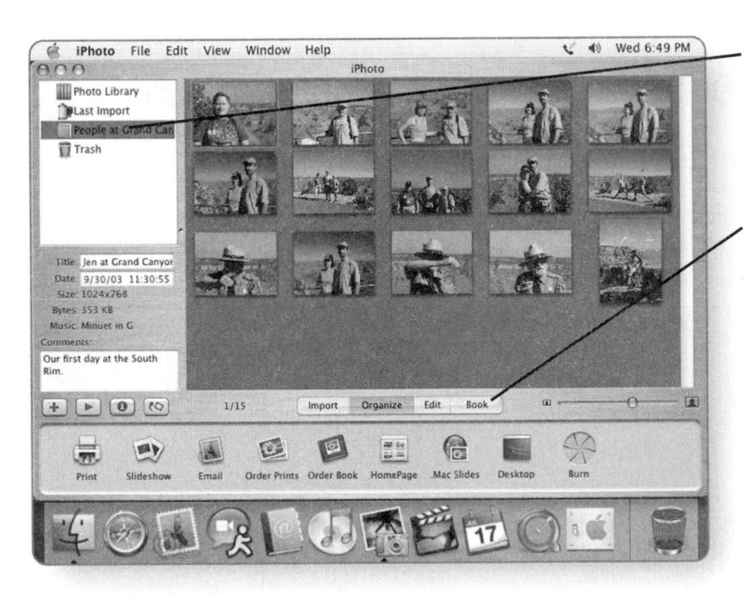

1. **Click** on the **album** in the list at the left. The photos in the album will appear in the right pane.

2. **Click** on the **Book button**. The Book pane will appear.

> **NOTE**
>
> A small exclamation mark indicator on a page in the Book pane means that the image has a relatively low resolution and may not print as clearly as other images. You can include more images on the page to alleviate this issue.

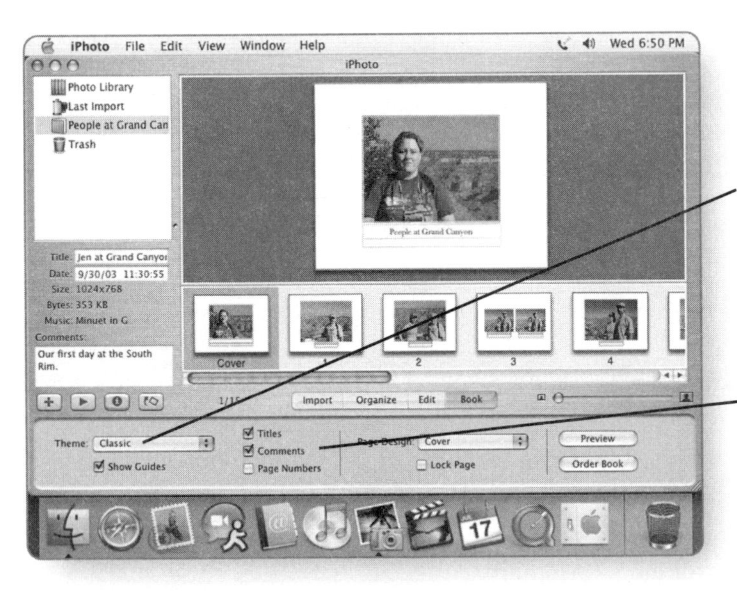

3. **Choose another theme** from the Theme pop-up menu. The layout of the book changes will change, based on the selected theme.

4. **Click** on the **Titles, Comments,** or **Page Numbers check boxes**. When a checkbox is checked, iPhoto will include the specified information on each book page.

> **TIP**
>
> Click on a text placeholder for the page shown to edit or change the text in it.

5. Scroll and **click** on a **page thumbnail**. The page will appear in the work area above the thumbnails.

6. Choose another page design from the Page Design pop-up menu. The layout of the page will change, based on the selected theme.

> **NOTE**
>
> The first page must always use the Cover page design. If you don't really want a cover page in a book printout, add a dummy photo and make it the first photo in your album. The Introduction Page design hides the photo and displays a large text placeholder so you can enter introductory text for your book.

Printing a Book

After you've created your book masterpiece, you can print it to share with others. Printing in iPhoto works a little differently than in some other applications, as you'll see next.

1. With the Book pane still displayed, **click** on **File**. The File menu will appear.

2. **Click** on **Print**. The Print dialog box will open.

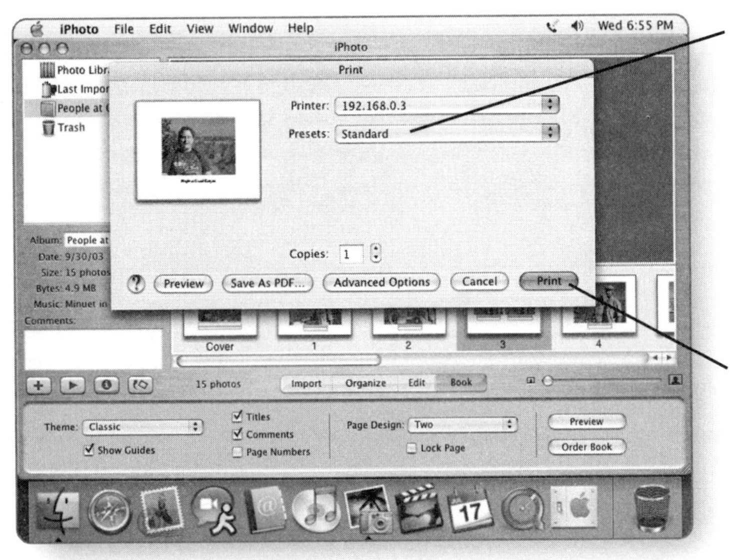

3. **Choose print settings. Click** on the **Advanced Options button** to see additional print settings. They will become the active settings. (See Chapter 10, "Working with Printers, Faxes, and Fonts," if you need help with print settings.)

4. **Click** on **Print**. Mac OS X Version 10.3 will send the book to your printer.

Choosing Another Publishing Method

In addition to printing your book of photos on your own printer, you can share or display the pictures in an album in a variety of ways. Start out by clicking on the desired album and then selecting one or more photos to share. (Use Shift+click or ⌘+click to select specific pictures within the album.) Then click on Organize and choose one of the sharing methods listed in the following table by clicking on its icon.

> **NOTE**
>
> Some of the sharing methods will require an Internet connection, so use Internet Connect to dial your Internet connection first, if needed. Some options also require an Apple ID or .Mac account.

Icon	Name	Description
	Print	Prints selected album (or selected images in the album).
	Slideshow	Displays your images as an on-screen slide show. You can select background music for the show and control how long each slide appears.
	Email	Resizes the selected images to 640 × 480, launches Mail, and inserts the images into a new, blank email message.
	Order Prints	Orders prints of the selected images via the Internet from the Kodak Print Service.

Continued

Icon	Name	Description
	Order Book	Assembles the book by using current template and settings, and enables you to order a bound copy of the book online via the Order Book service. (Note that the smallest book size is 10 pages, and you must have an Apple ID to Create a 1-Click account for ordering.)
	HomePage	Selects up to 48 images in the album. Creates a home page from them, specifying the text and design you want, and then publish them as your .Mac home page. (Requires .Mac account; your home page can be found at *http://homepage.mac.com/membername/Personal1.htm*.)
	.Mac Slides	Creates a slideshow by using your .Mac account; you can then select the slideshow as the Mac OS X screen saver.
	Desktop	Displays the selected image on the desktop.
	Burn	Burns the selected album or images to a CD-R.

18

Managing Your Movies with iMovie 3

Editing video used to be a job for the pros only. It required tens of thousands of dollars' worth of equipment, as well as a significant amount of technical expertise. Not so anymore. With the iMovie 3 application in Mac OS X Version 10.3 and your digital video camera, you can create great productions right in your home. In this chapter, you'll learn how to:

- Start a new movie project.
- Capture movie clips in iPhoto.
- Build a movie.
- Choose transitions between clips.
- Add titles and effects.
- Work with sound.
- Export the finished movie.

Starting iMovie and Creating a Project

When you work with iPhoto, you create each movie as a project file and then export the project to a finished movie file. This gives you the opportunity to go back to the project and make additional changes when you don't like how the movie turned out. So, to get started, launch iMovie and create a project file.

> **NOTE**
>
> Your Mac's screen resolution must be set to 1024 x 768 or better to use iMovie. If it isn't, iMovie will prompt you to change the resolution. Do so using the Displays pane of System Preferences, as described in Chapter 9, "Changing Essential System Preferences."

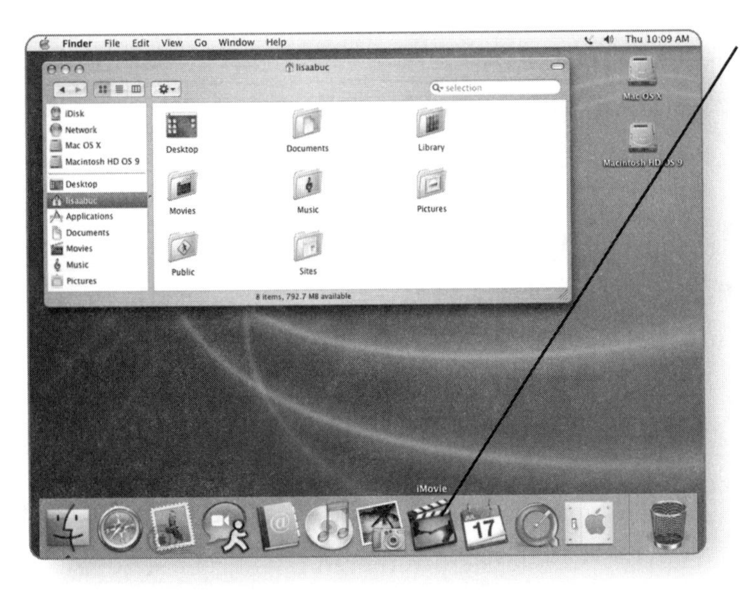

1. **Click** on the **iMovie icon** on the Dock. The iMovie application window and menu bar will appear with a dialog box prompting you to start a new project. (If you were working on a project previously, it will open automatically.)

2. **Click** on **Create Project**. A sheet for creating the project will appear.

> **NOTE**
>
> To create a new project when you've already been working in iMovie, choose File, New Project.

3. **Type** a **name** for the new project. The name will appear in the Save As text box.

4. **Click** on **Save.** iMovie creates the new project file. By default, it creates a new folder for each project within the Movies folder of your Home folder.

> **TIP**
>
> Starting iMovie may turn on automatic hiding for the Dock, to give you more room to work with the clip viewer at the bottom of iMovie.

Capturing Movie Clips

Mac OS X Version 10.3 supports a number of digital camcorders directly, but for others you may have to install the appropriate driver software. To verify whether Mac OS X Version 10.3 can work directly with your digital camera, visit the following page on Apple's Web site: *http://www.apple.com/macosx/upgrade/camcorders.html.*

Connect the camera to your system via the Firewire port and turn it on. iMovie will recognize the camcorder. You can then start the camcorder's playback or VCR feature to start capturing clips.

NOTE

iMovie also can import QuickTime video clips, clips you've previously captured, and images from any disk attached to your system. Choose File, Import File and select the image to import. It appears as a clip in the clip inspector pane in the upper-right area of iMovie.

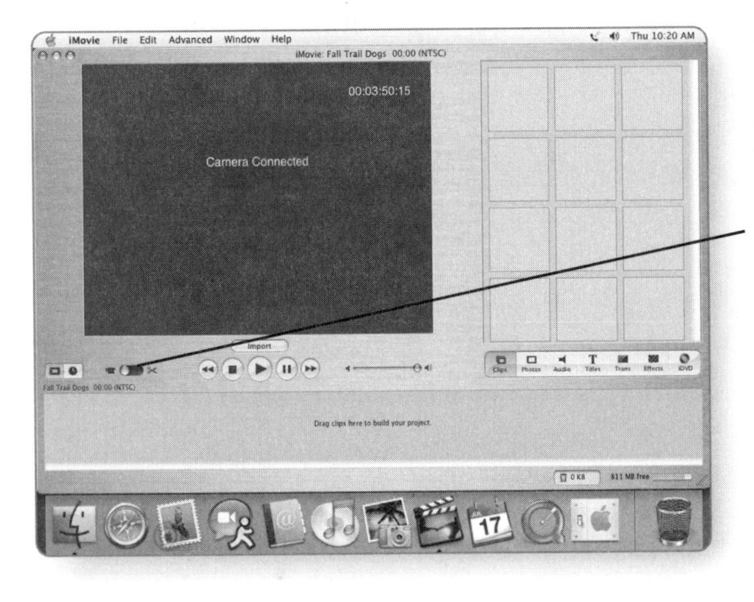

1. **Connect** the **camcorder** to the system, **turn it on** or **plug in** its **power source**, and **switch** to its **playback** or **VCR mode.**

2. **Drag** the **Mode Switch to Camera Mode.** A Camera Connected message will appear in the iMovie monitor.

3. **Rewind** the **tape** in the camcorder if needed and then **press** the **Play button** to start playing the video from the camera. The video will appear onscreen in iMovie.

4. When you see the section you want to import, **click** on **Import** in the monitor. iMovie will start capturing the clip.

5. Click on the **Import button** again to stop Importing. The new clip will appear in the clip inspector.

6. Repeat Steps 4 and 5 as needed to add clips to the project. The clips will appear in the clip inspector. You can then stop the camera playback and disconnect the camera.

> **TIP**
>
> Use the File, Save Project command periodically to save your ongoing changes.

Organizing Clips into a Movie

After you've captured all the clips you want, you can sequence them in the proper order for your movie. You do so by dragging clips from the clip inspector to the desired location on the clip viewer.

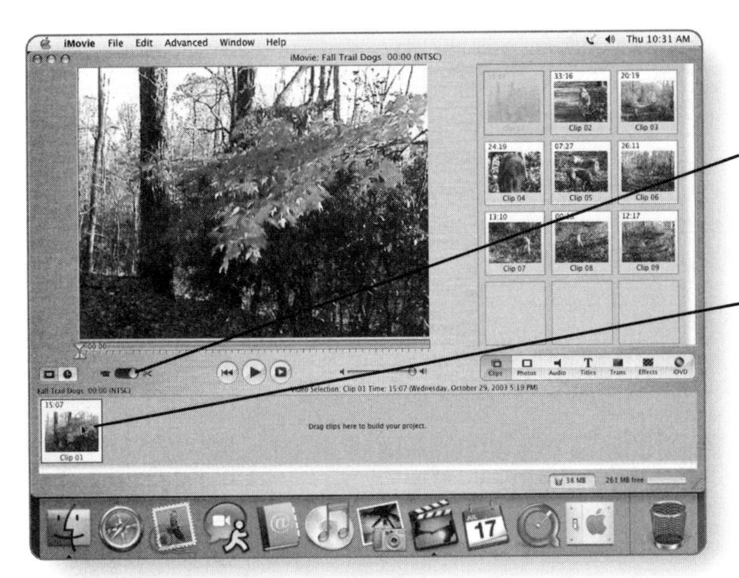

1. **Drag** the **Mode Switch to Clip Mode**. The monitor will change to a black screen.
2. **Drag** the **clips** from the clip inspector to the clip viewer. When you release the mouse button, the clip you're dragging will move to the clip viewer.

3. To rename any clip, **click** on **its name**, **edit** the **name**, and **press Return**. The new name will appear.

4. To reposition any clip, **drag** it on the **clip viewer**. The clip will move to the new location.

> **TIP**
>
> You can select a clip and use the Copy and Paste commands on the Edit menu to duplicate a selected clip.

Adding Transitions

Adding transitions really lends a professional effect to your movies. A transition eliminates an abrupt change between clips, substituting gentler fading or dissolving instead.

1. Click on the **Trans button** in the clip inspector. The available transitions will appear there.

2. Click on the **desired transition**. A preview of the transition will play.

3. Drag the **desired transition** from the clip inspector to the appropriate location (such as to the left of a clip when you want to apply the transition to the beginning of the clip) on the clip viewer. A preview of the transition will play.

Adding Titles

While your movie may include great audio, explanatory titles sometimes provide a nice courtesy for the viewer, or a way to inject additional humor and fun into your movie.

1. Click on the **clip** for which you want to add a title in the clip viewer. The clip will be selected.

2. Click on the **Titles button** in the clip inspector. The title settings will appear there.

3. Choose desired settings for the title. They will become active.

4. Type the **titles** in the text boxes at the bottom of the clip inspector. The titles will appear there.

5. Click on **Preview**. The monitor will play the selected clip with titles, so you can make additional formatting changes, if required.

6. Drag the **selected title type** from the list in clip inspector to the location just to the left of the desired clip on the clip viewer. iMovie will render the title and add it to the clip.

> **TIP**
>
> You also can add a video effect or additional sounds to your movie. Select a clip, click on Effects in the clip inspector, choose the desired effect settings, and click apply. iMovie applies the effect to the clip, but does not alter the original video. So you can use the Restore Clip button later to remove the effect. Click on Audio in the clip inspector to select a sound to add to a clip or to record voice or music.

Exporting the Finished Movie

You can click the play button in the monitor to preview a selected clip. After you've gotten your movie in order, it's time to export the finished video file.

1. **Click** on **File**. The File menu will appear.
2. **Click** on **Export**. The iMovie Export dialog box will appear.

3. **Click** on the **Export pop-up menu** and then **click** on **To QuickTime**. The dialog box will display the options for QuickTime Export.

4. **Click** on the **Formats pop-up menu** and then **click** on the **desired format**. The desired format will appear.

5. **Click** on **Export**. A saving sheet will appear.

TIP

The Formats pop-up menu offers formats optimized for the Web, email, streaming video, and full quality video, as wells as an Expert Settings choice that you can use to specify settings in greater detail.

6. **Type** a **name** for the movie. The name will appear in the Save As text box. Optionally, also specify a save location using the Where drop-down list.

7. **Click** on **Save**. iMovie will render the finished movie and place it in the Movies folder of your Home folder unless you specified otherwise. Depending on the length of your movie, this process may take several minutes.

Part V Review Questions

1. How do I create my own digital music files? *See "Making Digital Files and Adding Them To Your Library" in Chapter 16.*
2. How do I buy music online? *See "Buying Music from the iTunes Music Store" in Chapter 16.*
3. How can I group my favorite songs together? *See "Building and Playing a Playlist" in Chapter 16.*
4. Can I create my own music CD? *See "Burning a CD-R of Your Tunes" in Chapter 16.*
5. How do I transfer photos from my digital camera to my computer? *See "Starting iPhoto and Importing Photos" in Chapter 17.*
6. What changes can I make to photos? *See "Creating an Album" in Chapter 17.*
7. How do I arrange and print photos? *See "Creating a Picture Book" and "Printing a Book" in Chapter 17.*
8. How do I get started editing movies? *See "Capturing Movie Clips" in Chapter 18.*
9. How do I build a movie from my clips? *See "Organizing Clips Into a Movie" in Chapter 18.*
10. What kind of movie formats can I export? *See "Exporting the Finished Movie" in Chapter 18.*

PART VI

Managing Your Life

19

Getting Organized with iCal and iSync

As if handling your music, digital photos, and movies isn't enough, Mac OS X Version 10.3 includes the iCal 1.5.1 application to enable you to manage your schedule, and the iSync 1.2.1 application to synchronize your schedule between multiple locations. I think I'm feeling more organized already. If you use this chapter and Mac OS X's tools to get a handle on your tasks and events, you'll learn how to:

- Start and exit iCal.
- Create and select your calendar.
- Add events and to dos.
- Change the calendar view.
- Synchronize a calendar with iSync.
- Publish a calendar with .Mac.

Starting and Quitting iCal

Apple first introduced iCal as a free, stand-alone application. However, to make Mac OS X a full-fledged business and productivity environment, Apple soon saw the wisdom of including iCal in the Panther release of Mac OS X. When you need to work with iCal and then later finish working with your calendar, follow these steps:

1. **Click** on the **iCal icon** on the Dock. The iCal program will open, and its menu and window will appear onscreen.

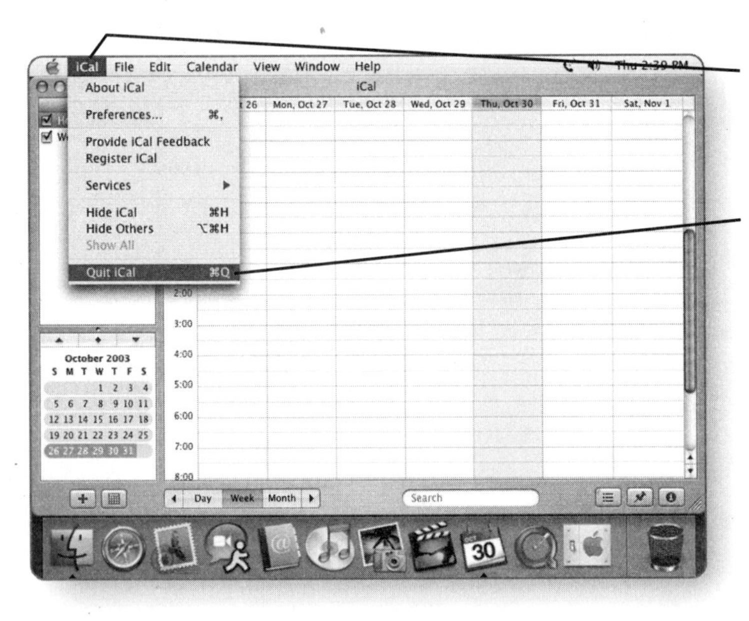

2. When you're ready to quit iCal, **click** on **iCal**. The iTunes menu will appear.

3. **Click** on **Quit iCal**. iCal will close.

Working with Calendars

Unlike some other scheduling applications, iCal actually enables you to track multiple calendars of information. For example, you could create a homework and activity calendar for each of your kids, or work, leisure, and medical calendars for you and your spouse. iCal gives you the total flexibility to create a calendar for any purpose that suits your planning needs.

Creating a Calendar

When you determine you need to create a new calendar, follow these steps to do so:

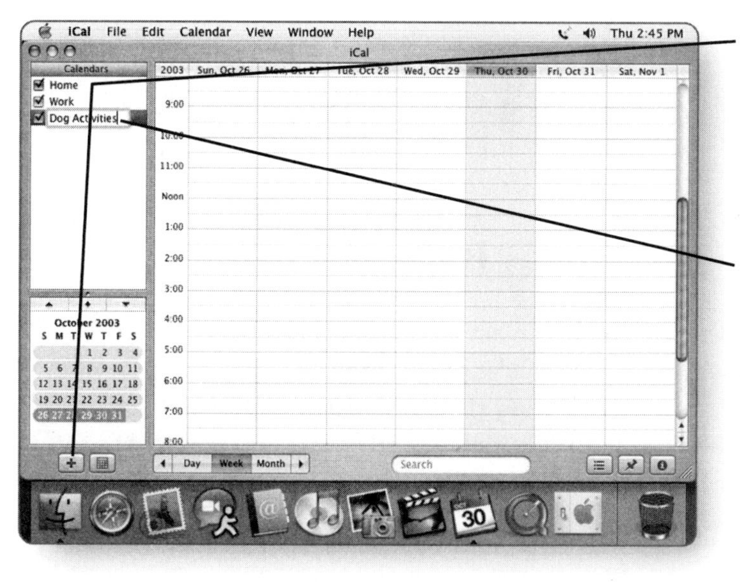

1. **Click** on the **Add a New Calendar (+) button**. (Or choose File, New Calendar). The new calendar will appear in the Calendars list.

2. **Type** a **name** for the calendar and **press Return**. The new calendar will be added to the Calendars list.

Choosing a Calendar

Use the Calendars list to choose the calendar to work with at any time.

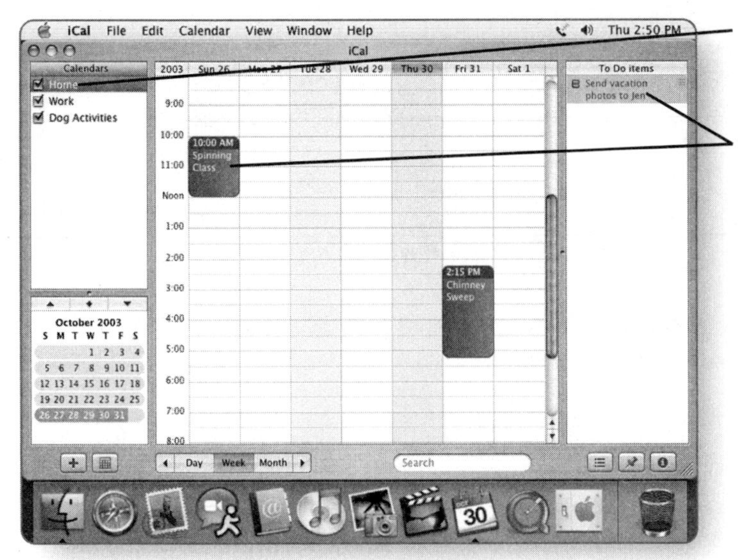

Click on the calendar to use in the Calendars list.

The events and to dos for that calendar will appear.

Notice that iCal automatically color-codes each calendar. The calendar name, as well as the events and to dos that it contains, all use the same color, such as blue or red. This helps you distinguish at a glance which calendar a particular event or to do list belongs to.

Scheduling Items

In iCal, an event is an action or activity that you need to schedule for a particular period of time, unlike a to do, which may be completed any time before a particular deadline. iCal makes it exceedingly easy to add new events and to dos to any calendar.

Adding an Event

You can add an event to the selected calendar for any future time, as follows:

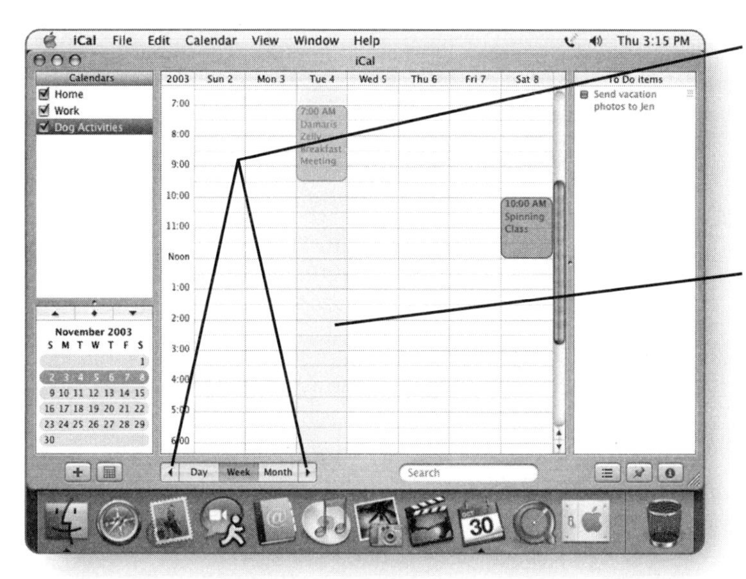

1. Click on the **Go back** or **Go forward buttons**. The date for which you want to add the event will appear in the calendar.

2. Double-click on the **event time** in the calendar. A new event will appear.

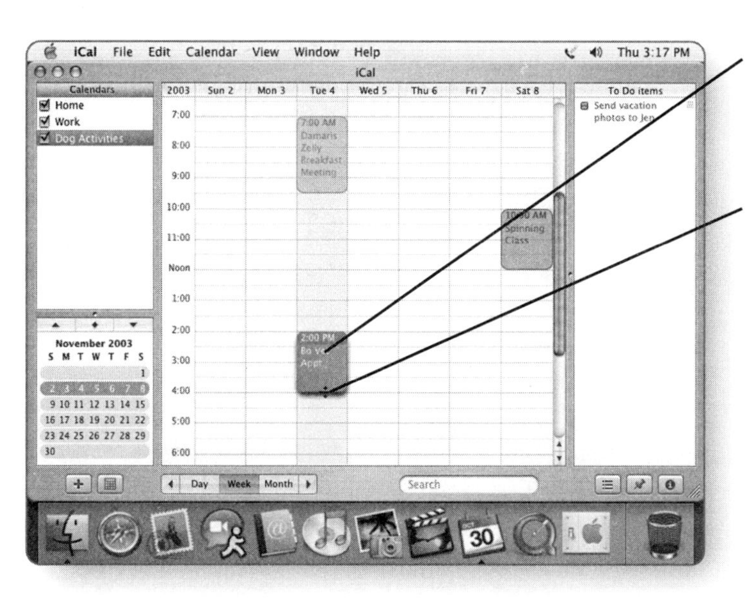

3. Type the **event name** and **press Return**. The event will be added to the calendar.

4. Drag the **top** or **bottom border** of the event. The starting or ending time for the event will be updated.

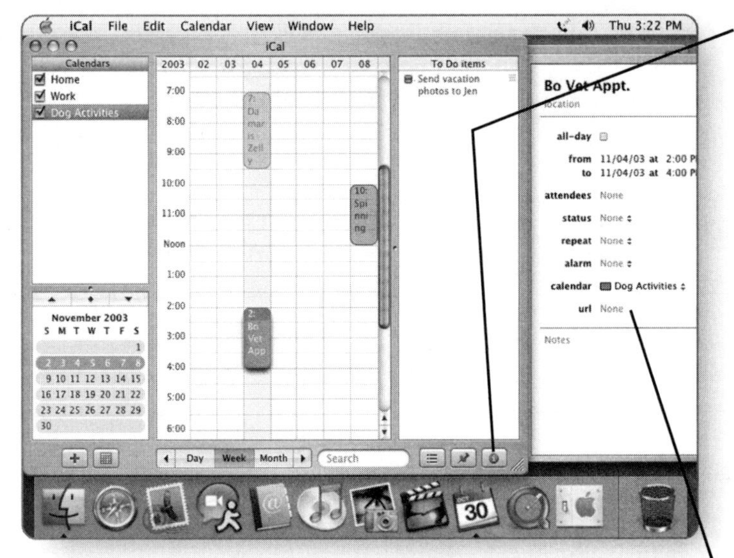

5. Click on the **event** to reselect it and then **click** on the **Show info button**. The info drawer or pane will appear at the right side of the iCal window.

> **TIP**
>
> If the info drawer doesn't appear, click on the green zoom button in the upper-left corner of the iCal window.

6. Specify other event settings. For example, **click** the **all-day check box** to mark an event as an all-day event, **use** the **repeat pop-up menu** to create a repeating event, or **use** the **alarm pop-up menu** to add an alarm for the event. The event will be updated.

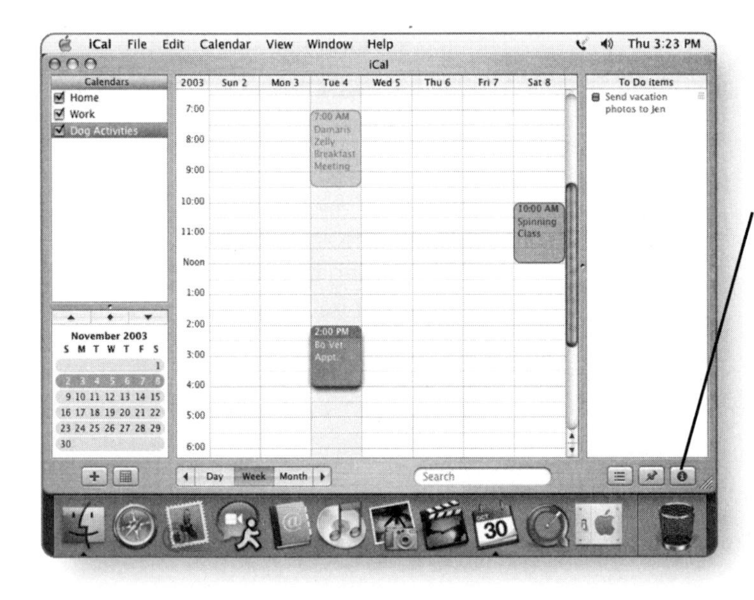

7. Click on the **Show info button** again. The info drawer or pane will close.

> **TIP**
>
> ⌘+click on an event or to do and then click on Cut to delete it.

Adding a To Do

iCal offers just as much ease and flexibility for building your list of to dos. Use these steps to add a to do to the selected calendar:

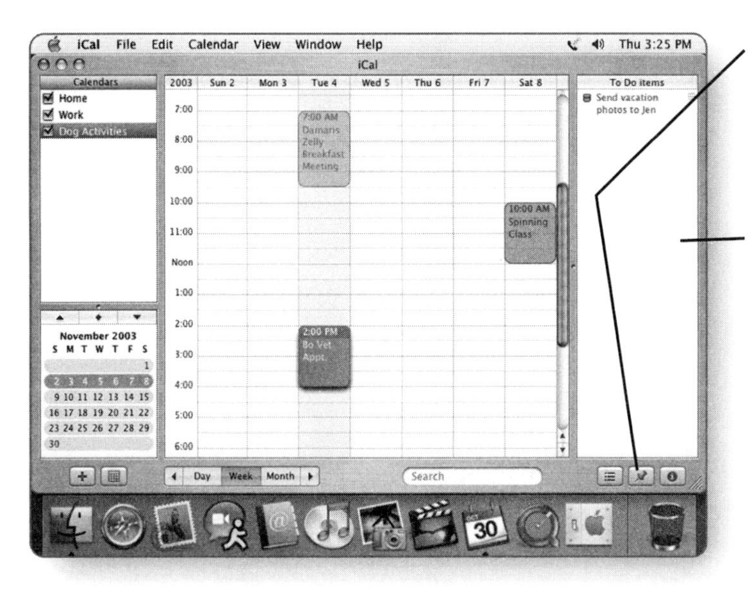

1. **Click** on the **Show or Hide the To Do List button** if the To Do items list isn't visible. The list will appear.

2. **Double-click** on the **To Do items list**. A new to do will appear.

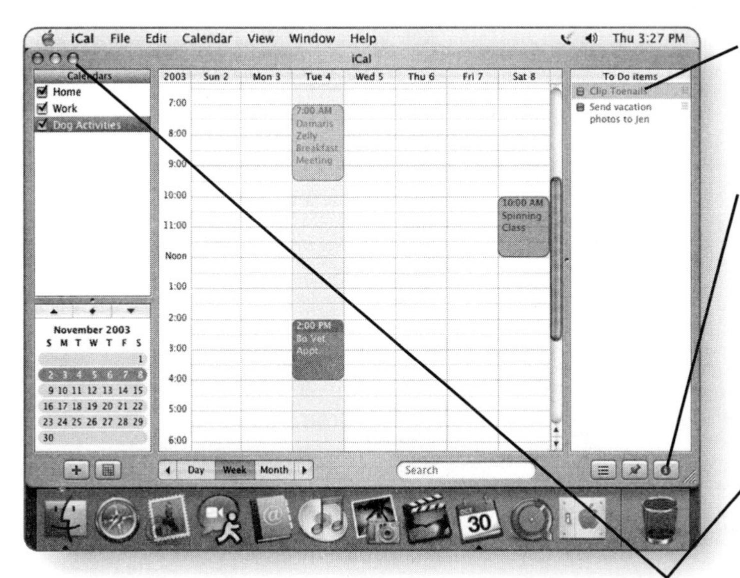

3. **Type** the **to do name** and **press Return**. The to do will be added to the list.

4. **Click** on the **Show Info button**. The info drawer or pane will appear at the right side of the iCal window.

> **TIP**
>
> If the info drawer doesn't appear, click on the green zoom button in the upper-left corner of the iCal window.

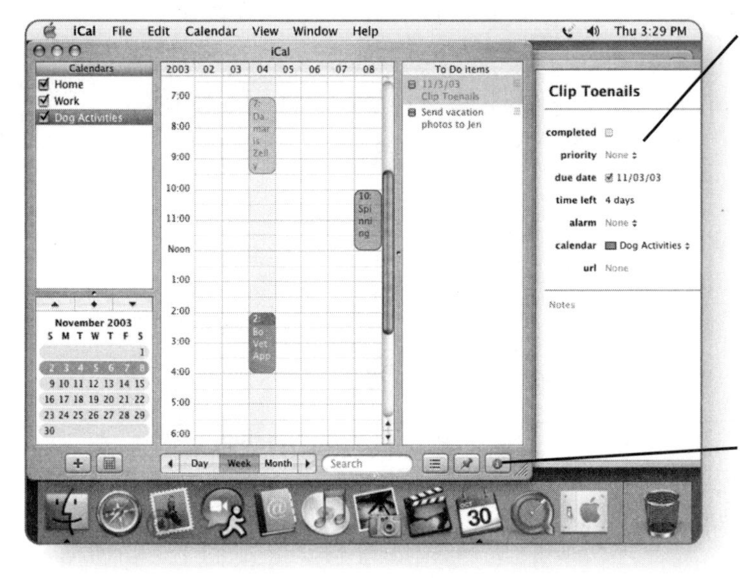

5. **Specify other event settings,** as needed. For example, use the priority pop-up menu to set a priority, check the due date check box and enter a due date, and so on. (Of course, use the completed check box to mark a to do as finished.) The to do will be updated.

6. **Click** on the **Show info button** again. The info drawer or pane will close.

Changing the View

iCal offers three different views for working with your calendar: Day view, Week view, or Month view. You can use one of two methods to choose another view:

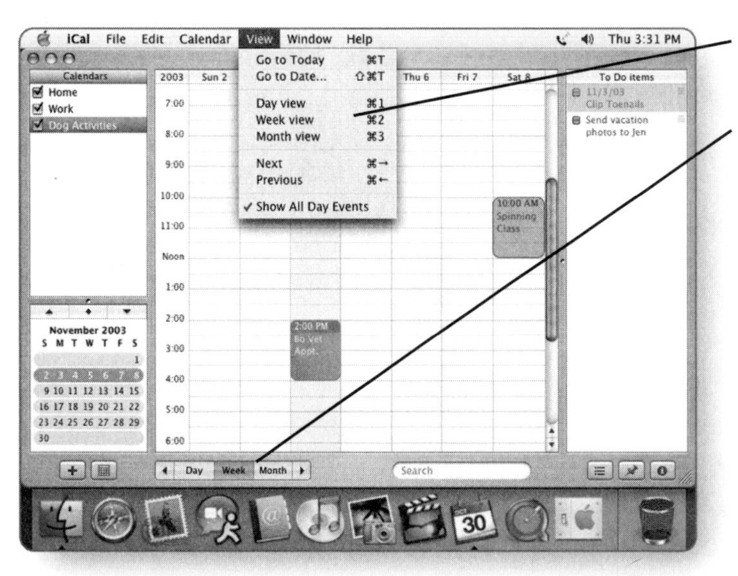

- Choose the desired view from the View menu.
- Click on the button for the desired view at the bottom of the iCal window.

> **TIP**
>
> Use the Go to Today command on the View menu to display the current date in the calendar. Use the Go to Date command to specify the date you want to see.

In addition, you can click on the Show or hide the mini-month button to display or hide the monthly calendar below the Calendar's list.

Synching a Calendar

You can use iSync 1.2.1 to synchronize your iCal calendar with another computer or with a device such as a mobile phone or iPod. For the process to work, both computers must have iCal and iSync installed. In addition, a device like an iPod must have its Calendar feature enabled. (If you're using a newer iPod, choose Settings from the iPod menu, Main Menu from the next menu, and then choose Calendar to enable the calendar. The Calendar choice will then appear on the iPod menu.)

While your specific steps for synching will vary depending on what you're synching, the following steps show an example of synching your iCal calendar with an iPod. iCal need not be running when you start these steps:

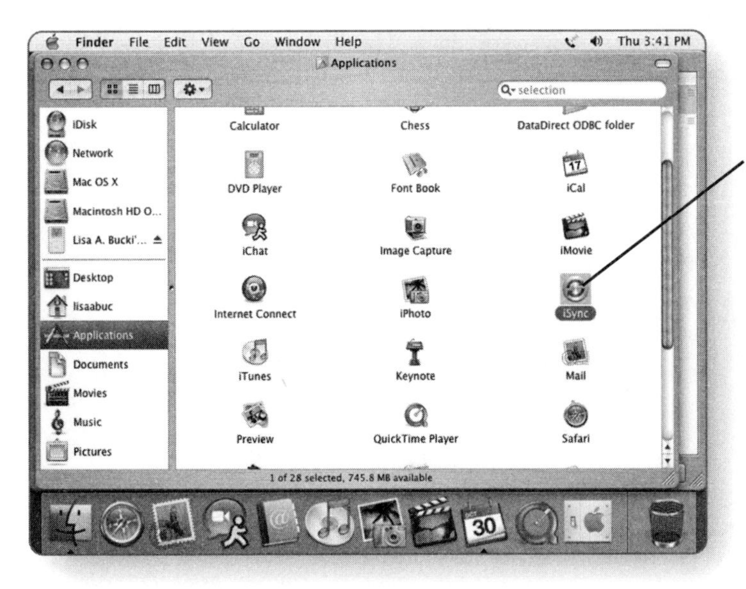

1. **Connect** your **iPod** via its cable or cradle. It will power up.

2. **Double-click** on the **iSync icon** in the Applications folder. iSync will start. (If iTunes starts, you can quit the iTunes application.)

3. **Click** on **Devices**. The Devices menu will open.

4. **Click** on **Add Device**. The Add Device window will appear, listing your device as a found device.

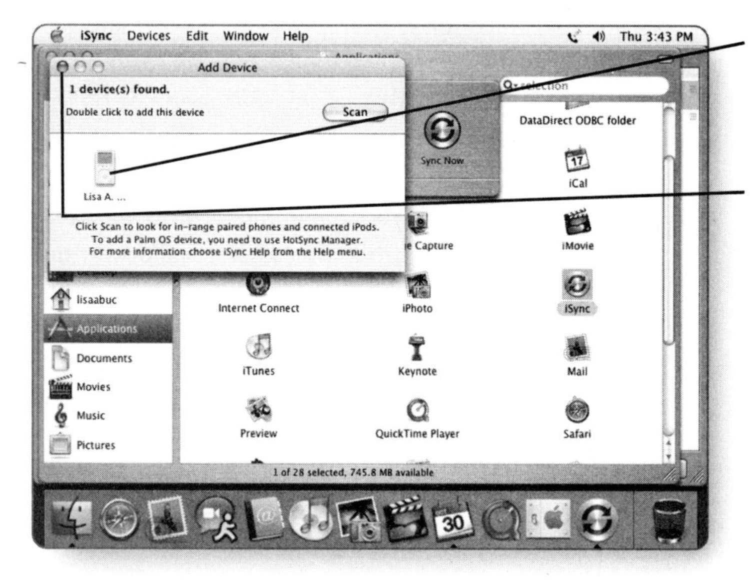

5. **Double-click** on **your device**. The device will be added to iSync.

6. **Click** on the **Add Device window Close button.** The window will close. The iSync window will show a list of synchronization settings.

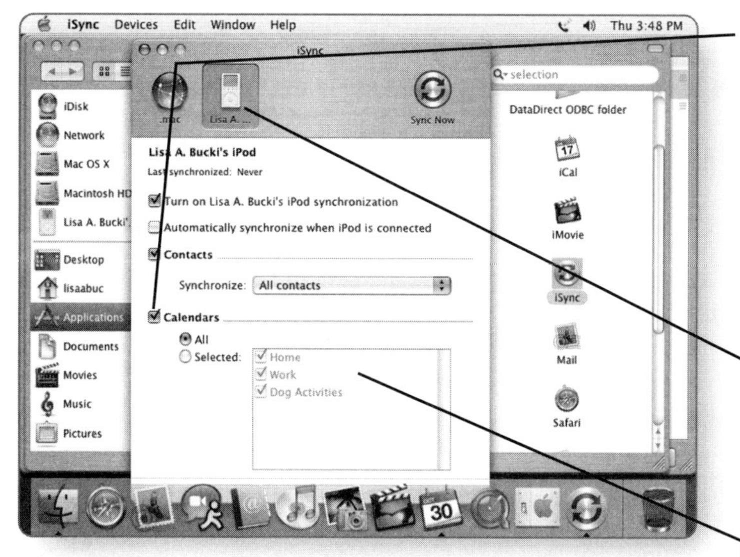

7. With the device icon selected at the top of the iSync window, make sure to **check** the **Calendars check box**. iSync will then be able to synchronize iCal information.

TIP

- For future synch operations, click on the device icon at the top of the iSync window to display the sync settings.
- Use the All or Selected option buttons to control which calendars to synchronize.

8. **Click** on **Devices**. The Devices menu will open.

9. **Click** on **Sync Now**. iSync will update the calendar information on the device.

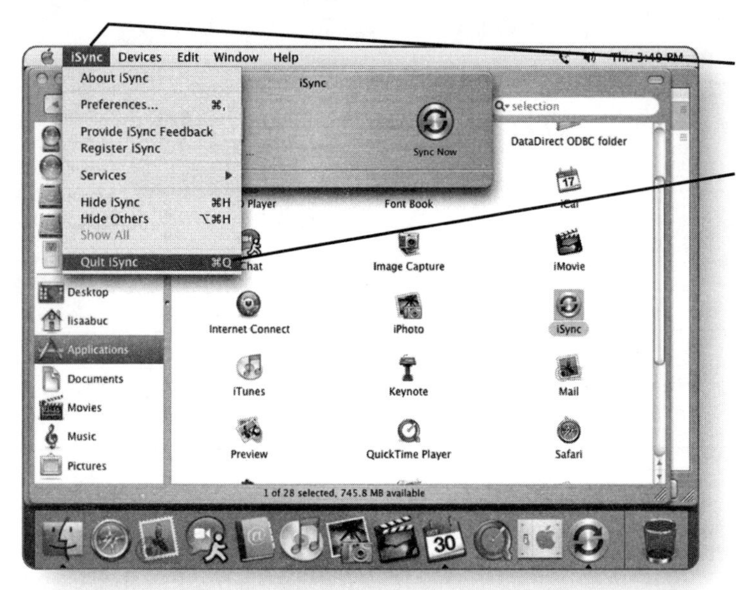

10. Click on **iSync**. The iSync menu will open.

11. Click on **Quit iSync**. iSync will update the calendar information on the device.

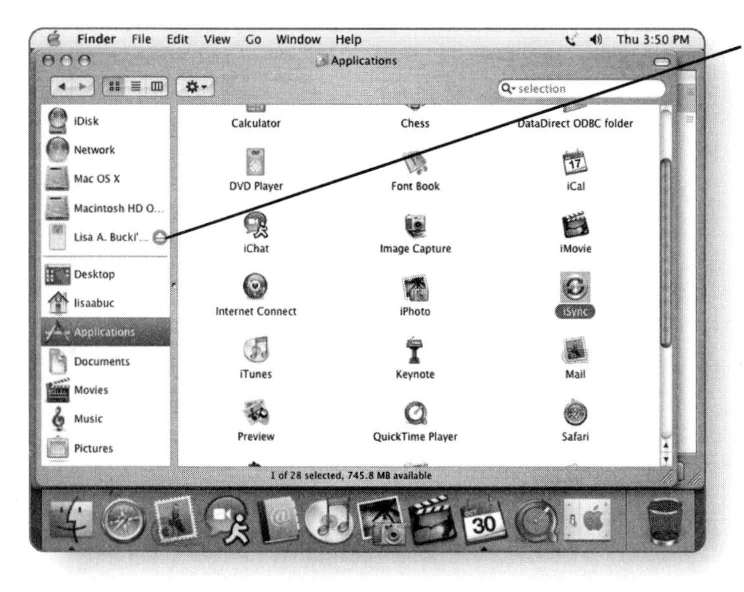

12. Click on the **Eject button** beside your device in a Finder window Sidebar. Mac OS X will unmount the device so that you can disconnect it from your system.

Publishing and Subscribing to Calendars

If you have a .Mac account, you can publish your calendar to your iDisk so that other users can log on and view it. To do so, those users must subscribe to the calendar. The following steps provide an overview of the publish/subscribe process:

1. **Connect** to the **Internet** by using Internet Connect. Your Mac will dial your Internet connection and log on.

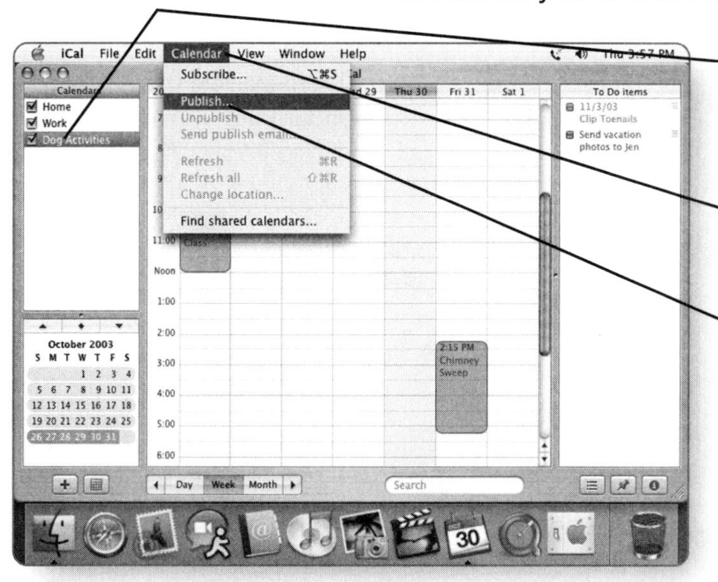

2. **Click** on the **calendar to publish** in the Calendars list. The calendar will be selected.

3. **Click** on **Calendar**. The Calendar menu will open.

4. **Click** on **Publish**. The Add Device window will appear, listing your device as a found device.

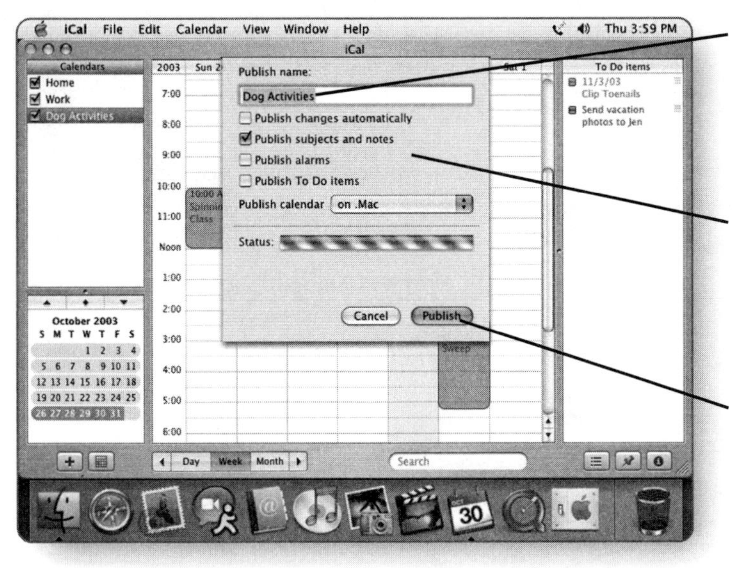

5. Edit the **online name** for the calendar in the Publish name text box. The new name will appear.

6. Choose additional publish settings. The specified settings will become active for the publish operation.

7. Click on **Publish**. iCal will connect to your iDisk, publish the calendar, and display the Calendar Published window.

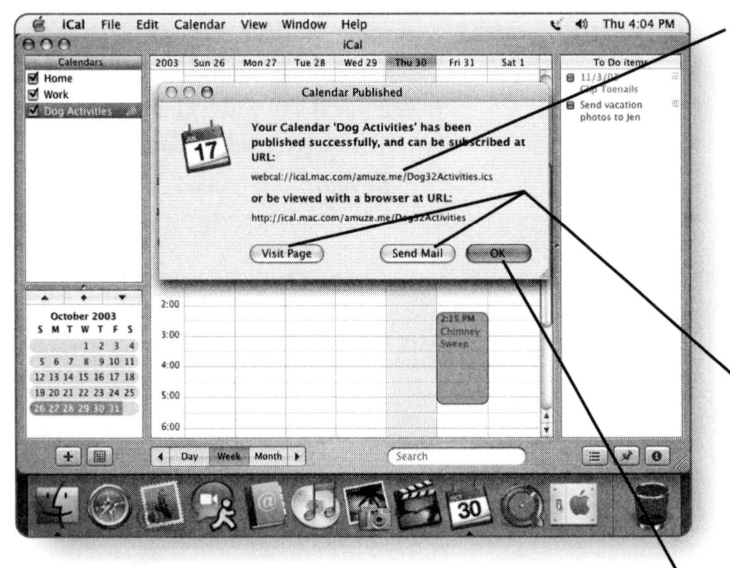

8. Take note of the **URLs** for subscribing to or browsing to the calendar. You will need to provide this information to other users who want to subscribe to or view your shared calendar.

> **TIP**
>
> Use the Visit Page button to see your online iCal, or Send Mail to send the URLs to potential visitors and subscribers.

9. Click on **OK**. The Calendar Published window will close.

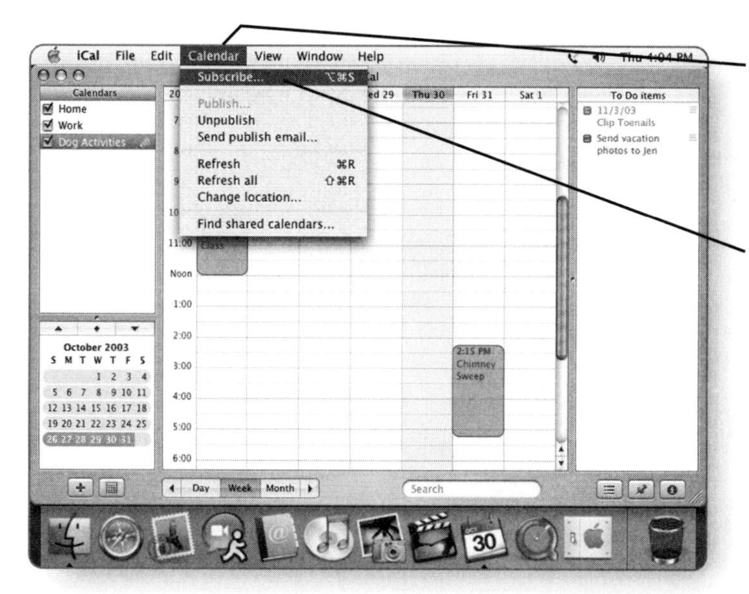

10. To subscribe to a calendar (you must be connected to the Internet), **click** on **Calendar**. The Calendar menu will open.

11. Click on **Subscribe.** A sheet will appear so that you can enter the subscription settings.

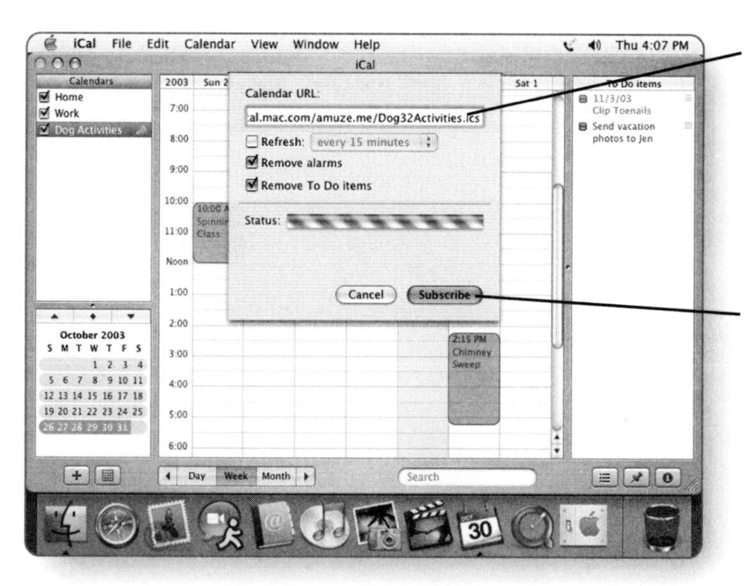

12. Enter the **precise** (case-sensitive) **URL** for the calendar to which you want to subscribe in the Calendar URL text box. The URL will appear. You can set other settings as desired.

13. Click on **Subscribe.** iCal will connect to the iDisk and download the information for the subscribed calendar.

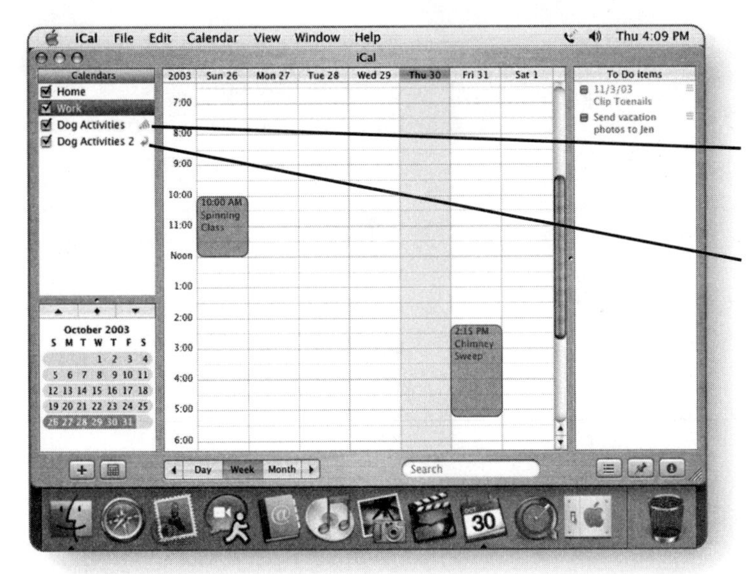

The subscribed calendar will appear in iCal's Calendars list.

This icon indicates a calendar that's been published.

This icon indicates a calendar to which you've subscribed.

> **TIP**
>
> You can unpublish a calendar. To do so, select the calendar and then use the Calendar, Unpublish command.

20

Working with Other Features

In addition to the applications that supply major areas of functionality within Mac OS X Version 10.3 Panther, a number of other applications supply other practical and fun functions. If you want to make a note to yourself, play chess, write a letter to a friend, and more, this is the chapter for you. In this chapter, you'll learn how to:

- Play digital movies.
- Create Stickie reminders.
- Create a text file.
- Take a picture of the screen.
- Use Preview to view graphics and .PDF files.
- Tackle other operations like creating your own PDF file.

Using QuickTime Player

QuickTime Player can open and display or play hundreds of different file types, including graphics files, audio files, movie files, and even virtual reality files that simulate a 3D environment. Most often, you'll want to use QuickTime to view various types of movie files that combine audio and video. In fact, movie files give rise to the term *multimedia*, which describes a computing experience that combines more than one media format.

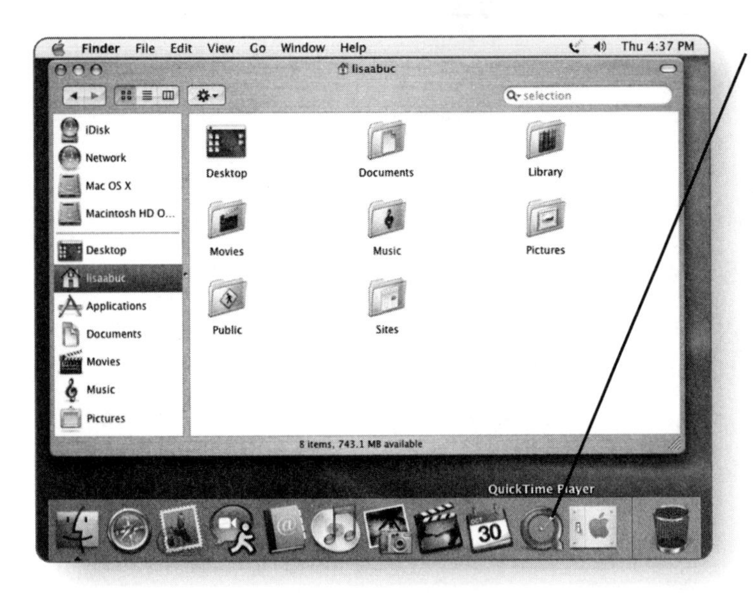

1. **Click** on the **QuickTime Player icon** on the Dock. The QuickTime Player application window will open and its menu and toolbar will appear.

> **NOTE**
>
> The first time you start QuickTime, a message box will ask you if you want to get QuickTime Pro. You can choose to do so, in which case you'll receive a code to activate the Pro features in QuickTime, or click Later to work with QuickTime as is.

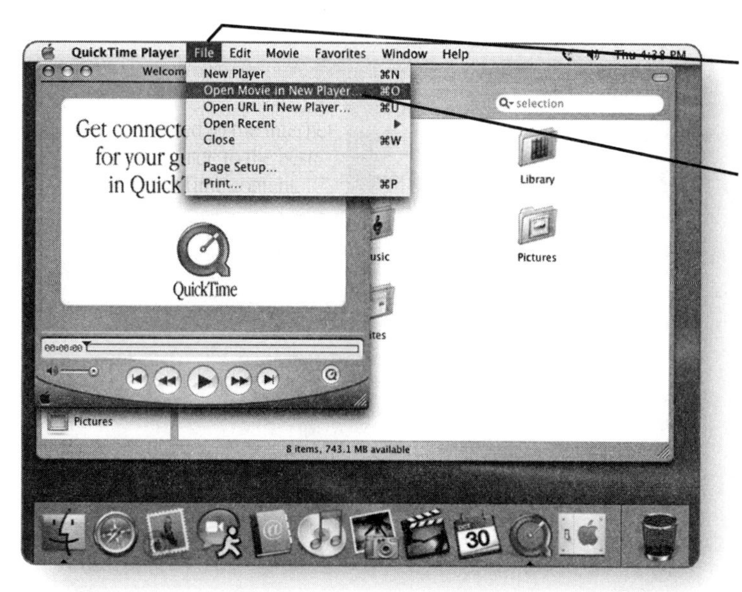

2. **Click** on **File**. The File menu will appear.

3. **Click** on **Open Movie in New Player**. The Open dialog box will open.

> **TIP**
>
> If you have a sound file that won't play in iTunes, open and play it in Quick-Time Player. Chances are that QuickTime Player can handle it.

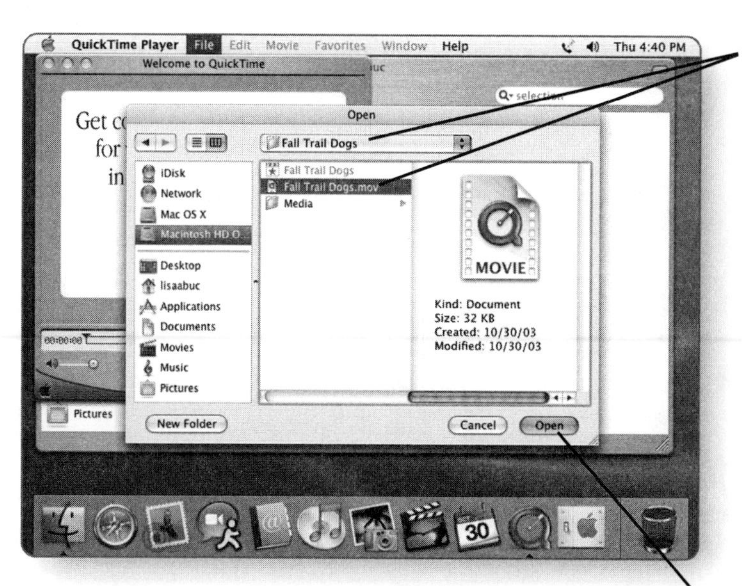

4. **Navigate** to the **disk** and **folder** that holds the movie to play and then **click** on the **movie**. Its preview will appear.

> **NOTE**
>
> When you click on a movie file in the list, the Open dialog box will display a preview frame if one is available. Often, the preview feature won't work for older movie files.

5. **Click** on **Open**. The movie file will open in the QuickTime Player window.

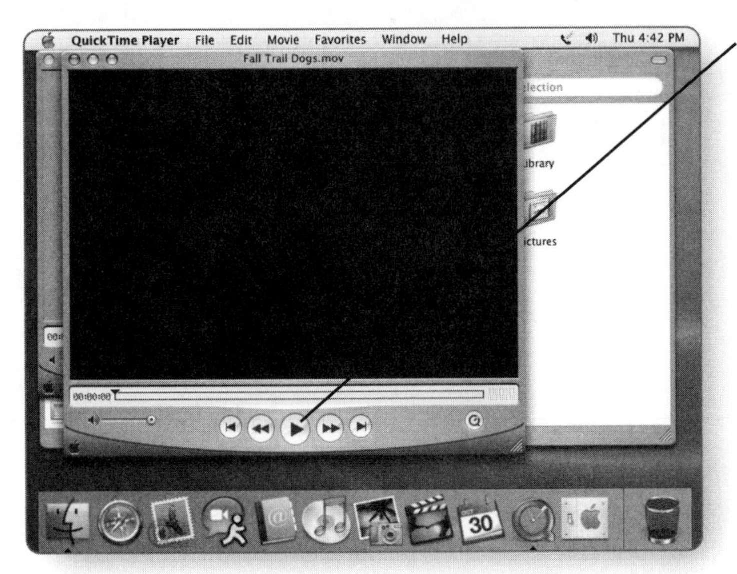

6. Click on the **Play button**. The movie will start playing. When you're finished watching the movie file, you can quit QuickTime.

> **NOTE**
>
> Of course, if the movie file that you want to start is on an inserted CD-ROM, DVD-ROM, or removable disk, you can open a Finder window for the media. Use Finder to display the folder that holds the movie file you want to play and then double-click on the movie file to start playback.

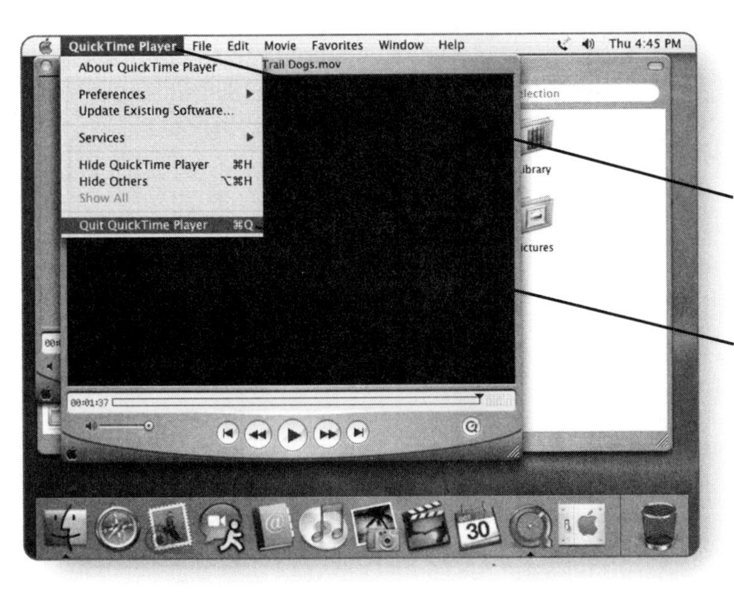

7. Click on **QuickTime Player**. The QuickTime Player menu will appear.

8. Click on **Quit QuickTime Player**. The QuickTime Player application will close.

Creating a Stickie

If you need to make a temporary note to yourself and place it in a visible location, create a Stickie. As long as the Stickies application is open, your Stickies stay on the desktop—right where they can be seen until you discard them. Follow these steps to create and remove a Stickie:

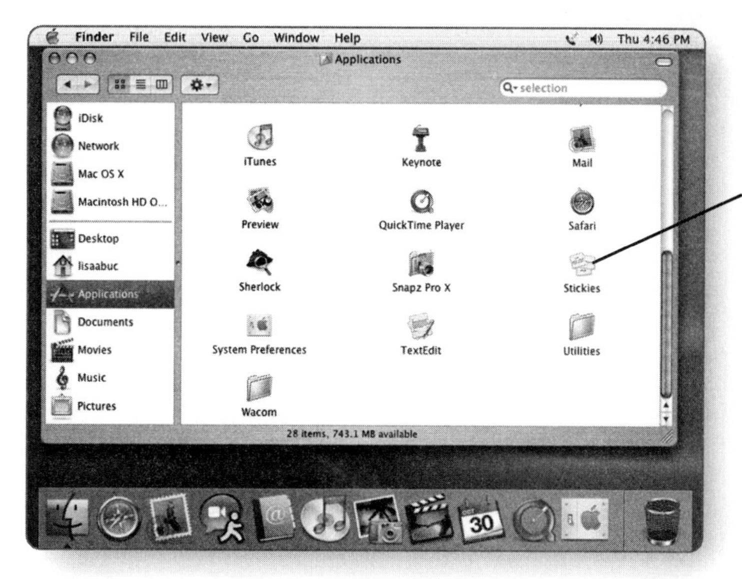

1. **Double-click** on the **Stickies icon** in the Applications folder. The Stickies application will start, and a blank Stickie will open. (The first time you open the Stickies app, it opens three sample notes. You can use File, New Note to create a blank Stickie.)

TIP

Once the Stickies application is open, choose File, New Note to add another new Stickie.

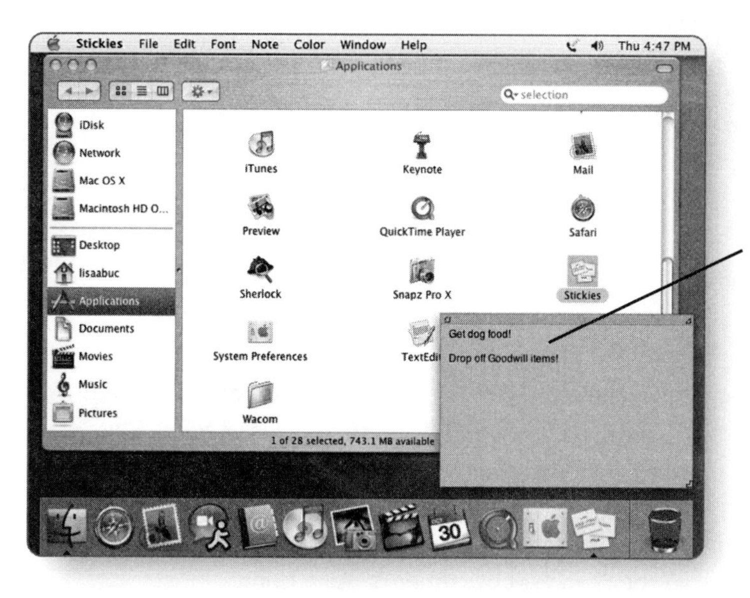

2. **Type** the **Stickie text, pressing Return** when needed.

TIP

Use the Floating Window and Translucent Window choices on the Note menu in Stickies to enable you to keep notes on top of other windows and to make them semi-transparent. Use the Color menu to choose a color for the Stickie.

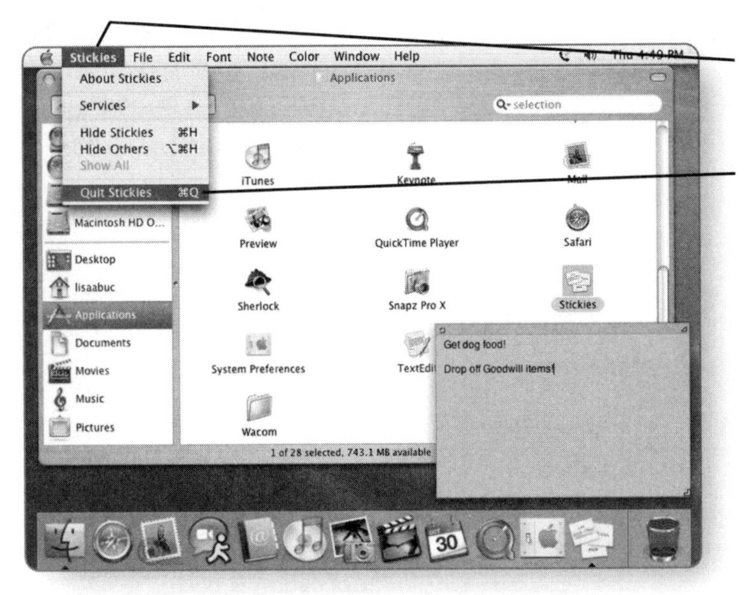

3. Click on **Stickies**. The File menu will appear.

4. Click on **Quit Stickies**. Stickies will close.

NOTE

Closing the Stickies application hides all of the Stickies without deleting them. Choose Stickies, Quit Stickies to close the Stickies application. To redisplay your Stickies, restart the application using the instructions in Steps 1 and 2.

Creating an RTF (Text) File

Mac OS X Version 10.3 includes the TextEdit application for creating basic documents. Although you can use TextEdit to create plain text (TXT) documents, by default it creates rich text format (RTF) documents. Rich text documents can include various text formats and graphics, capabilities that aren't available for plain text documents. As a bonus, most commercial word processors can open and read rich text format documents, so virtually any other user to whom you email an RTF file will be able to open and use it. While TextEdit offers features too numerous to cover in this section, follow these steps to learn the basics:

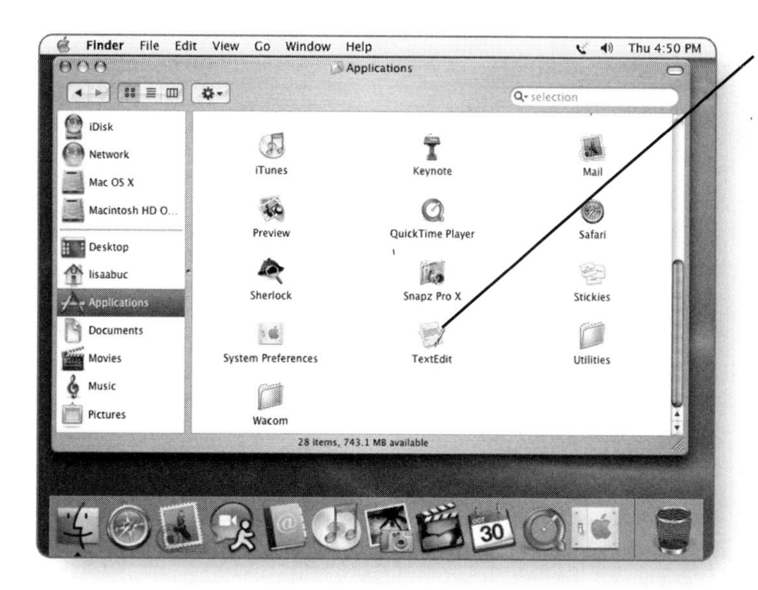

1. Double-click on the **TextEdit icon** in the Applications folder. The TextEdit application will start, and a blank document window will open.

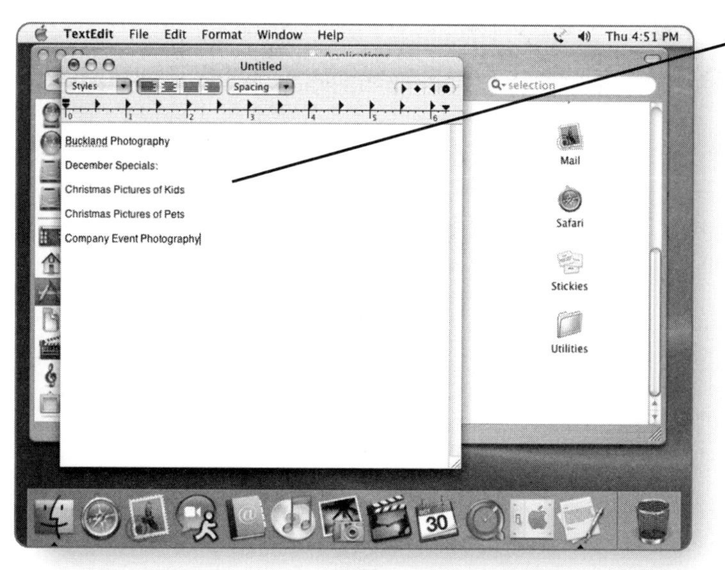

2. Type the **document text, pressing Return** when needed. The text will appear in the document window.

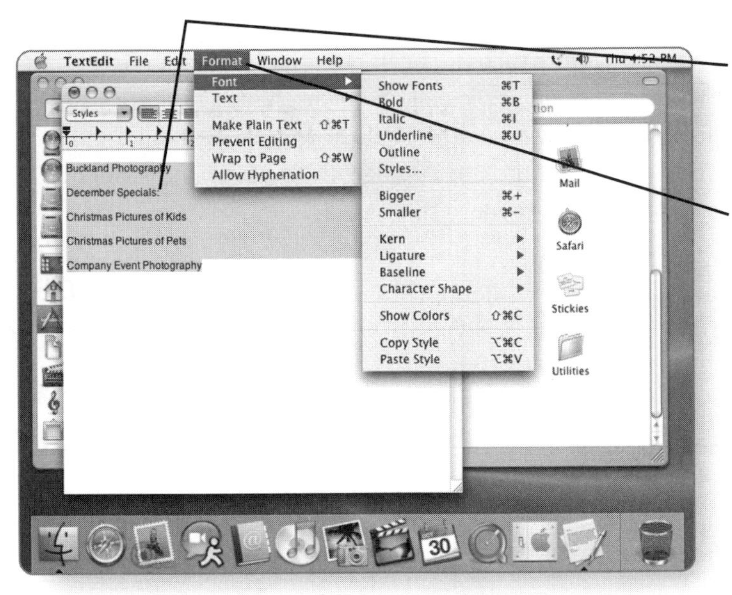

3. **Drag** over **text** in the document. The text will be selected (highlighted).

4. **Use Format menu commands** to format the text. The new formatting will appear.

> **TIP**
>
> If you make a mistake when creating a document, use the Edit, Undo command. (The command name changes to reflect the last action you performed in TextEdit.) TextEdit offers multiple undo levels, meaning that you can use the command repeatedly to undo multiple prior changes.

5. **Save** and **print** the **document**. These functions will work just as in other applications. Refer to the section "Saving a File in an Application" in Chapter 5 to learn more about saving, and see the "Selecting a Printer and Printing" section in Chapter 10 to learn how to print. You can then quit TextEdit.

Viewing a Graphic or PDF File

So many graphics applications, so many file types. The Preview application in Mac OS X helps you view graphics files in a variety of formats, including TIFF, JPEG, PICT, Photoshop (PSD), Graphics Interchange Format (GIF), MacPaint, Silicon Graphics, Targa, BMP (bitmap), and more. In addition, the Preview application enables you to view Adobe PDF (Portable Document Format) documents. PDF has become a standard format for documents that include text and graphics. In fact, many downloadable electronic books (ebooks) use the PDF format. Follow these steps to open a graphic or PDF file in Preview:

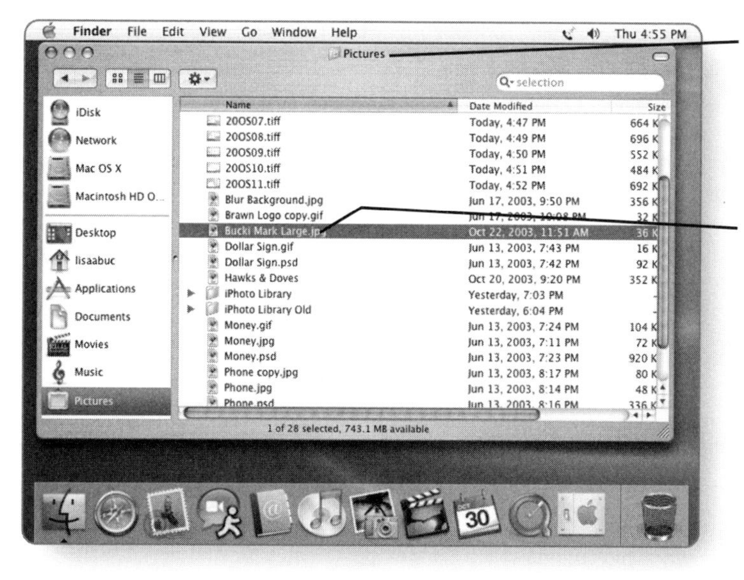

1. **Navigate** to the **folder** that contains the graphic or PDF file. The Open dialog box will list the files in that folder.

2. **Double-click** on a **graphic** or **PDF file**. The graphic or PDF file will open in the Preview window.

NOTE

If a PDF file was created in or for a Classic application, such as Adobe Acrobat Reader 4.0, double-clicking the file icon will start the Classic Environment and launch (or try to launch) Acrobat. To avoid this, start Preview by double-clicking on its icon in the Applications folder and then use the Open command on the File menu to open the desired file.

3. When you're finished working with graphics and PDF files, **click** on **Preview**. The Preview menu will appear.

4. **Click** on **Quit Preview**. The Preview application will close.

TIP

To add a picture to a TextEdit file, open the desired graphic in Preview. Choose Edit, Copy. Switch to the TextEdit document, click to position the insertion point where you want the graphic to appear, and then choose Edit, Paste.

CREATING A BASIC PDF FILE

Because of the increasing popularity of the PDF format, the Mac OS X Version 10.3 Print sheet enables you to save documents from a variety of applications as PDF files. To do so, choose File, Print. Click on the button for the Copies & Pages pop-up menu. The pop-up menu will appear. Click on Output Options. The Print dialog box will change to display the output options. Click on the Save as PDF File check box and then click on Save. The Save dialog box will open. Specify a file name and save location; then click on Save. Mac OS X will save the PDF file in the specified location. You can use the Preview application to view the PDF file.

Glimpsing Other Features

Panther includes so many great features that it's not realistic to expect to cover them all in a short beginner book like this. However, this last section gives you a look at a few more of the applications you can use to get your work done in Panther.

Using Your Ink

If you have a Wacom Graphire 2 graphics tablet (which is the only tablet recommended for use with and fully supported by Mac OS X Version 10.3), the new feature will become available automatically. Inkwell enables you to use the stylus to write text and commands, which your Mac can then recognize. You can write directly in an application or in the Inkpad window. Start by turning on the Ink recognition.

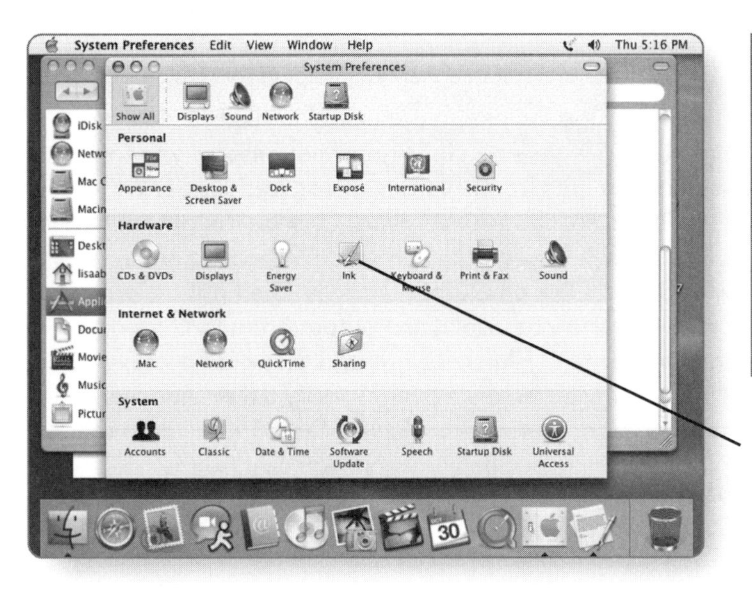

> **NOTE**
>
> Depending on when you purchased your tablet, it may not have shipped with Mac OS X drivers. You can download the latest drivers from *http://www.wacom.com*.

- Use the Ink choice in System Preferences to turn on handwriting recognition and display the Ink window.

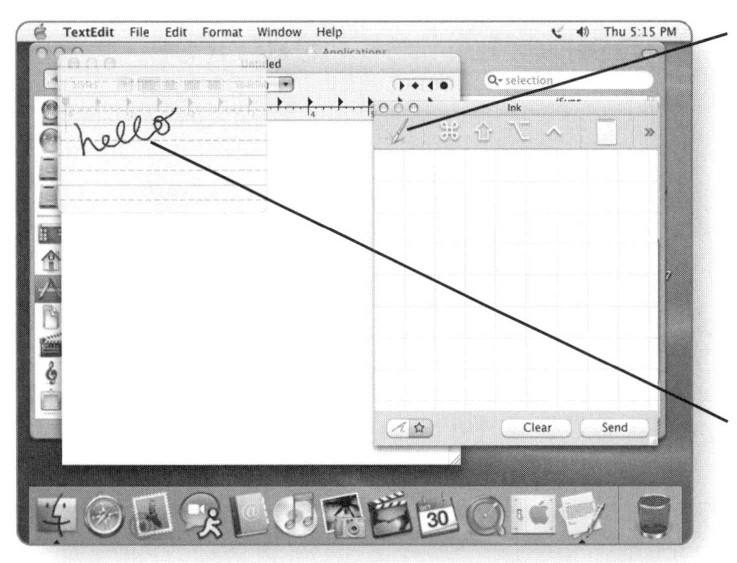

- Click on the Turn recognition on and off icon at the left end of the Ink window. This button will toggle between using the stylus as a writing pen or mouse. When the button shows an arrow, the stylus functions as a mouse. When it shows a pen, the stylus functions as a pen.
- Then begin writing over a document, such as a TextEdit document. A lined yellow note area will appear. After you finish a word and pause, it will appear in the TextEdit document.

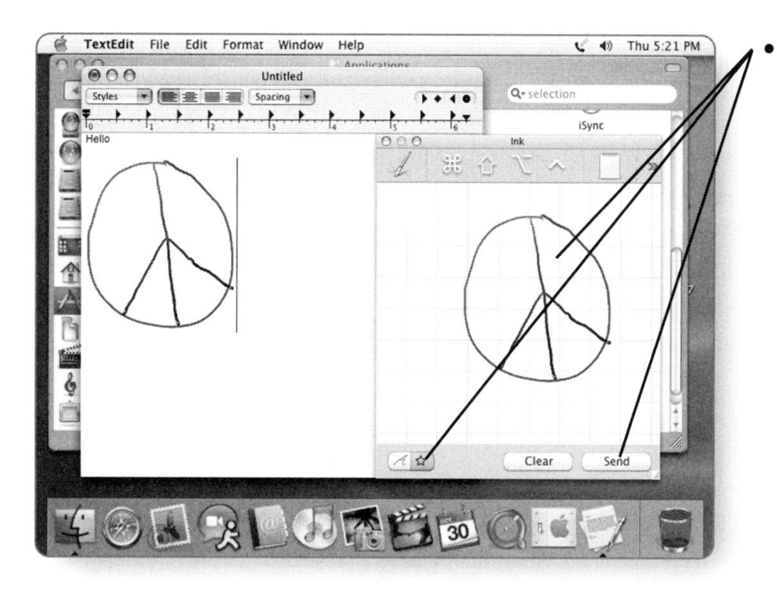

- You also can use ink to draw in a document. After positioning the insertion point in the document, click on the Show InkPad icon at the right end of the Ink window to expand it. Click on the draw button in the lower-left corner of the window. Draw in the Ink window and then click on Send.

Performing a Calculation

Double-click on the Calculator icon in the Applications folder to open the Calculator.

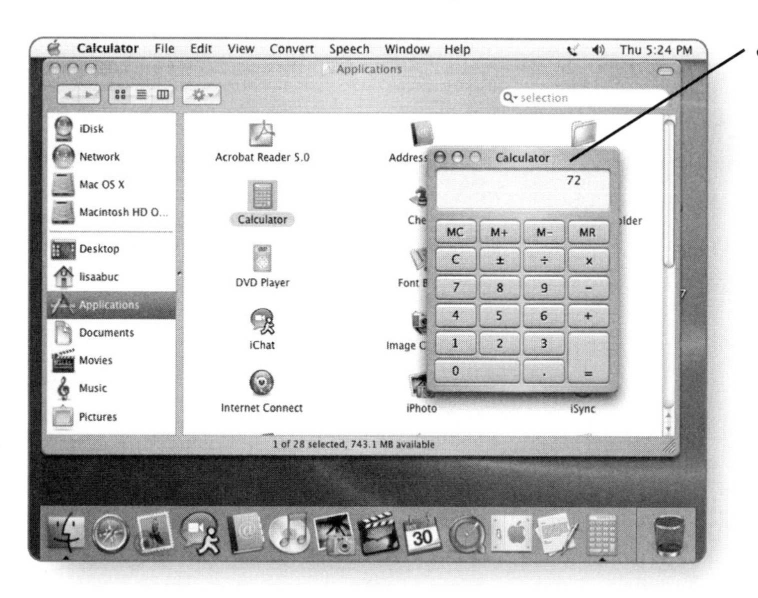

- Enter your calculation, either by clicking on the buttons in the Calculator window or by pressing keys on your keyboard's numeric keypad. Click or press = to complete the calculation, displaying the result at the top of the Calculator window. You can use Edit, Copy to copy the result; then use Edit, Paste to paste it into a document.

Shooting a Picture of Your Screen

There may be times where you want to take a picture of what's onscreen in Mac OS X, such as to show a friend an idea or procedure. Or you may be having a problem with an application. You can take a screen shot of the problem or error message and then email the image or fax a printout to a tech support representative.

Use the Grab utility built into Mac OS X to shoot the screen and save the shot as a TIFF graphic file. Start Grab from the Applications Utilities folder.

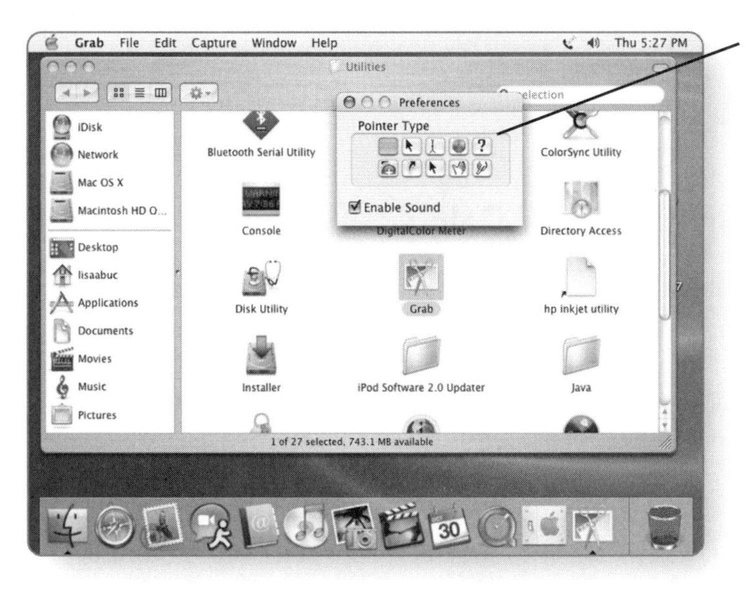

- Choose Grab, Preferences to open this window with the settings. Choose a pointer and then close the window. Press Shift+⌘+Z to start a timed countdown to save the screen.

Snooping for Content with Sherlock

Sherlock is a powerful application that you can use to search the Internet. Start your Internet connection and double-click on the Sherlock icon to start Sherlock.

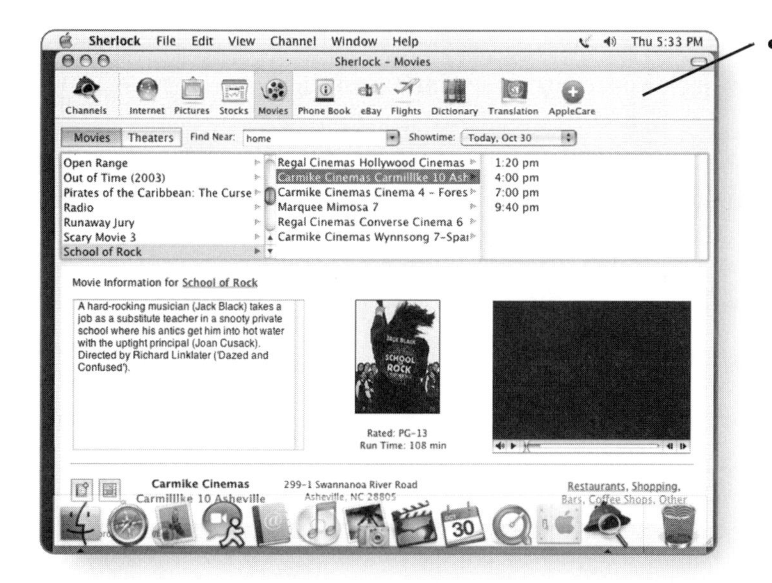

- The icons on the Sherlock toolbar enable you to perform a number of specialized searches. For example, here I clicked on the Movies icon and made a few choices from the lists Sherlock presented. Sherlock then presented show times for the movie and cinema I selected. (The first time you use Sherlock, it may prompt you to enter information about where you live so that such a feature will work.)

Whenever you need to find some information quickly, give Sherlock a try!

Part VI Review Questions

1. How do I set up a calendar? *See "Creating a Calendar" in Chapter 19.*
2. How do I schedule an activity in my calendar? *See "Scheduling Items" in Chapter 19.*
3. I heard I can carry my calendar on my iPod. Is that true? *See "Synching a Calendar" in Chapter 19.*
4. I have a .Mac account. Can I give others access to my calendar via .Mac? *See "Publishing and Subscribing to Calendars" in Chapter 19.*
5. How do I play a movie? *See "Using QuickTime Player" in Chapter 20.*
6. I want to leave a note for myself on my desktop. *See "Creating a Stickie" in Chapter 20.*
7. How do I create a letter? *See "Creating an RTF (Text) File" in Chapter 20.*
8. How do I view a graphic file? *See "Viewing a Graphic or PDF File" in Chapter 20.*
9. How do I save a PDF file? *See "Creating a Basic PDF File" in Chapter 20.*
10. How do I perform special searches on the Web? *See "Snooping for Content with Sherlock" in Chapter 20.*

PART VII

Basic Maintenance and Troubleshooting

21

Emergency Startup Measures

Macs enjoy an excellent reputation in terms of system reliability. They tend to be very stable with few instances where the system locks up or otherwise goes on the fritz. Despite such stability, you may encounter situations where Mac OS X Version 10.3 hangs up. In such a case, you can try various techniques to restart the system. If you have both Mac OS X Version 10.3 and OS 9.2 installed on separate disks, you also may encounter situations where you need to boot from the disk with the older operating system and then return to the Mac OS X Version 10.3 boot disk. In this chapter, you'll learn how to:

- Restart the system when it hangs.
- Start up the system from your Mac OS X CD-ROM.
- Boot the system from an OS 9.X disk (volume).
- Return to booting the system from the Mac OS X disk (volume).
- Rebuild the Classic Desktop if it hangs.

Restarting the System

In the process of writing the original edition of this book, I spent many hours using the Public Beta version of Mac OS X. Even its test version worked reliably, with few, if any, instances where the system crashed. Nevertheless, all systems hang at some point or another. For example, you could install a piece of shareware that causes a problem or open a corrupt file that the system can't handle.

> **TIP**
>
> The terms "crash," "hang," and "freeze" are generally interchangeable. Each refers to an instance where the system has stopped responding partially or totally to your keyboard and mouse input.

When the system freezes, you have a few ways to deal with the situation and restart (reboot) the system:

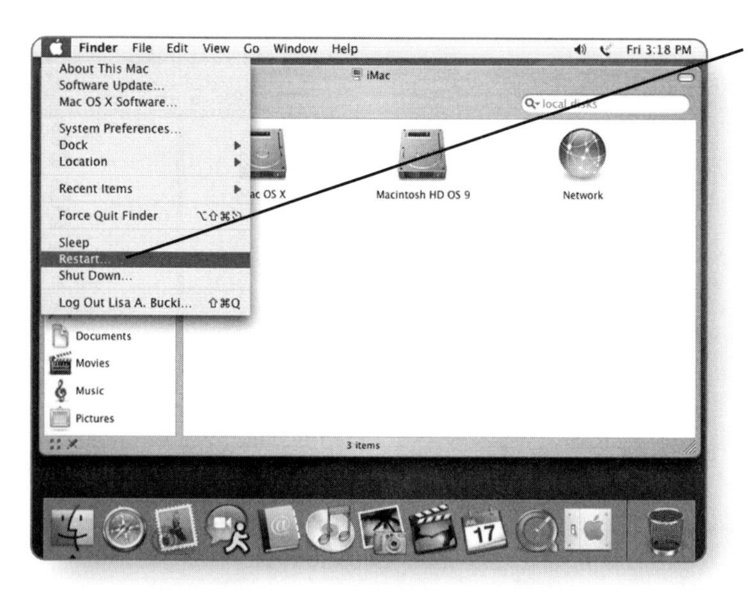

- If something goes wrong but you still can use the mouse, **click** on the **Apple menu**; then **click** on **Restart**. If you are prompted to confirm the restart despite a file sharing connection, click on OK. Click on the Restart button in the message box that appears. The system should restart.
- If the mouse doesn't work, try the keyboard next. **Press ⌘+Control+Power (the Power button)**. For some systems, you may need to **press ⌘+Option+Shift+ Power**.

- If you have an iMac, you can **press** the **Reset button**. It's a small round button imprinted with a left arrow and is located along with the other buttons and ports on the system—approximately below the modem port.
- **Press ⌘+Option+Esc** to open the Force Quit dialog box. (See the section called "Forcing an Application to Quit" in Chapter 5 to learn more.) If an application's name appears in red, it means there is a problem with that application. Force it to quit, and Mac OS X may be able to resume normal operations. Sometimes, forcing the Finder to quit will enable you to restart the system.
- **Press Shift+⌘+Q** to attempt to log out and then log back into Mac OS X Version 10.3.
- If none of the other methods works, **press** and **hold** the **Power button** to turn the system off. Let it power all the way down until you can hear that the hard disk has stopped spinning. Then press the Power button again to restart the system.

> **TIP**
>
> As a reminder, the Command key is also called the Apple key or the Clover key because it is designated with apple and clover symbols on some keyboards.

Starting from a CD-ROM

You may encounter situations so severe that Mac OS X Version 10.3 won't boot at all from a hard disk. Or you may have forgotten the password for the system. If you encounter such a problem, you may need to start the system from the Mac OS X CD-ROM. Follow these steps to do so:

1. **Insert** the **Install Disk 1 CD-ROM** of the Mac OS X Version 10.3 software into the CD-ROM or DVD-ROM drive. (If a

window with the CD's contents appears, you can ignore it and go on with Step 2.)

2. Use the method of your choice to **restart** the **system**, **pressing** and **holding** the **C key** down as soon as you can. (If you use a keyboard combination to restart, press and hold the C key as soon as you release the key combination.) Holding the C key forces the system to boot from the CD-ROM.

3. After you hear the CD-ROM spinning, you can **release** the **C key**. The system will continue restarting, and the Installer will reappear.

> **NOTE**
>
> Because most systems read data more slowly from a CD-ROM or DVD-ROM, restarting from the CD-ROM will take longer than starting normally.

4. At this point, you can **take one** of the **following actions**:

- **Click** on the **Continue button** and **rerun** the **Installer** to reinstall Mac OS X Version 10.3, which should help any serious problems with the system. (During the installation process, you may click on the Options button after choosing the install disk. Choose Archive and Install to archive your network settings and perform a clean reinstall, or Erase and Install to completely blow away your old OS X installation. Note that you will lose documents when you choose a clean reinstall option, but that may be your only choice if the OS has been damaged extensively.) After the Installer sequence finishes, the system restarts automatically.

OR

- **Open** the **Installer menu**; then **use** the **Reset Password** or **Open Disk Utility commands**. Use Reset Password to create a new password, which is handy if you've forgotten the system password. Choose Open Disk Utility to verify (check) or repair the system's boot hard disk. (Chapter 22, "Tackling Disk Issues," covers how Disk Utility works.) Be sure to quit each utility when you finish with it. Then choose Quit Installer from the Installer menu and click on Restart in the resulting dialog box.

Changing the Startup Disk

If you have Mac OS X Version 10.3 and Mac OS 9.2 (or an earlier version) installed on separate disks or disk partitions, you can choose the disk or partition from which you want the system to boot. Of course, booting from an OS 9.x disk starts your Mac with the OS 9.x operating system and booting from the Mac OS X Version 10.3 disk starts your system with the Mac OS X Version 10.3 operating system. This section covers how to reboot from disk to disk and system to system.

NOTE

As of this writing, Apple had announced that it intended to discontinue the ability to boot into older operating systems on Macs shipping with Mac OS X Version 10.2 Jaguar during 2003. So, whether or not you will be able to boot to a startup disk with an older operating system will depend on the age of your Mac and how you installed Mac OS X Version 10.3 (and prior Mac OS X versions).

Changing to an OS 9.x Disk

You may want to boot to OS 9.2 if the Classic environment won't work correctly or if you want to work with an OS 9.x application that won't work through the Classic environment for some reason. Follow these steps to boot into OS 9.2:

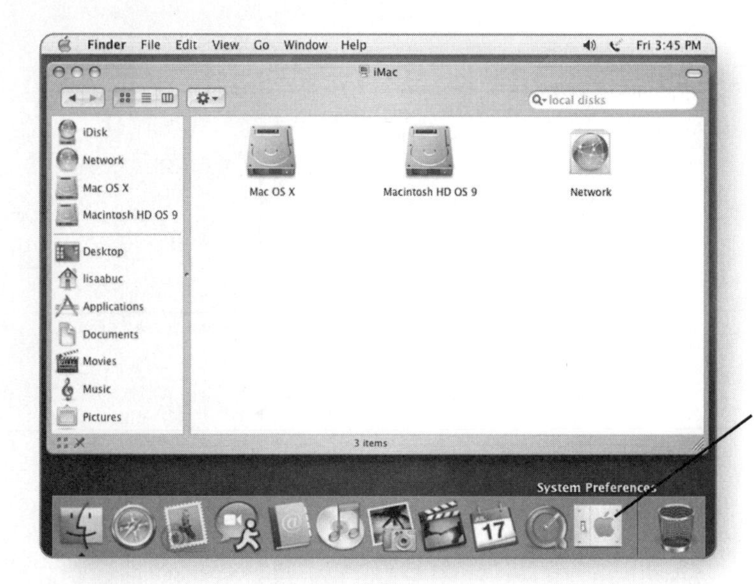

NOTE

You also can press and hold the Option key while restarting the system to boot to a screen that enables you to choose which startup disk to use.

1. Click on the **System Preferences icon** on the Dock. System Preferences will open.

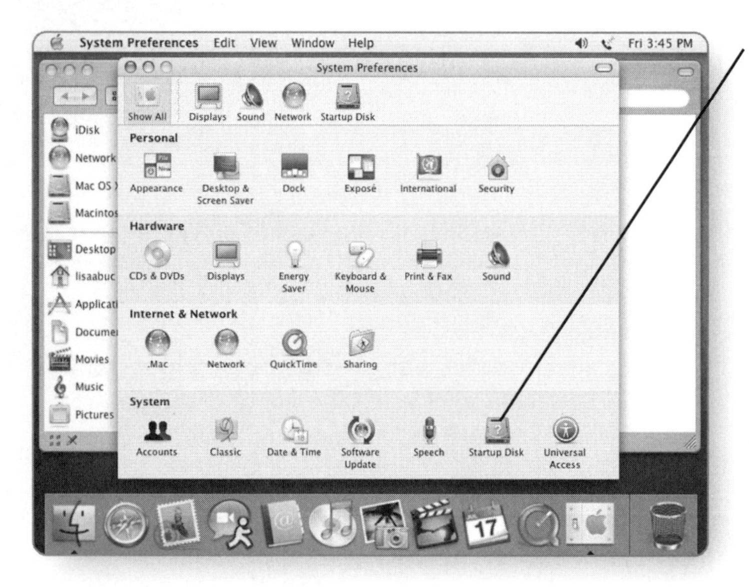

2. Click on the **Startup Disk icon**. The Startup Disk pane will appear.

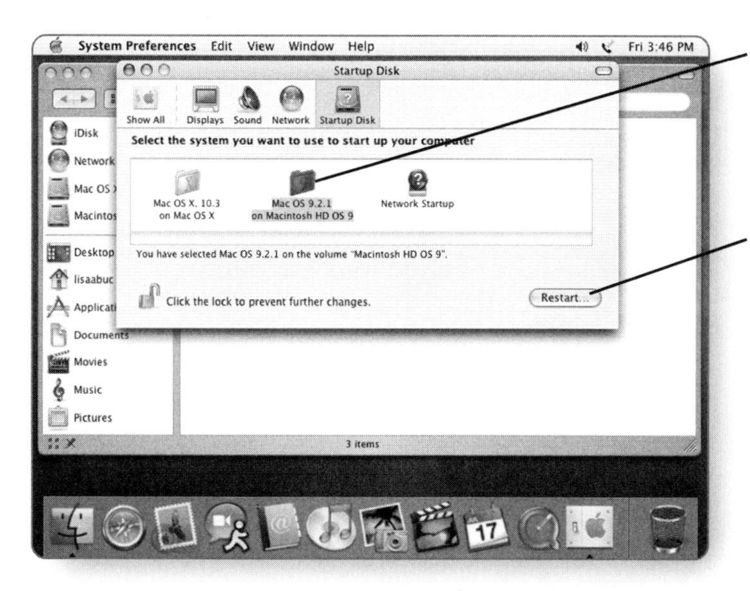

3. Click on the **icon** for the disk that holds the OS 9.2 system files in the Startup Disk pane. The icon will be selected.

4. Click on **Restart.** A sheet will open to prompt you to save the change and restart the system.

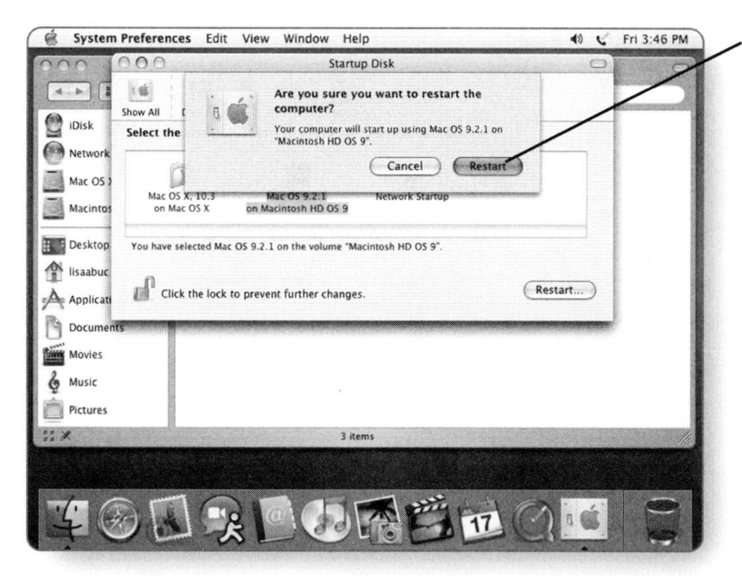

5. Click on **Restart.** The system will restart, rebooting into OS 9.2.

NOTE

When the system reboots, you may see a message telling you that Disk First Aid checked your hard disk. Click on Done to close the message and finish restarting the system.

Changing Back to an OS X Disk

Rebooting into Mac OS X Version 10.3 works a little differently from OS 9.2, as you might expect due to the significant differences between the systems. Follow these steps to return to Mac OS X from Mac OS 9.2:

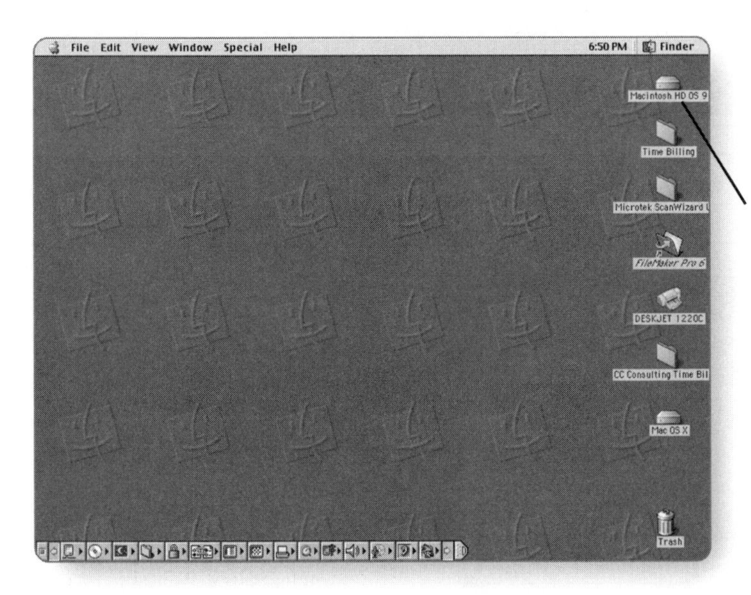

1. **Double-click** on the **icon** for the hard disk that holds OS 9.2 on the desktop. A Finder window will open.

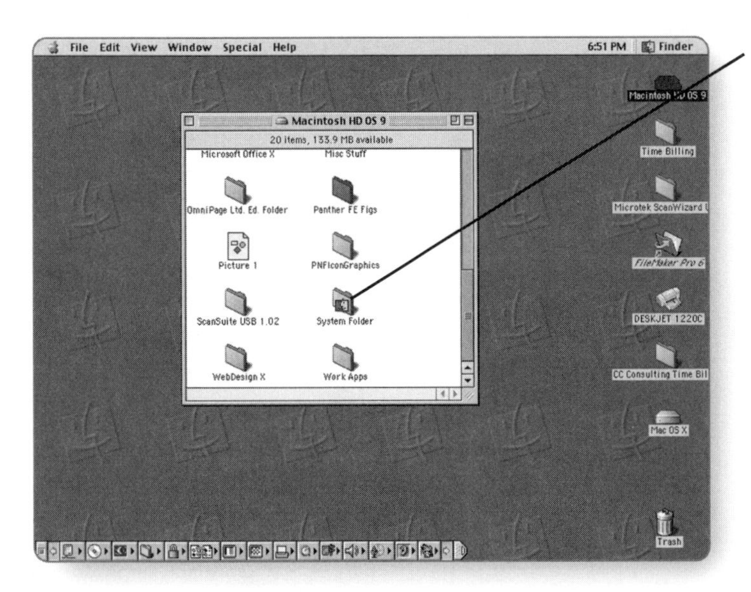

2. **Double-click** on the **System Folder icon**. A Finder window for the System Folder will open.

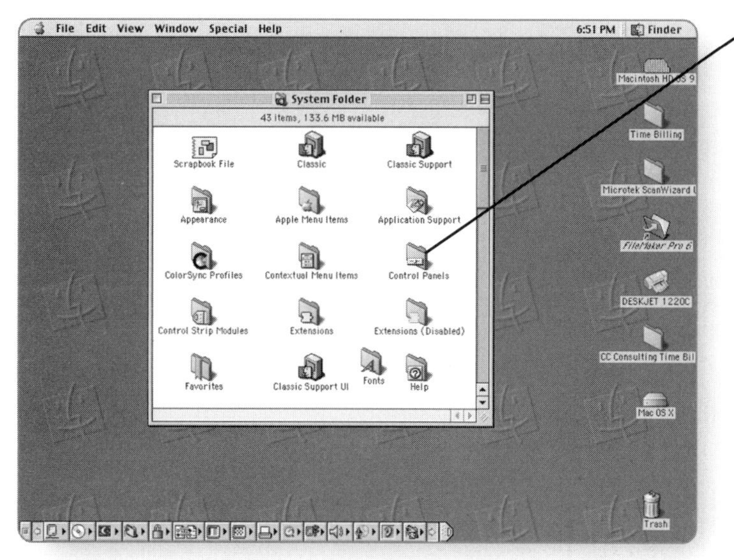

3. **Double-click** on the **Control Panels icon** (you may need to scroll the window contents). A Finder window for the Control Panels window will open.

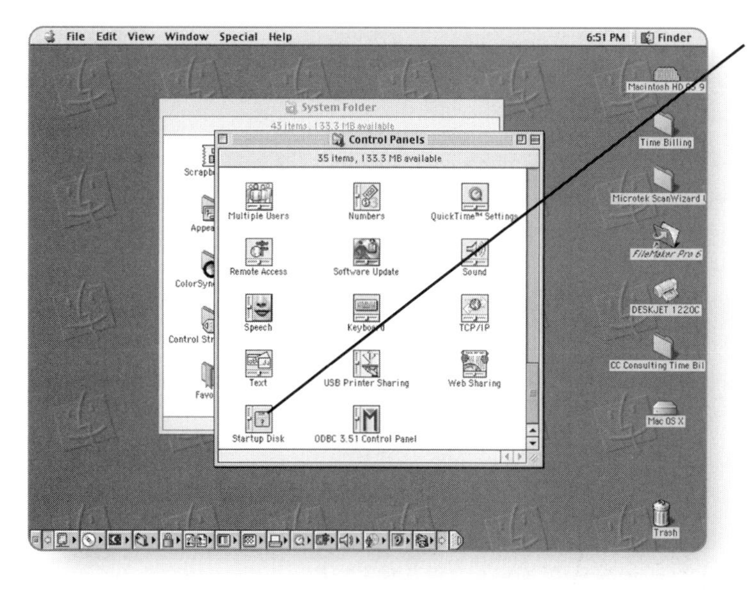

4. **Double-click** on the **Startup Disk icon**. (Similarly, you may need to first scroll the window contents to locate the Startup Disk icon.) The Startup Disk window will open.

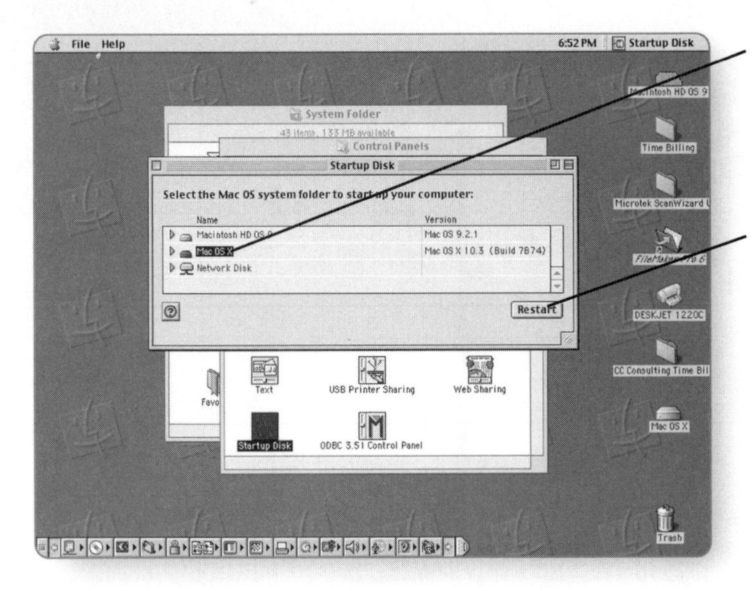

5. Click on the **hard disk** that holds the Mac OS X system in the list. The hard disk will be selected as the boot disk.

6. Click on the **Restart button**. The system will restart, booting to Mac OS X.

Rebuilding the Classic Desktop

There may be times when you're working in the Classic environment and its programs start malfunctioning. In such a case, rebuilding the Classic Desktop within OS X Version 10.3 can cure some of the problems.

Note that Classic typically causes problems when it sleeps, so set Classic to never sleep on the Advanced tab of the Classic pane in System Preferences. Also choose Turn Off Extensions under Startup Options on that tab to start Classic without system extensions that may cause problems. Further, once you've launched a Classic application, choose Control Panels from the Apple menu and use the Extensions Manager control panel to disable any Control Panels that you suspect might be causing problems with Classic under Mac OS X.

Follow these steps to rebuild the Classic Desktop:

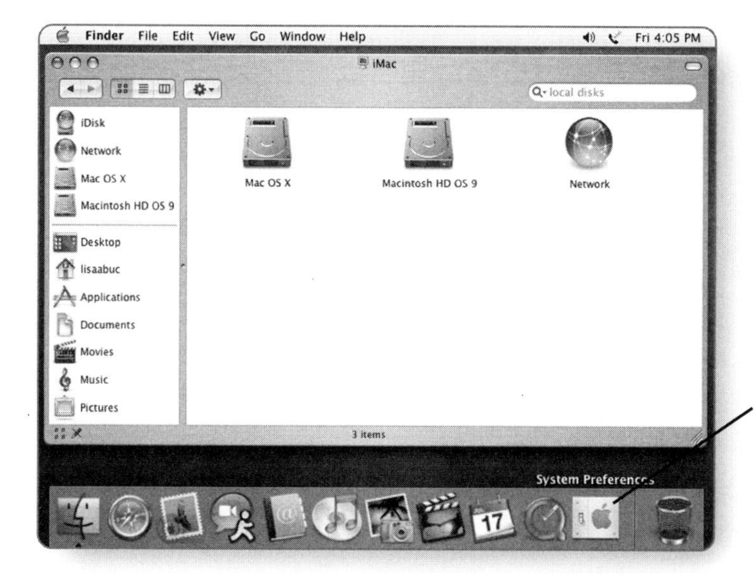

NOTE

This process may change the application used by default to open certain types of files under Mac OS X Version 10.3, so use the process with caution.

1. **Click** on the **System Preferences icon** on the Dock. System Preferences will open.

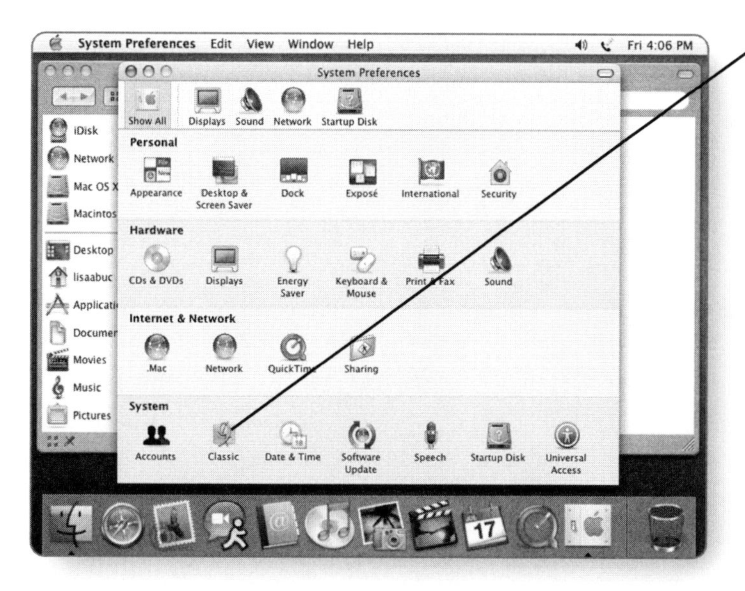

2. **Click** on the **Classic icon**. The Classic pane will appear.

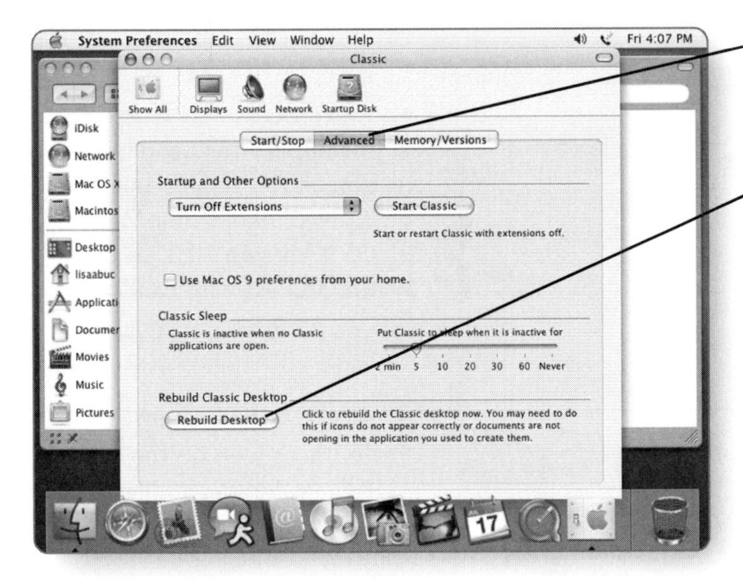

3. Click on the **Advanced button**. The Advanced choices will appear.

4. Click on **Rebuild Desktop**. The Desktop will be rebuilt, a process that takes a few minutes on most systems. Then you can either close the System Preferences application or continue working.

22

Tackling Disk Issues

While the Mac OS X Version 10.3 software offers a great deal of stability, sometimes you may not be as lucky with the disk media that you use. The surface of both hard and removable disks consists of magnetic material that can be damaged. If dust somehow gets in the disk case, it can cause damage. If the read/write head in a drive malfunctions, it can cause damage. Other magnetic matter placed too close to the disk can also cause damage. In this chapter, you'll learn how to:

- Start and exit Disk Utility.
- Check a disk for errors.
- Repair a disk.
- Erase a disk.

Starting and Exiting Disk Utility

Earlier Mac operating systems also offered the Disk Utility application to enable users to eliminate disk problems. In Mac OS X Version 10.3, Disk Utility can verify and repair disks formatted as one of the following volume (mountable disk) types:

- Mac OS Standard
- Mac OS Extended
- UFS Formatted

Each time you start Mac OS X Version 10.3, Disk Utility verifies the system's hard disk and repairs it, if needed. You also can run Disk Utility whenever you suspect there's a problem with a disk.

Before you use Disk Utility, you should close all open applications. If you are not logged on as an administrator (using the original User Name you entered or another administrator User Name created as described in Chapter 23, "Managing Users"), you will need to unlock the Disk Utility settings. Alternatively, you will be prompted to log in as an administrator. The following steps lead you through the overall process of starting Disk Utility, unlocking its settings, and exiting when you've finished using the utility:

NOTE

Some Disk Utility repairs are not allowed on a hard disk that is the current startup volume. In such a case, start up from the OS X CD (as described in the section called "Starting from a CD-ROM" in Chapter 21) and click on Open Disk Utility in the Installer application menu. On the other hand, Disk Utility will only repair disk permissions on a startup volume.

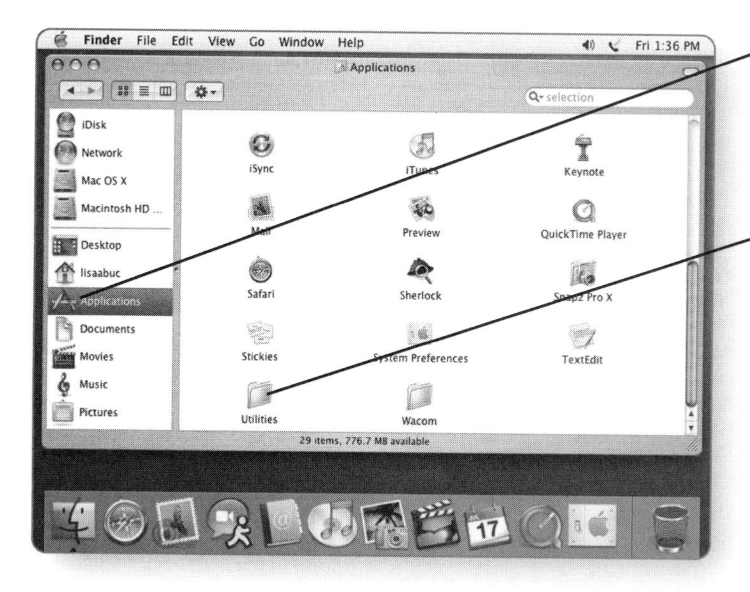

1. **Click** on **Applications** in the Finder Sidebar. The contents of the Applications folder will appear in the Finder window.

2. **Scroll down** and **double-click** on the **Utilities icon**. The contents of the Utilities folder will appear in the Finder window.

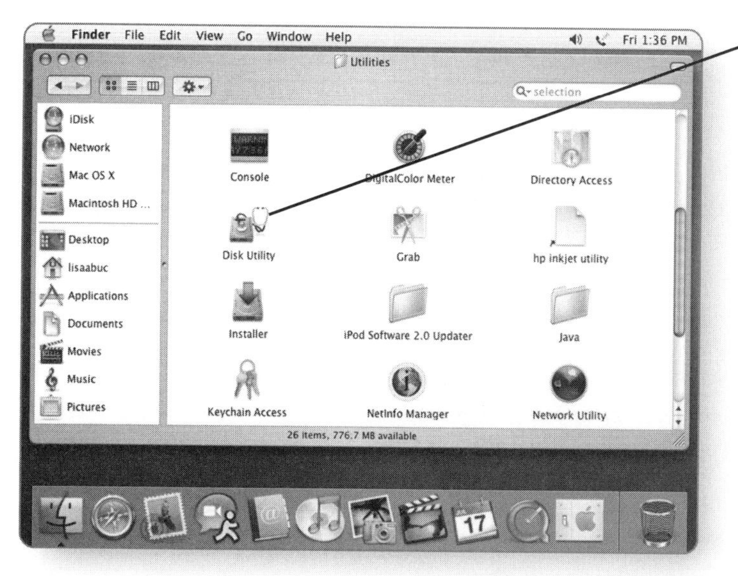

3. **Scroll down** and **double-click** on the **Disk Utility icon**. Disk Utility will start, and its window and menu bar will appear.

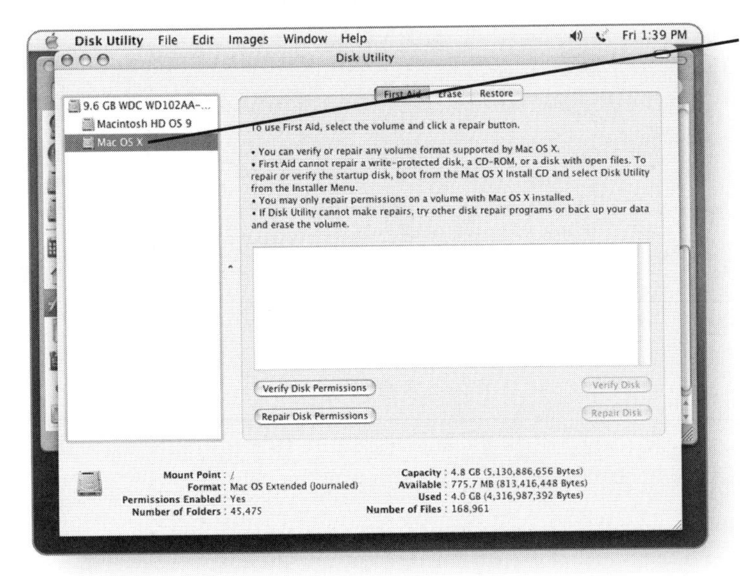

4. Click on a **disk** or **volume** in the list at the left. The First Aid choices will appear.

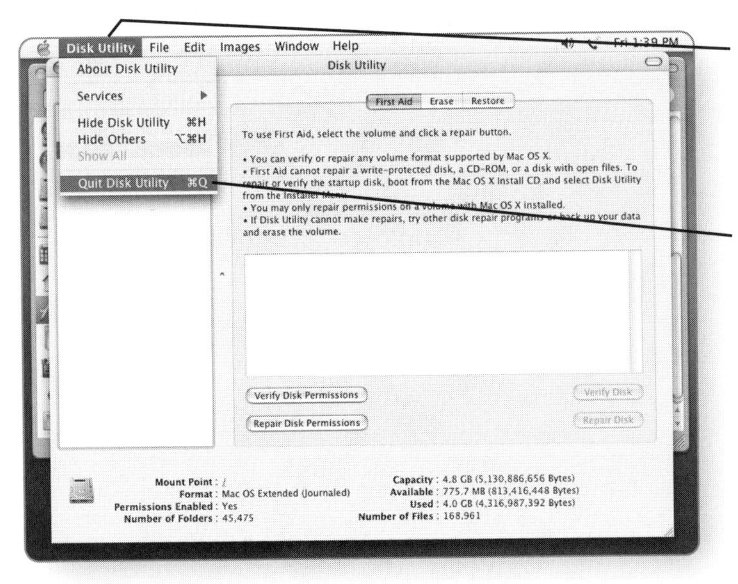

5. After you've finished working in Disk Utility, **click** on **Disk Utility**. The Disk Utility menu will appear.

6. Click on **Quit Disk Utility**. The Disk Utility application will close.

Verifying a Disk

Symptoms of a disk problem may vary. For example, using a particular document file or application may cause the system to hang or crash. Or, perhaps the system is experiencing slight problems when starting. If you ever suspect that you have a disk problem, use the Disk Utility application right away to check the disk. Follow these steps to verify a disk in Disk Utility:

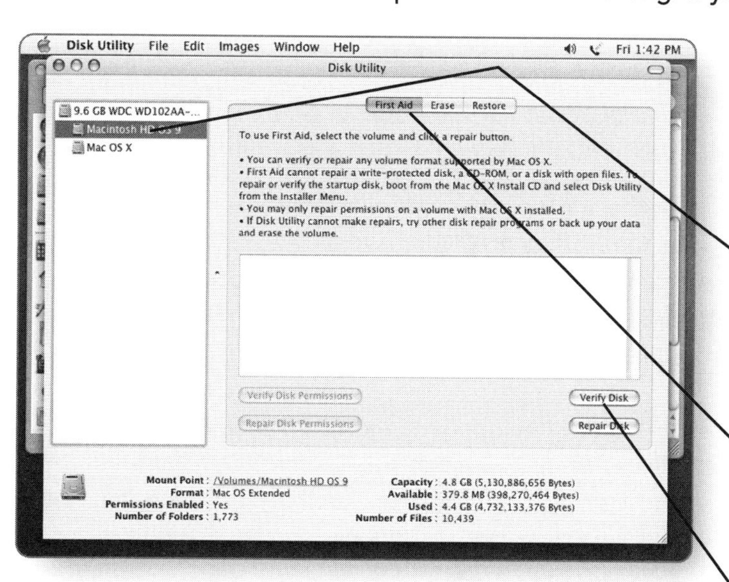

1. **Click** on the **disk** or **volume icon** in the list at the left side of the Disk Utility window. The icon will be highlighted.

2. **Click** on **First Aid**. The options for verifying and repairing a disk will appear.

3. **Click** on **Verify Disk**. Disk Utility will verify the disk and display a list of results.

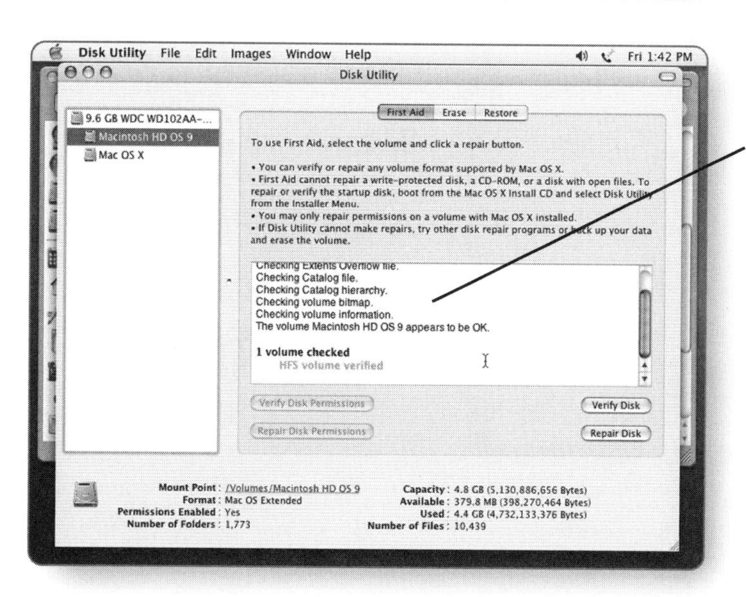

4. **Review** the **results** in the list at the bottom. If Disk Utility finds a disk error, it will be included on the list. If any errors are listed, you should repair the disk as described in the next section.

Repairing a Disk

If you verify a disk and find that it has problems or are advised by a technical support representative to repair a disk, then you can use Disk Utility to do so. However, Disk Utility does have a few limitations in this regard. It cannot:

- Repair a write-protected disk or CD-ROM.
- Repair a disk that has files open in other applications. Close all open applications and files to eliminate this problem.
- Repair the startup disk (boot disk or startup volume). To repair the startup disk, you have to use a third-party application, such as Norton Disk Doctor (part of Norton Utilities), or boot from the Mac OS X CD-ROM and choose Installer, Open Disk Utility.

To repair a disk when needed (and when none of the above conditions exist), follow these steps:

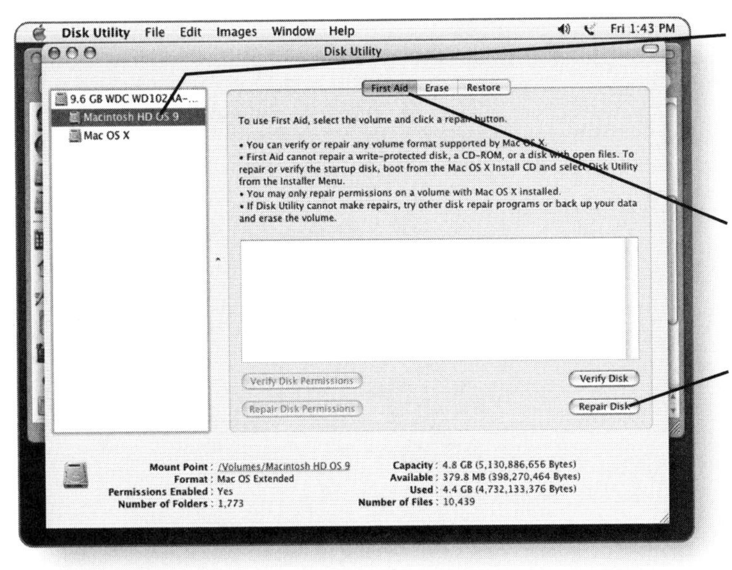

1. **Click** on the **volume icon** in the list at the left side of the Disk Utility window. The icon will be highlighted.

2. **Click** on **First Aid**. The options for verifying and repairing a disk will appear.

3. **Click** on **Repair Disk**. Disk Utility will repair the disk and display a list of results.

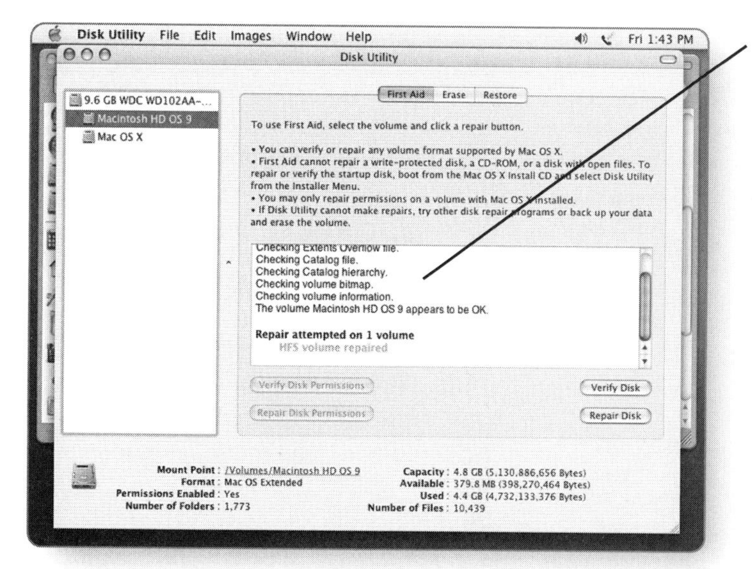

4. Review the **results** in the list at the bottom. If Disk Utility finds a disk error, it will be listed along with the corrective action that was taken.

> **TIP**
>
> If you click on the Partition tab in the Disk Utility window, Disk Utility displays options for repartitioning the system hard disk—that is, dividing the physical disk into multiple logical or functional disks. Avoid using this capability unless you have expert help or are confident that you have a recent backup of your system.

Erasing a Disk

You can erase a disk if you no longer need its contents and want to reformat it. Typically, you'll only want to erase some types of external disks: a floppy or Zip disk, an external hard disk, or a CD-RW. You cannot erase the current startup disk (volume). After you verify that you've identified the proper disk to erase, follow these steps to complete the process:

1. Insert the **disk** into the drive.

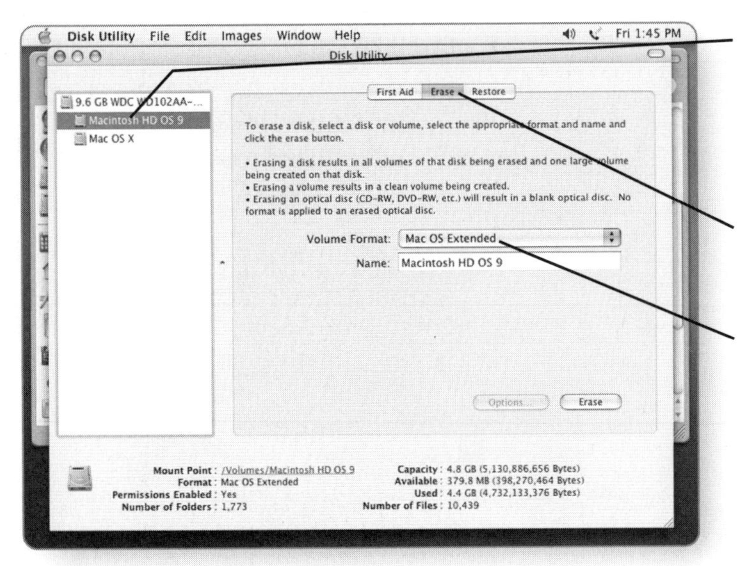

2. **Click** on the **volume icon** in the list at the left side of the Disk Utility window. The icon will be highlighted.

3. **Click** on **Erase**. The choices for erasing the disk will appear.

4. If needed, **choose** another **disk format** from the **Volume Format pop-up menu**. The new format choice will appear.

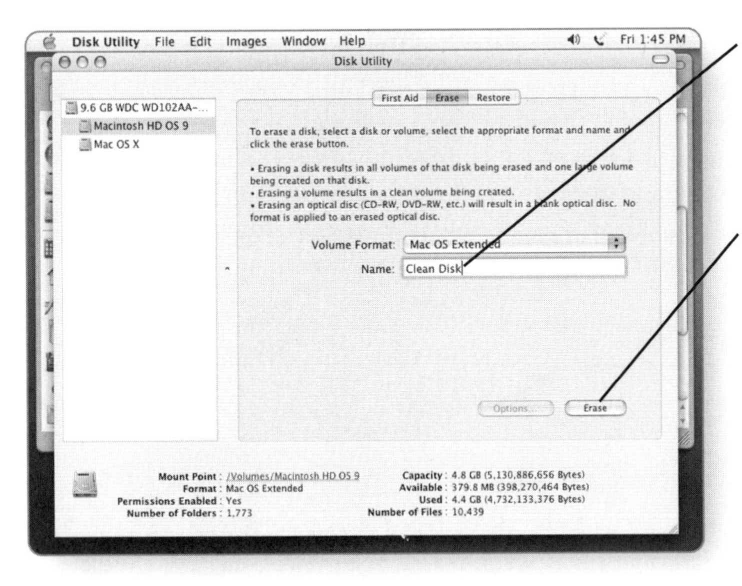

5. **Type** a **new name** for the disk volume, if required, in the Name text box. The new name will appear.

6. **Click** on **Erase**. Disk Utility will erase and reformat the disk.

> **CAUTION**
>
> You can't undo a disk format operation, so be sure that you've selected or inserted the proper disk before you proceed with Step 6.

23

Managing Users

You learned in Chapter 1 that Mac OS X was designed to accommodate multiple users. As you set up each new user on the system, Mac OS X Version 10.3 creates separate home folders for each user and basically restricts that user's hard disk access to his or her own home folder and its subfolders. By employing this and other special features in Mac OS X Version 10.3, not only do you protect each user's files but you also streamline each user's ability to operate his or her system. In this chapter, you'll learn how to:

- Add or delete a user.
- Change a user's password.
- Change a user's administration privileges.
- Use keychain access.
- Turn automatic login on or off, and working with fast user switching.

Starting Multiple Users

To add and work with multiple user features in Mac OS X Version 10.3, you will use the Accounts pane in System Preferences. To work with user information, you must be logged on as an administrator, or you must unlock the Accounts pane by providing an administrator's user name and password. The following steps show you how to access and enable the Accounts settings:

1. **Click** on the **System Preferences icon** on the Dock. The System Preferences application starts, and its menu and window open.

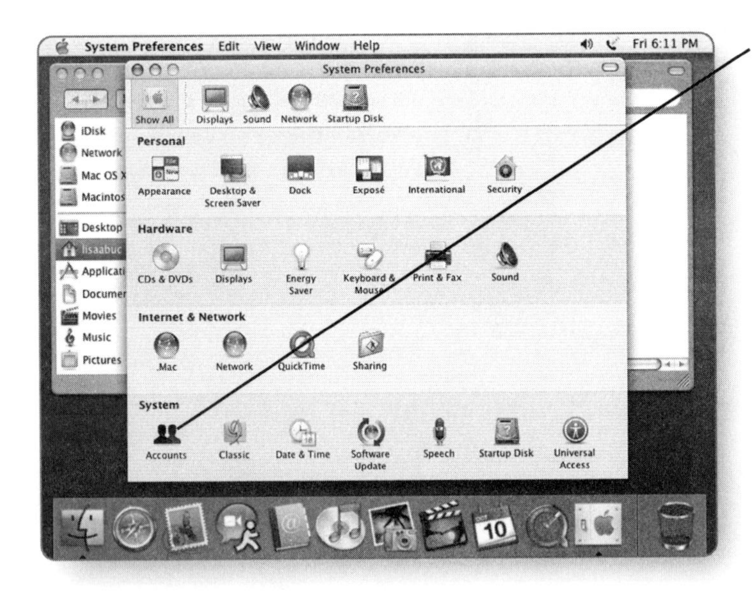

2. **Click** on the **Accounts icon**. The choices on the Accounts pane appear in the System Preferences window.

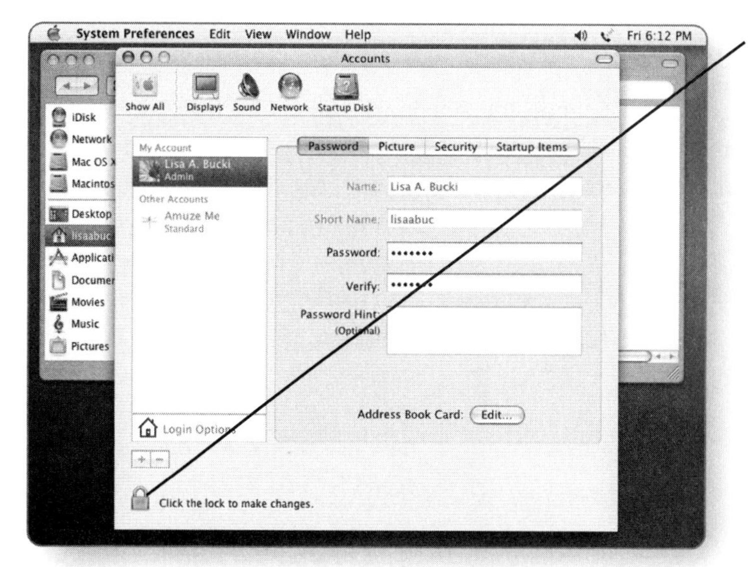

3. If the Accounts preferences are locked, **click** on the **small lock icon** on the lower-left corner of the window. The Authenticate dialog box will open, prompting you to enter the administrator password or phrase.

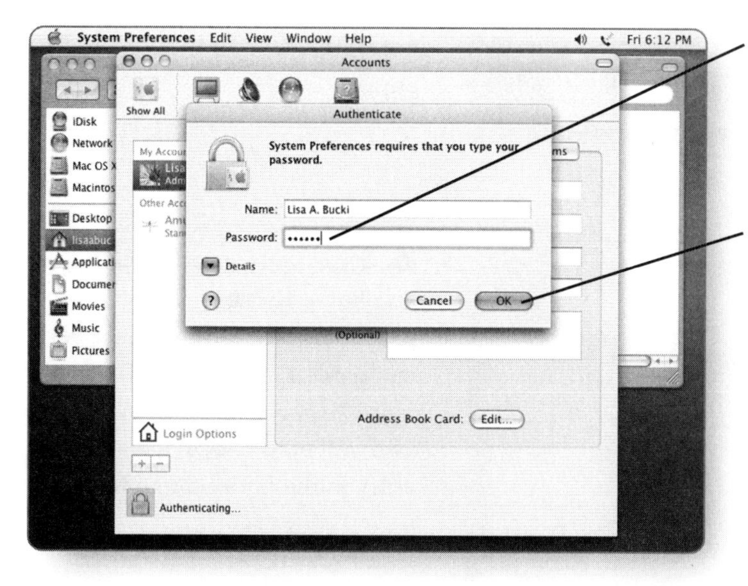

4. Type the **password** into the Password text box. A dot appears in the text box for each letter you type.

5. Click on **OK**. Mac OS X Version 10.3 will verify that you have administrator privileges and will then unlock the user's preferences. The lock icon will change to an unlocked state, and you can change settings on the pane.

NOTE

When you've finished working with User settings, choose System Preferences, Quit System Preferences to close the System Preferences application.

Adding a User

Once you've opened the Accounts pane in System Preferences and have unlocked its settings, you can set up additional users. For each user, you'll specify a separate user name and password, as well as additional, optional information. The user can then use the assigned user name and password to log in to the system and access his or her new home folder. Follow these steps to add a user:

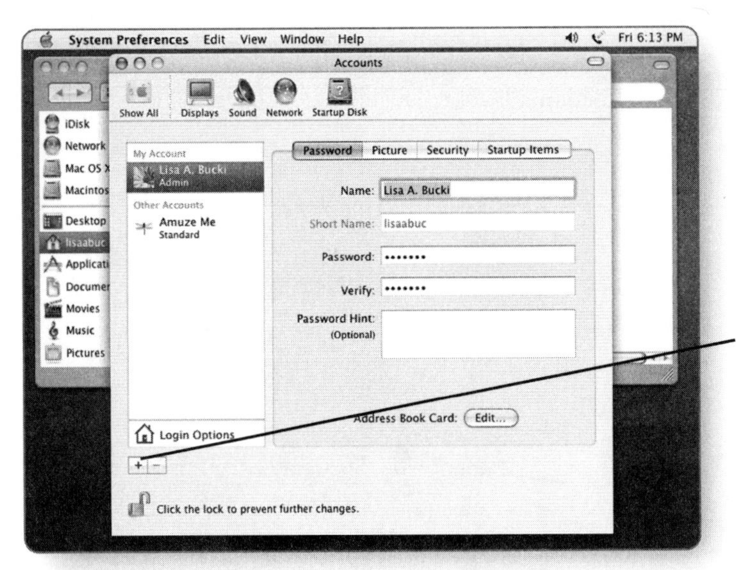

1. **Click** on the **Add (+) button.** A new user will be added to the list at the left and text boxes for entering user information will appear.

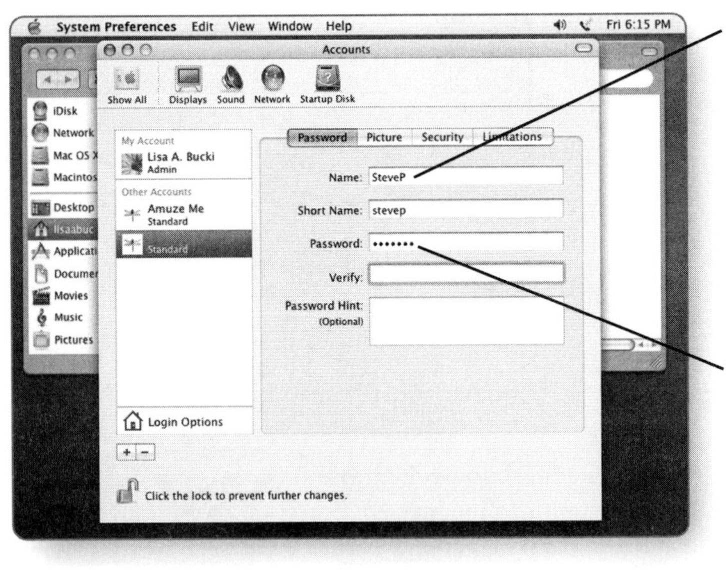

2. **Type** a **new user name** in the Name text box and then **press Tab twice.** The new user name will appear in the Name text box, and Mac OS X Version 10.2 will automatically make an entry in the Short Name text box.

3. **Type** a **new password** in the Password text box and **press Tab.** The insertion point will move to the Verify text box.

NOTE

Remember that user names and passwords are case- and punctuation-sensitive, so the user must enter the name and password exactly as you did. Also, it is highly recommended to create a password with more than three characters. Passwords that are three characters or less in length have been known to cause serious startup or login problems in Panther.

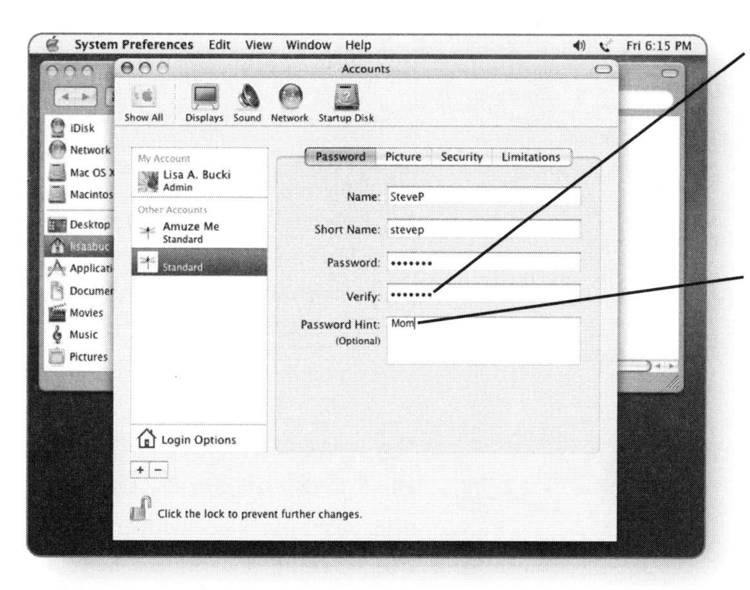

4. **Type** the **password again** in the Verify text box and **press Tab.** The insertion point will move to the Password Hint text box.

5. **Type** a **hint** in the Password Hint text box. If the user tries to log in to Mac OS X Version 10.3 and fails three times, the password hint will appear to help the user.

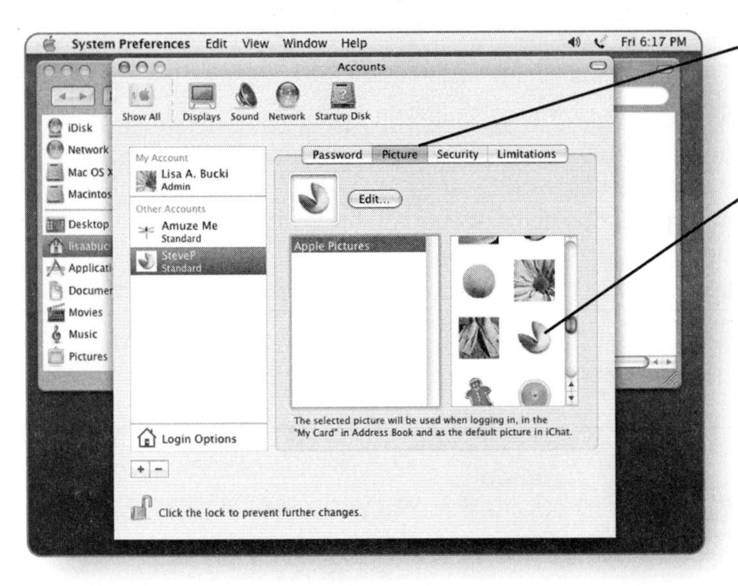

6. Click on **Picture**. The pictures available to assign to the new user will appear.

7. Scroll through the **available pictures** and **click** on a **picture** to represent the user. That picture will appear beside the user's name when the user logs on.

> **NOTE**
>
> You can use the Edit button to select an alternate digital picture. However, make sure you prepare the picture beforehand, cropping it to focus the image.

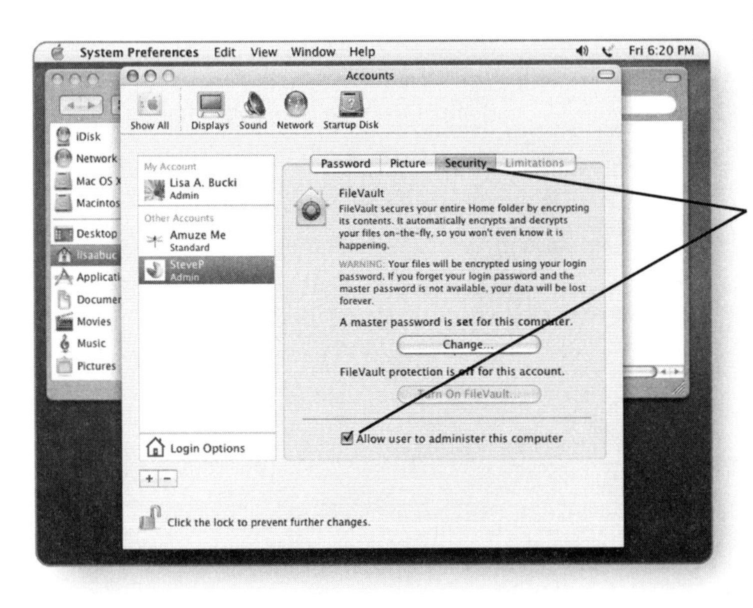

8a. Click on **Security**; then **click** on the **Allow user to administer this computer check box** to select it. The user will have administrator privileges and will be able to change key system settings when logged in.

OR

8b. Click on **Limitations.** Choices for restricting the user's access to the computer will appear.

9. Click on **Some Limits.** The specific limitations you can apply will appear.

10. Click on the **desired options.** Options will be set accordingly. Then close System Preferences.

Deleting a User

If a user no longer needs to work on the system, you can delete that user's login information. (The only user that you cannot delete is the first user created under Mac OS X Version 10.3.) The user's files will not be deleted. Instead, they will be placed in a file in the Deleted Users folder for later access.

1. Click on the **user name** in the list at the left side of the Accounts pane. The user will be selected.

2. Click on the **Delete (-) button.** A sheet opens and prompts you to verify the deletion.

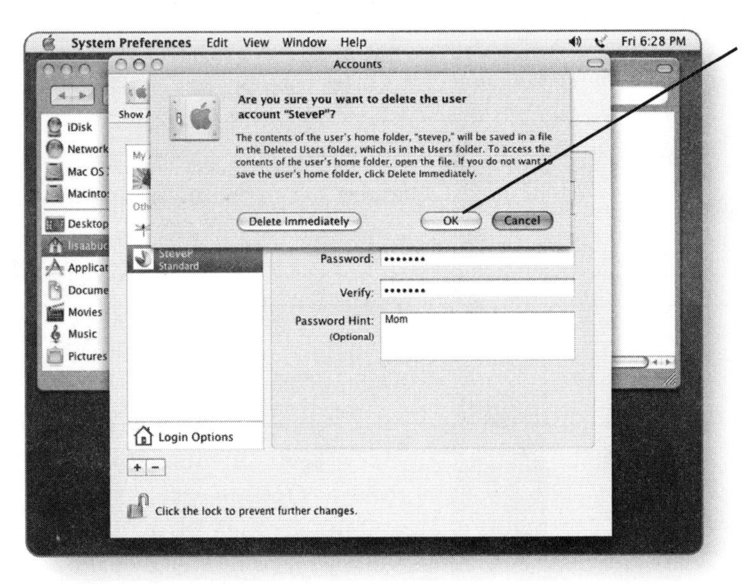

3. Click on **OK.** Mac OS X deletes the user.

> **NOTE**
>
> Mac OS X gives no further warning about deleting the user, so be careful when deleting users.

Setting User Capabilities and Updating User Information

User information isn't set in stone. You can change which features of the system and applications the user can work with. You also can update a user name, password, and administration privileges at any time. Follow these steps to update information about a particular user:

1. Click on the **desired user name** in the list at the left side of the Accounts pane. The user will be selected.

2. Click on **Limitations.** Choices for restricting the user's access to the computer will appear.

3. **Click** on **Some Limits**. The specific limitations you can apply will appear.

4. **Change options**. Options will be set accordingly. You can then close System Preferences.

NOTE

Choosing Simple Finder places the greatest restrictions on the user. When you choose Simple Finder, you can give the reader access only to certain applications on the system.

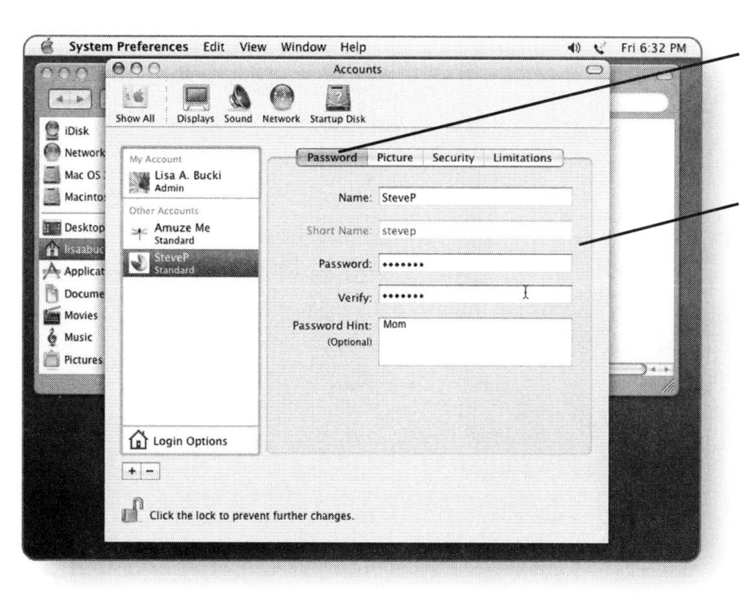

5. **Click** on **Password.** Login and password settings will appear.

6. **Make** any **needed changes** to the user's login. The changes will appear in the pane. You can then close System Preferences.

Working with Keychain Access

Keychain Access existed in previous Mac operating systems, so you may already be familiar with it. Basically, you can use the keychain file to track passwords, such as a password for a particular Web site, application, or network server. When you go back to the location that requires the password, Keychain Access enters the password for you automatically, assuming that the software in use (such as your Web browser) is keychain-enabled.

Mac OS X Version 10.3 automatically creates a basic keychain access file for each user you add. Each file stores the necessary password information, listed by kind of password. You can then use Keychain Access to modify keychain information.

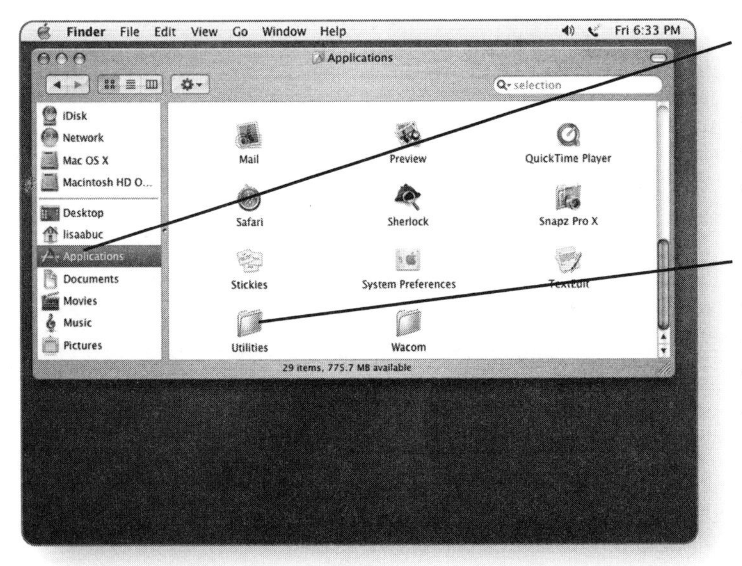

1. **Click** on **Applications** on a Finder window Sidebar. The contents of the Applications folder appear in the Finder window.

2. **Scroll down** and **double-click** on the **Utilities icon**. The contents of the Utilities folder will appear in the Finder window.

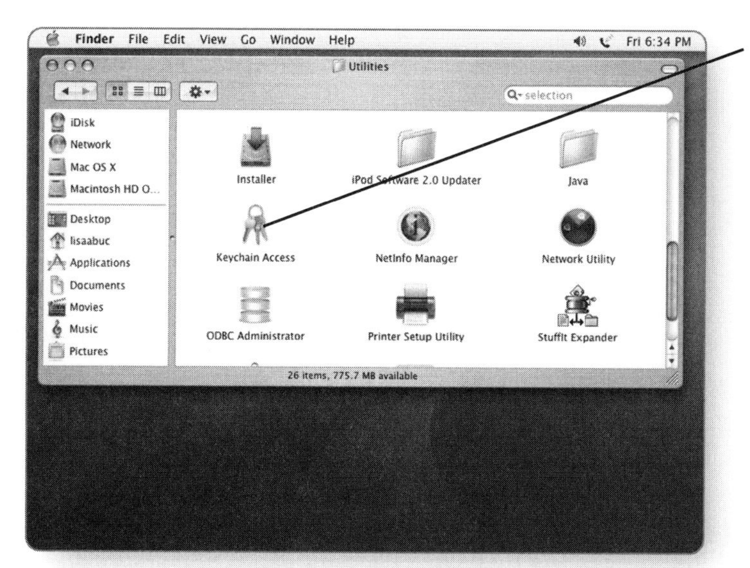

3. Scroll down and **double-click** on the **Keychain Access icon**. The Keychain Access application will start.

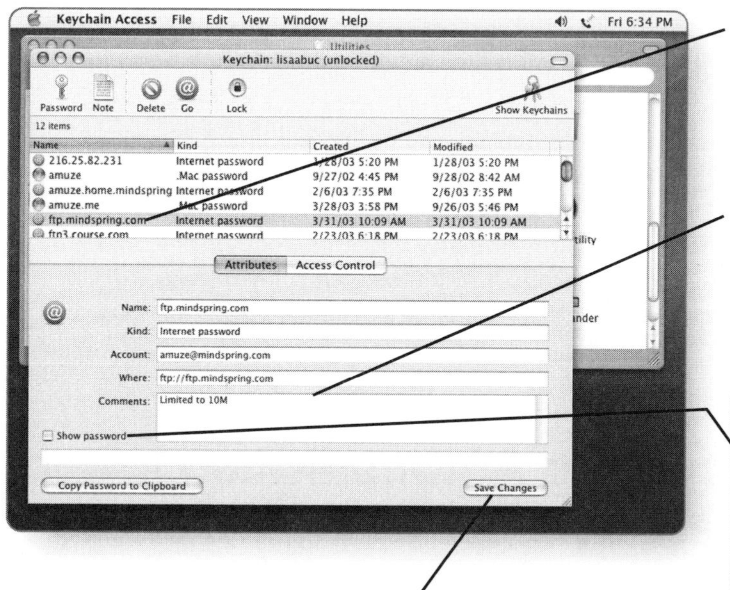

4. Click on the **desired keychain item**. It will be selected, and its options will appear.

5. Make changes, such as adding a Comment or working with Access Control. Your changes will appear.

> **TIP**
>
> Check the Show password check box; then edit the password that appears.

6. Click on **Save Changes**. Your changes will be saved, and the keychain will be deselected.

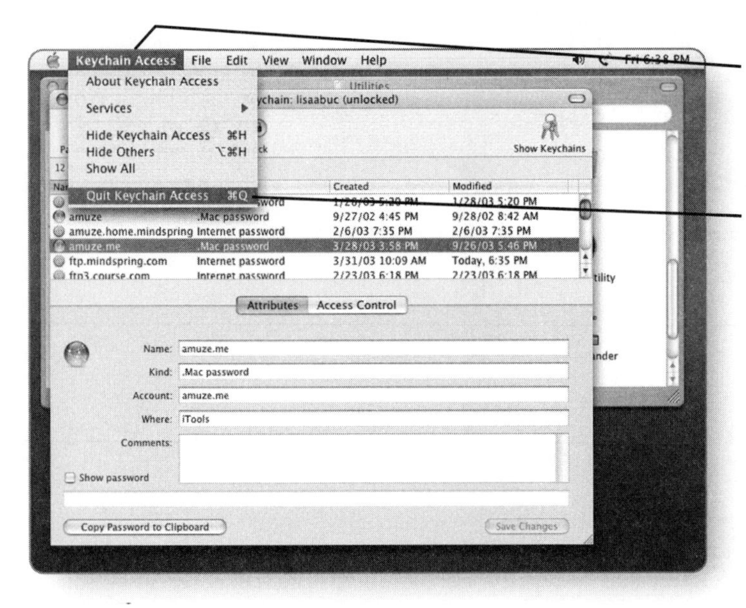

7. Click on **Keychain Access.** The Keychain Access menu will appear.

8. Click on **Quit Keychain Access.** The Keychain Access application will close.

NOTE

The Keychain Access application creates a file to hold your keychain items. The file uses your eight-character user name (such as lisaabuc, short for Lisa A. Bucki) as the file name. You can typically find this file in the Library: Keychains subfolder of your home folder. If you copy this file to the same folder on another Mac that also uses Mac OS X, the Mac to which you copy the file can also use the keychains you've set up.

Enabling Automatic Log In and Fast User Switching

If you're the only user on your system or are the primary user, you can enable the automatic login feature, so that you no longer need to type your user name and password each time you start the system. Mac OS X Version 10.3 also offers a new feature called *fast user switching*. This feature enables multiple users to remain logged in to the system, so that you can quickly switch between accounts. Be aware, however, that enabling fast user switching is less secure because others can access your account information.

> **NOTE**
>
> If you choose not to set up automatic login, you still can change some aspects of the login process, such as whether all the users are listed. To do so, start System Preferences, click on the Accounts icon, and click on Login Options.

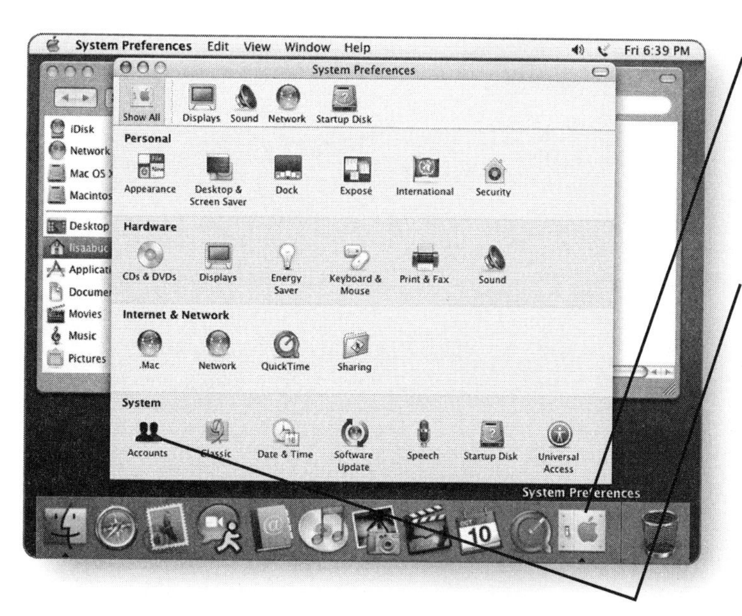

1. Click on the **System Preferences icon** on the Dock. The System Preferences application starts, and its menu and window open.

2. Click on the **Accounts icon.** The choices on the Accounts pane will appear in the System Preferences window.

> **NOTE**
>
> If the small icon in the lower-left corner of the pane is locked, click on the icon, enter an administrator user name and password, and click on OK to continue.

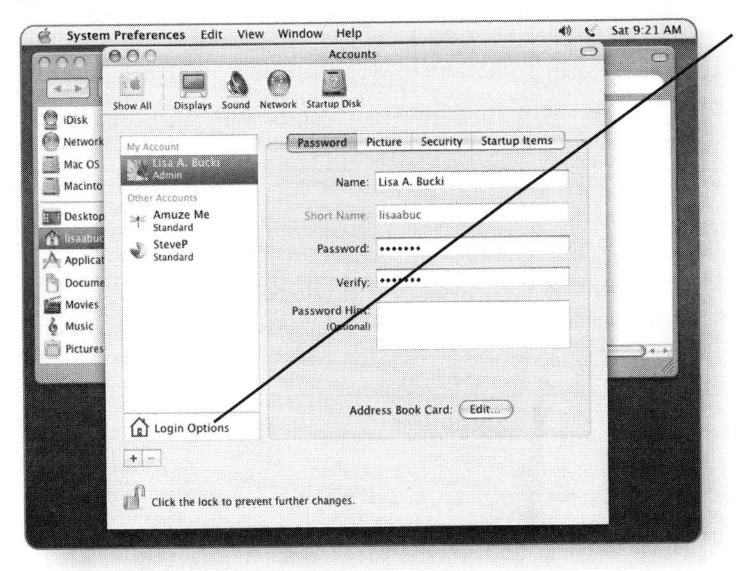

3. Click on **Login Options**. The right side of the Accounts pane will display log in options.

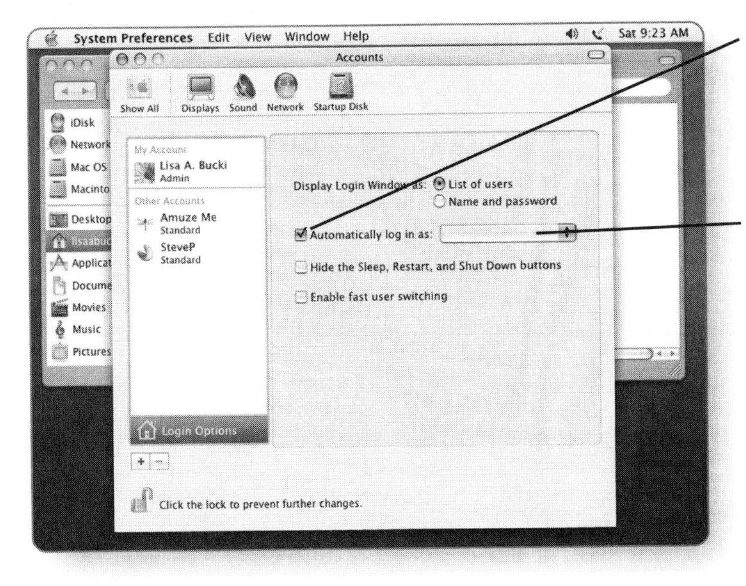

4. Click on the **Automatically log in as check box**. The accompanying pop-up menu will be enabled.

5. Select the **user to log in as** from the pop-up menu. A sheet will prompt you to enter that user's password.

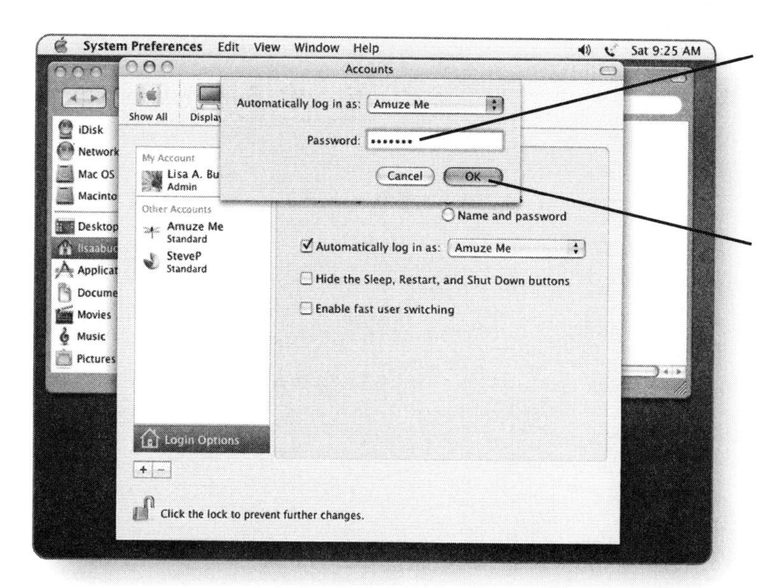

6. **Type** the **user's password** into the Password text box. A dot will appear for each character you type.

7. **Click** on **OK**. Automatic login will be enabled.

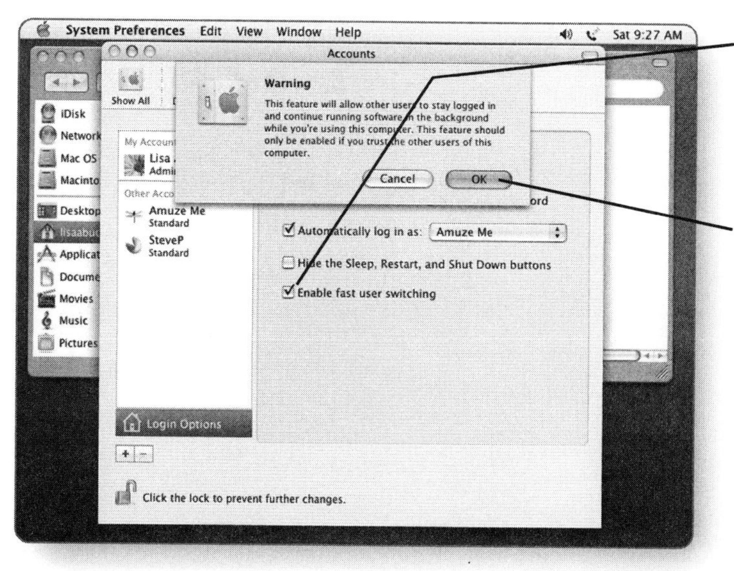

8. **Click** on the **Enable fast user switching check box**. A warning sheet will prompt you to verify enabling the feature.

9. **Click** on **OK**. Fast user switching will be enabled.

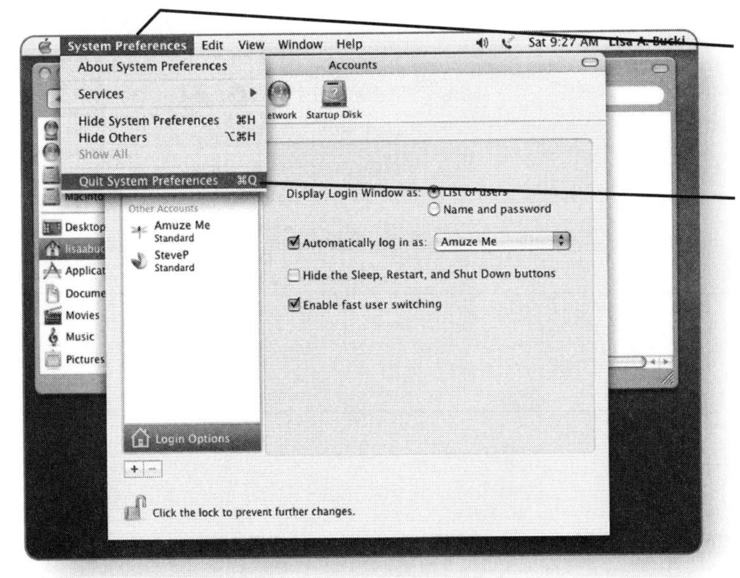

10. Click on **System Preferences.** The System Preferences menu will appear.

11. Click on **Quit System Preferences.** The System Preferences application will close.

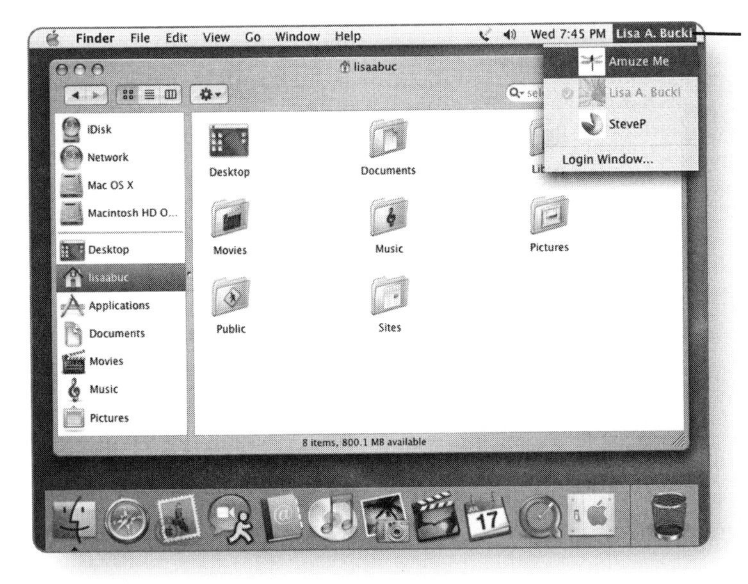

Once you've enabled fast user switching, your user name will appear at the right end of the Finder menu bar. When another user wants to log on, he or she can click on the current user name, and then click on his or her own user name. The user can then enter his or her password when prompted, and click on Log In.

This ends *Mac OS X Version 10.3 Panther Fast & Easy*. Thank you for choosing this book to guide you through your learning curve with Mac OS X.

Part VII Review Questions

1. How do I restart my Mac? *See "Restarting the System" in Chapter 21.*
2. What if I can't start from the hard disk? *See "Starting from a CD-ROM" in Chapter 21.*
3. I have OS 9.2 and OS X Version 10.2 on separate partitions. How do I boot from one or the other? *See "Changing the Startup Disk" in Chapter 21.*
4. How do I repair a disk? *See "Repairing a Disk" in Chapter 22.*
5. How do I authorize more Mac OS X Version 10.3 system users? *See "Adding a User," in Chapter 23.*
6. How can I prevent a user from running certain programs? *See "Setting User Capabilities and Updating User Information" in Chapter 23.*
7. How do I change a password? *See "Setting User Capabilities and Updating User Information" in Chapter 23.*
8. Can I log on automatically? *See "Enabling Automatic Log In and Fast User Switching" in Chapter 23.*
9. What's fast user switching and how do I use it? *See "Enabling Automatic Log In and Fast User Switching" in Chapter 23.*

Installation Notes

The Mac OS X CD-ROM includes both the Mac OS X Version 10.3 Panther program files and an installer program that walks you through the installation process. To complete the installation process, you boot by using the installation CD-ROM (see the section "Starting from a CD-ROM" in Chapter 21 "Emergency Startup Measures") and then follow the onscreen instructions. While *that* part of the process is simple, there are some issues to consider before and after you install Mac OS X Version 10.3 Panther.

Considering System Requirements When Upgrading

If you're installing Mac OS X on a system that already uses an older Mac operating system, you need to verify that your system can handle the upgrade before you begin the installation process. You can install Mac OS X Version 10.3 on the following systems: Power Mac G4, Power Mac G3 (Blue and White), PowerBook G4, PowerBook G3 with built-in USB, iMac, eMac, and iBook. In addition, the system should have 128MB or more of system memory and must use an Apple-supplied video card or built-in display. Finally, the system will need at least 2GB of free hard disk space to handle the standard upgrade.

After that, consider your options before diving into the installation process. Here are the key points you should consider:

- Before you do anything, open and read the Read Before You Install.pdf file on the Mac OS X CD-ROM. This document covers important considerations such as the system requirements for Mac OS X, where to check to see if you need to upgrade your firmware before installing Mac OS X, and more. This document also reviews how to start up the Mac OS X installer.
- Before you can install Mac OS X, you need to upgrade any OS 9.x version to Mac OS 9.1 or later. That's because Mac OS X requires a later OS 9.x version to run any non-OS X (now called Classic) applications. Apple recommends that you upgrade to Mac OS 9.2 before installing Mac OS X Version 10.3 Panther, with the OS 9.2.1 and 9.2.2 updates providing the best Classic performance and compatibility.

- You need to decide whether to install Mac OS X over your current Mac OS 9.1 installation, or whether to partition the disk and install Mac OS X in a separate partition. Taking the latter approach, for example, makes it easier to reinstall either OS if needed. Plus, it gives you the opportunity to install Mac OS X on a clean partition—rather than installing over a prior OS—which typically results in fewer problems when running Mac OS X.
- If you do want to partition the hard disk, be aware that the partitioning process erases everything currently on the disk. Therefore, you'll need a good backup of your data files. You should also record any important information (such as TCP/IP settings, Internet connection and email account settings, and dial-up connection settings) before beginning the partitioning process. If you use a good backup program, you should be able to restore all information to the Mac OS 9.x partition after you partition the disk.
- If you're not sure how to partition your hard disk, you can get help from *http://www.apple.com*. On the Web site, click first on the Support tab and then search for Article ID (article number) 19286 so that you can read instructions for partitioning the disk in prior Mac OS versions. (You'll have to click on a link to 19286 in article 106025, which the search actually returns.)
- Once you start the Installer, it will prompt you to select the partition in which you want to install Mac OS X. Be sure to select the proper partition.
- Consult Chapter 21 "Emergency Startup Measures" to learn how to boot between the two partitions (and operating systems).

Completing the Mac OS Setup Assistant

After the Installer program finishes copying files, it launches the Setup Assistant. The Setup Assistant gathers additional information from you to help configure the Macintosh OS X Version operating system. All you need to do is respond to each of the Setup Assistant screens.

NOTE

If you're installing Mac OS X Version 10.3 Panther over a prior Mac OS X installation, the Setup Assistant will not run. You can run it at a later time to update information about your Internet connection. The Setup Assistant utility is found in the System: Library: CoreServices folder of the disk where Mac OS X Version 10.3 is installed.

After you establish the initial user name and password information, the Setup Assistant will prompt you to establish other key settings, such as setting up your Internet account. Respond to each screen, as required, to complete the Setup Assistant.

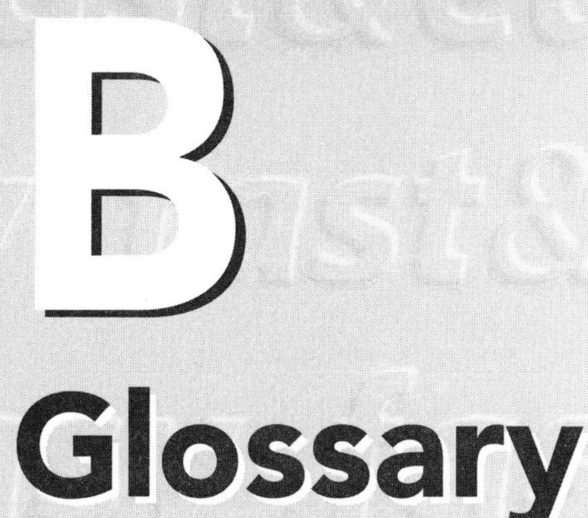

Glossary

Active Window. The window in which the insertion point appears. Click on a window to make it active.

Alias. A shortcut that helps you jump to a file or folder stored in another location. For example, an alias might be on the Desktop, while the file or folder to which it refers is in the Documents subfolder of your Home folder.

Alt Key. *See Option key.*

AppleTalk. A networking and device sharing technology included in current and previous versions of the Macintosh operating system.

Application (Program). A software program that adds specific functionality to your computer, such as a particular game or word processing program.

Aqua. The name for the user interface featured in all versions of Mac OS X.

Archive File. A file that holds a number of files, which may be compressed. Mac OS X Version 10.3 Panther enables you to create an archive file with a .zip extension, and you also can use special compression software such as DropStuff from Aladdin Systems. Archive files enable you to send email more quickly or download a number of files, because you can "group" all of those files within a single archive file.

Auto Hide. A feature that, when enabled, hides the Dock until you move your mouse pointer over it.

Bookmark. In Safari, a Web page that you use frequently and therefore mark for easy access.

Bounce. The Mail application's capability to return a junk email message in such a way that the original sender thinks your email address is invalid. This technique discourages further junk mailings.

Browser. *See Web browser.*

Check Box. In a window or dialog box, a check box element allows a user to enable or disable an option. To use a check box, click in the box to place a check mark in it, which enables or selects that setting. Click on a check box again to remove the check mark, which disables, unchecks, or clears the setting.

Classic Application. An application written for Mac OS 9.2 or earlier. The Classic Environment must load in Mac OS X so that you can use a Classic application.

Classic Environment. The Mac OS 9.2-based environment that loads to run applications written for earlier Mac OS versions.

Click. To press and release the mouse button.

Column View. A Finder window (or Save or Open dialog box) view that displays information in multiple columns. Generally, the leftmost column indicates upper-level locations (disks) and the rightmost column identifies a single file. The columns in between identify the folders and subfolders leading to the file.

Command Button. In a window or dialog box, you click on a command button to perform a command. In some instances, a subsequent dialog box is displayed.

Command ⌘ key (also called **Apple key**). A modifier key on Mac keyboards used in shortcut key combinations and in making selections.

Command Key Combination. *See shortcut key combination.*

Contextual Menu. In Mac OS X, a menu that appears when you Control+click on an item.

Control key. A modifier key on Mac keyboards that's typically used in combination with the mouse, as described in *Contextual Menu.*

Crash. *See hang.*

Current Window. *See active window.*

Delete. *See also Trash.* To remove an item from a folder or disk and place it in the Trash, from which you can permanently delete or retrieve the item.

Desktop. The working screen area of Mac OS X, from which you launch applications and use the Finder to manage files.

Disabled. An item that is dimmed onscreen indicating that it's not available for selection or use.

Disk Image. A special type of file that represents a disk volume. The Disk Copy utility typically mounts any disk image file after you double-click on the file. A removable disk icon for the disk image appears on the Desktop. You can use the Finder to navigate to folders on the disk image just as you would navigate to folders on a physical hard disk.

Disk Utility. An application that enables you to check and repair disks.

Dock. The bar that appears at the bottom of the Mac OS X desktop. The Dock contains icons for launching applications. You also can minimize an open file and window to an icon on the Dock; then click the icon on the Dock to reopen the window.

Document. See file

Double-click. To press and release the mouse button twice in quick succession.

Downloads Window. This utility works in conjunction with Safari to display the progress of a file being downloaded from the Web.

Drag. To drag, move the mouse pointer over an item, and then press and hold the mouse button as you move the mouse on your desk. When the mouse pointer (or the item you're dragging) reaches the desired location, release the mouse button.

Driver. A file that provides extra functionality to your system, such as a file needed to enable Mac OS X to use a particular printer.

Email. A means of sending messages electronically over the Internet, sometimes including attached files.

Email Rule. A means of specifying how the Mail program should handle messages from a particular source, such as instantly deleting a message from a source that sends junk mail.

Ethernet. A system for creating Local Area Networks that includes standards for hardware and cabling, as well as a communications protocol (or standard).

Exposé. A new feature in Mac OS X Version 10.3 Panther that enables you to organize windows on the desktop with a single function key.

File. The named set of information that you create in an application. For example, you use the TextEdit application to create RTF files, such as letters and memos.

File Name Extension. A period plus an identifying suffix that appears at the end of a file name. The extension typically identifies the file type. While extensions weren't necessary in older Mac operating systems, they are used in Mac OS X because it's based on new UNIX source code.

Finder. The application that helps you manage system disks, folders, and files.

Finder Menu. In the Classic Environment and older Mac operating systems, this menu appears at the far right of the Desktop menu bar and allows you to switch between applications.

Folder. Similar to a physical file folder, a folder is a named location on a disk in which you typically store files that are related in some way.

Font Book. A new application in Mac OS X Version 10.2 Panther that enables you to manage the fonts installed on the system.

Freeware. Software written by a programmer for free distribution. You typically download freeware from the Web or receive it on a demo disk.

Freeze. *See hang.*

Graphical User Interface (GUI). A computer operating system user interface that is graphics-based, including elements such as pull-down menus and icons that enable you to interact using a mouse. Because a GUI enables you to give commands by working with items that you can see onscreen (rather than having to remember obscure commands), GUIs are considered to be more user-friendly than command-line interfaces.

Hang. To have an application or the operating system stop responding to input for some reason.

Hard Disk. A computer component that consists of a sealed metal box housing spinning disks coated with magnetic material for data storage.

Help Button. A button labeled with a question mark found on some Help screens. Clicking a Help button displays the main Help Center screen.

Help Viewer. The application that enables you to browse for Help in Mac OS X.

Highlight. *See select.*

Home Folder. The folder set up to store the files for your user name. The home folder contains a number of subfolders. Each user has access only to his or her home folder contents as well as one Shared folder that all users can access.

Home Page. The page that, by default, loads first when you start Internet Explorer.

iCal. A new application included with Mac OS X Version 10.3 Panther that enables you to track appointments and to-do lists.

Icon View. A Finder window (or Save or Open dialog box) view that represents each file and folder as an icon.

Internet Service Provider. A company that sells Internet time via a dial-up (phone line), DSL, or other broadband connection.

iMovie. An application that enables you to edit and enhance your digital movies.

iPhoto. An application that enables you to import images from a digital camera or folder, arrange the images into an album or book, and print or share the images in a variety of ways, including making a slide show or Web page, having photo prints made, or even creating a screen saver.

iSync. Another application just added to Mac OS X Version 10.3 Panther, iSync enables you to synchronize Address Book and iCal information with a Bluetooth-equipped mobile phone, an iPod, or a Palm handheld computer.

iTunes. An audio application that enables Mac users to play audio CDs, create MP3 files, and build playlists.

IP Address. A number in the format 000.000.000.000 that uniquely identifies each system connected to a TCP/IP network.

ISP. *See Internet Service Provider.*

Junk Mail (spam). Unwanted solicitation emails, typically sent by a user who attempts to disguise his or her identity.

Keyboard Repeat Rate. When you hold down a key, this rate controls how quickly the system duplicates the character.

Local Area Network (LAN). A group of computers connected with special hardware and cabling for purposes of sharing files and devices, such as printers. A LAN exists in a single location.

Link (Hyperlink). A connection to another location (typically a Web page) on which you can click to jump to the destination page or location. On Web pages, a link can appear as specially formatted text, a graphic, or a button.

List View. A Finder window (or Save or Open dialog box) view that lists each file and folder along with basic information about the file or folder, such as the date it was last modified.

Log In. To enter your user name and password to gain access to Mac OS X after you start up your system.

Magnification. A Dock feature that causes an icon to increase in size when you move the mouse pointer over the icon.

Menu. *See pull-down menu.*

Menu Bar. The list of menus that appears at the top of the screen when you start a particular application.

Minimize. To reduce an open window to an icon on the Dock.

Mount. Occurs when the Disk Copy utility opens a disk image file and creates an icon for it on the Desktop.

Mouse. An input device for your system, which is designed to work with the graphical user interface. You move the mouse on your desk to move the mouse pointer in the corresponding direction and distance onscreen. Then use the mouse button to click, double-click, and drag.

MP3. (**MP**eg Audio Layer **3**). A technology resulting in a special music file format with a compact file format yielded by discarding frequencies and tones not perceptible by the human ear. (MPEG stands for Moving Pictures Expert Group, an ISO group that develops and regulates digital video and audio compression standards and formats.)

Navigating. Moving between disks and folders in the Finder or in a sheet for opening, saving, or selecting files.

Operating System. The software that enables computer system components to communicate and accomplish tasks, as well as enabling the user to give input to the computer.

Option Button (Radio Button). In a window or dialog box, a round button on which you can click to select an option. Typically, option buttons appear in groups and are mutually exclusive, meaning that only one option in the group can be selected at any time.

Option Key. A modifier key on Mac keyboards that's typically used in shortcut key combinations.

Pane. Displays a collection or group of preferences pertaining to particular system functions in System Preferences.

Panther. The code name for Mac OS X Version 10.3.

Password. A secret word or group of characters that you enter to log in to Mac OS X, certain Web sites, and other locations. Passwords limit access to authorized users (those with the password).

Path. The full list of folders and subfolders that identify a file's location.

Playlist. In iTunes, a custom list of songs that you create to control playback order.

Program. *See application.*

Pop-up Menu. A menu that opens after you click on a double-arrow button in a window or dialog box.

Printer Setup Utility. The Mac OS X application that enables you to install and remove printers and control printing.

Print Queue. The list of documents being sent to the printer by Printer Setup Utility.

Pull-down Menu. A menu that appears when you click on a menu name on a menu bar.

Quartz Extreme. Built-in graphics technology that enables Mac OS X Version 10.3 to render text and images more clearly and quickly onscreen.

Repair Disk. To use Disk Utility to find and fix problems on a disk.

Rendezvous. New networking technology built into Mac OS X Version 10.3 that enables the system to more easily discover other computers and some devices on a network.

Resolution. The size of the screen or of an image, stated in the number of pixels (dots) in width and height.

Rich Text Format (RTF). The default type of document created in TextEdit. RTF documents can include text formatting and some graphics, unlike plain text (TXT) files.

Root. The base location on a disk outside of any folders contained on the disk.

Rule. *See email rule.*

TCP/IP. Protocols (standards) that enable communication over the Internet and a Local Area Network (LAN).

Tracking Speed. When you move the mouse on your desk, correspondingly the tracking speed refers to how far and fast the mouse pointer moves onscreen.

Safari. Apple's new Web browser program included with Mac OS X Version 10.3.

Scroll Bar. A bar at the right side or bottom of a window or list that enables you to view other sections of the window or list contents. For example, click on the up arrow on a vertical scroll bar to scroll up in a document or list.

Search Engine. An application that searches for information (data) based on criteria generally supplied by the user. Typically, search engines are Web-based services that catalog Web pages, so that you can search the pages by topic. After you run the search, the search engine presents a list of links to potentially matching pages.

Select. To choose an icon by clicking on it or to choose text by dragging over it.

Shareware. Software distributed on the honor system. You typically download shareware from the Web or receive it on a demo disk, and are expected to send a modest fee to the developer if you plan to continue to use the software.

Sheet. A listing of options that drops down from the title bar of a window or dialog box. Unlike a dialog box, a sheet remains attached to the title bar from which it originated, so it can't be moved independently.

Shortcut Key Combination. Multiple keys pressed simultaneously to execute a command or action. Typically, these combinations include the use of the Control, Shift, Option, and/or Command (Apple) keys. In some cases, one of these keys is pressed while clicking with the mouse to execute the shortcut. The right side of most menus lists the shortcut key combination associated with a particular command.

Shut Down. To open the Apple menu and choose the Shut Down command to close the Mac OS X software and power down your Macintosh.

Sidebar. The pane at the left side of a Finder window that provides icons for navigating to frequently used disks and folders.

Signature. Closing information that the Mail application can automatically append to each of your outgoing email messages.

Sleep (Sleep Mode). A power-conserving mode that can activate for your system's screen, hard disk, or both after a period of inactivity (when you haven't used the system at all).

Slider. In a window or dialog box, a knob or *thumb* that you drag to the left or right to increase or decrease a setting.

Spring-Loaded Folder. A new feature in Mac OS X Version 10.3. When you hover the mouse pointer over a folder icon in a Finder window, the folder opens automatically.

Stickies. Desktop notes that you can create and view using the Stickies application.

Stuffed. Another term for a compressed archive file.

Tab. In a window or dialog box, a graphical element representing another page (collection) of settings. Click on a tab to display its settings.

Text Box. In a window or dialog box, a rectangular area in which you type an entry.

Trash. The Mac OS X feature that enables you to temporarily or permanently delete files from disks. You move a file to the Trash to delete the file temporarily. Empty the trash to permanently delete its files.

URL (*Uniform Resource Locator*). The Internet address for a Web page, usually in the format *http://www.domainname.ext/foldername/filename.html*.

USB (*Universal Serial Bus*). A type of port that enables you to connect and set up attached devices (like a printer) quickly and easily.

User Interface. The means of communicating with the operating system and your computer.

User Name. The name that you use to log in to Mac OS X and that is used to identify your Home folder.

Utility. A program or feature that typically performs some kind of system maintenance or repair feature.

Verify Disk. An activity performed by Disk Utility to check for problems on a disk.

Web Browser. An application that enables you to view pages on the World Wide Web.

Web Page. A document on the World Wide Web coded in HTML (HyperText Markup Language). Web pages are viewed using a Web browser.

Web Site. A collection of related Web pages published by a single source on the World Wide Web.

Window. A frame that holds a document or collection of options onscreen.

Word Processor. A program that creates text-based documents, such as letters, memos, and reports. TextEdit is a basic word processor.

World Wide Web. A collection of servers on the Internet that store and distribute interactive, graphical content in the HTML format.

Index

A

G

H

I

J

K

L

N

Q

R

S

T

U

Z

THOMSON
COURSE TECHNOLOGY
Professional ■ Trade ■ Reference

Mac OS X and iLife: Using iTunes, iPhoto, iMovie, and iDVD
ISBN: 1-59200-101-7 ■ $39.99

We love your Mac® almost as much as you do!

You're not the only one who recognizes the power of your Mac. That's why we offer books that show you how to use your Mac for everything from organizing home movies to setting up a Mac-based home recording studio. Are you ready to unleash the power of your Mac?

Keynote Fast & Easy
ISBN: 1-59200-129-7 ■ $19.99

iMovie 3 Fast & Easy
ISBN: 1-59200-098-3 ■ $19.99

iPhoto 2 Fast & Easy
ISBN: 1-59200-071-1 ■ $19.99

iDVD 3 Fast & Easy
ISBN: 1-59200-099-1 ■ $19.99

Mac Home Recording Power!
ISBN: 1-59200-051-7 ■ $29.99

Mac OS X and the Digital Lifestyle
ISBN: 1-931841-74-8 ■ $39.99

Mac Game Programming
ISBN: 1-931841-18-7 ■ $59.99

Mac OS X Power User's Guide
ISBN: 1-931841-44-6 ■ $39.99

THOMSON
COURSE TECHNOLOGY
Professional ■ Trade ■ Reference

Call 1.800.842.3636 to order
Order online at www.CoursePTR.com